City and Regional Planning

City and Regional Planning provides a clearly written and lavishly illustrated overview of the theory and practice of city and regional planning. With material on globalization and the world city system, and with examples from a number of countries, the book has been written to meet the needs of readers worldwide who seek an overview of city and regional planning.

Chapters cover the history of cities and city and regional planning, urban design and placemaking, comprehensive plans, planning politics and plan implementation, planning visions, and environmental, transportation, and housing planning. The book pays special attention to diversity, social justice, and collaborative planning. Topics include current practice in resilience, transit-oriented development, complexity in planning, spatial equity, globalization, and advances in planning methods.

It is aimed at U.S. graduate and undergraduate city and regional planning, geography, urban design, urban studies, civil engineering, and other students and practitioners. It includes extensive material on current practice in planning for climate change. Each chapter includes a case study, a biography of an important planner, lists of concepts and important people, and a list of books, articles, videos, and other suggestions for further learning.

Richard T. LeGates is Professor Emeritus of Urban Studies and Planning at San Francisco State University where he taught for 40 years before retiring in 2010. He was Summit Professor of Urban Planning at Tongji University in Shanghai from 2015 to 2017. He has a joint Master's of City and Regional Planning (MCRP) degree and Doctor of Laws degree (JD) from the University of California, Berkeley. He is a member of the California Bar.

Professor LeGates has also taught city and regional planning at the University of California, Berkeley, Renmin University of China, the American University of Sharjah, and Charles University.

He is the co-editor of *The City Reader*, now in its seventh edition (Routledge, 2020), and books and articles on spatial analysis, planning history, regionalism, housing policy, planning law, and planning in China.

Professor LeGates has received research support from the U.S. National Science Foundation, the U.S. Department of Housing and Urban Development, the California Legislature, the California State Department of Housing and Community Development, the San Francisco Foundation, the Brookings Institution, the Higher Education Funding Council of England, and the Ford Foundation. In 2015 he was Writer in Residence at the Rockefeller Foundation's Villa Serbelloni in Como, Italy.

City and Regional Planning

Richard T. LeGates

Routledge
Taylor & Francis Group
NEW YORK AND LONDON

Cover image credits: Transect: Metropolitan Government of Nashville and Davidson County Planning Department. Vibrant Northeast Ohio 2040 Planning Workshop. Courtesy of Sasaki Associates. National Capital Planning Commission sketch of South Capital Street. Washington National Capital Commission.

First published 2023
by Routledge
605 Third Avenue, New York, NY 10158

and by Routledge
4 Park Square, Milton Park, Abingdon, Oxon, OX14 4RN

Routledge is an imprint of the Taylor & Francis Group, an informa business

© 2023 Richard LeGates

The right of Richard LeGates to be identified as author of this work has been asserted in accordance with sections 77 and 78 of the Copyright, Designs and Patents Act 1988.

All rights reserved. No part of this book may be reprinted or reproduced or utilised in any form or by any electronic, mechanical, or other means, now known or hereafter invented, including photocopying and recording, or in any information storage or retrieval system, without permission in writing from the publishers.

Trademark notice: Product or corporate names may be trademarks or registered trademarks, and are used only for identification and explanation without intent to infringe.

Library of Congress Cataloging-in-Publication Data
Names: LeGates, Richard T., author.
Title: City and regional planning / Richard T. LeGates.
Description: New York, NY : Routledge, 2022. | Includes bibliographical references and index. |
Identifiers: LCCN 2021055116 (print) | LCCN 2021055117 (ebook) | ISBN 9781032050584 (hardback) | ISBN 9781032050577 (paperback) | ISBN 9781003195818 (ebook)
Subjects: LCSH: City planning. | Regional planning.
Classification: LCC HT166 .L444 2022 (print) |
LCC HT166 (ebook) | DDC307.1/216–dcundefined
LC record available at https://lccn.loc.gov/2021055116
LC ebook record available at https://lccn.loc.gov/2021055117

ISBN: 9781032050584 (hbk)
ISBN: 9781032050577 (pbk)
ISBN: 9781003195818 (ebk)

DOI: 10.4324/9781003195818

Typeset in Sabon
by Newgen Publishing UK

*Dedicated to
Joanne Fraser LeGates.
Without whose help this book would never have been possible.*

CONTENTS

List of Figures	ix
List of Case Studies	xiii
List of Biographies	xv
About the Author	xvii
Advance Praise	xix
Acknowledgements	xxiii

Chapter 1	The Art and Science of City and Regional Planning	1
Chapter 2	The Evolution of Cities and City and Regional Planning, 1607–1933	15
Chapter 3	Urban Design and Placemaking	45
Chapter 4	The Politics of City and Regional Planning	65
Chapter 5	Planning Theory	87
Chapter 6	Visions	107
Chapter 7	General Plans	133
Chapter 8	Implementing Plans	155
Chapter 9	Community Planning, Citizen Participation, and Social Justice	183
Chapter 10	Regional and National Planning	205
Chapter 11	Planning for an Urban Planet	229
Chapter 12	The Evolution of Cities and City and Regional Planning, 1933–Present	249
Chapter 13	Environmental Planning	283
Chapter 14	Transportation Planning	311

Chapter 15 Housing Planning and Policy   339

Chapter 16 Economic Development and Revitalization Planning   367

Chapter 17 Climate Change and Energy Planning   395

    Bibliography   421

    Acronyms   459

    Figure Credits   465

    Index   471

FIGURES

0.1	Richard LeGates	xvii
1.1	Multiple Flows: London Tube, Rail, and Flickr Networks	2
1.2	Urban Design Concept for South Capitol Street, Washington, D.C.	3
1.3	U.S. City and Regional Planning Specializations	8
1.4	Jane Jacobs (1961)	11
2.1	Kingsley Davis's Urbanization S Curve (England)	17
2.2	Kingsley Davis's "Family" of Urbanization S Curves	18
2.3	Boston Harbor, 1774	20
2.4	Geneva, Illinois (1869)	22
2.5	L'Enfant Plan for Washington, D.C. (1792)	24
2.6	Crowded Lodging in a Bayard Street Tenement by Jacob Riis (1889)	28
2.7	Dumbbell Tenement	29
2.8	Robert Fulton's Steamboat *Clermont* (1807)	30
2.9	Horse-Drawn Streetcar (Hamilton, Virginia, circa 1874)	31
2.10	"Big Red", Los Angeles Electric Streetcar (circa 1930)	32
2.11	Pacific Electric Railway Streetcars Awaiting Dismantling for Scrap Metal (Los Angeles, California, 1956)	33
2.12	Patrick Geddes	36
3.1	Andrés Duany's Transect	47
3.2	Kevin Lynch's 5 Image of the City Elements	50
3.3	Strøget (Copenhagen, Denmark, 2013)	51
3.4	Computer-Generated Street Network Created by Geoff Boeing	53
3.5	False Creek Waterfront (Vancouver, BC, Canada)	54
3.6	Louisville Waterfront Park	58
3.7	Hargreaves Jones Rendering of Louisville Waterfront Park	59
4.1	Members of Boston's City Council (2021)	69
4.2	Julian Castro	71
4.3	Anti-Fracking Protest (Hollywood, California, 2014)	79
4.4	Pro-"Dreamers" Rally (Ann Arbor, Michigan, 2017)	80
4.5	Protester at the United States Capitol (2006)	83
5.1	John Friedmann	90
5.2	The Rational Planning Model	92
5.3	Brasília, Brazil (2015)	96
5.4	Miscommunication in Planning	101
6.1	New Lanark, Scotland, circa 1825	109
6.2	New Lanark, Scotland Historic District (2021)	110
6.3	Ebenezer Howard's Three Magnets	112
6.4	Ebenezer Howard's Group of Slumless Smokeless Cities	113
6.5	The Lagoon and Agricultural Building at the World's Columbian Exhibition (Chicago, Illinois, 1893)	118
6.6	Proposed Civic Center Plaza and Buildings from the *1909 Plan for Chicago*	118
6.7	Le Corbusier's Plan for a Contemporary City of 3 Million (1929)	119
6.8	Pudong District, Shanghai, China (2012)	120
6.9	Frank Lloyd Wright with His Broadacre City Model (1935)	121

6.10	Arturo Soria y Mata's Linear City Plan (Madrid, Spain, 1894)	123
6.11	Clarence Perry's Neighborhood Unit (1929)	124
6.12	North End and Downtown Vision from Boston Vision Plan (2019)	128
7.1	*NashvilleNext* Growth and Preservation Concept Map (Nashville, Tennessee, 2018)	139
7.2	Madison County, Tennessee, Community Plan Transect Map	140
7.3	Madison County, Tennessee, Community Plan Transect Illustration	142
8.1	Allan Jacobs	156
8.2	City of Falls Church, Virginia Zoning Map (2021)	164
8.3	Typical Zoning Building Envelope, Height Limit, and Setbacks for a Single-Family House	165
8.4	Floor Area Ratio (FAR)	166
8.5	Columbia Pike Form-Based Code Building Envelope Standards for Neighborhood Sites (Arlington, Virginia, 2013)	170
8.6	Gary Hack	171
9.1	Sherry Arnstein's Ladder of Citizen Participation	184
9.2	Black Lives Matter (Albany, New York, 2020)	188
9.3	June Thomas	191
9.4	1934 Map of Boston Area Showing Redlined Neighborhoods	195
10.1	Tennessee Valley Authority Dam Construction Workers (1943)	208
10.2	Patrick Geddes's Valley Section	210
10.3	Illustration of Central Place Theory by Walter Christaller (1933)	211
10.4	Urban Sprawl	212
10.5	Catherine Ross	216
10.6	Metro's 2040 Growth Concept Map (Portland, Oregon, 1980)	220
10.7	*Vibrant Northeast Ohio 2040 Plan* Workshop	223
10.8	*Vibrant Northeast Ohio 2040 Plan* Digital Dashboard Dial	223
10.9	Regional Plan Association Projected U.S. Megaregions 2050	224
11.1	United Nations World Population Estimate 2020 and Projections to 2050	230
11.2	NASA "Black Marble" Night Sky in Western Europe and Northwest Africa	232
11.3	Hyderabad, India (2012)	234
11.4	Charminar Bazaar, Hyderabad, India	234
11.5	La Défense Business District (Paris, France)	235
11.6	Ekurhuleni Aerotropolis, Ekurhuleni, South Africa	236
11.7	Global Network Connectivity according to the Global and World Cities Network	237
11.8	Flooding in Jakarta, Indonesia (2013)	240
11.9	Eugenie Birch	244
12.1	Ann Forsyth	251
12.2	Tennessee Valley Authority Programs	256
12.3	Community Leaders Reviewing a Model of the Pruitt–Igoe Public Housing Project (St. Louis, Missouri, circa 1953)	262
12.4	Demolition of the Pruitt–Igoe Project (1972)	263
12.5	Pike Place Market (Seattle, Washington, 2019)	276
13.1	Map Layers Illustrating Ian McHarg's Design with Nature Method	296
13.2	Geographical Information System Map Layers	298
13.3	Biophilic Design, Eindhoven, the Netherlands (2021)	298
13.4	Industrial Wasteland	301
13.5	Cornell Dubilier Superfund Site (South Plainfield, New Jersey)	302
13.6	U.S. Army Corps of Engineers Map Showing Areas of San Francisco Bay "Susceptible to Reclamation" (1960)	305
14.1	Complete Streets Design	318
14.2	Janette Sadik-Kahn	320
14.3	New York City Pedestrianized Street at Broadway and 34th Street	321

14.4	Bus Rapid Transit, Curitiba, Brazil (2006)	325
14.5	Ciclovia, Bogotá, Columbia (2015)	326
14.6	Autonomous Rapid Transit System Design (2021)	328
14.7	Woonerf (Lodz, Poland, 2014)	330
14.8	Magnetic Levitation Train (Shanghai, China, 2006)	331
14.9	Proposed Sydney to Melbourne, Australia Hyperloop (2020)	332
15.1	Homeless and Hungry	341
15.2	Sears, Roebuck and Co. Mail Order House "The Magnolia" (1926)	344
15.3	Housing Efficiency	349
15.4	Jackson Gardens Public Housing Project (Boston, Massachusetts)	357
15.5	Robert Weaver	358
15.6	Paraisópolis, São Paulo, Brazil	363
16.1	Abandoned Packard Automobile Assembly Plant (Detroit, Michigan, 1955)	373
16.2	Renaissance Center (Detroit, Michigan, 2014)	374
16.3	Concert at Levitt Pavilion, SteelStacks Arts and Cultural Center (Bethlehem, Pennsylvania, 2020)	376
16.4	Falls Creek, Virginia Comprehensive Planning Opportunity Area Priority Schedule (2021)	378
16.5	Canary Wharf (London, England)	385
16.6	River Walk (San Antonio, Texas)	389
17.1	Global Mean Atmospheric Temperature 1880 to 2020 Relative to 1951–1980 Mean	397
17.2	Silicon Ranch Farm Combining Solar Energy Generation and Regenerative Agriculture (Millington, Tennessee, 2020)	399
17.3	Storm Surge Barrier (Rotterdam, Netherlands)	402
17.4	Kongjian Yu	403
17.5	Puyang River Ecological Corridor (Zhejiang Province, China)	404
17.6	Chicago City Hall Green Roof	415

CASE STUDIES

1.1	The Centre for Advanced Spatial Analysis (CASA)	3
2.1	Early U.S. Industrial Cities	26
3.2	The Louisville Waterfront Park Plan	57
4.2	Liberal, Neoliberal, Conservative, and Progressive Ideology in Planning	73
5.2	Complexity in Cities (CIC) Theory and the COVID-19 Pandemic	102
6.2	Ecotopia	125
7.2	The *NashvilleNext Plan* (Nashville, Tennessee)	139
8.2	The Columbia Pike Form-Based Code and Plan (Arlington, Virginia)	169
9.1	The Dudley Street Neighborhood Initiative	186
10.2	The *Metro 2040 Concept Plan* (Portland, Oregon)	219
10.3	The *Vibrant Northeast Ohio 2040 Plan*	221
11.1	Jabodetabek: The Jakarta, Indonesia Megaregion	240
12.2	The Cabrini–Green Homes and Pruitt–Igoe Public Housing Projects	261
12.4	Pike Place Market (Seattle, Washington)	275
13.2	The San Francisco Bay Conservation and Development Commission	304
14.2	Magnetic Levitation and Hyperloops	331
16.1	SteelStacks Arts and Cultural Center (Bethlehem, Pennsylvania)	375
17.2	Davis, California's *Climate Action and Adaptation Plan*	412

BIOGRAPHIES

1.2	Jane Jacobs	10	10.1	Catherine Ross	216
2.2	Patrick Geddes	35	11.2	Eugenie Birch	243
3.1	Kevin Lynch	49	12.1	Ann Forsyth	251
4.1	Julian Castro	71	12.3	Catherine Bauer	273
5.1	John Friedmann	89	13.1	Ian McHarg	295
6.1	Ebenezer Howard	111	14.1	Janette Sadik-Khan	319
7.1	T.J. (Jack) Kent	134	15.1	Robert Weaver	358
8.1	Allan Jacobs	156	16.2	Peter Hall	383
8.3	Gary Hack	171	17.1	Kongjian Yu	403
9.2	June Thomas	190			

ABOUT THE AUTHOR

Richard LeGates is Professor Emeritus of Urban Studies and Planning at San Francisco State University where he taught for 40 years before retiring in 2010. He served as Department Chair for 12 years. He was Summit Professor of Urban Planning at Tongji University in Shanghai from 2015 to 2017.

As a visiting professor he has taught at the University of California, Berkeley's Department of City and Regional Planning, Stanford University's Urban Studies Program, Renmin University of China's Department of Urban Planning and Management, the American University of Sharjah's Urban Planning Department in the United Arab Emirates, and Charles University's Geography Department in Prague, Czech Republic.

Professor LeGates is the co-editor with Frederic Stout of *The City Reader*—an urban studies and planning anthology first published in 1995 and now in its seventh edition (Routledge, 2020), the author of *Think Globally, Act Regionally: GIS and Data Visualization for Social Science and Public Policy Research* (ESRI Press, 2005), co-author with ZHANG Li and ZHAO Min of *Understanding Chinese Urbanization* (Edward Elgar Press, 2016), and co-author with Yumin YE of *Coordinating Urban and Rural Development: Learning from Chengdu* (Edward Elgar Press, 2013). He is the co-editor with Frederic Stout of the *Routledge Urban Reader Series*—ten anthologies related to urban studies, urban and regional planning, urban design, global cities, sustainable urban development, cities of the global south, city cultures, cybercities, urban geography, urban sociology, and urban politics published between 2003 and 2020. He co-edited a ten-volume series of reprints of classic books and articles on the history of city and regional planning titled *Early Urban Planning 1890 to 1950* with Frederic Stout.

Professor LeGates has published articles in the *Journal of the American Planning Association*, *Journal of Planning Education and Research*, *Journal of Urban Affairs*, *Habitat International*, *Cities*, *The Urban Lawyer*, and *Urban Law Annual*. Two articles co-authored with ZHANG Tingwei that were published in Chinese in *Urban Planning Forum* won the Urban Planning Society of China and the Jin Jingchang Urban Planning Education Foundation award as the third-best article in a Chinese urban planning journal in 2007 and the best article in 2009.

Professor LeGates received a U.S. National Science Foundation Course, Curriculum, and Laboratory Improvement/

Figure 0.1 Richard LeGates.

Educational Materials Development (CCLI-EMD) grant from 2003 to 2008 to develop teaching materials on spatial analysis and data visualization.

He has received research support from the United States Department of Housing and Urban Development, the California Legislature, the California State Department of Housing and Community Development, the Ford Foundation, the Rockefeller Foundation, the San Francisco Foundation, the Brookings Institution, the Higher Education Funding Council of England, Renmin University of China, and Tongji University. In 2015 he was Writer in Residence at the Rockefeller Foundation's Villa Serbelloni in Como, Italy.

Professor LeGates served as a Fulbright Senior Specialist at the University of Leicester, University College London, and University of Dundee, Scotland in 2006, the American University of Sharjah, United Arab Emirates in 2010, and the Technical Institute of Bandung, Indonesia, in 2012. In 2007 he taught a summer class to Erasmus Programme students at Charles University in Prague.

Professor LeGates was the first person to receive a joint Master's of City and Regional Planning (MCRP) degree from the University of California's Department of City and Regional Planning (1969) and Doctor of Laws degree (JD) (1968) from Berkeley Law School in 1969 when the University of California, Berkeley's joint MCRP/JD degree program was just beginning. He is a member of the California Bar. He graduated cum laude from Harvard in 1965 with a BA in Government, specializing in International Relations.

Professor LeGates welcomes feedback on this book. His e-mail address is: dlegates@sfsu.edu.

ADVANCE PRAISE

"Richard LeGates has written the most complete and comprehensive survey of city and regional planning by any author in the past twenty years. It will be the standard for the coming decades." Michael Teitz, Professor Emeritus of City and Regional Planning, University of California, Berkeley, USA

"LeGates has perfectly captured city and regional planning in its many applications from local to global and offers an excellent portrait of the international scope of urbanization from the past to the present." Eugenie Birch, Lawrence C. Nussdorf Professor of Urban Research and Education, University of Pennsylvania, USA

"This book is a refreshing, inclusionary, beautifully illustrated, and readable overview of a complex profession. It pays special attention to important issues of social inequality and justice." June Thomas, Professor Emerita of Urban Planning, University of Michigan, USA

"Eminent planning scholar Richard LeGates presents a beautifully crafted story of city and regional planning that will fascinate planning students worldwide. Full of masterly insights, this book is a planners' must-read." Ben Davy, Professor of Land Policy, Land Management, and Municipal Geoinformation, Technical University of Dortmund (retired); President of the Association of European Schools of Planning, 2017–2021

"This wide-ranging volume offers undergraduate and graduate students an overview that is U.S.-focused but globally engaged; historically grounded yet attuned to recent exemplary practice; concentrated on places, projects, policies, and techniques, yet aware of human agency." Lawrence Vale, Ford Professor of Urban Design and Planning, Massachusetts Institute of Technology, USA

"I can think of no better way to learn about the state of the art of designing and planning cities than Richard LeGates's *City and Regional Planning* textbook. It explains concisely the techniques planners use in creating and improving the quality of places, and offers avenues for further study to those who wish to pursue subjects in greater depth." Gary Hack, Professor Emeritus of Urban Design, Massachusetts Institute of Technology and University of Pennsylvania, USA

"*City and Regional Planning* is a very timely, refreshing text on solving complex contemporary urban challenges including climate change. LeGates's textbook will appeal to planners in Australia and New Zealand, as well as the USA and other countries." Professor Barbara Norman, Chair and Professor of Urban and Regional Planning, University of Canberra, Australia

"LeGates's broad overview of key planning concepts is readily accessible and engaging, laying the groundwork for both an informed planner and thoughtful citizen." Margaret Wilder, Executive Director, Urban Affairs Association, USA

"The editor of seven editions of *City and Regional Planning*, Richard LeGates has long been a leader in charting the domain of planning knowledge. In *City and Regional Planning*, LeGates thoughtfully articulates the history and current practice of urban planning in accessible language aiming to engage a new generation of planners." Ann Forsyth, Professor of Urban Planning, Harvard University, USA

"This sweeping introduction to American urban planning by one of the field's most perceptive observers does a wonderful job of highlighting key issues and debates. The up-to-date material on sustainable urban development and climate action planning is a welcome addition." Steven Wheeler, Professor of Human Ecology, University of California, Davis, USA

"Richard LeGates investigates the complete history of city and regional planning thoroughly in this milestone encyclopedic book. It will be a source of inspiration for many generations of planners." Fulong Wu, Bartlett Professor of Planning, University College London, UK

"*City and Regional Planning* is a veritable almanac of American planning from 1607 to the present, covering landmarks in styles, approaches, theories, visions, visionaries, scholars and scholarship, and much more. LeGates's wide experience as an international and interdisciplinary writer, teacher, and practitioner lends authority at every turn. The reader has the sense of being taken on an epic tour through a vast and rather overwhelming city by someone who sees significance in each of its buildings and spaces, and uses their stories to explain how the city started and what may become of it. Superb." Chris Webster, Dean, Faculty of Architecture; Chair Professor in Urban Planning and Development Economics, University of Hong Kong

"This long overdue textbook is a gift for planning students, educators, and scholars in Australia, China, and other countries—developed or developing. For the first time, it places urban planning and design in a global context and makes planning theory and practice accessible worldwide. The exhaustive and up-to-date references are a wonderful resource." Richard Hu, Professor of Urban Planning and Design; Director, Globalization and Cities Research Program, University of Canberra, Australia

"LeGates integrates planning scholarship and practice better than any previous text, across the full range of planning topics and issues. It is a major step forward in introducing the field." Michael Hibbard, Professor Emeritus of Planning, Public Policy, and Management, University of Oregon, USA

"An energetic, fact-filled overview of contemporary challenges combined with a wide-ranging survey of planning past and present. LeGates's accessible text reinforces crucial interconnections with broader social imperatives of sustainability, equity, and respect." Robert Freestone, Professor of Planning, University of New South Wales, Australia

"Professor LeGates's *City and Regional Planning* is a masterpiece. Its intellectual depth and clear explanations will make it an indispensable reference for academics in China and everywhere in the global south as well as the global north." Bo Qin, Professor of Urban Planning and Management, Renmin University of China

"This book is a comprehensive panorama of city and regional planning by a highly qualified author with a longstanding track record of seminal collections in urban studies." Ali

Madanipour, Professor of Urban Design; Director of the Global Urban Research Unit (GURU) at Newcastle University, UK

"*City and Regional Planning* covers all the concepts and knowledge an urban planning student needs to know. Understanding how urban planning has evolved in the United States will provide students in other parts of the world a framework to understand the evolution of urban planning concepts and systems in their own city." Anthony Yeh, Chair Professor, Department of Urban Planning and Design, University of Hong Kong; Founding Secretary General of the Asian Planning Schools Association

"Professor LeGates has produced a remarkably readable, detailed, and useful textbook for everyone studying urban planning, urban design, and all related academic fields. With admirable clarity and precision, he captures the full scope of how planning cities and urban regions guides the ongoing development of human civilization. It is a magisterial contribution to our understanding of the history, theory, and best practices of an enormously consequential profession." Frederic Stout, Lecturer in Urban Studies, Program on Urban Studies, Stanford University, USA

"*City and Regional Planning* provides an excellent introduction to the rapidly evolving field of city and regional planning. Its rich collection of international examples provides readers current planning ideas and paradigms, new roles for planners and communities, and the diversity of specialized programs and practices in internationally unique contexts." Sun Sheng Han, Professor of Urban Planning, University of Melbourne, Australia

"An essential starting-point for anyone wanting to understand the American planning system, including the history and theory behind why we plan, and the difficult planning challenges facing communities today. LeGates's textbook provides impressive depth and detail on the key issues facing cities today. I can't think of another single volume that so effectively and fully delivers what planners need to know." Timothy Beatley, Teresa Heinz Professor of Sustainable Communities, School of Architecture, University of Virginia, USA

"This text addresses the foundations of city and regional problems brilliantly, but also what planning should be, which is the art and science of effecting change." Ivis Garcia, Assistant Professor of City and Metropolitan Planning, University of Utah, Australia

"Our views of city planning originate from the observations and the writings of the early pioneers such as Patrick Geddes and Lewis Mumford. LeGates does a magnificent job in setting the contemporary development of city and regional planning with respect to this history. *City and Regional Planning* is built around the way urbanists and planners have developed their science and art in response to the evolution of cities. It is a wonderful description of the challenges facing society in dealing with contemporary problems of urbanism." Michael Batty, Chair, Centre for Advanced Spatial Analysis, University College London, UK

"Richard LeGates's textbook synthesizes an entire urban and regional planning curriculum maintaining a thoughtful theoretical and social justice perspective that elevates it into a platform for many scholarly debates. A true magnum opus." Rachelle Alterman, Professor Emerita of Planning and Law, Technion—Israel Institute of Technology, Israel

"LeGates captures the robust scope of urban planning from urban sprawl to climate change. Biographical briefs punctuate the narrative with exemplary tales showing how individual contributions matter. Passionate artistry and cool analysis combine to make good plans for places." Charles Hoch, Professor Emeritus of Urban Planning and Public Affairs, University of Illinois at Chicago, USA

"This comprehensive journey through the history and contemporary practices of city and regional planning offers insights for us all. A must-read for students of planning worldwide." Matthew Carmona, Professor of Planning and Urban Design, The Bartlett, University College London, UK

"This book is more than a 'must-read' for anyone who wants to see the enormous diversity of the planning discipline presented in its context. It tells the story with ease, elegantly drawing its path dependence and presenting the fine balance between all the issues that matter, including complexity, non-linearity and transformation, the latest advances in the field." Gert de Roo, Professor of Spatial Planning, University of Groningen, the Netherlands

"*City and Regional Planning* will be of interest to both students and practitioners of urban and regional planning, and to the general public who want to understand how planning impacts their lives and communities. It will be of interest to people outside of the USA who want to understand the American planning system." Penny Gurstein, Professor of Community and Regional Planning, University of British Columbia, Canada

"In this introductory textbook, Richard LeGates incorporates all of the genre's desired qualities: extensive coverage of the field, general concepts accompanied by concrete examples and illustrations, easy-to-read and up-to-date text, and succinct descriptions of substantive interests and procedural concerns. This book is a welcome introduction for those considering a career in city and regional planning." Robert A. Beauregard, Professor Emeritus of Urban Planning, Columbia University, USA

"A comprehensive view of what city and regional planners do in that part of the world (the USA) that has influenced planning internationally, and a source for reflection for southern planners." Vanessa Watson, Professor of City Planning, University of Cape Town, South Africa

"*City and Regional Planning* now for the first time provides an extensive integration of the work of the Association of Collegiate Schools of Planning's Planners of Color Interest Group on a range of challenges facing workplaces, institutions, and communities, racial equity-based policy solutions and culturally competent community planning." April Jackson, Associate Professor of Urban Planning and Policy, University of Illinois at Chicago, USA

"*City and Regional Planning* is an excellent addition to the literature on city and regional planning theory and practice in the United States. It provides a solid basis for scholars and planners in Canada and other countries who wish to undertake a comparative analysis to other planning systems." David Amborski, Professor of Urban and Regional Planning, Ryerson University, Canada

ACKNOWLEDGEMENTS

Many people provided advice, encouragement, and information without which this book would not have been possible.

My deepest gratitude is to my wife, Joanne Fraser LeGates, who encouraged and supported this three-year project, and carefully read and critiqued every chapter. Joanne's constant insistence that I simplify and clarify the text and ruthless editing are reflected in every page of the book.

Kate Schell and Sean Speers at Routledge who enthusiastically tackled a much longer and more complex planning book than usual and patiently guided me through Routledge's editorial process. Megha Patel, a Routledge editorial assistant, meticulously prepared the manuscript for production, Graham Frankland who did a first-rate job of copyediting the manuscript, and Adam Guppy whom guided the book through the production process.

Special thanks are due to colleagues who provided inspiration and advice on the manuscript and critiqued draft chapters. Professor Michael Hibbard a Professor of Urban Planning, Public Policy, and Management at the University of Oregon carefully reviewed the entire manuscript. Alex Schwartz, a Professor of Urban Policy at the New School, provided much of the information in the housing chapter. Tom Jacobson, a Professor of Urban and Environmental Planning at Sonoma State University, critiqued the plan implementation and environmental planning chapters. Roger Caves, Professor of City Planning at San Diego State University, provided invaluable guidance from the earliest formulation of how to organize the book through successive drafts of many chapters.

I am grateful to many people who took time out of their busy schedules to carefully read and mark up parts of the book and provided ideas, references, and corrections by e-mail, phone, and Zoom meetings. Carl Abbot (University of Oregon), Jim Buckley (University of Oregon), Scott Campbell (University of Michigan), William Issel (San Francisco State University), Deborah and Phillip LeVeen (San Francisco State University), David Morley (American Planning Association), Nelson Peng (Calthorpe Associates), Jasper Rubin (San Francisco State University), and Frederic Stout (Stanford University) read and critiqued multiple draft chapters in their areas of expertise. Courtney LeGates provided insightful advice on Chapter 9, and Rebecca LeGates offered advice on book design.

I extend my heartfelt gratitude to others who provided advice and reviewed materials including Roger Alford (Metro, Portland, Oregon), Shlomo Angel (New York University), Jonathan Barnett (University of Pennsylvania), Michael Batty (University College London), Timothy Beatley (University of Virginia), BO Qin (Renmin University of China), Erin Bradford (University of North Carolina Library), Maggie Brownstone (Hargreaves Associates), Fernando Burga (University of Minnesota), Gloria Chin (Regional Plan Association of America), Christina Day (planokc, Oklahoma City, Oklahoma), David Eifler (University of California, Berkeley), Fred Etzel (University of California, Berkeley), Brian Falk (Center for Applied Transect Studies), Anthony Flint (Lincoln Land Institute), John Forester (Cornell University), Ann Forsyth (Harvard University), Robert Freestone (University of New South Wales), Ivis Garcia

(University of Utah), Edward Goetz (University of Minnesota), Gary Hack (University of Pennsylvania and the Massachusetts Institute of Technology), Molla Hadley (University of California, Berkeley), Chester Harvey (University of California, Berkeley), April Jackson (Florida State University), Allan Jacobs (University of California, Berkeley), Tom Jacobsen (California State University, Sonoma), Christina Kata (Regional Plan Association), Michael Larice (University of California, Berkeley), Ali Madanipour (Newcastle University), Robin McElhey (Harvard University Archives), Beth McMahon (Canadian Instiute of Planners), Ali Modarres (University of Washington, Tacoma), Christina Paul (Petaluma, California Planning Department), Rolf Pendall (University of Chicago Champaign-Urbana), Zhang-Ren Peng (University of Florida), Roberta Rewers (American Planning Association), Sandra Rosenbloom (University of Texas, Austin), Catherine Ross (Georgia Institute of Technology), Jasper Rubin (San Francisco State University), Bill Siembieda (California State Polytechnic Institute, San Luis Obispo), Chris Silver (University of Florida), Nick Smith (Barnard College), Mark Twedyr-Jones (University College London), June Thomas (University of Michigan), Steven Ward (Oxford Brookes University), Sarah Weber (planokc, Oklahoma City, Oklahoma), Chris Webster (University of Hong Kong), Steven Wheeler (University of California, Davis), Karna Wong (University of California, Los Angeles), and Anthony YE (University of Hong Kong).

Thanks also to the many people who helped identify figures and generously granted permission to use their photographs, maps, tables, and data graphics. Tara Singh (University of California, Berkeley) drew the data graphics. Anna Ma prepared several figures and helped with technical issues with the text and figures. Others who assisted with the figures include Matthew Arielly (Saski Associates), Michael Batty (University College London), Catherine Brinkley (University of California, Davis), Anna Chu at the Forum News Group, Gary Claxton (Metropolitan Government of Nashville and Davidson County Planning Department), Siobhan Donnelly at the Artists Rights Society, Katherine Eschel and Stacia Sheputa at Boston City government, Brian Falk (Center for Applied Transect Studies), Larry Goldzband at the San Francisco Bay Conservation and Development Commission, Justin Helm (Saint Francis Square Cooperative Apartments Inc.), Charles Hoch (University of Illinois, Chicago), Paul Jutton, Stephen Staudigl, Laura Griggs, Kim Cooper-Hart, and Geoffrey Butler at the National Capital Planning Commission, Sylvia Lew (Saint Francis Square Cooperative Apartments Inc.), Elizabeth Macdonald (University of California, Berkeley), Robin McCallum at the University of California, Los Angeles Department of City and Regional Planning, Helen Meller (Montpellier, France), Aya Satoh (Massachusetts Institute of Technology Press), Nelson Peng at HDC Partners, Pamela Quick (Massachusetts Institute of Technology Press), Kathleen Richards at the City of Henderson, Nevada, Christine Sala at Avery Drawings & Archives at the Columbia University Library, Seth Solomonow (Bloomberg Associates), Margo Stipe and Frederick Prozzillo at the Frank Lloyd Wright Foundation, Allison Stoddard (National Archives of Scotland at George IV Bridge, Edinburgh), Roseanne Tye (Geddes Centre), Luis Vasquez (Boston Housing Authority), YU Kongjian (Turenscape), and Margaret Wilson at the National Museum of Scotland Image Library.

Richard LeGates, Oakland, California, January 2022

CHAPTER 1

The Art and Science of City and Regional Planning

INTRODUCTION

In Chicago, city and regional planners are helping low-income residents of public housing projects move to affordable housing in neighborhoods of their choosing. In New York City they are implementing plans for a million cool roofs to mitigate the impact of global warming. In Portland, Oregon, planners manage a regional urban limit line to control urban sprawl. In Savannah, Georgia, they protect historic neighborhood parks that were laid out in the 1730s. Planners are working to revitalize older neighborhoods in Akron, Ohio and to design lively streetscapes in Miami, Florida using innovative form-based codes that visually illustrate them. Planners are at work on hundreds of coastal zone management plans, and thousands of bicycle plans, environmental impact statements, city and county general plans, habitat conservation plans, and plans for replacing coal- and oil-powered energy plants with clean ones using solar and wind energy that emit no greenhouse gases (GHGs).

What links all of these disparate and exciting activities is a distinct way of thinking, and a body of theory and practice on both the art and science of city and regional planning.

SCIENTIFIC AND CREATIVE PLANNING THINKING

City and regional planners sometimes view planning as primarily requiring rational scientific thinking, and sometimes view it as primarily requiring creative, artistic thinking. A recurring theme in this book is that both are important in city and regional planning.

The scientific method was developed first in the natural sciences—physics, chemistry, and biology—during the Enlightenment, a period of intense exploration of natural phenomena that began in the 17th century. It is based on empiricism—the theory of knowledge that holds that knowledge comes from sensory experience and close observation of real-world phenomena rather than *a priori* reasoning (reasoning independent of experience), intuition, or faith.

Modern planning emerged as a professional field in England and the United States in the early 20th century. The first U.S. National Conference on City Planning took place in 1909. At that time creative, artistic city-planning-as-civic-architecture-writ-large approaches dominated the field. Most members of the nascent planning profession called themselves civic designers.

A minority view of city-planning-as-science immediately challenged the conception of city planning as an art. George B. Ford (1879–1930)—a municipal engineer and city planner—led the "city scientific" movement from the early 20th century until his death in 1930. At the fifth national U.S. planning conference in 1913, Ford famously declared that "city planning is rapidly becoming as definite a science as pure engineering".

By the 1950s, scientific thinking was dominant in city and regional planning, and creative thinking approaches receded. Planning professors taught their students to gather and analyze data, specify alternatives, and then select "the best" alternative based on the rational planning model. Planners drew on systems analysis. Quantitative geographers developed location theory and input–output

DOI: 10.4324/9781003195818-1

analysis to help planners understand and guide the location of economic activities. Planners began to use computers to model traffic, land use, and other urban systems on huge, clunky mainframe computers.

In the late 1960s and 1970s the pendulum swung back away from planning as a science. First-generation computer models did not deliver on the promise of scientific transportation and land use planning.

In the 1960s and 1970s, some planning theorists turned to theory developed by Karl Marx (1818–1883) and Friedrich Engels (1820–1895) for a thorough critique of capitalist society and capitalism-serving planning. They are referred to as neo-Marxists (neo- means "new" in Latin). Appalled by the war in Vietnam and racial turmoil in American cities, neo-Marxist planners urged all city and regional planners to critique capitalism and address normative issues of equity and social justice rather than advance city and regional planning as either an art or a science.

By the 1990s the pendulum swung back towards scientific planning using geographical information systems (GIS) software and improved modeling. At the same time, improvements in computer-assisted design (CAD) reinvigorated the creative approach to planning. A new, more powerful brand of urban design emerged.

Today a promising new science of cities is developing. Microcomputers with vastly more memory, better software, and much easier-to-use graphical user interfaces (GUIs) have overcome many of the technical limitations of early computers. Transportation and land use models have improved. Big data and new analytics make it possible to mine vast amounts of information and analyze it in complex new ways. City and regional planners now routinely use computerized statistical packages like the Statistical Package for the Social Sciences (SPSS) and Stata, computer-assisted design (CAD) software like AutoCAD, Rhino 3D,

a) Peak Hour Demand on the London Tube

b) Peak Hour Supply of Tube Trains

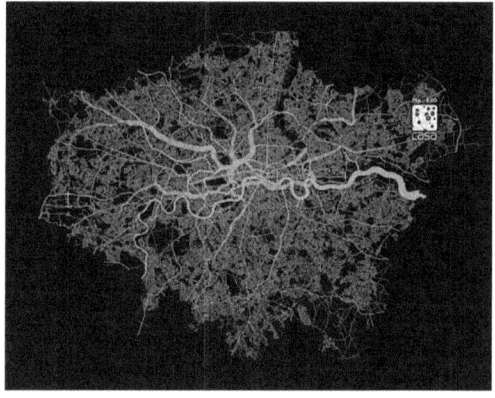
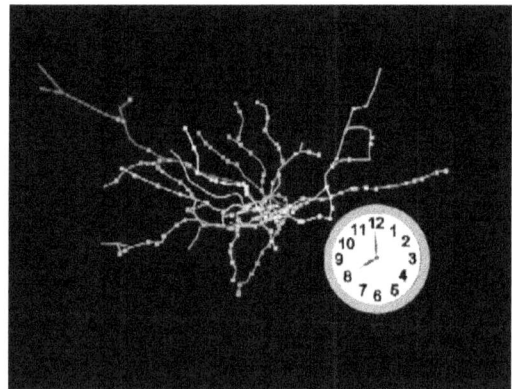

c) The Trains Network Including the Tube

d) One of Many Geotagged Flickr Networks

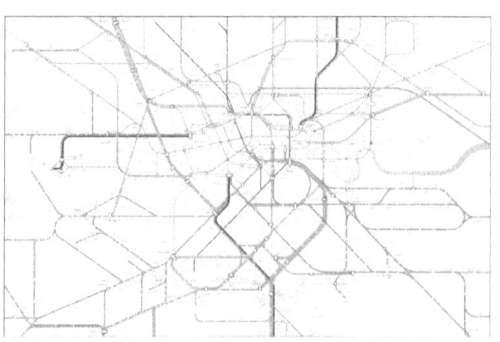
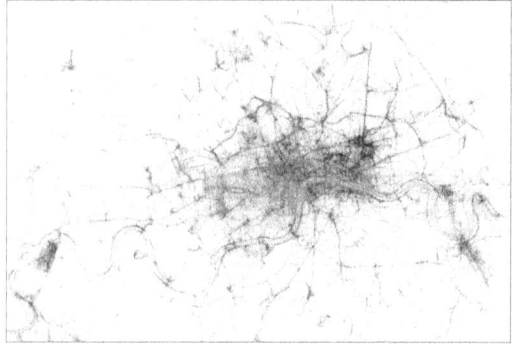

Figure 1.1 Multiple Flows: London Tube, Rail, and Flickr Networks.

Figure 1.2 Urban Design Concept for South Capitol Street, Washington, D.C.

and SketchUp, and GIS software like ArcGIS. Tools and theory based on the artistic approach to planning are also thriving today. Augmented and virtual reality, animations, and complex 3D CAD drawings are both useful and easy for clients to understand.

London's Centre for Advanced Spatial Analysis (CASA) illustrates these exciting developments in quantitative city and regional planning. Box 1.1 describes CASA.

Figures 1.1 and 1.2 illustrate scientific and artistic city and regional planning. Figure 1.1 shows visualizations of peak hour supply and demand for London tube (subway) trains in relation to London's existing trains network and Flickr networks. Flickr is an online photo management application that allows individuals to share photographs. Figure 1.1 was created by Michael Batty at University College London's Centre for Advanced Spatial Analysis (CASA). Figure 1.2 is a rendering of an urban design concept for South Capitol Street in Washington, D.C. by the National Capital Planning Commission.

BOX 1.1 THE CENTRE FOR ADVANCED SPATIAL ANALYSIS (CASA)

The Centre for Advanced Spatial Analysis (CASA) at the Bartlett School, University College London (UCL), has been a leading interdisciplinary center for developing and applying new technology and new analytics to city and regional planning since 1995.

CASA plays a central role in advancing the "new science of cities"; building concepts and tools to use new digital technologies in planning; and developing methods in modeling, complexity, visualization, and computation that can exploit big data in real time.

CASA's research is multidisciplinary. Staff and students at CASA include city and regional planners, geographers, mathematicians, physicists, architects, and computer scientists. Despite developing sophisticated theory, CASA prides itself on applied research. It produces findings and tools that are widely used. It illustrates the way in which geographical information systems and city and regional planning can mesh.

In 2020 as well as projects involving its core mission to develop a new science of cities, CASA had a dozen active projects including: (a) emergency work on the COVID-19 pandemic, (b) an ongoing urban dynamics laboratory, (c) creating a memory map of the Jewish East End of London, (d) designing a website on the history of the Whitechapel neighborhood in London in collaboration with artist and writer Rachel Lichtenstein and others, (e) studies with Transport for London on freight traffic delivery schedules, algorithms, and business models to improve carrier coordination and reduce energy demands, (f) a study with the African Centre for Population Health mapping HIV/AIDS in real time, (g) a project named "Colouring London" with the UK Ordnance Survey to gather crowd-sourced data on building age, use, type size, designation status, and rebuild history coded into 12 colors in order to create a useful and easy-to-understand interactive digital map of London for the general public, and (h) a project with the Bodleian Library at Oxford University and the Victoria and Albert Museum of Childhood to integrate accounts of play from 20,000 UK children in the 1950s and 1960s and interviews of the study participants (now in their 70s) to better understand how physical games, rituals, songs, and chants are passed on from one generation to the next in different cultures, and how children use play to negotiate membership of communities and their place within them. The information will be used to help design two experimental playgrounds that incorporate smart objects linking physical play to historic objects in the archives of libraries.

CASA receives its funding from the UK Government, European Union (EU), national governments, local governments in the UK and Europe, research councils, and charitable foundations. It collaborates with government organizations such as Transport for London—London's Transportation Agency—and the UK Ordnance Survey—the UK'S census and mapping agency—other universities, neighborhood groups, planning practitioners and artists. In addition to its research projects, CASA offers PhD and master's degree programs and engages in applied consulting projects.

U.S. city and regional planning departments learn from CASA's experiments. Many academic and applied planning entities worldwide send some of their best staff to study at CASA and incorporate the knowledge they bring back into their ongoing operations.

WHAT IS CITY AND REGIONAL PLANNING?

Planning is a pervasive human activity. Individuals, corporations, governments, and nonprofit organizations all plan to a greater or lesser extent, more or less consciously. Definitions of planning emphasize thought before action, systematic thinking, a process continuum, and the linkage between plans and actions.

City and regional planners constitute only a small percentage of all planners. In neo-liberal capitalist countries—countries that favor private market solutions rather than government planning—most planning is strategic and economic planning that takes place in the private sector. Big aerospace, automobile, and high-tech companies and the military employ hundreds or thousands of planners.

Public domain institutions like the United States Department of Housing and Urban Development (HUD), the U.S. Environmental Protection Agency (EPA), and the U.S. Office of Management and Budget (OMB) make plans related to their missions in areas such as urban revitalization, protecting the natural environment, and policy for funding urban programs. National, state, regional, and local governments make plans about everything from filling potholes in local streets to fracking oil shale by injecting water, sand, and chemicals under enormous pressure to release oil and gas deposits. Private corporations and nonprofit agencies make all manner of plans to guide their activities.

Cities and regions perform different functions that require very different types of plans. Omaha, Nebraska is dominated by the insurance industry, Mountain View, California's economy is based on high tech companies, and Anaheim, California and Orlando, Florida by Disneylands. Planning for Fayetteville, North Carolina adjacent to the giant Fort Bragg military base is very different from planning for a university town like Ann Arbor, Michigan, cities in agricultural regions, retirement communities, or mining towns.

In the *Encyclopedia Britannica* Harvard professor of city and regional planning, Susan Fainstein (2021), offers one of the best definitions of urban planning:

> [Urban planning is the] design and regulation of the uses of space that focus on the physical form, economic functions, and social impacts of the urban environment and on the location of different activities within it. Because urban planning draws upon engineering, architectural, and social and political concerns, it is variously a technical profession, an endeavor involving political will and public participation, and an academic discipline.

PLANNERS' ROLES

According to the United States Bureau of Labor Statistics (BLS), urban planners mainly do the following nine things:

- Meet with public officials, developers, and the public regarding development plans and land use;
- Administer government plans or policies affecting land use;
- Gather and analyze data from market research, censuses, and economic and environmental studies;
- Conduct field investigations to analyze factors affecting community development and decline, including land use;
- Review site plans submitted by developers;
- Assess the feasibility of proposals and identify needed changes;
- Recommend whether proposals should be approved or denied;
- Present projects to communities, planning officials, and planning commissions; and
- Stay current on zoning and building codes, environmental regulations, and other legal issues.

Planning jobs require people with a range of skills. Large planning organizations need analysts, designers, political strategists, and staff with technical and people skills. There are jobs for people with backgrounds and passion in transportation, land use, environment, climate change, housing, social justice, recycling, historic preservation, economic development, the arts, and other specialties.

THE CITY AND REGIONAL PLANNING PROFESSION

City and regional planning is a relatively small, new, rapidly growing profession. It is arguably evolving from a minor profession like secondary education or social work to a major profession like medicine, law, and engineering.

Planners working exclusively at the city, district, or neighborhood scale are commonly referred to as city planners. Planners working in geographic areas larger than the political boundaries of a city such as a metropolitan area or a wilderness area may be called regional planners. Planners working in rural areas, villages, and small towns are often identified as rural planners. The term city and regional planner reflects the reality that many planners blend roles or shift from one planning role and one scale to another.

The U.S. Bureau of Labor Statistics (BLS) enumerated 39,100 urban and regional planners—their term for city and regional planners—employed in the United States in 2019.[1]

About eighty percent of U.S. planners are White. Nearly half are women. The absolute number and percentage of city and regional planners in the United States who are women has increased rapidly in the last 30 years. A slight majority of planning students are women. People of color are underrepresented among students and in the planning profession. The Association of Collegiate Schools of Planning (ACSP) Planners of Color Interest Group (POCIG) and planning schools are working to increase the number of planners of color in academic degree programs, teaching in academia, and practicing in the planning profession. Since there were very few city and regional planners until recently, most planners are young. There are fewer mid- and late-career planners than practitioners in more established professions such as law and medicine.

Since most of the planning for cities and regions in the United States is done at the city and county level, many planners work for city or county planning departments. These are headed by a planning director reporting to a city or county planning commission, which in turn reports to the local city council or county board of commissioners as described in Chapter 4. Most staff of city and county planning departments are full-time civil servants protected by a local civil service commission.

The American Planning Association (APA) is the professional association of practicing city and regional planners for the United States.[2] It has 22 divisions including divisions for housing and community development, transportation planning, sustainable communities, technology and planning, and women and planning. The APA holds conferences, sets standards, publishes the *Journal of the American Planning Association*, and works to advance the theory and practice of city and regional planning. The Planning Accreditation Board (PAB) accredits city and regional planning degree programs in the United States. The PAB may also accredit Canadian planning programs. However as of Spring, 2022 the University of British Columbia was the only PAB-accredited planning program in Canada. The Canadian Institute of Planners (CIP) performs a role similar to APA. Canada has its own standards and processes for accrediting Canadian City and Regional Planning programs independent of PAB.[3]

Practicing planners meet to discuss their professional interests and learn current planning practices from each other and outside experts at the APA's annual conference and meetings of 47 geographically based APA chapters. Their emphasis is on applied knowledge that will be directly useful to practicing planners. The APA's website has links to research reports; memos; QuickNotes prepared by the APA's Planning Advisory Service (PAS); a zoning practice archive; a research KnowledgeBase; policy guides; statements on equity, diversity, and inclusion and other material of use to practicing planners and planning students.

Practitioners in medicine, engineering and other professions must pass state professional licensing examinations to practice their profession. They often have to have additional training and must pass examinations to be licensed to practice a specialty like eye surgery or structural engineering. This is not true for planners. The APA has an institute which examines and credentials planners—the American Institute of Certified Planners (AICP). Successful applicants may describe themselves as certified planners.[4] However, with the exception of New Jersey, the AICP exam is not a legally required licensing exam. New Jersey is the only state that requires planners to have a state license to practice planning. The test for the New Jersey planning license is the AICP exam.

More than two-fifths (43%) of APA's members are AICP-certified. A small number of people who have distinguished themselves by service to the planning field are inducted into the AICP as Fellows of the American Institute of Certified Planning (FAICP). This is the AICP's highest honor.

Many states and many local planning departments encourage planners to be members of APA and AICP-certified because the APA and AICP provide members access to valuable training, planning resources, and the professional planning community that supports their work. Some city and county planning departments and other public and private sector employers give hiring preference to AICP-certified applicants.

The United States Bureau of Labor Statistics reports that the median annual salary for urban and regional planners in the United States is lower than salaries for architects, civil engineers, lawyers, or surgeons. Medians do not adequately describe salary distributions based on differences in planners' education level, years of experience, specialization, or the type of jurisdiction where they work. Salaries of planners with graduate degrees, AICP-certified planners, planners with years of experience, planners with strong quantitative and computer skills, and planners working in big city planning departments earn considerably higher salaries, which may be higher than some doctors, lawyers, or engineers.[5]

PLANNING EDUCATION

City and regional planning is taught at the graduate level, leading to a Master's of City and Regional Planning (MCRP) or similarly named degree, and the undergraduate level, leading to a BA or BS degree. In the United States most city and regional planning education takes place at the master's level. In other countries planning education is mostly at the undergraduate level. University departments of city and regional planning are generally located within professional schools or colleges that include architecture, city and regional planning, landscape architecture, and sometimes other professional fields such as construction management. Some are within schools of public policy or public affairs.

North American universities' city and regional planning curricula follow standards established by the Planning Accreditation Board (PAB).[6] The PAB requires planning programs to teach specified professional knowledge, skills, and values. It specifies topics that planning curricula must cover.[7] PAB standards require that each graduate student be educated as a generalist "able to demonstrate the knowledge, skills, and values necessary for competent professional planning in diverse occupational and institutional settings" (PAB, 2017). Core courses in accredited city and regional planning programs typically provide an overview of the field, planning history, statistics, research methods, planning theory, urban design, planning ethics, studio and other practicum courses, and a capstone thesis or final project course. They require students to complete elective courses on topics like land use, transportation, environmental planning, housing, community development, infrastructure, citizen participation, planning administration, modeling, and spatial analysis using GIS. Planning students can usually take planning-related elective courses taught in other departments.

The Association of Collegiate Schools of Planning (ACSP) is a consortium of North American university programs offering degrees in city and regional planning. As of 2021, 103 U.S. schools were full ACSP members, 19 academic units that offer planning degrees were corresponding members, and 20 schools in other countries were affiliate members. ACSP also includes individual and student members.[8] Just before the COVID pandemic about 1,000 people attended ACSP's annual conference.[9]

Tracks at ACSP conferences bring participants with common interests together to present and discuss scholarly papers and share information. ACSP publishes the *Journal of Planning Education and Research* and facilitates communication among its members via webpages, listservs, and newsletters. The ACSP website describes ACSP activities, specializations within the organization, and information about city and regional planning.[10]

An ACSP interest group—the Planners of Color Interest Group (POCIG)—advances the interests and concerns of people and communities of color within academia and the planning profession. Members of POCIG meet at annual ACSP conferences. POCIG maintains a website, compiles a book with resumes of people of color seeking faculty positions teaching planning, and funds one-year memberships to the National Center for Faculty Development and Diversity (NCFDD) for junior faculty of color. POCIG presents an award—the Edward Blakeley Award—named for distinguished Black scholar-practitioner Edward Blakeley.[11] The Blakeley Award honors scholars who support the cause of social justice—particularly in planning or development for communities of color. ACSP's Faculty Women's Interest Group (FWIG) performs a similar function for women in planning and a new ACSP interest group named INCLUSION PLUS performs a similar role for LGBTQ planners and their allies.

The Urban Affairs Association (UAA) is an organization of professionals whose work is closely related to city and regional planning.[12] Most UAA members were educated in political science or public administration. The UAA publishes the *Journal of Urban Affairs*.

There are nearly 200 English-language journals related to city and regional planning, urban affairs, and urban studies. Most are published in the United States. There are additional city and regional planning and related journals published in other languages.

The Planetizen website provides information on unfolding developments in city and regional planning. The Next City website also has links to many current city and regional planning topics.

City and regional planning is also taught in degree programs in urban design, geography, public policy, urban affairs and urban studies. Urban design is taught as a subfield within city and regional planning or architecture degree programs and in graduate urban design programs. There are sixteen Master's of Urban Design (MUD) programs in the United States, typically offering a degree called a Master's in Urban Design (MUD).

Many geography departments offer courses and some offer tracks, certificates, or degrees in city and regional planning. A small number of departments of fine arts and departments of public administration offer city and regional planning degrees.

Urban studies is an interdisciplinary field that teaches students about cities. Urban studies programs' curricula may include courses about the history, economics, politics, sociology, and culture of cities combined with courses in city and regional planning, urban design, transportation, environmental planning, and sometimes other urban-related courses in the social sciences, humanities, and architecture. Almost all U.S. urban studies programs are at the undergraduate level.

Other professions related to city and regional planning are architecture, landscape architecture, and civil engineering. They all have professional organizations similar to ACSP.[13] U.S. academic organizations of geographers, political scientists, sociologists, economists, historians, and anthropologists have interest groups for members interested in urban issues.[14]

PLANNING SPECIALIZATIONS

Almost all graduate U.S. city and regional planning programs offer planning specializations. The PAB does not require accredited planning programs to have any specializations. However, it provides guidelines for specializations and reviews and approves applications to certify specializations if they satisfy PAB guidelines.[15]

The number of city and regional planning specialties has grown as the field has expanded. A recent study by University of California, Davis Human Ecology Professor Catherine Brinkley and University of Illinois, Chicago Urban Planning Professor Charles Hoch concluded that in 2016 U.S. city and regional planning programs offered 332 different specializations, which Brinkley and Hoch clustered into 129 specialization themes. Nearly half of the 129 specialization themes that Brinkley and Hoch identified are unique and offered only in one university. The themes are as varied as golf course design, watershed management, sustainable food systems, and tribal planning. Figure 1.3

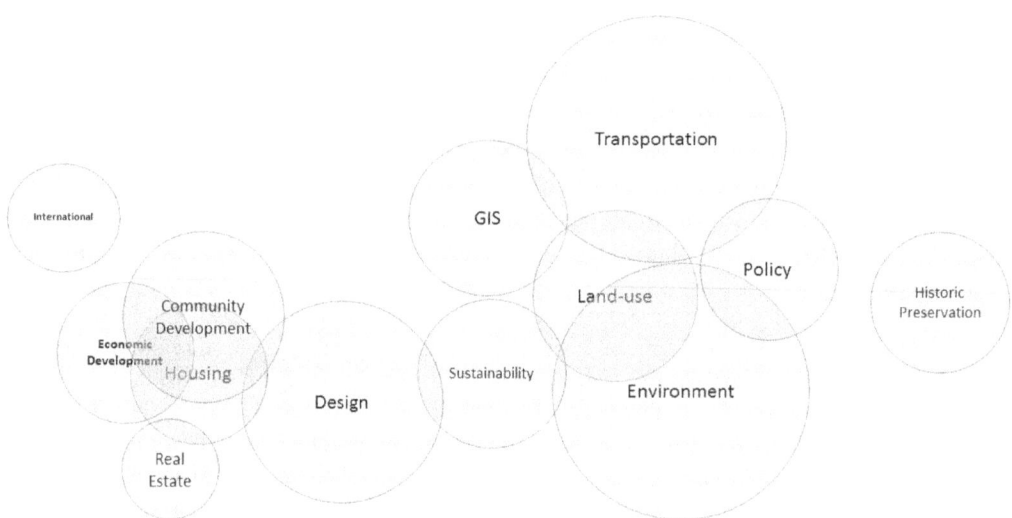

Figure 1.3 U.S. City and Regional Planning Specializations.

is a Venn diagram showing the frequency, alignment, and overlap among the 13 most common city and regional planning specialization themes. The size of the circles visually represents how many there are.

Some universities have graduate-level dual-degree programs, so that a student may complete a degree in city and regional planning and law, public health, civil engineering (most commonly in transportation), public policy, environmental studies, or another professional field. Some have dual-degree programs with foreign universities so that U.S. students can study abroad, and foreign students can study in the United States and receive degrees from both universities in less time than if they took the degrees sequentially.[16]

Until the 1960s most academic city and regional planning departments in the United States were staffed almost entirely by faculty with degrees in architecture. Now, many planning faculty have PhD degrees in city and regional planning or other disciplines and professional fields. A few have an advanced degree in one of the natural sciences.

Regardless of their background and education, planners—like other professionals—continue to develop their professional expertise on the job, learning from mentors and their own experience. They engage in self-education and perhaps structured lifelong learning. The American Institute of Certified Planners (AICP) requires certified planners to engage in 32 hours of professional development every two years by completing continuing education courses, attending conferences, or maintaining their certification in other ways.

CITY AND REGIONAL PLANNING RESEARCH AND ANALYTIC METHODS

The PAB requires accredited planning programs to teach research methods. Graduate planning students learn research methods in core and elective courses. They develop their research skills under faculty supervision, and must demonstrate proficiency in research in their thesis or capstone project. City and regional planning methods courses teach research design and quantitative and qualitative research methods developed in the social and natural sciences. Urban research designs often triangulate on research questions using an array of quantitative and qualitative social science and public policy research methods.

Quantitative research methods require using mathematics and statistics to analyze numeric data. Michael Batty's analysis of flows in the London tube network (Box 1.1) is an example.

Qualitative research methods rely on observation, interviews, and other methods that do not require numeric analysis. William Whyte's observations and time lapse photography of how people use public plazas and parks in New York City described in Chapter 3 is an example of skillful use of qualitative research methods.

Most city and regional planning programs' methods courses emphasize statistical analysis of quantitative data and spatial analysis methods. Almost all graduate planning programs in the United States require their students to take a course in descriptive and inferential statistics. Some offer a number of spatial analysis and modeling courses. These may include coursework on simulations and new methods to mine big data. A few offer a PAB-approved specialization in spatial analysis. Planning programs may introduce students to qualitative methods such as observation and archival research. A few planning students take an urban-oriented sociology or anthropology course in qualitative research methods.

Almost all planning students take some coursework in spatial analysis methods and learn how to generate two- and three-dimensional analytic maps from numerical values. They learn to use geographical information systems (GIS) software like the Environmental Systems Research Institute (ESRI)'s ArcGIS or public domain GIS software.

The way in which research results are presented is critical to how they are received. In addition to text, planners use PowerPoint presentations, images, tables, and data graphics to communicate their plans.

One good way to understand city and regional planning is by reading biographies of notable planners. Box 1.2 is a biography of Jane Jacobs.

BOX 1.2 JANE JACOBS

Jane Jacobs (1916–2006) was one of the most original and influential city planning thinkers of all time despite the fact that she hated planners. As an author, critic, activist, and lover of cities Jacobs had a profound influence on planning. The book that made her famous—*Death and Life of Great American Cities*—was a frontal attack on orthodox city and regional planning as it was practiced in the 1960s.

Jacobs was a superb empirical observer as well as a critic of scientific thinking. She carefully observed micro-level human interactions on Hudson Street in New York City's Greenwich Village where she lived, and used inductive reasoning to construct a body of bottom-up anti-planning theory, acerbic critiques, and common-sense prescriptions for better city and regional planning and urban design.

Jane Butzner was born in 1916 into a middle-class family in the mining city of Scranton, Pennsylvania. After graduating from high school, she moved to Greenwich Village in New York City in 1934—then a low-rent bohemian neighborhood—where she lived with her older sister, Betty. She began writing about New York City and eventually became the editor of *Iron Age*—a steel industry trade magazine.

During the Second World War Jacobs got a job as a feature writer for the U.S. Office of War Information, where she became the editor of *Amerika*—a magazine describing American life that was translated into Russian for distribution in the Soviet Union. The Soviet Union was then a U.S. ally. In 1944 she married Robert Hyde Jacobs, an architect, and changed her name to Jane Jacobs.

After World War II, Jacobs's journalism increasingly focused on architecture and planning, especially after she joined *Architectural Forum* magazine in 1952. A 1958 article in *Fortune* magazine titled "Downtown Is for People" caught the attention of the Rockefeller Foundation, which provided her a 3-year grant to write a book. The result—*Death and Life of Great American Cities*—was published in 1961. It became a bestseller. Jacobs became an icon. She devoted the rest of her life to writing and political activism. Mainstream planners worldwide have now embraced her ideas.

Jacobs (1961) conflated and condemned all planners, proclaiming: "As in the pseudoscience of bloodletting, just so in the pseudoscience of city rebuilding and planning, years of learning and a plethora of subtle and complicated dogma have arisen on a foundation of nonsense." She dismissed three of the most important city and regional planners—the modernist LeCorbusier, the inventor of the garden city Ebenezer Howard, and Daniel Burnham, the great American "city beautiful" planner. Despite the fact that they were famous and their ideas were radically different from each other, Jacobs lumped the three together as "radiant garden city beautiful" planners! She dismissed all of their ideas as useless or counterproductive.

Jacobs argued that over-scaling, superblocks, uniformity, and concern only with efficiency were causing the death of cities. In contrast she argued that humane, livable, messy, largely unplanned working-class urban areas like New York City's Greenwich Village, near the tip of Manhattan, where she lived, were full of life. Greenwich Village had a comfortable neighborhood scale, mixed land uses, and a diverse population. The neighborhood had lively streets and sidewalks, affordable restaurants, and community-serving businesses. As a result, flows of residents and regular and periodic visitors of all ages and occupations were out and about in the neighborhood from early morning until late at night. This included what Jacobs called a diurnal "street ballet" as people went about their morning and late afternoon routines, provided "eyes on the street"—which Jacobs argued reduced crime—and a friendly and stimulating human environment.

Jacobs's second notable accomplishment was leading grassroots movements in New York City to stop large-scale highway and urban renewal projects by New York

City's power broker, Robert Moses. Moses held no elective office, but made most of the important planning decisions for New York cities for over four decades from the mid-1920s through the 1960s.

The late 1950s and 1960s were the high point of the federal urban renewal program—which cleared entire low-income neighborhoods—and the national federal-aid highway program that provoked a "highway revolt" in which angry citizens organized to stop segments of highways that disrupted urban neighborhoods. Moses was an enthusiastic practitioner of urban renewal and highway building in New York City and the New York City region.

Jacobs's Greenwich Village neighborhood and other New York neighborhoods she loved were threatened by Moses's urban renewal and highway projects. She became a principal voice in neighborhood movements opposing Moses's vision and projects. Her most notable battle was to save Washington Square Park—an iconic New York City park that Moses proposed to bisect with a freeway to link highways running along the east and west sides of New York City. Jacobs was arrested in one protest. Eventually Moses's plan was abandoned. Washington Square remains closed to all traffic today. Figure 1.4 shows Jacobs holding up documentary evidence of Moses's plans at a meeting of her supporters meeting at a restaurant on Hudson Street in 1961.

Jacobs's take-no-prisoners attack on all planners and city planning was unfair. Lewis Mumford—who also championed humane cities and opposed Moses and top-down planning—dismissed Jacobs's ideas as "home remedies for urban cancer". However, her attack on top-down urban renewal and highway planning as it was practiced in the 1960s and 1970s was right on target. *The Death and Life of Great American Cities* was an excellent wake-up call for city and regional planners to critically question the science behind all planning proposals, demand transparency and collaborative planning, and respect neighborhoods and their residents. Above all Jacobs energized planners to consider livability and human values. Her activism translated her values into reality in New York City. It remains an inspiration today.

Figure 1.4 Jane Jacobs (1961).

SUMMARY

Fundamental approaches to city and regional planning at every scale apply worldwide, but need to be operationalized consistently with the planning culture of the country or region where plans are being made. All plans should be "grounded"—based on empirical data. They should follow social and natural science methodology rather than intuition or political expediency. They should reflect citizens' and policy makers' normative visions of what constitutes a good city or region. While logic is important, it is never a substitute for creativity.

City and regional planning is an important, robust, and rapidly expanding profession. In the last three decades it has moved rapidly from a minor profession towards a status like medicine, law, and engineering.

Digital technology and new analytics have greatly improved planning as a science. Innovative urban design concepts and powerful new urban design software tools have revolutionized the art of city and regional planning.

City and regional planning is now a global phenomenon with at least 550 city and regional planning degree programs in 71 countries. It is growing most rapidly in the developing world.

While they are still mostly generalists with a specialty, planners in the United States are increasingly mastering specialized tools and knowledge to prepare transportation, environmental, urban design, climate change and other plans. Academic accreditation standards are becoming much more rigorous, though planning has no licensing system comparable to more established professions.

City and regional planning is a big tent with room for people with many different interests and skills. Techies, managers, visionaries, and activists are needed and welcome. Almost half of the new generation of U.S. planners are women. Minority planners are in high demand, and their numbers are increasing. City and regional planning is an important profession for the future of the world. Planners are change agents who can make the world a better place.

CONCEPTS

American Institute of Certified Planners (AICP)
American Planning Association (APA)
Association of Collegiate Schools of Planning (ACSP)
City Scientific Movement
Journal of Planning Education and Research (JPER)
Journal of the American Planning Association (JAPA)
Master's of City and Regional Planning (MCRP)
Master's of Urban Design (MUD)
Planning Accreditation Board (PAB)
Planners of Color Interest Group (POCIG)
Urban Affairs Association (UAA)

PEOPLE

Jane Jacobs

NOTES

1   The BLS reported that in 2016, 68% of U.S. urban planners worked in local government, excluding education and hospitals, 12% in architectural, engineering, and related services, 11% in state government, 3% in management, scientific, and technical consulting services, and 2% for the federal government. Most had master's degrees from accredited city and regional planning programs. Eighty-one percent were White, and 60% were men. Blacks and Latinx were seriously underrepresented in the profession.

2   The APA was created in 1978 by combining predecessor professional planners' associations which had been created in 1917 and 1934. This occurred much later than the creation of professional associations for medicine (1847), civil engineering (1852), and law (1878).

3   Canada's Professional Standards Board (PSB) administers the certification process of professional planners on behalf of the Provincial and Territorial Institutes and Associations (PTIAs), except in Québec. However, regulatory responsibilities are held by the PTIAs. In Quebec L'Ordre des Urbanistes du Québec (OUQ) accredits and administers three planning schools.

4   To become an AICP-certified planner, an applicant must be a current APA member, pass a 3½ hour examination consisting of 170 multiple-choice questions testing their city and regional planning skills and knowledge, be engaged in professional planning either currently or in the past, pledge to

uphold ethical standards, and have a high enough level of planning experience. For certification, the FAICP require that planners with a Planning Accreditation Board (PAB)-accredited graduate planning degree have 2 years of planning experience. They must have 3 years of planning experience if they have a PAB-accredited bachelor's degree in planning or a graduate degree in planning from a program that is not accredited by the PAB, 4 years if they have a postgraduate degree in a discipline other than planning, and 8 years if they have no college degree (AICP, 2021).

5 The BLS reported that the median salary for urban planners in 2019 was $74,350 (BLS, 2020). The median salary for architects was $80,750, civil engineers $80,060, lawyers $119,250, and surgeons $208,000 (ibid). Average salaries were higher for planners with advanced degrees, working in higher levels of government and private firms, and working in large cities (APA, 2018). In 2018 AICP reported that members' salaries were $17,000 more on average than APA members who were not certified (ibid). Some of the salary difference is likely because certified members generally have 15 to 18 years of experience and are more likely to work in large cities. Even controlling for these differences FAICP planners earn higher salaries on average than non-members (ibid).

6 The Planning Accreditation Board (PAB) requires city and regional planning programs to submit extensive self-studies and conducts site visits to confirm that a program meets their standards. Initial accreditation is a complex, lengthy, and costly process. Re-accreditation also requires a great deal of effort. Programs that fail to maintain PAB standards lose their accreditation. Without accreditation a city and regional planning program is at a competitive disadvantage. It will likely have a hard time attracting students.

7 The PAB defines general planning knowledge as the comprehension, representation, and use of ideas and information in the planning field, including appropriate perspectives from history, social science, design, and allied fields. They state that topics in city and regional planning degree programs should include the purpose and meaning of planning, planning law, human settlements, and history of planning. They should help students think about the future and global dimensions of planning. The PAB requires education related to six planning skills: research; written, oral, and graphic communication; quantitative and qualitative methods; plan creation and implementation; planning process methods; and leadership. Required education in ethics and values includes professional ethics and responsibility, equity, diversity and social justice, governance and participation, sustainability and environmental quality, growth and development, and health and the built environment.

8 Faculty and students of institutions that are full members of ACSP have voting rights. Faculty and students in affiliated and corresponding schools may serve on and chair ACSP committees, but may not vote or hold office at the association level. Individual members may attend ACSP meetings, participate in discussions and deliberations, and serve on or chair committees, but may not vote or hold office.

9 Most attendees at recent ACSP conferences have been faculty and graduate students from U.S. and Canadian planning schools. Some faculty and students from other countries and some practitioners attend. Attendees present and critique academic papers, listen to keynote addresses, and visit local sites of planning interest. The boards of major city and regional planning journals, the Planning Accreditation Board, interest groups of women, minority planning faculty, and people interested in planning for LGBTQ communities, global planning educators, the International Association for China Planning, and other organizations meet at the ACSP conferences. There is an awards ceremony recognizing faculty and student achievements. PhD students seeking faculty positions have job interviews at the conferences.

10 The ACSP website www.acsp.org has information on the ACSP's governing board; committees; affiliated organizations; accreditation; membership; job openings; annual and other conferences and events; awards; publications; careers; and resources. There is a list of member, affiliated, and corresponding schools. Text and a video titled *What Is Planning?* provide the ACSP's introduction to the planning profession. The ACSP website provides links to descriptions of other planning organizations.

11 Edward Blakeley chaired the Department of City and Regional Planning at the University of California, Berkeley, served as Dean of the School of Urban Planning and Development at the University of Southern California, and Dean of the Robert J. Milano Graduate School of Management and Urban Policy at the New School in New York City. He is the co-author of the leading local economic development textbook, nine other books, more than one hundred scholarly articles and dozens of essays and opinion pieces. Blakeley was the "planning Czar" appointed to help plan New Orleans' recovery from Hurricane Katrina. He has served as an adviser to the Organisation for Economic Co-operation and Development, governments in Korea, Japan, Sweden, Indonesia, New Zealand and Vietnam and state and federal governments in Australia and the United States.

12 Urban affairs is an interdisciplinary academic social science/public policy field that overlaps city and regional planning, urban politics, and urban studies (UAA website, 2021). In North America the Urban Affairs Association (UAA) has over 700 members. Most are faculty and students from political science, city and regional planning, and other academic disciplines and professional fields related to urban affairs and planning. Most UAA members are from the USA but individual UAA membership

is open worldwide. The UAA holds an annual conference, publishes the *Journal of Urban Affairs*, lists jobs, and has an international, multidisciplinary honor society—Upsilon Sigma.

13 Other professional organizations involved in city and regional planning include the American Institute of Architects (AIA, 2021), American Society of Landscape Architects (ASLA, 2021), and the American Society of Civil Engineers (ASCE, 2021).

14 The principal social science disciplinary associations related to city and regional planning are the Association of American Geographers (AAG), American Political Science Association (APSA), American Sociological Association (ASA), American Economic Association (AEA), American Historical Society (AHS), and the American Anthropology Association (AAA).

15 Some graduate programs offer, but do not require, specialization(s) (Brinkley & Hoch, 2021). Others require students to complete at least one specialization. Some encourage students to take more than one specialization. Only three PAB-accredited planning schools do not offer any specialization. Most PAB specializations consist of three to five graduate courses with a thesis or final project related to the specialization (ibid). They may require as few as two courses.

16 A common pattern for U.S. planning master's students is a 2+1 program in which students complete one year at their home university, a year abroad, and then complete both degrees back at their home university. For example, U.S. graduate students at Georgia Institute of Technology (Georgia Tech) may complete part of their graduate planning degree at Georgia Tech and part at Tongji University in Shanghai and vice versa. Students typically write a thesis or complete a capstone project related to their experience in the country where they studied abroad. Dual degree programs typically permit double counting some courses. This can reduce the total time necessary to get two master's degrees by one or two semesters or a two-year planning degree and a three-year law degree in 4 years.

SUGGESTIONS FOR FURTHER LEARNING

Overviews: John Seeley, What is planning? (2008). Peter Hall, *Cities of tomorrow*, 4th ed (2014). ACSP, What is planning? (2021). **Textbooks:** John Levy, *Contemporary city and regional planning*, 11th ed (2017). Barry Cullingworth & Roger Caves, *Planning in the USA*, 5th ed (2021). **Anthologies:** Rachel Weber & Randall Crane (eds), *The Oxford handbook on urban planning* (2015). Gary Hack, Eugenie Birch, Paul Sedway, & Mitchell Silver (eds), *Local planning* (2009). **The Centre for Advanced Spatial Analysis (CASA):** CASA [website] (2021). **The U.S. City and Regional Planning Profession:** American Planning Association (APA) [website] (2021). American Institute of Certified Planners (AICP) [website] (2021). U.S. Bureau of Labor Statistics (BLS), *Urban and regional planners* (2021). Rick Wilson, How to launch your planning career [video] (2019). Rachelle Alterman, From a minor to a major profession (2017). John Seeley, What is planning? (2008). Lloyd Rodwin and Bishwapriya Sanyal, The profession of city planning (2000). **Planners of Color:** Andrew Greenlee, April Jackson, & Ivis Garcia-Zambrana, Where are we going? Where have we been (2018)? April Jackson, Ivis Garcia-Zambrana, Andrew Greenlee, & C. Aujean Lee, All talk no walk (2018). Ivis García, April Jackson, Stacy Harwood, Andrew Greenlee, C. Aujean Lee, & Benjamin Chrisinger, Like a fish out of water (2018). **City and Regional Planning Education:** Andrea Frank & Chris Silver, *Global planning education* (2018). *Planetizen guide to graduate planning programs* (2021), Planetizen [website] (2021). Planning Accreditation Board [website] (2021). Christina Brinkley and Charles Hoch, The ebb and flow of planning specializations (2021). Global Planning Educators Interest Group (GPEIG) [website] (2021). **Plan Making:** Lew Hopkins, *Urban development* (2001). John Forester, *City planning in the face of conflict* (2013). Allan Jacobs, *Making city planning work* (1980). Charles Hoch, Making plans (2015). International Society of City and Regional Planning (ISOCARP), *International manual of planning practice*. **City and Regional Planning Research Methods:** Richard LeGates, How to study cities (2020). Barbora Lipovská & Roberta Stepankova, *Research methods in urban and regional planning* (2 vols) (2016). Elisabete Silva (ed), *The Routledge handbook of planning research methods* (2016). American Planning Association Research KnowledgeBase [website] (2021). Stuart Farthing, Research design in city and regional planning (2016). Michael Batty, *The new science of cities* (2013). **Planning Journals:** *Journal of Planning Education and Research (JPER)*. *Journal of the American Planning Association (JAPA)*. *Urban Studies*. *Cities*. *Habitat International*. *Journal of Planning Literature*. *Journal of Urban Affairs*. **Magazines:** *Planning*. **Websites:** Planetizine. Next City.

CHAPTER 2

The Evolution of Cities and City and Regional Planning, 1607–1933

INTRODUCTION

Every place in the United States contains physical reminders of different times in its past. Buildings, ruins, and archeological sites augment the written record of how places came to be what they are like today.

At Cahokia on the outskirts of St. Louis, Missouri, a visitor atop Monks Mound—once a stepped pyramid larger than the Great Pyramid at Giza, Egypt—can look out over dozens of ceremonial mounds over a 6-square-mile site that was once home to 20,000 "Mound Builder" Indians.

At Plymouth, Massachusetts, visitors can walk through a full-scale replica of "Plimoth Plantation" as it was in 1621 when the first group of Pilgrims from England completed their first tiny settlement. They can visit a replica of the Mayflower that departed from Plymouth, England on Christmas day, 1620 bound for the New World with 102 men, women, and children.

The street grid laid out in 1682 for Philadelphia is still mostly intact. Modest brick row houses where craftsmen, their wives and children, indentured servants, and sometimes slaves lived and worked still line some of Philadelphia's streets.

Buildings, ruins, and museum artifacts in St. Louis and St. Joseph, Missouri, preserve evidence of what frontier settlements were like. Moving west, abandoned ghost towns and fragments of early western settlements that grew into cities are reminders of the great western migration to settle the American frontier. Many settlements in the American Southwest still show evidence of planning according to Spanish city planning law dating to 1593.

Planners can see physical evidence of the rise of industrial cities in Patterson, New Jersey and Lowell, Massachusetts and remains of the great industrial enterprises from the heyday of the industrial city in Pittsburgh and Bethlehem, Pennsylvania.

WHAT IS A CITY?

The census's umbrella term for a concentration of population is a place. A place must have a name, be locally recognized, and not part of any other place. Places expand or contract over time as population and commercial activity increases or decreases. They include neighborhoods and unincorporated villages as well as counties and incorporated cities. The census provides data grouped for different kinds of places, the most important of which are cities and counties defined by their political boundaries.

States have the power to create political subdivisions called counties and grant them power to make important local decisions, including planning. Counties are called boroughs in New York and parishes in Louisiana.

States also have the power to incorporate cities as municipal corporations—granting them the legal authority to govern themselves consistent with state law. Every state except for Hawaii has done so.

The U.S. Census Bureau defines a city as "a type of incorporated place", but takes 33 pages to describe what that means. Politically, cities are the third tier in the U.S. federal system, below the federal and state governments. Once they are incorporated, cities have the power to plan land use within their borders, zone land, regulate land uses, and pass municipal ordinances to implement their plans.

For census purposes a place can qualify as a city with a population as low as 2,500 if it meets census area and density standards. New York City—the largest city in the United States—has over eight million residents. State laws vary as to the minimum population and other standards necessary to qualify as a city. Some permit places with fewer than 2,500 residents to be incorporated. Oregon has 78 incorporated cities with populations under 1,000. Industry, California's population as of spring, 2022 was 373.

City and regional planners often use data for an entire city or county where they are working. Fine-grained census data is available for small census units called blocks, block groups, census tracts, and transportation analysis zones (TAZs) within cities and counties. Planners can group data from small census units into units of analysis such as a commute shed or air basin that fit a specific analytic need better than standard census units. The census also summarizes data for large places including metropolitan and micropolitan areas—which may include multiple cities and counties—states; and the entire United States.

The census draws a binary distinction between urban and rural areas. However, neither city political boundaries nor the binary census rural/urban dichotomy distinguish areas very well. Most U.S. cities do not have an urban limit line that sharply distinguishes urban from rural areas. Patches of urban land sometimes lie beyond the boundaries of incorporated cities' limits. Cities may contain land classified as rural that remain after the city engulfed them. Fringe areas often contain a jumble of urban and rural features.

Land that is not within cities lies in counties—political subdivisions of the state where they are located. Land beyond city limits falls under county jurisdiction for planning purposes.

URBANIZATION

Urbanization is the process by which rural places such as villages, towns, and sparsely settled countryside become urban. About 81% of the U.S. population lives in urban places. Worldwide about 57% of earth's inhabitants live in areas the United Nations classifies as urban.

Urban population growth and urbanization usually occur simultaneously. They are often confused, but they are not the same. Population is expressed as a number of people. Population growth of a city refers to an increase in the absolute number of people in the city. Urbanization describes the process of change in the *percentage* (proportion) of the total population of a geographic area such as a country living in areas classified as urban as opposed to rural.

There were about 5 million people in the United States in 1800, 76 million in 1900, 281 million in 2000, and there were approximately 331 million in 2022. About seven percent of all humans who have lived are alive today.[1] Earth's population growth is a power curve—growing faster than exponentially.

Stanford University sociologist/demographer Kingsley Davis (1908–1977) found that urbanization generally follows an attenuated S curve. The Davis S curve has a long left tail as the proportion of an area's population living in urban areas begins at a very low level and slowly increases. It has an inflection point when urbanization begins to grow rapidly as an area industrializes, and then a flattening right tail as the area becomes fully urbanized.

England was the first country to urbanize. Urbanization curves in the United States

Urbanization

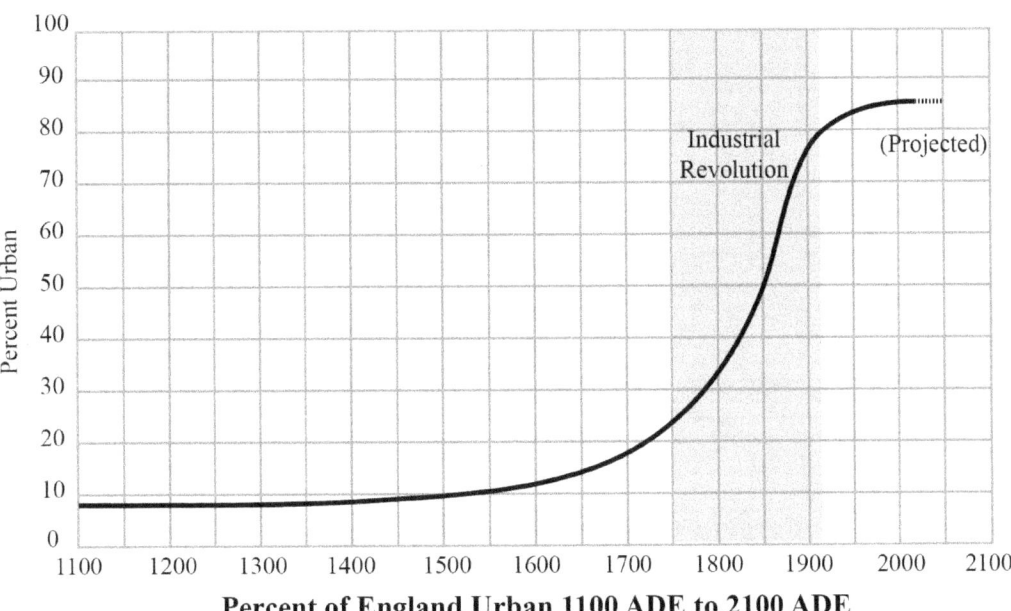

Figure 2.1 Kingsley Davis's Urbanization S Curve (England).

and other Western European countries lag England, but follow similar attenuated S curves. Demographers expect the percentage of the population of the United States that is urban to remain nearly flat in the future, though they expect the total population of the U.S. to grow. Many developing countries are still in the rapidly increasing segment of their S curves.

Kingsley Davis uses the term "family of S curves" to describe urbanization patterns in different countries. This is an excellent metaphor for understanding world urbanization. Figure 2.2a shows the S curve of urbanization in the United States. It starts later than in England, but has now reached about the same percentage. Figures 2.2b, and 2.2c show urbanization S curves for China and Cambodia.[2]

Since Davis defined urbanization as a percentage, it has an end. Urbanization can never exceed 100%. The United Nations classifies a few countries as already 100% urbanized—but these are unusual cases such as Singapore and small Caribbean and Pacific Island countries.

Population growth in an area (including an entire country) occurs when the number of live births exceeds deaths, the average age of the population increases, in-migration exceeds out-migration, or if refugees fleeing from war and economic, political, health, or environmental crises move into the area, or as a combination of several of these factors.

Urbanization occurs as agriculture becomes more efficient, so that fewer people need to farm to support the population; economies industrialize so that there are more (and often better paying) jobs in urban areas; and as rural–urban migration occurs as rural households are either pushed out of rural areas because there is not enough land for them to farm or pulled into cities by the real or perceived advantages they offer. Apparent—but false—population growth or urbanization may occur on paper if the legal boundaries of urban areas are enlarged or if countries relax the definition of what qualifies as urban.

a) Percent of the U.S Population Urban
1790–2050

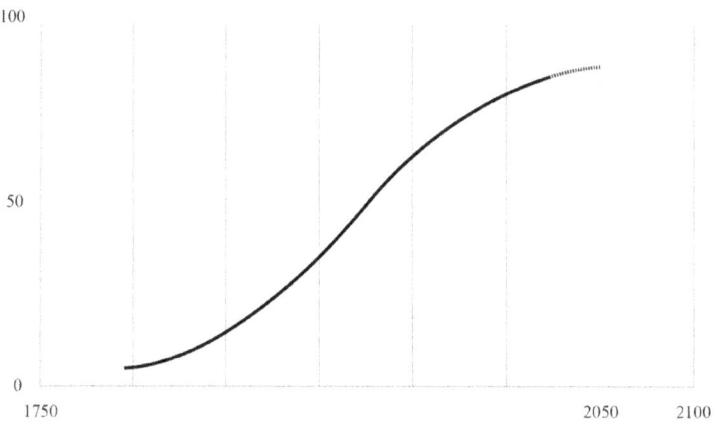

b) Percent of the Chinese Population Urban
1950–2050

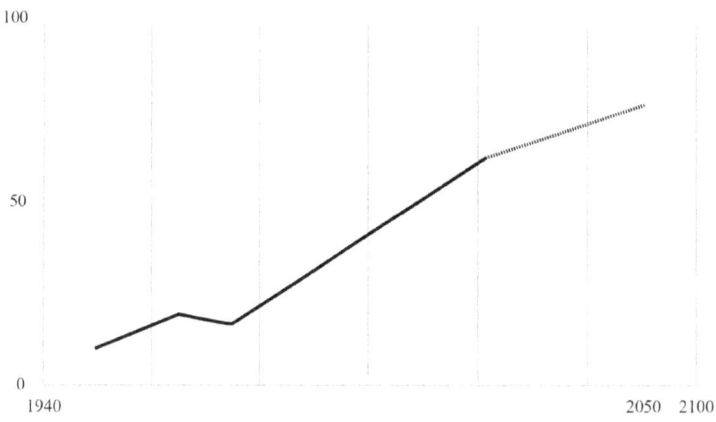

c) Percent of the Cambodian Population Urban
1950–2050

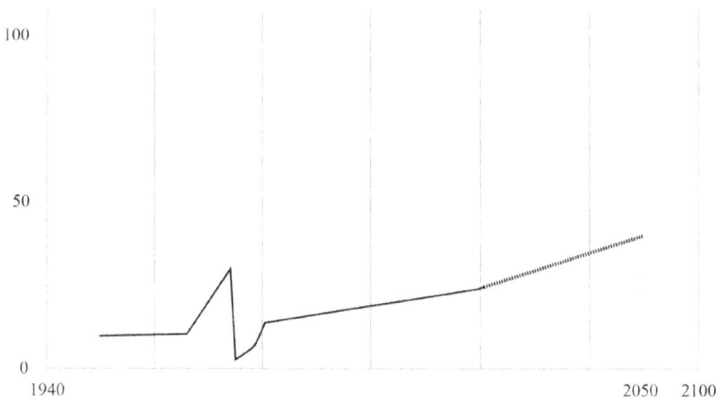

Figure 2.2 Kingsley Davis's "Family" of Urbanization S Curves.

U.S. URBAN HISTORY

In order to understand cities in the present and plan for their future, it is essential to understand their past. In the words of U.S. Supreme Court justice and author Oliver Wendell Holmes: "A page of history is worth a pound of logic."

History is sometimes considered a humanity and sometimes a social science discipline. Urban history has developed over the last 90 years as a subfield of history. Cornell city and regional planning professor John Reps (1921–2020) was a leading urban planning historian. Reps's major text—*The Making of Urban America* (1965)—and more than two dozen of his other books provide reproductions of many historical U.S. physical plans, illustrations, and primary source texts describing what cities were like during different historical periods.[3]

AMERICAN INDIAN SETTLEMENTS

Two American Indian settlements in what is now the United States had large enough populations at sufficient density to arguably qualify as cities. Both were modest compared to the spectacular planned Aztec capital of Tenochtitlan (present day Mexico City) and the Inca capital city of Cuzco in present-day Peru at their height in the 15th century.

Cahokia, on the outskirts of St. Louis, Missouri, was the largest North America Indian settlement. It was built by the Mound Builder Indians. Cahokia consisted of many enormous stepped pyramids built for religious ceremonial purposes, residential areas, and a market. It was largely built after 1050 CE. By the 12th century Cahokia covered more than 6 square miles, included over 120 mounds, and may have had a population of 20,000 at its peak. Cahokia was abandoned about 1350 CE. Today the archeological remains of Cahokia are a U.S. National Historic Landmark and a United Nations Educational, Scientific and Cultural Organization (UNESCO) world heritage site.

Pueblo Bonito ('beautiful settlement' in Spanish) is in the Chaco Canyon National Historical Park in present-day New Mexico. It was the largest Ancestral Puebloan Indian settlement. Pueblo Bonito is a 3-acre site with approximately 800 rooms in a religious and residential complex that was sometimes five stories high. It was planned and constructed in stages between 850 CE and 1150 CE by ancestral Puebloan peoples. Pueblo Bonito is a spectacular architectural creation and arguably qualifies as a small city.

EAST COAST COLONIAL CITIES

Colonial cities are offshoots of their mother country. Even the largest colonial cities along America's East Coast began as small settlements of a few dozen people. U.S. East Coast colonial cities were built by settlers from England and other European countries beginning in the early 17th century for commercial, religious, philanthropic, and military reasons. Migration to the East Coast of the United States from the 16th through the early 20th century came mainly from Western, Southern and Central Europe. The Spanish settled Saint Augustine, Florida in 1565 as a fort and military town, but did not build other permanent settlements in what is now the United States. Spain ceded Florida to the United States in 1819.

The first English settlement in America occurred in 1607 at Jamestown, in present-day Virginia, built by entrepreneurs eager to start tobacco plantations. In 1620 Protestant religious dissenters (Pilgrims) seeking freedom to practice their religion and prosper economically arrived at "Plimoth Plantation" (Plymouth in present-day Massachusetts). In addition to English settlements, there were French, Dutch, Spanish, and Swedish colonial settlements along the East Coast of the United States. They reflected the architectural style, planning norms, and culture of the colonizing countries. The Dutch colonial city of New Amsterdam looked like a Dutch town—complete with windmills—before it was acquired by England in 1664 and renamed New York.

Despite high mortality rates, the early East Coast colonies succeeded economically and grew rapidly in the 17th and 18th centuries.[4] Still, by the time of the American Revolution, even the largest East Coast cities were what historian Carl Bridenbaugh (1938) called "specks in the wilderness". In 1775, only five East Coast colonial cities—New York City, New York; Philadelphia, Pennsylvania; Boston, Massachusetts; Charleston, South Carolina; and Newport, Rhode Island had populations of 5,000 or more. The biggest cities—New York and Philadelphia—had about 25,000 people each.

All of the major and most of the smaller U.S. East Coast settlements were on the Atlantic Ocean or on bays or tributaries that flowed into it. Goods and people moved by ocean-going ships, and along the coast and into the interior by foot, horse, or small boats. Roads and paths connecting cities and towns were sparse and rudimentary.

What University of California, Los Angeles (UCLA) History Professor Gary Nash (1986) calls a "web of seaport life" existed among the East Coast colonial cities. Much of the economy centered on the waterfront where warehouses were located, and stevedores loaded and unloaded goods to and from ships that sailed up and down the coast, on to the Caribbean, and to English and other European ports. There was a high ratio of men to women in the East Coast colonial settlements. Cheap rooming houses, pubs, and houses of prostitution were concentrated along the waterfronts. Figure 2.3 is a 19th-century engraving based on an original print by Paul Revere published in 1774 to protest the arrival of British warships just before the outbreak of the American Revolution. It illustrates how important the waterfront and maritime activities were to colonial Boston.

A principal reason for the existence of American East Coast colonial cities was economic—to export raw materials such as beaver and other animal skins, salt cod-fish, and timber from the northern colonies and tobacco, indigo, and rice from the southern colonies. There was a brisk "triangle trade" between Africa (slaves), the Caribbean (sugar), the northern colonies (rum manufactured from Caribbean sugar), and England (imports of raw materials and exports of finished products).

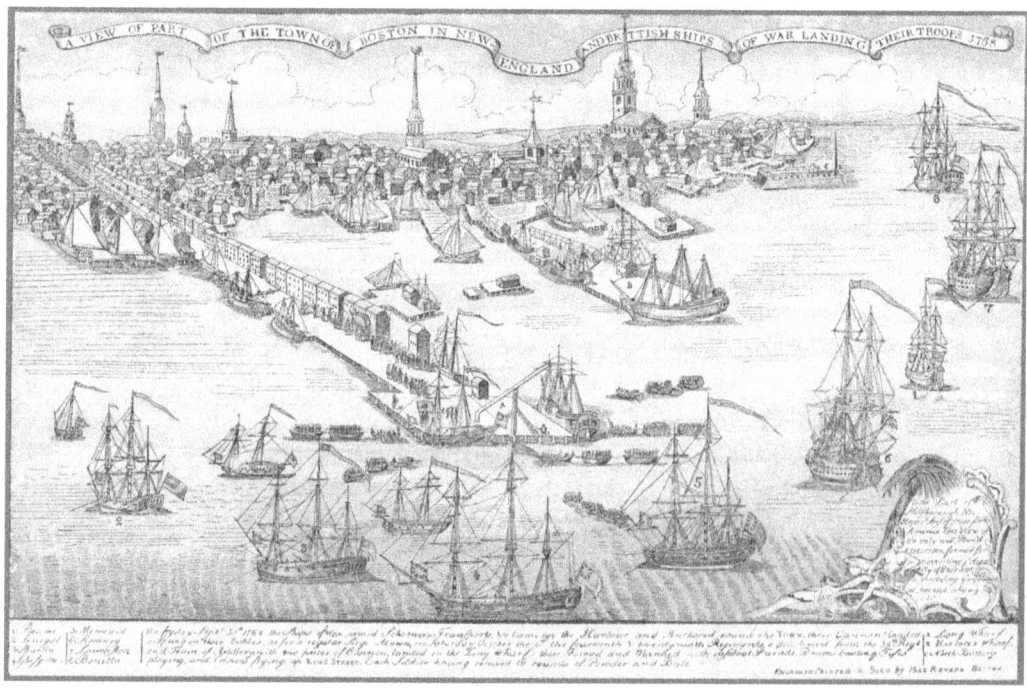

Figure 2.3 Boston Harbor, 1774.

Religious freedom and philanthropy for debtors from British debtors' prisons were other fundamental reasons for the existence of Philadelphia, Pennsylvania; Boston, Massachusetts; New Haven, Connecticut, Savannah, Georgia and other U.S. colonial cities.[5]

All the American colonial cities were "walking cities"—compact cities where most residents walked to get to destinations within the city. Wealthy residents sometimes traveled by horse or in horse-drawn carriages. Pedestrians shared space with horses and carriages. There were few sidewalks, little or no streetscaping, street furniture or trash receptacles. Main streets were often paved with cobblestones—great for horses, not so great for people to walk on. Streets were often fouled with manure and trash.

Philadelphia in 1775 was what Massachusetts Institute of Technology and University of Pennsylvania planning historian Sam Bass Warner (1968) called a "private city"—with many small entrepreneurs and little government involvement in the economy. Modest two-story, wood or brick row houses with a workshop on the ground floor and sleeping quarters for the family (and often indentured servants and sometimes slaves) on the second floor were common. Craftspeople produced chairs, silverware, hats, and other goods in their homes. There was a lively produce market in Philadelphia and one pub for every 120 residents!

Crowding, jumbled land uses, and the absence of rudimentary sanitation made the early colonial cities unhealthy places. Shortly after independence, the yellow fever pandemic of 1793 killed a quarter of the population of Philadelphia. Infant mortality rates were high. Many women died in childbirth. New York and other of the largest American cities began sanitary reforms in the mid-19th century, but waste disposal and poor health remained urban problems.[6]

THE PARKS MOVEMENT

The parks movement, led by Frederick Olmsted (1822–1903)—the designer along with Calvert Vaux (1824–1895) of New York City's Central Park—led to the creation of many of the great U.S. urban parks during the second half of the 19th century. Urban parks provided fresh air, places to exercise, and greenery. They had water fountains—demanded by temperance advocates—where working-class men could drink water rather than going to a tavern to drink beer, whiskey, gin, and other hard liquor.

American English colonial society was socially stratified. The top stratum consisted of prosperous farmers with a house in town, merchants, sea captains, and the clergy. Next were free laborers with a craft specialty like silversmithing. These were followed by indentured servants bound for a period of years (usually seven), who received room and board and learned a trade in exchange for their labor. Free Blacks formed a Black elite, but faced great discrimination. The lowest stratum of American colonial society were Black slaves.

Women were relegated to childrearing and domestic work or helping their husbands in handcraft manufacturing. Widows sometimes continued their husband's work, took in boarders, were paid for washing, or worked as domestic servants.

Colonial cities had little spatial segregation. Planning historian Sam Bass Warner has documented that in Philadelphia wealthy merchants, farmers, craftspeople, free laborers, indentured servants, and slaves all lived in close proximity in the small, dense settlement.

FROM SPECKS IN THE WILDERNESS TO CITIES IN THE WILDERNESS

After the American Revolution the population of the United States grew rapidly as a result of immigration and natural increase. It continued to grow rapidly throughout the 19th and 20th centuries and is still growing today.

In the early 19th century there were virtually no restrictions on immigration and no process required to obtain U.S. citizenship. Virtually anyone who arrived in the United States, with the exception of slaves, indentured servants, people identified as having a transmissible disease, and in a few cases in some states some other categories of "undesirables" could simply get off the boat and become a citizen.

Immigrants to the East Coast of the United States after American independence came mostly from Great Britain, Ireland, and Germany. Most came seeking cheap farmland. As the first factories emerged in the early 19th century, some came for factory work. Conditions in American factories were better than in factories in Europe—though hours were long and conditions very harsh by later standards. There was little net immigration in the first decades after independence, but immigration to the East Coast increased rapidly after 1820.[7]

Between 1845 and 1849 the Irish potato crop failed. Much of the crop rotted in the fields before the potatoes were edible. Potatoes were the main source of food in Ireland. As potatoes rotted many people starved to death or emigrated. The numbers are debated, but it appears likely that at least a million or more people in Ireland starved to death and as many, or more, migrated to the United States during the "Great Famine" Large numbers of destitute, poorly educated, Irish Catholics flooded into Boston, New York, and other cities. Unskilled Irish workers supplanted young women in New England textile mills and built a majority of the canals and railroads in the Eastern United States

Attempted revolutions in Europe failed in 1848. Many intellectuals and political radicals then fled to the United States to avoid persecution.

One of the first tasks of the new nation was to sort out land claims and encourage settlement of the interior. The Northwest Ordinance of 1787 created new territories west of the Appalachian Mountains in the area around the Great Lakes.[8] New settlements grew into what historian Carl Bridenbaugh called "cities in the

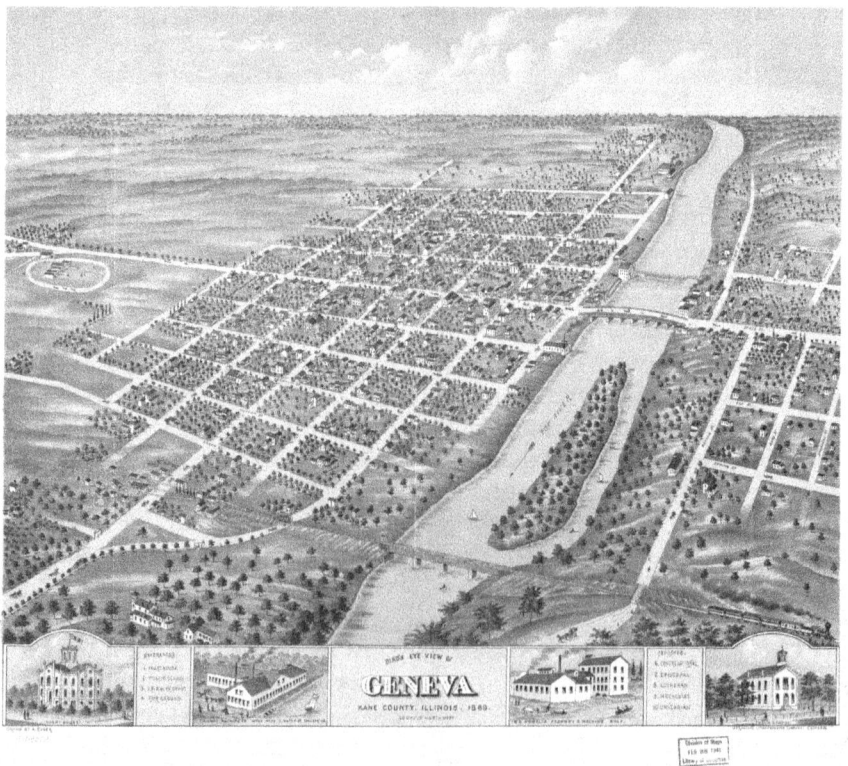

Figure 2.4 Geneva, Illinois (1869).

wilderness" in this region. The Northwest Ordinance imposed an enormous grid on the region consisting of 6-square-mile townships, 1-square-mile (640-acre) sections, and half, quarter, half-quarter, and quarter-quarter sections. Land for a house and farmland, called a homestead—usually 160 acres per household—was granted free to Revolutionary War veterans. Most of the rest of the land was sold in large parcels for $1 an acre or less. The resulting spatial structure is evident in Figure 2.4.

SPANISH SETTLEMENTS IN THE AMERICAN WEST

A second set of specks in the wilderness developed independently in the northwestern region of New Spain—now the Western United States. Spain had claimed the land in 1513 (indeed all land touched by the Pacific Ocean)! It remained under Spanish control until Mexican independence in 1821. Mexico ceded most of this land to the United States in 1848 after Mexico's defeat in the U.S.–Mexican War.

Spanish settlements (*pueblos*) were laid out according to 148 planning regulations that are part of the Laws of the Indies established by Philip II of Spain in 1573.[9] Many Spanish settlements in New Mexico conformed to Laws of the Indies standards. Santa Fe, New Mexico—the largest of these settlements—was established by migrants from New Spain who walked overland from Mexico City in 1610. The governor's palace—much altered—is still in Santa Fe's historic district as well as a Catholic church and other Spanish buildings dating to the early 17th century. Santa Fe's plan did not follow the Laws of the Indies.

After Mexico achieved independence from Spain in 1821, building footprints and street grids continued to reflect the Laws of the Indies. However, the physical and social structure of the settlements changed. Church lands were secularized. Local military and civilian elites acquired giant ranchos—enormous ranches mainly used to raise long-horned cattle for their hides and tallow. Overland trade with the USA from St. Joseph, Missouri, began in 1821 via the Santa Fe trail. After the United States acquired this region, the settlement patterns grew more like settlements in the Eastern United States.

PLANNING WASHINGTON, D.C.

After independence, political leaders wanted a new capital to symbolically knit the new country together and manifest its importance to the world. In 1791 President George Washington appointed three commissioners to select a site for a new capital city, and appointed Major Charles Pierre L'Enfant—a French engineer who had served in the continental army during the American Revolutionary War—to prepare a plan for the new capital. For political reasons, the new capital was located on the Potomac River just north of Virginia, the most northerly and most important of the southern states. The site was low-lying swampy undeveloped land. The commissioners named the capital Washington, D.C. (District of Columbia). L'Enfant proposed a grand European baroque city design.

The L'Enfant plan (Figure 2.5) is a highly political document that used city planning and design to symbolically represent the pride of a revolutionary new country and the aspiration to knit southern and northern states together into a more perfect union. It laid out the new city as a grid. Broad diagonal avenues (now named after states) intersect north–south and east–west streets at circles. L'Enfant laid out plazas to provide open space, and for statues and other historic monuments. One of the plazas was named L'Enfant Plaza in 1954. To symbolically emphasize the structure of the new U.S. federal democracy, L'Enfant placed the sites for "Congress House" and the newly created federal Supreme Court higher than the "President's House" and linked Congress and the Supreme Court by the hypotenuse of a large triangle (present-day Pennsylvania Avenue). Along the east–west line of the federal triangle the L'Enfant plan proposed a 400-foot-wide "grand avenue" containing a public walk that is now the capitol mall.

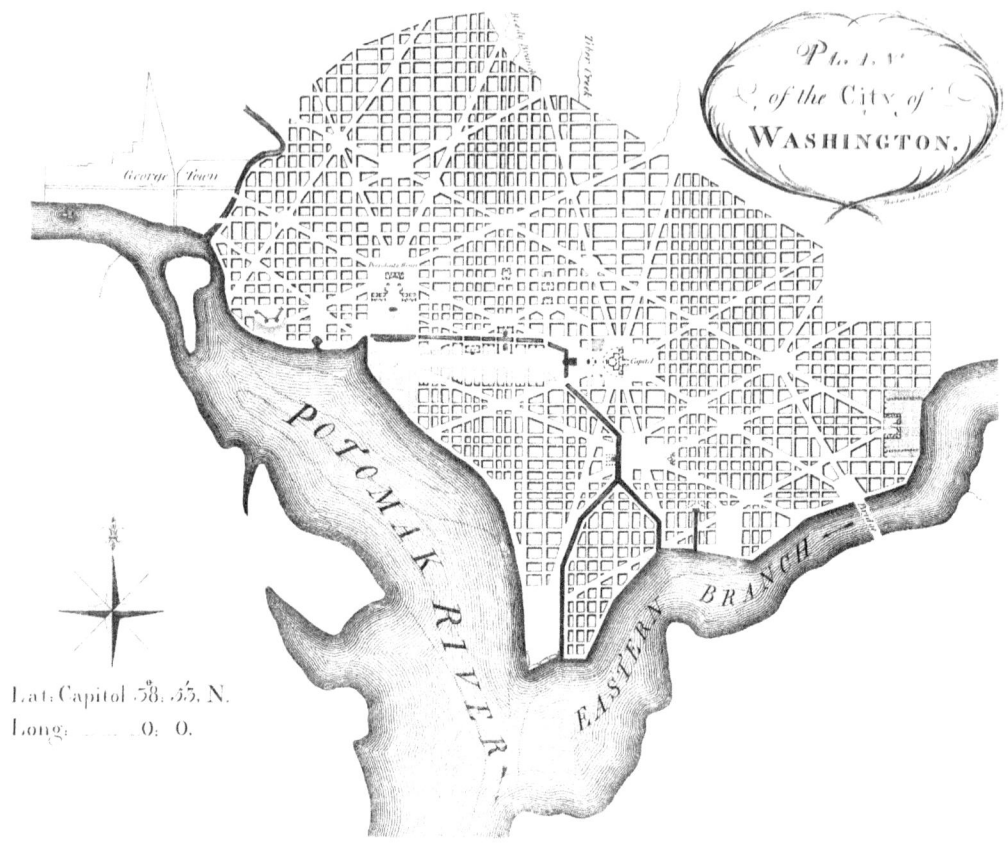

Figure 2.5 L'Enfant Plan for Washington, D.C. (1792).

Details were changed and L'Enfant's plan was adjusted by the surveyor assigned to survey the site—Andrew Ellicott. It received a major update as the result of a 1902 study by the McMillan Commission that altered the design of the area around Union Station and the Supreme Court. However, the core features of L'Enfant's plan are still evident in Washington, D.C. today.

WESTWARD EXPANSION: FRONTIER AND INSTANT CITIES

The United States acquired the balance of the land in what is now the continental United States by the Louisiana Purchase from France in 1803; annexation of the Republic of Texas—which had become independent from Mexico in 1836—in 1848; the Treaty of Guadalupe Hidalgo at the conclusion of the Mexican–American war in 1848; purchase of Alaska in 1868; and other acquisitions.

San Francisco and Denver sprang up as "instant cities". They mushroomed quickly into large cities with banks, hotels, opera houses, mansions, and substantial populations as a result of the gold rush in California that began in 1849 and the Colorado silver rush that began in 1858.

An important impetus for westward migration and the growth of cities in the west was the Homestead Act of 1862. The Homestead Act provided 640 acres of public domain land free to any head of household 21 years old or older who had not borne arms against the United States, was willing to live on the land, build a home, make improvements, and farm it for a minimum of five years.

Until 1890, the U.S. census showed a demarcated frontier moving westward in each successive census. Frontier settlements were mostly unplanned mining, ranching, and agricultural hubs with population that consisted mostly of single men. They were vernacular settlements that used local building materials. The frontier cities were built without architects. In 1890, the census declared that the frontier no longer existed.

Nearly a million migrants from Asia and the Pacific Islands came to the West Coast of the United States in the second half of the 19th century and the early 20th century, despite blatant racial discrimination against them. In addition to settling on the West Coast of the continental United States some settled in Hawaii—which the United States had acquired in 1898. The Asian and Pacific Islander (AAPI) migration is well documented by University of California ethnic studies professor Ronald Takaki.

The first and largest group of Asian immigrants to the West Coast consisted of 430,000 Chinese who arrived between 1849 as a result of the gold rush and 1882 when the Chinese Exclusion Act banned further Chinese immigration. Initially most Chinese immigrants settled in rural areas, working in mining, railroad construction, and agriculture. By 1900, a majority of Chinese immigrants lived in cities. Chinese immigrants clustered in "Chinatowns" for mutual support and because of racial discrimination. During the gold rush a foreign workers' tax aimed primarily at the Chinese miners made it financially impossible for them to legally mine for gold. Chinese women were barred from immigrating to the United States by the Page Act of 1875. The flow of legal male Chinese immigrants was suspended between passage of the Chinese Exclusion Act in 1882 and its repeal in 1943, when China became a U.S. ally during World War II.

Japanese immigration to the Western United States began later and was more gradual than Chinese immigration. It continued after 1882.

Most of the 150,000 Filipinos who migrated to the Western United States before World War II arrived after the United States effectively took possession of the Philippines at the conclusion of the Spanish–American War in 1898. A second wave of Filipino immigrants came after World War II.

About 8,000 Koreans and 8,000 Indians immigrated to the Western United States in the late 19th and early 20th century. Many settled in cities.

Between 1905 and 1940 legal Asian migrants to the West Coast were processed at the Angel Island immigration station in San Francisco—a much smaller-scale equivalent of the Ellis Island immigration station in New York City that processed immigrants from Europe. Planners in the Western United States work with Chinese, Japanese, Filipino, Indian, Korean, and other Asian-American and Pacific Islander (AAPI) communities that began to form over 170 years ago and are still receiving AAPI migrants.

U.S. INDUSTRIAL CITIES

British historian Arnold Toynbee coined the term "industrial revolution" to describe the radical change in technology and economic and social relations that began in England about 1750. There was a continuum of U.S. industrial cities as technology evolved from small water-powered factories in the early 19th century to Andrew Carnegie's large coal-powered steel mills in Pittsburgh, Pennsylvania in the late 19th century, and Henry Ford's River Rouge automobile assembly plant in Dearborn, Michigan that employed 100,000 workers assembling Model T Ford automobiles by the early 20th century. Box 2.1 describes the early U.S. industrial cities of Paterson, New Jersey and Lowell, Massachusetts.

Innovations in energy technology—waterwheels, steam generated from burning coal, and then electrical energy from coal- and oil-powered plants, altered the mode of industrial production from pre-industrial to industrial production across many different industries during the 19th and early 20th centuries. By 1933, when this chapter ends, America was already becoming a post-industrial nation where services were becoming as important as industrial activities.

BOX 2.1 EARLY U.S. INDUSTRIAL CITIES

When the United States declared its independence from England in 1776, it was still a pre-industrial society. There were no factories. The largest manufacturing operations, such as shipyards and manufacturers of masts, spars, sails and other maritime products employed a few dozen workers, working without significant machinery. The new nation was dependent on importing many manufactured goods from Europe, including textiles produced in Great Britain. Most energy came from renewable sources—human and animal power, waterwheels, and windmills. Greenhouse gas (GHG) emissions and global warming were insignificant and unrecognized. There was no systematic governmental energy planning.

In 1791, Alexander Hamilton, the first U.S. Secretary of the Treasury established what was effectively a national economic development corporation—the Society for the Establishment of Useful Manufactures (SUM)—to nurture infant U.S. industries and wean the new nation from the economic domination of England. Hamilton appointed Pierre Charles L'Enfant (1754–1825)—the architect and planner who created the plan for Washington, D.C.—as SUM's first planner. L'Enfant selected the 77-foot Great Falls in New Jersey as a promising site for water-powered industry. SUM began constructing raceways—canals to provide waterpower for factories—in 1791. The Great Falls site became the city of Paterson, New Jersey. SUM failed to build its own publicly owned mills, but the dam, canals and water raceways it built provided waterpower for private entrepreneurs to build cotton and later steel mills as well as the Colt Firearms Factory, silk, and locomotive manufacturing factories.

Francis Cabot Lowell and members of the extended Lowell family created the model for early U.S. water-powered industry based on designs copied from English examples. England forbade export of textile machinery or even drawings. Lowell—an American textile merchant—committed to memory textile machinery designs he observed in England in the early 1800s. In 1813 he created a successful water-powered cotton mill on the Charles River in Massachusetts based on the British designs. Lowell died in 1817, but in 1823 his relatives and business partners shifted operations to a site in Massachusetts with falls that could produce much more energy. This site became the city of Lowell, Massachusetts. Lowell's mill produced cotton textiles. The mills in Lowell relied largely on a labor force of young women from rural New England who were housed in dormitories, given religious instruction, and chaperoned to keep their morals intact. Many of the young women mill workers accumulated a dowry and returned to their villages of origin to become New England farm wives. Working conditions in the Lowell textile mills were austere, but much better than the dreadful conditions Friedrich Engels described in Manchester, England in the 1840s.

THE GROWTH AND DISPERSION OF MIGRANTS OF COLOR 1607–1933

Between 1607 and 1933 Black, Latinx, and Asian-American and Pacific Islander (AAPI) populations in the United States, as well as the White population, all grew enormously. However, the growth of the Black, White, Latinx, and AAPI population in the United States occurred for different reasons, in different ways, and in different parts of the United States.

Detailed census figures by race are available from 1790, but in different, inconsistent, and questionable categories.[10] Since racial categories are socially constructed, many Americans are mixed-race, and many people either refuse to reveal their race or lie to the U.S. census, historical estimates of the racial composition of the U.S. population are uncertain and highly subjective.

The first slaves in what was to become the United States arrived in Jamestown in 1607. The U.S. census of 1790 enumerated half a million Blacks in the United States—mostly in Maryland, Virginia, North Carolina, South Carolina, and Georgia. It reported 32,162 free Blacks in the North and 27,032 in the South. Until 1808 when importation of slaves was banned and became a felony, the Black population of the United States was augmented by Blacks from Africa and the Caribbean as well as natural increase. The 1810 census reported approximately 1.2 million Black slaves in the United States and 200,000 nominally free Blacks. After 1808, all the legal increase in Black population is attributable to natural increase—the excess of live births over deaths. In 1860, the southern states that seceded from the union had 3,754,304 enslaved people, and 250,787 Blacks who were classified as free.[11] Border states that stayed with the union had 317,655 slaves.[12] There were 226,961 African Americans who lived in the northern states in 1860—all of whom were nominally free.

Important factors in the spatial distribution of racial and ethnic groups in the United States between 1607 and 1933 are decimation of the indigenous population through war, epidemics, and forced migration; migration of people of color from east to west as the frontier expanded; growth of the Latinx population, particularly along the U.S.–Mexican border; great waves of Black migration from the South to the North after the Civil War, World War I, and World War II; and ebbs and flows of Asian and Pacific Islander migration as a result of international politics and changing immigration law.

EARLY LAND USE, HOUSING, ENVIRONMENTAL, AND NATURAL RESOURCE PLANNING AND POLICY

Land use, housing, environmental, and natural resource planning and policy in America before the New Deal (beginning in 1933) were very rudimentary. Land was surveyed and subdivided, deeds established ownership rights, and streets were laid out. The size and physical arrangement of residential building lots and the street grids on which they were located were precisely mapped for many U.S. colonial and 19th-century towns and cities, as documented by Cornell University planning historian John Reps. New York City Commissioners established New York City's street pattern and grid in 1810.

In 1787 the Northwest Ordinance established a uniform grid pattern in the Northwest United States around the Great Lakes region and provided cheap land to settlers willing to live on the land and develop it. The 1862 Homestead Act expanded the homesteading policy that began with the Northwest Ordinance by providing free land in the Western United States to people willing to settle and improve it.

During the first half of the 19th century virtually all residential construction was privately financed, unplanned, and unregulated vernacular building—building that uses local materials and folk wisdom, without architects. Primitive building codes prohibited extremely dangerous practices such as wooden chimneys!

In the first half of the 19th century most households paid for their housing themselves or with money borrowed from relatives. They did not borrow money for their housing from financial institutions and had no mortgages. In the 19th and early 20th century savings and loan banks (S&Ls) which paid interest on individual saving accounts and lent money for home mortgages and other purposes grew in number and size. S&Ls typically lent money to homebuyers with a very high lump sum down payment amount—50% or more—and a very short mortgage term— typically five years. Most early mortgages were interest-only loans with a "balloon" payment at the end of the term that repaid all of the loan principal. In 1933 there was no government-provided housing even for what later came to be called "the worthy poor"—such as widows and orphans— except for dreadful almshouses, lunatic asylums, orphanages and jails (sometimes combined!).

Zoning ordinances began to impose local regulations on the height, bulk, and setback of houses, apartment buildings, and commercial buildings in the United States in the early 20th century. New York City adopted a zoning ordinance in 1916. Zoning became widespread after the U.S. Commerce Department promulgated a recommended Standard Model State Zoning Enabling Act (SSZEA) in 1922, and even more widespread after the U.S. Supreme Court declared zoning constitutional in the *Euclid vs Ambler Realty Company* case in 1923.

There was essentially no systematic federal, state, or local environmental planning and policy until after 1933.[13] A few pioneering environmentalists raised consciousness about the environment and the need to protect it. Scottish naturalist John Muir wrote eloquently about the marvels of the unspoiled natural environment of the American West. President Theodore Roosevelt succeeded in establishing Yellowstone National Park. Gifford Pinchot—Roosevelt's Chief of the Forestry Service from 1905 to 1910—worked tirelessly to establish stewardship over natural resources.

TENEMENT HOUSE REFORM

New York City was the center of early housing planning and policy because of its large population and many multi-family tenement buildings—poorly constructed, dense apartment buildings rented to multiple low-income households.

By 1867 there were 18,000 tenement house buildings in New York City. Most were cheaply built three- and four-story wood or brick buildings. The tenements had no running water or indoor toilets. They were constructed on almost the entire land area of 25×100-foot lots that had been laid out by New York City's Commissioners in their great 1810 plan for all of Manhattan. The early tenements typically contained "railroad flats"—apartment units with a

Figure 2.6 Crowded Lodging in a Bayard Street Tenement by Jacob Riis (1889).

series of rooms connecting to each other in a line similar to the layout of passenger train cars. Families and individuals that could not afford to rent even a tenement unit or a shared room in a tenement house lived crowded together in windowless basements, dilapidated farmhouses partitioned for many households, or five-cents-a-night beds in flophouses. Some slept in shifts in beds shared with people who worked at other times of the day or night, or were homeless.

Lawrence Veiller (1872–1959) emerged as the principal advocate of tenement reform. Jacob Riis's (1849–1914) iconic photographs of squalid conditions in New York tenements such as Figure 2.6 supported Veiller's tenement reform campaigns.

Unlike European socialists or later New Deal housing reformers, who focused on public ownership and subsidies to make modern housing affordable to millions of low- and moderate-income households, Veiller accepted that it was politically impossible to fundamentally change the private housing market in late 19th-century America, but sought to temper its worst abuses through regulation of building design. He was instrumental in getting tenement acts passed in New York City in 1867 and 1879, and a New York State tenement act that applied to New York City passed in 1901. Figure 2.7 illustrates the New York City "dumbbell tenement" design created by the 1879 Tenement Act—so named because it looked like a weight-lifting dumbbell. The dumbbell tenement had more space for households than older tenements and also had indoor toilets, but was still cramped and dangerous.[14] Dumbbell tenements are now also referred to as old law tenements.

New York City's tenement museum is in an old law tenement building constructed in 1863 that has been designated a National Historic Landmark. Apartments in the museum have been restored as they were at different periods in the building's past, and furnished with former tenants' original furniture and possessions. The surrounding area is a National Historic Site.

TRANSPORTATION AND COMMUNICATIONS TECHNOLOGY AND THE EMERGENCE OF THE U.S. CITY SYSTEM

Beginning in the early 19th century, a rapid succession of new technologies augmented transportation by foot, boat, and horse. The increased mobility altered the spatial pattern of metropolitan areas and regions of the United States.

Steamboats were the first disruptive transportation technology. Steamboats initially utilized wood and later coal to power a steam engine originally designed by Scottish inventor James Watt and manufactured by Matthew Boulton, which drove back- or side-paddle wheels. In 1807 American engineer and inventor Robert Fulton (1765–1815) and Robert Livingston (1746–1813)—a wealthy and politically connected entrepreneur who

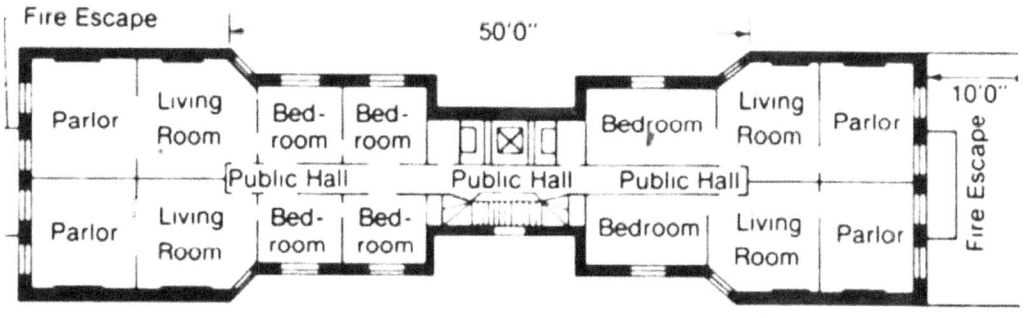

Figure 2.7 Dumbbell Tenement.

Figure 2.8 Robert Fulton's Steamboat *Clermont* (1807).

held the monopoly on steam transportation on the Hudson River—launched a steamboat that succeeded in making it much faster to travel between New York City and the New York state capital in Albany than by foot or horse. Their steamboat was originally named the *North River*, but it was later named the *Clermont* after Livingston's estate on the Hudson River. The *Clermont* was 150 feet long by 12 feet wide. It was powered by a custom Watt–Boulton steam engine and carried both passengers and freight. The *Clermont* could make the 150-mile trip between New York City and the New York State capital in Albany in about 36 hours each way. Figure 2.8 is a contemporary sketch of the *Clermont*.

Steamboats proliferated along the East Coast. They were soon going up the Mississippi River against the current—making St. Louis a principal hub, and by some measures the richest city in America before the Civil War. Transatlantic steamships were operating within a decade. The first steamboat on the West Coast of the United States began operation in 1849.

Horse- or mule-drawn streetcars running on wooden rails began operation in New York City in 1832, providing transportation between fixed destinations more quickly than it took to walk. Soon, two streetcars drawn by two horses and double-decker streetcars running on steel rails were common. By the mid-1880s, there were 415 street railway companies in the USA operating over 6,000 miles of track and carrying 188 million passengers per year. A horse could only pull a streetcar for four or five hours a day, was expensive to feed and care for, and produced prodigious amounts of manure.

Primitive wood-burning railroads began carrying freight and risk-tolerant passengers for short distances in the United States as early as the 1820s. The basic railroad network east of the Mississippi River was completed by 1840.[15] Congress passed legislation in 1862 to link the Union States to California and other Western states and territories. The first Railroad Act provided land grants and bond financing to private railroad companies, but the railroads were built almost entirely by private capital.[16]

Cable cars use an underground steel cable moving at a constant speed to haul passenger cars. A hand grip operated by a brakeman on

Figure 2.9 Horse-Drawn Streetcar (Hamilton, Virginia, circa 1874).

the car stops and starts the cars. The first cable car line began operation in San Francisco in 1873. It was built by an entrepreneur named Andrew Smith Hallidie (1836–1900) to go up and down San Francisco's hills. Other cities quickly adopted cable car technology. The largest and most successful cable car system in America was in Chicago. Construction of new cable car lines ended about 1890 as electric streetcar systems proved less expensive and more efficient.

Electric street railway systems use electricity from overhead wires to power streetcars. The first successful large electric street railway system was developed by Frank J. Sprague (1857–1934) in Richmond, Virginia in 1887. By 1895 there were about 900 electric street railways and nearly 11,000 miles of electric streetcar track in the United States.

"Streetcar suburbs" that relied on electric streetcars to transport commuters to and from suburbs to work in a nearby core city grew rapidly, beginning in the 1880s. Private entrepreneurs built electric streetcar lines out to cheap suburban land. The typical five-cents-a-ride fare did not cover construction, operating, and maintenance costs. However, developers made large profits by purchasing cheap land where new housing could be built near stations before the lines were built and then selling the land for a large profit when the lines were completed. In addition to streetcar suburbs there were intra-urban and inter-urban electric streetcar lines.

The first streetcars in Los Angeles began operation in 1887. By 1945 Los Angeles had the largest electric streetcar system in the world. In 1898 most of the lines were consolidated into a system controlled by Henry E. Huntington called the Pacific Electric Railway Company. At its peak, the Pacific Electric Railway Company operated over twenty streetcar lines with 1,250 streetcars. The system included lines serving different purposes both within the core of Los Angeles and interurban lines that connected communities over low-density Los Angeles City and parts of Los Angeles County. Streetcars were identifiable by their color. Figure 2.10 shows one of LA's "big red" streetcars about 1920.

Electric streetcars were increasingly replaced by automobiles and trucks during the first half of the 20th century. However, many streetcar lines continued in operation until after World War II. San Francisco, Boston, New Orleans, Philadelphia, Pittsburgh, Cleveland, and Newark have functioning streetcar systems in parts of the city operating with technological improvements. In the United States here are heritage streetcar

Figure 2.10 "Big Red", Los Angeles Electric Streetcar (circa 1930).

lines retained for nostalgia and tourism and a limited number of new light rail systems.

General Motors (GM) and other auto-related corporations operating through a subsidiary named National City Lines acquired, downgraded, and eventually eliminated major electric streetcar systems between 1937 and 1955. Huntington's estate sold his Los Angeles streetcar system to American City Lines in 1944. Figure 2.11. shows Los Angeles streetcars stacked for disposal by American City Lines.

An anti-trust attorney named Bradford Snell devoted his life to proving that GM and other auto-related companies had conspired to destroy the U.S. streetcar system in violation of U.S. anti-trust laws. The popular media sensationalized Schnell's conspiracy theory. However, most scholars conclude that electric streetcar systems disappeared mainly because auto and bus technology was superior and consumers preferred cars and buses to fixed rail systems that were never economically viable apart from the initial land sales.

The first great spike in automobile usage occurred early in the 20th century. There were fewer than 200,000 motor vehicles registered in the United States when the first Model T Ford was completed in 1908. Before the Model T Ford, automobiles were essentially toys for the rich—produced by several hundred small manufacturers. The Model T Ford was the first affordable, mass-produced automobile. The four-cylinder, twenty-horsepower model Henry Ford (1863–1947) introduced in October 1908 sold for $825— affordable to middle-class farm families. Between 1908 and 1927, Ford produced 15 million Model T Fords—nearly half of all the automobiles built in the United States during that time. By 1920 there were over nine million Model T Fords in operation, and in 1930 nearly 27 million. Increased mobility made it possible to greatly expand urban areas. People were no longer dependent on

Figure 2.11 Pacific Electric Railway Streetcars Awaiting Dismantling for Scrap Metal (Los Angeles, California, 1956).

fixed railroad and streetcar lines. They could live anywhere there was a road a Model T Ford could use.

A series of advances in communications technologies began during the second half of the 19th century. The telegraph and telephone linked U.S. cities, helped create a national system of cities in the United States, and connected cities in the U.S. to the world city network. In 1844 Samuel Morse (1791–1872) invented the technology to communicate by electric pulses representing letters as a series of dots and dashes (Morse code) traveling electronically on telegraph lines. A transatlantic cable connecting the East Coast of the United States to Europe was completed in 1854. A network of telegraph wires quickly linked cities east of the Mississippi River, and a transcontinental telegraph line linking the East and West Coasts was completed in 1861. In 1876 Alexander Graham Bell made the first successful telephone call, and the U.S. telephone network grew in extent and quality throughout the rest of the 19th and 20th centuries.

THE WORLD'S COLUMBIAN EXHIBITION OF 1893

World's fairs have been held periodically since the Great Exhibition of the Works of Industry of All Nations—also known as the Crystal Palace Exhibition—in London in 1851. Exhibitions illustrating cities have become increasingly important parts of world's fairs. In 2005 more than 75 million people attended a world's fair in Shanghai, China with the theme "better city better life" and exhibits on innovations in sustainable urban development.

The World's Columbian Exhibition, held in Chicago in 1893 to commemorate the four-hundredth anniversary of Christopher Columbus's voyage to the New World was a landmark event in early U.S. city and regional planning. It gave Chicago architect and planner Daniel Burnham and other leading architects and landscape architects the opportunity to demonstrate their vision of what a city might be like. The exhibition highlighted ideas of the "city beautiful" movement that Daniel Burnham led.

The city beautiful movement is discussed in Chapter 6.

ORIGINS OF THE U.S. PLANNING PROFESSION

While the 1893 World's Columbian Exhibition introduced city beautiful planning to the public, and both modern city planning and modern regional planning have earlier roots in Europe and America, 1909 is the watershed year in the early evolution of city and regional planning. In 1909 the first U.S. conference on city planning took place in Washington, D.C, the first U.S. course in city planning was offered at Harvard, the first U.S. city planning textbook—by Benjamin Clark Marsh and George B. Ford—was published, and Daniel Burnham and Edward Bennett's *Plan of the City of Chicago*—a "city beautiful" plan funded by the Chicago Commercial Club—was released. In Great Britain the first planning courses and degree programs began at the University of Liverpool, and the British parliament passed the first national planning law in 1909.

Only a handful of the 40 people who attended the first U.S. conference on city planning in 1909 called themselves city planners. The rest were landscape architects, architects, housing advocates, public health workers, and lawyers. Almost all were white, native-born men reflecting the gender and racial profile of the embryonic planning profession. Two women made important contribution to the conference. Jane Addams—the leader of the U.S. settlement house movement argued that planners should address issues of poverty and inequality and help acculturate and assimilate foreign immigrants to cities. Mary Simkovitch—a prominent housing reformer and leader of the settlement house movement—urged the conference participants to emphasize affordable housing in their plans.

Participants at the first U.S. conference on city planning debated fundamental questions about planning—who should prepare a city plan? approve it? What purpose should it serve? Should it be a secret document intended only for the mayor, city council, or an independent planning commission? Should it be for a specific time period or open-ended? Should the plan focus only on physical development or also economic and social issues. Participants even debated whether cities should have any plan at all.

Annual U.S. city planning conferences continued and grew. At the 9th conference in 1917, participants created a professional association named the American City Planning Institute (ACPI)—the predecessor of the American Planning Association (APA).[17]

Before he became president, conservative Republican Herbert Hoover (1874–1964), a brilliant civil engineer, catalyzed the next big step forward in city planning in the United States. As Secretary of Commerce, Hoover appointed an exceptionally talented 11-member committee to draft a model Standard State Planning Enabling Act (SSPEA). Landscape architect and ACPI president Frederick Law Olmsted Jr, attorney Edward Bassett—who had drafted New York City's zoning ordinance in 1916—and housing reformer Edward Veiller served on Hoover's SSPEA committee. SSPEA was advisory—a model act that states could adopt as written, modify, or ignore. If a state adopted it, the SSPEA enabled (authorized) cities and counties to prepare a comprehensive plan; it did not require them to do so. SSPEA stimulated a great wave of state enabling legislation during the 1920s and 1930s, followed by creation of planning commissions and a proliferation of city and county comprehensive plans. These were usually called master plans.

University of California, Berkeley planning professor T.J. (Jack) Kent—whose concept of the urban general plan is dominant today—blames the SSPEA for causing 20 years of confusion between zoning and planning between 1930 and 1950. On the one hand the act stated that a city master plan should be general and long-range, and on the other hand, that a detailed zoning ordinance, controlling short-term decisions, should be a major element of the master plan. Chapters 7 and 12 discuss Kent's role in sorting out this confusion.

EARLY U.S. CITY AND REGIONAL PLANNING EDUCATION

The first city planning programs were undergraduate civic design programs housed in schools of landscape architecture and architecture. Harvard College introduced the first college course in city planning in its landscape architecture department in 1909. In 1913 the University of Illinois Urbana-Champaign began offering courses in civic design. Harvard started a three-year graduate city planning program in 1923 and created a School of City Planning in 1929.

Early U.S. planning education was strongly influenced by the University of Liverpool, England, which initiated two different three-year undergraduate civic design programs in 1909. Civic design students in the United States and England studied classical Greek and Roman and European beaux arts city designs, and learned how to draw two-dimensional urban plans. They were exposed to Patrick Geddes's ideas described in Box 2.2 and Ebenezer Howard's vision of garden cities surrounded by greenbelts described in Chapter 6. By the 1920s, planners drew on empirical research and theory developed by Robert E. Park, Roderick McKenzie, Ernest W. Burgess, and other sociologists at University of Chicago. A number of city planning texts were published in England and the United States between 1909 and 1933. Clarence Perry's idea of the neighborhood unit, Le Corbusier's modernist vision of a contemporary city of 3 million consisting of enormous megastructures, and Frank Lloyd Wright's model of a low-density, urban-rural broadacre city described in Chapter 6 influenced early U.S. city and regional planning education in the 1920s and 1930s.

PATRICK GEDDES AND LEWIS MUMFORD

The eccentric Scottish polymath and activist, Patrick Geddes (1854–1932; Box 2.2) and his devoted friend Lewis Mumford (1895–1990)

BOX 2.2 PATRICK GEDDES

Patrick Geddes (1854 – 1932) was the great prophet of modern city and regional planning. More than a century ago he developed a unified vision of city and regional planning that identified many of the issues that concern city and regional planners today.

Geddes studied biology at the Royal School of Mines (Imperial College) in London from 1874 to 1877 under the tutelage of Thomas Henry Huxley, a disciple of Charles Darwin. While he was a laboratory assistant at University College London, Geddes met Darwin in person. Darwin's theory of evolution became central to Geddes's conception of how cities and regions evolve.

Geddes held teaching positions related to botany, civics, and sociology at the University of Edinburgh; biology and gardening at the University of Dundee, Scotland; and sociology and civics in Bombay, India. Shortly before his death he founded and taught in Scots College in Montpellier, France. Geddes believed that city and regional planning should enrich human life experience. He famously declared that "A city is more than a place in space, it is a drama in time."

In 1886 Geddes and his (wealthy) new wife purchased a row of tenement houses in Edinburgh, Scotland's worst neighborhood. They moved into the neighborhood and Geddes worked as a community organizer, affordable housing developer, and neighborhood planner. He plunged enthusiastically into organizing his neighbors to plant window flower boxes, rehabilitate salvageable houses, and widen the narrow alleyways between buildings into courtyards to bring in sunlight and clean air. Geddes purchased a house in this neighborhood where Sir Thomas More—the author of *Utopia*—had met with the great Dutch humanist educator Erasmus and turned it into a student dormitory!

Figure 2.12 Patrick Geddes.

Between 1887 and 1897 Geddes ran a summer school in Edinburgh to teach visiting intellectuals and local residents about urban planning and civics. His eclectic faculty included geographers, sociologists, artists, and anarchists.

Observing that greater London was engulfing other cities, Geddes coined the term conurbation to refer to areas where older cities and towns were merging with a sprawling city. He predicted that more conurbations would emerge in the future. He proposed the term megalopolis to describe emerging giant city regions 46 years before French geographer Jean Gottmann popularized the term by applying it to the urbanized Atlantic Seaboard of the United States.

Geddes's approach to studying the natural and built environment of city-regions together prefigured the "design with nature" approach that Scottish-American landscape architect Ian McHarg developed in the late 1960s. Geddes anticipated the vision of sustainable development Gro Harlem Brundtland's influential United Nations Commission report *Our Common Future* advanced in 1984, and planners engaged in sustainable urban development continue to pursue today.

Geddes created the world's first urban planning museum—the Watchtower Museum in Edinburgh, Scotland—in 1892. Visitors could ascend a watchtower next to Edinburgh Castle to view Edinburgh through a device called a camera obscura on the top floor that showed parts of the city in real time They then descended through four floors of exhibits showing physical, social, economic, and cultural aspects of Edinburgh, the Edinburgh region, Scotland, Europe, and—at the ground floor—the world. Geddes exhibited material from his Watchtower Museum in Europe, India, and the Middle East. The original exhibits were lost in 1914 when the ship transporting them to India was torpedoed by a German submarine. Geddes created new exhibits and carried on. The Watchtower Museum closed when Geddes died in 1932, but the Outlook Tower still has a one-room Geddes exhibit on the fourth floor.

Geddes made major contributions to city and regional planning research methodology. He is often quoted for his aphorisms "survey before plan" and "diagnosis before treatment", urging planners to do comprehensive background studies before preparing plans. By survey, Geddes meant a systematic study of the natural, cultural, and built environment by immersion in the local culture and ways in which communities and neighborhoods had developed in the past and could be developed in the future. He was not referring to telephone or mail surveys or surveying land parcels.

Geddes designed the Hebrew University in Jerusalem and a plan for part of the emerging metropolis in Tel-Aviv, Israel. A commission to make a plan for Dunfermline, Scotland where Andrew Carnegie was born that was generously funded by the Carnegie Endowment illustrates his approach to planning, but was not implemented.

Between 1915 and 1925 Geddes lived in India, where he studied Indian cities, promoted local city plans, and worked to improve public health. Astride an elephant, he led teams of sweepers to clean up cholera-ridden neighborhoods a century before today's healthy city movement.

Geddes's energy was always scattered across multiple projects. He was a terrible writer and never took the time to organize and clearly express his many prescient ideas. Fortunately, the American social critic Lewis Mumford became his friend and life-long collaborator. Mumford was a brilliant writer and introduced Geddes's ideas to U.S. and world audiences.

maintained one of the most fruitful intellectual collaborations in city and regional planning history. Geddes was formally educated as a biologist, self-educated in the social sciences, humanities, and the arts, considered himself a sociologist, and taught civics and gardening as well as biology, sociology, and city and regional planning. He was knighted for his contributions to education. Mumford was a self-educated polymath and public intellectual—a prolific and forceful writer who tirelessly propagated Geddes's ideas.

Geddes's approach was shaped by Charles Darwin's theory of evolution, but drew on the social sciences, arts, and humanities. Geddes (1915) famously said that "A city is more than a place in space, it is a drama in time." He applied biological concepts—particularly evolution—to cities and regions. Geddes pioneered, and Mumford developed, the interdisciplinary study of cities across natural and social sciences, humanities, and the arts. Together they invented the culture studies approach: an interdisciplinary way of viewing culture as the product of historical, political, and sociological forces. Culture studies provides useful background for city and regional planners.

THE GREAT REGIONAL PLAN DEBATE: THE NEW YORK REGIONAL PLAN ASSOCIATION (RPA) VERSUS THE REGIONAL PLANNING ASSOCIATION OF AMERICA (RPAA)

Geddes's and Howard's ideas clashed with mainstream planners' ideas in an epic battle between the U.S. planning establishment and an 18-member band of dissident regionalists with no official status or funding named the Regional Planning Association of America (RPAA). Lewis Mumford—the brilliant polymath who championed Patrick Geddes's ideas—and architect/planner Clarence Stein organized the RPAA in 1923.

Stein had planned the Sunnyside Garden's neighborhood in New York City and the new town of Radburn, New Jersey based on Ebenezer Howard's garden city ideas, discussed in Chapter 6.[18] Sunnyside Gardens was built between 1924 and 1928. Radburn was only partially built as planned because of the Great Depression.

The RPAA had only 18 members, no funding, and no formal status. However, the RPAA members were deeply versed in innovative European planning ideas, passionate, and strongly motivated to apply the ideas of Patrick Geddes, Ebenezer Howard, and other progressive European planners to planning in the United States. Housing advocates Catherine Bauer (Box 12.3) and Edith Elmer Wood, naturalist Benton MacKaye, and architect/planner Henry Wright were RPAA members.

The conflict pitted two formidable planners—Thomas Adams, an Anglo-American planner who was the Director of Plans and Surveys for the New York-based Regional Plan Association (RPA), and Lewis Mumford as the principal spokesperson for the RPAA. Adams had been the secretary of the Garden Cities Association in England and had taught urban planning at Harvard and Columbia universities. He had generous funding from the Russell Sage Foundation to develop a plan for New York City and the New York City region. The leaders of the U.S. planning profession worked with Adams and the RPA. The RPA produced a monumental multi-volume *Regional Plan of New York and Its Environs* in 1929. The plan covered a 5,528-square-mile region with a population of 10 million people. It cost $1.2 million to produce. Only 300 square miles were in New York City itself; the balance was in New York state, and parts of New Jersey and Connecticut.

The RPA envisioned New York as a city of towers consistent with European modernist visions. It proposed re-ordering density and transportation to make the region function more efficiently. The New York City economy would be enhanced as the vibrant hub of the region. Political power would be centralized to provide transportation, housing, and park and open space systems, on a regional basis. A central business district in Manhattan would be zoned for skyscrapers, surrounded by concentric rings of residences with zones for industry and recreation, connected by circumferential and radial rail lines and parkways.

While The 1929 Regional Plan for New York and its Environs did not originate the terms slums, blight, overcrowding, density, concentration, mobility, and traffic jams, The Regional Plan Association was the first to look at these issues regionally and make recommendations to address them in the New York metropolitan area. This helped educate other city leadership and citizens. It has had an enormous influence on the development of the New York region—particularly the region's park and highway system. Plans for other large metropolitan regions were based on it. The RPA is alive and well today with visionary plans for American regions in 2050.

While Thomas Adams and the RPA were preparing the *Regional Plan of New York and Its Environs*, the RPAA was meeting informally to discuss Patrick Geddes's regional planning philosophy (Box 2.2) and Ebenezer Howard's garden cities ideas, which are discussed in Chapter 6. Howard envisioned human-scale garden cities of about 32,000 people surrounded by greenbelts organized into a system of social cities in stark contrast to a megalopolis with a very dense core and power concentrated at the center as Adams and the RPA proposed. The RPAA met with Geddes in person while he was touring America.

The RPAA ferociously attacked the RPA for ignoring or muddling serious regional planning of the natural and built environment and failing to plan them together as Geddes proposed. They considered the RPA a pro-big-city betrayal of Howard's principles. Mumford (1930) savaged the plan in an article in the *New Republic* magazine titled "The booby prizes of 1929" and two other articles. He derided the RPA's reliance on metropolitan commuting to define the New York region as arbitrary and rationally indefensible, serving only the shortsighted needs of commuters and suburban speculators. Drawing on Geddes, Mumford proclaimed that a city and a region should be defined by their natural systems and cultural history. Mumford and the RPAA referred to New York City as a dinosaur city and a necropolis (city of the dead) and opposed resuscitating it. They attacked the modernist vision of office towers in the RPA plan. They proposed an alternative vision to decentralize activities of the core over a much larger region. Beyond Manhattan, the RPAA proposed a system of cities separated by greenbelts along the lines Howard proposed. About the only area on which the RPA and RPAA agreed was sociologist Clarence Perry's concept of the neighborhood unit, described in Chapter 6.

Ultimately Adams succeeded in having a large impact on the New York region. The system of parks and freeways he proposed was largely built and adds greatly to the region. While Mumford and the RPAA may have lost the battle, they arguably won the intellectual war about what city and regional planning should be like. Many planners are critical of over-centralization in New York and are sympathetic to the ideas Geddes, Mumford, and the RPAA advocated.

HISTORIC PRESERVATION PLANNING

Preservation of historic buildings, districts, artifacts, and tangible and intangible cultural heritage are important considerations in city and regional planning. In the United States, historic preservation initially focused on saving buildings associated with patriotic figures such as the home of the Revolutionary War leader and first U.S. president George Washington (Mount Vernon) near Washington, D.C., and historic events, such as Independence Hall in Philadelphia where the Declaration of Independence was drafted. There is growing recognition of the importance of preserving the cultural contribution of diverse racial, ethnic and religious groups, women, and LGBTQ communities.

There are many ways of preserving old buildings and historic districts. Buildings and artifacts may be simply saved from destruction. Minor repairs and refurbishing may protect and restore deteriorating structures. Buildings may be moved to save them or make them more accessible. Sometimes individual buildings or other parts of an old site or even the entire site are rebuilt as copies of the original. There are many museum villages like Old Sturbridge Village near Boston, which mixes original buildings with buildings moved from all over New England to show what a New England village in the early 19th century was like. Many cities have walking tours of historic districts and architecturally significant buildings such as Boston's Freedom, Black Heritage, and Women's History trails.

Most city and county planning departments lack funding for even one full-time historic preservation planner. However, one or more staff members may be assigned to work on historic preservation planning part-time. Some planners work or volunteer for public, nonprofit, or private historic preservation organizations. Architectural historians—educated to understand the historic significance of buildings and districts—play an important role in historic preservation planning.

SUMMARY

The past is prologue. Historians, planners, demographers, and others have produced empirical information on the evolution of individual cities; theory about how cities evolve; and histories of urban form, transportation, planning law, and other topics. All graduate students in Planning Accreditation Board (PAB)-accredited planning programs study the growth and development of places over time.

There is an excellent body of scholarship on the history of colonial, 19th-, and 20th-century U.S. cities, and recent U.S. urban history. The history of planning in the United Kingdom is well documented and there is a rapidly increasing body of scholarship on cities and city planning in other parts of the world. Planning historians have mined a wealth of primary material about the origins and growth of modern city and regional planning. Contributions of indigenous people, women, people of color, and LGBTQ individuals to cities and city and regional planning have been neglected, but are now being increasingly acknowledged and documented.

Experts continue to debate what constitutes a city. Census metrics and concepts developed by academics provide different answers to this important question. Fifty-seven per cent of the world's 7.9 billion inhabitants now live in urban places. World population and urbanization will likely continue to increase until the end of the 21st century. The population of the United States is now a little over 80% urban. The absolute urban population is expected to grow, but the percentage of the U.S. population living in urban areas is not projected to increase very much. Most of the world's urbanization for the balance of the 21st century will be in developing countries.

There was little concern with social justice in cities before the New Deal. Until recently women, people of color, and members of the LGBTQ community were largely absent from the planning profession and their concerns barely considered in city and regional plans. Women are now well represented among planning students and in the profession. The number of people of color in planning is increasing, but is still much too low. Few city or regional plans include a gender perspective, or adequately consider Black, Latinx,

AAPI, indigenous, LGBTQ, and other diverse communities or their concerns.

Patrick Geddes was right: "A city is more than a place in space, it is a drama in time." Studying the past is critical for planning the future. The urban drama is continuing today.

CONCEPTS

Cable Car
City Scientific Movement
Colonial City
Congestion Movement
Dumbbell Tenement
Electric Streetcar
Homestead Act
Industrial City
Model T Ford
Northwest Ordinance
Pre-industrial City
Regional Plan Association (RPA)
Regional Planning Association of America (RPAA)
S Curve of Urbanization
Standard State Planning Enabling Act (SSPEA)
Steamboat
Streetcar Suburb
Society for Useful Manufactures (SUM)
Tenement
U.S. Conference on City Planning (1909)
Walking City
Web of Seaport Life

PEOPLE

Thomas Adams
Kingsley Davis
Henry Ford
Robert Fulton
Peter Hall
Andrew Smith Hallidie
Herbert Hoover
Ebenezer Howard
Lewis Mumford
Frederick Law Olmsted
Frederick Law Olmsted Jr
John Reps
Sam Bass Warner

NOTES

1 In 1800 there were about 1 billion people on earth, in 1900 about 2 billion, and today nearly 7.9 billion (UN, 2019). Earth's population was no greater than 20 million in both 10,000 and 5,000 BCE, 400 million in the first year of the Common era (CE), 345 million in 1000 CE and 2.54 billion in 1950 (United States Census, 2018). There are approximately 7.9 billion people on earth today (World Population Clock, United States Census Bureau, 2021).

2 Only 10% of the Chinese population was urban when the People's Republic of China was founded in 1949. The percentage nearly doubled by 1958, until a combination of bad harvests and chaotic policies during the Great Leap Forward (1958–1962) and sending millions of city dwellers to the countryside during the Cultural Revolution (1966–1976) slowed urbanization. From the late 1970s—when Deng Xiao Peng and a new pragmatic leadership initiated reforms—China's urbanization rate has grown very rapidly. It is about 61% today and may be 75% or more by 2050. Cambodia—one of the poorest countries in the world with a tragic history of war and genocide—was only about 10% urban in 1950, but soared to 29% as terrified villagers streamed into Cambodia's capital—Phnom Penh—to escape revolutionary Khmer Rouge violence and U.S. bombing. It then plummeted to 4% when the Khmer Rouge drove the urban population to rural work camps and murdered an estimate 1.5 to 2 million Cambodians. After the Khmer Rouge were overthrown. Cambodia's urbanization rate recovered, but about 75% of Cambodians still live in rural areas today.

3 Other of Professor Reps's books—listed in the references to this chapter—describe the planning history of Washington, D.C., tidewater towns in Virginia, Delaware, and Maryland, Western cities and towns, Mississippi River towns, St. Louis, bird's-eye views of cities, and the lithographers who produced historic U.S. city plans.

4 In 1610 there were only 350 European settlers in what is now the continental United States—all in Virginia (U.S. Census, 2018). By 1620 there were 2,302—in Virginia and New England (Greene & Harrington, 1932). By 1700 there were 250,000 in the 13 British colonies. In 1775 there were 2,500,000 in what was to become the United States (ibid).

5 William Penn founded Philadelphia as a refuge for Quakers in 1682. English Protestant Puritans settled Boston and other towns and cities in the Massachusetts Bay Colony in the 1730s. British philanthropist James Oglethorpe founded Savannah, Georgia in 1733 as a place for convicts from British debtors' prisons to begin a new life.

6 Chicago continued to dump its sewage into and draw its water from Lake Michigan until the Chicago Sanitary and Ship Canal opened in 1900, reversing the course of the Chicago River to protect the Lake Michigan water supply. Most of Chicago's

7 sewage then flowed into the Mississippi River, alleviating Chicago's water pollution problem, but creating problems for human settlements downstream along the Mississippi.
7 Some loyalists who had sided with England during the Revolutionary War moved from the United States to Canada during and after the war. In the 1820s 143,000 immigrants came to the United States from Europe. Between 1831 and 1840 immigration to the USA more than quadrupled to a total of 599,000; 207,000 were Irish, 152,000 German, 76,000 British, and 46,000 French. Between 1841 and 1850, immigration nearly tripled again, totaling 1,713,000 immigrants; at least 781,000 Irish, 435,000 German, 267,000 British, and 77,000 French.
8 The Northwest Ordinance defined all of the land between British North America—the territory now known as Canada—and the U.S. border around the Great Lakes as the Northwest Territory (U.S. Congress, 1787). It extinguished pre-existing state land claims and provided that new territories could be formed once a territory achieved a population of 5,000 free male inhabitants. Once the population of a territory reached 60,000 it could be admitted to the union as a state. Eventually the states of Ohio, Indiana, Michigan, Illinois, Wisconsin, and part of Minnesota were created from Northwest Territory land.
9 The Laws of the Indies specified that a site for a settlement (*pueblo*) should have a healthy location away from lagoons or marshes, adequate fertile soil and water, fuel, timber, and other resources. It was supposed to have a native population to supply slave labor. The *pueblo* itself should have a main plaza (*plaza mayor*) large enough for horse racing, with covered arcades for market activities. Twelve straight streets were supposed to radiate from the plaza to form a grid. A Catholic church was to be located on an imposing site. Each household was to receive a plot of land in the *pueblo* and a second plot to farm within easy walking distance. Some Spanish settlements in North, South, and Central America followed the Laws of the Indies specifications. Others—including Santa Fe, New Mexico—did not.
10 There was no systematic effort to count Latinx in the U.S. census until 1970. In 1970 approximately 9 million people reported that they were of Mexican, Puerto Rican, Cuban, Central or South American, or Other Spanish descent. Estimates of the number of indigenous people living in what is now the United States before 1492 are as high as 60 million. By 1930 only 330,000 people self-identified as American Indian. The actual numbers of Latinx, mixed-race, and indigenous Americans were almost certainly much higher, as many respondents were afraid to report their race.
11 The slave states were Alabama, Arkansas, Delaware, Florida, Georgia, Kentucky, Louisiana, Maryland (which included Washington, D.C. in 1860), Mississippi, Missouri, North Carolina, South Carolina, Tennessee, Texas, and Virginia.
12 The border states that had slaves, but did not secede were Kentucky, Delaware, and Maryland (including Washington, D.C.).
13 Private developers clear-cut timber and extracted minerals with no thought of pollution or damage to the environment, and harvested fish and wildlife without any regard for long-term sustainability of species. Sportsmen (and women) could rent a rifle and shoot buffalo from train windows as they took the new transcontinental railroad across the great plains in the 1870s leaving thousands of buffalo carcasses to rot. The great American ornithologist James Audubon described people clubbing millions of passenger pigeons that migrated along the East Coast in flocks that blackened the sky. Their corpses were used as pig food. The last passenger pigeon died in the Cincinnati zoo in 1913.
14 The 1867 New York City Tenement House Act required buildings it covered to have fire escapes, one toilet for every 20 tenants, and to be connected to city sewers "if possible". The dumbbell tenements built after the 1879 New York City Tenement House Act are based on the winning design in a contest offered by *Plumber and Sanitary Engineer* magazine in 1878 (Lubove, 1963: 31). The Dumbbell Tenement footprint was limited to 65% of the lot. Figure 2-7 shows one floor of a dumbbell tenement. There were 4 families on each floor, each with four 7' x 8 ½' bedrooms (barely enough for a single bed), and a separate 10½-foot-by-11-foot living room and parlor. An 18" indentation on each the side of the building was supposed to provide light and air to the bedrooms. Not only were the indentation inadequate, they were often filled with trash and acted as chimney flues if they caught fire.
15 Before 1840 there were less than 3,000 miles of railroad track in the United States—mostly in the Northeast (Pred, 1980: 6). Between 1840 and 1860 railroad mileage quintupled to 30,600 miles. In 1860 there were still over 300 independent railroad lines in operation in the United States and eleven or more different gauges of track (ibid: 6).
16 The First Pacific Railway Act (1862) granted the Union Pacific and Central Pacific Railroads 400-foot rights-of-way and 5 square miles of land for each mile of track built. Congress doubled the amount per mile in 1864. Between 1862 and 1973 the federal government gave railways 250,000 square miles of federal land either directly or indirectly through the states. Federally backed bonds provided cheap construction financing for the railroads. The transcontinental railroad was completed in 1869.
17 Frederick Law Olmstead Jr. was the first president of ACPI. Planning directors, planning commissioners, and staff created a separate organization named the American Society of Planning Officials (ASPO) in 1934. The ACPI was renamed the American Institute of Planners (AIP) in 1939. In 1978 AIP and ASPO were consolidated into the American Planning Association (APA).

18 Sunnyside Gardens consists of nine rows of townhouses and nine four- to six-story apartment buildings. Seventy-two percent of the 77-acre site is open space. Stein conceived of Radburn as "a town for the motor age". The plan for Radburn had a greenbelt, "superblocks", and a pedestrian path system separating automobiles and pedestrians. Stein remained a champion of new towns for America until his death in 1975.

SUGGESTIONS FOR FURTHER LEARNING

Overviews of U.S. Urban History: Howard Chudakoff, Judith Smith, & Peter Baldwin, *The evolution of American urban society*, 8th ed (2014). Raymond Mohl and Roger Biles, *The making of urban America*, 3rd ed (2012). Steven Corey & Lisa Boehm (eds), *The American urban reader*, 2nd ed (2020). John Reps, *The making of urban America* (1965). Sam Bass Warner, *The private city* (1968). Lisa Boehm & Steven Corey *America's urban history* (2014). Charles Glaab & A. Theodore Brown, *A history of urban America* (1967). Timothy Gilfolyle, *Oxford encyclopedia of American urban history* (2019). **Planning History Timelines:** American Planning Association (APA), American planning history since 1900 [slideshow] (2021). Skillshare, A brief history of U.S. city planning (2020). Scott Campbell, Planning history timeline [website] (2021). **Urbanization:** Kingsley Davis, The urbanization of the human population (1965). John Palen, *The urban world*, 11th ed (2018). Paul Knox & Linda McCarthy, *Urbanization*, 3rd ed (2014). Shlomo Angel, *Planet of cities* (2015). United States Census, *Historical estimates of world population* (2018). Carl Haub, How many people have ever lived on earth? (2011). **Cities and Civilization:** Lewis Mumford, *The city in history* (1962). Peter Hall, *Cities in civilization* (1998). **American Indian Cities:** Roger Kennedy, *Hidden cities* (1994). Cahokia Mounds State Historic Sites [website] (2021). Robert Silverberg, *The Mound Builders* (1986). Eric Skopec & Christopher Skopec, *The ancestral Puebloan primer* (2010). Lewis Henke, *Aristotle and the American Indians* (1959). **U.S. Urban Planning History:** Donald Krueckeberg (ed), *Introduction to planning history in the United States* (1982). Richard LeGates & Frederic Stout (eds), *Early urban planning 1870–1940*, 3 vols (1998). Mellior Scott, *American city planning since 1890* (1969). Christine Boyer, *Dreaming the rational city* (1983). American Planning Association (APA), National planning pioneers (2021). **The 1909 U.S. Conference on City Planning:** United States Senate Committee on the District of Columbia National Conference on City Planning (1909). **American Colonial Urban History:** Gary Nash, *The urban crucible* (1986). Samuel Bass Warner, *The private city* (1968). **Frontier Cities:** Frederick Jackson Turner, *The frontier in American history* (1893). Carl Bridenbaugh, *Cities in the wilderness* (1938). John Reps, *Town planning in frontier America* (1981). Gunther Barth, *Instant cities* (1975). **The Northwest Ordinance and the Homestead Act:** United States Congress, An ordinance for the government of the territory of the United States, north-west of the river Ohio (1787). United States Congress, United States Homestead Act (1862). **The L'Enfant Plan for Washington, D.C. (1791):** John Reps, *Washington on view*. **Spanish City Planning in North America:** Dora Crouch, Daniel Garr, & Axel Mundigo, *Spanish city planning in North America* (1982). **Transportation Planning History:** Sam Bass Warner, *Streetcar suburbs* (1962). **General Motors, American City Lines, and Bradford Snell's Streetcar Conspiracy Theory:** Christopher Slater, General Motors and the demise of streetcars (1997). George Hilton, General Motors and the demise of streetcars: A comment (1998). Martha Olson & Jim Klein, *Taken for a ride* [video] (1996). **U.S. Immigration:** Oscar Handlin, *The uprooted* (1952). Ron Takaki, *Strangers from a different shore* (1998). **U.S. Environmental History:** William Cronin, *Nature's metropolis* (1997). **U.S. Black Urban History:** W.E.B. Dubois, *The Philadelphia Negro* (1899). Saint Claire Drake & Horace Caton, *Black metropolis* (1945). Gary Nash, *Forging freedom* (1991). Ira Berlin, *Slaves without masters* (1992) and *The long emancipation* (2018). Erin Bradford, Free African American population in the U.S., 1790–1860 (2008). Ira Berlin The Long Emancipation (2018). U.S. Bureau of the Census *A century of population growth: From the first to the twelfth census of the United States*. Washington, D.C.: United States Bureau of the Census. **19th-Century Cities:** Adna Weber, *The growth of cities in the 19th century* (1899). Jacob Riis, *How the other half lives* (1890). Roy Lubove, *The progressives and the slums* (1963). **The Regional Plan Association (RPA)–Regional Planning Association of America (RPAA) Conflict:** Regional Plan Association (RPA), *Regional plan of New York and its environs* (1929). David Johnson, *Planning the great metropolis* (2015). Lewis Mumford, The booby prizes of 1929 (1930), The plan of New York (1932), and The plan of New York, II (1932). **History of U.S. Suburbs:** Kenneth Jackson, *The crabgrass frontier* (1985). Becky Nicolaides & Andrew Wiese (eds), *The suburb reader*, 2nd ed (2016). **Historical U.S. Urban Statistics:** U.S. Census Bureau, *Historical statistics of the United States 1790–1970* (1975). Inter-university Consortium for Political and Social Research, *Historical, demographic, economic, and social data: The United States, 1790–1970* [computer file] (1997). United States Census Bureau, *Historical census statistics on population totals by race, 1790 to 1990, and by Hispanic origin, 1970 to 1990, for large cities and other urban places in the United States* (2005). **Patrick Geddes:** Patrick

Geddes, *Cities in evolution* (1915). Walter Stephen (ed), *Think global, act local: The life and legacy of Patrick Geddes* (2016). Philip Boardman, *Patrick Geddes* (2017) and *The worlds of Patrick Geddes* (1978). Volker Weller, *Biopolis: Patrick Geddes and the city of life* (2002). Helen Meller, *Patrick Geddes* (2017). Marshall Stalley, *Patrick Geddes* (1972). **Journals:** *Journal of Planning History*. *Urban History*.

CHAPTER 3

Urban Design and Placemaking

INTRODUCTION

In the 5th century BCE the great Greek philosopher Socrates declared that the understanding of "how to plan and beautify human communities is by far the greatest and most admirable form of wisdom". Urban design is a well-established professional field. It is a central feature of U.S. planning education and planning practice. Design education helps planning students develop innate design skills and master computer-assisted design (CAD) and other tools.

Placemaking combines design with a wide range of other considerations and ongoing processes to make places succeed—particularly public places. Sittable spaces like steps, ledges, and movable chairs are important placemaking design elements. Placemaking involves attention to social inclusion, security, public facilities management, and public relations. Many urban designers consciously strive to include diverse populations.

Site planning applies urban design and placemaking principles at the site level, where most urban design occurs. Urban designers design highway corridors, windfarms, habitat conservation areas, parks, and many other spaces, as well as residential, commercial, and industrial sites. They often develop design standards for a project or a specific area.

This chapter describes what urban design and placemaking are and gives examples of good urban design and placemaking practice. It describes form-based codes and transects—visual representations of form elements that some local governments are beginning to use in addition to or in place of zoning. The chapter include a biography of Massachusetts Institute of Technology planning professor, Kevin Lynch, and describes his influential ideas about five elements that help people form their image of the city.

Since space between buildings and streets is such an important urban design element, sections describe the relationship of urban design to the space between buildings, street and sidewalk design, and pedestrianized streets. Different individuals and communities require different urban design solutions. A section describes designing with diversity. The last sections of the chapter describe important urban design movements—the New Urbanism, design with nature, creating defensible space, and crime prevention through environmental design.

URBAN DESIGN

Urban design is a specialty that falls somewhere between architecture and city and regional planning. According to University of Pennsylvania planning professor Jonathan Barnett (1982) urban design "occupies the substantial middle ground between city planners who are primarily concerned with the allocation of resources according to projections of future need … and architects [who] design buildings".

Some U.S. planning schools offer urban design specializations. Sixteen offer graduate Master's of Urban Design (MUD) degrees. While The Planning Accreditation Board (PAB) does not have accreditation standards for urban design programs, it reviews the adequacy of urban design programs that seek accreditation as part of its overall accreditation process for PAB-accredited degrees. Some U.S. undergraduate planning, architecture, and other students take urban design courses.

Urban design professionals have often completed undergraduate degrees in architecture or design before getting an MUD degree or an MCRP degree with an urban design specialization. Urban design is widely taught in other countries—usually at the undergraduate level. Urban design education involves studio work in which individual students and student teams produce and critique urban designs in the same way that architecture students learn to design buildings through studio work.

Urban design requires theoretical and applied understanding of how different spaces relate to each other and the technical ability to accurately render two- and three-dimensional space. Planners and policy makers need to understand how the height, bulk, and setback of each building on each parcel in a site plan—the detailed plan for a specific site—will affect views, privacy, safety, and the activities that the development generates. The urban designers must consider the relationship of the site's streets to each other and the surrounding area and infrastructure. Urban design requires holistic thinking. It synthesizes material from multiple fields.

Computer-assisted design (CAD) software allows urban designers to create and manipulate two- and three-dimensional designs and their associated values. An urban designer in Dortmund, Germany can use CAD software to design a 3D site plan and upload it to the internet. Then, an urban designer in Shenzhen, China can download the design, tweak it to have Chinese characteristics, and print it out on paper or—using a 3D printer— as a three-dimensional plastic, wood, resin, powder titanium, or steel model.

Architects have designed cities for millennia. "Civic design" was a well-established field of architecture in Europe and America by the end of the 19th century.[1] The term "urban design" originated at a conference at the Harvard Graduate School of Design in 1956. The first university programs named "urban design" were created in the late 1950s. The New York City Urban Design Group, formed in 1967, was the first city-level urban design group in the world. The number of urban design firms proliferated during the late 1970s and early 1980s and has grown and matured since that time.

The urban design process for a single site with one or more buildings like a mall or shopping center is similar to the way architects plan a building or a civil engineer designs a dam. Local governments rarely formally adopt urban design standards, unlike plumbing, electrical, and other standards that they formally adopt and that have the force of law. Urban designers refer to urban design standards for detailed advice on specific parts of the built environment such as exactly how wide parking spaces for a public library should be.

Urban design issues are complex—they involve architecture, land use, transportation, and the natural environment. They require interdisciplinary understanding of the social, economic, and political culture of communities they are intended to serve. Urban design requires normative decisions, not just technical skills. Aesthetics and beauty are important, but good design should also contribute to efficiency, resilience, equity, and other values. Changing the mix of building heights, bulk, shapes, or floor area ratios (FARs) will produce alternative designs that will meet some criteria better and others less well.

Renderings of two- and three-dimensional images of alternative urban designs are important for planning communications. Government officials, private clients, and citizens often respond to visual representations of alternative futures more easily than written ones. Few non-experts have the time or expertise to master engineering and budget details for a proposed development, but paper, digital, and physical models showing different designs allow stakeholders to understand alternatives and permit decision-makers to make more informed choices during the planning stage before implementation begins.

PLACEMAKING

Placemaking involves a range of tangible and intangible ingredients. Sociologist William Whyte (1946–2014) developed an approach to placemaking over a 20-year period in the 1960s and 1970s by studying the relationship between design and the social life of parks and plazas in New York City.[2] Whyte worked with Hunter College students and staff of New York City's excellent Urban Design Group on what he called the "Street Life Project".

Whyte's findings in the Street Life Project were often surprising. He found that the amount of "sittable space"—any place where people can sit in a park or plaza—is much more important than either the total space or the shape of the space. Grass, ledges, and other areas can provide sittable space, in addition to benches or chairs. Movable chairs make a huge difference in how much people use and enjoy an urban space. Other elements that Whyte found contributed to places that people enjoy include food vendors, water, public art, festivals, trees, inviting entrances, sunlight (even reflected sunlight), shade, protection from wind, and connectivity to the street (no steps). The New York City Planning Commission adopted many of Whyte's suggestions as requirements or guidelines for new park and plaza development.

The New York City based Project for Public Spaces (PPS) continues to carry out the placemaking work Whyte pioneered. PPS has completed projects in more than 3,500 communities in all 50 U.S. states and over 50 countries. PPS is a national and international hub for placemaking information.

While much placemaking is for public spaces, many urban designers work on private projects which are not open to the public. Planners can impact the design of private spaces in many ways. Zoning—including design review—and other implementation tools can help create attractive and lively places by encouraging mixed uses and facilitating uses at street level like cafes that will attract people and encourage them to linger. New York and other cities offer private office building developers density bonuses allowing them to build taller buildings or increase the amount of floor space in new office buildings if, in exchange, the owners agree to build a park or plaza open to the public at ground level—a privately owned public open space (POPOS).

FORM-BASED CODES AND TRANSECTS

Form-based codes are a recent innovation in city planning and urban design that visually illustrate permissible alternatives. Duany Plater-Zyberk (DPZ)—a New Urbanist urban design firm headed by the husband-and-wife team of Andrés Duany and Elizabeth Plater-Zyberk—has developed standards for transects—visual representations of the nature of development at different levels from undeveloped rural land to dense urban areas. Transects are increasingly widely used in form-based codes. DPZ and the Congress of the New Urbanism (CNU), which Duany and Plater-Zyberk helped create, collaborate in a teaching program on form-based code planning at the University of Miami.

Figure 3.1 shows an updated version of Andrés Duany's original transect design.

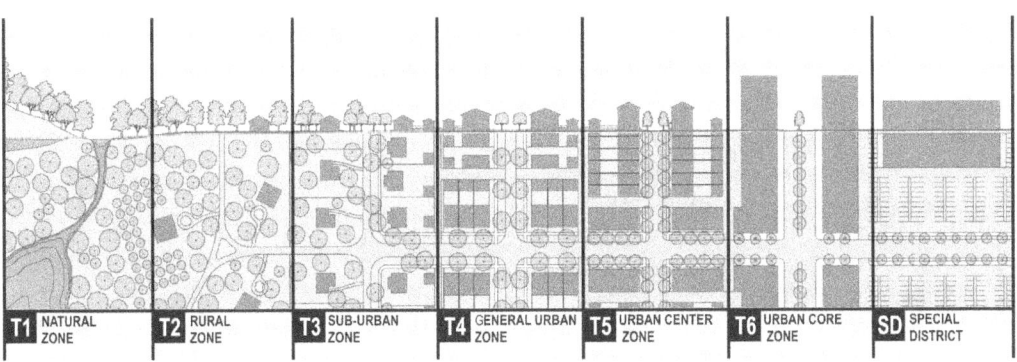

Figure 3.1 Andrés Duany's Transect.

There is a continuum from T1 (Natural Zone) on the left to T6 (Urban Core Zone) and SD (Special District) on the right.

The Form-Based Codes Institute (FBCI) is a nonprofit corporation that does research, sets standards, and engages in outreach and education to advance the knowledge and use of form-based codes. It makes available a model SmartCode that illustrates current form-based code practices. The Center for Applied Transect Studies (CATS) is a source of information about form-based codes. CATs distributes a model transect based on the SmartCode.

The Form-Based Codes Institute (2021) defines a form-based code as: "a land development regulation that fosters predictable built results and a high-quality public realm by using physical form rather than separation of uses as the organizing principle for the code". The form-based code approach contrasts with conventional zoning's focus on the micromanagement and segregation of land uses. Zoning is a blunt instrument that does not match buildings to sites or each other well. It controls development intensity through tools such as floor area ratios (FARs), the number of dwellings per acre, setbacks, parking ratios, and traffic levels of service (LOS) rather than focusing on an integrated built form.

Form-based code regulations and standards are presented in words, diagrams, and visual images. They are keyed to a regulating plan that designates the appropriate form and scale (and therefore, character) of development, rather than only identifying the boundaries of residential, commercial, industrial, and other areas like zoning does. Form-based codes address the relationship between building facades and the public realm, the form and mass of buildings in relation to one another, and the scale and types of streets and blocks for an area. They may specify street and building types, including mixes of types, build-to lines, the number of floors, and the percentage of the building frontage to be used in certain ways. They regulate development to give unity, efficient organization, social vitality, and walkability to cities, towns, and neighborhoods. Form-based codes may include architectural, landscaping, signage, and environmental resource standards. They are generally regulatory—not advisory like design guidelines or vague statements of design policy. The Form-Based Codes Institute (2021) defines five main components of form-based codes:

1) Building Standards: Regulations controlling the features, configurations, and functions of buildings that define and shape the public realm;
2) Administration: A clearly defined and streamlined application and project review process;
3) Definitions: A glossary to ensure the precise use of technical terms;
4) Regulating Plan: A plan or map of the regulated area designating the locations where different building form standards apply;
5) Public Standards: Standards specifying elements in the public realm such as sidewalks, travel lanes, on-street parking, street trees, and street furniture.

The FBCI maintains a library of examples of exemplary U.S. and foreign form-based codes. It gives an annual award for achievement in the writing and implementation of form-based codes—the Driehaus award.

THE IMAGE OF THE CITY

Theory by Massachusetts Institute of Technology city planning professor Kevin Lynch (Box 3.1) about how people perceive cities helps planners and urban designers understand and clarify universal form elements to make cities more psychologically and emotionally satisfying. Lynch sought to understand how people perceive urban environments and how planners and design professionals can respond to their psychological and spiritual needs while also designing efficient, beautiful, culturally appropriate sites, cities, and regions. Lynch's profoundly humane writings weave together a unique blend of theory and

BOX 3.1 KEVIN LYNCH

Kevin Lynch (1918–1989) is a towering figure in 20th-century urban design—the founder of the modern field. Lynch's 1961 book—*The Image of the City*—is the most widely read urban design book of all time. Lynch was a scholar-practitioner with extensive professional experience in urban design and site planning. He was a superb theorist who described precise, practical ways to implement his ideas clearly in text and drawings. Lynch was an excellent artist. The margins of his notebooks, books, and journal articles are illustrated with sketches capturing essential form features he observed and detailed design solutions at different scales.

Lynch studied architecture at Yale University and apprenticed himself to the great American architect Frank Lloyd Wright for a year and a half at Wright's Taliesin Teaching Studio. He transferred to the Massachusetts Institute of Technology (MIT) where he received a bachelor's degree in urban planning. After serving in World War II, Lynch joined the MIT faculty in 1947 at age 30. He taught courses at MIT in urban design and site planning for 41 years.

Lynch was a principal in the urban design firm Carr, Lynch Associates. After *The Image of the City* cemented his reputation, Lynch lectured and consulted worldwide. He continued to write original and brilliant books on site planning, good city form, regionalism, and historic preservation by himself and co-authored with his talented PhD students—many of whom became leaders in the fields of urban design and planning. Lynch's integration of psychology into design helped spawn the subfield of urban psychology in the 1960s. There are urban psychology degree programs and research centers in Europe, but urban psychology is little taught, researched, or practiced in the United States today.

Lynch was a sophisticated methodologist. Rather than starting from a theory and reasoning from it about how people perceive cities (deductive logic), Lynch started by gathering empirical information from people themselves and then constructed theory that explained the patterns he found (inductive logic). He pioneered the research method of asking people to draw mental (cognitive) maps showing how they perceived the image of the city and analyzing the maps to understand how people perceive their surroundings. Lynch found that the maps people drew were distorted—expanding space they knew or liked and shrinking or omitting spaces they disliked, did not know well, or had never visited. Recurring patterns in the cognitive maps helped Lynch formulate his theories about what basic elements of city form people find most satisfying.

In *The Image of the City* Lynch argues that people perceive cities as consisting of underlying city form elements: "paths" (along which people and goods flow), "edges" (which differentiate one part of the urban fabric from another), "landmarks" (easily recognized features that help orient people), "districts" (that people perceive as physically or culturally distinct places even if their boundaries are fuzzy), and "nodes" (centers of activity where paths often intersect). Lynch believed that humans have an innate desire to understand their surroundings. Lynch was convinced that urban environments would be more psychologically satisfying as well as more aesthetically appealing and efficient if urban designers understand how people perceive the elements he identified and use them to design cities that are more imageable.

Thousands of city planners, urban designers, and architects all over the world have prepared plans that clarify paths, edges, nodes, landmarks, and districts in cities as diverse as San Francisco, Cairo, Havana, and Ciudad Guyana, Venezuela based on Lynch's ideas and proposed designs to strengthen elements of good city form based on his suggestions and illustrations.

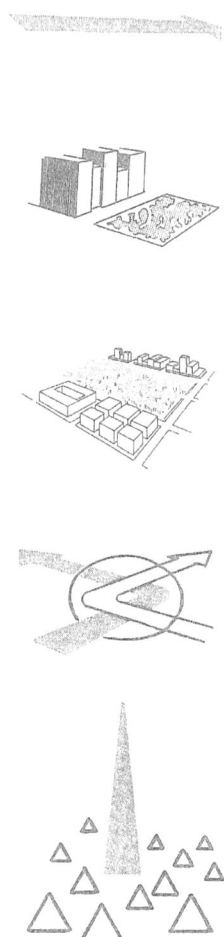

Figure 3.2 Kevin Lynch's 5 Image of the City Elements.

practical design suggestions drawn from his voluminous reading in the social sciences and humanities as well as planning and architecture. Lynch's approach is a model for interdisciplinary work and uniting theory and practice.

THE SPACE BETWEEN BUILDINGS AND PEDESTRIANIZED STREETS

Danish urban designer/architect Jan Gehl (born 1936) has developed an influential approach to designing the space between buildings. Gehl was instrumental in Copenhagen's 1962 plan to pedestrianize the city's main shopping street—Strøget—banning cars so that Strøget is used only by pedestrians. The Strøget plan was the first major pedestrian street design. Strøget is now the longest pedestrian-only street in the world.

Gehl's studies and design recommendations convinced the Copenhagen municipal government to make the very controversial change. Many merchants with stores on Strøget initially opposed pedestrianization. However, Strøget was an astonishing success and is a highly used and much-loved feature of Copenhagen today. Other cities have replicated pedestrian streets closed to cars and trucks. Figure 3.3 shows a section of Strøget today.

Gehl's Strøget success and his first book—*Life Between Buildings* (1971)—brought him international recognition. For

URBAN DESIGN AND PLACEMAKING | 51

Figure 3.3 Strøget (Copenhagen, Denmark, 2013).

50 years, Gehl's urban design firm—GEHL Architects, headquartered in Copenhagen—has designed pedestrianized streets and other projects reflecting Gehl's design philosophy. They have prepared urban design plans in 39 countries for cities as diverse as London, Lille, Melbourne, Cork, San Francisco, Chongqing, Belgrade, Moscow, Muscat, and Rabat. City planners and urban designers have incorporated Gehl's ideas into many more plans and projects.

Buildings occupy less than half the land in most cities.[3] Gehl is concerned with how to design "the space between buildings" so that it is used and enjoyed. He argues that contact among people is important at any level, from simply seeing, hearing, and being among other people, to complex and emotionally involved interactions such as public mourning or attending a political rally. He considers human interaction in outdoor public spaces essential to enrich human lives.

Gehl distinguishes between necessary and optional outdoor activities. He believes good urban design should draw people outside for optional activities like attending a festival or political rally, sitting in an outdoor cafe, or simply walking and people watching. Good urban design can also encourage people to spend more time outdoors on necessary trips like going to work or school. People will engage in more optional outdoor activities rather than staying at home, work, or inside another building if they enjoy the space between buildings.

Gehl favors designs that assemble rather than disperse, integrate rather than segregate, invite rather than repel, and open up rather than close in. His designs seek to bring people of different genders, ages, races, incomes, and sexual orientation together and concentrate them in spaces where they will interact. He has operationalized principles to accomplish these goals.[4]

Many of Gehl's suggestions for the design of outdoor spaces are based on his empirical research about how people interact with each other and the space around them at the micro scale.⁵ Gehl likes narrow buildings with many doors and curving, rather than straight, streets. He notes that active, thriving commercial streets worldwide tend to have narrow facade widths. He recommends "soft edges" without walls and fences and active ground floors with shops and cafes rather than windowless office building walls at street level because he observed people using and enjoying spaces with soft edges. Since most outdoor human activities occur on streets and sidewalks, Gehl urges planners to design short, logical routes with easy-to-navigate sidewalks. He encourages street designers to think of what makes a good city at eye level—as viewed by pedestrians. Gehl's empirical studies of pedestrian behavior help urban designers operationalize design strategies that encourage walking such as making wider sidewalks and designing light signals that will not cause unnecessary stops. Gehl believes pedestrian underpasses and bridges should be used only as a last resort. He has found that even a few feet of elevation will discourage pedestrian use and urges urban designers to eliminate or reduce stairs and steps wherever possible.

Gehl favors designs to encourage people to pause and linger, such as niches in facades. Like William Whyte, Gehl likes movable chairs and other sittable space. If people are to stay outdoors, urban designers have to reduce negative effects of cold, rain, sun, shade, snow, and wind—particularly at the base of large buildings. Beautiful outdoor city spaces between buildings with public art, green space, lively shopping, soft edges, easy-to-navigate pedestrian paths, and events, festivals, and performances will encourage people to linger outdoors.

Denmark lies close to the Arctic circle and Gehl suggests from experience that in cold climates designers need to make cities as walkable as possible in winter by incorporating design features like roof overhangs that keep snow and ice off sidewalks and heating elements that can melt snow and ice.

The verb "Copenhagenize" is not yet in common parlance. However, Gehl uses it to describe the design principles he hopes to export from his native city.

STREET AND SIDEWALK DESIGN

Streets and adjoining sidewalks occupy a great deal of land and impact the physical form and quality of life of surrounding areas. Jane Jacobs observed that streets designed so that residents can keep "eyes on the street" deter crime. Complete street designs consider sidewalks, benches, trash receptacles, street trees, and other features related to streets and the needs of bicyclists and pedestrians as well as motorists. Pedestrianized streets, traffic calming, and street/sidewalk designs that encourage use of the space between buildings are urban design approaches that impact much more than mobility.

How many streets there are, how wide, and their design affect how humans interact with each other and the quality of community life. Architects and urban designers sometimes prepare figure/ground drawings—drawings with a background in one color and a feature of interest in another to schematically illustrate the essential features they are designing without distracting the viewer with extraneous details. University of California, Berkeley City and Regional Planning Professor Allan Jacobs observed streets worldwide and created figure/ground drawings showing street networks at identical scales with a black ground and white streets. Jacobs's street drawings illustrate how varied street patterns are and how much or little opportunity for interaction among people they offer. From these images, Jacobs constructed theory about how to design great streets.

Figure 3.4 looks like one of Jacobs's drawings, but it is not. It was generated by computer using a tool developed by University of Southern California urban planning and spatial analysis professor Geoff Boeing. This nicely illustrates the synthesis of art and science; observation and analysis; and theory and practice. Jacobs, an urban design planning and design practitioner, artist, and skilled observer developed a methodology for observing and illustrating street patterns from hundreds of hours observing life on the world's great streets. From his empirical research, he constructed theory about how to

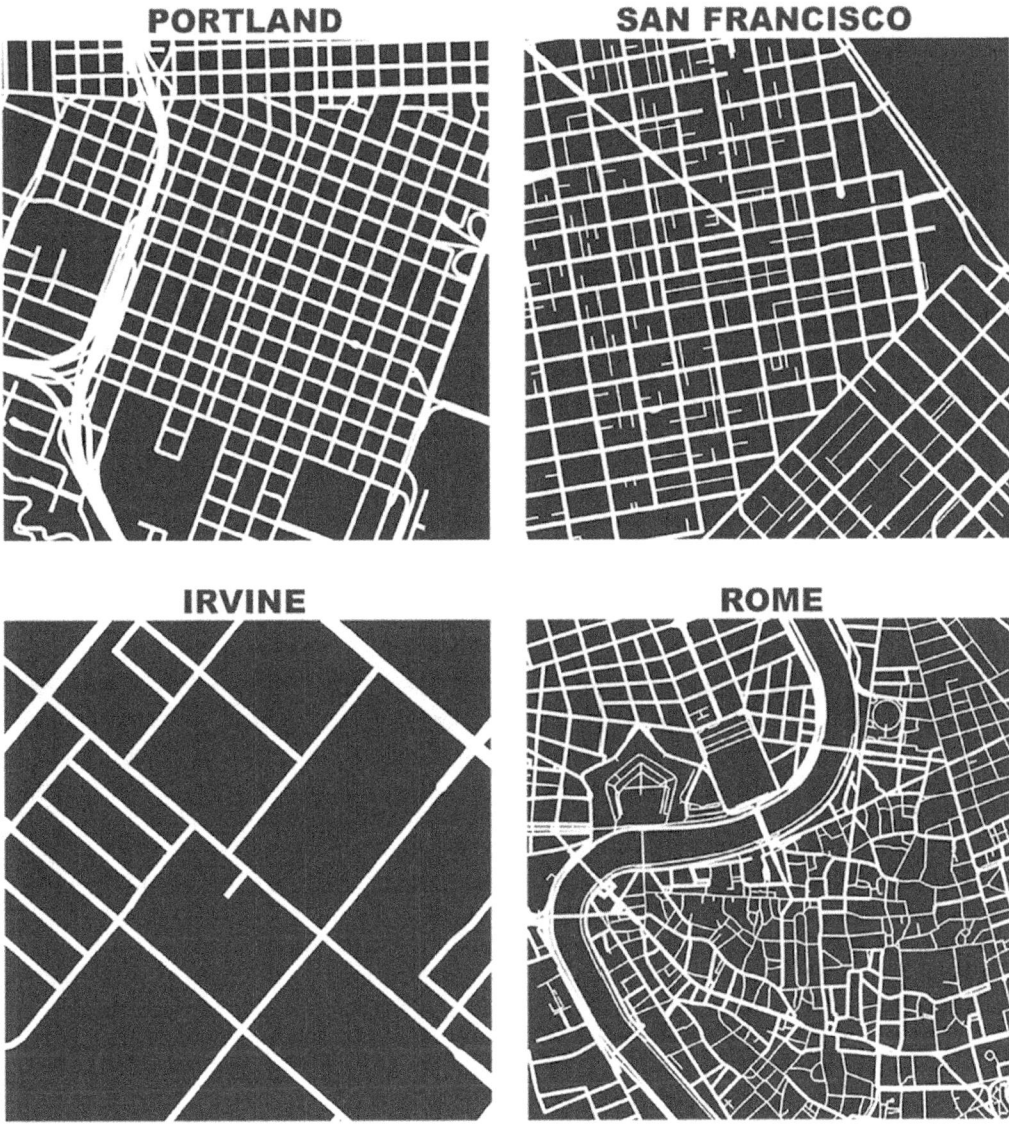

Figure 3.4 Computer-Generated Street Network Created by Geoff Boeing.

design great streets. Boeing, an urban planner and designer with advanced computer skills, invented a tool to help practitioners replicate Jacobs-like street patterns as a starting point for doing their own observations and applying Jacobs's theory.

Canadian architect/planner/urban designer Larry Beasley has developed a model for achieving lively human-scale street life in high-density developments. He played a major role in the urban design of the False Creek area of Vancouver, Canada. Beasley calls the design philosophy that guided development of the False Creek Project and other innovations in Vancouver "Vancouverism".

The False Creek area combines high building density near the waterfront and lively streets (Figure 3.5). Many of the False Creek buildings are designed with two- to four-story buildings at street level with stores, restaurants, cafes, and other uses that attract people and generate street life. Much taller buildings are set back behind the buildings fronting on the street and waterfront, so that they do not harm

Figure 3.5 False Creek Waterfront (Vancouver, BC, Canada).

the pedestrian landscape with shade, wind, uninviting facades, or uses unrelated to enjoyment of the streetscape. Tall slender towers provide necessary density but allow waterfront views and reduce wind and shade on streets. The False Creek waterfront area is a walkable residential, commercial, recreational area with housing, shopping, a farmer's market, and marina. The Vancouver model has been imitated in Dubai and other cities.

Vancouver's approach is totally different from the so-called Brasília syndrome named after Brasília, the capital of Brazil. Brasília was planned based on modernist planning and architectural principles. The approach to Brasília's design was developed by European theorists beginning in the 1920s and emphasizes large scale, rapid transportation, modern building materials, and efficiency. Brasília looks well-organized from the air (Figure 5.3) but works poorly for many day-to-day human activities on the ground in the space between buildings.

"Complete streets" planning is an approach to street planning that integrates mobility and other functions of streets and the area functionally related to them such as sidewalks and median strips. The concept was developed in Boston, Massachusetts beginning in 2010. Complete streets plans consider bicyclists and pedestrians as well as motorized vehicles. They are concerned with the quality of life streets can provide as well as mobility.[6] Many U.S. cities and counties now either have complete streets plans or incorporate complete streets planning concepts into their general plan and transportation-related plans.

Boulevards are an important feature in some large cities. Most boulevards are in capital cities like Paris, where Baron Haussmann built boulevards between 1853 and 1870. Most boulevards are wide and tree-lined. Bi-directional main roads for through traffic are separated by medians. In addition to the main road, boulevards often have frontage roads that may provide parking and medians. In the twentieth century, many older boulevards were modified to accommodate large numbers of automobiles traveling faster than horse-drawn vehicles or electric streetcars that ran in their centers at the time they were built. Planners and urban designers have developed ways of adapting boulevard design to both achieve much of the charm of historic boulevards and meet modern traffic needs. Urban design professors Allan Jacobs, Elizabeth MacDonald, Michael Larice, and Yodan Rofe have studied and written about boulevard design.

DESIGNING FOR DIVERSITY

Urban design seeks to meet the needs of people and communities with diverse racial, ethnic, gender, sexual orientation, citizenship, age, and disability statuses. Ethnic communities have culture-based design preferences. Their residents may not value some norms of the dominant culture. The theory and practice of design to overcome discrimination and better meet the needs of different groups is rapidly improving. Planners and urban designers work to keep toxic uses away from residential areas and vice versa, provide infrastructure in diverse communities to the same standards as more affluent areas, put in street lighting to make outdoor spaces safer, build or adapt buildings, stairs, curbs, and other parts of the built environment to accommodate people with disabilities, provide public toilets that people with different gender orientations find acceptable, and provide for murals, statues, paintings, and other public art that reflects contributions of different cultures.

Communities with household incomes lower than city or county averages need less expensive housing on smaller lots that require different zoning, and include more rental units. They may need different housing and building codes, transects, or other standards. Communities with many recent immigrants may require different kinds of public facilities than other communities. Extended Asian-American multi-generational households and double income no kids (DINK) households need housing designs that fit their household needs. So do households with members with disabilities. Gender and sexual orientation affect people's planning preferences.

University of Virginia planning professor Daphne Spain describes how city planners and urban designers can include a gender perspective in all their work. Dolores Hayden, a Yale Professor Emerita of Architecture and American Studies, describes what a non-sexist city might be like. Hayden has also written about historical feminist designs for American homes, neighborhoods, and cities, and the relationship between gender, housing, and family life. Petra Doan, a Professor of Urban and Regional Planning at Florida State University, writes about planning for LGBTQ communities. Doan describes the social dynamics as LGBTQ households transform neighborhoods and the way in which public spaces may be made more acceptable to queer users.

Vernacular architecture produced without architects, planners, or other design professionals often meets the needs of the people who created it as well as or better than designs and plans produced by outsider professionals. Planners in the United States and other countries are increasingly recognizing the value of folk wisdom in design for different cultures.

THE NEW URBANISM

The New Urbanism is a neo-traditional urban design movement that emerged during the 1980s. The Congress of the New Urbanism (CNU)—an association of architects, planners, urban designers, and their supporters—has worked to advance New Urbanism since 1993.[7] The CNU now has 19 state, regional, and local chapters and more than 3,000 members, including international members. The CNU holds annual congresses. It has education and training projects and an accreditation program in connection with the University of Miami.

New Urbanist principles are described in the *Charter of the New Urbanism*. The charter advocates building communities that encourage neighborhood interaction, mixed-use districts, more pedestrian and bicycle and less automobile use, conservation of the natural environment, and historic preservation. The New Urbanism advocates compact, city-centered development rather than poorly planned suburban sprawl. It draws on Ebenezer Howard's garden city and Clarence Perry's neighborhood unit ideas described in Chapter 6 and the theory and practice of urban growth management described in Chapter 8. The charter's 27 principles include structuring development around neighborhoods, districts, and corridors and the space along streets, roads, and other transportation infrastructure; clear metropolitan boundaries; infill development; definition of streets and public spaces as places of shared use; safe and comfortable streets and squares for pedestrians; and preservation and renewal of historic buildings, districts, and landscapes. New Urbanists blame the loss of community and lack of walkability in post-World War II suburban and exurban developments on what they consider excessively low densities and over-reliance on automobiles. New Urbanists find much to admire in compact small towns built before the widespread use of automobiles.[8]

Critics of the New Urbanism consider it a backward-looking movement built on nostalgia for a small-town America that was never as good as New Urbanists imagined. They fault New Urbanist developments for failing to provide enough housing for low-income households. Many critics of the New Urbanism argue that the density in the New Urbanist developments that have been built is still too low.

DESIGNING IN HARMONY WITH THE NATURAL ENVIRONMENT

The natural environment is an important component of urban design and placemaking. "Design with nature"—a term University of Pennsylvania landscape architecture professor Ian McHarg originated that is described in Box 13.1—begins planning at any scale with analysis of the natural environment. It makes preservation of environmentally important features of the natural landscape a paramount goal. Ecological design, eco-design, and green city design are other closely related terms for planning approaches that emphasize protecting and utilizing natural features.

The United States Green Building Council (USGBC) is a nonprofit organization that promotes energy-efficient design. They have Leadership in Energy and Environmental Design (LEED) standards for energy-efficient design. The LEED standards provide a silver, gold, and platinum rating system that architects, planners, landscape architects, and urban designers use to improve energy efficiency in buildings and neighborhoods. There are similar rating systems in other countries and a World Green Building Council helps with energy efficiency design wordwide.

Design is a critical element of climate change planning. Extraction and consumption of coal, oil, and natural gas disrupts natural environments, causes pollution, and is the principal source of global climate change. Urban design can reduce the impacts of resource extraction, processing, and consumption and help provide alternative sustainable energy solutions. Trees; green roofs and walls with living vegetation; and white or reflective roofs that absorb less heat can reduce pollution and the emission of greenhouse gases (GHGs) that contribute to global warming.

A new movement called "landscape urbanism" originated in landscape architecture. It is contributing to an expanded view of the connection between the built and natural environment in city and regional planning, architecture, and urban design as well as helping to revitalize landscape architecture practice.[9] Landscape urbanism seeks to discover the potentials and opportunities in landscapes. It views the natural landscape at any scale as a context within which to place infrastructure designed by civil engineers, buildings designed by architects, and land uses shaped by city and regional planners. While landscape urbanism began as a criticism of architectural and planning practice, many architects, planners, urban designers, and civil engineers have embraced the concept. Landscape urbanism strategies in the USA are now widely used in waterfront development; redevelopment and infill of vacant urban land; urban agriculture; green infrastructure; and other urban designs. The Louisville Waterfront Park case study in Box 3.2 reflects landscape urbanism theory and practice. It illustrates the relationship between city planning, urban design, site planning, and landscape architecture.

DEFENSIBLE SPACE AND CRIME PREVENTION THROUGH ENVIRONMENTAL DESIGN (CPTED)

Defensible space and crime prevention through environmental design (CPTED) are design philosophies that respond to the regrettable reality that crime is a problem in the USA and other countries. Design strategies can reduce crime. However, poverty, inequality, racism and other structural societal problems and personal psychological challenges, not good or bad design, are the root cause of crime.

CPTED is a sensitive issue. Surveillance in the United States is intertwined with issues of race and income. On the one hand, many people want video evidence of police misconduct from surveillance cameras and police body cameras. On the other hand, they are suspicious of too much police and state surveillance.

BOX 3.2 THE LOUISVILLE WATERFRONT PARK PLAN

The Louisville, Kentucky Waterfront Park was a substantial project combining urban design, placemaking, and site planning to transform an 85-acre parcel of land on the Ohio River into an attractive waterfront park to serve as a gateway to Louisville, Kentucky. The Louisville Waterfront Development Corporation (WDC) was responsible for the park design. The WDC selected Hargreaves Jones—a New York landscape architecture firm that specializes in transforming derelict urban areas—from among 85 firms that responded to their request for qualifications (RFQ) to prepare the park plan.

Louisville Metro (a merged city and county) has a population of 1.27 million, about 75% of whom are White, 22% Black, and 3% Latinx. During the 19th and 20th centuries industry disfigured and polluted the Louisville waterfront. By the mid-1980s the waterfront was occupied largely by vacant lots, abandoned buildings, gravel companies, and scrapyards that compressed junked cars. Three interstate highways intersecting at "spaghetti junction" formed a visually dominant barrier between downtown and the river. A road bisected the site, making access to the waterfront difficult. Flood control infrastructure blocked access to the water.

Planning for the project began in 1986. The scale, complexity, and particularly the financing of the project dictated incremental construction. It took 20 years before the park was essentially complete.

Hargreaves Jones articulated a number of goals for their plan including:

- Reconnecting the city to the Ohio River;
- Making a place where all races, ages and social classes feel comfortable together;
- Cleaning up the industrial wasteland along the river to create an attractive approach to Louisville;
- Incorporating elevated roads and flood control infrastructure into the park; and
- Catalyzing the revitalization of downtown areas adjacent to the waterfront.

When planning for the park began in 1986 the WDC held ten public meetings to solicit input on proposed development of the site. Hargreaves Jones made involving the community and fostering a feeling of community ownership of the project core goals of the planning process.

The Hargreaves Jones design called for cleaning contaminated soil and using it to create landforms that define separate sites in the park and retention basins for drainage control and collecting water for irrigation. This required input from civil engineers. One of the elevated highway ramps was removed, land was graded downward towards the river, and lighting and tree systems were designed to reduce the visual impact of the highways. The road bisecting the site was relocated to take surface traffic out of the park area.

The Hargreaves Jones design features a great lawn and adjoining water features at its center to draw people from downtown Louisville to the Ohio River's edge. It provides multiple performance venues, picnic areas, walking and running paths, two marinas, and a dock for the only steam-powered paddlewheel riverboat still in operation. The park is organized along the river as a series of settings for diverse activities and group sizes ranging from very large to intimate, with differing geometries, surfaces, plantings, and supporting facilities. The design consciously fosters social inclusion. While the park consists of 85 acres, WDC's planning and design review influences 35 additional acres of development sites in the Louisville Downtown Waterfront District. The Louisville Slugger Field, a minor league baseball stadium, is located there. The Park and stadium are generating further development.

The Louisville Waterfront Park design is an urban design plan that reflects the contemporary emphasis on placemaking. It required site planning for many different areas as each was developed. The park is large enough that there are detailed sub-site plans for different areas within the park. The activity areas Hargreaves Jones planned include sites for food and entertainment, sittable space, and other elements that William Whyte and the Project for Public Spaces (PPS) recommend.

In addition to design, the planning process considered financing, security, public facilities management, and public relations. The planners used computer-assisted design (CAD), illustration, and other software to develop the plan.

Hargreaves Jones is a landscape architecture firm, but drew on urban designers, civil engineers, and city and regional planners to help prepare the plan. Civil engineers were involved in removing the freeway ramp, redesigning flood control systems, and cantilevering part of the park over the Ohio River. Urban designers did the design work for sites within the park. Planners helped define the process. The design reflects Jan Gehl's design principles of assembling rather than dispersing, integrating rather than segregating, inviting rather than repelling, and opening up rather than closing in. Street design—rerouting a road that bisected the site to the periphery and reducing the visual impact of it and the spaghetti-junction elevated freeways—was critical. The Park was designed with nature consistent with principles University of Pennsylvania landscape architect professor Ian McHarg developed.

Louisville Waterfront Park now attracts 1.5 million visitors a year. It hosts more than 120 concerts, walks for charities, sports events, a Fourth of July celebration, and other festivals and events each year. In 2013 the Louisville Waterfront Development Corporation (WDC) received a silver medal from the Rudy Bruner Foundation for excellent park design.[10] Figure 3.6 illustrates Louisville Waterfront Park. Figure 3.6 is the Hargreaves Associates rendering of the park plan.

Figure 3.6 Louisville Waterfront Park.

Figure 3.7 Hargreaves Jones Rendering of Louisville Waterfront Park.

Architect/planner Oscar Newman (1935–2004) revolutionized design of potentially dangerous public housing and other crime-prone residential projects by developing theory and practice about how to design defensible space. Criminologist C. Ray Jeffries coined the term Crime Prevention Through Environmental Design (CPTED).[11] In 1977 Oscar Newman embraced the term and philosophy of CPTED. There is now an international CPTED association.

Newman developed his defensible space theory based largely on data provided by the New York City Housing Authority.[12] He was able to analyze before-and-after studies of experiments that the NYC Housing Authority conducted when they altered existing buildings and built new ones to test hypotheses about reducing crime and increasing safety through design.

The most problematic New York City public housing projects: (a) were very large (1,000 or more residents), (b) were high-rise (seven or more stories), (c) covered a large site (the equivalent of four to six city blocks), (d) were in superblocks, and (e) were on buildings sites that provided easy access between residential buildings and streets. The high crime buildings were typically slab or cruciform towers with a single lobby. Long floors with double-loaded corridors—one apartment on each side of a corridor running the entire length of a floor—had the highest number of robberies and assaults. Newman found that many crimes occurred where no one could observe crimes as they were being committed. Violent crimes were most likely to occur in specific places within buildings, like elevators and fire stairs leading to secondary exits. Well-intentioned designers had designed elevators in high-rise public housing that would skip floors, making it quicker for people in the higher floors to reach their units from ground level. But "skip-stop" elevators inadvertently gave criminals enough time to commit crimes in elevators between floors. So-called "scissors" fire escapes—stairs located on either side of elevators to meet building code requirements that fire exits be within 100 feet of elevators—were high crime areas. Criminals could trap victims in windowless stairwells. Enclosed laundry rooms, playgrounds, and auto-repair facilities that existed in some public housing projects also provided opportunities for crime. In the most dangerous family public housing projects, the only defensible space was in apartment interiors. Newman describes all other space as a "no man's land". Similar high-rise public housing projects in Chicago (Cabrini–Green) and St. Louis (Pruitt–Igoe) had even worse crime problems and were eventually demolished (Box 12.2).

Newman confirmed the common perception that there is a positive relationship between density and crime. Row houses he studied were less crime-prone than high rise buildings with the same demographics. Smaller projects with multiple individual doors were less crime-prone than larger ones with a single entrance. Having a doorman or security guard made a big difference, but that is too expensive for public housing projects.

Crime was concentrated in family public housing projects. There was little crime in high-rise 100% elderly public housing projects where there were no families with children—even if they had all the design elements present in family projects with high crime rates. Accordingly, Newman recommended against mixing units for the elderly and families in the same building. However, Newman concluded that both elderly and family buildings in the same public housing complex could work and might provide positive synergies depending upon the tenant population and good defensible space design.

Newman argued that humans are inherently territorial and designs that help create real or symbolic zones of territorial influence reinforce inhabitants' willingness and ability to prevent crime in their territory. He argued that designs that encourage residents to take responsibility for crime prevention work much better than designs that off-load the responsibility for crime prevention to the police. He agreed with Jane Jacobs that "eyes on the street" can reduce crime, but extended this idea to all exterior and interior space where crimes might occur. Newman concluded that surveillance by the residents themselves—the ability of residents and others to casually and continually survey their non-private indoor and outdoor living environments—can greatly reduce crime. He proposed a number of alternative designs to make surveillance of public space by the residents easier even in large high-rise public housing complexes. Locating mailboxes in areas with a steady flow of residents and locating elevators in lobbies with a lot of activity are two examples.

Design that reduces perceptions that a project is unique, isolated, and vulnerable can reduce crime. The geographical juxtaposition of safe zones and activities in a residential environment can help. So can physical barriers such as gates, walls, fences, setbacks, and symbolic barriers such as raised front door stoops and landscaping that delineate private from public and semi-public areas. Newman drew on semiotics—the study of how nonverbal signs and symbols communicate meaning. Degrading design to reduce maintenance costs such as installing heavy glazed tiles (easy to clean) and steel doors (difficult to break) send the message that a project is a crime area. They subconsciously suggest to residents that the building where they live is more like a hospital or prison than a home.

Today, surveillance cameras have made it easier for police in control rooms—rooms where police or other observers can observe what is happening in different parts of a building in real time—to monitor crime hot spots and deploy officers to a crime scene quickly. This is quite different from direct observation of spaces by the tenants themselves. Planners need to be sensitive to what tenants consider acceptable tradeoffs between crime reduction and intrusion into their private lives.

SUMMARY

Urban design and placemaking are central to city and regional planning. They are based on differing views about the importance of traditional and modern design and modern practice; livability and efficiency; beauty; and functionality. Both urban design and placemaking are humanistic practices—emphasizing human interaction and community building.

Design of the three-dimensional physical form of the built environment largely determines how well it will meet users' needs. However, unless good urban design is supported by effective placemaking strategies such as good facilities management, rules about what activities can occur where, and assuring that access to a space will be inclusive, even the best-designed space will fail to meet its potential.

As human settlements become larger, denser, and more complex, urban design and placemaking are becoming increasingly important. Most U.S. local governments now incorporate design standards into their general plans, zoning ordinances, building codes, and other land use regulations. Some have separate urban design plans or design review boards. Urban designs increasingly use form-based codes to visually represent design possibilities as a supplement to or alternative for conventional zoning,

Creating good urban design requires mastering computer-assisted design (CAD) and other modern digital design tools. Augmented and virtual reality are making it possible to illustrate design alternatives and allow people to interact with the designs. Three-dimensional printers are making it possible to create physical models or entire elements of the built environment directly from digital designs.

Theory developed by urban designers like Kevin Lynch, Gary Hack, William Whyte, Jan Gehl, Ian McHarg, Oscar Newman, and Allan Jacobs can guide the design of sites, neighborhoods, parks, plazas, streets, sidewalks, highway corridors, boulevards, the space between buildings, and regions. More and more local governments in the United States are seeking to "Copenhagenize" pedestrian streets to create lively areas for human interaction and design the space between buildings so that pedestrians will use and enjoy it. Some urban designs "Vancouverize" dense areas to retain light, air, views, and street-level vitality.

Local governments and other planning bodies are using urban design and placemaking in many ways. Urban designs can help to preserve the past, draw people to interact in the space between buildings, create great streets, reduce crime, adorn and embellish cities with public art, harmonize the built and natural environment, and heighten the human drama.

CONCEPTS

Computer-Assisted Design (CAD)
Congress for the New Urbanism (CNU)
Copenhagenize
International Congress of Modern Architecture (CIAM)
Landscape Urbanism
Modernism
New Urbanism
Pedestrianized street
Placemaking
Privately Owned Public Open Space (POPOS)
Project for Public Spaces (PPS)
Sittable Space
Site Planning
Space Between Buildings
Street Life Project
Transect
Urban Design
U.S. Green Building Council (USGBC)
Vancouverism

PEOPLE

Donald Appleyard
Jonathan Barnett
Oscar Newman
Jan Gehl
Kevin Lynch
Gary Hack
Allan Jacobs
Charles Waldheim
William Hollis Whyte

NOTES

1 Austrian architect Camillo Sitte developed an approach "to city planning according to artistic principles" that operationalized design principles to preserve historic areas in 1889 (Sitte, 1889; Collins & Collins, 1981). American architect/planners Werner Hegeman and Elbert Peets

popularized Sitte's approach in the United States (Hegemann & Peets, 1922). Civic design was the principal focus of the first modern urban planning courses and degree programs at Harvard University, Columbia University, and the University of Illinois Champaign-Urbana.

2. Whyte was a sociologist and journalist with no formal education in city and regional planning, landscape architecture, architecture, or urban design. He was an advisor on environmental issues to Laurance Rockefeller—a wealthy New York financier and developer—and a planning consultant for major U.S. cities.

3. Land in cities not occupied by buildings includes open space, streets, sidewalks, parking lots, transit corridors, parks, squares, plazas, and outdoor markets. Some cities have large amounts of publicly or privately owned undeveloped land. Every city has odd bits of unused space and vacant lots. Front, back, and side setbacks require space surrounding buildings on individual lots.

4. Five of Gehl's principles for assembling activities are: (1) carefully locate the city's functions to ensure shorter distances between them and a critical mass of people and events, (2) integrate functions in cities to ensure versatility, wealth of experience, social sustainability, and a feeling of security in individual city districts, (3) design city space so it is inviting and safe for pedestrians and bicycling traffic, (4) open up the edges between the city and buildings so life inside buildings and outside in city spaces can work together, and (5) work to strengthen the invitations to invite longer stays in city spaces because a few people spending much time in a place provide the same sense of lively space as many people spending only a short time there (Gehl, 2010: 232).

5. Gehl's research shows that 16–25-foot facades can contain 15–20 shops every 328 feet. He calculated that these facade widths generate new activities and sights every five seconds at ordinary walking speed (Gehl, 2010: 77). Gehl found that it is possible to see a person at 328 feet, but the person becomes interesting and exciting only at a distance of less than 33 feet (ibid: 34). Historic European city squares that work very well for human interaction are rarely larger than 12,000 square yards.

6. A complete streets plan considers sidewalks, median strips, crosswalks, curbs and gutters, and street furniture. Complete streets plans based on form-based codes or transects consider building facades, height and bulk, views, and other form-related aspects of the entire street environment. Complete streets provide for private and public transportation options by automobile, other motorized vehicles, bicycles, and pedestrians. They consider safety, health, crime, pollution, and quality of life as well as efficient transportation.

7. Architects Andrés Duany, Elizabeth Plater-Zyberk, Peter Calthorpe, Leon Krier, and others pioneered the New Urbanism to improve design of new suburban development on the fringe of existing cities and exurban communities. Duany, Plater-Zyberk, Calthorpe, the California Local Government Commission (LGC)—a California state agency that oversees local governments—and other New Urbanists formed the Congress of the New Urbanism in 1993.

8. Traditional small towns were compact. It was possible to walk anywhere within five minutes. They had substantial jobs–housing balance. Commuter rail and streetcar lines linked many small towns to job centers, so commuters did not have to drive to work. Most houses were for single families. There were also small multi-family apartment buildings; affordable "granny flats" (for renters as well as grandparents and other kin); multi-family rental apartment units built over garages; and back yard *casitas* (little houses). Most residential building lots were small, and many houses were modest and affordable to middle-income households. Narrow streets shaded by trees were charming and calmed traffic. Front porches encouraged human interaction. There were neighborhood parks, playgrounds, bandstands, and other accessible open spaces. Traditional small towns had grocery and other retail stores in a defined city center within five minutes' walk of houses.

9. Australian Peter Connolly originated the term landscape urbanism in the late 1980s. Landscape urbanism theory and practice developed rapidly after a 1997 conference in Chicago sponsored by the Graham Foundation. They have been further developed by landscape architects at the Harvard Graduate School of Design, University of Pennsylvania's Departments of Architecture and City and Regional Planning, London's Architectural Association, and other academic programs and practitioners. Landscape urbanism now includes a range of concepts reflecting a desire for more ecologically sensitive practice than is currently common in architecture and planning.

10. The Bruner Foundation is a New York-based philanthropic foundation that gives an annual award for urban excellence and development in American cities (Bruner Foundation, 2021; Langdon, Shibley, & Welch, 1990; Saunders, 2009).

11. Crime prevention through environmental design (CPTED) emphasizes natural surveillance such as placing windows to overlook sidewalks; lighting along pathways at proper heights to light faces of potential attackers; natural access control such as maze entrances to bathrooms; and natural territorial reinforcement strategies such as motion sensor lights at all entry points. CPTED practitioners also recommend use of security cameras and closed-circuit television and other types of surveillance by authorities and the police. Some U.S. urban designers rely on information about CPTED practice from an unusual source—the Singapore National Crime Prevention Council (NCPC)'s 68-page *Crime prevention through environmental design guidebook* (NCPC, 2003). Singapore is an authoritarian state. It has a low crime rate, but is justifiably criticized for much greater intrusion into the lives of its citizens than most Americans consider acceptable.

12 Newman directed a three-year research project at New York University studying security design of urban residential areas that was funded by the U.S. Department of Justice's National Institute of Law Enforcement and Criminal Justice (Newman, 1972: xiv). The New York City Housing Authority maintained detailed longitudinal data on the buildings, tenants, and crimes in the 169 NYC Public Housing projects housing 528,000 residents, which existed at the time Newman did his research. The Authority's 1,600-person police force documented the exact location where different types of crime in a huge variety of building sizes and designs took place—a unique resource for Newman's empirical research.

SUGGESTIONS FOR FURTHER LEARNING

Introduction to Urban Design: Jonathan Barnett, *Introduction to urban design* (1982). Peter Bosselmann, *Urban transformation* (2008). Brent Ryan, *The largest art* (2017). **Jane Jacobs:** Jane Jacobs, *The death and life of great American cities* (1961). Anthony Flint, *Wrestling with Moses: How Jane Jacobs took on America's master builder and transformed the American city* (2011). **Urban Design History:** A.E.J. Morris, *History of urban form before the industrial revolution* (1979). Spiro Kostoff, *The city shaped* (1991) and *The city assembled* (1992). **Urban Design Textbooks:** Matthew Carmona, Tim Health, Taner Oc, & Steve Tiesdell *Public places urban spaces*, 2nd ed (2010). William Saunders, *Urban design* (2009). **Urban Design Anthologies and Overviews:** Elizabeth MacDonald & Michael Larice (eds), *The urban design reader*, 2nd ed (2006). Tridib Banerjee & Anastasia Loukaitou-Sideris (eds), *Companion to urban design* (2011). **Placemaking:** Linda Schneekloth & Robert Shibley, *Placemaking* (1995). Laurie Olin et al., *Placemaking* (2008). Project for Public Spaces, What is placemaking? (2015) and *Placemaking and the future of cities* (2015). William Whyte, *City: Rediscovering the center* (1988) and *The social life of small urban spaces* [video] (1988). **Urban Design and Placemaking in the Global South:** Tridib Banerjee, *In the images of development: City design in the global south* (2021). **Street Design:** Allan Jacobs, *Great streets* (1993). Donald Appleyard, Sue Gerson, & Mark Lintell, *Livable streets* (1982). Donald Appleyard, Kevin Lynch, & John Myer, *The view from the road* (1964). Michael Southworth & Eran Ben-Joseph, *streets and the shaping of towns and cities* (1996). **Feminist Urban Design:** Dolores Hayden, *The grand domestic revolution* (1982) and *Redesigning the American dream* (2002). Daphne Spain, *Gendered spaces* (1992) and *Constructive feminism* (2016). **Form-Based Codes:** Daniel Parolek, Karen Parolek, & Paul Crawford, *Form-based codes* (2008). **Transects:** Brian Falk & Andrés Duany (eds), *Transect urbanism: Readings in human ecology* (2020). **The Space Between Buildings:** Jan Gehl, *Life between buildings* (1980), *Cities for people* (2010), and *In search of the human scale* [video] (2015). **Kevin Lynch:** Tridib Banerjee & Michael Southworth, *City sense and city design: Writings and projects of Kevin Lynch* (1995). Kevin Lynch, *The image of the city* (1961), *Managing the sense of a region* (1976), *Good city form* (1984), and *What time is this place?* (1976). **Design with Nature and Ecodesign:** Ian McHarg, *Design with nature* (1961). Jonathan Barnett and Larry Beasley *Ecodesign for cities and suburbs*, 2nd ed (2015). Frederick Steiner, Richard Weller et al. *Design with nature now* (2019). **Defensible Space and Crime Prevention through Environmental Design (CPTED):** Oscar Newman, *Defensible space* (1972) and *Creating defensible space* (1996). Randall Atlas, *21st century security and CPTED* (2013). Singapore National Crime Prevention Council, *Crime prevention through environmental design guidebook* (2003). **Landscape urbanism:** Charles Waldheim, *Landscape and urbanism* (2016). Dean Almy & Michael Benedict (eds), *Center 14: On landscape urbanism* (2007). **Louisville Waterfront Park:** Richard Werner, Jay Farbstein, Anne-Marie Lubenau, & Robert Shibley, *Louisville Waterfront Park* (2014). **The New Urbanism:** Congress of the New Urbanism, *Charter of the New Urbanism*, 2nd ed (2013). Andrés Duany, *Principles of New Urbanism* [video] (2015). Peter Calthorpe, *Seven principles for building better cities* (2017) [video]. **Journals:** *Environment and Planning B: Planning and Design.*

CHAPTER 4

The Politics of City and Regional Planning

INTRODUCTION

Bicycle enthusiasts jam a city planning commission hearing to demand more bicycle lanes. A planner from an oil-producing state distributes factual information that contradicts a right-wing state senator's assertion that climate change is a hoax. A recent Master's of City Planning graduate working for a neighborhood Housing Development Corporation in the predominantly Black neighborhood where she grew up networks with former classmates in the city planning department and state Housing Finance Agency to get approvals for an affordable housing project. A county planner shuttles between environmentalists, developers, and county officials, in order to hammer together a habitat protection plan to save enough land and water where red-legged frogs live to protect them from extinction as a species. In Glasgow, Scotland, a U.S.-educated planner from Bangladesh whispers advice to the Bangladeshi Environmental Minister at a UN conference on global climate change.

City and regional planning is profoundly political. It takes place in the face of conflict. Planners must understand the nature of the political system within which they operate and the role that planning plays in governance at every level of government. Planning practice is not easy, but it is exciting and meaningful work that makes a difference. Political theory helps city and regional planners place the politics of planning in context and understand it more deeply.

Political scientists, sociologists, journalists, urban planners, and others have studied local government politics by closely examining community power in different American cities. They have produced a rich body of theory about urban politics.

This chapter begins by describing the legal framework of the United States within which planning takes place. It describes the separation of powers among the legislative, executive and judicial branches of the federal government. A biography of former Secretary of Housing and Urban Development Julian Castro illustrates how an activist federal official can impact planning. The chapter describes the nature and powers of counties, general law and charter cities, and special districts. It describes the difference between Dillons Rule states that sharply limit local government discretion and Cooley doctrine states which grant city and county government great "home rule".

A section describes the relationship of private and nonprofit planning to government planning within the United States. Another gives examples of how international treaties affect planning at the planetary scale.

A section describes how conservative, liberal and neo-liberal political ideology impact planning and the ideological orientation of successive administrations in the United States since the New Deal. Another explains how elitist, pluralist and regime theory illuminate the nature of local government politics.

Final sections discuss how planners get things done in the face of conflict. This section includes a discussion of "speaking truth to power", transparency, and theory and practice of negotiating and mediating in planning conflicts.

THE LEGAL FRAMEWORK OF U.S. GOVERNMENT PLANNING

City planning in the United States takes place within a legal framework dividing federal, state, and local government power. Within states, political power is fragmented among many local governments. There are multiple counties and often dozens or even hundreds of separate cities within metropolitan areas. Political scientists refer to metropolitan areas as "Balkanized" because there are many competing jurisdictions that tend to fight with each other, just as countries on the Balkan peninsula have done for centuries.

The basic units of local government are counties, which are legal subdivisions of the state itself, and cities that are incorporated by the state. Cities granted the status of municipal corporations under the state's general law are called general law cities. Cities that operate under a state charter that describes the powers they have are called charter cities.

Legally, cities are municipal corporations authorized to act as a legal personality in the same way that business corporations do, but for the purposes of governing rather than making a profit in business. State law defines their powers, duties, and liabilities, including the power to engage in city and regional planning. Counties have powers that are similar to cities. Special districts—governmental units that are separate from cities and counties—are often empowered to provide water, sewer, or other services.

County boundaries are established by states. Most county boundaries were established at the time the states were established. They were sometimes changed long ago, but are now well established and are virtually never changed.

Once incorporated, cities are almost never dissolved. In some metropolitan areas essentially all of the land has been annexed, so city boundaries are stable and do not change. In growing cities with unincorporated fringe land that is not part of any city, land continues to be annexed. City and regional planners are often involved in city annexation matters. Special districts change more frequently. They may be created, abolished, or consolidated with other special districts or with a city or county government. City and regional planners may be involved in special district formation, dissolution, or boundary or function changes.

Policies made at the federal government level are shaped by international law and treaties. Some international treaties form the basis for plans that transcend national borders, such as plans to manage resources that cross national borders, maritime and aviation plans that affect U.S. transportation policy, and laws regarding oceans that affect coastal zone planning. It is difficult to get the 197 sovereign countries in the world to agree or, once they have agreed, to fulfill their international treaty obligations. There are many breaches of international law and failures of countries—including the United States—to meet their treaty obligations. This is a particularly pressing problem with respect to climate change.[1]

Federal and state courts play an important role in city and regional planning. Decisions prepared by planning departments and approved by city or county governments may be appealed to the courts, which ultimately decide whether a planning decision will stand.

The Planning Accreditation Board (PAB)—the body that accredits academic planning degree programs in North America—requires graduate programs to teach city and regional planning students about the legal system and planning law. Many city and regional planning law courses are taught by lawyers using law school case study pedagogy and law school land use planning casebooks that contain the text of legal decisions and other legal materials.

City and regional planning in the United States is decentralized and largely bottom-up. There is a long tradition of anti-urbanism in America. Thomas Jefferson (1743–1826)—the third U.S. President—famously commented "The mobs of great cities add just so much to the support of pure government, as sores do to the strength of the human body" (Jefferson, 1787).

There is an ideological and political division between rural states and rural areas within states versus metropolitan areas. Strongly Democratic "blue states" favor city and regional planning more strongly than

Republican "red states". The red/blue divide is evident at the metropolitan, city, and even the neighborhood level. Core precincts and zip codes in metropolitan areas tend to be blue (Democratic); peripheral ones red (Republican). Decisions about general plans, zoning, takings of private property, stewardship of resources, and many other planning matters reflect this red/blue divide.

The U.S. federal government intervened in local planning during World Wars I and II, the Great Depression of the 1930s, and the global economic crisis that began in late 2007. However, they shifted back to encourage mostly bottom-up planning when the wartime and financial crises subsided. This bottom-up tradition contrasts with top-down planning in what are called "welfare" or "developmental" states in Scandinavia and elsewhere in the world, where the central government plays a much larger role in steering the economy than it does in the United States.

In the United States, power—including the authority to plan cities and regions—is shared between the national government and states. States in turn share power to plan with cities and counties and also with special districts. The federal government plays an important role in establishing policy and providing funding to state and local governments, but most urban planning decisions are made and implemented by local city and county governments. Highway programs and other programs of statewide significance are exceptions. They are generally carried out by state agencies.

Since the New Deal began in 1933, the federal government approach to urban programs has been to require states to pass enabling acts that authorize the state to establish governmental entities that can receive federal funding and manage programs. For example, state enabling acts may authorize formation of regional air quality districts (AQDs) or permit cities and counties to establish local public housing authorities (PHAs). State enabling acts authorize state and local government to accept federal funding for housing, air and water quality, environmental, transportation, revitalization, endangered species, and other programs.

Metropolitan councils of government (COGs) and metropolitan planning organizations (MPOs) do regional planning at the metropolitan level. Other regional planning entities such as regional park districts, regional transit authorities, and coastal zone management districts do regional planning for regions defined in different ways.

Nonprofit organizations and civil society institutions like labor unions and churches play important roles in city and regional planning. Neighborhood organizations influence plans that affect them. Most goods and services in the United States are provided by the private sector.

The U.S. Constitution is based on the theory that separation of powers between the executive, legislative, and judicial branches of government will produce better governance than consolidating power at the national level or vesting too much power within one branch of the federal government. The separation of powers model differs from the fusion of powers model in parliamentary systems where the executive and legislative branches overlap and from authoritarian regimes governed by a single political party or a dictator.

At the federal level, power in the United States is divided among three branches, each with separate and independent powers and areas of responsibility. The U.S. Constitution attempts to keep powers of one branch of the federal government from conflicting with powers of either or both of the other branches. However, conflict among branches of government in the United States can be intense and bitter.

Congress is divided into two chambers—the Senate and House of Representatives—which constitute the legislative branch. The President presides over the executive branch of government. The Supreme Court sits at the top of the judicial branch of government.

The Supreme Court decides federal constitutional questions and matters of federal law. For example, a controversy about the federal Constitution's prohibition of governments' taking of land by eminent domain unless it is for a public purpose and just compensation is paid, may be appealed to the U.S. Supreme

Court. Planning controversies involving only state law, such as whether or not a state recycling law applies to recycling of automobiles, and municipal ordinances such as a controversy involving a local bicycle ordinance are decided by state courts. Planning controversies that involve only state law end at the state's supreme court and may not be appealed to the U.S. Supreme Court if there is no U.S. constitutional or federal question to be decided.

States cannot pass laws that violate the U.S. Constitution or are in conflict with laws the federal government has preempted—laws Congress intends to apply uniformly to all states, rather than allowing many different state variations. Article 10 of the U.S. Constitution—the reserved powers clause—provides that powers not specifically assigned to the federal government are reserved to the states.

The U.S. Constitution makes no mention of local government. However, it is now well established that the power to create local governments is among the powers reserved to the states. All U.S. state constitutions authorize the state to create cities and counties, or their equivalents—boroughs in New York state and parishes in Louisiana.

Counties are "creatures of the state". States have the legal power to create, alter, or eliminate them. County planning departments are responsible for planning land use within unincorporated county land and regulating development that is not within the border of an incorporated city.

In contrast to counties, cities are municipal corporations created or chartered by the state. The legal requirements to create or charter cities vary from state to state. Once a city is incorporated it becomes responsible for most functions and services previously provided by the county, including land use planning and regulation of development. All states now enable their counties and cities to create planning commissions and planning departments.

Counties are governed by an elected county board of commissioners—usually five to seven commissioners elected for four-year terms with two term limits. Cities are governed by city councils, also usually with five to seven members elected for four-year terms with two term limits. City council members are usually elected at large from the entire jurisdiction. In some large cities, city council members are elected in district elections to represent a specific geographic district. Most local elections are non-partisan, but in some states county commissioners and city council members run as members of a political party.

Whether or not local government elections are non-partisan, the political orientation of local elected officials—as pro- or anti-development, environmentalists, champions of minority rights, or with some other special interest—will affect the elected officials' political base and how they vote on planning issues. County commissioners and city council members are unpaid or receive only token salaries except in a few large cities. Local elected officials reflect a broad variety of backgrounds. Figure 4.1 shows six of the 17 members of the Boston City Council.

SPECIAL DISTRICTS

City and regional planners in the United States often work with another type of political entity—special districts. Special districts are independent governmental units that exist separate from city and county government. They provide services that the local government does not provide. Different state laws provide for a large variety of different types of special districts responsible for services as diverse as sewers, parks, rapid transit, and mosquito control and abatement.[2] Most special districts provide a single service, but some provide several related types of services. Special districts have their own sources of revenue such as a portion of the local property tax and user fees. State limits on municipal debt—how much the state permits cities and counties to borrow—are a main reason for special districts' existence.[3]

Special district boundaries may be larger or smaller than a city or county and may cross city and county boundaries. The boundaries of a small sewer district, for example, may

Figure 4.1 Members of Boston's City Council (2021).

be within a fraction of a square mile, entirely within one city. Large air, water, transit, or regional park districts may overlap dozens of cities and counties in a metropolitan area. Small special districts rarely have planning staff, but large districts may have substantial planning staffs.

Planners in city and county planning departments, the private sector, or nonprofit organizations need to consider special districts' activities and plans and work with them. Transit, park, water, air quality, and other districts can have a large impact on city and regional planning. If water is not available from a water district at the time a subdivision is completed, for example, occupancy permits will not be issued and people cannot legally live in completed units.

Many political scientists and urban planners are critical of the additional fragmentation special districts create. They opposed the proliferation of special districts because it complicates planning and delivery of coordinated services. Others accept special districts as a reasonable way to finance and provide some needed services.

GROUP IDENTITY AND URBAN POLITICS

Either by what they say or what they fail to say, plans reflect conceptions of, and policies to respond to, different groups based on race, gender, income, sexual orientation, citizenship status, disabilities, and other statuses. In the United States explicit social planning or social engineering is anathema. However, planners and government officials implicitly engage more or less consciously in social planning. An important normative consideration in all planning at every scale is social justice for diverse groups.

Political aspects of planning involve spatial considerations. General plans, zoning ordinances, and other land use regulations impact spatial segregation by income. They may indirectly increase or decrease segregation by race, ethnicity, migrant status, or age, because income is so closely related to these demographic variables. If a city general plan and zoning ordinance designates one area of a city for multi-family housing and all other residential areas for single family housing, low- and moderate-income households will likely be disproportionately spatially concentrated in the multi-family area. The low-income area may be populated primarily by people of color. The city is indirectly practicing exclusionary land use. A city planner may be able to change the city general plan or zoning to allow more economically mixed residential areas with multi-family housing, small as well as large lots for single family homes, or small separate living units within single family houses (sometimes referred to as in-law units or granny flats). He or she may be able to develop an inclusionary housing program requiring a specified percentage of units in new developments to be set aside for low- and moderate-income households. Staff of a city planning department, local housing authority (LHA), or nonprofit housing development corporation (HDC) can help provide affordable housing. That can reduce class and racial segregation. For example, a planner may develop plans and programs to retain and rehabilitate the existing low-rent housing stock and legacy public housing units and get new affordable housing built, subsidized by federal, state, local, nonprofit, and private subsidies as described in Chapter 15.

FEDERAL GOVERNMENT URBAN PLANNING AND POLICY

The United States has no national urban plan. However, the ideology and politics of national political parties shape national urban policies.

At the federal level the U.S. Department of Housing and Urban Development (HUD) is the agency most directly involved in urban affairs. The U.S. Environmental Protection Agency (EPA), Department of Transportation (DOT), Department of Commerce (DOC), and other federal agencies also develop plans and make policy that impact cities and regions.

HUD was established in 1965. It has never received funding adequate to its mission. HUD was badly crippled during Republican administrations.[4] The Biden administration has announced its intent to rebuild HUD, but has limited funding and many competing priorities. Box 4.1 is a biography of Julian Castro—the Secretary of Housing and Urban Development during the Obama administration. It illustrates how an activist political leader at the federal level can affect urban plans and policies at every level of government.

For more than a century, U.S. national politics have been a contest between the Democratic and Republican parties. During a 20-year period between the election of Franklin Roosevelt in 1932 and the election of Dwight Eisenhower in 1952, Democrats controlled the presidency. Since then, the two major parties have alternated control of the presidency. Control of both branches of Congress has also alternated between the parties.

Lobbying organizations for cities—the National League of Cities (NLC)—and counties—the National Association of County Officials (NACO)—represent local government interests. City managers are the governmental equivalent of chief executive officers (CEOs) of private corporations. The International City Management Association (ICMA) represents city managers. The American Planning Association (APA) represents city and regional planners. NLC, NACO, the ICMA, and the APA all maintain offices and deploy lobbyists in Washington, D.C.

IDEOLOGY AND POLITICAL PARTIES

Political ideology affects how governments approach city and regional planning and policies they adopt. The Republican Party is ideologically committed to less intervention by federal and other levels of government than the Democratic Party. In the decades following the New Deal Democratic and Republican administrations promised a Fair Deal, Dynamic Conservatism, New Federalism, a New Frontier, a War on Poverty, and a Great Society.

BOX 4.1 JULIAN CASTRO

Julian Castro is a Democratic political leader who is knowledgeable about and has played a role in local planning. As mayor of San Antonio, Texas Castro initiated and oversaw a vision planning process for the city. As Secretary of the U.S. Department of Housing and Urban Development (HUD) from 2014 to 2017, he helped stabilize the U.S. housing market, preserve HUD housing, rebuild resilient communities after natural disasters, and implement proactive fair housing rules. In 2020, Castro was a top contender for the Democratic Party's nominee for U.S. President.

Castro was born in San Antonio, Texas in 1974. His parents were political activists. His mother was the founder of the Hispanic political party La Raza Unida (Our United People). As children, Castro and his twin brother Joaquin (now a U.S. congressman) attended rallies and political events with their parents. Julian received a BA in Political Science and Communications from Stanford University in 1996 and a JD from Harvard Law School in 2000. While at Harvard, Castro worked as a White House intern during Bill Clinton's presidency. After working as an attorney for nine years he was elected mayor of San Antonio, Texas in 2009. He served as San Antonio's mayor for five years until President Obama appointed him Secretary of HUD in 2014.

Castro is a visionary activist who believes in evidence-based collaborative planning to serve diverse populations. The vision planning process in San Antonio that Castro led in 2010 produced a vision plan named SA2020. Castro formed a nonprofit organization with the same name—SA2020—to help implement the plan's stated goals. SA2020 now works with over a hundred community partner agencies to achieve the vision. A digital data dashboard tracks progress towards 61 indicators showing progress to make San Antonio a thriving, creative community, safe, healthy, and informed; a livable and engaged community with cohesive, connected neighborhoods linked by mass transit and improved infrastructure complemented by smart growth; where all residents can reach their full potential.

Figure 4.2 Julian Castro.

Castro's record in San Antonio and his selection as the first Latinx speaker to deliver a keynote address at a Democratic National Convention in 2012 gave Castro national recognition. Two years later President Obama named him Secretary of HUD. Castro brought new energy, vision, and a passion for public service to this role. He helped revive HUD under exceedingly difficult conditions. Castro successfully lobbied for funding for HUD's public housing program, housing vouchers, and other housing assistance and created a public–private rental assistance demonstration (RAD) program to attract private sector investment in the public housing stock (Chapter 15).

When Castro became HUD secretary, private mortgage lending in the United States—particularly to subprime homeowners—who had limited income and high loan-to-value ratio mortgages—was in deep trouble. Millions of low- to moderate-income homeowners had lost or were in danger of losing their homes. Castro oversaw a series of Federal Housing Administration (FHA) programs that helped ten million homeowners reduce or defer mortgage payments. In 2012, under Castro's leadership, HUD, along with the Department of Justice (DOJ), and 49 state attorneys general—the head government lawyer for each state—reached the National Mortgage Servicing Settlement—a $25 billion agreement with five large mortgage providers. The settlement prevented hundreds of thousands of additional foreclosures by getting the mortgage lenders to reduce premiums, help homeowners refinance their loans, and in other ways.

Hurricane Katrina and Superstorm Sandy had occurred before Castro became Secretary of HUD, but many areas affected by them had not recovered. Castro drew on his collaborative planning experience in San Antonio to help communities that had been badly damaged by these extreme weather events recover. During his tenure, HUD invested more than $18 billion in disaster recovery. Castro worked collaboratively with the Federal Emergency Management Agency, state and local governments, and the nonprofit Rockefeller Foundation.

Castro drew on resilient planning theory in the Rebuild by Design Program he created. He oversaw a National Disaster Resilience competition for resilient housing and infrastructure projects that awarded nearly one billion dollars in HUD Disaster Recovery Funds to 13 states and communities to help communities respond to climate change, save public resources, revitalize and modernize infrastructure, and improve access to opportunity for vulnerable populations.

Castro made federal fair housing more proactive. Until his tenure, most HUD fair housing activity had been reactive. Castro issued the Affirmatively Furthering Fair Housing Rule that encourages communities to do evidence-based planning to assess housing discrimination, set fair housing goals, and implement strategies to meet the goals. He oversaw adoption of new HUD rules to strengthen protections for residents of HUD-assisted housing who were victims of domestic violence, make it easier for women to obtain relief under the 2013 Violence Against Women Act, protect transgender individuals seeking emergency shelter, and facilitate emergency housing transfers among federally assisted housing units. Castro directed his staff to develop a "prosperity playbook" in order to help local leaders plan regionally to expand affordable housing opportunity and increase economic mobility.

Other innovative HUD projects Castro oversaw include: efforts to reduce the digital divide by proving high-speed internet in public housing projects and American Indian reservations through the Connecthome Initiative; a project to provide data to help people find affordable housing near jobs and transportation; launching a National Housing Trust Fund; creating lead and smoke-free spaces in public housing; and creating programs for homeless families, youth, and veterans.

In the 1960s, Democratic President John Kennedy's New Frontier and President Lyndon Johnson's Great Society programs were the most pro-urban in U.S. history—devoting a great deal of attention to cities and providing large amounts of federal funding to address urban poverty, housing, transportation, and other issues. Democratic presidents Jimmy Carter, Bill Clinton, and Barack Obama had urban agendas that were philosophically similar to presidents Kennedy and Johnson's urban agendas, but because of the political climate and other crises and priorities, they were less focused on urban issues and were never able to garner as much funding for them as Kennedy and Johnson. Conservative Republican president Richard Nixon pursued a policy of "benign neglect" towards urban problems—essentially ignoring them. Nixon favored the new federalism—providing federal funding to state and local governments mostly through flexible block grants with few strings attached—rather than categorical grants directing federal urban aid towards specific problems and with detailed federal regulations and oversight. President Ronald Reagan and both Presidents George H.W. and George W. Bush followed suit. Under President Donald Trump, the federal government pursued an extreme anti-urban agenda.

Ideology affects how much government intervention in urban affairs political parties and individuals favor. Box 4.2 describes how political ideology affects city and regional planning.

BOX 4.2 LIBERAL, NEOLIBERAL, CONSERVATIVE, AND PROGRESSIVE IDEOLOGY IN PLANNING

The terms liberal, neoliberal, conservative, and progressive refer to ideological orientations that affect how people think and feel about government and government policies. The terms are important in all aspects of politics, including city and regional planning. Planning students and practicing city and regional planners will encounter them frequently in their academic studies and planning careers.

The difference between a liberal and a neoliberal is confusing. Both terms contain the word "liberal", but they refer to belief systems that are at nearly opposite ends of the ideological spectrum. A little history will help clarify these two important concepts. The terms "liberal" and "neoliberal" occur frequently in this book, so it is imperative to understand the difference. It will be helpful to re-read this box as you encounter examples of how liberals and neoliberals feel about plans and policies related to land use, housing, transportation, the environment, revitalization, and climate change in the last five chapters.

A majority of people in the United States are neoliberals. "Neo" means "new" in Greek, so a neoliberal is a new liberal. The reason neoliberals are called "new" liberals is because Adam Smith used the term liberal in his 1776 treatise *Wealth of Nations*, and contemporary issues are different than they were at the time Smith first articulated the concept. What Smith described is sometimes referred to as "classical" liberalism. Smith argued that the "invisible hand of the market" unfettered by government intervention would produce the greatest good for the greatest number of people. Accordingly, Smith argued that the private sector should be large and unregulated and that government should be small and the role of government very limited. He opposed government planning. Smith's examples mostly refer to international trade and to kinds of regulation and government programs that were important in the 18th century. However, the basic anti-government philosophy he developed can be applied to other issues and other time periods, including the present. Neoliberals are towards the right end of the political spectrum in the United States.

In the 1970s and 1980s Margaret Thatcher—the British prime minister from 1979 to 1990—and Ronald Reagan—the U.S. president from 1981 to 1989—resurrected classical liberal ideology as a philosophical justification for programs to reduce government planning, regulations, subsidies, and other intervention in the private market and to eliminate or radically downsize government at every level. Thatcher and Reagan were politically powerful. Their successors in office continued their neoliberal policies. Thatcher privatized publicly owned council housing (public housing for low- and moderate-income households) in the UK and had the units sold off to the tenants as condominiums. She stopped or greatly reduced government benefits to coal miners and railway workers. She reduced the number of civil servants in the UK. President Reagan ended the U.S. public housing program, cut public welfare expenditures, and reduced federal land use, environmental, and other regulations. He took the position that government should provide assistance only to the "truly disadvantaged", which he defined very narrowly. During Democratic president Bill Clinton's presidency, the "Washington Consensus" favored neoliberal policies. Clinton was a moderate liberal, but went along with the consensus. The U.S. government, World Bank, International Monetary Fund, and almost every government in the world accepted neoliberal policies in the 1980s, and the great majority still do.

The word "liberal" has quite a different meaning than neoliberal. Liberal, used alone without an adjective, refers to someone who favors an active role for government. Liberals favor more government spending and regulation—exactly the opposite of neoliberals. A liberal might support the federal government spending more money to aid the homeless, build public housing, repair roads, improve air quality, and extend medical coverage to people with pre-existing medical conditions. He or she would likely favor strong government regulation of banks' mortgage lending policies, enforcement of fair housing laws, regulation of private property with habitat critical to endangered species, and closing coal-powered energy plants that emit carbon dioxide. Liberals are towards the left end of the political spectrum in the United States.

The term "conservative" is generally used to describe individuals' social values. Conservatives are ideologically inclined towards traditional values, established social and religious norms, respect for government authority, and family values. They oppose what they consider excessive individualism. Most conservatives have neoliberal political values, but that is not necessarily the case. A "neo-conservative" is a contemporary conservative.

The term "progressive" refers to individuals and organizations that are left-leaning, but not as far left as socialists and communists. In the United States members of progressive planners' organizations like Planners for Equal Opportunity in the 1960s and 1970s and the Planners Network today share progressive ideology and work to make city and regional planning more progressive. They are politically liberal. In the 1960s and 1970s Paul Davidoff, Sherri Arnstein, and Norman Krumholz were leading progressive planners. Today the Poverty and Race Research and Action Council (PRRAC) conducts research and engages in advocacy for progressive causes such as the right to the city, gender equity, fair housing, inclusionary zoning, and anti-racism.

STATE AND LOCAL POLITICS AND PLANNING

City, county, and regional planning are largely governed by state law. How much planning is permitted or required varies, depending on the perceived need for planning and the political culture of each state. Rural states like North Dakota (population 755,000)—with only five cities with populations over 25,000—have limited city planning. Pro-planning, politically liberal states—such as Oregon, Washington, New Jersey, and California—have strong state planning laws requiring a great deal of city and regional planning. They describe in detail what kind of planning cities and counties within the state may or must do.

Once a city is incorporated, the responsibility for land use planning, public infrastructure, parks and recreation, police and fire protection, libraries and other local matters, shifts from the county board of commissioners to the city council. State laws explicitly provide, or court opinions have determined, that zoning, subdivision, environmental, growth management, and other planning-related ordinances are sufficiently related to local government police power purposes. Housing and building codes are also permitted under the police power. All of these kinds of municipal ordinances are constitutional so long as: (1) there is a rational basis for them, (2) they are not arbitrary or capricious, (3) they do not violate a federal constitutional provision, and (4) they do not conflict with federal or state law that preempts them (takes precedence over them).

Immediately after independence from England, U.S. cities had limited functions and did limited planning for three reasons: they were small, had little public revenue, and chose not to engage in planning because of America's anti-government philosophical orientation. New York, Chicago, and other big cities took on more functions that required planning during the 19th and early 20th centuries. Still, no state granted any city or county the express power to plan itself until the late 1920s. The handful of city plans that existed before the 1920s were created by private business elites such as the Commercial Club of Chicago and the Regional Plan Association in the New York City region or by a few private planning consultants working for city or county governments. Oddly, initially, many cities began to regulate land use through zoning before they had a comprehensive plan—a remarkable example of putting the cart before the horse.

DILLON'S RULE AND THE COOLEY DOCTRINE

Two competing legal doctrines govern the authority of a city or county to pass ordinances: Dillon's rule and the Cooley doctrine. The two are nearly diametrically opposed.

Dillon's rule greatly restricts local government discretion. In a celebrated 1868 Iowa Supreme Court opinion—*Clinton vs Cedar Rapids*—Judge Forest Dillon held that a municipal government has authority to act only when to do so is:

Granted in the express words of the law creating the municipal corporation;
Necessarily or fairly implied in, or incident to the powers expressly granted; or
Essential to the declared objects and purposes of the corporation.

Judge Dillon declared that

Municipal corporations owe their origin to, and derive their powers and rights wholly from, the legislature. It breathes into them the breath of life, without which they cannot exist. As it creates, so may it destroy. If it may destroy, it may abridge and control.

Dillon's rule goes on to state that powers expressly granted to a municipality should be narrowly construed and that courts should resolve ambiguities in the legislative grant of power against the municipality.

In contrast, the Cooley doctrine—the doctrine of municipal home rule—expresses the theory that local governments have an inherent right to local self-determination. In a concurring opinion in an 1871 Michigan Supreme Court—*People vs Hurlbut*—Michigan Supreme Court judge Thomas M. Cooley famously stated, "local government is a matter of absolute right; and the state cannot take it away".

In 1907 the U.S. Supreme Court made it clear that interpretation of state constitutional law regarding the establishment of cities and counties was entirely up to the states.[5] Unless there is a conflict with a federal constitutional provision, state courts decide issues related to the balance of state and local power.

There are 39 Dillon's rule states and 11 Cooley doctrine states. Nine states that follow Dillon's rule also permit the state to grant jurisdictions home rule by approving a charter that gives them greater planning authority than state general law.

BALLOT BOX PLANNING

Many states authorize direct democracy in which registered voters can pass or repeal state or local laws through "ballot box planning"—voting on laws and whether to remove local elected officials from office. Each state has its own law regarding state and local initiatives, referenda, and recall. If a state law permits it, voters can accept or reject a planning-related law passed by a state or local government by voting on a referendum, or propose a new planning-related law through an initiative. They may recall—remove immediately from office—elected state and local officials, including county commissioners and city council members, before their term of office is over, based on state law. If a specified percentage of registered voters sign a petition for an initiative, referendum, or recall, the government must hold a special election. Usually a simple majority is sufficient, though measures to amend the state constitution require a supermajority in some states. If passed, the measure usually takes effect immediately, regardless of the wishes of the elected officials. This has the advantage of holding elected officials accountable and expressing the popular will when elected officials fail to act, or act in ways contrary to what a majority of voters want. It has the disadvantage of creating uncertainty and provoking conflict been election cycles.

Initiatives and referenda must be "legislative acts"—proposing laws that the city council or county board of commissioners has the legal authority to enact. They may not be "quasi-judicial" acts like lawsuits. States do not want citizens to replace the state judicial system in conflicts involving individual disputes. "Ministerial acts", such as granting a building permit if an applicant has met requirements of the local building code may not be decided by ballot box planning. They are considered matters of right.

Many political scientists and planners oppose ballot box planning. They are concerned that people tend to vote because of a vague preference. They may vote to stop all building over a certain height, based largely on emotion rather than empirical research or good planning practice. In contrast planners and urban designers can draw on expertise and a body of experience. For example, in deciding about appropriate height limits they can tailor sophisticated land use regulations such as form-based codes that visually describe design alternatives, Floor area ratios (FARs) that specify how much floor space a building can have in relation to its lot size, and planned unit developments (PUDs) to the physical environment and local context. The details of planners' proposals can be evidence-based and thoroughly vetted.

CONFLICT AMONG LEVELS OF GOVERNMENT

Since 2000, a great deal of innovative planning and urban policy has come from state and local governments. President Trump's anti-urban policy bias, budget cutting, and deregulation prompted many states to develop their own state-level urban policy. Many cities and counties filled the urban policy vacuum with imaginative policies of their own.

Cities and counties in Dillon's rule states have a long tradition of opposing state limitations on their power to innovate. Resentment of states stifling innovation has grown recently. Neo-Marxist geographer David Harvey describes how "rebel cities" have begun pursuing alternative social justice, environmental, and other policies. Experiments with municipal socialism and neoliberal urban policies are popping up. San Francisco, Oakland, and Berkeley, California; Portland, Oregon; and Seattle, Washington have recently enacted notable local urban legislation on issues such as climate action plans, inclusionary zoning, and pro-bicycling laws. Whether this proves to be a short-term aberration or an ongoing trend remains to be seen. In states where neoliberals have power at the state level, state governments have lashed back, reversing liberal and progressive local government reforms and preempting local government decisions. The conservative and mainly corporate-funded American Legislative Exchange Council (ALEC) helps local governments controlled by neoliberals to draft conservative laws.

THE ELITIST/PLURALIST DEBATE

In the 1950s and 1960s polar opposite narratives about community power emerged reflecting the researchers' ideology and the research methods they used, as well as the communities they studied. In *Community Power Structure* (1953) progressive activist sociologist Floyd Hunter developed the concept of community power structure—the way in which power to make things happen is distributed at the city level. Hunter concluded from a study of Atlanta, Georgia, that community power was highly centralized. He found that a small interlocking elite group of White businessmen made all the really important decisions in Atlanta. Hunter's theory of local government community power is called elitist theory. Hunter used a reputational method of community power research based on interviews of people who informants told him were influential. He asked knowledgeable first-round informants about how much political power other people within and outside of government had on important local decisions and then interviewed them. From the second round he got additional names and went on to interview them. Sociologists Harvey Molotch and John Logan have contributed to elitist theory. They argue that business-dominated urban growth machines hold local political power—not a broad base of citizens.[6]

In *Who Governs?* (1961) Yale University political science professor Robert Dahl reached a conclusion that was the opposite of Hunter's, based on his study of New Haven, Connecticut. New Haven is an older, medium-sized, ethnically diverse, East Coast city. Dahl concluded that, in New Haven in the 1950s, ordinary citizens dominated city government and local decision-making. Local elected officials and local decision-makers who were not part of government were mostly middle-income working-class or lower-middle-class Irish, Italian, and East European immigrants or their descendants who lacked wealth or social position. Based on this evidence, Dahl developed a pluralist theory of community power to describe local government decision-making in the United States. Dahl used a research method called decision analysis. He looked carefully at exactly how key local decisions were made and by whom. Dahl and his students observed city council meetings, read newspaper accounts of planning issues, interviewed decision-makers, and studied documents about big local decisions like designating an urban renewal project site and building a hospital. Dahl concluded that many different groups of people were involved in different types of local city plans and decisions. For example, redevelopment decisions were made by one group of people, a different group of people were influential in education-related decisions, and a still different group of people made the key decisions about building the new hospital.

REGIME THEORY

Regime theory describes how coalitions of interest groups form, obtain, and use local political power. *Regime Politics* (1989) by George Washington University and University of Maryland Political Science Professor Clarence Stone is based on his analysis of urban politics in Atlanta, Georgia, from 1946 to 1988. Stone's description of how local government political regimes actually work has informed scholarship on urban politics for three decades. It has helped city and regional planners, local government officials, academics, and citizens better understand urban politics. Stone's approach to regime analysis has been replicated, critiqued, and adapted by other scholars.

Stone's regime analysis focuses on how the internal features of a governing arrangement fit together to allow a coalition to pursue an agenda. He pays special attention to the internal dynamics of political regimes. Stone concluded that in Atlanta between 1946 and 1988, a cohesive regime formed largely around a federally funded redevelopment agenda. He described the workings of a biracial (White and Black) coalition of governmental and non-governmental actors who worked together to govern Atlanta during that time. This is quite different from Floyd Hunter's depiction of a dominant White power elite governing Atlanta in the

1950s or Robert Dahl's depiction of broad citizen decision-making in New Haven in the 1950s and 1960s.

Stone's description of what he calls "the iron law of an urban regime" is that any governing arrangement must have the resources to sustain itself. This requires a stable coalition with participation by civil society actors such as local businesses, the media, organized religion, and labor unions. To understand a regime, Stone argues, it is important to understand how different elements of a common agenda mutually support each other to provide the glue holding the regime together. The lesson for planners is that to be effective, they must understand the local context, how interest groups relate to each other, and long-term political change.

Stone believes that the core elements of his original regime approach are valid, but that the urban context has changed, so that regime dynamics are different today than during the era he studied from 1946 to 1988. The large federal urban renewal, highway construction, and anti-poverty programs of that era are over. Accordingly, Stone argues that today, local governing arrangements have to be built around less sharply defined, more localized agendas. He argues that exogenous structural forces affect, but do not dictate local politics. Stone recognizes that American urban regimes are now shaped by knowledge-based services and information processing in a global economy. In his view, market hierarchies and political relationships in American cities, work against a level playing field and a truly pluralistic democracy.

CITY AND COUNTY PLANNING DEPARTMENTS

Most local government planning in the United States is performed by planners in city and county planning departments. Planners at the local level make plans for land use, transportation, open space, capital improvements, housing, and climate change action as well as preparing the local general plan, developing and overseeing zoning, deciding on land subdivision, and reviewing current development proposals. Making and implementing these plans is shared with local public works, parks and recreation, transportation, and other city and county departments.

City planning commissions, analogous to boards of directors of private corporations, oversee city planning departments. There are typically five to seven planning commissioners. In most cities, planning commissioners are appointed by the city council. Some may be appointed by the mayor, serve *ex officio*—based on an elected or appointed office that they hold—or get their position in some other way. Planning commissioners are unpaid except in a few large cities where they receive a low salary. Most have other full-time paying jobs. Some planning commissioners have a background in city and regional planning, law, architecture, civil engineering, public finance, or another planning-related specialty, but many have no such expertise.

City planning departments are headed by a planning director. The planning director is usually appointed by the city council and serves at their pleasure. Ordinarily the planning director is not a civil servant. He or she can be fired by the city council at any time without cause. It is no disgrace for a planning director to quit or be fired based on ideological or policy disagreements with the city council or county board of commissioners. The director of the San Francisco City Planning Department between 1967 and 1975, Allan Jacobs, said he always kept his bags packed so he could quit if he disagreed strongly enough with the San Francisco board of supervisors or mayor. To make city planning work, Jacobs often came close to doing that as described in Box 8.1.

Planning staff are generally members of the civil service—hired and promoted by competitive examinations with job security protected by a local civil service commission. This is arguably an improvement over the days of local government boss rule where political machines organized blocks of voters largely based on their national origin and appointed loyalists regardless of their qualifications. However, the civil service system favors seniority, and may keep the most able and imaginative planning staff from advancing

Figure 4.3 Anti-Fracking Protest (Hollywood, California, 2014).

rapidly over mediocre staff who have seniority and play by the rules. San Francisco Planning Director Allan Jacobs was constantly at odds with the San Francisco Civil Service Commission. Chapter 8 describes a parody he wrote imagining what would have happened to the San Francisco Giants baseball team if a clever lawyer discovered that they were protected by the San Francisco Civil Service Commission. The commission made it virtually impossible to hire or retain qualified baseball players or manage the team.

Most of city planning staff's day-to-day work is current planning—reviewing plans for proposed developments. Developers bring plans to the planning department for review and meet with staff to discuss their plans. Staff analyze the plans and make recommendations to the planning director, who in turn makes recommendations to the planning commissioners. Staff present their views orally at public hearings before the planning commission and the city council or county board of supervisors. Some planners work on advance planning, preparing a city or county's general plan, making long-range forecasts, formulating policy, and making climate change, resilience, or other long-range plans.

City and regional planning takes place in the face of conflict. Figure 4.3 shows a protest by activists in Hollywood, California opposed to fracking—injecting water, sand, and chemicals under high pressure to fracture shale that contains deposits of oil and natural gas in order to release them. Figure 4.4 illustrates a rally by demonstrators supporting "Dreamers".

Dreamers are about 650,000 young immigrants who have grown up as Americans, but do not have legal U.S. citizenship status. A program called DACA—Deferred Action for Childhood Arrivals—created by President Obama in 2012 by executive order protected Dreamers from deportation. President Trump rescinded DACA in 2017. President Biden reinstated it and opened it to new first-time applicants. Ultimate resolution is still in the courts and subject to national politics congressional Presidential and congressional elections. The fate of the Dreamers is still uncertain.

Cornell city and regional planning professor John Forester is a scholar-practitioner who has written extensively about the politics

Figure 4.4 Pro-"Dreamers" Rally (Ann Arbor, Michigan, 2017).

of planning at the local level. Forester identifies four main roles planners play in the face of conflict: as resource people, rule enforcers, shuttle diplomats, and negotiators/mediators.

As resource people, planners provide information and interpretations that help with decision-making. Interest groups vary in their sophistication and command of factual information. Some include skilled professionals who are well informed, while others consist entirely of people with little or no expertise about a planning issue that is being debated. Virtually every group can benefit from detailed and objective information about a specific planning issue.

As rule enforcers, planners describe the law to citizens, stakeholders, and elected officials. They channel dialogue to options that are legally possible. To the extent that they can, they shift discussion away from ideas which can never be implemented because of legal constraints. This helps keep conflicting parties from wasting time fighting about impossible options.

As shuttle diplomats, planners move back and forth among competing stakeholders, informing interest groups what other groups want and suggesting possible compromises. Negotiations are similar to mediation, but usually involves sequential separate meetings. Shuttle meetings may set the stage for face-to-face negotiations. They can save time and facilitate dialogue.

As negotiators and mediators, planners listen to all sides' demands, try to help each side see what the other side wants, and encourage all sides to compromise. A mediator is neutral—managing the process of consensus-building. A negotiator is an active participant—representing the position of the planning department, city council, or other employer.

PLANNING MEDIATION AND NEGOTIATIONS

Because planning decisions are controversial, city and regional planners often become involved in negotiations or mediation to resolve planning disputes. Virtually every planning process involves negotiations among parties—including parties on the same side of an issue—to reach compromises. Activists who agree that their city needs to adopt a local climate action plan that will achieve net zero carbon emissions by 2035 may disagree strongly about how much emphasis to give to tree planting, all-electric municipal vehicles, or shifting to solar, wind, or other clean renewable energy sources. Once they achieve consensus, the local climate activists will face push-back from stakeholder groups with other priorities, voters who know or care little about climate change, and climate change deniers.

Change is unsettling. There is always opposition to locally unwanted land uses (LULUs). NIMBYs want nothing built in their back yard. Elected officials who say "not in my election year" are called NIMEYs. City and regional planners have two other colorful terms for intransigent parties: CAVE people (Citizens Against Virtually Everything) and BANANAs—people who want to Build Absolutely Nothing Anywhere Near Anything.

Planners acting as negotiators serve as point people, accountable to a "back table" of people who need someone to represent their position with other stakeholders. Ultimately the local elected officials decide local policy.

Planners acting as mediators have a different role than negotiators. They may be appointed to try to resolve a conflict or because conflicting parties turn to them to do so. They listen to each side and try to get the parties to agree upon a compromise solution that will work based on scientific evidence and current planning practices.

A ground-breaking 1981 book by Roger Fisher, William Ury, and Bruce Patton at Harvard Law School's Negotiation Project, titled *Getting to Yes*, revolutionized approaches on how to conduct negotiations and resolve conflicts. Before *Getting to Yes*, negotiations were generally viewed as adversarial. Most of the theoretical and applied literature on negotiating focused on strategies to "win" a conflict. Fisher, Ury and Patton's approach represented a paradigm shift. It moved the focus away from conventional, time-consuming, and often unsuccessful negotiation processes. They opposed both initially taking a hard line and then giving up a series of positions or alternatively initially taking a soft line and then opposing other parties before reaching an agreement. In contrast, their negotiating principles include not bargaining over positions, separating people from the problem, using objective criteria, focusing on interests, and inventing mutual gain options. Thoughtful city and regional planners who are involved in planning negotiations analyze their own as well as their opponents' strengths and weaknesses (Strength, Weakness, Opportunity, and Threat—SWOT—analysis), develop strategy, build alliances, protect terrain they control, look for strategic opportunities, only attack when necessary, and limit the extent and duration of direct conflict with opponents along lines Fisher and Ury recommend.

A teaching program at Harvard Law School named the Program on Negotiation builds on and applies approaches developed by Fisher, Ury, and Patton. Lawrence Susskind—a city and regional planner at the Massachusetts Institute of Technology teaches in the Harvard Program on Negotiation. He has written practical and lively books and articles on how to conduct negotiations to resolve planning conflicts. Susskind notes that it is important that all parties feel an agreement benefits them, so they feel good accepting it and can sell it to their supporters. He uses the acronym GFTGFY (Good For Them, Great For You) as shorthand for a settlement that will leave other parties feeling they have gotten a good deal while getting an even better outcome for the planner's constituency. Susskind argues that during a negotiation a planner should make sure people at his or her "back table" will be satisfied with the outcome. This is one of Susskind's three most important principles for conducting a successful negotiation. Two others are convincing other parties to the negotiation that they have been treated fairly, and generating as much value as possible during the negotiation and sharing it to produce an agreement.[7]

Susskind's approach involves gingerly establishing a trading zone—a domain in which both sides can make, reject, and modify components of what may ultimately become a resolution to the conflict. Having more parking near her fitness studio than in comparable areas appears rational to a small businesswoman and building expensive tunnels for red-bellied newts to safely cross a road appears rational to an environmentalist. Rather than immediately getting into a fight, Susskind counsels a negotiator to get the other parties to agree to first find facts, then jointly map the terrain, choose expert advisers, and define appropriate methods of analysis. The parties might fruitfully discuss how to determine how much parking can be made available near the fitness studio or what research methods will provide alternative designs to protect newts from traffic on the road. Susskind recommends that parties assess tentative findings together and communicate the results clearly.

All sides in a negotiation value certain things. Creating more value widens the possibility that all parties can get enough out of a deal to agree. Susskind suggests playing "what if", bringing more parties to the table, creating public–private partnerships, and possibly using agents. Conflict resolution negotiations are full of surprises. Susskind urges negotiators to be prepared for surprises, improvise, and perhaps surprise other parties themselves. One chapter of Lawrence Susskind's book *Good for You, Great for Me* is titled "Write their victory speech". Thinking how opponents can describe what that have been able to negotiate as a success to the people they represent is critical to a successful resolution.

In addition to advice on handling individual conflict resolution negotiations Susskind emphasizes the importance of building group decision-making capacity. Long-term relationships are important to implement settlements and to avoid future conflict.

TRANSPARENCY AND SPEAKING TRUTH TO POWER

Planning, public administration, and business administration texts enshrine the concept of transparency—the principle that the government and other institutions should accurately describe their plans and policies to citizens in a timely manner. They urge professionals to speak truth to power. They agree that lower-level officials or citizens should be free to express their disagreements with government candidly without fear of retaliation.

These are important ethical principles. There are many examples where they have (or have not) been applied throughout this book. It is easy to declare the principles, but applying them in practice often presents planners with serious moral issues.

The rationale for transparency is that even if the process is painful, full disclosure may lead to fruitful dialogue and compromise that will produce a better plan. A transparent process may also make it easier to implement the plan than failing to provide transparency. The rationale for speaking truth to power is that decision-makers should hear dissenting voices which may sway them to modify their plans and policies or at least think more deeply about the consequences of what they propose and adjust the plan.

In practice planners often face moral dilemmas about how much information to release as plans are formulated. Of course, insiders profiting from information about plans and public investment before they are disclosed—what corrupt late 19th-century New York City political boss George Washington Plunkitt called "honest graft"—is unethical and illegal. Declaring that part of a neighborhood is planned for renewal that will involve demolishing old apartment buildings may create "planners' blight". Apartment owners may stop maintaining buildings that provide affordable housing. Releasing information about a proposed new highway when planners have determined only the general outline of where the highway will go may provoke confusion and fruitless controversy. On the other hand, once planners have narrowed the plan to a relatively small corridor, premature release of this information may provoke land speculation and drive up the cost of acquiring the highway right of way. James Rouse, the planner of the most successful new town in the United States (Columbia, Maryland) and Ebenezer Howard, the visionary responsible for the most successful new town in Great Britain (Letchworth, England) kept plans for the new towns secret while they assembled

Figure 4.5 Protester at the United States Capitol (2006).

land for the new towns. Providing honest and accurate information about plans in a timely manner is always good policy, but how to do it requires political skill.

SUMMARY

City and regional planning in the United States is not a passive, technical process. Big planning decisions involve dozens of stakeholder and hundreds or thousands of individuals who feel passionately about what the plan should be. Even decisions about a single site, such as how it will affect views or parking, raise political passions. At the margin, NIMBYs, NIMEYs, CAVE people, and BANANAs are unwilling to compromise on any reasonable solution to a planning issue. However, for the most part, the politics of city and regional planning in the United States is a healthy democratic process that ultimately produces better results than less conflictual plan making.

There is a long tradition of checks and balances in American government. This avoids tyranny and overreaching from the top down, but it also assures that it will take time and energy to get plans completed and things done.

Power to make city and regional plans in the United States is divided functionally both vertically and horizontally. Vertically the power to plan is divided among federal, state, and local governments. Horizontally it is divided among states and within states among counties, cities, and special districts.

Planning politics is context-specific. It reflects the great variety of places and where the local political culture falls along the liberal-to-conservative spectrum. It often reflects ethnic, racial, and interest group dynamics. Functionally, different entities planning for transportation, infrastructure, air quality, land use, the environment, and other matters are jealous of their own turf. Making city planning work in this complex environment requires political savvy. Planners serve as resource people, rule enforcers, shuttle diplomats and negotiators or mediators.

Ultimately politics—including planning politics—is about values. Ethical principles such as transparency and speaking truth to power should guide city and regional planning.

CONCEPTS

Annexation
Back Table (Negotiations)
Best Alternative to a Negotiation (BATNA)
Balkanization
Ballot Box Planning
Board of Supervisors (County)
Charter City
City
City Council
Civil Service
Community Power Structure
Cooley Doctrine
County
Decision Analysis
Dillon's Rule
Elitist Theory
General Law City
Good for Them, Great for You (GFTGFY)
Home Rule
Incorporation
Initiative
Municipal Corporation
Planner's Blight
Planning Commission
Planning Department
Planning Director
Pluralist Theory
Police Power
Recall
Referendum
Regime Theory
Reputational Method of Community Power Research
Reserved Powers Clause
Special District
State Enabling Act
Urban Growth Machine
Win–Win Negotiation

PEOPLE

Julian Castro
Thomas Cooley
Robert Dahl
Forest Dillon
Roger Fisher
Floyd Hunter
Allan Jacobs
Clarence Stone
Lawrence Susskind

NOTES

1 The UN-sponsored Paris climate agreement is the principal international climate change treaty. Treaties with Mexico and Canada impact planning along the U.S. border. Cross-border plans for oil pipelines affect energy and environmental planning. International maritime and aviation law impact U.S. national transportation plans and policy. Laws regarding oceans, fishing rights, and maritime law impact coastal zone planning. Laws regarding refugees impact migration into the United States.

2 Special districts may also be responsible for water, irrigation, sanitation, utilities, airports, libraries, community services, harbors, ports, open space, lighting, fire protection, veterans' memorials, cemetery upkeep, and other specialized purposes. The U.S. Census Bureau treats school districts as a separate governmental type distinct from other special districts for statistical purposes.

3 During the Great Depression many local governments were unable to pay their debts. As a result, states established city and county borrowing limits to make sure that would not happen in the future. Cities became more risk averse. After World War II, the U.S. economy was very strong. The risk of local government insolvency decreased, and pressure for additional public infrastructure increased as cities expanded and needed more infrastructure. However, states were cautious and slow to relax limits on local government borrowing for fear of a repeat of their terrible experience during the Great Depression when many local governments were unable to provide for basic needs of their residents, had to impose deep cuts to essential services, and faced the threat (and sometimes the reality) of bankruptcy. Special districts are usually not covered by state general purpose government borrowing limits. Accordingly, many special districts were created to borrow money, build and manage infrastructure, and provide services that cities and counties could not legally provide due to state borrowing limits or feared to add to their other obligations.

4 President Nixon imposed a moratorium on virtually all new HUD funding at the start of his second term of office in 1972. He initiated the Section 8 housing voucher and Community Development Block Grant (CDBG) programs. Ronald Reagan (1981–1989) massively cut what was left of New Deal, New Frontier, and Great Society urban programs. George H.W. Bush (1989–1993) and George W. Bush (2001–2009) continued the Nixon/Reagan neoliberal, anti-government, new federalist approach. Democratic Presidents Bill Clinton (1993–2001) and Barack

Obama (2009–2017) were pro-city presidents who tried to revive HUD, but never got as much support from Congress as Presidents Kennedy and Johnson had received. Each year the Trump administration issued budget proposals that called for massive cuts to the Department of Housing and Urban Development's budget, but Congress pushed back and rejected many of the proposed cuts (Schwartz, 2021: 385–387; NLIHC, 2020).

5 *Hunter vs Pittsburgh*, 207 U.S. 161 (1907) established the supreme sovereignty of a state over its municipalities. The supreme court stated: "The number, nature, and duration of the powers conferred upon [municipal] corporations and the territory over which they shall be exercised rests in the absolute discretion of the state. ... We have nothing to do with the policy, wisdom, justice, or fairness of the act under consideration ... those questions are for the consideration of the courts of the state, and their decision of them is final."

6 The term "machine", applied to local politics, refers to an organization with no legal basis that *de facto* controls local government decisions. Irish, Italian, and other ethnic urban political machines were prevalent in U.S. cities in the 19th and early 20th century.

7 Susskind's six principles for a successful negotiation are:

> Reframe your negotiating partner's mandate and priorities;
> Propose packages that they will consider good for them which will be great for you;
> Use contingent offers;
> Help the other side sell your deal to their back table;
> Insulate agreements against predictable surprises;
> Build your organization's negotiating capabilities.

SUGGESTIONS FOR FURTHER LEARNING

Urban Politics: Edward Banfield & Martin Meyerson, *Politics, planning and the public interest* (1964). Myron Levine, *Urban politics* (2019). Dennis Judd & Annika Hinze, *City politics* (2018). Steven McGovern, *Urban politics* (2016). Robert England, John Pelissero, & David Morgan, *Managing urban America* (2014). Mark Davidson & Deborah Martin, *Urban politics* (2013). Peter John, Karen Mossberger, & Susan Clarke, *The Oxford handbook of urban politics* (2015). **Anti-Urbanism in American Thought:** Morton & Lucia White, *The intellectual versus the city* (1962). **"Honest Graft":** George Washington Plunkitt & William Riordain, *Plunkitt of Tammany Hall* (1905). **Julian Castro:** Julian Castro, *An unlikely journey* (2018). **Planning Politics:** Allan Jacobs, *Making city planning work* (1980). John Forester, *Planning in the face of power* (1988) and *Planning in the face of conflict* (2013). **Federal–State Conflicts:** Gerald Frug & David Barron, *City bound: How states stifle urban innovation* (2008). Harold Meyerson, The revolt of the cities (2014). David Harvey, *Rebel cities* (2013). **Planning Law:** David Callies, Robert Freilich, & Shelley Saxer, *Cases and materials on land use law* (2017). Daniel Mandelker, *Planning and control of land development* (2011). Julian Jurensmeyer & Thomas Roberts, *Land use planning and development regulation law* (2018). **The Elitist/Pluralist Debate:** Floyd Hunter, *Community power structure* (1953). Robert Dahl *Who governs?* (1961). Peter Bachrach & Morton Baratz, Two faces of power (1962). **Regime Theory:** Clarence Stone, *Regime politics* (1989) and Reflections on regime politics (2015). Clarence Stone & Robert Stoker, *Urban neighborhoods in a new era* (2015). Harvey Molotch & John Logan, *The political economy of place* (1987). Richard DeLeon, *Left coast city* (1992). **Negotiation and Conflict Resolution:** John Forester, *Planning in the face of conflict* (2013). Lawrence Susskind, *Good for you, great for me* (2014). Roger Fisher, William Ury, & Bruce Patton, *Getting to yes* (2011).

CHAPTER 5

Planning Theory

INTRODUCTION

Consider what three planners actually do. The first planner is beginning to prepare a habitat conservation plan to protect an endangered sparrow that lives in patches of coastal scrub along parts of the California coast. Drafting a work program, she writes "**GOALS**", in all caps and bolded. Below and indented, she writes "Protect sparrow habitat", and indented under that "Increase coastal scrub cover", "Provide nesting boxes", and six related items. On the next page she writes "**COLLECT DATA**" followed by "Field observation", "Analyze Landsat images", and "Check 2015 Audubon Society study". The next pages list major tasks like "**DEVELOP ALTERNATIVES**", "**SELECT BEST ALTERNATIVE**", and "**IMPLEMENT PLAN**" with a sub- and sub-sub-topics. The major headings on the last pages are **MONITOR PLAN** and **CONTINUALLY ADAPT PLAN**.

The second planner is beginning work on a city bicycle plan. He opens a layer showing the city's streets in ArcGIS—the geographical information systems software most city and regional planners use—and adds layers showing park-and-ride lots, rental bike locations, and census data from the most recent U.S. census transportation analysis zones (TAZs) for the city. From the existing data he creates new layers designating streets where bike lanes might be added, and prints out a draft map. This is a start. He is confident that over the coming weeks he can complete a draft plan backed by data that he can defend. He will present his plan as a series of maps.

A third planner works for a regional fair share housing coalition that helps provide residents of low-income communities greater housing choice. Drafting a memo for the next meeting of the board, his ideas for a plan include "get information from tenants on what housing they want", "identify city council supporters", "get developers on board", and "prepare for an exclusionary zoning lawsuit".

These are all valid planning approaches. They reflect very different conceptions of what planning is and how to go about it. All three planners can benefit from reflecting on how they are approaching planning and theories of plan making.

The Planning Accreditation Board (PAB)—the body that accredits city and regional planning programs in the United States (and one program in Canada at the University of British Columbia)—requires city and regional planning programs to teach planning theory in order for their degrees to be accredited. Many city and regional planning degree programs include a required course on planning theory. Others teach planning theory as one or more modules in other courses.

This chapter grounds planning theory in a discussion of theories of knowledge. It describes shifting paradigms in planning theory since the advent of modern city and regional planning at the first U.S. city planning conference in 1909, and the divorce between practitioners and academic planning theorists. Sections of the chapter cover major planning theories, including the rational planning model, modernism, systems analysis, disjointed incrementalism, mixed scanning, strategic planning, neo-Marxist and progressive planning, welfare economics, communicative action planning, and complexity in cities theory. Sections address normative planning theory and planning ethics.

DOI: 10.4324/9781003195818-5

THEORIES OF KNOWLEDGE

Theory in planning and other of the social and policy sciences draw heavily upon scientific method that developed initially in physics, chemistry, biology, and other natural sciences during the "Age of Reason"—the Enlightenment—in the seventeenth and eighteenth centuries.[1]

Scientific theory is grounded in empiricism—the philosophical view that all concepts originate in experience of the real world. It consists of principles formulated by measuring phenomena empirically rather than relying on intuition, faith, or pure logic. It calls on scientists to formulate hypotheses based on observations and construct theory by a process of inductive reasoning that produces useful generalizations. Rigorous data collection, precise observation and measurement, and value-free analysis undistorted by the observer's preconceptions are central to all science including the applied social science of city and regional planning.

Once developed, theory allows practitioners to draw conclusions by deductive reasoning—understanding what is true or how probable it is, by reasoning logically from general theoretical principles. Unlike the natural sciences, where many phenomena can be isolated and observed in a laboratory setting, social science theory requires looking at cities, using scientific methods to capture and analyze data, and reflecting on empirical evidence.

PARADIGM SHIFTS

One good way to understand planning theory is as a roughly chronological series of paradigm shifts. A paradigm is a framework containing basic assumptions, ways of thinking, and methodology commonly accepted by members of a scientific community. Sometimes, there is only one dominant paradigm in a subject matter area, but there may be competing paradigms at the same time. Old paradigms are discarded, linger on, or are replaced by new ones. Paradigms often overlap with each other.

Physicist and historian of science Thomas Kuhn (1922–1996) distinguishes a "scientific revolution" in which a major scientific breakthrough occurs from "normal science" in which scientific knowledge advances slowly and incrementally. Kuhn's examples are drawn from the natural sciences, but his insights apply to social and policy sciences including city and regional planning. A theory that planting dune grass will reduce coastal flooding from storm surges is an example of normal science. It builds on an accretion of knowledge. In contrast, the idea—introduced in the early 1960s—that highway planning should be done using computer models rather than by drawing two-dimensional route maps by hand is an example of a fundamental paradigm shift about how transportation planning should be done.

Anglo-American Planning and Geography Professor Peter Hall—an eminent planning academic whose biography is in Box 16.2—has summarized the evolution of planning theory as a series of paradigm shifts. Nigel Taylor—a British planning academic who specializes in planning theory—agrees with most of Hall's descriptions of changes in planning theory. However, Taylor calls them significant developments rather than true paradigm shifts.

Hall and Taylor agree that in the late 19th and early 20th century urban planning was initially conceptualized as civic design and that after World War II the rational planning model became dominant. They also agree that the period dominated by the rational planning model was followed in the 1960s by a quantitative revolution in economic geography, regional science, and systems analysis. During the systems revolution planners began to analyze cities as a related set of transportation, park, water, and other systems. Both Hall and Taylor describe a series of other chronological developments in planning theory. As a result of such a variety of conflicting approaches, a humbler, more pluralistic, more realistic, and flexible hybrid urban planning theory has emerged.

Paradigms in planning specialties evolve. We have already encountered paradigms related to early U.S. urbanization and urban planning in Chapter 2, based on concepts of the walking city, web of seaport life, specks in the wilderness, and the Turner thesis about the role of the frontier in American history. Chapter 3 on urban design and placemaking introduced civic design theory, William Whyte's theory of placemaking, and Le Corbusier's modernist theory.

UNIFYING PLANNING THEORY AND PRACTICE

Peter Hall ends his tour of planning theory with critical comments on the divorce between planning theory and practice. He argues that, as graduate programs in city and regional planning have grown in number and size, and as a formal body of planning theory has developed, too often planning professors merely debate each other's academic theories with little attention to planning practice or the needs of planning practitioners on the front lines. Hall (1982) states that around 1955 city planning "split into two separate camps: the one, in the schools of planning, increasingly and exclusively obsessed with theory; the other, in the offices of local authorities and consultants, concerned only with the everyday business of planning in the real world". As a result, practitioners considered much of the planning theory that academics developed sterile and irrelevant and planning academics looked down on practitioners for failing to ground their practice in theory. Hall called for an improved, reciprocal relationship between the two—theory informed by and relevant to planning practice and planning practice informed and improved by relevant theory. Partly as a result of Hall's critique, the chasm between academics and practitioners has closed somewhat, but not entirely.

An important theoretical approach to unifying planning theory and practice is encouraging practitioners to engage in reflective practice. A "reflective practitioner" reflects on a course of action as it is underway or after it is partially or fully completed.

Massachusetts Institute of Technology professor Donald Schön recommends two types of reflective practice—reflecting on an experience that has already occurred and considering what could have been done differently (reflection-on-action), and reflecting on actions in real time as a practitioner is doing them (reflection-in-action). Cornell University professor of city and regional planning John Forester has applied theory about reflective practice to city and regional planning.

Many of the best planning theorists have also been practicing planners, planning commissioners, planning consultants or planning directors, who qualify as reflective practitioners.[2] Box 5.1 is a biography of John Friedmann—a pre-eminent city and

---

BOX 5.1 JOHN FRIEDMANN

John Friedmann (1926–2017) was a leading 20th-century urban planning theorist. From his participation as a student in the world's first planning theory seminar at the University of Chicago in the early 1950s until his death in 2017, Friedmann was passionately engaged in planning practice and planning education. He participated in planning projects and planning education all over the world. Friedmann participated in, and helped drive the growth of, planning theory into a body of knowledge that is regularly taught in city and regional planning degree programs in the United States and other countries. He wrote 27 books and more than 100 peer-reviewed articles. In addition to planning theory Friedmann is best known for his work on regional development planning, the world city hypothesis, and empowerment in planning.

Friedmann's most important planning theory book is *Planning in the Public Domain* (1987). Many city and regional planners worldwide have adopted Friedman's classification of planning in the public domain to define the boundaries of the field of city and regional planning and its relation to other disciplines and professional fields. Friedmann also wrote notable books on social justice, world cities, empowerment, urban futures, and planning in China.

Friedmann read voluminously in many disciplines and fields. He had a great capacity to anticipate, articulate, and promote new ways of thinking about urban planning theory and practice and to synthesize and critique the work of other planning scholars. He was a profound humanist who believed planning theory should reflect normative values—not merely the planning process and technical matters. Friedmann believed that radical change was necessary to make the world a better place and that planners should play an active role in that change.[3]

Friedmann argued that in the last 50 years three big shifts in planning theory have occurred. The first has been toward making planning more of a whole-society process rather than primarily a technical one. The second shift has turned planning increasingly into a political art. A third shift has been the direct engagement of planners with getting things done. In Friedmann's opinion, today's planners are no longer merely analysts advising politicians; they have become—or have the potential to become—political actors in their own right.

Friedmann was born in Austria and taught and practiced urban planning in the United States, Australia, Canada, and a number of Latin American countries. He taught planning theory at UCLA and served as the head of the UCLA Department of Urban Planning for 14 years at several different time between 1969 to 1996. Friedmann also taught at Melbourne Institute of Science and Technology (MIST) and was an Honorary Professor in the School of Community and Regional Planning at the University of British Columbia.

Figure 5.1 John Friedmann.

regional planning theorist and scholar-practitioner who unified planning theory and practice in his own work. Reflecting on decades of thinking about planning theory, in 2008—at age 82—Friedmann argued that three tasks that are central to planning theory are: evolving a humanist philosophy to guide planners in their work, adapting planning practices to the continually changing course of human affairs, and translating knowledges and concepts from fields other than planning into planners' language.

THE PLANNING AS CIVIC DESIGN PARADIGM

In the first half of the 20th century city and regional planning was conceptualized and taught as civic design. Civic design was a mixture of art and architecture—elitist, ivory-tower design at the city scale. First-generation physical plans were often like architectural renderings—detailed visual representations of an idealized future, hand-drawn in excruciating detail. Planning theory was preoccupied with the idealized physical form for cities. Its principal normative concern was aesthetics. Even though many of the pioneering urban planning professors at the first planning programs in the United States and England had been practicing planners, they did not teach much about the politics and economics of planning, equity, citizen participation, collaboration, or plan implementation.

Hall describes the first-generation planner as arrogant and serenely sure of his technical capacities. He (White, upper class, male) produced new town plans strongly influenced by Greek and Roman architecture, French neoclassical designs, and city plans reflecting the garden cities and city beautiful movements described in Chapters 2 and 6. The first generation of planning professors taught students to prepare architectural drawings extended to city scale—particularly end-state physical plans for an entire new town like Raymond Unwin's plan for the garden city of Letchworth, England, described in Chapter 6. Planners were viewed as a privileged elite who were not expected to interact with the people for whom they were planning. Once a well-crafted, aesthetically pleasing, functional plan was on paper, the first generation of planning theorists naïvely assumed that a city could be built just as a house is built from architectural drawings. Because early planners were divorced from the messy, political world of cities and gave virtually no thought to plan implementation, their plans were almost never followed.

Few planners actually get to plan a whole new town from scratch. Rather, they have to make plans to integrate new housing, streets, commercial and retail districts, industrial areas, parks, individual buildings, and infrastructure into existing cities and suburbs. They mostly plan sites, neighborhoods, and transportation systems or make city-level plans to influence incremental future development. Nor is the urban planning process value-neutral, in which an educated elite can pick a technically good design solution to a planning problem and have the client meekly endorse it. Effective urban planning is conflictual and requires planners to interact with citizens.

Despite its shortcomings, the planning-as-civic-design model represented an advance over non-planning. Ebenezer Howard's garden cities idea was a powerful paradigm that would produce one model of efficient, livable, healthy, green, sustainable, equitable, nearly carbon-neutral small cities appropriate to early 20th-century industrial society. The idea of designing new towns was visionary. Design is an important planning skill. Working with talented faculty and students taught the first generation of planning students teamwork and professionalism. However, this ivory-tower planning approach was never very practical and Hall concludes that it was no longer defensible after World War II, as the pace of urban development and urban change accelerated.

The term urban design began to replace the term civic design in the mid-1950s. Kevin Lynch at the Massachusetts Institute of Technology, and planners and architects at the University of Pennsylvania and elsewhere launched urban design courses at that time. Contemporary urban design is much more sophisticated, practical, and influential than early civic design.

THE RATIONAL PLANNING MODEL

The rational planning model assumes that city and regional planning goals can be accomplished by breaking planning into a number of discrete sequential steps and proceeding step-by-step to address each step in a linear fashion. The first planner described in the introduction to this chapter is following the rational planning model to develop a habitat conservation plan. The rational planning model reflects scientific thinking. The number of steps and what they are called varies. Figure 5.2 is a typical schematic diagram of the rational planning model.

The rational planning model became a dominant urban planning paradigm from the late 1950s through the mid-1960s. According to Peter Hall (2014 [1988]): "It was a happy, almost dream-like, world. But, increasingly, during the 1950s, it did not correspond to reality."

Planning theorist Michael Brooks (2002) states categorically that by the turn of the millennium: "Planning theorists [had] … thoroughly discredited the notion of planning as an exercise in rationality." However, Brooks goes on to say that while the rational planning model was trashed in theory classes, it continued to be taught in methods courses and is "still the dominant paradigm in planning practice".

City and regional planners now understand that city and regional planning will never be like branches of the natural sciences where research may disclose one true solution. They know that planning problems are "wicked" problems—in which any solution to part of the problem will inevitably create other problems—and that planning is inherently conflictual. It is never possible to gather (even specify) all the data that bears on any planning problem. All planning requires normative, value-based decision-making. Pure rationality is impossible. There is never one "best" solution to a planning problem.

Rational city and regional planning is now generally based on what Nobel Prize-winning Carnegie Institute of Technology political scientist Herbert Simon calls "bounded" rationality. Practitioners doing

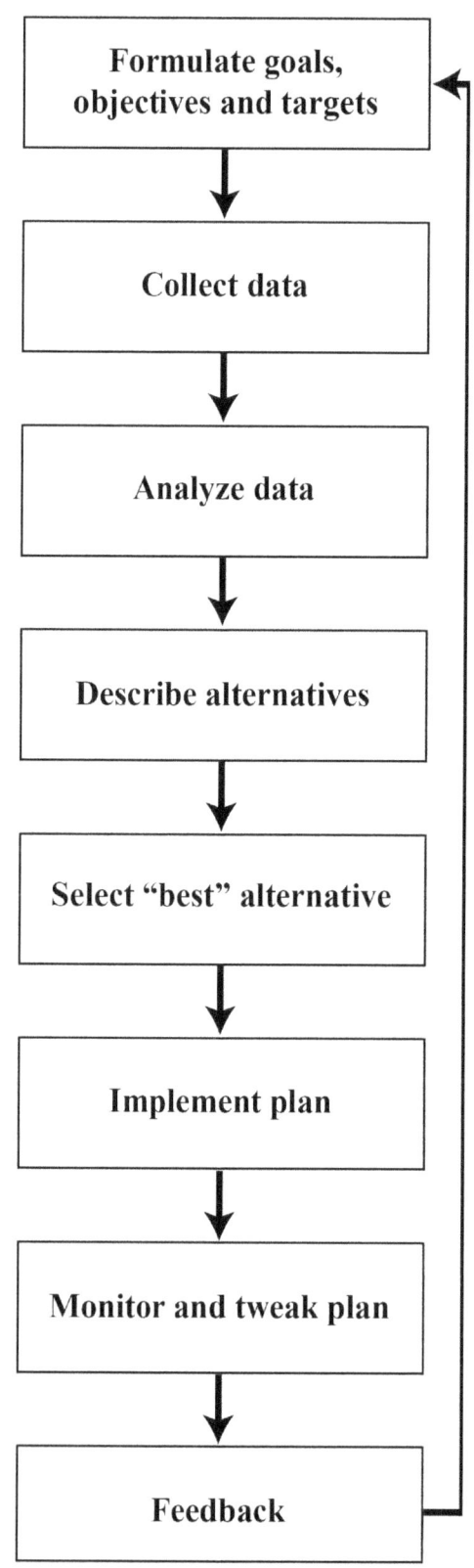

Figure 5.2 The Rational Planning Model.

city and regional planning based on Simon's model collect a manageable amount of data through evidence-based empirical research, analyze it using a reasonable number of appropriate social and policy science research methods, apply logical and structured decision-making to specify and prioritize plan alternatives, and pick an alternative that appears to be best. They don't get drowned in data, lost in analysis, agonize over too many alternatives, or pretend that their decision is the only right one. They present their recommended course of action to decision-makers and the public as their chosen alternative in a collaborative planning process and defend the choice with evidence that it is superior to alternatives they considered and rejected. They are sensitive to complexity, and constantly remain aware of changes in the planning environment. They are open to adapting a plan in progress in response to input from citizens and experts, and as unanticipated changes and shocks occur and interaction effects become apparent. They are reflective practitioners following reflection-in-action.

The simplistic first-generation rational planning model was naïve. Rationality-based fads from business, engineering, and economics were over-hyped as definitive ways to do city and regional planning, giving the rational planning model a bad name. However, so long as planners pursue bounded rationality and are aware of its limitations, the rational planning model is a valid approach in many situations.

SYSTEMS ANALYSIS AND URBAN PLANNING

An important, recurring theory of city and regional planning conceives of cities as comprised of multiple "systems" such as transportation, water, and park systems that each need to be planned, and together form a city system that is in turn part of a system of cities—"systems within systems of cities" in urban geographer Brian Berry's artful phrase.

Systems analysis was widely taught in schools of business administration and engineering in the late 1950s and 1960s. It was widely practiced in the military and the aerospace and automobile industries where tens of thousands of decisions needed to be coordinated. Systems analysis is a valid planning approach. However, it was often poorly executed, and fell out of favor. Today many professionals, including planners, use improved systems analysis.

Systems analysts developed a paradigm of planning as the application of computerized mathematical models to empirical data about highway, street, rail, subway, park, water, sewage, and electrical systems. In the 1970s city and regional planners began to input mountains of data into mainframe computers and to write computer programs to model traffic flows, land development, and the relationship between different city and regional systems. They analyzed data about land use, transportation, and employment using spatial interaction models to create city spatial structure plans.

A first-generation planner educated in civic design at the University of Liverpool in the 1920s could produce a carefully drafted paper design for a new town. However, he would not understand the equations and mathematical computer models showing how land should be subdivided, roads built, and parks dedicated if it was presented as the town plan by a systems planner educated by systems-oriented faculty at the University of Pennsylvania or the University of Sheffield, England in the 1970s. The first-generation big models were oversold. By the early 1970s enthusiasm for the systems paradigm had waned.

Today, city and regional planners routinely use spreadsheets, computerized statistical packages, and computer-assisted design (CAD) software in their work. Many city and regional planners use geographical information science concepts and geographical information systems software such as the Environmental Systems Research Institute (ESRI)'s ArcGIS to do spatial analysis as they develop plans. The student described in the introduction to this chapter whose approach to creating a bicycle plan was to create draft maps using GIS and spatial analysis illustrates the application of spatial analysis to city and regional planning.

Scientific research and analytic methods and technology are essential planning tools, but planners must ultimately decide what to recommend to decision-makers in their plans based on community values, politics, and the planner's knowledge of current planning practices as well as the results of rational analysis using these analytic tools. Planning, like politics, is the art of the possible.

DISJOINTED INCREMENTALISM

In a classic 1959 article titled "The science of 'muddling through'", Yale University political science professor Charles Lindblom (1917–2018) developed an anti-planning paradigm called disjointed incrementalism. Lindblom believed that in in pluralistic societies, as contrasted with top-down master planning in totalitarian societies, policy makers generally make many unrelated (disjointed) decisions in small steps (increments) unconnected by an overarching plan. He considered disjointed incremental decision-making both inevitable and the best way to make decisions. Lindblom's paradigm was strongly influenced by the free competition model in economics. He believed that mutual adjustment between stakeholders would provide a measure of coordination and compensate at the societal level for the inadequacies of individual incremental decision-making. Lindblom summarized six primary aspects of the disjointed incrementalism paradigm as follows:

- Rather than attempting a comprehensive survey and evaluating all alternatives, the decision-maker focuses only on those policies which differ incrementally from existing policies;
- Only a relatively small number of policy alternatives are considered;
- For each policy alternative, only a restricted number of "important" consequences are evaluated;
- The problem confronting the decision-maker is continually redefined: incrementalism allows for countless ends–means and means–ends adjustments which make the problem more manageable;
- Thus, there is no "right" solution but a "never-ending series of attacks" on the issues at hand through serial analyses and evaluation;
- Incremental decision-making is remedial, geared more to the alleviation of present, concrete social imperfections than to the promotion of future social goals.

Disjointed incrementalists argue that, since values cannot be scaled and summarized, "good" decisions cannot be defined. Hence evaluation is not really possible.

Lindblom's frontal assault on rational planning was a whack on the head that provoked city and regional planners and made them think. It led to more sophisticated approaches to planning theory that addressed legitimate aspects of his concerns.

MIXED SCANNING

Amitai Etzioni—a sociology professor at Columbia University proposed mixed scanning as a bridge to close the divide between the rational planning model and disjointed incrementalism. Mixed scanning emphasizes moving forward with a plan with limited information and continuously adapting the plan as conditions change. It provides both a realistic description of the strategy used in most decision-making and a theoretical model of how to do it.

Mixed scanning begins by differentiating fundamental decisions from incremental decisions. Scanning may be divided into multiple levels with varying degrees of detail and coverage based on available assets and the time available. Incremental decisions are made within contexts set by fundamental decisions.

Etzioni argues that decision-makers can summarize and rank their values, at least on an ordinal scale. Accordingly, he concludes—contrary to Lindblom—that evaluation is possible.

Decisions can never be made on either a fully ordered set of values or exhaustive information. They are largely determined by power relations among decision-makers. Mixed scanning works best in large planning processes where the situation is changing rapidly such as addressing climate change or pandemics. It is less necessary when conditions are stable and the planning environment is changing slowly. For example, during the COVID-19 pandemic, as understanding of the virus increased, guidance from the World Health Organization (WHO) and the U.S. Centers for Disease Control (CDC) regarding face masks, touching parcels, indoor dining, and social distancing changed rapidly. A carefully thought out plan about how to respond to the pandemic based on the rational planning model could be out of date a few weeks or even days after it was completed. Many health planning organizations followed the mixed scanning model to good advantage. Initially they formulated a plan based on the rational planning model. Then they then constantly scanned the changing environment and modified the plan as necessary.

STRATEGIC PLANNING

City and regional planners sometimes prepare strategic plans. A strategic plan differs from a comprehensive city-level general plan and specialized transportation, environmental, open space, and other plans in format and purpose. Strategic plans describe an approach to achieving stated objectives rather than operationalizing details of the plan in great detail. They may be for an entire city, a region, or city or regional system, such as a transportation or park system. Some states have strategic plans.

Theory about strategic planning is well developed in business and military applications. Michael Porter, a professor of business administration at the Harvard Business School and his colleagues at Harvard's Institute for Strategy and Competitiveness, which he directs, have produced influential books and articles on corporate competitive strategy.

MODERNISM

From the 1920s through World War II and beyond, modernism was a broad intellectual movement among artists, philosophers, writers, and social theorists as well as architects and city and regional planners. Modernists struggled to respond to the enormous changes they were witnessing in industrial society and the transformation of social relations by technology. They emphasized the ability of humans to improve and reshape their environment using modern science and technology. Modernists favored planning at large scales; functional designs; new materials; and efficiency. They had little nostalgia for the past.

In architecture and planning, the Congress of Modern Architecture (Congrès Internationaux d'Architecture Moderne (CIAM)—founded in 1928 and disbanded in 1959—organized a series of congresses in Europe attended by leading architects, landscape architects, industrial and urban designers, and planners. A leading figure in the CIAM was the Swiss-French architect/planner Le Corbusier. Le Corbusier drafted the Athens Charter (*Charte d'Athènes*)—the CIAM's manifesto on urban planning—in 1922.[4]

In 1922 Le Corbusier exhibited a 300-square-meter model for a contemporary city of 3 million at the Salon d'Automne—an annual arts festival in Paris—and continued to revise and refine his concept for the rest of his life. He called variations on his original design for a contemporary city of 3 million the "Radiant City". Figure 6.7 in Chapter 6 is Le Corbusier's rendering of his contemporary city of 3 million from *The City of Tomorrow* (1929). In the rendering, two great highways, north–south and east–west, intersect at the exact center of the city. The center is a transportation hub for superhighways, a subway system and an airport. Surrounding the central terminal are 24 glass-and-steel skyscrapers—vertical neighborhoods, each sixty stories high. Each skyscraper has as much usable space as a neighborhood, but occupies little more land than the old buildings that had previously been on the site. Le Corbusier was never able to get a Radiant City built, but his approach was very influential at smaller scales. Brazil's capital—Brasília—is a modernist city, built on Le Corbusier's principles. Figure 5.3 illustrates the layout of Brasília.

Figure 5.3 Brasília, Brazil (2015).

NORMATIVE PLANNING THEORY

Planning theorists have long sought to specify what a "good" city is and what constitutes a good city and regional planning process. This is normative planning theory. Massachusetts Institute of Technology planning professor Kevin Lynch crystalized the idea of normative planning theory and explored whether or not there are universal principles of "good city form". Planning professors Allan Jacobs at the University of California, Berkeley and Alexander Garvin at Yale University have described their views of what makes a city "good" or "great". The balance of this book introduces hundreds of specific normative ideas about what constitute good practices in city and regional land use, transportation, urban design, environmental, housing, and other plans and planning processes. It discusses the relationship between planned outcomes and normative theory regarding efficiency, beauty, social justice, equity, resource stewardship, livability, and other normative planning values.

In *Good City Form*, Lynch identifies three fundamental models of what constitutes a good city: the cosmic model, the model of the city as a machine, and the model of the city as an organism.[5] Lynch's theory of good city form addresses vitality, sense, fit, access, control, efficiency, and justice. Lynch and his students identified a remarkably relevant list of normative city and regional planning values in 1964 that include efficiency; beauty; safety; equality; justice; government responsiveness; diversity of people, jobs, housing, activities, densities, recreation, shopping, and lifestyles; tolerance and appreciation of diversity; support of social interaction including small group activity and identity; a clean, healthy, pollution-free environment; a solid, stable, and diverse economic base; accessibility; public transport and ease of pedestrian movement; expression of time, history, and tradition; responsive, accessible government; and adaptability (Lynch, 1964: 367–369). Normative planning values which have crystalized since Lynch's pioneering attempt to define a general theory of good city form include sustainability, livability, resilience, transit-oriented development, collaborative planning, and carbon neutrality.

Planning ethics is an important consideration in normative city planning. Ethics involves moral beliefs about right and wrong. Planning ethics inform city and regional planners about what is moral professional planning practice. The Planning Accreditation Board (PAB) requires all students in accredited graduate city and regional planning programs to study planning ethics.

Four ethical issues that planning professor Michael Brooks considers particularly critical for urban planners include:

1) loyalty to their employer versus loyalty to a broader principle or group interests;
2) the control and release of information;
3) the accuracy and integrity of information; and
4) conflict between what one deems right and what will sell.

Professional associations' codes of conduct define ethical conduct for their members. The American Institute of Certified Planners (AICP) *Code of Ethics and Professional Conduct* (2016) is the code of conduct for AICP-certified planners.

Many city and regional planning practices now viewed as unethical were accepted normative planning practice in the past. Planners wince at the racist theory that Black residential areas should be segregated from White areas to protect property values which was once Federal Housing Agency policy and which many planners accepted as good planning practice. Some planners helped justify bulldozing viable low-income communities to expand businesses, build offices, or provide high-income housing during the era of urban renewal and highway construction. Their uncritical acceptance of the mantra that land should always be developed to its "highest and best use" justified unethical practice.

NEO-MARXIST, PROGRESSIVE, AND EQUITY PLANNING

Beginning in the 1960s, the civil rights movement and civil unrest shook the United States. There were riots in many Black neighborhoods. Opposition to the Vietnam War radicalized a generation of young people. The 1960s and 1970s were a period of intense reflection on social justice in city and regional planning. Planning theory took a sharp turn to the left. Neo-Marxist geographers like Henri LeFebvre at the University of Paris; David Harvey at Johns Hopkins, Oxford, and the City University of New York; sociologist/planner Manuel Castells, then teaching at the University of California, Berkeley; and Columbia University City and Regional Planning Professor Peter Marcuse critiqued city and regional planners' failure to address social inequality. The neo-Marxist planning theorists modernized Marxist theory to consider inequality based on race and gender rather than inequality based on class as developed by 19th-century communist theorists Karl Marx and Friedrich Engels. Castells emphasized that by the 1960s social conflicts were mostly about consumption of goods and services rather than control of the means of production that had been Marx and Engels's principal concern. Neo-Marxist planning theorists also developed theory based on Karl Marx's *Das Kapital* (1867) and Vladimir Lenin's *Imperialism as the Highest Stage of Capitalism* (1917) criticizing the capitalist neo-colonial system. They described how rich capitalist nations in Europe and North America were exploiting poor countries in Latin America, Asia, and Africa.

While not drawing explicitly on Marxist theory, progressive planners in the 1960s agreed that radical change in the United States was imperative and that planners should be change agents. The very idea of progressive planning is that the present is not nearly as good as it can be, and that planning can and should make progress towards a better future. Progressive U.S. Department of Housing and Urban Development official Sherri Arnstein (1930–1997) developed a theoretical "ladder" of citizen participation describing how citizens can participate effectively in neighborhood planning. Norman Krumholz (1927–2019) developed and practiced equity planning while he was Cleveland, Ohio's planning director. Equity planning makes social equity the guiding principle behind every planning decision.

Progressive lawyer/planner Paul Davidoff (1930–1984) developed theory about advocacy planning, arguing that planners should act more like lawyers representing clients—not value-neutral technocrats. The third planning student in the introduction to this chapter who is developing a regional fair share housing plan to help provide residents of low-income communities greater access to affordable housing is a progressive planner engaged in advocacy planning. Arnstein's ladder of citizen participation, Krumholz's theory of equity planning, and Davidoff's ideas about advocacy and pluralism in planning are described in Chapter 9.

WELFARE ECONOMICS THEORY

Welfare economics is a branch of economics that provides theory designed to improve social welfare by intervening in free markets. City and regional planners draw heavily on welfare economic theory. In the United States welfare economics concepts are ideologically acceptable as a modest departure from the dominant neoliberal paradigm. The neoliberal paradigm holds that the law of supply and demand will cause the invisible hand of the market to allocate goods to achieve maximum human happiness more efficiently than top-down planned government direction. In the United States welfare economics concepts are perceived as less threatening than socialist planning ideas that have been widely implemented in other countries.

A key concept in welfare economics is the idea of market failure. Welfare economists argue that the governments should intervene only in a limited number of instances when markets fail. Market failure may occur because people cannot individually provide a public good like a highway, or indigent people are at risk of great harm or death without a redistribution of wealth in the form of government aid. When market failure occurs, planners and policy makers turn to tools like regulation, subsidies, and taxation to alter free-market behavior. For example if a coal-powered electrical power plant is releasing harmful greenhouse gases (GHGs) emissions into the atmosphere, a planner drawing on welfare economics theory might propose a carbon tax or a regulation prohibiting the release of GHGs. The polluter may realize that it is in his economic self-interest to pay for a scrubber to clean the emissions, which would eliminate the externality. Government may use the money they collect from a carbon tax to mitigate the damage that GHG gas emissions are causing. After a hurricane a planner might justify temporarily providing free food to disaster victims if the local market makes it impossible for them to pay for food themselves.

The tragedy of the commons is a compelling metaphor for a situation where individual users of a shared resource harm the common good of all users by acting independently based only on their own self-interest. University of California, Santa Barbara biologist Garrett Hardin invented the concept, using grazing land in early New England village commons to represent a generic problem. Grazing land on the commons could feed the community's sheep and cows indefinitely if managed wisely by everyone in the community. Since it was in the short-term economic self-interest of individual farmers to allow their animals to eat more than their fair share of grass, eventually the commons in many New England villages were destroyed by overgrazing and could no longer be used for that purpose. Long-term, everyone in the community lost from the unregulated short-term self-interested behavior of some people. Hardin used the tragedy of the commons as a metaphor that can be applied to many contemporary planning problems. For example, the failure of nation states to collectively protect earth from global warming can be conceptualized as the most important instance of the tragedy of the commons that humankind has faced. If individual nation states fail to implement policies to reduce release of carbon into the atmosphere because none is willing to pay their fair share of the cost of becoming carbon-neutral and each wants the other nation states to make costly changes that will benefit everyone, humankind faces the imminent danger of catastrophic change in the global commons that is the climate of planet earth.

When an individual or an entity impacts others, welfare economists refer to the impact as an externality. Externalities may be positive or negative, or have both positive and negative impacts. For example, if the Tesla automobile company locates a new automobile assembly plant in a community, the plant will create jobs, increase municipal tax revenue, and increase the number of customers at local businesses—positive externalities. The plant will likely increase traffic congestion, may create problems with noise, and might ruin the views of some residents near the plant—negative externalities. An economic development planner may recommend a welfare economics solution requiring Tesla to "internalize the externalities". The local government might require Tesla to install technology to reduce carbon emissions; pay for a shuttle from a park-and-ride lot on the edge of town to the plant in order to reduce traffic congestion; pay an impact fee to the community which can be used to landscape the area near the plant; compensate owners whose views have been ruined; or a combination of these and other solutions.

Development may create "free riders"—people or entities that pay nothing for a public good, but benefit from it. For example, if residents of a coastal town use their own revenue to build a seawall that will protect all the property on a long stretch of the coast, their neighbors who pay nothing get a "free ride". When there is a possibility that someone else will pay for a service, individuals and governments have an incentive not to pay for it. This arguably leads to under production of some needed goods. The planner's solution, based on welfare economics theory, is to make everyone pay their fair share for public goods.

City and regional planners sometimes use a pair of colorful terms to describe another common welfare economics problem: windfalls and wipeouts. A windfall occurs when an individual receives a large benefit through no effort of their own. For example, if a local Vision 0 program, which seeks to eliminate traffic deaths, decides to require all drivers to complete a defensive driving course this may create an economic windfall. If there is only one parcel of land where a defensive driving course can be built, the owner receives a windfall, because the value of their land will increase.

American socialist Henry George referred to the gain in land value that is not attributable to the owner's investment, labor, or risk-taking as the "unearned increment" in land value. George argued that the government should "capture" 100% of the unearned increment in land value. A politically more palatable solution in neoliberal countries is to make sure that the property owner benefits from any effort or investment he has made and shares some of the increase in land value, but that the government is compensated for at least some of their investment that produced the windfall. For example, if land next to a new $500 million subway station increases in value by $100 million as a result of the new station, capturing most of that money could go a long way towards paying for the enormous public investment to build the station. The local government that paid for the subway station may decide to capture most of the $100 million increase in value by taxes or fees to cover part of the cost of constructing the station. For political reasons they will likely allow the owner to keep part of the windfall profit. Hong Kong and Singapore finance huge subway and other transportation infrastructure projects through land value capture.

Alternatively, if the city decides to locate a landfill (dump) next to someone's house, the value of the owner's land will decline. They will have experienced a wipeout. When wipeouts occur, property owners sometimes seek money damages in court based on nuisance law—state common law that allows one private party to bring a lawsuit to enjoin an activity that reduces use of his property, get money damages, or both. If the wipeout is severe enough, a landowner may try to force the offending government to pay just compensation and take title to the property based on a legal doctrine called inverse condemnation. A well-designed and fairly administered land value capture system may reduce litigation like this, insulate the government from inverse compensation liability, and produce fair outcomes for all parties.

Specific applications of the tragedy of the commons, free rider theory, internalizing externalities, capturing windfalls, and compensating for wipeouts are described throughout this book—particularly in the chapters on environmental, transportation, housing, urban development, revitalization, and climate change planning.

COMMUNICATIVE ACTION PLANNING

Communicative action planning is a theoretical and applied approach to engaging a wide range of stakeholders in planning. It seeks to bring together affected citizens, government entities, and other individuals and organizations that may be affected by a plan during the planning process.

Communicative action planning reflects a distinct epistemology (philosophy of knowledge) and empirical research on how collaboration does and does not occur. Communicative action theory conceptualizes social reality as constructed by communication among people and groups with different perceptions and goals. It seeks to describe and explain how people jointly construct social reality (collaborative rationality) and to equip city and regional planners with practical ways to encourage collaboration.

Communicative action theory was initially developed in the 1960s at a very high level of philosophical abstraction by Jürgen Habermas. Habermas is a philosopher and critical social theorist associated with the Frankfurt School of critical social theory at Goethe University in Frankfurt, Germany. Habermas had an interest in epistemology that was not directly related to city and regional planning. Patsy Healey, a leading European planning theorist and Professor Emeritus of Town and Country Planning at Newcastle University in England began to apply Habermas's theory to city and regional planning in the late 1970s.[6] Healey urged planners to recognize that identity and knowledge are produced in social contexts and are always limited by human capacity. She shifted attention away from the search for objective laws that govern social behavior towards the social dynamics through which norms and practices are produced, legitimated, become hegemonic, and are transformed. Communicative action planners focus on the micro dynamics of planning—how decisions are actually made. While it is sometimes referred to as a theory, Healey calls communicative action planning a fully-fledged package of principles, hypotheses, and prescriptions.

Figure 5.4 is a light-hearted illustration with a serious message. It shows how miscommunication between people who are the intended users of a plan and planners can lead to disastrous results.

Communicative action theory is a well-established strand of planning theory. In the United States, John Forester at Cornell University and Judith Innes at the University of California, Berkeley have developed communicative action planning theory that builds on Habermas's and Healey's theory.

COMPLEXITY IN CITIES (CIC) THEORY

Complexity in cities (CIC) theory is a new paradigm in city and regional planning theory. Complexity theory explores topics such as non-linearity, adaptivity processes, self-organization mechanisms, and transition management. It is a particularly fruitful approach to very large planning issues such as financial crises, pandemics, and climate change.

The Working Group on Complexity and Planning is an Association of European Schools of Planning (AESOP) thematic group. The group's leader Gert de Roo, a professor of spatial planning at the University of Groningen in the Netherlands, and members of the group have applied complexity theory to city and regional planning. Michael Batty and others at the Centre for Advanced Spatial Analysis at University College London have contributed to the quantitative aspects of complexity theory by applying cellular automata models, agent-based models, fractals, and other advanced analytics to understanding and planning cities.

Many recent shocks and surprises illustrate the relevance of CIC theory. Policy makers and planners did not anticipate that the core

How the people described what they wanted

How the planner understood it

How the urban designer designed it

What was built

Figure 5.4 Miscommunication in Planning.

of nuclear reactors at the Fukushima nuclear power plant near Tokyo could melt down, a storm as strong as Superstorm Sandy would wipe out entire communities on the New Jersey shore, what the human toll of the COVID-19 pandemic would be, or the boiling anger evident in the Black Lives Matter movement. However, CIC theory is highly relevant to planning in each of these situations.[7]

How local, state, and national planners in the United States can anticipate and respond to future financial crises, climate change, terrorism, oil price shocks, and other unforeseen events depends on the way in which global systems change and what other state and non-state actors do. Without planned interventions, already bad situations can become much worse. Complexity theory is beginning to provide some much-needed guidance on planning in turbulent environments.

BOX 5.2 COMPLEXITY IN CITIES (CIC) THEORY AND THE COVID-19 PANDEMIC

University of Groningen, Belgium professor of planning Gert de Roo and other complexity in cities (CIC) theorists argue that planning needs to respond to the reality that discontinuous change and transformations are constant factors in the world. Change is often non-linear and full of surprises. There will always be tensions, frictions, mismatches, and breaks in the way in which development occurs and policies are implemented. City and regional planners know a great deal about approaches to purposefully intervening in situations that are more or less stable or developing in a predictable linear fashion. The rational planning model—identifying a problem, gathering data on it, selecting a "best" solution and implementing a plan—works reasonably well in many normal situations if planners set bounds to the model (bounded rationality). Planners know far less about how to deal with non-linear dynamic change, that is full of spontaneous developments, disruptions, shocks, breaks, and mismatches such as occur during a pandemic. Accordingly, de Roo and other CIC theorists argue that city and regional planners need to reconsider how to adapt plans for a static world to the reality of constant flux. CIC theory sees complex adaptive systems as interdependent and multi-level relationships among their parts and with their environment. Systems adapt both on their own and in response to planned human interventions. Intentional change by purposeful planned interventions is necessary in turbulent environments.

Historians, epidemiologists, and policy makers are well aware of catastrophic prior epidemics like the bubonic plague—which may have killed as much as 60% of the population of Europe between 1346 and 1353 and the Spanish flu that killed 15 million people between 1918 and 1920. Recently the world has experienced Ebola, swine flu, and other pandemics. The World Health Organization (WHO), U.S. Centers for Disease Control (CDC), Bill and Melinda Gates Foundation and other institutions had done important planning to anticipate and prepare for how to respond to pandemics before the COVID-19 outbreak.

As COVID-19 evolved, the pandemic produced a series of shocks to individual countries and to the global system. Italy's decision to close large sectors of the economy and require people to shelter in place was a wrenching one. Other countries quickly followed suit. Policy was discontinuous with stops and starts—lockdowns during surges and opening back up as new cases, hospitalizations, and deaths declined. New variants of the virus appeared. Many jurisdictions established standards and had linear plans—triggering actions when indicators such as hospitalization rates reached established levels. This reduced rates of infection and hospitalizations and saved lives compared to jurisdictions that chose not to plan responses to the pandemic. However, planning a response to the pandemic was mostly non-linear. Given the urgency and uncertainty, rather than invest in one effort to develop a vaccine, the U.S. and other governments invested in multiple vaccine development efforts. They knew that they needed to get an effective vaccine and that the value of one successful vaccine greatly outweighed the cost and financial waste of failed attempts or producing more vaccine than was needed.

The pandemic made it clear that systems have interdependent and multi-level relationships among their parts and with their environment. If New York City banned public gatherings and required people to wear face masks, but Florida did not, travel from Florida to New York could undermine New York's efforts.

Responses to the pandemic were discontinuous—initially the CDC recommended against individuals wearing face masks and then changed course; it recommended using gloves to bring packages into a house, but then decided that was not necessary; it set one standard for when indoor gatherings could occur and then revised the standard as new information became available.

There were mismatches—many countries including the United States temporarily stopped using a vaccine developed by the Johnson & Johnson pharmaceutical company when a small number of recipients died from a rare blood clotting disorder, then after further studies they lifted the ban, but required a warning about the blood clotting risk on the vaccine label.

The early phases of the pandemic produced friction and tensions. The Trump administration tried to label COVID-19 the "Chinese flu", but that label did not stick. The United States banned travel from the United States to China, and China quickly banned travel from the United States to China.

The COVID pandemic makes clear the relevance of complexity in planning. It will undoubtedly drive further refinement of a promising new line of theory.

SUMMARY

Consciously or not, all planners base their practice on some theory of what planning is and how plans should be made. City and regional planning academics have developed a body of theory both about the planning process and substantive plan content. There is a divide between city and regional planning practitioners who want practical guidance for their practice and consider academic theorizing irrelevant, and planning theorists who look down on practitioners, but the divide is closing. Planning scholar-practitioners who have reflected on their experience and derived theory from the school of hard knocks are increasingly producing sophisticated theory that practitioners find relevant—including theory about reflective practice.

There is value in many different lines of planning theory, but also in the critiques leveled against them in their purest form. Planning should be grounded—based on scientific evidence—as well as creative artistic thinking. It should be an applied social science, using scientific methods. While critics of the rational planning model are correct that plans rarely follow their initial formulation, the core ideas of the rational planning model are sound. Bounded rationality is an appropriate approach to planning. Planning beats muddling through. Mixed scanning, following a scaled-down version of the rational planning model and continually scanning the changing context within which a plan operates, is often a good approach. The real world is messy, but not incomprehensible. It is complex, but tools and concepts to better manage complexity in city planning are evolving rapidly.

Planning is much more than a technical matter. Normative planning theory is important.

City planners should be change agents making cities more efficient, prosperous, beautiful, accessible, pedestrian-friendly, eco-friendly, adaptable, resilient, inclusive, safe, clean, healthy, pollution-free, and carbon neutral. They should help cities express their history, tradition and culture and reflect other normative values of their residents.

CONCEPTS

Communicative Action Planning
Complexity in Cities (CIC) Theory
Deductive Reasoning
Disjointed Incrementalism
Empiricism
Equity Planning
Inductive Reasoning
Mixed Scanning
Neo-Marxist Planning
Normative Planning Theory
Paradigm
Planning Ethics
Progressive Planning

Rational Planning Model
Reflective Practitioner
Scientific Method
Scientific Revolution
Strategic Planning
Systems Analysis
The Science of "Muddling Through"

PEOPLE

Sherri Arnstein
Paul Davidoff
Amitai Etzioni
John Friedmann
Jürgen Habermas
Patsy Healey
Judith Innes
Norman Krumholz
Thomas Kuhn
Charles Lindblom
Karl Marx
Gert de Roo

NOTES

1 Galileo Galilei (1564–1642) revolutionized astronomy by proposing a heliocentric (sun-centered) theory of the solar system based on empirical observations with a telescope he invented rather than the prevailing earth-centered theory based on Christian theology. Sir Isaac Newton 1642–1726) pioneered the natural science discipline of physics by observing how physical objects with different weights and masses behaved when they were dropped, collided with each other, or their states were altered by changes in temperature. Antoine Lavoisier (1743–1794) advanced the discipline of chemistry by discovering the role of oxygen in combustion, classifying elements, and proving that the mass of matter remains constant. Antonie van Leeuwenhoek (1632–1723) pioneered the discipline of biology by observing "wee beasties" (microbes) with a microscope he designed and built.

2 Planners profiled in the biographies in this book who combined teaching and practice include Catherine Bauer, Eugenie Birch, Ann Forsyth, John Friedmann, Patrick Geddes, Gary Hack, Peter Hall, Allan Jacobs, Janette Sadik-Khan, T.J. Kent, Kevin Lynch, Ian McHarg, Catherine Ross, June Thomas, Kongjian Yu, and Robert Weaver.

3 In "The uses of planning theory" (2008) Friedmann rejects the notion that planning is a value-free activity guided by scientific or professional standards. He is critical of the rational planning model. He argues that planning is profoundly political, and planners must make normative judgments. Outcomes, not just process, matter. Friedmann goes on to argue that the world's major challenge in an increasingly materialist, individualist world, largely indifferent to humans' impacts on the natural environment, is to develop a human-centered philosophy. This will help build sustainable and livable cities that will allow individuals to flourish to their full potential. He challenges the assumption that unlimited cumulative growth in material consumption will lead to human happiness. Participation, deliberative democracy, and collaborative planning are necessary to reach humanistic goals.

4 The Charter of Athens was drafted and adopted at the fourth Congrès Internationaux d'Architecture Moderne (CIAM) conference in 1933. The conference was held on an ocean liner traveling from Marseille to Athens, Greece.

5 Lynch's four models are described in *Good City Form* (Lynch, 1984: 73–98). The Cosmic model guided the physical form of the American Indian settlements such as Cahokia and Pueblo Bonito using axes, grids, centers, and polarities to represent powerful psychological archetypes and serve as magical religious and ceremonial centers. The model of the city as a machine is the basis for Le Corbusier and CIAM theorists' conception of the city as a collection of autonomous, but linked and often moving parts. The model of the city as an organism depicts the city center as the city's heart, highways and roads as arteries and veins, and parks the lungs of a city. Viewed as an organism, a city can be considered healthy or sick. Cites can be conceptualized as progressing through life cycles—birth, maturation, and death. Lynch himself did not consider cities organisms, but argued that the model of the city as an organism, and city health as a normative goal for a city are powerful and recurring metaphors. The metaphor of cities as healthy or sick is different from the 19th-century concern to improve public health in cities and the contemporary "healthy cities" movement's quest to build cities to promote healthy people by strategies like increasing walkability and promoting bicycling to reduce obesity and lower the rate of diabetes (Corburn & Gottlieb, 2009; Sarkar & Webster, 2016).

6 Healey was the founding editor and remains a senior editor of the journal *Planning Theory*. *Planning Theory* is a leading international planning theory journal and has served as a vehicle for articles developing collaborative planning theory.

7 The 2008 global financial crisis disrupted existing plans for building new affordable housing and financing the existing affordable stock. Presidents Bush and Obama, the U.S. Congress, the U.S. Federal Reserve Board, the Secretary of The Treasury, and U.S. Department of Housing and Urban Development Secretary Julian Castro had to quickly devise new plans to stabilize the mortgage system. Local planners and housers had to radically change local housing plans on short notice. The unexpected nature of the mortgage crisis, the non-linear foreclosure

pattern, and how what was happening was linked to many simultaneous changes called for planning of a qualitatively different kind. Similarly, climate change is complex and its implications are only partially understood. Planners and policy makers knew that New Orleans was vulnerable to flooding and that there was some risk that some old levees might fail in a big hurricane. However, they did not anticipate the magnitude of the devastation Hurricane Katrina caused or all the many physical, economic, and social interaction effects that followed.

SUGGESTIONS FOR FURTHER LEARNING

Introductions to Planning Theory: Peter Hall, The city of theory in *Cities of tomorrow* (2014). Michael Brooks, *Planning theory for practitioners* (2002). Nigel Taylor, *Urban planning theory since 1945* (1998). Robert Beauregard, *Advanced introduction to planning theory* (2020). Michael Gunder, Ali Madanipour, & Vanessa Watson, *The Routledge handbook on planning theory* (2018). **Urban Planning Theory Anthologies:** Philip Allmendinger (ed), *Planning theory*, 3rd ed (2017). Susan Fainstein & James DeFilippis (eds), *Readings in planning theory*, 4th ed (2016). Seymour Mandelbaum, Luigi Mazza, & Robert Burchell (eds), *Explorations in planning theory* (1996). **John Friedmann's Contribution to Planning Theory:** John Friedmann, *Planning in the public domain* (1987), The uses of planning theory (2008), and *Insurgencies* (2011). Haripriya Rangan, Mee Ng, Libby Porter, & Jacquelyn Chase, *Insurgencies and revolutions: Reflections on John Friedmann's contribution to planning theory and practice* (2017). *Journal of the American Planning Association* Symposium: John Friedmann Retrospective—particularly Sandra Rosenblum, Introduction: John Friedmann and links to planning practice (2018). **Urban Planning Paradigms:** Thomas Kuhn, *The structure of scientific revolutions* (1962). Peter Hall, The city of theory in *Cities of tomorrow* (2014). Nigel Taylor, *Anglo-American town planning theory since 1945* (1999). Michael Brooks, A plethora of paradigms? (1993). **The Rational Planning Model:** Michael Brooks, *Planning theory for practitioners* (2002). Herbert Simon *Models of man: Social and rational-mathematical essays on rational human behavior in a social setting* (1957). **Reflective and Deliberative Planning Practice:** Donald Schön, *The reflective practitioner* (1982). Chris Argyris, *Reasoning, learning and action* (1982). John Forester, *The deliberative practitioner* (1999). **Planning Ethics:** American Institute of Certified Planners, *AICP code of ethics and professional conduct*. Carol Barret, *Everyday ethics for practicing planners* (2002). **Urban Systems Theory:** Brian Berry, Cities as systems within systems of cities (1964). Walter Isard, *Methods of regional analysis* (1960). **Neo-Marxist planning:** William Tabb & Larry Sawers (eds), *Marxism and the metropolis* (1984). Manuel Castells, *The urban question* (1977). David Harvey, *Social justice and the city* (1973). Henri Lefebvre, *The production of space* (1992). **Advocacy planning:** Paul Davidoff, Advocacy and pluralism in planning (1965). **Citizen participation:** Sherri Arnstein, A ladder of citizen participation (1969). **Equity Planning:** Norman Krumholz, A retrospective view of equity planning (1982), *Making equity planning work* (1990), and *Reinventing cities* (1994). Norman Krumholz & Kathryn Hexter *Advancing equity planning now* (2019). **Disjointed Incrementalism:** Charles Lindblom, The science of "muddling through" (1959). **The Tragedy of the Commons:** Garrett Hardin, The tragedy of the commons (1968). **Mixed Scanning:** Amitai Etzioni, Mixed scanning (1967). **Corporate Strategic Planning:** Michael Porter, *Competitive strategy* (1998). **Land value capture:** Henry George, *Progress and poverty* (1879). Donald Hagman & Dean Misczynski, *Windfalls for wipeouts* (1978). Vivian Ho & Eddie Hui, Land value capture in Hong Kong and Singapore (2004). **Conflict Resolution:** John Forester, *Planning in the face of conflict* (2013). Lawrence Susskind, *Good for you, great for me* (2014). **Collaborative and Communicative Action Planning:** Jürgen Habermas, *Moral consciousness and communicative action* (1990). Patsy Healey, *Collaborative planning* (1997) and The communicative turn in planning theory and its implications for spatial strategy formation (2006). Judith Innes, Information in communicative planning (1998), Consensus building and complex adaptive systems (1999), and Collaborative rationality for planning practice (2016). **Complexity in Cities (CIC) Theory:** Gert de Roo *The Routledge handbook on complexity* (2020). Gert De Roo, Jean Hillier, & Joris Van Wezemael, *Complexity and planning* (2012). Judith Innes & David Booher, *Planning with complexity* (2010). **Journals:** *Planning Theory. Planning Theory and Practice*.

CHAPTER 6

Visions

INTRODUCTION

Visions often anticipate and sometimes shape reality. Descriptions of ideal cities by planners, philosophers, revolutionaries, and novelists have driven paradigm shifts in planning theory and influenced planning practice.

Descriptions of what their proponents consider elements of a radically better city reflect broader visions of society. They are based on a combination of ethical principles such as eliminating class distinctions, living harmoniously with nature, gender equality, and work–life balance. In addition to descriptions of a better built environment they reflect ideas for improving society's economic and social foundations.

Early utopian visions of cities reflected Christian ethics, socialistic and anarchist views about how to organize the industrial labor force, the role of the state in childrearing, and other issues that transcend physical city planning.

In the early 16th century English philosopher Sir Thomas More described an imaginary society he called Utopia. Utopia became a noun and utopian an adjective. Dozens of fictional accounts of other utopias and experiments to actually build them followed. The opposite of a utopia is a dystopia—a terrible anti-utopia.

By the early 19th century Scottish industrialist Robert Owen had built New Lanark—an industrial town in Scotland that became a model for utopian socialist experiments. A century later planners, policy makers, and the curious public flocked to Letchworth, England—the world's first "garden city" to admire a human-scale alternative to the great unplanned sprawling cities or stagnating rural areas where they lived. More recently the vision of ecotopia—an environmental utopia—reflects a vision of how to live in harmony with nature.

This chapter discusses utopian and dystopian visions of what future cities could be like. It begins with a description of Thomas More's original Utopia. Sections describe ideal cities in utopian fiction and their opposites in dystopian fiction; 18th- and 19th-century utopian socialists' visions; garden cities invented by English visionary Ebenezer Howard; Chicago architect Daniel Burnham and the city beautiful movement; the modernist movement led by Swiss-French architect/planner Le Corbusier; post-modernist approaches to city planning that arose in reaction to the modernist movement; and environmental utopias.

The chapter describes American architect/planner Frank Lloyd Wright's low-density, auto-centered broadacre city that called for blending city and countryside; Spanish architect Alberto Soria y Mata's vision of a linear city—built along a transit corridor; and American educator/planner Clarence Perry's concept of how to design neighborhood units. The final sections describe Ernest Callenbach's vision of an environmental utopia he called Ecotopia and vision planning—a distinct type of big-think planning intended to get citizens and decision-makers to think outside of the box.

In his classic study of 18th- and 19th-century European utopian political economists, *The Worldly Philosophers*, New School of Social Research economics professor Robert Heilbroner observed that: "He who enlists a man's mind wields a power even greater than the sword or the scepter." Utopian thinkers have enlisted many planners' minds. While none of the great urban utopian visions discussed in this chapter has been implemented exactly as

DOI: 10.4324/9781003195818-6

imagined by their inventors, their inspiration to create better cities and better societies has profoundly affected city and regional planning practice.

SIR THOMAS MORE'S UTOPIA

The word utopia comes from English philosopher, lawyer, statesman, and humanist Sir Thomas More's 1516 book *Of a Republic's Best State and of the New Island Utopia*.

More's *Utopia* describes an imaginary community of abundance and harmony. Utopia is an island nation with a capital (Amarout) and 54 cities of 6,000 people each. The population is periodically redistributed to maintain balance. The Utopians found new colonies on the mainland if necessary. There is no private property. People are given what they request. Houses are rotated every ten years. There are no locks on the doors. Every able-bodied resident works both in farming and a trade such as weaving or carpentry. The residents of Utopia balance work and leisure time. They wear similar simple clothing and take turns cooking basic, healthy meals, which they eat in communal dining halls. The Utopians tolerate different religions. Wealth is of little importance. Gold is used for chamber pots and criminals' chains. There are free hospitals. Euthanasia (mercy killing) is permitted. Divorce is legal. Priests can marry. There is no capital punishment. Every household has two slaves—criminals or captives from other countries. The slaves are treated well and can be released for good behavior. Women do the same farm work as men, but there is gender inequality in the trades. Carpenters are male; weavers are female. Women are responsible for child rearing. Utopia is ruled by a popularly elected prince who governs for life. Utopians engage in war only when forced to do so, never go to war to aggrandize themselves, and try to avoid bloodshed even when they are at war. Only men participate in war games and serve in the military.

The word utopia (lower case) has come to stand for any idealized society. The adjective utopian is often used pejoratively to characterize and ridicule ideas people who disagree with them deem impractical. Many utopian and dystopian novels and films depict cities of the future reflecting positive and negative urban trends that concerned people at the time they were produced.[1]

Contemporary urbanists include both optimists who believe the urban future will be better—if not achieving the level of a utopia—and pessimists who believe future cities will be worse, but not as bad as they are depicted in dystopian fiction. Edward Glaeser—a Harvard economist—calls cities "our greatest invention" and predicts "the triumph of the city" (Glaeser, 2012). Bruce Katz—a scholar at the Brookings Institution argues that cities and metropolitan areas are "fixing our broken politics and fragile economy" (Katz & Bradley, 2014). Author and social critic Mike Davis describes a future planet of slums, but is enthusiastic about how Latinx are reinventing the American city.

ROBERT OWEN AND THE UTOPIAN SOCIALISTS

Colorful and eccentric European thinkers referred to as utopian socialists imagined ideal societies and described visions of what cities might become. Most were theorists, but some tried to build utopian communities themselves or inspired others to do so.[2]

Robert Owen (1771–1858) was the most important of the 19th-century utopian socialists. Owen built the community of *New Lanark, Scotland* between 1788 and 1817 on the River Clyde, about 25 miles from Glasgow (Figure 6.1). New Lanark was the most successful 19th-century utopian socialist community.

New Lanark included brick textile mill buildings, tidy rows of tenement housing for millworkers, a progressive primary school, and an institute for the formation of character. The streets were free of garbage, and the air and water were relatively clean.

Owen's workers had consistent work, and were paid regularly. They worked long hours by today's standards, but shorter hours than workers in other British textile factories.

Figure 6.1 New Lanark, Scotland, circa 1825.

When one of the mills burned, Owen continued to pay the workers. Children under the age of ten were educated at Owen's expense—receiving instruction in music, dance, reading, arithmetic, geography, and Christian morals. Owen helped his workers set up a cooperative store to sell fresh farm produce.

Owen made a personal fortune from New Lanark. He became a celebrity to businessmen and social reformers. Economic historian Robert Heilbroner (1953) reports that 20,000 people, including Grand Duke Nicholas, who later became the Tsar of Russia, and "a whole covey of parish deputations, writers, reformers, sentimental ladies, and skeptical businessmen" signed the guestbook at New Lanark between 1815 and 1825.

Owen's achievement stands in stark contrast to conditions in what poet William Blake called England's "dark Satanic mills" in other early 19th-century cities in Great Britain. In *The Condition of the Working Class in England in 1844* Friedrich Engels—Karl Marx's lifelong collaborator and the co-author of *The Communist Manifesto*—described Manchester. Smoke blackened the air and crusted Manchester's buildings with soot. The River Irk was a bubbling green miasma of industrial waste. Multiple households (and their animals) crowded into single dark rooms in flimsy houses with dirt floors. Manchester had no sewer system. When it rained (frequently) the floors of the factory workers' wretched houses were covered by the stinking overflow from communal backyard cesspools. In Manchester the working class—whom Marx and Engels called the proletariat—included children as young as eight. When a worker lost an arm in the textile spinning machinery, her wages stopped. There was no medical or income security net. Many of the factory owners—whom Marx and Engels called the bourgeoisie—lived in country estates insulated from the squalor of the city.

Owen sold his interest in New Lanark in 1825 and moved to the Indiana frontier with his four sons and father-in-law, Chester Dale. He purchased 20,000 acres of land on the Wabash River. A utopian community named Harmony had been started on the site 11 years earlier. Owen renamed the settlement New Harmony. Unlike New Lanark, New Harmony was not a mill town. Its residents were mostly intellectuals interested in Owen's social experiment of creating a utopian community. New Harmony failed economically. The European and American intellectuals it attracted could not agree with each other or manage the economy. Owen lost 80% of his fortune. He returned to England in 1828 and spent the remainder of his life

Figure 6.2 New Lanark, Scotland Historic District (2021).

working with embryonic working-class trade unions in the Grand National Model Union of the Productive and Useful Classes. Today the remains of New Harmony are a U.S. national historic district. Some of the original harmonist buildings and others built by Owen have been restored.

Capitalists applaud Owen for demonstrating that capitalism could be both profitable and humane. Socialists revere him for his devotion to bettering the lives of workers. The United Nations has designated New Lanark a UN World Heritage site. It is largely intact as it was in the 1820s. Figure 6.2 shows the New Lanark World Heritage Site today.

GARDEN CITIES

The most influential urban planning vision of all time—the garden city—was invented in 1898 by Ebenezer Howard—a modest British social reformer. Garden cities were intended as an alternative to vast, sprawling, unplanned city-regions like London in which formerly separate towns and villages were being engulfed as the conurbations expanded. The concept has worldwide relevance as urban areas have expanded since Howard formulated his ideas.

In a celebrated diagram titled "The three magnets", subtitled "Where will the people go?" Howard drew three horseshoe-shaped magnets labeled "town", "country" and "town-country" pulling "the people" in competing directions (Figure 6.3). Towns had "more high money wages", but also "higher rents". The country had "fresh air", "an abundance of water", and "the beauty of nature", but "land lying idle" and "lack of amusement". The pull of Howard's new town-country magnet—a garden city—would be stronger than either of the other two magnets. Howard listed only positive features that would attract rural migrants including "the beauty of nature", "social opportunity", "low rents", "high wages", "pure air and water", and "plenty to do" in the garden city.

Howard proposed locating garden cities on inexpensive agricultural land about forty miles from the existing urban fringe of expanding cities like London. Their target population was 32,000 residents—enough people at a high enough density to form a real community. Most of the population would live within a 1,000-acre core. Garden City would be walkable with only a three-quarter-mile radius.

The core of garden city would be surrounded by a 5,000-acre greenbelt—a term Howard invented, and which has become extremely important worldwide.[6] Most of the greenbelt would consist of farms—providing locally sourced fresh

BOX 6.1 EBENEZER HOWARD

Ebenezer Howard (1850–1928)—a modest man with little formal education—is the most influential visionary city and regional planner of all time. A slim little book Howard self-published in 1898—*Tomorrow: The Peaceful Path to Real Reform* which was commercially republished in 1902 as *Garden Cities of Tomorrow*—galvanized British philanthropists to build a new kind of city—a "garden city". It sparked a worldwide garden city movement that is still relevant and influential today.

Howard came from a lower-middle class family. He left school at age 14. At age 21 he emigrated to the United States where he resided for 12 years from 1871 to 1883. Howard failed as a farmer in Nebraska and then spent four years in Chicago working as a stenographer. He returned to England in 1876, where me made his living as a court reporter for the rest of his life.

As Howard was formulating his garden city ideas, utopian, socialist, anarchist, communist, and philanthropic capitalist approaches to rural depopulation and how to solve "the social question" were much discussed. Howard borrowed freely from anarchist and socialist sources and utopian fiction, but retained his independence from rigid movements.[3] He termed the garden city his "invention"—convinced that what was important was the combination of proposals he had put together. Howard produced a subtle balance of innovative ideas that were carefully crafted to be acceptable to his wealthy backers. While no garden cities that fully follow his ideas have been built, Letchworth and Welwyn, England—built during his lifetime—reflect his vision and are radically different from other cities of the era. The garden city idea has influenced hundreds of developments worldwide.

When Howard published *Tomorrow* he was 48 and still an unknown clerk. While it sold only a handful of copies, *Tomorrow* immediately caught the attention of powerful backers and launched the most celebrated experiment in city and regional planning history—construction of Letchworth Garden City.[4]

Howard was an excellent writer and speaker. He was shrewd, dogged, and passionately sincere—always ready to present his illuminated lantern slides to any labor, church, settlement house, temperance union, or debating club that invited him to speak. He was effective because he radiated empathy and kindness for the rural poor and working class rural–urban migrants.

Howard was directly involved in the planning and development of two garden cities—Letchworth and Welwyn, England—just beyond the outskirts of London. Both incorporated many of his principles. He lived in both of them when they were partially built.

Howard was knighted in 1927. Two decades after his death, Howard's vision played an instrumental role in England's post war new towns program. Since *Tomorrow* was published in 1898 hundreds of cities or parts of cities inspired by the garden city concept have been proposed and sometimes built all over the world.

Howard's vision inspired more than three dozen garden cities, garden suburbs, and garden city-inspired developments in the UK,[5] three U.S. garden cities partially built early in the New Deal in the 1930s—Greenbelt, Maryland; Greenhills, Ohio; and Greendale, Wisconsin, Australia's capital city of Canberra, and hundreds of developments that claim to be garden cities in other countries. Most are garden suburbs or "overspill estates"—the British term for settlements built to rehouse people displaced by slum clearance projects.

Howard's vision of building entire new towns on greenfield land at some distance from the urban fringe, a human scale alternative to urban sprawl, unity of the built and natural environment, greenbelts, a system of social cities, jobs–housing balance, and municipally owned land to provide revenue, remain a source of inspiration that is still impacting city and regional plans.

farm produce for the residents of garden city, woodlands, and other rural uses. The greenbelt would provide a clear urban limit line separating developed land from undeveloped rural land. It would protect clean air and water and provide recreational opportunities. New industry on the fringe of the core would provide jobs with wages high enough that factory workers could afford to purchase houses in garden city. There would be enough jobs for the local workforce and enough housing for them and their families that there would be what planners now call "jobs–housing balance". Land prices would be cheap to begin with and would remain comparatively affordable, helping solve the housing problem. Land would be publicly owned. As other garden cities grew, the greenbelt would create a buffer between the individual garden cities. Howard's diagrams were illustrative only. He was careful to put a bold disclaimer ("N.B. DIAGRAM ONLY Plan cannot be drawn until site selected") on the illustrations in the 1902 second edition.

Howard proposed clusters of "social cities" that would form a system of cities—essentially a small metropolitan area, but with a structure quite different from the metropolises that were arising at that time and that are common worldwide today. Together

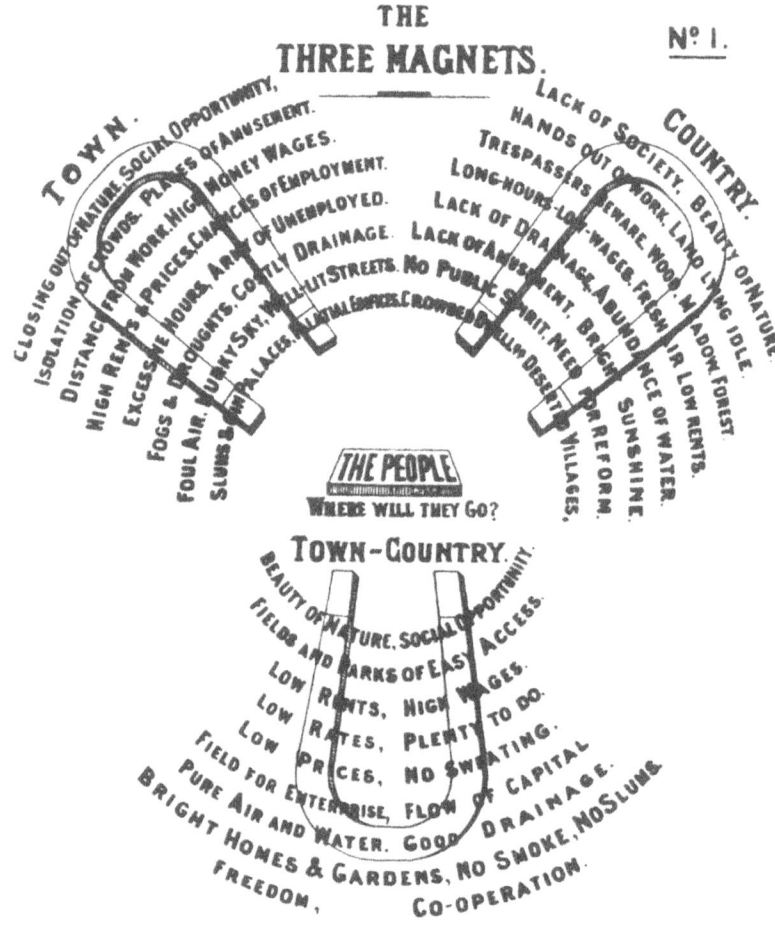

Figure 6.3 Ebenezer Howard's Three Magnets.

seven garden cities would form a single social city with a population of 250,000 people on 66,000 acres of land—about eight times as large as a single garden city. An important diagram that appeared in *Tomorrow* in 1898 but was omitted from *Garden Cities of Tomorrow* in 1902—what planning professor Peter Hall and British urbanist Colin Ward call "the lost diagram" (1998)—shows "a group of slumless smokeless cities" surrounding a larger central garden city that collectively form a social city (Figure 6.4).

According to Howard "Each inhabitant of the whole group ... would in reality be living in, and would enjoy all the advantages of, a great and most beautiful city; and yet all the delights of the country would be within a few minutes' walk."

Howard's physical planning idea that has proven most influential—and most misunderstood—is the idea of a greenbelt. Howard envisioned the greenbelt as a continuous 5,000-acre ring around each garden city. The greenbelt would be a working

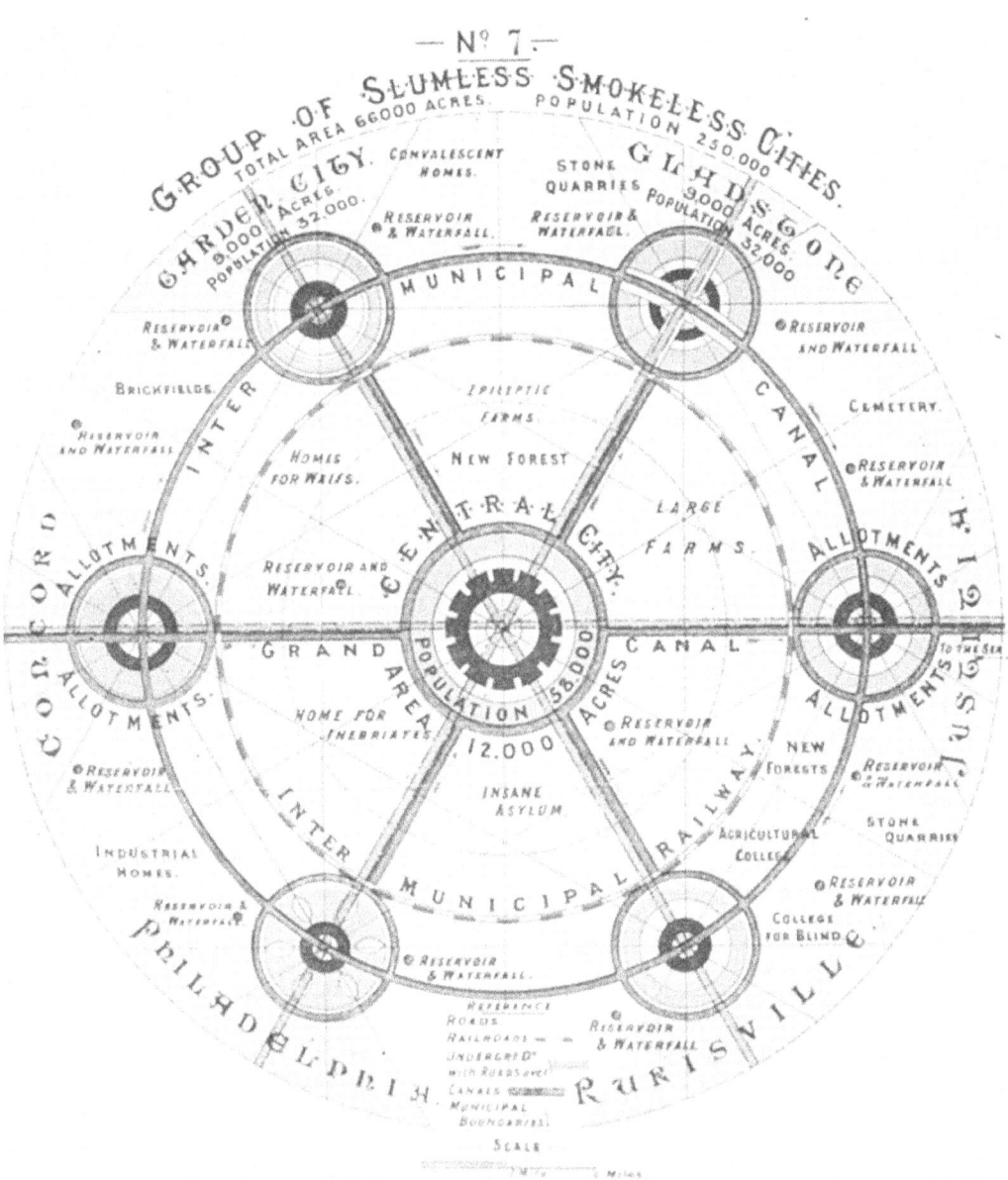

Figure 6.4 Ebenezer Howard's Group of Slumless Smokeless Cities.

landscape with farms, gardens, fruit trees, forests, and cow pastures. It would also have institutions for epileptics, the deaf and blind, and orphans. The greenbelt would contain appropriate uses such as brickyards to manufacture and store bricks. A small percentage of the population—mostly farmers and residents and staff of the institutions—would live in the greenbelt. Farmers could earn a reasonable living because transportation costs for getting agricultural products to consumers in the garden city core would be nearly non-existent. Leasing public land in the greenbelt would create competition and be a source of municipal revenue.

In each 6,000-acre garden city there was to be a 5-acre public garden at the center, surrounded by a ring of public buildings including a town hall, museum, picture gallery, library, theater, and concert and lecture halls. These would look out onto a 150-acre central park.

England is cold and damp in the winter, so Howard proposed a cast-iron and plate glass "crystal palace" around the central park that would serve as a combination exhibition hall, shopping center, and winter garden. Howard's crystal palace was modeled on the crystal palace exhibition building in Hyde Park built in 1851 for the first world's fair—the Great Exhibition of the Works of Industry of All Nations.

Beyond the crystal palace lay garden city's residential district and parks organized into neighborhood wards defined by avenues and streets.[7] Howards's original diagrams in *Tomorrow* suggest that terraced (row) housing would be used. As built, Letchworth contained a mixed range of housing including detached and semi-detached houses.

The density even of the core of garden city was low. Average households in Great Britain at the time were much larger than in the UK or the United States today. Including the sparsely populated greenbelt, the average density of garden city would be only five people per acre—accommodating about one average nuclear family per acre.

Factory jobs would be located in a belt on the edge of the garden city core. Since automobiles were almost non-existent and the density was too low to support an electric streetcar network, factory workers would walk or bike to work. Howard proposed a circular railroad to connect the factories and rail lines to link one garden city to others to form the network of social cities and to connect the network to other cities.

While Howard, himself, favored cooperative ownership of factories, he was careful to leave the choice of what mix of private and cooperative enterprises each individual garden city would have to the Garden Cities Association board in consultation with the residents. Initially large factories would almost certainly be private, but Howard believed that over time the superiority of cooperatives would be so obvious that all enterprises would eventually be cooperatively owned.

Eight months after the publication of *Tomorrow*, philanthropic British capitalists who had built the model company towns of Port Sunlight (soap magnate William Heskith Lever), and Bournville (chocolate magnate George Cadbury) backed Howard and joined together with other prominent and wealthy supporters to form the Garden Cities Association (GCA).

Howard's vision included a specific model for financing a garden city by continuing to capture increased land values as ground rents increased—the precursor of land value capture policies today, described in Chapter 16.

Land acquisition and the initial infrastructure would be paid for by debentures—a type of loan unsecured by collateral—purchased by Garden City Association board members and other wealthy investors. Fundamental was the idea that garden cities would be located on land far enough from large conurbations—sprawling agglomerations around large cities—that land prices would be low. In Howard's time, agricultural land prices in rural England were depressed. Howard was sure that as garden cities succeeded, land prices would rise. One of Howard's most important diagrams is rarely discussed in descriptions of garden cities. It shows "the vanishing point of rent" and explains how, after 30 years, landlords' interests in land would be paid off and revenue from ground rents could all go to the municipality to pay for art, music, drama, and—most importantly—pensions which Howard put in large ornamental Victorian script at the bottom of his diagram.[8]

The Garden City Pioneer Society (GCPS)—an organization of members of the Garden Cities Association interested in implementing Howard's ideas—purchased depressed agricultural land in Letchworth about 40 miles from London in 1902. Lever, Cadbury, and other progressive industrialists became trustees and they and other investors purchased debentures, that promised to pay a 5% annual dividend to finance purchase of the land and construction of infrastructure. Five percent was a modest dividend at the time, and dividend payments could be deferred for a long time. Howard proselytized among labor unions and radical groups but got no significant labor or radical support for his garden city invention.

Construction began immediately and Letchworth Garden City formally opened in 1903. It had only 1,000 residents in its first two years.

Neither Letchworth, nor any of the other early garden cities, exactly followed Howard's physical planning ideas. In Letchworth the crystal palace was replaced by a curving street of shops. There was no grand avenue or circular railway. A large greenbelt almost entirely circled Letchworth, but it was smaller and occupied a smaller percentage of land than Howard envisioned—1,200 acres for the city proper, 2,800 for the greenbelt, rather than 5,000 acres of greenbelt surrounding the 1,000-acre city proper.

Howard's original diagrams in *Tomorrow* suggest that most housing in Letchworth would be terraced row housing. Letchworth's architects, Raymond Unwin and his cousin Barry Parker, designed and built a range of row houses, attached units, and single family detached cottages. The units were beautifully designed with a combination kitchen/living room and access to sunlight. They were inspired by the charming medieval German city of Rothenberg ob der Tauber that Unwin admired and arts and crafts architecture that sought to create beautiful buildings from natural materials. Unwin and Parker's beautiful, orderly arts and crafts look and feel of Letchworth's housing, inspired by Rothenberg and arts and crafts designs, convinced visitors to try to replicate garden cities perhaps as much as Howard's underlying political, social, economic, and design strategies.

One Letchworth cooperative—Garden City Tenants—built a small number of model workers' houses for an exhibition in Letchworth in 1904. The exhibition houses were sold at prices that Letchworth construction and factory workers could afford. However, the rest of Letchworth's housing was too expensive for working-class households. Almost all of Letchworth's workers lived in less expensive rental housing and bicycled in to work in Letchworth. Many of the units in Letchworth were occupied by intellectuals and artists attracted by the visionary concept or Unwin and Parker's design.

Letchworth struggled economically. There was one significant co-partnership—the Garden City Press and several smaller co-partnerships in Letchworth. Co-partnerships differ from cooperatives in which every owner has an equal share in the enterprise. Co-partnerships allow members to own different stakes in the enterprise. Eventually a major London printer/bookbinder and a corset manufacturing plant located factories in Letchworth. War industry developed in Letchworth during World War I. Dividend payments on the debentures used to finance construction of Letchworth were not made for many years, and dividend arrears were not paid off until 1945.[9]

By 1910 Letchworth appeared at least a limited success, but not on a scale sufficient to stop growth of the London conurbation. University of Michigan planning historian Robert Fishman points out that London added 450,000 new residents—a population equivalent to 14 fully built-out garden cities of 32,000 each—between 1900 and 1910.

Between 1904 and the end of World War I, the GCA did not try to launch other new garden cities. After the war there was popular support in Great Britain for subsidized housing for veterans—a "Homes for Heroes" movement. Despite his bottom-up, anti-national government philosophy, Howard agreed that the Garden Cities Association should participate in the program. However, only one additional garden city—Welwyn—was started supported in part by the Homes for Heroes program.[10]

After Howard's death in 1928, his disciple, Frederick Osborn, continued to proselytize for garden cities in Great Britain. Lewis Mumford tirelessly promoted Howard's ideas in America. A 1940 report by the Royal Commission on the Distribution of the Industrial Population that had been established in 1937—*The Barlow Report*—reinvigorated the garden city idea. The *Barlow Report* proposed policy to reduce the concentration of England's industry and employment in the South East and South Midlands of England, both to reduce economic disparity and to reduce the threat from bombing industrial concentrations. While the report was published too late to be implemented during World War II, it—combined with other of what are now called the British wartime reports—shaped policy for both Britain's postwar planning machine and the British welfare state, implemented by the Labour (Attlee) government in the period 1945 to 1951 and later Labour governments—including construction of new towns. Ten British new towns strongly influenced by garden cities ideas were started in England in 1948, five more during a second wave beginning in 1961, and six more during a third wave between 1967 and 1970.

Recent UK Labour and Conservative governments have proposed additional eco-friendly carbon-neutral sustainable new towns that draw on garden cities ideas, but progress has been limited by the global financial crisis, Brexit, the COVID-19 pandemic, and political disagreements.

In the United States new communities inspired by the garden cities movement were built during the 1920s and 1930s. Architect Clarence Stein planned and oversaw construction of a development in New York City named Sunnyside Gardens between 1924 and 1928. Sunnyside Gardens was inspired by Howard, but was very different from his vision. It had only 6,000 units—less than one-fifth as many as Howard proposed. It had an unusual percentage of open space for any American city at the time—72%—but not in the form of a greenbelt. The housing in Sunnyside Gardens consisted of row houses as Raymond Unwin and Barry Parker designed and built in Letchworth and six apartment buildings. Still Sunnyside Gardens was a remarkable achievement—an entire new community with abundant open space, retail, and business areas as well and ownership and rental housing. Stein planned a larger community—Radburn, New Jersey, that would have more closely paralleled the British garden city concept. Construction on Radburn began in 1929, but the Great Depression made it impossible to complete Radburn as Stein envisioned it.

During the Great Depression, President Roosevelt created a greenbelt town program. The program was expensive, politically unpopular, and soon aborted. Scaled-down versions of three greenbelt towns—Greenbelt, Maryland; Greenhills, Ohio; and Greendale, Wisconsin—were completed, and a few units in a fourth were built.[11]

When an entire new community is built on raw land it is often referred to as a new town or a new community. Most new towns and new communities are not garden cities. Title IV of the U.S. Housing Act of 1968 authorized $50 million in loan guarantees for new communities. It was a costly failure. Of a dozen Title IV new communities, only Woodlands, Texas was completed. All of the other new communities funded by Title IV went bankrupt. Many other private or public–private new towns have been proposed and sometimes started in the United States. Most were never built; were really garden suburbs; or morphed beyond recognition as they were built. Only Columbia, Maryland; Reston, Virginia; and Woodlands, Texas qualify as true U.S. new towns. Like Sunnyside Gardens and Radburn, they have garden city-like features, but do not have the physical or economic features of garden cities as Howard proposed. The People's Republic of China has built thousands of new towns and new cities since the mid-1980s. Some other countries have successful new towns programs.

Jane Jacobs—the uncompromising anti-planner who conflated Ebenezer Howard with Patrick Geddes and Daniel Burnham (Box 1)—is one of Ebenezer Howard's few critics. Jacobs concludes that virtually all modern city planning has been adopted from what she calls the "silly substance" of garden city planning. In her words (Jacobs, 1961):

> Howard set spinning powerful and city-destroying ideas: He conceived that the way to deal with the complex functions was to sort and sift out of the whole certain simple uses and arrange each of these in relative containment. ... He conceived of good planning as a series of static acts ... the plan must anticipate what is needed and [after it is built] protect it against all but the most minor subsequent changes. ... He conceived of planning as ... essentially paternalistic."

Garden cities are too low-density to succeed in most parts of megacities—cities with over ten million residents—that are now emerging worldwide or the even more populous megacity regions of which they are part. Howard's economic model relied on hard-to-replicate support from wealthy patrons. Other attempted garden city and new town ventures have found it hard to attract private capital or industry. The British garden cities were never able to provide enough housing affordable for low-income workers. Howard's schematic physical design was never followed and is now out of date.

Howard's legacy includes the continuing appeal of his vision of systematic planning for entire new towns, cooperation, land value capture, livability, greenbelts for fresh produce and protection of air and water quality, jobs–housing balance, pedestrian-friendly neighborhoods, and attractively designed modest ownership housing. Today, Letchworth is an attractive, economically solid city reflecting Howard's ideas.

THE CITY BEAUTIFUL MOVEMENT

The city beautiful movement was an important late 19th- and early 20th-century planning movement. It was led by Chicago architect-planner Daniel Burnham (1846–1912).

The 1893 World's Columbian Exhibition gave Burnham and other city beautiful planners a platform to demonstrate their ideas to a large audience. They built a "white city" of temporary structures with beautiful buildings, exhibition halls, boulevards, roundabouts, gardens, canals, lagoons, reflecting pools, fountains, and statuary. Twenty-seven million people visited the exhibition during the course of six months. Figure 6.5 shows the lagoon, agricultural building, and other exhibition halls in the World's Columbian Exhibition.

Burnham's *Plan for Chicago 1909*, co-authored with Edward Bennett is the leading example of a city beautiful plan. It was funded by and represents the interests of the powerful private Chicago Commercial Club. The *Plan for Chicago 1909* is a work of art—lavishly illustrated by pastel paintings of what Chicago might become. Burnham hired French watercolorist Jules Guérin to paint lovely watercolor drawings for the plan. Chicago institutionalized a committee to implement the Burnham Plan which became the Chicago Planning Commission. Burnham and Bennett proposed transforming Chicago's waterfront on Lake Michigan into an enormous park filled with museums and cultural institutions; "embellishing and adorning" the city with statues and fountains; creating European-style boulevards and roundabouts; and improving transportation. Figure 6.6 is an illustration of a proposed Civic Center Plaza and Buildings from the *1909 Plan for Chicago*.

Burnham's imprint is visible in Chicago today. Much of the lakefront of Lake Michigan was reclaimed and redesigned as Burnham proposed. Michigan Avenue has evolved into the "magnificent mile"—Chicago's main high-end shopping street. Chicago has boulevards and roundabouts and is "adorned and embellished" with fountains, statues, and public art to a greater extent than any other American city with the exception of Washington, D.C.

Burnham is criticized as an elitist whose plans served the interests of wealthy businessmen. He is attacked for being concerned mostly with aesthetics rather than social justice and for promoting backward-looking

Figure 6.5 The Lagoon and Agricultural Building at the World's Columbian Exhibition (Chicago, Illinois, 1893).

Figure 6.6 Proposed Civic Center Plaza and Buildings from the *1909 Plan for Chicago*.

classical Greek and Roman prototypes and lavish French beaux arts ideas. There is truth to these criticisms, but Burnham made many positive contributions. He is a model of a doggedly determined visionary who urged planners to "make no little plans". Burnham used modern materials and technical innovations to good advantage. The *1909 Plan for Chicago* included consideration of the whole region. It improved Chicago's transportation pattern and helped rationalize the location of industry. Burnham advocated government-supported public housing long before that became a mainstream idea in the United States. He was a superb city booster who conducted what is still one of the most successful city branding campaigns of all time. Walter Moody, the executive director of the Chicago Plan Commission, orchestrated an extraordinary public relations effort to promote the *1909 Plan for Chicago* including distribution of information on the plan to virtually all Chicago residents and a manual about the plan that was required reading by every 8th-grade Chicago schoolchild.

MODERNISM

From the end of the 19th through the first half of the 20th century, modernism was a dominant philosophy in city and regional planning, architecture, and the arts and humanities. The modernist vision influenced city planning and architecture worldwide.

Paris-based Swiss architect/planner Charles-Édouard Jeanneret (1887–1965)—who went by the name of Le Corbusier—was the intellectual leader of the modernist movement in architecture and planning. Between 1922 and 1935 Le Corbusier's principal intellectual preoccupation was designing a modern city. He initially called his vision "a contemporary city of 3 million" and later "the radiant city". Figure 6.7 is Le Corbusier's 1933 rendering of a city of 3 million.

Le Corbusier believed modern technology made it possible to radically decongest the city center by building upwards to increase its density. He proposed eliminating a large percentage of city streets and leaving 85% of central city land open. Land around the high-rise megastructures would be occupied by parks, gardens, cultural and sports facilities, restaurants, and cafes on a fine-grained lattice of streets.

Le Corbusier initially proposed housing the elite in high-rise apartment blocks in the city center and workers in suburban cities he called garden cities—but with high-rise megastructures very different from Howard's garden city vision. Later he advocated all classes living in high-rise apartments in the city itself.

Le Corbusier and modernism are out of favor. Planners attack Le Corbusier's vision for its emphasis on efficiency and speed over livability. They criticize his lack of respect for history; overwhelming scale; linearity; elitism; lack of ornamentation; disdain

Figure 6.7 Le Corbusier's Plan for a Contemporary City of 3 Million (1929).

for incorporating rivers and other natural features; and absence of fantasy and playfulness in design. As implemented, modernist Le Corbusian projects do not work well for pedestrians and small businesses. Superblocks—the very large blocks necessary for Le Corbusier's megastructures—are too big for pedestrians to navigate. Street-level facades are uninviting. Highways chop up neighborhoods. Despite these flaws, aspects of Le Corbusier's thinking remain a powerful vision for how to accommodate huge numbers of people on limited land. The very dense Pudong District of Shanghai—mostly built in the last 30 years and illustrated in Figure 6.8—looks very much like Le Corbusier's renderings of a radiant city. Residents in tall residential buildings have light, air, spectacular views, and amenities like exercise rooms. They can walk to green space along the Huangpu River, and are minutes away by foot from office jobs in the business district of Pudong.

Many criticisms of Le Corbusier are caricatures that quote him out of context. They simplify and misstate his arguments. A visitor to Le Corbusier's radiant city would experience a green city. She could walk along an elevated pathway at tree canopy level looking at a vast expanse of green foliage pierced by enormous steel and glass megastructures. At ground level, there would be cafes, public spaces, and some remaining historic buildings—not just empty space. Even a middle-income housing unit would have light, air, and views. The mechanical systems would work better than many multi-million-dollar apartment house units in New York or London today. Once on a subway, a resident of radiant city could get to other destinations within radiant city quickly and comfortably.

Le Corbusier's ideas remain valuable for their audacity and uncompromising clarity. They are particularly important for planners in megacities in the developing world that require vertical building and solutions to housing and transportation at megacity scale.

BROADACRE CITY

American architect Frank Lloyd Wright (1867–1959) developed a vision of Broadacre City—the clearest 20th-century disurbanist vision. Broadacre City is a vision of an extremely low-density alternative to 20th-century cities. Figure 6.9 shows Wright with a 12 x 12-foot model representing a hypothetical 4-square-mile Broadacre City he unveiled in 1935.

Just as Ebenezer Howard's vision was really about a better society—not just a better city form—Wright believed that the automobile made possible a new democratic

Figure 6.8 Pudong District, Shanghai, China (2012).

Figure 6.9 Frank Lloyd Wright with His Broadacre City Model (1935).

urban society that would be truly representative of individualistic American values. By 1935, there were nearly 23 million privately owned automobiles in the United States—nearly one for every household.

Wright valued a society of strong, proud, family-oriented individualists drawing strength from their ownership of land. He argued that broadacre city would strengthen individualism, build self-reliance, and engage citizens. Each person would own a minimum of one acre—a huge amount of land per capita, requiring extremely low densities.

Wright located farms, small factories, schools, churches, hospitals, stores, professional buildings, and cultural institutions throughout broadacre city. Hundreds of separate, single-family detached homes and dozens of factories are distributed among fields. A community center in broadacre city would be an "attractive automobile objective" with a golf course, racetrack, zoo, aquarium, planetarium, art gallery, theaters, and restaurants. Wright envisaged "a great roadside market" for retail activities—a permanent county fair. Each retailer would have his own stall selling machine-made products and crafts as well as farm produce.

Urban and rural land uses in broadacre city blend together. Farming would contribute to the economy of broadacre city, but Wright also saw part-time manual agricultural work as a psychological and social benefit. This echoes Russian anarchist Pëtr Kropotkin's 1898 vision of "factories and workshops combining industry with agriculture and brain work with manual work". Broadacre city would have no elected city government. A county architect would be the only government official!

The overwhelming consensus among Western planners today is that low-density development mixing agriculture, residences, industry, offices, and other uses is undesirable on many grounds. It wastes scarce agricultural land; consumes natural resources;

is expensive to serve with infrastructure; and may be socially divisive by segregating affluent households who can afford to live in a broadacre city environment from less affluent households who will continue to live in core cities. Most planners favor "smart growth"—compact city-centered growth that leaves land on the urban fringe undeveloped for as long as possible. However, there is a minority group of "smart growth contrarians" who do not agree with smart growth advocates. Smart growth contrarians include Robert Bruegmann—Professor of Art History, Architecture, and Urban Planning at the University of Illinois, Chicago—and University of Southern California planning professors Peter Gordon and Harry W. Richardson.

THE LINEAR CITY

Spanish architect-planner Arturo Soria y Mata (1844–1920) originated the idea of building linear cities—long narrow cities along transportation corridors. He designed and began construction of a 29-mile-long linear city that would have circled Madrid if it had been completed. While Soria's implementation of the linear city in Madrid was small-scale and at a low density, he believed the linear city idea could be applied at much larger scales. He envisaged "a single street unit 547 yards wide, extending … from Cadiz to St. Petersburg, from Peking to Brussels". Fragments of Soria's linear city are still discernible in Madrid's urban fabric. Figure 6.10 illustrates a four-mile section of Soria's linear city in Madrid and shows how it could be continued to circle the city.

The linear city that Soria started in Madrid was at least a partial success. Building lots sold well, and housing was built. By 1930 about four miles of the linear city had been completed. The development was very green, had public transit, and was somewhat economically diverse.[12]

Soria's experiment in Madrid was small-scale, relatively short-lived, low-density, and reflected a specific set of design, economic, and social features appropriate to early 20th-century Madrid. Only one segment was completed. There are no pure examples of successful planned linear cities in the West, but Soria's vision of linear development sparked a worldwide movement that has inspired dozens of linear city experiments at different scales.

In 2021 Mohammed bin Salman—the Crown Prince of Saudi Arabia—announced plans to spend 48 billion dollars to construct a string of car-free cities strung along a linear transportation system "like beads on a necklace". The system will be named "The Line". Bin Salmin has declared that The Line will be built by Saudi Arabia's NEOM company—an acronym for "new beginnings" in Arabic—which bin Salman chairs. Schools, medical clinics, leisure facilities, and green spaces would be within a five-minute walk for any of the cities along the Line. If built as planned, the new communities would have no cars or streets and the entire system would emit zero carbon.

Many urban planners advocate transit-oriented development and there are many transit-oriented developments in the United States and other countries. Transit-oriented development usually refers to projects to increase density around existing transit hubs such as subway and bus rapid transit (BRT) stops. About thirty U.S. cities have built light rail systems and encourage development along light rail corridors. Since 2010, large linear cities have developed along segments of China's high-speed rail (HSR) lines.[13] Soria's extravagant claim that a linear city could stretch from Peking to Brussels may become a reality. China has even formulated embryonic plans to extend high-speed rail lines across the Bering Sea into North America.

THE NEIGHBORHOOD UNIT

American architect, planner, and education theorist Clarence Perry (1872–1944) developed an approach to the planning and design of neighborhood units in 1929. Perry's vision has had a profound impact worldwide.

In the late 1920s, Perry observed large patches of undeveloped land isolated by freeways that were developing haphazardly. Families with children settling in these areas

Figure 6.10 Arturo Soria y Mata's Linear City Plan (Madrid, Spain, 1894).

experienced little sense of community. Perry believed that the primary school was the central institution to which families with young children related, and accordingly that "neighborhood units" should be built around primary schools. Perry's neighborhood unit was aimed at nuclear families consisting of a husband, wife, and several children—the conventional nuclear U.S. family unit in 1929. Perry also prepared designs for denser areas and strategies to redevelop existing areas within cities into neighborhood units.

Perry argued that schools should also function as community centers with adult education classes and cultural events in the evening, sporting events on weekends, and festivals throughout the year. The average size of nuclear households in 1929 was much larger than it is today. To support a primary school, Perry calculated that the residential land in a neighborhood unit should be large enough to house families with between 800 and 1,500 children.

Perry argued that streets in a neighborhood unit should serve two different groups: neighborhood residents and people passing by the neighborhood. Residential streets, designed for use by neighborhood unit residents and delivery vehicles, are in the interior. Perry proposed residential street widths and designs within the neighborhood unit to assure that traffic would move slowly enough that pedestrians—even young children going to or returning from school to their nearby homes—would be safe within the residential areas. This was an early form of traffic calming. Perry's design would allow neighborhood residents to reach schools, neighbors, and convenience stores safely by foot on interior sidewalks and streets. Drivers on the arterials could stop to shop—helping generate enough sales to make neighborhood-serving businesses economically viable. Through traffic could pass the neighborhood unit on arterials at the edges of the neighborhood unit, without slowing down. Perry proposed locating small commercial businesses such as convenience stores at the edge of the neighborhood unit on the arterials. He proposed setting aside generous amounts of land for neighborhood parks and open space. Figure 6.11 is an illustration from *The Neighborhood Unit* that illustrates the basic plan for a neighborhood unit.

One of Perry's few critics is Jane Jacobs. Without mentioning Perry by name, she called neighborhood units within cities "a silly and even harmful ideal" and "a fittingly

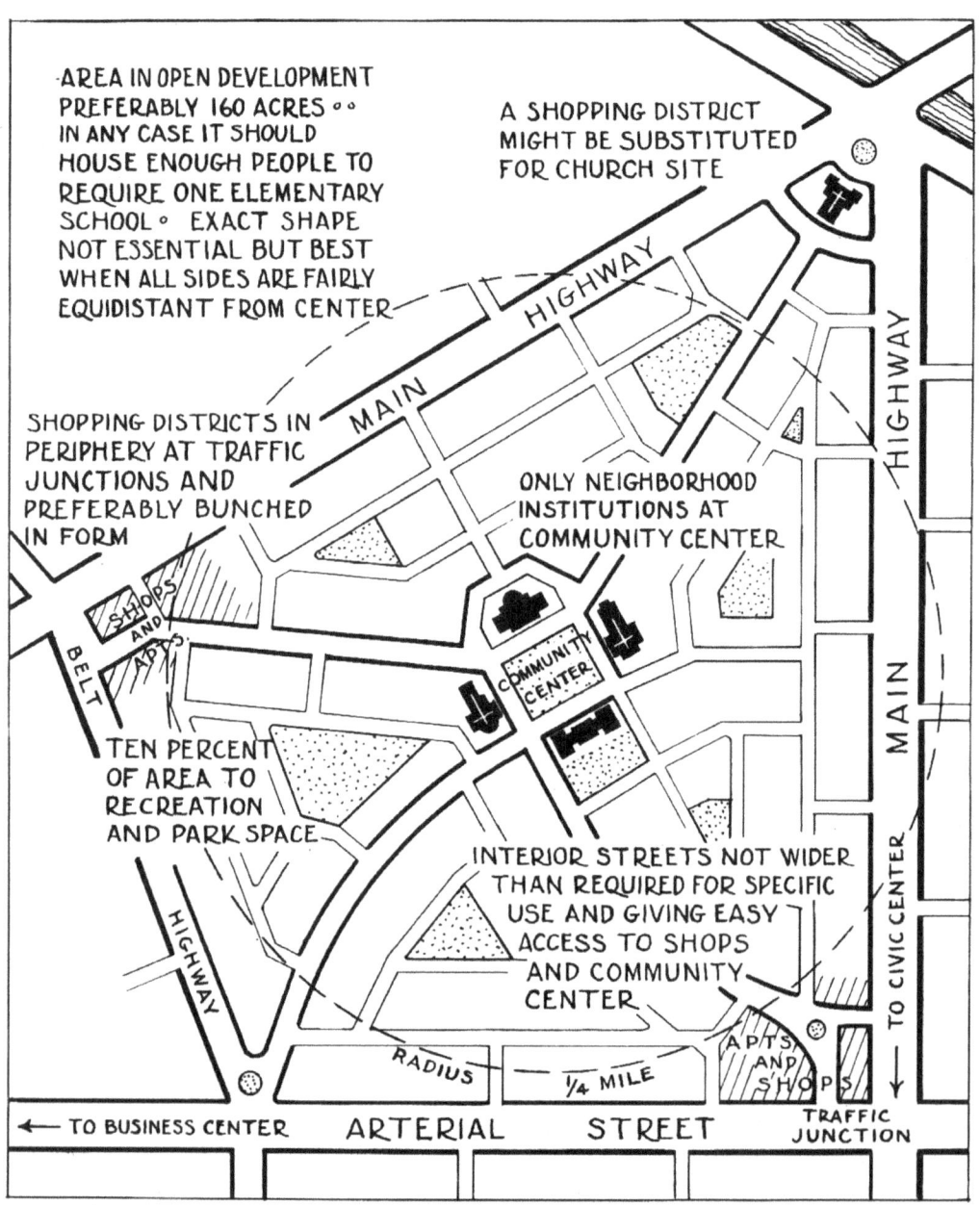

Figure 6.11 Clarence Perry's Neighborhood Unit (1929).

nauseating term for an old ideal in planning theory" that "solves easy problems for an easy kind of population but fails to work even on its own terms with any other kind of population" (Jacobs, 1961).

Hundreds of developments in the United States are designed more or less according to Perry's neighborhood unit design. Russian planners in the Soviet Union embraced the idea, and hundreds of neighborhood units adapted to Russian conditions were built in the Soviet Union beginning in the 1930s. When the Chinese Communist Party created the People's Republic of China (PRC) in 1949, they imported the idea of neighborhood units from the Soviet Union, and thousands of neighborhood units with Chinese characteristics have been built in the PRC. Modern adaptations of the neighborhood unit continue to be built worldwide today.

ENVIRONMENTAL UTOPIAS

Modern environmental utopias began to appear with the turn towards environmental planning in the early 1970s. Biophilia—an innate love of nature—is arguably inherent in all humans.

Ernest Callenbach (1929–2012) was one of the earliest and remains the most influential of the environmental utopian visionaries. His 1975 fictional book, *Ecotopia*, reflects what were fringe green and counterculture values at that time—many of which have become mainstream today. Callenbach imagined an ecologically sound alternative lifestyle and describes the physical and social environment that would produce it in humorous and specific detail.

Callenbach worked at the University of California Press in Berkeley, California from 1955 to 1991. As an editor of UC Press's natural history guides, he became familiar with the emerging literature on ecology, conservation biology, soft energy paths, and design with nature. Callenbach was sympathetic to radical ideas about the environment, society, gender roles, and alternative counterculture lifestyles.

Ecotopia is set in 1999—25 years in the future from the time Callenbach wrote it. It purports to be diary entries and reports to the *Times-Post* by journalist William Weston—the first American to visit the new country of Ecotopia since it broke away from the United States 19 years earlier in 1980. Box 6.2 describes Ecotopia.

BOX 6.2 ECOTOPIA

Ernest Callenbach's ecological utopia—Ecotopia—consists of what was formerly Northern California, Oregon, and Washington state. The Ecotopians value and have become a part of a sustainable ecosystem. They have achieved stable-state ecological food production, producing organic food locally in sustainable ways. They have banned chemicals in food. There is no packaged food. Farm animals are all free-range. Ecotopia's population is declining, so there is plenty of affordable fresh organic food for everyone.

Unlike the consumer-oriented, wasteful United States of 1999, Ecotopians practice sustainable urban development. They sort and recycle everything. Food containers are all biodegradable—quickly breaking down into natural substances. Ecotopians think nothing of squashing a beer can and leaving it on the ground, knowing it will quickly decompose. All food wastes, sewage, and garbage are turned into organic fertilizer. The Ecotopians show William Weston—the first journalist to visit Ecotopia since its secession from the United States—recycling bins for metal, glass, and paper—which were rare in the United States in 1999.

The Ecotopians have cleaned up polluted air and water. There are no more deaths from air and chemical pollution. They have restored streams and other natural systems and value and protect sustainable forests.

Many objects in Ecotopia are built with natural products. Clothing is casual, imaginative, and funky. Cotton and other natural substances have replaced synthetics.

The Ecotopians use green building construction materials and techniques. They prefer wood for houses, but most housing is assembled from extruded modular tubes made entirely from biodegradable plant-based plastics. Four people can lift whole room modules 13 feet wide by 10 feet high with 6-inch-thick flat floors. The Ecotopians glue these modules together in many imaginative configurations. Housing built this way is cheap and easy to produce, solving Ecotopia's affordable housing problem. No one in Ecotopia is homeless. If they are no longer needed, the housing modules can be broken up and thrown into biovats, digested by microorganisms, and the resulting sludge recycled into fields from which the plants that made them came as fertilizer.

San Francisco's office buildings have been turned into apartments—providing both affordable housing and a family-friendly city. The total population of San Francisco has declined. The demographics have changed. There are many children in the city—many more than comparable cities in the United States.

The oil industry in Ecotopia was shut down after Ecotopia gained its independence in 1975. Ecotopia uses renewable solar, wind, wave, geothermal, and other energy sources almost exclusively. It is phasing out nuclear fission reactors. Restructuring the economy was disruptive, and Ecotopia's gross domestic product (GDP) declined. It is still much lower than the U.S.'s 1999 GDP. However, the Ecotopians consider this a small price to pay for the ecological society they have created.

Ecotopians invest heavily in public transportation. Once William Weston—the fictional *Times-Post* journalist who is describing Ecotopia—crosses the border into Ecotopia, he travels to San Francisco on a bullet train traveling smoothly at 225 miles per hour. In San Francisco walking and bicycling are the main forms of transportation. San Francisco's main street—Market Street—has become mostly pedestrianized. It is planted with thousands of trees bordering a restored creek, with only two lanes for electric taxis, free minibuses, and delivery carts. The wide sidewalks have mini gardens and benches. The streets are filled with entertainers. There are free bicycles everywhere. Ecotopians travel short distances by bicycle and foot. For longer distances they use custom slow-moving vehicles they have made themselves by combining front and back electric modules with wood and other materials.

Weston visits new human-scale Ecotopian garden cities. Most of Ecotopia's economy consists of cooperative enterprises owned by the workers—very like the cooperatives 19th-century anarchists espoused and that Ebenezer Howard hoped would emerge in the garden cities he proposed.

The Ecotopians embrace new technologies so long as they are used to further their social values. They connect crude visual phones to their televisions to communicate. (The internet had not been invented.)

Ecotopia has both racial segregation and integration. Black separatists formed their own separate mini nation of Soul City. Blacks who prefer to live elsewhere are welcomed throughout Ecotopia. The Ecotopians tolerate other separatist movements.

Culturally, Ecotopians value a lifestyle radically different from the dominant lifestyle in the United States in 1975. They embrace sexual freedom and accept multiple gender roles and alternative forms of education, health, research, sports, and media. Marijuana is legal and widely used. Monogamy is the exception. Gender equality prevails, though only men participate in war games. A female president heads the ruling Survivalist Party.

The Ecotopians are not pacifists. They have weapons of mass destruction to maintain their independence from the United States and other hostile foreign powers. The males engage in violent war games.

Despite their concern for humans' devastating impact on the planet, the Ecotopians are not aware of global climate change. Their alternative energy program is mainly intended to conserve nature and reduce air pollution.

Ecotopia was a literary and commercial success. Callenbach followed it up with a prequel—*Ecotopia Emerging*—and the *Ecotopian Encyclopedia*.

The word ecotopia has entered the American lexicon, and ecotopian ideas continue to inspire idealists. The Ecotopia 2021 Project promotes Callenbach's vision. The project has identified more than a hundred future cityscapes that are or arguably could become ecofriendly utopias.

A new generation of environmental fiction books and movies address dystopian futures that could result from global climate change. They are concerned with catastrophic damage to earth rather than pollution or consumption of resources, which were environmentalists' main concerns at the time Callenbach wrote *Ecotopia*. This shift in emphasis is exemplified by UC Davis Professor of Urban and Environmental Planning Steven Wheeler's description of earth in 2500. In *Climate Change and Social Ecology* (2012) Wheeler imagines that humans have adapted to the impacts of global warming and achieved a sustainable—but far from ideal—alternative sustainable society on a badly damaged earth. The human communities Wheeler imagines represent a much smaller footprint in 2500 than they do today. Cities are on high ground set back from the much higher oceans and waterways. Humanity has been forced to abandon most once-temperate regions because of heat and drought. The remaining cities are clustered near the North and South Poles. Vast ecosystems have reverted to their pre-human status. There has been some human-led ecological restoration. Human settlements no longer sprawl. Cities have dense urban centers no more than 5 miles in diameter. They are surrounded by 10- to 20-mile-wide greenbelts with organic farms and ponds for aquaculture. Most buildings are 5 stories high, though there are some 20- and 30-story buildings. Each building is clad with a thin photovoltaic skin to generate energy. Rooftops are green. Vegetated corridors meander through the communities, tying the cities into the natural landscape around them. Freeways, power lines, reservoirs, and other infrastructure are gone, as are mines and quarries. Gas-powered automobiles and other 21st-century artifacts are in museums.

VISION PLANNING

City and regional planners sometimes engage in vision planning to engage citizens and stimulate creative ideas at a high level of generality. Unlike a detailed site plan, a vision plan lays out an inspirational picture of what a city or region might be like in the future in broad strokes. The vision planning process brings diverse stakeholders together to imagine different futures. Vision planning is a form of communicative action planning.

Planners sometime organize vision planning exercises in the early stages of preparing a new or revised general plan to gather ideas from a broad segment of community; educate the planners about people's ideas; and to energize the public to pursue the vision. Many city and county general plans begin with a vision statement which may be informed by vision planning. Sometimes planners facilitate vision planning for a state or region.

A state-wide citizens' organization in Oregon named 1000 Friends of Oregon pioneered vision planning in 1973. Their vision planning was a bottom-up, citizen-oriented process. Over the course of two years 1000 Friends of Oregon led a planning process called Envision Oregon at town hall forums for over 2,200 participants from 146 cities in 16 locations across the state. The key components of the resulting *Blueprint for Oregon's Future* are economic security, improved health, and protection of special places. Key strategies the blueprint proposed are to: (a) make towns and neighborhoods healthier and safer, (b) invest in farming and forestry, (c) protect special places, (d) plan for transportation, given climate threats, and (e) provide more parks, trails, and natural areas. *Blueprint for Oregon's Future* contains dozens of specific proposals to implements the blueprint's goals.

Figure 6.12 is an illustration from Boston, Massachusetts's 2019 vision plan. It illustrates a vision of a resilient design for the north end and downtown of Boston.

Figure 6.12 North End and Downtown Vision from Boston Vision Plan (2019).

A vision plan can help build consensus. The wildest and most utopian ideas in a vision plan may never come to pass, but thinking outside the box may lead to more imaginative plans. Vision planning ideas can cascade down to become imaginative components of comprehensive, specific, neighborhood, site, and other kinds of plans. Vision planning is particularly important for planners working in the advance planning section of city or county planning departments at the outset of major general plan revisions and for activist planners in nonprofit planning and environmental organizations seeking to mobilize their constituencies.

SUMMARY

Planners imagine future cities and regions that are better than present ones, and ones that are much worse. Utopian visions serve as inspirations, and dystopian visions caution planners and policy makers what to avoid. Both utopian and dystopian plans provide insights about how the physical form, social organization, economy, gender relations, social control, health, policing, surveillance, and the relationship between the built and natural environment of cities and regions might be different from current conditions.

Sir Thomas More's *Utopia* (1516); 18th- and 19th-century utopian socialist visions; Ebenezer Howard's garden city vision; the city beautiful, modernist, and linear city movements; Clarence Perry's articulation of what a neighborhood unit should be like; and Ernest Callenbach's description of Ecotopia have all had profound impacts on city and regional planning in the United States and worldwide.

Vision planning engages citizens and stimulates creative ideas. A vision plan lays out an inspirational picture of what a city or region might be like in the future. Mobilizing citizens and stakeholders to envision alternative futures for their community educates both them and the planners working on the plan and helps build community consensus.

Social theorists, utopian writers, and great visionary urban planners provide inspiration for city and regional planning. They help planners, policy makers, and citizens think outside the box.

CONCEPTS

Anarchism
Broadacre City
City Beautiful Movement
Dystopia
Garden City
Greenbelt
Letchworth, England
Linear City
Neighborhood Unit
New Lanark, Scotland
One Thousand Friends of Oregon
Radiant City
Socialism
System of Social Cities
Three Magnets (Howard)
Unearned Increment in Land
Utopia
Utopian Socialist
Vision Plan

PEOPLE

Daniel Burnham
Ernest Callenbach
Ebenezer Howard
Le Corbusier
Sir Thomas More
Robert Owen
Clarence Perry
Alberto Soria y Mata
Steven Wheeler
Frank Lloyd Wright

NOTES

1 In addition to Ernest Callenbach's *Ecotopia* (1975), utopian novels of particular interest for city and regional planners include Edward Bellamy's *Looking Backward* (1888), Charlotte Perkins Gilman's *Herland* (1915), H.G. Wells's *Men like Gods* (1923), and B.F. Skinner's *Walden Two* (1948). Dystopian novels of particular interest for city and regional planners include Henrik Ibsen's *An Enemy of the People* (1882), Jack London's *The Iron Heel* (1908), Aldous Huxley's *Brave New World* (1932), Arthur Koestler's *Darkness at Noon* (1940), and especially George Orwell's *Nineteen Eighty-Four* (1949).

2 Henri de Saint-Simon (1760–1825) was a French utopian socialist who distinguished the working class from the parasitic "idling class" (Saint-Simon, 1816–1817). Saint-Simon advocated a meritocracy based on talent and work rather than family and inherited wealth. Étienne Cabet (1788–1856) was a French utopian socialist who first used the terms communist and communism.

3 Howard was impressed by Robert Owen's success at New Lanark, Edward Bellamy's utopian romance *Looking Backward* (1888), American socialist Henry George, British Fabian socialists who believed in a gradual and peaceful path to socialism, and Russian anarchist Pëtr Kropotkin and French anarchist Élisée Reclus who envisioned a society of small workers' cooperatives combining agriculture and industry.

4 Howard obtained a £50 loan to self-publish 300 copies of *Tomorrow* and drew and colored diagrams in the original copies himself by hand. He distributed most copies to family and friends for free. A one-shilling paperback published by a commercial London publisher—Swan Sonnenschein—had sold 3,000 copies by 1900 (Howard, Hall, & Ward, 2006: 3).

5 In the 1920s and 1930s Howard's ideas inspired *overspill estates* in or on the outskirts of London and Manchester, England and Glasgow, Scotland, which were built to house households displaced by slum clearance projects.

6 Since the 1950s 13% of England (6,454 square miles) has been reserved for 14 greenbelts (Hack, 2018: 42). There are another 63 square miles of greenbelt in Scotland (ibid). Tokyo, Seoul, Bangkok, and hundreds of smaller cities worldwide have what they call greenbelts. These greenbelts are larger, smaller, irregularly shaped, incomplete, or otherwise different from what Howard proposed. Some take the form of green fingers, hearts, strips, girdles or patches. Some cities have blue belts—planned watercourses for drainage and recreation (Beatley, 2014: 88–89; Al, 2018: 61).

7 Howard proposed a 750-foot-wide residential zone between pairs of radial streets along five circumferential avenues. A 420-foot-wide "grand avenue" would divide the residential area into two equal belts; effectively an additional 3.75-mile-long 118-acre park within 240 yards of every resident in the city core.

8 Howard calculated that more than half of the money from rent and local rates (property taxes) of British cities with an average population equal to what he proposed for garden city at the time went to the landlord, leaving less than half for municipal purposes. He estimated that in a garden city rents and ratables would be only about half that amount. Initially, expenditure for municipal services would be low in the new city. After landlords received rent there would be a balance left over. Howard suggested that this go into a sinking fund to eventually buy out landlords' interest in land so that all the land would be municipally owned, and ground rent would become the main source of municipal revenue. There would be little money for the sinking fund at first, but as garden city prospered economically there would be more and more. After 30 years,

rent to landlords would vanish and in Howard's words "this being obtained all the funds hitherto devoted to that purpose may be applied municipally or to the provision of OLD AGE PENSIONS" (capitalization in the original).

9. The trustees were not able to pay debenture holders a dividend until 1913 and then only 1% (Thomas, 1997). They did not begin paying the full 5% dividend until 1923, and payment of dividend arrears was not completed until 1945 (ibid).

10. In 1919 Howard learned that 1,000 acres in Welwyn, about 30 miles from London, were about to be auctioned. He cobbled together support and submitted a winning bid. Welwyn had housing subsidies for servicemen from the "Homes for Heroes" program. A Quaker organization leased a large tract in the greenbelt to divide into small holdings for ex-servicemen. Howard was 70 years old when construction of Welwyn began. He lived his final years in Welwyn, trying to perfect a new stenographic machine and dabbling in spiritualism—faithfully transcribing messages from his dead wife. Howard died in 1928 at age 78.

11. As head of the Resettlement Administration Rexford Tugwell ("Rex the red")—the most left-leaning of senior New Deal officials—oversaw construction of three greenbelt towns—Greenbelt, Maryland; Greendale, Wisconsin; and Greenhills, Ohio—and started a fourth—Greenbrook, New Jersey. Initial portions of the new towns were completed in 1937 and 1938. The greenbelt towns program was expensive and aroused a firestorm of criticism from conservatives who considered the program socialistic. Roosevelt dismantled the Resettlement Administration in 1937. A different New Deal Agency—the Farm Security Administration—closed out work on the towns. There were 885 row houses and apartment units in Greenbelt, Maryland, 676 in Greenhills, Ohio, and 572 in Greendale, Wisconsin at the time the program was closed out.

12. In Soria y Mata's linear city in Madrid at least 80% of every lot was devoted to open space and plantings. Buildings were no more than three stories high and were separated from the street by a 15-foot strip of greenery and from each other by vegetation. Initially horse-drawn trams provided public transit. Later they were replaced by electric streetcars. Individual parcels varied in form (rectangular, square, and trapezoidal), size, and price. Some lots were priced for low- and moderate-income homeowners. Large parcels for luxury villas faced the principal street and other major thoroughfares. Smaller lots for moderate- and some low-income households were located on parallel secondary streets. Maximum net density was very low—3.16 houses per acre. Construction stopped at the outbreak of the Spanish Civil War in 1936 and the Compañía Madrileña de Urbanización ceased to exist during the war.

13. China's belt and road initiative is a huge program to fund transportation infrastructure within China and to connect other countries to China. It is inspired by the historic overland silk road(s) from China to Europe and the maritime routes from China to Arabia and beyond that existed from 130 BCE to 1453 CE. Portions of the land portion of the belt and road system already bring goods to Europe by rail.

SUGGESTIONS FOR FURTHER LEARNING

Overviews: Peter Hall, *Cities of tomorrow* (1994). Robert Fishman, *Urban utopias in the twentieth century* (1982). Robert Heilbroner, *The worldly philosophers* (1953). **Utopia:** Sir Thomas More, *Utopia* (1516 and many modern editions). **Utopian and Dystopian Literature:** Utopian and dystopian novels website (2021). Carl Abbott, *Imagining urban futures* (2016). **Garden Cities:** Ebenezer Howard, *Tomorrow: The peaceful path to real reform* (1898), and *Garden cities of tomorrow* (1902). Peter Hall & Colin Ward, *Sociable cities* (1998). Ebenezer Howard, Peter Hall, & Colin Ward, *Tomorrow: The peaceful path to real reform, annotated edition* (2006). Robert Fishman, *Urban utopias in the twentieth century* (1982). Robert Beevers, *The garden city utopia* (1988). Stanley Buder, *Visionaries and planners: The garden city movement and modern community* (1990). Standish Meacham, *Regaining paradise: Englishness and the early garden cities movement*. Kermit Schuyler (ed), *From the garden city to green cities* (2002). **American Greenbelt Towns:** Joseph Arnold, *The New Deal in the suburbs*. **Daniel Burnham and City Beautiful Planning:** Daniel Burnham & Edward Bennett, *Plan of Chicago 1909*. Walter Moody, *Wacker's manual of the plan of Chicago* (1911). Carl Smith, *The plan of Chicago: Daniel Burnham and the remaking of the American city* (2009). Thomas Hines, *Burnham of Chicago: Architect and planner*, 2nd ed (2008). Judith McBrien, *Make no little plans* [video] (2010). **Geddesian Planning:** Patrick Geddes, *Cities in evolution* (1915). Walter Stephen (ed), *Think global, act local: The life and legacy of Patrick Geddes* (2016). Philip Boardman, *Patrick Geddes* (2017) and *The worlds of Patrick Geddes* (1978). Volker Weller, *Biopolis: Patrick Geddes and the city of life* (2002). Helen Meller, *Patrick Geddes* (2017). Marshall Stalley, *Patrick Geddes* (1972). **Anarchist Visions:** Pëtr Kropotkin, *Fields, factories and workshops: Or industry combined with agriculture and brain work with manual work* (1898). **The Radiant City:** Le Corbusier, *The city of tomorrow* (1929) and *The radiant city* (1935). Robert Fishman, *Urban utopias in the twentieth century* (1982). **The Linear City:** Alberto Soria y Mata, *The linear city* (1882). Ivan Boileau, La ciudad lineal: A critical study of the linear suburb of Madrid. George Collins, The ciudad lineal of Madrid (1959). **Broadacre**

City: Frank Lloyd Wright, *Broadacre city* (1935). Robert Fishman, *Urban utopias in the twentieth century* (1982). Ada Louise Huxtable, *Frank Lloyd Wright* (2004). Meryl Secrest, *Frank Lloyd Wright* (1998). **The Neighborhood Unit:** Clarence Perry, *The neighborhood unit* (1929). **Ecotopia:** Ernest Callenbach, *Ecotopia* (1975) and *The Ecotopian encyclopedia for the 1980s* (1980). Allan Marshall, *Ecotopia 2021* (2016). **Journals:** *Journal of Planning History. Urban History.*

CHAPTER 7

General Plans

INTRODUCTION

City and regional planners are optimists. They choose the planning profession because they are motivated to make life better for members of the communities they plan for. Comprehensive city and county plans provide local government planners the opportunity to make the world a better place by helping invent alternative urban futures.

Virtually every city and county in the United States has a comprehensive plan that establishes goals, policies, objectives, standards, and implementation strategies to achieve a vision of their future. Some comprehensive plans are called master plans, or simply the city's plan, but most are now called general plans. General plans establish the broad outlines of the jurisdiction's intended future for a period of 20 years or more. This provides planners the opportunity to think big about what the community might become several decades in the future.

Preparing and overseeing the implementation of general plans provides planners the time and funding to carefully assess what the community they are planning for is like—its unique physical features, demographics, and economy. Planners can step back and see how a city or county fits into the region, state, country and the world city system. They can think deeply about the community's strengths and weaknesses. General plans require planners to deploy the full array of their professional skills and to use all of the tools at their disposal. Planners get the opportunity to use all of the research methods the profession uses. In the process, planners engage in continuing education about current planning practices and educate citizens and policy makers about what they know. Preparation of a general plan provides planners the opportunity to interact with and learn from all manner of people. It requires them to use their advocacy and political skills.

Substantively, general plans can be the vehicle for promoting any agenda or vision for the future of the community that prepares it from increased bikeability, to net zero carbon emissions, to the elimination of homelessness. Planners can craft ways to make the community more beautiful, efficient, diverse, resilient, green, transit-oriented, healthy, carbon-neutral or to reflect other values they and the community believe in.

Planners, policy makers, developers, and citizens turn to general plans for information and guidance on decisions about land use, transportation, housing, infrastructure, urban design, open space, the environment, and other matters. General plans help guide planning for residential and commercial development, streets, neighborhoods, parks, open space, historic buildings, and many other aspects of the community.

This chapter begins by describing what "comprehensive" means in the comprehensive plan context. It describes how general plans are prepared, amended, and updated, the purposes they serve, and how they communicate information in the digital age. It traces the evolution of comprehensive plans from early master plans to modern general plans. It describes the elements that make up a general plan and plan visions, goals, objectives, standards, implementation, monitoring, and revision. The chapter describes four general plans that have recently received awards from the American Planning Association. It provides a biography of T.J. (Jack) Kent—the scholar-practitioner most responsible for developing the theory and practice of preparing general plans dominant in the United States today. A case study

DOI: 10.4324/9781003195818-7

describes the *NashvilleNext Plan*, Nashville, Tennessee's general plan, which won a Burnham Award for excellence in comprehensive planning in 2018.

COMPREHENSIVE, MASTER, AND GENERAL PLANS

"Comprehensive" suggests that a plan covers all aspects of the plan for a city or county. This is a bit deceptive. Modern general plans have evolved from the 1928 Standard State Planning Enabling Act (SSPEA) that conceptualized planning mostly in physical terms. They are strongly influenced by T.J. (Jack) Kent (Box 7.1) who also felt that general plans should be essentially physical plans, and that economic, social, and other matters should mostly be planned by other governmental, nonprofit, and private entities. Even though they deal primarily with physical planning, general plans indirectly impact a community's economy, social structure, and character because these are all closely related to its land use pattern and physical development.

BOX 7.1 T.J. (JACK) KENT

Thomas J. ("T.J." or "Jack") Kent (1917–1998) was a notable planning educator, practitioner, local elected official, and activist. Mild-mannered and soft-spoken, Kent was a lifelong champion of principles he believed in—local physical planning, regional planning, grassroots democracy, civic engagement by academics, protection of open space, and academic freedom.

Kent received a BA in Architecture from the University of California, Berkeley in 1938 and a Master's Degree in City Planning from the Massachusetts Institute of Technology in 1943. His lifelong commitment to democracy and freedom of speech was shaped by a year-long traveling fellowship to Germany in 1939 at the outbreak of World War II where he observed Nazi tyranny firsthand.

Kent served as a practicing planner in San Francisco and a planning commissioner in Berkeley, California. He played a leading role in city and regional planning and environmental design education at the University of California, Berkeley. He helped create the Association of Bay Area Governments—the San Francisco Bay Area's Council of Governments. Kent was a national leader of local planning officials.

Kent was deeply involved in local politics and planning. Between 1946 and 1948 he was San Francisco's second city planning director. He was the principal author of San Francisco's first comprehensive plan. He served as a member of the Berkeley city planning commission from 1948 to 1957. He helped prepare Berkeley's first general plan—which is based on his ideas. Berkeley's first general plan figures prominently as a model in his writings. From 1957 to 1965 he served on the Berkeley city council.

Kent was the founder of the University of California, Berkeley's Department of City and Regional Planning (DCRP), which was established in 1948. He taught city and regional planning in the DCRP for 26 years until he retired in 1974. He was the DCRP's first department chair—serving for 12 years. Kent was instrumental in organizing Berkeley's College of Environmental Design that houses Berkeley's departments of Architecture and Landscape Architecture as well as City and Regional Planning.

Between 1969 and 1970 Kent served as President of the American Society of Planning Officials (ASPO)—a national organization of planning officials that later merged into the American Planning Association (APA). Kent helped organize an influential Bay Area grassroots open space organization—originally named People for Open Space and now called the Greenbelt Alliance. He served as president of People for Open Space from 1974 to 1978.

Kent is best known for defining what an urban general plan should contain. In contrast to Edward Basset, Kent used the term "general" rather than "master" plan. He argued that general plans should be long-term physical plans, leaving economic, social, and other matters to other plans. He is largely responsible for the separation of zoning from general plan elements. Kent successfully argued that planning departments should serve as staff to city councils and county boards of commissioners—not independent planning commissions divorced from messy real-world politics.

Shortly after Kent died at age 81 in 1998, the Berkeley Department of City and Regional Planning celebrated it 50th anniversary. Kent's proposal for the DCRP had resulted in one of the leading centers of city and regional planning education in the world. UC Berkeley's College of Environmental Design that Kent proposed and helped create had become a model for environmental design education. The little band of planning directors he presided over at ASPO had merged into The American Institute of Planners (AIP) which in turn merged into the The American Institute of City Planning which later merged into the American Planning Association (APA) which in turn merged into the the American Planning Association (APA) in 1978.

The handful of volunteers Kent presided over at People for Open Space had grown into the established, respected, and effective Greenbelt Alliance, which is still going strong. The Association of Bay Area Governments (ABAG)—that he envisioned and helped create—had grown into a large Council of Governments (COG)—though neither ABAG nor most other COGs did regional planning as Kent conceived it.

During the 34 years between publication of Kent's *The Urban General Plan* in 1964 and his death in 1998 Kent's position on what a general plan should be like became standard practice in California, was becoming mainstream in the United States, and influenced general plan making in other states. After his death, his ideas of what a general plan should be like became even more widely adopted in the United States and other countries.

Kent is significant for city and regional planners today both as a model of a successful academic practitioner who bridged the divide between academics and practicing planners and because much day-to-day physical planning in the United States conforms to his ideas.

General plans typically begin with an explicit vision statement. They usually include plan elements, goals, policies, and objectives. They may include benchmarks and standards. General plans typically contain sections on implementation and perhaps a list of action items.

Since local government in the United States is fragmented and regions are Balkanized—divided into many small competing jurisdictions, there are usually general plans for dozens of cities and counties within metropolitan regions. General plans almost always cover all the land within a city. They usually cover all the unincorporated land within a county. This is different from zoning ordinances, which may leave parts of a city or county unzoned. General plans guide public land and infrastructure and also impact private land use.

Most states do not have a state plan and do not review local general plans prepared by their cities and counties. Only a few states' planning laws require much, or even any, coordination among comprehensive plans of adjacent or nearby cities or between a city's general plan and the general plan of the county where the city is located. Oregon and New Jersey are exceptions. Oregon requires its cities and counties to coordinate their comprehensive plans—which they call comp plans—with the comp plans of any other cities or counties that share a common border with them. Oregon has 19 state planning goals. The Oregon state Office of Land Conservation and Development reviews and has the authority to approve or disapprove all local general plans for consistency with the 19 state goals. It can refuse to approve a plan if it conflicts with the state goals. New Jersey has a cross-acceptance policy that requires local governments to review each other's general plans and negotiate agreements to make sure they are consistent with each other. The New Jersey Office of State Planning mediates cross-acceptance disputes.

General plans in the same geographic area often conflict. Jurisdictions compete to attract the most desirable land uses like clean high-value-added tech companies and try to externalize less desirable land uses such as landfills (dumps) onto neighboring jurisdictions. One city may zone an area for agricultural use and a neighboring city may zone adjacent land for a residential subdivision. Many jurisdictions want an auto mall on the outskirts of the main road because auto malls produce a large amount of property and sales tax revenue and do not require much municipal expenditure. So jurisdictions often compete to attract and retain auto malls.

As the number of different types of plans at all levels of government in the United States proliferate, planners at the city and county level are spending more and more time conforming general plans to other state and regional transportation, land use, air quality, housing, economic development, climate change and other plans. They do this either because the state requires them to do so or because they consider this good planning practice.

City councils and county boards of commissioners are legally responsible for general plans. Before a general plan becomes final, the local elected officials must approve it. If a court finds that a general plan violates the law, it is up to the city council or county board of commissioners to fix it.

Planners and local elected officials use many tools to implement general plans. Local zoning, subdivision, and growth management ordinances, housing and building codes, and environmental impact assessment can help implement general plan visions and goals.

General plans are now in digital as well as hardcopy formats. Basic ones are simply PDF versions of paper plans. However most general plans now take advantage of the ability to present words, photographs, data graphics, maps, videos, and other content in imaginative ways; permit users to search for information digitally; and link summaries to more detailed material, including the data and background reports that underlie the plan.

Paper and digital general plans vary in length. A digital plan will usually have links to other material, including background studies, ordinances, and explanatory material. Oklahoma City's general plan is 426 pages long. Kauai County's hardcopy general plan runs to 568 pages. The online *NashvilleNext* plan starts with just a 20-page summary, but links lead to 5 volumes and 14 community plans. The elements and community plans in the *NashvilleNext Plan* in turn link to hundreds of pages of addition material such as the text of ordinances, reports, visual images, meeting records, videos, and other plans.

It is difficult to define the boundary between some digital general plans and supporting material or even to specify how many pages are in the plan itself. Many links are dynamic, making modern general plans fluid. This keeps them up to date, but requires readers to make sure they are relying on the current version.

THE VARIETY OF GENERAL PLANS

Since local governments are defined by state law, each state has the power to specify what their local governments' general plans may, should, or must contain. What state laws require is shaped by the state's history, geography, economic development level, degree of urbanization, and political culture. The relationship between state and local government differs depending on whether the state follows Dillon's rule—which strictly limits local governments planning—or the Cooley doctrine that grants cities and counties broad power to plan, as described in Chapter 4. It also depends on whether a city is a general law city governed only by the state's planning law or a charter city whose authority to plan is specified in a written charter from the state.

North Dakota has a total state population of 755,000 residents and only one city with a population over 100,000 (Fargo) for a land area of 71,000 square miles. In contrast, California has a population of almost 40 million people and 73 cities with populations between 100,000 and more than four million (Los Angeles City). The population of New York city is 8,500,000. Understandably California's and New York's state general plan laws are much more extensive and detailed than North Dakota's. The Fargo comprehensive plan—*Go 2030*—is 268 pages long; the *Los Angeles City General Plan* is thousands of pages long.

Growing communities have very different needs than older stable or declining communities. Growing communities' general plans are intended primarily to manage growth, while stable or declining communities' general plans often mainly focus on revitalizing older neighborhoods, economic development planning to retain existing industry and attract new industry, planned shrinkage and managing decline.

In addition to strategies to retain existing industry and attract new industry, declining communities' general plans may include plans for projects to redevelop blighted land, revitalize older neighborhoods, and re-train the local workforce. They may include plans to maintain the older housing stock, remediate dangerous environmental conditions, clean up brownfields contaminated by toxic waste, preserve historic buildings and districts, and perhaps deal with housing abandonment, arson, and social pathologies.

Growing communities' plans typically separate incompatible land uses, specify the spatial distribution of desired future density, seek to contain sprawl, lay out the pattern of new streets, provide for access to recreational, educational, shopping, and other facilities, detail plans for public facilities, parks and open space, and describe housing plans and policies. They usually address how they plan to protect the natural environment, sensitive natural region habitat, and endangered species. Some specify plans for traffic calming, "complete streets", zero traffic fatalities (Vision Zero planning), pedestrianized streets, bicycle ways, and reducing global warming.

SOCIAL JUSTICE AND GENERAL PLANS

General plans are primarily physical plans. They differ in the extent to which they address social issues. They almost always describe the racial composition of the city or county using U.S. census categories. The current U.S. census racial categories are White; Black or African American; American Indian or Alaska Native; Asian; and Native Hawaiian or Other Pacific Islander. The U.S. Office of Management and Budget permits the Census Bureau to use a sixth category—Some Other Race. Respondents may report more than one race. Race is a social construct, and many academics and organizations of racial and ethnic groups question these categories.

General plans usually report the income ranges and the number of households in poverty as defined by the federal government. They may report other demographics such as the population age distribution. In addition to cross-sectional census data, they discuss demographic trends and projections. Most general plans explicitly say that they value diversity and racial equity. Since planning for social justice is a sensitive topic, some planning departments choose to leave planning and policy to alleviate poverty, eliminate racial discrimination, or address migrant needs to other city departments or nonprofit organizations and focus strictly on physical planning. In politically conservative and predominantly White jurisdictions, general plan content related to social justice is often vague and there may be no operational details on what the city or county actually intends to do to overcome inequality, improve the status of disadvantaged groups, enforce fair housing laws, or otherwise address social justice.

Of the four general plans described in this chapter, the Nashville and Kauai plans clearly state their commitment to diversity. These jurisdictions worked hard to include diverse groups in preparing their general plans and include operational policies to address needs of different populations. Nashville created a committee to provide input about diversity in the *NashvilleNext Plan*. Nashville's existing City Offices of Neighborhood and Community Engagement and New Americans (recent immigrants) involved people of color and immigrants in the general planning process. There is a Spanish-language version of the *NashvilleNext* plan.

Kauai County also had a very inclusive general planning process. Nine percent of respondents to recent U.S. Census Annual Community Surveys of Kauai self-described themselves as native Hawaiian. The Kuai County general plan succeeded in involving many ethnic Hawaiians in the planning process. The resulting plan reflects native Hawaiian values and includes policies to protect sacred native Hawaiian sites.

A small number of cities explicitly practice equity planning as it was practiced in Cleveland, Ohio in the 1970s—making social equity the top priority in every planning decision. Many of the planners who develop general plans are now women. However, general plans rarely adopt an explicit gender perspective or operationalize action plans and programs explicitly for women. Almost no general plans address the special needs or concerns of lesbian, gay, bisexual, transgender, queer (LGBTQ) communities or even acknowledge that LGBTQ communities exist.

BURNHAM AWARD COMPREHENSIVE PLANS

The American Planning Association (APA) presents annual awards for the best comprehensive plan, named the Burnham Award in honor of Daniel Burnham—the influential Chicago architect and city beautiful planner described in Chapter 6, who famously declared "make no little plans". Four recent Burnham Award recipients are the Plano, Texas *Plano Tomorrow* general plan in 2015; the Nashville, Tennessee, consolidated city-county *NashvilleNext* metro region plan in 2016; the Oklahoma City, Oklahoma *planokc* general plan in 1918; and the Kauai, Hawaii County *Kaua'I Kākou* general plan in 2019. These four plans are representative of city and county comprehensive plans that the APA considers excellent. Box 7.2 describes the Nashville, Tennessee general plan. It is followed by overviews of the Kauai, Plano, and Oklahoma City general plans. The following sections summarize commonalities and differences among the four plans.

PLANO TOMORROW, PLANO, TEXAS

Plano, Texas is a prosperous "boomburg"— a fast-growing community located in Collin County, Texas 17 miles north of Dallas. Plano's 2015 general plan—*Plano Tomorrow*—won the APA's Burnham Award in 2015. The *Plano Tomorrow* plan is notable for its innovative use of web links.

Early settlers chose the Spanish word *plano* (flat) for the city's name in the 1840s because Plano lies on flat, nearly treeless land. Plano was incorporated in 1873. Today Plano is surrounded by other incorporated cities, so it can no longer expand by annexing unincorporated county land. Plano has a land area of 72 square miles and a population of 290,000. The U.S. census reports that in 2019 83% of Plano's population was White alone, not Hispanic or Latino; 9% Hispanic; 3% Asian Alone; 2% Black; and the remaining 3% other races or two or more races.

The headquarters of the J.C. Penny Corporation, Toyota North America, the Frito-Lay Company and other major corporations are located in Plano. Plano has high-quality residential neighborhoods, a commercial district, and significant commercial development along four regional expressways. It has a historic downtown, recognized by the American Planning Association (APA) as "a great neighborhood in America", two international-caliber business parks, and various mixed use and traditional suburban shopping and dining centers.

Plano's population grew from 3,695 in 1950 to 17,872 in 1960, to 72,000 in 1980, 222,030 in 2000, and an estimated 2,854,537 in 2021. The city is 95% developed, and

BOX 7.2 THE *NASHVILLENEXT PLAN* (NASHVILLE, TENNESSEE)

Nashville, Tennessee's general plan—the *NashvilleNext Plan*—won an American Planning Association (APA) 2016 Burnham Award. Nashville is the capital of Tennessee, and Tennessee's largest city. It is the center of America's country and western music industry. Nashville is one of the 27 consolidated city-county governments in the United States. In 2019 the population of the Nashville-Davidson County metro area was 669,053. The U.S. census reported that its population was 56% white, 28% Black, 10% Hispanic, and 4% Asian.

The NashvilleNext Plan contains five volumes titled: (1) Vision, Trends, and Strategy, (2) Elements, (3) Communities (with 14 community plans), (4) Actions, and (5) *Access Nashville 2040*—Nashville's transportation plan. Links from the *NashvilleNext* website provide access to other Nashville-Davidson County metro area city, county,

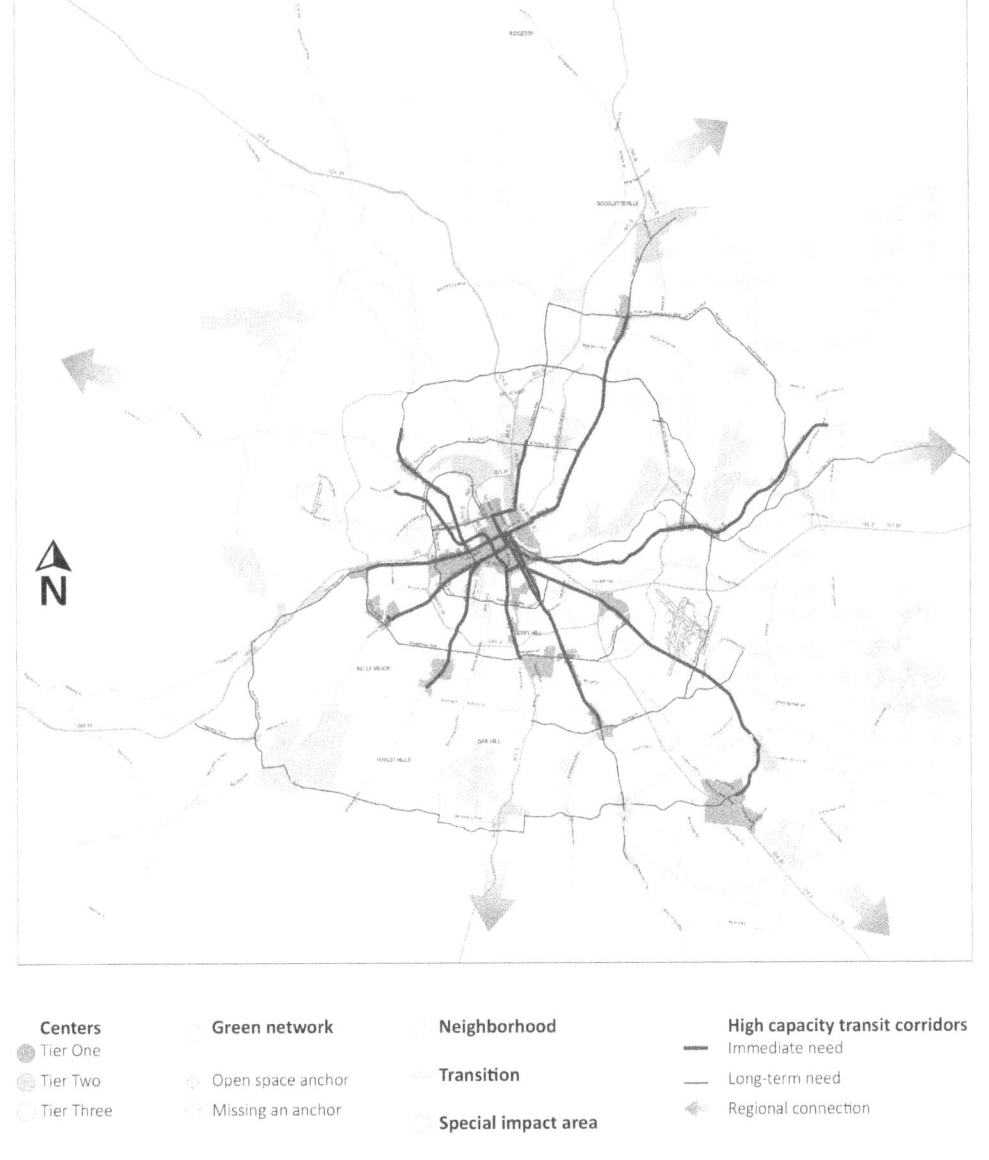

Centers	Green network	Neighborhood	High capacity transit corridors
Tier One			Immediate need
Tier Two	Open space anchor	Transition	Long-term need
Tier Three	Missing an anchor	Special impact area	Regional connection

Figure 7.1 *NashvilleNext* Growth and Preservation Concept Map (Nashville, Tennessee, 2018).

and regional plans, including an urban design plan for Music Row where many of Nashville's music-related establishments are located.

Volume 1 contains seven guiding principles for the plan's vision: (1) ensure opportunity for all, (2) expand accessibility, (3) create economic prosperity, (4) foster strong neighborhoods, (5) advance education, (6) champion the environment, and (7) be Nashville.

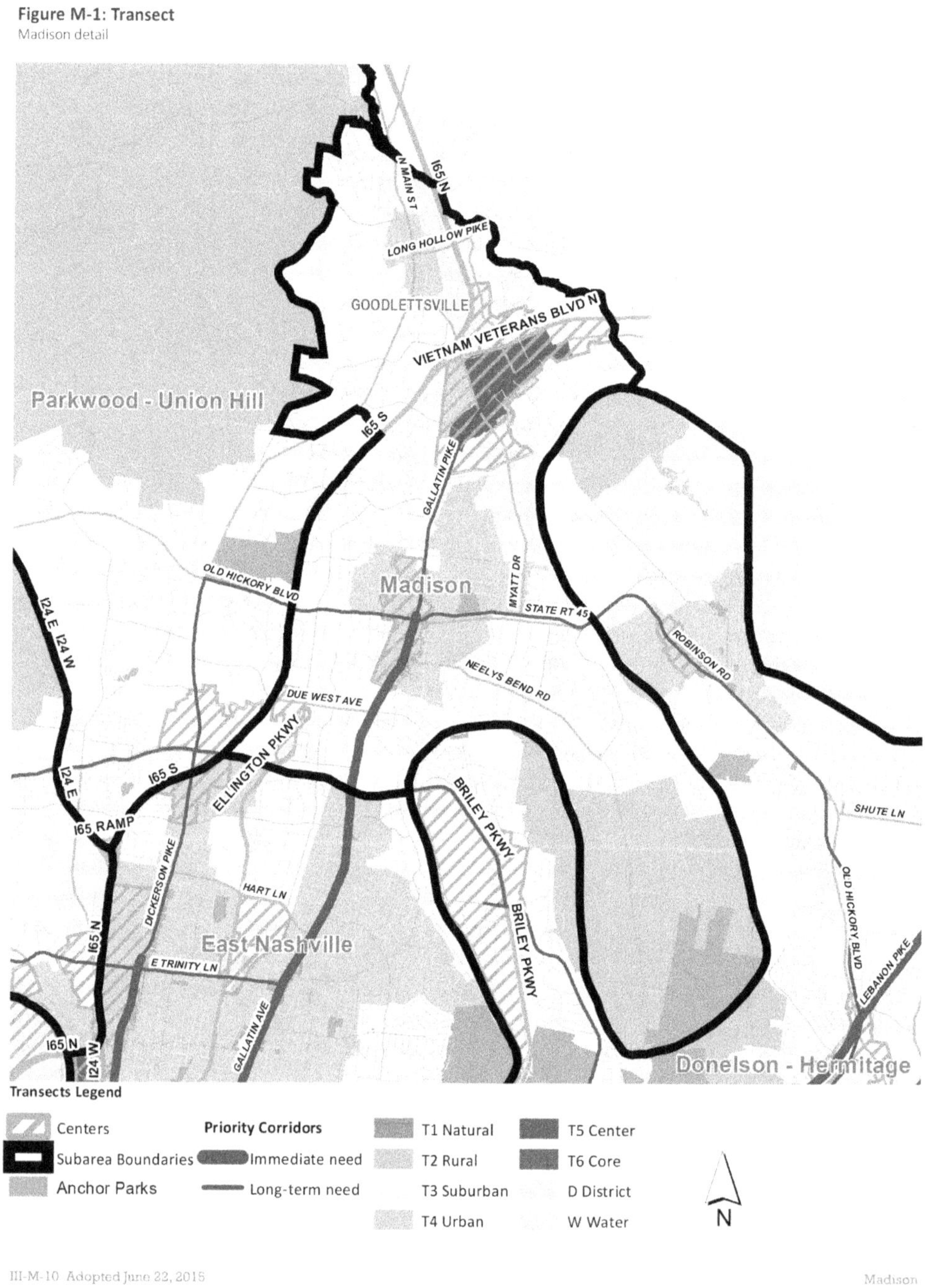

Figure 7.2 Madison County, Tennessee, Community Plan Transect Map.

Volume 2 operationalizes the *NashvilleNext* plan principles in seven elements that contain specific goals applying the seven guiding principles to each of the seven plan elements. (1) land use, transportation and infrastructure, (2) arts, culture, and creativity, (3) economic and workforce development, (4) education and youth, (5) health, livability, and the built environment, (6) housing, and (7) natural resources and hazard adaptation. This way of organizing the plan follows Edward Bassett's and T.J. Kent's view that plans should be divided into elements, but uses categories that fit the Nashville context. They reflect contemporary U.S. city and regional planning practice rather than dated elements that Bassett proposed in 1933 and Kent proposed in 1974. While this way of organizing the plan contents into elements fits Nashville's perception of how best to organize their plan, elements of other general plans group their plan content in other ways.

Volume 3 describes Nashville's vision. It updates and brings together descriptions, issues, and strategies for 14 community planning areas. Detailed community character maps illustrate visions for the different communities. Figure 7.2—The *Madison County Infrastructure, Land Use, and Transportation Concept Plan* map—identifies a green network, centers, neighborhoods, transition areas, special impact areas, and high-capacity transit networks in Madison County—one of the counties in the Nashville Metropolitan Area. Figure 7.3 is a transect—a visual representation of development—in Madison County. It illustrated the continuum from undeveloped natural areas to dense areas in the downtown.

Volume 4 describes specific tasks for metro departments and partners to undertake to implement the *NashvilleNext* plan. It is regularly updated based on monitoring and annual reports describing what activities were begun or completed during the preceding year. For example, the 2016 *NashvilleNext Annual Report* describes activities such as a Nashville walls project to create public art on city walls; an inclusionary housing ordinance to increase the county's supply of low- and moderate-income housing units; and committees which were created during 2016 to oversee how well the plan is meeting each of its seven stated guiding principles and 34 action items.

Volume 5, titled *Access Nashville 2040*, is the metro region's transportation plan. It is a transportation framework plan that describes Nashville's plans for infrastructure for walking and bicycling paths, mass transit, and street networks. It includes descriptive material and case studies describing Nashville's transportation vision including a "complete streets" plan covering the pedestrian environment; bicyclability; mass transit; travel lane management; strategic connections; a description of how the region plans to maintain its existing transportation infrastructure; and a Vision Zero plan describing how Nashville intends to achieve zero traffic fatalities.

The *NashvilleNext Plan* was developed over the course of three years, with citizen participation involving over 18,500 participants. To assure community inclusion, planners received input from a diversity advisory committee. Nashville's Mayor's Office of Neighborhoods and Community Engagement, and Nashville's Office of New Americans that works with immigrants helped with this process.

Citizen participation that led to the plan included a community survey, interviews with 100 community leaders, and "blue sky" visioning to encourage thinking big, followed by more focused visioning to define 34 key issues for Nashville's future. By "blue sky visioning" Nashville meant big think brainstorming. (This a different use of the term than "blue sky" laws designed to prevent fraudulent subdivisions discussed in Chapter 8.) Growth and preservation mapping with citizen input identified priority areas for growth and areas to preserve. With this background, the process assessed alternate futures for Nashville and selected a preferred future. Draft community plan maps were reviewed by citizens and changed to reflect citizens' views of the preferred future.

142 | GENERAL PLANS

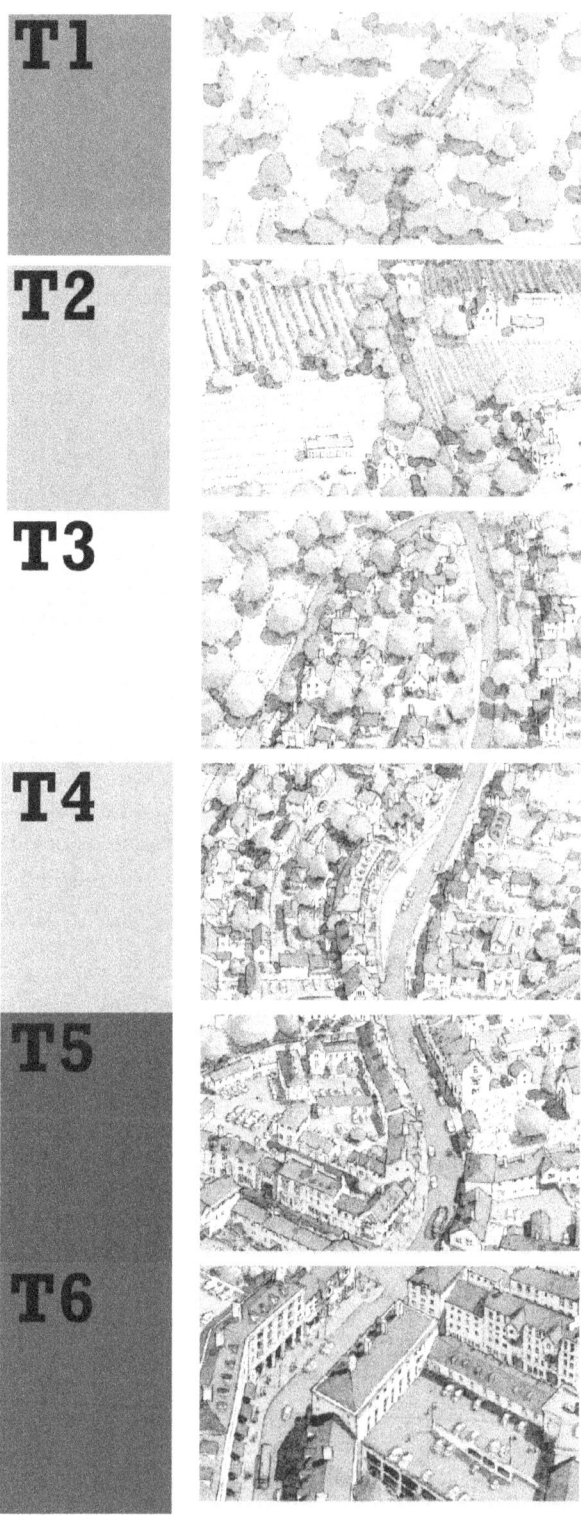

Figure 7.3 Madison County, Tennessee, Community Plan Transect Illustration.

The Nashville Leadership Council provided "healthy city" input. A booklet by the Nashville Civic Design Center titled *Shaping the Healthy Community* describes design strategies to improve public health. Nashville's 2017 *Community Character Manual* is a 68-page manual that describes the relationship of 11 types of communities to the *NashvilleNext Plan*.[1] Appendices in the manual summarize community character policies and describe how they are to be put into practice. The manual includes a glossary. Maps, photographs, and sketches describe the different types of communities clearly and text describes policies for them. The growth and preservation concept map and transect (Figures 7.1 and 7.2) are essential elements of the manual.

The *NashvilleNext* plan is a good example of bounded rational planning. it proceeded through conventional steps in the rational planning model, but with much greater interconnectivity and flexibility than most plans developed that way. The *NashvilleNext Plan* places much greater emphasis than most general plans on implementing and adjusting the plan as needed.

population growth has slowed. However, Plano's flat land, thriving economy, and proximity to Dallas make it a prime location for further development. A central feature of the *Plano Tomorrow* plan is to increase density in the city.

Texas is a Dillon's rule state vesting power to plan in local governments. Plano is a charter city, so the state charter describes Plano's authority to plan. Politically, Plano is a conservative Republican city.

The *Plano Tomorrow* plan that won a Burnham Award proved controversial. A group opposed to the number of new high-density apartments that the plan permitted (or was perceived to permit), and the process by which it was developed, gathered enough signatures for a referendum to overturn the plan. A lawsuit contesting the legality of the referendum resulted in the city council repealing the plan. As of winter 2021, a draft plan prepared by a citizens' committee, modifying controversial sections on transportation, future land use, density, and growth management was under consideration by the Plano city council.

PLANOKC (OKLAHOMA CITY, OKLAHOMA)

Planokc—Oklahoma City's 2016 general plan—was the city's first new comprehensive plan in 38 years. It won a Burnham Award in 2018. The APA based the award on the depth of background research that preceded it, smart land use, and notable bicycle, historic preservation, and arts plan elements.

Oklahoma City is the capital and largest city in Oklahoma. In 2019, 68% of Oklahoma City's 655,057 residents classified themselves as White alone, 20% Hispanic or Latino, 14% Black or African American, and 4.5% Asian alone. Oklahoma City is a low-density city with a land area of 62 square miles. It is in the middle of an active oil field. Its economy is based largely on extracting and processing oil and gas. Petroleum products and related industries are the largest sector of the city's economy. Oklahoma City is also an important livestock center. Because it is Oklahoma's state capital, Oklahoma City has many state government jobs. The city extends into Canadian, Cleveland, and Pottawatomie counties and is part of the Oklahoma City-Shawnee Combined Statistical Area with a population of 1.46 million people.

Oklahoma City is extremely auto dependent. Transportation accounts for an unusually high percentage of Oklahoma City's air pollution and 64% of its greenhouse gas (GHG) emissions. Sixty percent of the area's forest has been eliminated since 1871, contributing to a city-wide heat island effect—causing severe air pollution on hot days. Health and fitness are serious problems. In a 2020 study of 100 cities, analysts at the American College of Sports Medicine ranked Oklahoma City's personal health 95th, community and environment 99th, and the city's overall health last—100th of 100 cities.

However, recently residents have shown a growing preference for biking, walking, and public transit. Oklahoma City has some low-income neighborhoods and deteriorated housing. An estimated 12,000 buildings had been vacant six months or longer in 2018.

Planokc discusses and updates major infrastructure plans that Oklahoma City has implemented over the last 25 years. In the late 1990s, Oklahoma City started a large public infrastructure program named the MAPS (Metropolitan Area Projects) program to renew the city's riverfront and build a ballpark, canal, and new cultural, entertainment, and arts facilities. Voters later approved an extension of the city's sales tax to fund school facilities. A new central park and modern streetcar system approved under the MAPS 3 program are nearing completion. In 2019 voters approved MAPS 4 with projects dedicated to neighborhood and human needs, quality of life, and job-creation initiatives. One of the challenges *planokc* identifies is maintaining the MAPS program's momentum and enhancing these assets.

THE KAUA'I KĀKOU PLAN, KAUAI, HAWAII

The 2017 Kauai County general plan is named *Kaua'I Kākou*, using the native Hawaiian spelling of the island name (*Kaua'I*) and the Hawaiian word for "ours" (*Kākou*)—"the plan for our island". The *Kaua'I Kākou plan* won a 2019 Burnham Award for its outstanding citizen participation process, level of detail, sensitivity to native Hawaiian culture, and environmental planning.

Kauai is the fourth largest of the Hawaiian Islands. It is a county with a land area of 619 square miles. Most of Kauai is open space. Kauai is a spectacularly beautiful tropical island with a varied and fragile ecosystem, strong tourist economy, distinct native Hawaiian culture, and many other assets. It faces significant challenges such as very high housing prices and the impact of rising sea levels and ocean warming on its coasts and coral reefs.

The census estimate of the racial composition of Kauai's 72,293 residents as of 2019—based on respondents' self-reporting using the (questionable) census categories—was 29% White alone Not Hispanic or Latino; 31% Asian alone; 9% Native Hawaiian and other Pacific Islander alone; 26% two or more races; 11% Hispanic or Latino; and a little over 1% either Black/African American or American Indian or Alaska Native alone. About 10% of Kauai's residents are in poverty as defined by the U.S. census. These percents exceed 100% because some respondents fall into more than one category.

Much of the *Kaua'I Kākou* plan focuses on preserving and protecting the island's environmental resources and native Hawaiian culture. Housing affordability is a major feature of the plan.

The *Kaua'I Kākou Plan* projects that the population of Kauai will continue to increase by a little over 1% per year on average during the 20-year life of the plan. Most population growth is projected to occur in Kauai's two largest settlements—Lihue (population 6,500), and Ka'a (population 10,000)—both of which are unincorporated places. Most other settlements in Kauai are small historical settlements on the coast.

Kauai's existing housing stock consists of a mix of single-family homes and condominiums in the two major urban areas, small towns, and rural areas of the county. Property prices per square foot are high. Much of Kauai's housing stock consists of second homes. Forty-five percent of the housing units on Kauai are owned either by people who live in on the U.S. mainland or in other countries. Forty-four percent of Kauai's households are cost burdened—paying more than 30% of their income for housing.

Tourism is Kauai's largest industry. More than a million visitors per year provide about one-third of the island's income. The *Kaua'I Kākou* plan projects that tourism will grow and does not try to slow that growth. More than a quarter of Kauai's 27,000 jobs are in accommodation and food services. About 15% each are in government and retail. Kauai has fertile land and produces guavas, coffee, sugarcane, mangos, bananas, papayas, avocados, pineapples, and other fruits and vegetables. The *Kaua'I Kākou* plan tries to strike a balance between economic development to provide jobs and revenue, protecting the island's unique character, and keeping some housing affordable to middle- and low-income resident households.

GENERAL PLAN MAKING

It typically takes two to three years to prepare a new general plan. A year or more of studies often precedes the kickoff of a general planning process. The *Kaua'I Kākou* general planning process took 23 months, the *Plano Tomorrow* process 26 months, *planokc* 31 months, and the *NashvilleNext Plan* 3 years. In California it usually takes an additional year for general plans to be completed because the California Environmental Quality Act (CEQA) requires a full environmental review of general plans.

General plans usually have a 20 to 25-year time frame before communities prepare a major update or a new general plan. Some cities adopt one or more new plan elements before they comprehensively update their general plans. There may be a gap between plans. The *Plano Tomorrow* plan was Plano's first comprehensive new general plan in 29 years, though the prior plan was regularly and frequently updated incrementally.

Almost all city plans are developed by the city planning department, most county plans by the county planning department, and most consolidated city-county plans by the metro government's planning department. Many planning departments rely on consultants to help prepare, monitor, and update the general plan. Large cities may hire consultants for political reasons so that they can point to expert external recommendations and let the consultants take the heat. Small cities often rely on consultants for staffing if they do not have enough staff qualified to prepare a general plan. In some small cities and counties, the general plan is prepared entirely by an outside consultant under the direction of the city or county planning department, the local planning commission, and local elected officials.

The way in which Plano, Texas developed their plan was unusual. It was prepared by city staff who were not in the planning department. There were no outside consultants and little citizen input. The Plano Planning and Zoning Commission acted only as an advisory committee. This created problems, because there were limited citizen advocates when the plan was challenged. Even though it won a Burnham award, Plano repealed the plan. As of winter, 2022, a 16-member committee is working preparing a revised general plan.

City and county planning departments generally distinguish advance planning, which deals with the general plan and other long-range planning, from current planning, which deals with review of current development proposals. If the department has an advance planning unit, its staff do most of the work on the general plan.

General plans use U.S. census and other federal, state, and local data. Planning departments may conduct their own background studies or commission studies to gather additional data on which to base the plan before they kick off the general planning process. Background studies typically focus on current conditions but may include longitudinal data from the past and projections to the future. If a city or county decides to do new background research before beginning a general plan process, it usually takes two or more years to decide on which new studies to do and to complete the background research. The studies are public.

The *Kaua'I Kākou* plan illustrates how a local government can make good use of existing information and supplement it with additional research on critical topics. Phase 1 of the *Kaua'I Kākou* planning process included preparation of six technical reports dealing with economics, climate change, health, agriculture, land use, and infrastructure. The *Kaua'I Kākou* plan used National Oceanic and Atmospheric Administration (NOAA) data and a NOAA visualization tool called the digital coast sea level rise viewer that allows users to simulate the extent of inundation likely at high tide after various amounts of sea level rise. Five tabs on the NOAA digital sea coast viewer show sea-level rise, confidence, marsh, vulnerability, and frequency. They allow viewers to visualize changes in each category on maps using a slider bar. The *Kaua'I Kākou* plan is based on the county's existing *Energy Sustainability Plan* (2010). It sets Kauai's target for reduction of greenhouse gas (GHG) emissions to zero, consistent with state policy. The Kauai planning department commissioned a new *Kauai Climate Change and Coastal Hazards Assessment* (2014) as one of the technical studies for the part of the plan describing likely coastal hazard impacts of climate change and policies for climate change adaptation, resiliency, and mitigation. Nashville and Oklahoma City also commissioned new studies for their general plans.[2]

CITIZEN AND STAKEHOLDER INPUT

Every city and county has some form of citizen participation and collaborative planning in preparation of their general plan. Most cities encourage degrees of participation in planning toward the top rungs of what Sherri Arnstein describes as a ladder of citizen participation in her classic article, described in Chapter 9. Advocacy planners representing different interest groups participate in some general planning. The State of California has developed a set of recommended tools for citizen participation in general planning in each of the state's 58 counties and 482 cities.[3] Kauai County's *Kaua'I Kākou* plan process involved 32 months of island-wide input.[4] Nashville, and Oklahoma City used many of the same citizen participation tools as Kauai.

Citizen participation related to general plans usually ebbs after the plan is completed. Philadelphia is notable for its efforts to educate its citizens in planning on an ongoing basis through a unique organization—the Philadelphia Citizens Planning Institute (CPI). CPI is the education and outreach arm of the Philadelphia City Planning Commission. The Institute offers eight-week evening courses each spring and fall for neighborhood residents to provide them with a greater understanding of city planning. The course includes seven classes on planning issues and principles; land use; zoning; and the development process and three electives, which change each session. Instructors include planning commissioners, planning department staff, city officials, developers, and neighborhood leaders. Nearly 600 participants have completed the program.

VISIONS

A vision is a very broad, slightly utopian statement of what the community hopes to become. General plans typically begin with an explicit vision statement. Sometimes the vision statement comes from a vision planning process as described in Chapter 6, but general plan vision statements often grow out of the general planning process itself.

Plano's vision statement is the single sentence: "Plano is a global leader, excelling in exceptional education, abounding with world class businesses, and vibrant neighborhoods." The *Plano Tomorrow* webpage contains a link to a video titled "Plano's future" that describes Plano's vision in detail. The *Kaua'I Kākou* plan articulates what it calls "a vision grounded in reality" with four key components, to make Kauai: 1) a sustainable island, 2) a unique and beautiful place, 3) healthy and resilient, and 4) equitable. The *NashvilleNext Plan* combines the city's vision with information on the city's trends and strategy. It operationalizes the vision, trends, and strategy with seven "guiding principles".[5] Oklahoma City summarizes its vision with seven "big ideas".[6]

Substantive visions are as varied as the communities themselves. Communities may envision themselves as residential towns, technology centers, mining centers, company towns, college towns, historic cities, global cities, or retirement communities among others. Planning for sustainability, walkability, bikeability, equity, and diversity are common themes. So are environmental stewardship, smart growth, resilience, beauty, and "healthy city" planning. Moving towards zero net carbon emissions, and net zero automobile fatalities are increasingly listed among general plan visions.

PLAN ELEMENTS

Edward Bassett and T.J. Kent—the planning pioneers who developed master and general planning—called parts of a master or general plan "elements". Many states use this terminology in their state planning laws.[7] California's list of general plan elements and the state's description of what they should contain is one of the most comprehensive. It includes:

- **Land Use:** designates the type, intensity, and general distribution of uses of land for housing, business, industry, open space, education, public buildings and grounds, waste disposal facilities, and other categories of public and private uses.
- **Circulation:** correlates with the land use element and identifies the general location and extent of existing and proposed major thoroughfares, transportation routes, terminals, and other local public utilities and facilities.
- **Housing:** assesses current and projected housing needs for all economic segments of the community. In addition, the housing element embodies policies for providing adequate housing and includes action programs for that purpose. By statute, the housing element must be updated every five or eight years, according to a schedule set by the State Department of Housing and Community Development (HCD).
- **Conservation:** addresses the conservation, development, and use of natural resources, including water, forests, soils, rivers, and mineral deposits.
- **Open Space:** details plans and measures for the long-range preservation and conservation of open space lands, including open space for the preservation of natural resources, the managed production of resources, agriculture, outdoor recreation, and public health and safety.
- **Noise:** identifies and appraises noise problems within the community and forms the basis for land use distribution determinations.
- **Safety:** establishes policies and programs to protect the community from risks associated with seismic, geologic, flood, and wildfire hazards, as well as from other concerns such as drought.
- **Environmental justice:** identifies objectives and policies to reduce pollution exposure, improve air quality, promote public facilities, improve food access, advance access to housing, and increase physical activity in identified disadvantaged communities.[8]

California general plan elements must be internally consistent and consistent with each other. Diagrams must be consistent with the plan text. Not all other states require this kind of consistency.

Preparation of a new general plan or a major update in California is considered a discretionary legislative action that requires an environmental impact assessment. Other states do not require environmental impact analysis when general plans are adopted or substantially revised.

While they are not required, cities and counties in California may include permissive elements of their choice in their general plans. The most common permissive elements California cities choose to include are parks and recreation, public facilities, design, and economic development/commerce. Counties often include an agricultural element. Coastal cities and counties may include an element to reduce smog (a mixture of fog and air pollution). Other permissive elements in California general plans include childcare, archeology, geothermal resources, arts, parking, trails, and—recently—anthropogenic (human caused) climate change.

GOALS AND OBJECTIVES

Most general plans operationalize their elements with goals. A goal is a statement of a desired end state—the object or purpose of part of the plan. French author Antoine de Saint-Exupéry called a goal without a plan "just a wish". San Francisco's general plan goals include:

Protection, preservation, and enhancement of the economic, social, cultural, and aesthetic values that establish the desirable quality and unique character of the city.
  Coordination of the varied pattern of land use with circulation routes and facilities required for the efficient movement of people and goods within the city, and to and from the city.
Coordination of the growth and development of the city with the growth and development of adjoining cities and counties and of the San Francisco Bay Region.

Goals may, in turn, be broken down into objectives. An objective is like a goal, but objectives are narrower and more specific than goals. San Francisco's general plan objectives include, among many others: development of adequate sites to meet the city's housing needs, especially permanently affordable housing; maintaining and enhancing a sound and diverse economic base and fiscal structure for the city; and meeting the needs of all residents and visitors for safe, convenient, and inexpensive travel within San Francisco and between the city and other parts of the region while maintaining the high-quality living environment of the Bay Area.

POLICIES AND STANDARDS

Policies in a general plan are descriptions of how to achieve the general plan's goals and objectives. The number of policies can vary greatly. The *Kaua'I Kākou* plan contains 18 policies that reflect Kauai's situation as a fragile tropical island with a strong native Hawaiian culture.[9] *Plano Tomorrow*'s plan elements—which they call "pillars"—have five to nine policies each—41 policies in all.

Standards operationalize goals and objectives. They describe minimum quantifiable targets that must be attained. For example, traffic level of service (LOS) standards are ordered from level A—in which traffic is flowing freely—to level F in which traffic is stop-and-go or does not move at all.

INITIATIVES AND ACTION ITEMS

General plans contain material on plan implementation that describe implementation tools the city or county will use and how they intend to achieve their vision, goals, and objectives. Implementation tools include zoning; subdivision control; site planning; growth management; transfer of development rights (TDRs); housing and building codes; form-based codes; transects and other tools described in Chapter 8.

Descriptions of how the local government intends to implement the plan may provide descriptions of action items the community intends to take to implement the plan's goals and objectives. These may specify benchmark dates by which goals and objectives are to be accomplished. They usually describe which parts of city government will be responsible for completing each action item and which agency will act as the lead agency coordinating work of all agencies involved if more than one agency is working to implement the action item. They may specify a budget for each action item.[10] Some cities include the names and contact information of individual city staff members responsible for specific implementation tasks so that it is easy for citizens and others to contact them. Other cities make contacting the appropriate staff person difficult.

The *Plano Tomorrow* plan includes 273 one-sentence action statements. These contain measurable objectives strategically linked to the broader, more aspirational goals in the *Plano Tomorrow* policies. The action statements have links to related and supporting material so that readers can drill down and understand how the policies and action statements were formulated. For example, the digital version of the *Plano Tomorrow* plan's transit-oriented development (TOD) subsection has links to six supporting resources such as the *Dallas Area Rapid Transit-Oriented Development Guidelines,* and fact sheets on two transit stations. The plan indicates the status of each action statement—pending, in progress, or completed. Illustrative *Plano Tomorrow* action statements include: "create an interactive undeveloped land map updated on a quarterly basis and post to the city's website for public use", "create end of trip amenity guidelines, such as bicycle parking and shower facilities to encourage bicycle transportation", and "work with area cities to develop a policy regarding high occupancy vehicle (HOV) access and congestion pricing".

The *Kaua'I Kākou* plan operationalizes actions by sector for each of ten sectors. For each sector the plan describes implementation tools—seven major ways in which actions will be implemented. Since Kauai is a global hot spot for biodiversity with a fragile environment, one of the actions Kauai proposes is to protect its watershed and threatened and endangered species. Six policy maps illustrate visually how implementation of these actions will affect Kauai County.[11]

Nashville operationalizes specific tasks for metro departments and partners to undertake each year. Volume four of their general plan is an action plan describing specific annual action items. The action plan is updated each year with progress reports and modifications as needed. Each of Nashville's action items is linked to one or more policies. Each action item includes a timeline. Items may be ongoing, immediate (with work to start immediately), near term (starting within one to three years), mid-term (beginning within four to seven years) or long term (with work delayed for seven to ten years). Unless the action is entirely in the private or nonprofit sector, each action item specifies the metro agency or agencies and partners most likely to carry out the action.

Planokc includes a policies and implementation matrix that lists all policies from each element of the plan, and the goals and initiatives each policy addresses. For example, the matrix shows that Oklahoma City's greenokc initiative #8 "enrich biodiversity and natural habitats in urban, suburban, and agricultural areas" will contribute to greenokc goals "(#1) valuing, protecting, and preserving the city's biological resources", "(#2) protecting safe drinking water, conserving waterways, wetlands and other water resources, and protecting water quality", and (#10) "pursuing green and sustainable development by context-sensitive development and redevelopment to support a healthy balance between the built and natural environments." The matrix includes columns describing the type of policy, the responsible parties, and a start-by date for the policy.

Plano, Texas's action statements are short and to the point. For example, four of eight transit- oriented development (TOD) action statements under Plano's land use and community design policies and actions operationalize Plano's TOD policy as follows:

Prioritize and prepare station area plans to guide development patterns within ½ mile of identified transit stations.
Rezone property within ½ mile of transit stations to encourage urban design and increase development opportunities.
Establish parking maximums in transit-served areas and identified compact complete centers.
Develop plans for the K Avenue/DART light rail and the 14th Street/Cotton Belt commuter rail corridors to address redevelopment of retail and multifamily sites and encourage new development around transit stations.

MONITORING, UPDATING, AND CHANGING GENERAL PLANS

Once a general plan is completed, three important issues are: how to monitor progress towards implementing the plan, when and how to update or change parts of the plan, and when to do a major update or prepare an entirely new plan.

Many cities and counties monitor progress on plan implementation and action items as frequently as once a year. If they see that they are falling behind, the following year they may focus more attention and resources on the action items that are not getting done on time.

General plan changes need to balance continuity and stability so that citizens, developers, and policy makers can rely on them against the need to change as conditions and opinions change. They need to be changed in an orderly and transparent way. Kent and Bassett envisioned paper general plans that would last 20 plus years with only occasion amendments. In 1955 Harvard law professor Charles Haar called general plans "impermanent constitutions" that he envisioned would "sit atop the pyramid" of zoning and other local land use regulations. Since Bassett, Kent, and Haar articulated their ideas, the world has become more complex, change more rapid, and perceptions of what cities and regions can be like more varied. Digital technology has made it easier to change plans. General plans still serve as impermanent constitutions for physical development. Conceptualizing their parts as elements is still helpful. However, when necessary, modern digital general plans can be changed frequently and all parts of the plan conformed to the changes immediately.

General plans are long-range documents. The *Kaua'I Kākou* and *NashvilleNext* plans have 20- and 25-year time frames respectively. The Plano and *planokc* general plans are open-ended—they do not specify an ending date. Even if a general plan specifies a time frame, it may not be completed or revised on schedule. Some cities and counties simply fail to adopt a new general plan at the end of the plan's time period. Oklahoma City's 2015 *planokc* was the city's first new general plan since 1977, adopted 18 years after the end of the city's original 1977 general plan. Some cities do a comprehensive revision of only one or a few elements at one time. For example, if a city council decides that the transportation element of their general plan is out of date, they may instruct the city planning department to prepare a comprehensive update of just the transportation element (and adjust other elements to be consistent if they consider that is important, or state law requires them to be consistent). Small changes to general plans are common. California law authorizes up to four general plan changes a year. The Oklahoma City Council amended the *planokc* plan 12 times in its first two years.

NEIGHBORHOOD PLANNING

Many cities and some counties have neighborhood plans. These may be part of the general plan or independent of it. Some are top-down plans that the city prepares in partnership with neighborhood associations; others are bottom-up plans that arise spontaneously from grassroots neighborhood activism.

Neighborhoods are defined in many ways based on their function, history, culture, architectural style, or the predominant race, gender, religion, or sexual orientation of their residents. The Vieux Carré (Old Quarter) in New Orleans; Greenwich Village in New York City; Back Bay in Boston, Massachusetts; Savannah, Georgia's Historic District; Monterey Park in Southern California; and San Francisco's Castro District are examples of neighborhoods defined by historic, cultural, ethnic, and gender orientations.

Some neighborhoods are officially designated by local governments with sharp boundaries. Others are not officially designated and have fuzzy boundaries. Preserving and strengthening neighborhood identity can provide support for diverse residents and add life and interest to places.

The *NashvilleNext* plan includes 14 community plans. Each community plan contains about 35 pages of text, maps, and diagrams, and references and links to much more material. Each describes the role the community plays in realizing the plan's overall vision.

Nashville's 2017 *Community Character Manual* provides the overall framework for all 14 of Nashville's community plans. Each is tailored to local conditions. Each community plan describes community character (land use) policies based on 11 categories in the manual. The plans form the basis for zoning and guide public and private investment in the community. All of the community plans contain a community profile, history of the neighborhood, a description of the community planning process, inventory of natural features and resources in the community, analysis of the community's role in the city and region, and goals, objectives, and implementation strategies for residential and economic development. They describe the community's streets, sidewalks, parks, stormwater collectors, and other public facilities.

SUMMARY

Having a comprehensive plan to guide the future of a community is a noble goal. What "comprehensive" means, how to decide what content it should contain, how it should be prepared and communicated, and ultimately the normative questions of what the community's vision and goals should be, go to the heart of city and regional planning. Historically many comprehensive U.S. city and regional plans were called master plans. Most today are called general plans.

Current general plans are important documents. They educate citizens, policy makers, and the planners themselves. They crystalize and operationalize the planning process. They provide a framework for other plans. General plans provide what University of North Carolina city and regional planning professors Edward Kaiser and David Godschalk (1995) call the "sturdy trunk" of planning's "stalwart family tree" from which not only local physical plans grow, but also provide a summary of a community's normative values from which "branches" such as strategic, design, and management plans may grow and flourish.

In the last three decades digital technology and new analytics have provided revolutionary new tools for formulating general plans. General plans' contents have become much more sophisticated and encompass a much wider range of issues than in the past. As the quality of general plans has improved, they are taken much more seriously. This has created a virtuous circle in which impactful general plans lead to ever better planning.

General plans' visions, goals, objectives, standards, and how well they are implemented impact people's lives. Preparing and implementing them are exciting city and regional planning activities—difficult, but rewarding, work.

CONCEPTS

Advance Planning
Comprehensive Plan
Current Planning
Element (of a General Plan)
General Plan
Master Plan

PEOPLE

Edward Bassett
Charles Haar
T.J. (Jack) Kent

NOTES

1 The community types are civic, conservation, open space, transition natural, rural, suburban, urban, center, downtown, and districts. Many of the community types include sub-types. For example the T2 category "rural" includes T2-RA "rural agriculture", T2-RCS "rural countryside", T2-RM "rural maintenance", and T2-NC "rural neighborhood centers".

2 Nashville updated pre-existing plans for 14 community planning areas and used an existing transportation plan—*Access Nashville 2040*—for the transportation element of the *NashvilleNext* general plan. Oklahoma City's background studies for *planokc* included a *Land Needs Assessment and Action Plan, Community Appearance Survey, Retail Plan, Employment Plan, Parks Master Plan, Housing Market Study, Health Impact Assessment*, and growth scenario analyses of three scenarios: past trends continued, trends+market+ efficiency, and market+ efficiency+revitalization.

3 The California Office of Planning and Research (OPR) describes ten recommended citizen participation engagement tools—meetings; workshops; events; activities; tours; open houses; surveys—particularly community image surveys; web-based meetings and engagement tools; postal and e-mail mailings; design charettes (a term architects use for intense review of a draft plan); and a tool called "Photo Voice" (a participatory method where users can capture elements about the environment and use them as a starting point for a discussion about their community) (California Governor's OPR, 2017: 35–39).

4 A 17-member citizen advisory committee (CAC) with county and state representatives oversaw Kauai's general plan process. The Kauai public engagement process had three phases: visioning, policy and land use outreach, and discussion draft outreach. Tools Kauai used to involve citizens included a website; e-mail list; Facebook and Instagram pages; a video; and newspaper articles and advertisements. Planning staff began the public participation process with a community-wide kickoff meeting. They held small group meetings

with 34 community organizations at schools, farms, bike paths, libraries, the local farmers' market, the county fair, and pop-up locations. The department created a *Kauai'I Kākou* logo and distributed T-shirts, pens, stickers, and water bottles to advertise the planning process and encourage participation. They involved the public in visioning sessions early in the planning process; bus and walking tours; mapping sessions; and discussions of the draft plan towards the end of the planning process. They reached out to involve young people in primary, middle, and high schools and the local community college. Outreach to youth included a *Keiki* (Youth) art contest on the theme "I love my island because …". The plan documents the citizen participation process and describes how citizen input was incorporated into the plan.

5   Nashville's seven general plan "guiding principles" are (1) ensure opportunity for all, (2) expand accessibility, (3) create economic prosperity, (4) foster strong neighborhoods, (5) advance education, (6) champion the environment, and (7) be Nashville.

6   Oklahoma City's seven "big ideas" are to (1) develop a transportation system that works for everyone, (2) increase housing choice and diversity for all lifestyles, (3) build an urban environment that facilitates health and wellness, (4) develop great places that attract people and catalyze development and innovation, (5) ensure stable, safe, attractive, and vibrant neighborhoods, (6) develop efficiently to achieve fiscal sustainability and improve our quality of life, and (7) and preserve the city's rural character and natural resources.

7   The *Plano Tomorrow* plan calls its plan elements "pillars". The five pillars are (1) built environment, (2) social environment, (3) natural environment, (4) economic environment, and (5) regionalism. The pillars are similar to Nashville's seven guiding principles, but call attention to the importance Plano attaches to regional planning and education. The *NashvilleNext* plan is organized into five parts they call volumes rather than plan elements.

8   California's environmental justice element's goals, policies, and objectives do not have to appear as a single standalone plan element. They may be integrated into other elements so long as they: (a) identify objectives and policies to reduce the unique or compounded health risks in disadvantaged communities by reducing pollution exposure, (b) identify objectives and policies to promote civil engagement in the public decision-making process and (c) identify objectives and policies that prioritize improvements and programs that address the needs of disadvantaged communities.

9   Kauai's 18 general plan policies are: design healthy and complete neighborhoods; make strategic infrastructure investments; reduce the cost of living; build a balanced transportation system; manage growth to preserve rural character; uphold Kauai as a unique visitor destination; protect Kauai's scenic beauty; help business thrive; help agricultural lands be productive; protect watersheds; complete Kauai's shift to clean energy; prepare for climate change; provide local housing; recognize the identity of Kauai's individual towns and districts; respect Native Hawaiian rights and *Wahi Pana* (sacred places); nurture *Keiki* (children); honor *Kūpuna* (elders); and communicate with *Aloha* (affection; compassion for others).

10 General plan policies include: actions to control urban sprawl, integrate water resource management programs, reduce air pollution from point and mobile sources, conserve critical habitat with a habitat conservation plan, designate 100-year flood plains, use hard and soft protect strategies to eliminate or reduce flooding, implement the Clean Air and Clean Water Acts, protect endangered or threatened plant and animal species, require U.S. Green Building Council Leadership in Energy and Environmental Design (LEED) building standards, calm traffic, improve the level of service (LOS) on streets, integrate multi-modal transit, implement complete street plans, improve street livability, provide adequate public facilities, add recharging stations for all electric Zero Emission Vehicles, improve walkability and bikeability, provide affordable housing, enforce fair housing laws, improve parks, increase and better manage open space, carry out community development with community development block grants (CDBGs) and other funding, support economic development, and neighborhood revitalization projects, and develop and implement climate action plans.

11 The *Kaua'I Kākou Plan* operationalizes actions in 11 areas including housing, critical infrastructure, heritage resources, energy sustainability, and opportunity and health for all. The plan groups Kauai's implementation tools into four categories: permitting and code changes, plans and studies, projects and programs, and partnership needs. It identifies the tools that can be applied to ten sectors such as watershed, housing, transportation, and heritage resources. For example, six permitting and code change action items include (a) avoiding development or land use intensification on critical habitats and in areas that are essential to the health, safety, and life of vulnerable native species, and (b) developing and adopting landscape guidelines that require non-invasive plant species to landscape newly developed areas, and public lands, and (c) roadways minimizing risks to threatened and endangered species in construction and development activity. Kauai's six policy maps illustrate future land use, heritage resources, hazards, infrastructure, public facilities, and transportation.

SUGGESTIONS FOR FURTHER LEARNING

Plan Making: Allan Jacobs, *Making city planning work* (1980). Lewis Hopkins, *Urban development: The logic of making plans* (2001). **Current**

Texts Describing General Plans: John Levy, *Contemporary urban planning*, 11th ed (2016). Barry Cullingworth & Roger Caves, *Planning in the USA*, 2nd ed (2022). Gary Hack, Eugenie Birch, Paul Sedway, & Mitchell Silver, *Local planning: Contemporary principles and practice* (2009). William Fulton & Paul Shigley, *Guide to California Planning*, 5th ed (2018). **Historical Material on Master and General Plans:** Edward Bassett, *The master plan* (1938). Charles Haar, The master plan: An impermanent constitution (1955). T.J. (Jack) Kent, *The urban general plan* (1964). U.S. Department of Commerce Standard City Planning Enabling Act (1928). Edward Kaiser & David Godschalk Twentieth century land use planning: A stalwart family tree (1995). **Digital General Plans:** Pete Sullivan, *Digital zoning codes and comprehensive plans* (2017). **The American Planning Association (APA) Burnham Awards:** APA national planning awards [website] (2021). **The *NashvilleNext* Plan:** *NashvilleNext plan* (2016), NashvilleNext [website] (2021). *NashvilleNext* [video] (2016). **Plano Tomorrow Plan:** *Plano tomorrow* (2017). Plano tomorrow [website] *(2021)*. American Planning Association, *Plano tomorrow comprehensive plan* [video] (2017). ***planokc:*** *planokc* (2015). planokc website (2021). American Planning Association, *planokc* [video] (2015). **Kaua'i Kākou Plan:** *Kaua'i Kākou plan* (2018). Kaua'I County, *Kaua'I Kākou plan*. American Planning Association, *Kaua'I Kākou plan* [video] (2018). **The Philadelphia Citizens Planning Institute (CPI):** CPI website (2021).

CHAPTER 8

Implementing Plans

INTRODUCTION

Like a skilled woodworker, the modern planner has a toolkit with many plan implementation tools. The art of plan implementation—like the art of woodworking—requires mastering which combination of tools to use for different purpose. Scientific methods are necessary, but not sufficient.

Plan implementation requires promoting the plan, navigating complex laws and regulations, overcoming bureaucratic and political barriers, meeting budget limits, and adjusting to financial surprises. It requires judgment about what is possible in a given context. Except for small site plans, the final design of transportation projects, and plans that will be completed by a single developer, plans are rarely implemented exactly as they were conceived. However, as American polymath, Benjamin Franklin quipped: "By failing to prepare, you are preparing to fail."

Planners need to understand the limits of their own competence and when to turn to experts for legal advice. A planner with good people skills or who is known and trusted in a community may become the lead person communicating with the community. Planners with a law degree or, better yet, both law and planning degrees, may take special responsibility for guiding a plan through the legal minefield. Planners involved with zoning, land subdivision, urban growth management, or plans that require taking land by eminent domain, need to be familiar with applicable law. Architects, urban designers, and planners with a design specialty work on design review. Civil engineers will likely do most of the infrastructure planning for a city or county.

Implementation tools are necessary, but they do not make a plan. That requires creativity, normative planning, and political skill. Box 8.1 is a biography of Allan Jacobs—a University of California, Berkeley professor of city and regional planning and former San Francisco planning director who wrote about his experiences making city planning work in San Francisco.

PLAN PROMOTION

Convincing the public, stakeholders, and government officials of a plan's merit and garnering their support are critical to making city planning work. Plan promotion involves a combination of education, politics, public relations, collaborative planning, and city branding.

Great plans have succeeded in part because of how they were promoted. Ebenezer Howard, Daniel Burnham, and Thomas Adams skillfully promoted the Letchworth and Welwyn garden city plans, the 1909 *Plan for Chicago* and the 1929 *Plan of New York City and Its Environs* discussed in Chapter 2. Ebenezer Howard's brilliant diagrams and lectures on garden cities to any group that would listen helped get Letchworth Garden City built. Daniel Burnham's distribution of *Wacker's Manual of the Plan of Chicago* to every resident and every 8th grader in Chicago helped him get public support that made it possible to implement parts of his city beautiful vision that are evident in Chicago today. Thomas Adams's and the Regional Plan Association (RPA)'s tireless promotion of the 1929 *Regional*

BOX 8.1 ALLAN JACOBS

Allan Jacobs (born 1928) is a distinguished planning educator and practitioner. He was San Francisco's planning director between 1967 and 1975 and taught at the University of California, Berkeley's Department of City and Regional Planning from 1974 to 2002. Jacobs is a world authority on street and boulevard design. His 1978 book, *Making City Planning Work*, alternates chapters describing Jacobs's day-to-day activities as planning director with case studies. Jacobs's classic case studies provide a blow-by-blow account of his most notable successes and failures. They are a unique firsthand account of how a principled planning director can defend his normative planning values in the face of political and bureaucratic opposition. Jacobs candidly discusses his own education as a planning director including failures and lessons learned. He reports that he always kept his bags packed in case he was fired or felt compelled to resign on principle.

A bumper sticker some planners favor says "the process is the plan". Jacobs disagrees. His suggested alternative is "the plan is the plan". Jacobs agrees that a good planning process is necessary, but concluded it is not sufficient. What really matter is the plan outcome—how well it actually meets the need the plan was intended to fill.

Initially Jacobs got along well with San Francisco's opinionated and strong-willed mayor, Joseph Alioto, despite Alioto's laissez-faire pro-development orientation and lack of enthusiasm for planning and planners. Relations became strained when Alioto considered running for governor of California or vice-president of the United States and pressured Jacobs to support his political ambitions. Jacobs refused to lend his reputation to Alioto's politicking.

Figure 8.1 Allan Jacobs.

San Francisco is a combined city-county and its governing body is the San Francisco board of supervisors. Jacobs developed good relations with members of San Francisco's board of supervisors—mainly because of his professionalism and quick and thorough responses to questions the supervisors posed. The supervisors supported his proposals for neighborhood planning and greater citizen participation, increasing open space, federally assisted code enforcement, and urban beautification projects. These were quite successful. However, his efforts to limit the height of buildings that he considered too tall or the bulk of buildings he felt were out of scale were controversial. The board of supervisors often failed to approve his recommendations on building heights and bulk.

Jacobs reports that his relations with the board of supervisors soured when the board refused to back his objections to a proposal to build a 55-story downtown corporate headquarters building—the Transamerica Pyramid Building—that had strong business backing and that the supervisors supported. The project required a street closure that Jacobs opposed. He considered the building out of scale. The proposed building would block views and change the fabric of the area. Jacobs's professional expertise as an urban designer clashed with the supervisors' concern with accommodating one of the city's most powerful corporations that provided jobs and property tax revenue to the city. Jacobs and the planning commissioners drew further apart when the commissioners failed to take Jacobs's professional advice on precedent-setting matters, gave more weight to other professionals than to planning department staff, ignored their own policies, and particularly when they voted on major planning and design issues for purely political reasons.

Jacobs got along well with the media. He often worked with neighborhood groups and professional organizations of architects and planners who agreed with him and were willing to serve as surrogates to support his views. He increased community participation. He successfully implemented visible and appreciated urban beautification projects.

Jacobs fought with San Francisco's large, powerful Public Works Department which could frustrate his projects by foot dragging. He developed the power to thwart public works projects he opposed by mobilizing citizen support and working with individual supervisors who agreed with him. Jacobs lost battles to protect views that he believed in preserving, based on principles Kevin Lynch, Donald Appleyard, and he had developed years earlier at the Massachusetts Institute of Technology.

Jacobs also fought with the San Francisco Civil Service Commission. The commission kept him from hiring staff he wanted. He felt that they wasted countless hours of his time with needless red tape. After leaving office, Jacobs wrote a parody imagining what it would have been like if a clever lawyer discovered that the San Francisco Giants baseball team was protected by the San Francisco Civil Service Commission. The commission made it almost impossible to hire and manage the team.[1]

Jacobs considers his greatest success to be San Francisco's *Urban Design Plan*, adopted in 1971. Few cities at that time had city-wide urban design plans, and the plans that existed dealt almost entirely with aesthetics. *The San Francisco Urban Design Plan* took three years to complete. Jacobs took time for field surveys and public discussion of a series of intermediate reports. The final *Urban Design Plan* included 4 objectives, 86 principles, and 45 policies that dealt with the physical and sensory relationships between San Franciscans and their environment. It operationalized Kevin Lynch's theories about the image of the city discussed in Chapter 3 and showed how Lynch's five urban form elements could be applied to strengthen San Francisco's image. Unlike other proposals that attracted little or no interest, Jacobs's initial presentation to the mayor, supervisors, department heads and other San Francisco notables was a smashing success. In a follow-up meeting 1,300 people enthusiastically watched a three-screen presentation. Jacobs attributes his success with the *Urban Design Plan* to the three-year planning process, multiple studies and reports, and a highly professional final plan.

Plan of New York and Its Environs is largely responsible for the freeway and park system in the New York region. City branding is an important activity of local governments and private city chambers of commerce.

THE LEGAL AND REGULATORY FRAMEWORK OF PLANNING

The United States is a litigious society. City and regional planners are critical players in implementing planning-related laws and regulations. The most important are U.S. Federal constitutional law and state constitutional and land use law.

Legal treatises on land use law summarize what the law is, and law school land use law casebooks contain the text of important legal decisions related to land use law. These are often used in graduate U.S. city and regional planning law courses. There are also treatises and casebooks on environmental, housing, and transportation law, and other legal topics of interest to planners.

The United States has no national city and regional planning law. Authority to define urban planning within a state is left to the states, so long as it is not preempted by the U.S. Constitution or a federal law. States, in turn, delegate responsibility for most planning to local governments. Cities and counties enact their own subdivision, zoning, building, housing, growth management, and other planning-related municipal ordinances consistent with state law.

The U.S. Constitution and federal laws preempt (override) state and local law that conflicts with them. A great deal of planning-related litigation involves whether or not state or local laws conflict with federal law and, accordingly, whether a federal law does or does not preempt them. If the federal government has passed a law that applies nationwide, state and local courts must follow it. Conflicts involving federal law are resolved in federal courts.

There is a robust property rights movement in the United States. Organizations representing private property owners monitor planning that impacts private property rights. They are well funded by conservative corporations and conservative foundations. Plans that arguably overreach government authority or take land without just compensation are likely to end up in court. Conservative private property rights organizations such as the Cato Institute, Pacific Legal Foundation, and the Goldwater Institute have developed pro-property rights legal theory and have won many lawsuits protecting private property rights since the early 1980s. For the last 45 years the U.S. Supreme Court has had a conservative majority. Key Supreme Court cases have defined property rights expansively limiting the power of government plans, regulations, and programs that conservatives feel encroach on private property rights.

Federal laws such as the National Environmental Protection Act (NEPA), Moving Ahead for Progress in the 21st Century (MAP-21) Act, Home Investment Partnership (HOME) program, Clean Air Act, Clean Water Act, Endangered Species Act, and the Empowerment Zone/Enterprise Communities (EZ/EC) Act influence state and local planning for the natural environment, transportation, housing, air and water quality, protection of endangered species, urban revitalization, and other planning issues. They specify rules that states and their legal subdivisions must follow. They often provide funding, and may make non-binding recommendations.

Local governments derive their legal authority to regulate land use from the police power—a doctrine imported from British common law. The police power grants local government the power to protect public health, safety, welfare, and morals. Zoning, subdivision, and growth management ordinances; housing and building codes; and other planning regulations are based on the police power. So long as there is a reasonable basis for a local ordinance, and it is not arbitrary or capricious, courts will uphold it if they decide that it is justified by one of the police power purposes.

The federal government owns millions of square miles of land—mostly in the continental Western United States, including Alaska. Federal government agencies directly manage some federally owned land.

However, Congress has delegated planning for most federal public land to states to manage in trust, jointly with the federal government—providing another area ripe for litigation to define the limits of federal and state authority.

Most states specify their cities' and counties' power to plan, but do not have a state plan. New Jersey and a few other states have adopted state-level urban development plans. They leave it to local governments to prepare general plans and devise and implement zoning, subdivision, and other land use regulations, and approve development consistent with the state plan. Oregon does not have a state-level urban development plan, but it has adopted 19 statewide planning goals which local (city and county) plans must meet.

Depending on their circumstances, history and political culture, different states have quite different planning laws. How pro- or anti-planning state law is changes over time depending on state-level politics. Texas, a politically conservative state with a long anti-government tradition. Sparsely populated, largely rural, North Dakota has weak planning laws. In contrast, the politically liberal, environmentally conscious states of Oregon, Washington, and New Jersey have strong state planning laws empowering their cities to plan and manage growth and requiring all local plans to be consistent with a state plan. Florida, Maryland, Vermont, and other states have had strong state level growth management laws and policies in the past.

INFRASTRUCTURE AND CAPITAL IMPROVEMENTS PLANNING AND PROGRAMMING

Plan implementation is shaped by the availability of infrastructure and completion of local capital improvements. Infrastructure is built, owned, and maintained by both government and the private sector. Sometimes it is built and operated by public-private partnerships or nonprofit entities.

Basic local infrastructure such as streets, sewers, storm drains, and water and electricity transmissions lines are referred to as capital improvements. At the local level, city and county public works departments implement capital improvement programs (CIPs). Projects to build or maintain public infrastructure are called public works projects. Some city and regional planners work for local public works departments on capital improvement planning and programming. Staff of local planning departments may contribute planning expertise to CIPs.

CIPs provide a framework for the infrastructure element of general plans and other plans. The may include congestion management; "complete streets" plans that include sidewalks and other construction related to streets; and other kinds of transportation plans. CIPs define what infrastructure related to land use, air and water quality, and housing the community will provide. Recently, some cities have passed adequate public facilities ordinances specifying standards for all types of public infrastructure.

City and regional planners are also involved in planning transportation, environmental, energy, communications, community facilities, and other types of infrastructure. Planners at the federal and state levels make plans for federal highways and other major infrastructure projects. At the regional and higher levels, infrastructure planning may involve planning for airports, rail systems, power plants, water distribution systems, the electrical grid, and other large-scale infrastructure. Infrastructure planning is discussed in Chapter 16.

NUISANCE LAW

Nuisance law provides private legal remedies if the activity of one landowner harms other property. Landowners who feel an adjacent or nearby land use is harming them may turn to state nuisance law to try to get a court to force the owner of the offending property to stop the harm and perhaps pay compensation for damage the nuisance has done. Nuisance law in the United States has existed since the early colonial period. In the English colonies nuisance law came from British common law.

If a property owner has a kiln to fire pots in her backyard and smoke blows into a neighbor's yard, the adjacent property owner might petition a state court for an injunction to make the potter stop emitting the smoke and perhaps force her to pay the cost of getting accumulated soot from the kiln off his house. The court will apply state nuisance law principles, which vary from state to state. If there was a lot of smoke and accumulated soot, or if the offended property owner can prove some soot was toxic, he would likely win. If there was just a little occasional smoke the property owner who brought the nuisance case would probably lose. Thousands of small nuisance cases are filed in the United States each year. Individual case-by-case resolution of land use conflicts by nuisance law is slow and costly. At a much larger scale, nuisance law may apply to oil spills, refinery accidents, warehouse explosions and other horrific intrusions on life and property. While nuisance lawsuits or the threat of them serve a purpose, plaintiffs usually rely on federal or state law regulating dangerous uses of land rather than nuisance law in big cases. Large, dense, modern, complex urban areas need systematic legislation to avoid problems that give rise to nuisance cases, so that catastrophic accidents do not occur, and hundreds of nuisance cases are never filed in the first place.

SUBDIVISION REGULATION

Subdivision is the process of surveying and defining the legal boundaries of land parcels before previously undeveloped raw land is developed. When it is time for a private or public developer or public–private partnership to develop a tract of raw land, basic decisions must be made about how many parcels the land will have, the exact parcel boundaries, the type and location of infrastructure needed, and infrastructure standards. Land needs to be surveyed, and precise lot descriptions determined and recorded. Local subdivision ordinances contain standards and engineering requirements and describe the process for converting raw greenfield land—land that has never been developed and is still in its natural state—into developable lots. Subdivision ordinances require local governments to notify nearby landowners and the general public before even tentative subdivisions are established. They specify how citizens can give input at public hearings as planners and local government officials review proposed subdivisions before they are finalized. City and county planning departments review and make recommendations about land subdivision to local elected officials who approve or disapprove subdivision maps.

Not all the land in a community that is planned for development needs to be subdivided initially. Subdivision occurs on a case-by-case basis—usually when the land is ripe for development. It is required if the land is to be sold, leased, or financed as individual parcels.

Subdivision ordinances typically also govern conversion of apartment units to condominiums, as that requires a change of ownership. When the land is converted, title must be transferred from whoever owned the land on which the apartment house rests to shared ownership by condo owners, who own their individual units and a fractional interest in the land. Small divisions of land dividing one parcel into two or more lots—called lot splits—can often be done by a simplified process.

State subdivision law establishes the framework and basic rules of subdivision planning. City and county subdivision ordinances detail local policies consistent with state subdivision law. Subdivision is particularly important for counties—where much of the raw land that will be developed in the future is located.

The subdivision map resulting from the subdivision process specifies the number of parcels, their location, size, and front, side, and rear lot lines. It shows where roads, sewers, electrical lines, storm drains and sites for schools and other public facilities will be located. Subdivision maps do not specify building height and bulk. That is left to the local zoning ordinance.

Legally, subdivision is what lawyers call a quasi-judicial act, similar to a court decision in an individual case, not a legislative act similar to a government passing legislation that applies community-wide. Subdivision is not subject to ballot box planning in which citizens may repeal a law passed by state or local government by a referendum or enact a subdivision ordinance of their own by an initiative. Property owners' rights that are guaranteed without the right of a government to deny them—such as granting a building permit if a property owner's plans comply with a local building code—are called ministerial acts. They are not subject to ballot box planning.

On their face, subdivision ordinances are not very exciting. The don't explicitly deal with sustainable development, climate change, social justice or other issues that citizens and planners care about. Only property owners who stand to make or lose money depending on the details of the subdivision and owners of property adjacent to the subdivision whose land may be impacted pay much attention to them. Their impacts will often not be felt for years. However, astute city and regional planners know that subdivision indirectly impacts important issues like biodiversity and economic segregation. A subdivision that assigns all the land to large parcels may perpetuate spatial segregation because large lots will usually have just one expensive single-family home only wealthy households can afford. Since race and income are correlated, subdivisions with only large lot zoning may indirectly impact racial segregation. A subdivision that reserves environmentally sensitive land as open space may preserve or increase biodiversity and vice versa. The intensity of development on a subdivision will affect its carbon footprint and global climate change.

Subdivision is generally a two-step process resulting first in a tentative and then a final subdivision map. Subdivision maps are sometimes called subdivision plats.

The final subdivision map shows exact individual parcel boundaries after they have been surveyed. It is a legally binding public record. Deeds showing who owns the land are based on the subdivision map. The final subdivision map specifies the types of streets the subdivision will contain—arterial, collector, and minor streets—and engineering standards such as street widths, grades, and center and side strips. The final subdivision map specifies the location of easements for public utilities such as sewers, water mains, and storm drains. Subdivision ordinances usually contain requirements for dedicating land for parks, school sites, police and fire stations, and other public buildings.

Local governments have the power to require developers to dedicate reasonable amounts of land for basic infrastructure and for parks and school sites as a condition for subdivision approval. If a local subdivision ordinance allows the developer to pay cash rather than dedicating land or providing an improvement, this is called an in lieu payment—from the French word "lieu" meaning "place"—literally an "in-place-of" (land) payment. In lieu payments are also called required dedications, exactions, or impact fees. The amount the developer pays must be roughly proportional in terms of benefits and burden to the value of the land that the developer would otherwise have had to dedicate. Local governments may require developers to grant easements on private land for water and electrical lines without paying for them. All of these devices are intended to mitigate negative impacts the development will have on the community.[2] The legal theory underlying them is that the new development will impose costs on the community that the developer should internalize, rather than externalizing them onto the community as a whole.

Local governments do not pay for land that developers dedicate or for easements they grant. The U.S. Supreme Court has held that reasonable exactions do not violate the fifth amendment of the U.S. Constitution's taking clause.[3] If local governments require exactions that overstep the line, a court will determine that they have "taken" the land through inverse condemnation even though they have not acquired title to it and do not want to own the land. In that case, the government must take title to the land and pay fair market value for it or nullify the subdivision. Inverse condemnation is the inverse (opposite) of a conventional condemnation, where a government wants title to land for a public purpose such as building a highway, and is willing to pay for it.

Having a preliminary subdivision map approved by the local planning commission and county board of supervisors or city council provides developers and people near the site greater certainty about what can be developed. This will almost certainly increase the value of the land. The entitlement to build according to the subdivision "runs with the land". If the land is sold, the new owners retain the entitlement.

Premature subdivisions can be problematic. A huge amount of land was subdivided in the financial frenzy that preceded the 1929 stock market crash. Many subdivisions approved at that time were not developed until the 1950s or later. Speculative subdivisions developed in Florida and other potential retirement venues after World War II also often remained undeveloped for many years. By the time old subdivisions were economically developable, many were out of date. They did not meet the standards of current subdivision ordinances.

Another subdivision issue—particularly in areas attractive to retirees—is fraudulent or extremely deceptive subdivisions that promise very unlikely or impossible development. Sometimes the developer cannot complete the roads, water, sewers, and electricity promised when a subdivision lot is sold because financing projections for the project were wrong or they flat out lied. In that case, the buyer will have a much less desirable building site than promised, lose property value, and perhaps not be able to build at all. State laws requiring developers to disclose financial details of their proposed subdivisions are called "blue sky laws" because otherwise the subdivision description is backed by nothing more than the blue sky. Subdivision blue sky laws are a concept imported into land use planning from securities regulation.

Some states permit local governments to approve subdivisions with a state guarantee that they can be built that cannot be reversed. California permits local governments to approve "vesting tentative subdivisions" with no expiration date.

ZONING

Every major city in the United States with the exception of Houston, Texas now has a zoning ordinance and zones all (or almost all) of the land within the city. Houston, has no zoning ordinance, but many private properties in Houston have legal covenants or deed restrictions have effects somewhat similar to zoning. Conservative legal scholar Bernard Siegen—an advocate of free markets and opponent of government regulation—argues that Houston's economic success and comparatively low housing costs are a result of the absence of zoning. Other experts point to Houston's traffic congestion, the city's failure to protect itself from flooding, and many disputes that lack of zoning causes. Most urban counties have zoning ordinances and zone at least some county land, but rural counties and counties in states that have weak planning laws may not have zoning ordinances or, if they do, may not zone all the land within the county. Counties in urban and pro-planning states like California, Oregon, Maryland, and Washington have the authority to zone, and most counties have zoning ordinances. Many Midwest and Northeast states don't enable county zoning, leaving it instead to towns and townships. Texas and Alabama bar county zoning and have no town or township zoning. Other states limit counties' power to zone, and many counties do not zone their land. Counties with zoning ordinances are most likely to zone urban land within the county and land on the urban fringe that may become urbanized. They may or may not zone rural land. There is no uniform and complete record of how county land is zoned. The National Longitudinal Land Use Survey and Data Base was developed by researchers at the Urban Institute based on surveys in 1994, 2003, and 2019. It provides the best available data on zoning in U.S. counties, but the researchers who created it could not determine the zoning status of some of the county land because local records were unavailable, and the survey has not been updated since 2019.

Zoning is based on the police power concerns of health, safety, welfare, and morals. A main legal justification for zoning is to protect public safety. Requiring residential areas to be separate from industrial areas and enforcing front, rear, and side setbacks can reduce the risk that a fire will spread. Zoning can promote health by isolating areas where there are toxic substances that may harm humans and animals. It can keep landfills away from populated areas and vice versa, and prohibit landfills near streams and where permeable soil may allow toxic substances to seep into aquifers. Zoning arguably promotes the public welfare by creating orderly, aesthetically pleasing districts that retain land value. In 1986 the U.S. Supreme Court upheld zoning restrictions on the location of adult movie theaters too close to schools, churches, and residential zones on the theory that this will help protect community morals in the *Renton vs Playtime Theaters* case.

State zoning enabling acts authorize cities and counties within the state to enact local zoning ordinances. Most state zoning enabling acts were originally derived from the 1922 model Standard State Zoning Enabling Act (SSZEA), but almost all have been updated and modernized over the years. Local zoning ordinances are sometimes free-standing municipal ordinances and sometimes bundled as part of an integrated city municipal code that may also include design review, subdivision, and other land use regulations. Virtually all local zoning ordinances are now available online.

Originally zoning ordinances were crude documents that simply divided the land area of a city or county into areas where only one kind of residential, commercial, industrial, or other specified use was permitted. This was called Euclidean zoning—a double pun based on the shape of zones and the name of the city where the case that established the constitutionality of zoning arose.[4] Over time Euclidean zoning has become more complex and more flexible. Most U.S. communities have modified their zoning laws to include many different kinds of zones, including zones for mixed-use developments and planned unit developments (PUDs). Most include zoning flexibility devices such as development agreements, growth management ordinances, and form-based codes in addition to variances and conditional use permits. Still, many planners and lawyers consider zoning a crude and blunt instrument for regulating land use.

A zoning ordinance consists of two parts: text and maps. The zoning map shows the boundaries of different kinds of zones in the city or county. A landowner (or anyone) can see which zone a parcel is in. Figure 8.2 is the Falls Church, Virginia zoning map.

The text of a zoning ordinance describes in words what uses are permitted in each zone in lawyerly detail. For example, the South San Francisco zoning law chapter on residential use classifications defines a single unit dwelling as:

> A dwelling unit designed for occupancy by one household, where all rooms are internally connected and internally accessible via habitable space and located on a separate lot from any other unit (except second living units, where permitted). This classification includes individual manufactured housing units installed on a foundation system pursuant to Section 18551 of the California Health and Safety Code.

Naming of zones is not uniform. Zoning district names generally use a combination of letters and numbers to identify zones, with the letter(s) indicating a land use category, and the number(s) indicating the intensity of use. For example, an R-1 (Residential 1) zone might permit only single-family homes. An R-4 zone might permit uses as intense as an apartment building with up to 15 units. A zoning district with a higher number ordinarily permits all of the uses permitted in zones with the same letter but a lower number. In an R-4 zone, for example, rather than build 15-unit apartment building, a parcel owner could choose to build a single-family home.

There has been a movement towards greater mixing of uses in zoning. In part this is a response to Jane Jacobs's criticism of sterile single-use districts in downtowns, described in Chapter 1. Mixed-use zones frequently allow streets with shops at ground level and housing above, and permit mixing housing, restaurants, and convenience stores adjacent

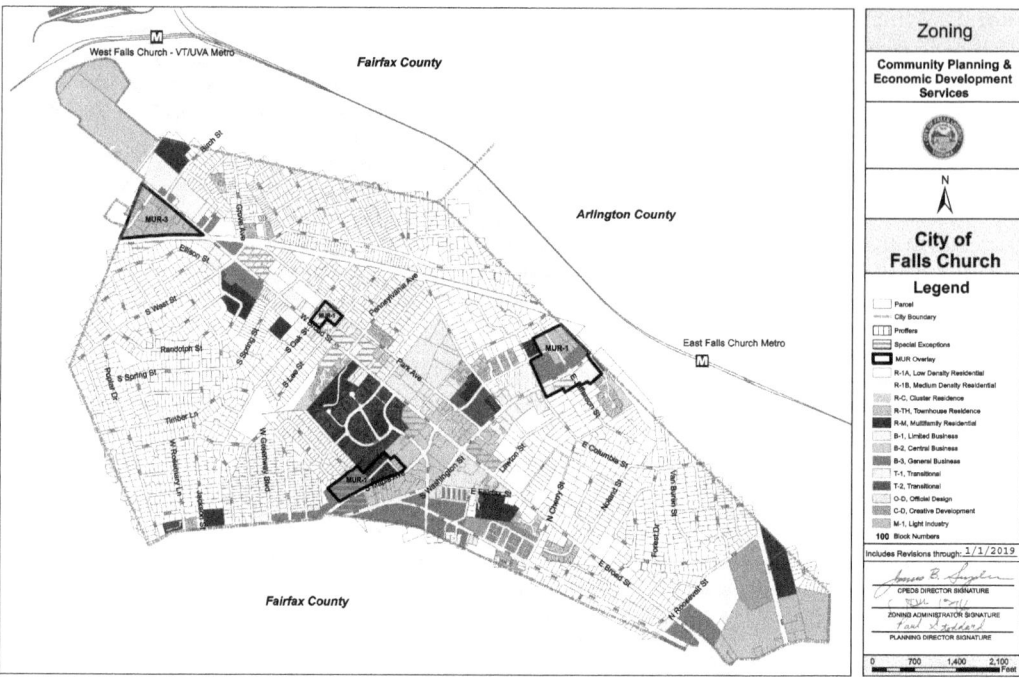

Figure 8.2 City of Falls Church, Virginia Zoning Map (2021).

to transit stops or parking garages. Combined retail/commercial/residential districts and permitting restaurants and exercise studios in industrial parks are other examples of mixed-use zoning. City and regional planners need to sort out what uses can be mixed, and which should be separated based on local conditions and input from stakeholders and residents.

In addition to the major permitted uses, zoning ordinances typically specify accessory uses permitted in different zones. For example, an R-1 residential zone that permits only single-family dwelling may also permit the owner to build a garage, gardening shed, gazebo, or other structure compatible with the residential use if it is listed as a permitted accessory use.

A small zone that is different from other zones is suspect. If land in a R-1 zone owned by the mayor's friend is upzoned to R-2, its value will almost certainly go up. This is called spot zoning. There may be reasons to create a small or oddly shaped zone sufficient to withstand a legal challenge, but most will not. If a court decides spot zoning has occurred, it will strike it down as illegal.

Zoning ordinances impact site planning. They typically specify setbacks prohibiting building too close to the street in front, the lot line to the rear (back), and the lot lines on either side of a building. The front setback is intended to assure enough separation from the street for safety, to reduce the negative impact of passing cars on the building occupants, and so that a street can be widened, if necessary, without destroying parts of the house, as well as for aesthetic and quality of life reasons. Side setbacks assure light and air between buildings and some privacy and quiet in individual houses. The rear setback provides separation from the house or accessory uses in the lot adjoining the back of the house.

Zoning ordinances usually also specify maximum building height and bulk limits. The buildable space on a lot is called the building envelope. For a single-family home, designing a house that will fit within the building envelope is usually straightforward. The house height cannot exceed a specified height limit and front, back, and side lot lines must be at least a specified distance from the house. Figure 8.3 illustrates setbacks and

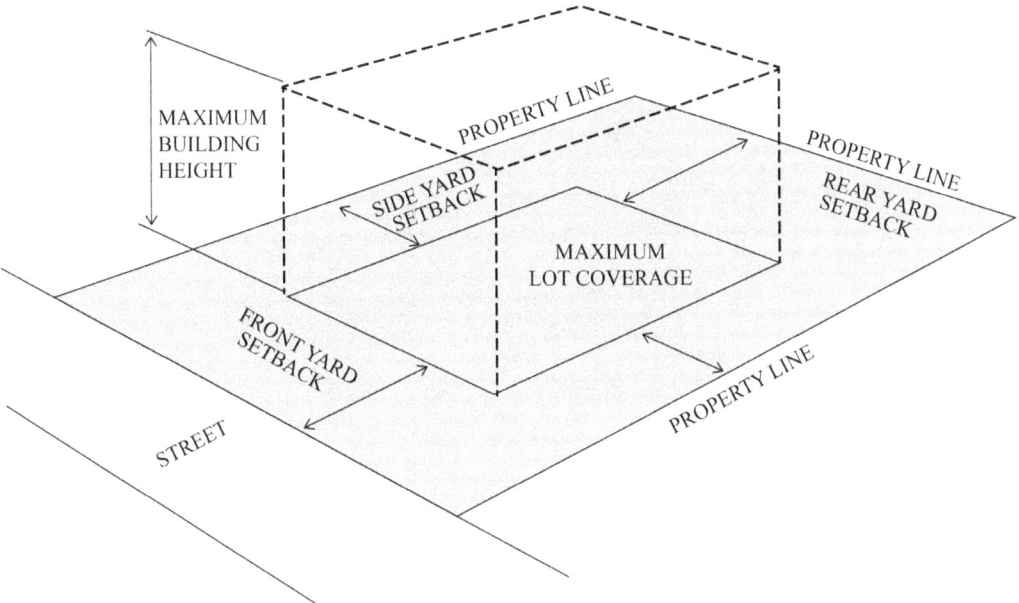

Figure 8.3 Typical Zoning Building Envelope, Height Limit, and Setbacks for a Single-Family House.

the building envelopes for a typical single-family house.

Zoning ordinances often express bulk limits for office buildings as floor area ratios (FARs) specifying how many square feet of floor space can be built on a parcel based on the parcel size. FARs take the form of a ratio of floor area in the building to the lot. A FAR with a ratio of 1:1 means that a one-story building can cover 100% of the lot, a two-story building half of the lot, or a four-story building one-quarter of the lot. Figure 8.4 illustrates FARs.

Designing a multi-story office building or large apartment complex to meet FAR requirements and optimize use and profit can be a complex planning, legal, and design challenge. Done properly, it can maximize light and air, protect views, minimize wind at street level, and perhaps provide privately owned public open space (POPOS), as well as optimizing usable floor area and the building's value. Urban designers designing buildings and planners reviewing building proposals, need design skills, technical expertise, legal advice, and political savvy for this kind of planning.

Once enacted, zoning ordinances are applied consistently and can only be changed after required procedures are followed. Governments do not want similarly situated lots to be treated in different ways. That would be unfair and cause endless politicking for special treatment. On the other hand, planners and policy makers recognize the need for flexibility in zoning ordinances. They want to be able to prohibit permitted uses if they feel they should no longer be permitted. They would like the ordinance to describe how hardship exceptions can be granted, and special standards applied to just some areas within a zone such as an unstable hillside subject to landslides or an environmentally sensitive area. Cities and counties generally want their zoning ordinances to allow uses that may be appropriate in some places within a zone, if the planning commission determines that they are appropriate at that location, even if they are inappropriate elsewhere. Examples include, daycare centers and convenience stores.

There are two main types of zoning changes—map changes and text changes. A map change simply re-draws zone boundaries but does not change the text describing what uses are permitted within zones. A text change does not change the map zone boundaries. Rather, it changes what uses

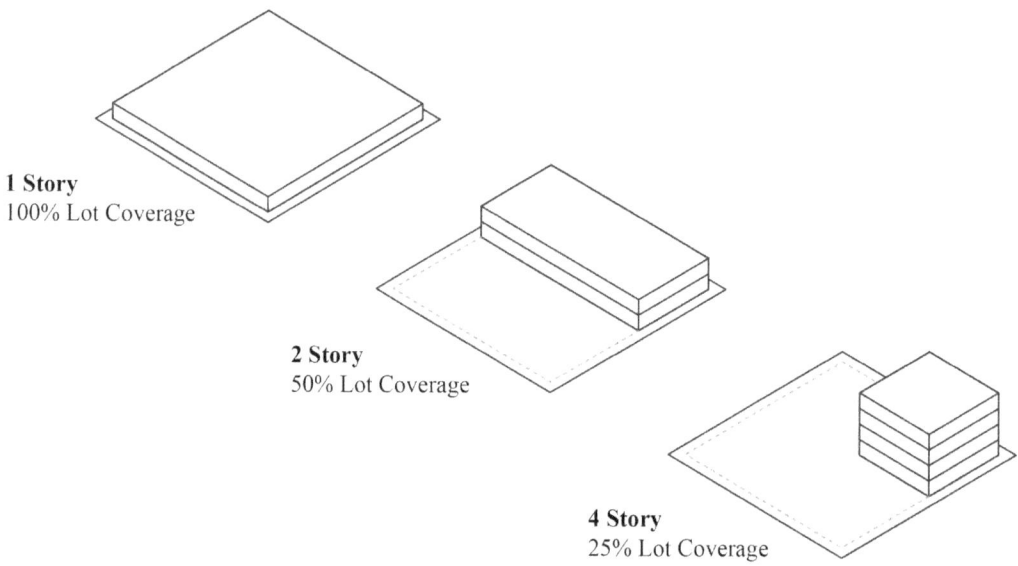

Figure 8.4 Floor Area Ratio (FAR).

are permitted within zone(s), definitions, or procedures. Intensity of uses may be increased (upzoning), decreased (downzoning), or varied in other ways. Map and text changes may be made separately or together. Occasionally local governments comprehensively change their entire zoning scheme. In states like California that require zoning to be consistent with the general plan, changing a zoning ordinance requires simultaneously changing the general plan. In California major zoning change in California requires an environmental impact analysis.

Since zoning ordinances can be changed, uses that were once permitted may no longer be legal after a change. They are called nonconforming uses—because they do not conform to the revised zoning law. A typical example is a mom-and-pop grocery store that was legal, but becomes a nonconforming use if the zone is revised so that the district where it is located becomes purely residential. The owners of uses declared nonconforming are usually strongly opposed to the change. It may be costly, disrupt a use they want to continue, or put them out of business. Planners and decision-makers are generally sympathetic to the owners—they don't consider their behavior or the uses bad per se—just in the wrong place as the community has developed and norms have changed. Planners encounter both a formal, legal side to this dilemma and an informal human side. Zoning ordinances typically amortize—phase out—nonconforming uses over time. For example, a text revision might grant owners of a mom-and-pop grocery store ten more years to operate their business before it becomes illegal (but not expand or rebuild if the property is destroyed). With a ten-year cushion, the owners have time to recover some of the investment that they have made in developing the business and to make other plans. The other approach is just to look the other way and not enforce the law unless neighbors complain. Planning offices do not devote much attention to inspections or enforcing zoning violations, so continuation of benign nonconforming uses is common.

There are two main ways to grant zoning hardship exceptions—through either a variance or a conditional use permit. A variance is a small exception to a zoning ordinance because something about the site would be a hardship if the law were strictly applied, and the change has no significant negative impacts. For example if a large rock in the back of a lot makes it impossible to comply with a zoning setback requirement, the owner might get a variance to have a slightly different building footprint, so long as it does not adversely affect neighbors or the character of the neighborhood.

A conditional use permit (CUP) is different from a variance. If the zoning ordinance specifies that the jurisdiction may grant a conditional use permit for a specified type of activity in a zone, the planning commission has discretion to grant or deny the permit. If they decide to grant permission for the use, it will be for a specified period of time and subject to conditions they impose. For example if a homeowner wants to start a daycare center in a residential area zoned R-1 for single-family houses and the zoning ordinance already lists a daycare center as a CUP there, she may apply for a CUP. If the ordinance does not already include daycare centers as one of the potential CUPs, she may not apply. The local planning department has the discretion to approve or not approve a permit for the daycare center, based on their consideration of the facts regarding the site. After notice to neighbors and a hearing, the planning commission may grant the permit. It will be for a limited time such as ten years and can be revoked if the homeowner does not comply with a specified condition, such as closing by 6:00 PM.

Some cities and counties permit "development agreements" for how land is to be used. Development agreements are typically used for very large projects. If Amazon.com or the Disney Corporation proposes building a mega-project, zoning and other conventional land use regulations will be inadequate. In that case the developer and the city council or county board of supervisors may negotiate a development agreement prepared by planners and lawyers that is tailored to the project. Development agreements are legally binding contracts between a local government and a developer.

Planned unit developments (PUDs) are a category of zone that establish performance standards for how the land is to be developed such as the total number of units or maximum density, but allow planners and urban designers to distribute buildings creatively in relation to the site characteristics. For example the PUD might allow developers to increase density on the top of a hill or change building envelopes or setbacks to protect views.

An overlay zone—also called an overlay district—is another zoning flexibility device. Overlay zones apply an additional layer of standards in addition to the underlying base zoning to areas within a defined overlay boundary. For example, part of an R-1 area with single-family homes might also be within a hillside overlay zone. The hillside overlay zone might require owners to get a geo-technical report and, if necessary, build a type of foundation capable of withstanding soil movement that is not required in other parts of the R-1 zone where that is not necessary. Flood plains, areas near earthquake faults, areas vulnerable to wildfires, and other hazard-prone areas are good candidates for overlay zones.

INCLUSIONARY AND EXCLUSIONARY ZONING

Planners sometimes use zoning and other land use regulations to promote social equity. Racists and NIMBYs may try to use zoning to exclude categories of people they consider undesirable. Exclusionary zoning is the deliberate attempt by a city or county to keep people they do not want from being able to live there. The opposite of exclusionary zoning is inclusionary zoning—a deliberate attempt to make it easier for households of different sizes and income to secure rental or owned housing that meets their needs within a community. Since income and race are correlated, inclusionary zoning can promote racial integration. In addition to eliminating egregious and overt instances of exclusionary zoning, planners can promote social inclusion in more subtle ways. How residential zone boundaries are drawn, permitted densities, lot sizes, and a myriad of what appear to be merely technical details can increase the income mix in residential areas, make affordable housing more accessible, and otherwise improve the life situation of lower-income households, communities of color, and immigrant communities.

The fourteenth amendment of the United States Constitution—adopted in

1868—prohibits states from denying any person within their jurisdiction equal protection of the laws. The U.S. Supreme Court has held that the equal protection clause applies to the "suspect classifications" of race, religion, and national origin. States and their political subdivisions—cities and counties—may not legally discriminate on the basis of race, religion, or national origin by zoning some residential areas only for Whites, Protestants, or native-born people.[5] The Supreme Court has not held gender or sexual orientation to be suspect classifications. However, the 1968 federal Fair Housing Act bans discrimination in housing on the basis of gender, sexual orientation, family status, or disability. Some state constitutions or state laws, and some local city and county ordinances explicitly prohibit discrimination based on gender, sexual orientation, or other categories.

In two epic decades-long cases in Mount Laurel, New Jersey, the New Jersey Supreme Court held that the New Jersey Constitution prohibits exclusionary zoning. They held that the New Jersey Constitution requires local governments to zone in such a way that builders can build housing suitable for the population of the region and that local governments in New Jersey must affirmatively zone to allow builders to build housing affordable to low- and moderate-income households. After 45 years of bitter litigation and political upheaval, the Mount Laurel cases have led to the production of some more affordable housing and some greater income and racial integration. No other state supreme court has followed the Mount Laurel precedent.[6]

A regional approach to reducing spatial economic segregation is to create "fair share" housing plans. Communities in a metropolitan area may agree to each accept their fair share of affordable housing. Fair share housing plans and programs promoted by the federal government or local governments in a metropolitan area have been episodic, small-scale, and rarely fully implemented for a substantial period of time.

One international example of a nation's effort to eliminate discrimination and achieve an integrated society merits mention.

Singapore—a small country at the tip of the Malaysian peninsula has a unique inclusionary land use and housing policy for Singaporean citizens. Most individual residential building in Singapore consists of condominiums that must by law be occupied by households in proportions to the Chinese, Malaysian, and Indian ethnic mix of Singapore's population. When a household of one ethnic group moves out, only a member of the same ethnic group can move in. Singapore's housing is deeply subsidized so that it is affordable to a much greater proportion of the population than is true for the United States and other countries.

FORM-BASED CODES

An alternative or supplement to zoning is use of form-based codes, which were introduced in Chapter 3. While they are called codes, form-based codes are a hybrid type of regulation that perform functions that overlap with both zoning and building codes. The basic idea of form-based codes is to provide a visual alternative that illustrates height, bulk, setback, facades, the relation of buildings to the streetscape, and other specifications with much more depth, subtlety, and flexibility than conventional zoning or building codes. Some jurisdictions with form-based codes also keep their zoning and building codes. Box 8.2 describes Arlington, Virginia's form-based code for the Columbia Pike area.

SITE PLANNING

Site planning—"the art of arranging structures on the land and shaping the spaces between" (Lynch & Hack, 1984: 1)—is an essential aspect of plan implementation. "Regardless of scale or the degree of deliberation, any human site is somehow planned, whether piecemeal or at one sweep, whether by convention or by conscious choice" (ibid).

Architects, urban designers, and city and regional planners typically plan sites at the project level just before a project is about to be implemented. Sites are often for a single building and its grounds, but may be for a cluster of buildings, park, highway corridor, or any other functionally related space. Sites are usually on a single parcel of land with a single owner. The site and the buildings that will be on the site are usually planned simultaneously, and development of the entire site is usually completed within a few years. Occasionally site planning extends to a neighborhood, district, community, or even an entire new town or city and can take decades to complete. The height, bulk, and setback of buildings on a site, the space between buildings, access, and infrastructure are all planned for efficiency, aesthetics, livability, and compliance with the law. Once projects are completed, they may require continuing site planning or planning to adapt the site to new uses.

Site planning is closely related to architecture, engineering, and landscape architecture, as well as land use, environmental, transportation, and other types of planning. Site plans are closer to architectural renderings or engineering schematics than general, strategic, or regional plans—particularly if they are made to guide immediate implementation, as is usually the case.

Massachusetts Institute of Technology urban planning and design professor Kevin Lynch originated the modern theory and practice of site planning. His colleague, Gary Hack, built on Lynch's foundation. Hack's *Site Planning International* (2018) is now the definitive work on site planning. Box 8.3 is a biography of Professor Hack.

BOX 8.2 THE COLUMBIA PIKE FORM-BASED CODE AND PLAN (ARLINGTON, VIRGINIA)

In 2002, Arlington County, Virginia adopted a plan for a 3.5-mile urban corridor immediately across the Potomac River from Washington, DC. The corridor was in the most underdeveloped area in Arlington County—an urban county that had seen explosive growth in recent decades and was built out with no remaining developable land elsewhere. A form-based code to implement the plan applies to portions of ten zoning districts that are located in the Columbia Pike Special Revitalization District. The code is an optional zoning tool. Property owners retain their rights under the county's existing zoning ordinance. The stated purpose of the plan and code are to:

Foster a vital main street for its adjacent neighborhoods through a lively mix of uses with shopfronts, sidewalk cafes, and other commercial uses at street level, canopy shade trees, and upper-story residences and offices;
Create transit, pedestrian, and bicycle-oriented development, dependent on density, diversity of uses, and design; and
Place greatest emphasis on design, or physical form, because of its importance in defining neighborhood character.

The code's regulating plan provides standards for the disposition of each property or lot and describes how each relates to its adjacent properties and streets, civic greens, pedestrian pathways, other public domain spaces and the surrounding neighborhood. Figure 8.5 shows the code's building envelope standards for neighborhood sites.

A property owner can see the buildable area of the lot; the side lot lines; heights permitted for the building as a whole; and heights and permitted uses on the ground and upper stories. The code illustrates parking structures; mezzanines; what the street facade should be like; fenestration requirements; balconies; and other building features. The Columbia Pike form-based code has detailed building envelope, architectural, and streetscape standards to ensure coherent building envelopes, building design, and streets. The standards require public art in accordance with the county's public art policy. Standards are consistent within a project and from project to project within an activity node such as the town center.

E. Building Envelope Standards: Neighborhood Sites

1. Height Specifications

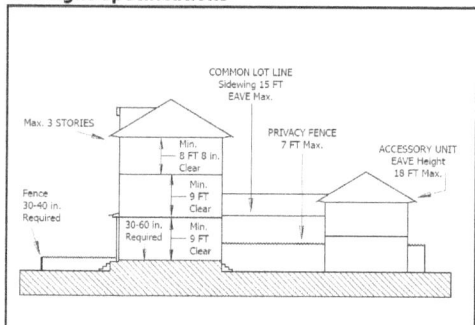

2. Siting Specifications

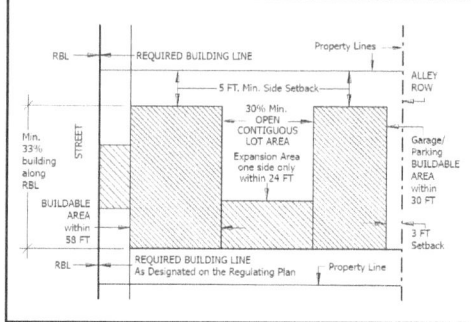

Building Height
1. Principal building height is measured in Stories.
2. The building shall be no more than 3 Stories in height.
3. No accessory building shall be more than 18 feet to its Eaves.

Ground Floor and Second Story Height
1. The Ground Floor finished elevation shall be between 30 and 69 inches above the average RBL elevation. [11F]
2. The maximum floor-to-floor Story Height limit for the Ground Floor Story is 14 feet.
3. The Ground Floor Story and second Stories shall have at least an 8 foot 10 inch clear height for at least 80 percent of the area of the particular Story. [11F, 18B]

Upper Stories Height
1. The maximum floor-to-floor Story Height for upper Stories is 10 feet.
2. Each Story above the second Story shall have at least 8 feet 8 inches in clear height for at least 80 percent of its area.

Mezzanines
Mezzanines greater than 2/3 of the floor area footprint shall be counted as full Stories.

Street Facade
1. The Street facade shall be built-to the RBL not less than 33 percent of the overall RBL.
2. That portion of a facade that is required to be built to the RBL shall be composed as a simple plane (limited jogs less than 18 inches are considered a simple plane within this requirement) interrupted only by Porches, Stoops, Bay Windows, shop fronts and Balconies. [11F]

Buildable Area
Buildings shall occupy only the area of the Lot specified on the Regulating Plan as Buildable Area. No part of any building excepting overhanging Eaves and BES permitted Balconies, Bay Windows, and Stoops, shall encroach into the Street beyond the RBL. No part of any building (excepting overhanging Eaves, Balconies, Stoops, and small and unroofed garden structures) shall occupy the remaining Lot area. The minimum Open Contiguous Lot Area shall comprise at least 30 percent of the total Buildable Area and can be located anywhere within the Buildable Area of the site.

Side Lot Line
The minimum side setback is 5 feet.

Garage and Parking Entrances
1. Designated Garage Entries shall be the sole means of automobile access to a site, unless otherwise approved by the County.
2. Garage doors shall not face (be at an angle of less than 90 degrees from the RBL or street) the RBL. Vehicle parking areas (except where a Street Wall exists or parking is enclosed within an ancillary building) on private property shall not be located within 25 feet of the RBL. These prohibitions are not applicable to on-Street parallel parking.
3. Any garage or parking for vehicles (autos, trailers, boats, etc.) shall be kept within the area designated on the Siting Specifications diagram Garage doors shall not face (be at an angle of less than 90 degrees from the RBL or right of way) the RBL.

Alleys
Where there is no Alley at the rear Lot line, there shall be a 12-foot setback.

Corner Lots
Corner Lots shall be treated as having Street Frontage on both the front and side Streets (or RBLs).

11F - Columbia Pike Form Based Code Amendment adopted on May 25, 2010
18B - Columbia Pike Form Based Code Amendment adopted on November 15, 2014

ARLINGTON, VIRGINIA   4.8   **BUILDING ENVELOPE STANDARDS**

Figure 8.5 Columbia Pike Form-Based Code Building Envelope Standards for Neighborhood Sites (Arlington, Virginia, 2013).

BOX 8.3 GARY HACK

University of Pennsylvania Professor Emeritus of Urban Planning Gary Hack established his reputation as an academic authority on site planning in 1984 by co-authoring the 3rd edition of *Site Planning* with his mentor, Massachusetts Institute of Technology (MIT) Professor Kevin Lynch. In 2018—after a hiatus of 34 years—Hack published *Site Planning International*. Like the first two editions of *Site Planning* by Kevin Lynch and Gary Hack, *Site Planning International* combines very specific applied material with theory. It blends information from the professional fields of urban planning, architecture, landscape architecture, civil engineering, and the natural sciences and draws on humanities and culture studies.

Gary Hack has had a distinguished academic career teaching city and regional planning and urban design at the Massachusetts Institute of Technology, the University of Pennsylvania, and other universities. He served as head of the Department of Urban Studies and Planning at MIT and dean of the School of Design at the University of Pennsylvania. Thousands of students and practitioners have taken his urban design Massive Open Online Course (MOOC). In addition to sole authoring *Site Planning International*, Hack is the co-editor of *Local Planning* with Eugenie Birch, Paul Sedway, and Mitchell Silver (2009) and *Global City Regions* with Roger Simmonds (2015).

Hack has had a notable career as a practitioner. He has been a principal in the Cambridge, Massachusetts urban design firm Carr, Lynch, Hack and Sandell, and an independent consultant preparing plans and designs for projects in New York City, Boston, Detroit, Philadelphia, and over 40 other cities in the United States and many cities in other countries. Hack led urban design for reconstruction of the West Side highway in New York City as an urban boulevard with 4.5 miles of adjacent parks and promenades. He oversaw design of Rockefeller Park at Battery Park City—an 8.5-acre park that serves as the key open space in Lower Manhattan. He has directed teams preparing downtown plans for Louisville, Kentucky and Knoxville, Tennessee, downtown development guidelines for the center of Portland, Maine, design review manuals for Hendersonville and Germantown, Tennessee, and guidelines for the development of the entrance corridors and downtown for Charlottesville, Virginia. Hack served

Figure 8.6 Gary Hack.

as chairman of the Philadelphia City Planning Commission. Perhaps the capstone to Hack's career was preparing the design guidelines as a member of the team tasked with reconstruction of the Twin Towers after they were destroyed in the 9/11 terrorist attack.

Hack's major international planning and design experience has been in Canada, Taiwan, and Thailand. He was the principal designer for the Hwa Shan cultural district in the center of Taipei, Taiwan and *The Bangkok Plan*—a strategic plan for the development of Bangkok. In the 1970s he oversaw the planning of Harbourfront in Toronto, the Vieux Port in Montreal, and other projects across Canada. He has served as an urban design consultant for projects in Japan, China, and Saudi Arabia. Many of his University of Pennsylvania and MIT PhD students have gone on to teach urban design and site planning in other countries.

Hack was educated in architecture at the University of Manitoba (B. Arch 1964) and University of Illinois (M. Arch 1966), and in planning at the University of Illinois (MUP 1967) and at MIT, where he received his PhD in 1976.

Practitioners—planners, urban designers, landscape architects, and civil engineers—confronting a site planning challenge refer to detailed chapters of *Site Planning International* for guidance about what they need to consider and issues that might arise. For example, material in Hack's book on assessing a site provides practical details about soil, slopes, grading, utilities, sanitary drainage, electricity, and lighting. Hack provides practical wisdom on the way site planning actually happens based on his experience in the school of hard knocks. His writings reflect his firsthand experience with huge and conflictual design projects and mediating disagreements among dozens of groups as well as the practical politics of planning for smaller cities. Hack emphasizes the psychological, almost religious "spirit of place". He is a model scholar-practitioner who was able to bring people to agreement on site plans that have contributed to successful places.

Lynch and Hack consider the first step in site planning—defining the problem to be addressed—the most difficult, because it contains the final design in embryo. Defining the problem is often given short shrift by developers eager to get on with a project, but Lynch and Hack urge planners to advise developers to give defining the problem to be addressed the attention it deserves.

During the site planning process, a site planner may observe the site multiple times, armed with maps to mark up; a journal for field notes; a camera to take photographs and videos from different angles at different times of day; and containers for soil samples. She may ask current and potential users to draw cognitive maps of how they use and perceive the site and what features they would like in a newly designed site. Site planners may get feedback from interviews, focus groups, and design charettes—intense working sessions in which citizens, stakeholders, and experts advise the designers on how to tweak their design before it is implemented.

A topographic base map (topo map) is essential for site planning—usually at a scale of 1:500 (1 inch = 50 feet) for moderate size sites. Site planners use the local property tax assessor's maps, aerial photos from airplanes and drones, GIS maps of sites and their surroundings, and maps prepared from remotely sensed spatial data from satellites. In the United States topo maps are usually U.S. Geological Survey (USGS) contour maps. Contour lines show the shape, slope, and elevation of the land surface through the relative spacing of the lines.

The top layer of soil on a site is critical for understanding the engineering aspects of what can be built on the site, how much soil compaction will be required, and what soil amendments may be needed for landscaping. The stability and characteristics of subsoil and the presence or absence of underground water are critical considerations for building foundation safety. The United States Department of Agriculture (DOA)'s National Cooperative Soil Survey (NCSS) provides soil information. If necessary, site planners send soil samples to laboratories for analysis.

Historical information on sites can be found on 700,000 large-scale Sanborn maps published between 1867 and 1977 by the private Sanborn map company. Sanborn maps are large-scale lithographed street plans at a scale of 50 feet to one inch (1:500) on 21×25-inch individual sheets of paper.[7]

Historical information on site characteristics and microclimates, annual temperature cycles, sun, wind, rain, snow, heat islands, and the occurrence and impacts of past extreme weather events such as flooding, hurricanes, and tornadoes is critical to planning resilient sites that can withstand extreme events and recover from them if damage is done.

In sophisticated site designs, particularly for large buildings, site planners consider technical aspects of albedo. Albedo is the proportion of the incident light that is reflected by a surface such as a building facade. Designs for large buildings also consider heat and sound conduction, and convection. Site planners use technology to measure these and other site characteristics or subcontract with firms qualified to do specialized studies of them.

Site planning requires analysis of the needs of both present and potential users—"all those who interact with the place in any way: live in it, work in it, pass through it, repair it, control it, profit from it, suffer from it, even dream about it" (Lynch & Hack, 1984: 67). Site planners consider both habitability (how people's bodies will be affected by the site) and perception (how people will perceive the site). A good site will fit both present and future user needs, actions, and perceptions. It will have what Patrick Geddes called "goodness of fit" and reflect what he called the "spirit of place".

There is a growing literature on green, sustainable, ecological, and carbon-neutral site design. The U.S. Green Building Council (USGBC)—a private U.S.-based nonprofit has been promoting sustainable building design, construction, and operations since 1993. The USGBC certifies buildings, sites, and neighborhoods that meet different levels of green design excellence with silver, gold, or platinum ratings. They publish a reference guide for neighborhood development and give awards for energy-saving neighborhood designs. The USGBC LEED rating system and green rating systems developed by other organizations provide dozens of standards as varied as orienting buildings to face the sun, preserving native ecosystems, using xeriscape plants that require almost no water, installing low-flush toilets, and reserving parking spaces for zero-emission vehicles.

BUILDING AND HOUSING CODES

Building and housing codes are top-down regulations that require builders to meet minimum standards for the construction of buildings. Building codes set standards for new construction. Housing codes require owners of residential buildings that have been completed to maintain them in a safe and habitable condition. Both are intended to protect people living or working in the building or visiting it. They are also intended to protect buildings in the immediate vicinity from fire and other dangers. The departments within local government responsible for housing and building code enforcement are organized differently in different cities. In some cases, one or both functions are incorporated within a larger local government department such as a local department of community development.

Housing and building codes are city- and county-specific. Each local government has the authority under the police power to pass their own building and housing codes. Local governments rely on model building and housing codes prepared by governmental and industry experts as templates for their individual city and county codes. The International Association of Plumbing and Mechanical Officials (IAPMO) develops the Uniform Plumbing Code (UPC). The U.S. National Fire Protection Association (NFPA) develops the National Electrical Code (NEC)—also called NFPA 70. Cities and counties borrow freely from their neighbors, perhaps altering small parts of their building and housing codes to fit local conditions.

Building codes for mobile homes are different from building codes for other dwelling units. The federal government promulgates and oversees enforcement of mobile home codes.

Oversight of new building construction to assure that the building complies with the local building code takes place at critical junctures during the construction process. It begins with a review of plans before construction starts and ends with a final inspection when the building is complete, just before the local government issues an occupancy permit allowing the building to be occupied.[8]

Local governments also inspect existing residential buildings to assure that they meet local codes. The applicable code regulating existing housing is called a housing code, rather than a building code. Cities and counties typically have a systematic process for addressing housing code violations. They usually target the most dangerous buildings first and work their way through as large a caseload of inspections and enforcement as time and money permit. If tenants or neighbors feel that a building is unsafe and report the danger to the local office responsible for enforcing the local housing code, that may trigger an inspection. If a building code inspector finds code violations, the local government will give the owner a specified amount of time to bring the building into compliance. If a re-inspection shows the violations have been corrected the case is closed; if not, the city attorney may take legal action to fine the owner, force the owner to comply with the building code, or even condemn the building and have it destroyed.

Owner-occupants of private homes (64% of the U.S. housing stock) have an incentive to purchase housing units that were designed to housing code standards when they were built and maintain them up to building code standards that apply after they have been built for two reasons. They want to live safely in properly built units, and they know that keeping their homes up to code will maintain the building's property value. Fewer than one percent of the owners who responded to the 2017 U.S. Census Bureau's Annual Community Survey (ACS) reported living in a housing unit they considered to have severe physical problems and fewer than three percent in units they considered to have moderate physical problems.

Most rental housing in the United States (36% of the residential housing stock) is well built and up to code. Fewer than two percent of renters reported living in rental units with severe physical problems in the 2017 ACS survey and fewer than six percent in units they considered to have moderate physical problems. Owners of rental property generally maintain their buildings because it is in their economic self-interest. Sometimes builders cut corners during construction of rental housing, and deliberately hide the fact that their work violates the building code. Older buildings may have been built when building codes standards were lower or there were no building codes. Buildings deteriorate over time. Sometimes owners do not maintain rental units to code because they cannot afford the expense, are negligent, or deliberately choose to maximize profit by neglecting maintenance and repairs. This is the source of many landlord–tenant disputes.

Buildings that clash with local aesthetics may disrupt the unity of a historic district or planned unit development (PUD), offend neighbors and other residents, and perhaps reduce nearby property values. Aesthetic standards in codes and design review by local planning design review boards can protect aesthetics. The police power justification for this is weaker than health or safety considerations, but proponents argue that good aesthetics contributes to the welfare of a community. Critics argue that top-down regulation of aesthetics may stifle creative or innovative designs or impose societal values on what should be individual choices.

Building and housing code inspections offer fertile ground for corruption, particularly in older and poorer jurisdictions. A landlord may slip a poorly paid housing inspector a bribe to overlook a code violation. A short-lived federal program in the mid-1970s to bring modest existing houses up to code and make them available for sale to very-low-income first-time homebuyers—the Section 235 program—became the poster child for this kind of corruption.

Building and housing code issues have become particularly important in the face of rapid technological change and the need to address global climate change. Housing and building codes may permit, encourage, or require the use of building materials and construction practices to save non-renewable resources, reduce use of water, conserve energy, and contribute to addressing climate change in other ways. Planners working on plans to reduce their community's carbon footprint—the amount of carbon dioxide (CO_2) and other greenhouse gases (GHGs) they release into the atmosphere—can help shape the myriad decisions that builders and homeowners make about individual buildings. Collectively, this can contribute to mitigating global climate change and the current unsustainable pattern of urban development described in Chapter 17.

DESIGN REVIEW BOARDS

Many cities now have design review boards with nearly unlimited authority to approve or disapprove plans for new buildings or substantial alteration of old buildings based on whether board members consider the building design to be appropriate in the context of the neighborhood and local values. Aesthetics and the law is the subject of lively and ongoing debate among architects, lawyers, and planners.

Design review boards usually consist of five to seven architects or other design experts. They may be separate from the local planning commission, part of a zoning appeal board, or fit into local government in some other way. For example, San Francisco authorizes the planning department to conduct design reviews that are then considered by the planning commission and board of supervisors to ensure that a proposed project meets general principles of good design and neighborhood compatibility. These principles include "supporting a project's compatibility with the neighborhood scale and character; encouraging site and ground-floor design to enhance San Francisco's walkable environment; and fostering architecture that is both reflective of its time and offers a sense of timeless presence for future generations".

A thorny question is under what circumstances a local design review board should have the power to reject a proposal for a design that differs from existing buildings—what Louisiana State University law professor John Costonis calls "aliens"—and only approve plans for conventional buildings—which Costonis calls "icons". A 1963 federal appeals court opinion—*Reid vs Architectural Review Board of Cleveland Heights*—upheld a decision of the Cleveland Heights Architectural Review Board to reject a plan for a large, expensive, architecturally imaginative custom single-family house that met zoning and building codes, was not visible from the street, and would not harm the health, safety, or welfare of the community or property values. The house involved in the *Reid* case was designed by an architect as his personal residence. It called for a U-shaped cluster of one-story modules with glass walls, hidden behind a 10-foot wall and landscaping in a neighborhood of older two- and one-half- story "dignified multi-story houses". The court deferred to the opinion of the architectural review board because they were architects "acting on proper architectural principles" even though the decision was based solely on aesthetic grounds and the designer of the house in question was himself an architect.

TRANSFER OF DEVELOPMENT RIGHTS (TDR)

A transfer of development rights (TDR) is an implementation tool that allows governments to regulate private property without taking title to it, even if the TDR significantly decreases the land's value or severely limits how the owner may use it. TDRs provide owners compensation for lost value by giving them valuable rights to develop elsewhere. If a court upholds a TDR, the regulating government is not forced to take the land by eminent domain (inverse condemnation). TDRs are most commonly used to compensate owners of historic buildings for the value they lose when local regulations prohibit demolishing or altering them in order to build something more profitable on the land, but can be used to protect environmentally important land and for other purposes.

Imagine a privately owned, beautifully preserved, Revolutionary War tavern in a mixed-use area of an East Coast city. Market forces make high-density development of the area profitable. If the owner sells the tavern to a developer who wants to demolish it and build a more profitable building, the community will lose a local treasure. The local government and nonprofit historical societies can't afford to buy the tavern. A TDR giving the owner a density bonus worth as much, or almost as much, as the proceeds from the sale of the tavern if it were developed to its "highest and best use" may provide a solution. The tavern is saved and the owner is not denied the profit he might have made if he sold it. If the TDR granted is priced so that it is valuable enough, the owner will not file a fifth amendment takings lawsuit claiming inverse condemnation or, if he does, will lose in court. The right to use additional density may be transferred and used somewhere else. For example, the TDR for the Revolutionary War tavern might give the owner a density bonus allowing him to add stories to a building that he owns somewhere else in town. He might be granted permission to sell the rights or "bank" them in a TDR bank so that they can be sold to someone else. In *Penn Central Transportation Company vs New York City*, the U.S. Supreme Court upheld New York City's right to designate the magnificent historic Grand Central Station—completed in 1913—protected landmark status, compensating them for loss of development value on the site with air rights to build over the building.

TDRs are complex and require sophisticated financial, design, and legal analysis. Properly used, they can be a creative tool to balance public and private interests.

URBAN GROWTH MANAGEMENT

Since the 1960s hundreds of cities and counties in the United States have adopted some form of urban growth management plan. Almost all urban growth management plans are for residential buildings. A few cities have growth management plans for commercial buildings.

Two pioneering cities—Ramapo, New York and Petaluma, California—were the first communities to implement urban growth management plans. Both are appealing small cities located close to major cities—New York City and San Francisco. Both adopted their urban growth management plans when they began to grow rapidly and residents feared growth was altering their small-town character.

Originally urban growth management was primarily concerned with tempo control—the timing of when new home building can occur. Cities limited the number of new housing units that could be built each year. They sought to achieve concurrency—specifying the timing of new residential construction so that adequate infrastructure was in place before residential units that need them were completed.

Tempo control and concurrency remain important concerns in urban growth management—particularly for rapidly growing suburban cities. Some communities set a maximum level or residential units at buildout, either explicitly or that will *de facto* occur based on annual absolute or percentage limits.

As urban growth management has matured, cities are increasingly focused on the location of different uses, density, and the quality of their built environment, rather than the tempo or pace of development. Urban growth management ordinances do this by including normative standards for what policy makers feel the built environment of the community should be like, such as establishing appropriate density for different areas, protecting the natural environment, producing more compact growth, encouraging superior design, providing for more open space, and providing more off-street parking spaces.

Another justification for growth management is to make sure property tax or other revenue from new developments at least covers their own costs and ideally increases net municipal revenue. Some communities abuse growth management by using it to protect their privileged economic status or to keep out lower income and minority households.

It is commonly assumed that growth management will result in less residential development. That is often the case in the short run. However, growth management can ultimately result in the same or more development at buildout.

The 1972 Ramapo plan used a very simple and straightforward point system. Points were awarded to a development proposal for proximity to five essential facilities or services such as roads and sewers.[9] Even if a parcel was zoned for development and an owner's plans complied with the local building code, Ramapo's urban growth management ordinance required the owner to have enough total points to get a building permit. A parcel near the built-up center of Ramapo where there were roads, storm drains, and a firehouse would get enough points to get a building permit. A parcel on the fringe, far from existing infrastructure, would not get enough points, and the owner could not get a building permit.

Ramapo's capital improvement program (CIP) called for spreading construction of new infrastructure that would service every parcel over an 18-year period—cold comfort for property owners who wanted to build immediately or sell their property for the price it would command if a buyer did not have to wait to build for as long as 18 years. Property owners in the infrastructure deserts were furious. The value of their property plummeted, as only buyers with deep pockets and patience would buy a site where building could not occur for such a long time.

In the inevitable lawsuit, the New York Court of Appeals (New York's supreme court) upheld the Ramapo plan. The court concluded that even restricting development for 18 years did not constitute an unconstitutional taking of property in violation of the fifth amendment of the U.S. Constitution.

They were impressed by the city's four-volume study and careful wording of the ordinance. They rejected the argument that, by limiting new housing construction, the plan discriminated against potential future homebuyers of color, who, on average, had lower incomes than Whites.

Petaluma is an attractive small city 29 miles from San Francisco. The center of Petaluma has 19th-century brick buildings and charming wooden houses with white picket fences. Petaluma is often a setting for movies about small town America.

In the early 1970s a new highway reduced travel time between San Francisco and Petaluma. Race-related conflict was driving White flight out of San Francisco and other Bay Area cities to communities like Petaluma. The number of applications for new residential building permits increased from 358 in 1969 to 591 in 1970, and 891 in 1971. Utilities were inadequate and schools had to move to half days for each student. Petaluma adopted the plan in 1971. The Petaluma plan was a much more sophisticated point-based plan than Ramapo's plan.[10]

Contrary to the nearly universal depictions otherwise, the original Petaluma plan permitted much more residential development—including multi-family housing suitable for low- and moderate-income households—than most other Bay Area communities. Petaluma just stretched out the time when the housing could be built. Petaluma has aggressively promoted affordable housing development since the mid-1980s. It works with a variety of local and regional affordable housing and homeless organizations to provide more than their "fair share" of affordable housing. Many cities and towns deserve criticism for using urban growth management selfishly to keep out people who should have the opportunity to reside there, but Petaluma is not one of them.

The Petaluma plan withstood legal challenges.[11] Other cities then considered it safe to follow Petaluma's lead. Since the Ramapo and Petaluma plans were adopted, many other cities and counties have developed their own variations of growth management plans. Most have a point system similar to Petaluma's. Many cities today have urban limit lines—also called urban growth boundaries—similar to the urban limit line that Petaluma pioneered. Washington, and New Jersey currently have notable state-level urban growth management plans and policies and Oregon has state level planning goals. Florida, Delaware and other states have experimented with urban growth management in the past.

SUMMARY

A good planning process or a glossy, nice-looking plan is a waste of time unless it produces concrete results. Plan implementation should be integral to planning—not an afterthought once a plan document is completed. Engaging citizens and stakeholders early on and really listening to them and incorporating their ideas into successive drafts of a plan lays the groundwork for getting the plan approved and ultimately implemented. Promoting the plan once it is written is essential. Describing the plan to different audiences in a variety of media can help get it implemented. Long-term relations with organizations that help educate the public and prepare them to participate effectively and realistically in plan making, such as Philadelphia's Citizens' Planning Institute, can lay the groundwork for plan implementation. Planning budgets should anticipate that promoting the plan and engaging citizens will take time and cost money. Communication—including use of modern communications methods via the web and social media—is critical.

Many tools can contribute to plan implementation. These include public education, advocacy, public investment in infrastructure, city branding, subdivision regulation, zoning, form based codes, building and housing codes, design review, TDRs, and urban growth management plans and regulations.

In the United States, federal, state, and local laws define what plans and policies are legally possible. Americans are litigious. Controversial planning decisions are often fought out in the courts. Most planning litigation takes place in state courts. Cases involving federal constitutional questions and federal legislation are adjudicated in federal courts. Planners need to consider legal mandates and constraints in the planning process. Since legal requirements are complex, planners need to understand the limits of their own competence and when to call on attorneys, in the same way that they turn to engineers, urban designers, or natural scientists to help with technical issues.

The fruits of a successful planning process are watching the results. One of planners' sources of greatest satisfaction is seeing the tangible results of their plans that have been successfully implemented.

CONCEPTS

Ballot Box Planning
Building Permit
Capital Improvement Plan (CIP)
Concurrency
Condemnation
Conditional Use Permit (CUP)
Contour Map
Design Review Board
Exaction
Exclusionary Zoning
Form-Based Code
Housing Code
Inclusionary Zoning
In Lieu Fee
Inverse Condemnation
Legislative Act
Level of Service (LOS)
Ministerial Act
Nonconforming Use
Petaluma Plan
Point System
Quasi-Judicial Act
Ramapo Plan
Required Dedication
State Enabling Legislation
Subdivision
Tempo Control
Transfer of Development Rights (TDR)
Urban Growth Boundary
Urban Growth Management
Variance

PEOPLE

Allan Jacobs
Gary Hack

NOTES

1. In Jacobs's parody, the manager, coaches, batboys, and groundskeepers all became San Francisco civil servants (Jacobs, 2011). The players had to take exams, live in the city, and could not be traded, optioned, or released. The commission kept the Giants' manager from firing a drunken third baseman who was having an affair with his wife and pushed all manner of unqualified players onto the team during the 1980 season. Jacobs's parody ends with no certainty when, if ever, the 1980 baseball season will ever end!
2. Common impact fees include money for streets and roads, parks, school sites, sewer and water facilities, curbs and gutters, sidewalks, and police and fire stations. Less common and more controversial are impact fees to cover additional school costs for the increased number of students from the subdivision; fund bus and streetcar systems that will be more widely used; soil investigations and reports; groundwater recharge systems; erosion control; jogging and bicycle paths; and daycare facilities.
3. The fifth amendment of the U.S. Constitution—part of the Bill of Rights—prohibits the federal government from taking private property unless it is for a public purpose and the owner is paid just compensation. Originally the takings clause only applied to takings by the federal government. In 1866, the fourteenth amendment to the U.S. Constitution provided that no state shall deprive any citizen of property without due process of law. The U.S. Supreme Court has held that substantive due process requires states, and cities and counties as subdivisions of states to accord property owners the same rights when a state takes their land as the fifth amendment taking clause requires when the federal government takes land.
4. First-generation U.S. land use zones often had shapes that looked like squares, rectangles, triangles, and other geometrical forms that were first defined by the Greek geometrician Euclid (300 BCE). The Supreme Court case upholding zoning—*Village of Euclid vs Ambler Realty Company* (1926)—originated in an Ohio village named Euclid, Ohio that is part of the Cleveland, Ohio metropolitan area.
5. The equal protection clause of the thirteenth amendment is applied to the states through another clause in the thirteenth amendment called the due process clause. The due process clause prohibits any state from depriving any person of life, liberty, or property, without due process of law. The U.S. Supreme court has held that discrimination on the basis of race, religion, or national origin is a violation of the due process clause.
6. The New Jersey Supreme Court found that Mount Laurel's zoning ordinance made it nearly impossible for builders to build housing for the full spectrum of households who could be "expected to reside" in Mount Laurel, including the low-income Black and Puerto Rican plaintiffs from both Mount Laurel and the nearby city of Camden, New Jersey who brought a class action lawsuit on behalf of people like themselves and other low-income people of color (*Southern Burlington NAACP*, 1975). The court held that local governments in New Jersey must use their zoning powers in an affirmative manner to provide a realistic opportunity for developers to build housing affordable to low- and moderate-income households. When Mount Laurel refused to comply, after years of local government dithering, in the second *Mount Laurel* opinion—*Southern Burlington NAACP vs Mount Laurel* (1987)—the New Jersey Supreme Court took drastic action. They set up a special category of trial courts to hear only cases challenging discriminatory local government land use and housing laws. They gave trial court judges power to quickly decide exclusionary zoning cases and force communities to be inclusionary. They established a presumption that discrimination exists if a community's plans and regulation do not allow a realistic opportunity for developers to build a variety of housing to meet needs of people expected to reside in the community (whether or not they are residents). In extreme cases, the second Mount Laurel case authorized the trial court judges to provide a "builder's remedy" simply permitting construction of housing regardless of local zoning rather than fining the city or pressuring them in other ways (*Southern Burlington NAACP*, 1983). This pressure from the New Jersey Supreme Court forced the New Jersey legislature to enact a Fair Housing Act in 1985 and to create a state Council on Affordable Housing (COAH). The combination of litigation and state legislative action has improved the low-income housing situation in New Jersey, but conflict continues. The COAH no longer exists.
7. The Sanborn Map Company had a virtual monopoly on publishing maps for fire insurance underwriters throughout the United States. Sanborn maps include property boundaries, house and block numbers, outlines of each building and outbuilding, the building use, and building materials. Sanborn maps are often available in local libraries or archives. A complete set is in the U.S. Library of Congress. The University of California, Berkeley Bancroft library has a large, indexed collection of Sanborn maps with an online index (UC Berkeley, 2018).
8. Before construction, a property owner or developer will submit blueprints for the building to the local building code department and meet with a building inspector. If the building inspector advises that parts of the building plan violate the local building code, the developer must change them to get a building permit. During construction the building inspector will make onsite inspections at critical stages to assure that the construction is up to code. When the

building is finished, a building inspector will do a final inspection and issue an occupancy permit only if everything meets the building code.

9 The five facilities that Ramapo considered in its residential tempo control system were: (1) public sanitary sewers or approved substitutes, (2) drainage facilities, (3) improved public parks or recreation facilities, including public schools, (4) state, county, or town major, secondary, or collector roads, and (5) firehouses. The plan exempted single-family homes and included hardship exemptions.

10 Petaluma set a maximum population of 55,000 at buildout, halted annexations of land on the city's fringe for 15 years and created an urban limit line establishing a clear division between land which could be developed immediately and land which could only be developed in the future. Unlike Ramapo's simple infrastructure-related point system, Petaluma awarded points for good design, building on in-fill lots, landscaping, controlling sprawl, providing extra parking spaces, and other development features the community valued. Petaluma did not adopt a points threshold. Rather, they specified an absolute number of 500 building permits they would grant each year. Petaluma required developers to submit proposals detailing how their development would meet the criteria in the Petaluma plan. A Site Planning and Architectural Review Committee (SPARC) of citizens and experts ranked proposals. The developer who submitted the top proposal received a permit to build all the units he or she proposed. These units were subtracted from the 500 total units. Then the developer with the second highest-ranked proposal got permits, and so on. As soon as the 500 units were allocated, no more permits were issued that year. Developers could re-submit a proposal the following year. They had an incentive to improve their proposals in order to increase their chances of approval. However, they would never know for sure if their proposal would be approved until competing applications were reviewed. Petaluma's urban growth boundary is still highly relevant. It reflects the city and community's high prioritization of Petaluma's rural setting. The city's growth management efforts are currently focused on transitioning towards a new, denser city form that respects Petaluma's history, the urban growth boundary, desire for walkable neighborhoods with a strong sense of place, and limiting the city's carbon impacts.

11 The U.S. District Court for the Northern District of California held that the Petaluma plan violated the U.S. Constitution's "right to travel" (Petaluma I, 1974). The U.S. ninth circuit court of appeals reversed that decision (Petaluma II, 1976). The Petaluma case did not decide a second issue—whether the plan violated the interstate commerce clause of the U.S. Constitution that prohibits states from passing laws that interfere with interstate commerce. A federal district court invalidated the plan because they concluded that it violated a constitutionally protected right to travel interstate because it would so increase housing costs that people from out of state could not afford to cross state lines into California. The ninth circuit reversed the district court's decision. The U.S. Supreme Court denied certiorari (chose not to hear) the case—leaving the matter unresolved. Application of the right to travel because of growth management is no longer a live issue, because of the more conservative composition of the federal judiciary, including the U.S. Supreme Court.

SUGGESTIONS FOR FURTHER LEARNING

Land Use Regulation: John Nolon & Patricia Salkin, *Land use law in a nutshell* (2017). David Callies, Robert Freilich, & Shelly Saxer, *Cases and materials on land use*, 7th ed (2017). Patricia Salkin, Julian Juergensmeyer, Thomas Roberts, & Ryan Rowberry, *Land use planning and development regulation law*, 4th ed (2018). Daniel Mandelker, Carol Brown, Stuart Meck, Dwight Merriam, & Peter Salsich Jr., *Planning and control of land development*, 10th ed (2020). William Fulton & Paul Shigley, *Guide to California planning*, 5th ed (2018). **City and County Planning:** Gary Hack, Eugenie Birch, Paul Sedway, & Mitchell Silver, *Local planning* (2018). John Levy, *Contemporary urban planning* 11th ed. (2016). Allan Jacobs, *Making city planning work* (1980). **City Branding:** Keith Dinnie, *City branding* (2011). Walter Moody, *Wacker's manual of the plan of Chicago* (1911). **Supreme Court Legal Decisions Related to Plan Implementation:** *First Evangelical Church of Glendale vs County of Los Angeles* (1987). *Nollan vs California Coastal Commission* (1987). *Golden vs the Town Planning Board of Ramapo* (1972). *Construction Industry Association vs City of Petaluma* (1974). *Construction Industry Association vs City of Petaluma* (1975). *Renton vs Playtime Theaters Inc.* (1986). (1986). *Kelo vs New London*. (2005). *Penn Central Transportation Company vs New York City*. **Vision Planning:** 1000 Friends of Oregon, *Blueprint for Oregon's future* (2008). **Property Rights:** Timothy & Christina Sandefur, *Cornerstone of liberty: Property rights in the 21st century*, 2nd ed (2015). **Zoning:** Richard Babcock, *The zoning game* (1966). Richard Babcock & Charles Siemon, *The zoning game revisited* (1985). Bernard Siegen, *Land use without zoning* (1972). California Governor's Office of Planning and Research, *Planning, zoning, and development laws* (2011). Daniel Mandelker, New perspectives on planned unit developments (2017). **Inclusionary and Exclusionary Zoning:** Nico Cavalito & Allan Mallach, *Inclusionary housing in international perspective* (2010). *Southern Burlington NAACP vs Village of Mount Laurel* (1975). *Southern Burlington NAACP vs Township of Mount Laurel* (1983). David Kirp, John Dwyer, Larry Rosenthal, *Our town: Race,* *housing, and the soul of suburbia* (1997). Sock-Yong Phang, *Policy innovations for affordable housing in Singapore* (2018). **Design Review:** San Francisco Planning Department, *Design review* (2021). *Reid vs Architectural Board of Review of City of Cleveland Heights* (1963). **Form -Based Codes and Transects:** Brian Falk & Andrus Duany (eds), *Transect Urbanism* (2020). Form-Based Codes Institute (FBCI), *Form-based codes defined* (2021). Form-Based Codes Institute (FBCI) [website] (2021). Center for Applied Transect Studies (CATS) [website] (2021). Daniel Parolek, Karen Parolek, & Paul Crawford, *Form -based codes* (2008). Korkut Onaran, Crafting form-based codes (2018). **Site planning:** Gary Hack, *Site planning international* (2018). **Urban Growth Management:** Douglas Porter, *Managing growth in America's communities*, 2nd ed (2007). Arthur Nelson, *Growth management and urban planning in the United States* (2015). Robin Boyle & Raymond Mohamed, *State growth management, smart growth and urban containment* (2007). Lincoln Land Institute, *Portland: Quest for the livable city* [video] (2009). National Center for Smart Growth [website] (2020). **Infrastructure Planning:** Vicki Elmer & Adam Leighland, *Infrastructure planning and finance* (2013). **The Unearned Increment in Land:** Henry George, *Progress and poverty* (1879). **Windfalls, Wipeouts, and Land Value Capture:** Donald Hagman & Dean Misczynski, *Windfalls for wipeouts* (1978). Eddie Hui & Vivian Ho, Land value capture mechanisms in Hong Kong and Singapore (2004). **LEED Standards:** United States Green Building Council, *Leadership in energy and environmental design (LEED)* green building standards (2013) and *LEED v4 for neighborhood development* (2021). **Aesthetics and the Law:** John Costonis, *Icons and aliens* (1988).

CHAPTER 9

Community Planning, Citizen Participation, and Social Justice

INTRODUCTION

There are thousands of communities in the United States with physical features and social institutions that residents of every income, race, gender, age, and sexual orientation find deeply satisfying. Each resident of the historic core of Savannah, Georgia, need walk only a few minutes to enjoy lovely parks—famous for their towering oak trees and Spanish moss. People of a variety of races and incomes enjoy the vitality of neighborhoods in Chicago where planners have helped low-income public housing tenants to move close to their jobs and to schools they prefer for their children. Residents of the Vieux Carré (old square) in New Orleans enjoy the look and feel of a historic Spanish-French neighborhood with iron balconies, Cajun cuisine, and jazz venues. Members of the LGBTQ community in San Francisco's Castro District meet with their friends at outdoor cafes. Hassidic Jewish couples stroll along the Hudson River in New York's Williamsburg neighborhood.

There also many troubled communities in the United States. Residents of inner-city neighborhoods in Flint, Michigan were poisoned by the local drinking water. Black residents of Ferguson, Missouri rioted after White police shot and killed an unarmed Black man and there have been similar riots in many other U.S. cities when police have killed Black residents. Entire blocks of Camden, New Jersey, and East Saint Louis, Missouri, are boarded up. Some Detroit neighborhoods have many vacant lots because of arson.

To plan for neighborhoods, city and regional planners need to understand different types of communities based on their geography, history, demographics, and culture. They need to relate planning at the neighborhood scale to planning at the scale of individual sites, cities and counties, and at higher levels up to the national and international levels.

Community planning poses issues of how to involve citizens and practice collaborative planning. It is entwined with issues of income and race. Community planning requires cultural sensitivity and anti-racist practice.

This chapter begins with a discussion of citizen participation and collaborative and communicative action in neighborhood planning. Sections describe opposition to locally unwanted land uses. Several sections of the chapter are devoted to race, diversity, equity, and social justice in city and regional planning. These include discussions about how planners can gain cultural competence to better understand the communities they are planning for, recognize and overcome White privilege, and pursue anti-racist policies and practice.

Sections describe how city and regional planners can act as advocate planners, representing the interests of the poor and powerless. The chapter discusses how equity planners make equity and social justice the key normative value in every city and regional planning decision in some cities.

DOI: 10.4324/9781003195818-9

CITIZEN PARTICIPATION AND COMMUNITY PLANNING

The dominant theory of citizen participation for over 60 years has been Sherry Arnstein's "ladder of citizen participation". Arnstein was an official of the United States Department of Housing and Urban Development. She oversaw neighborhood citizen organizations in communities funded by the federal model cities program, which distributed flexible funding to low-income neighborhoods in 150 cities in the late 1960s and early 1970s.

In a classic article in the *Journal of the American Institute of Planners*, Arnstein used the metaphor of a ladder with rungs of citizen participation (Figure 9.1). She saw planning as a tool to redistribute power from haves to have-nots by empowering the poor and

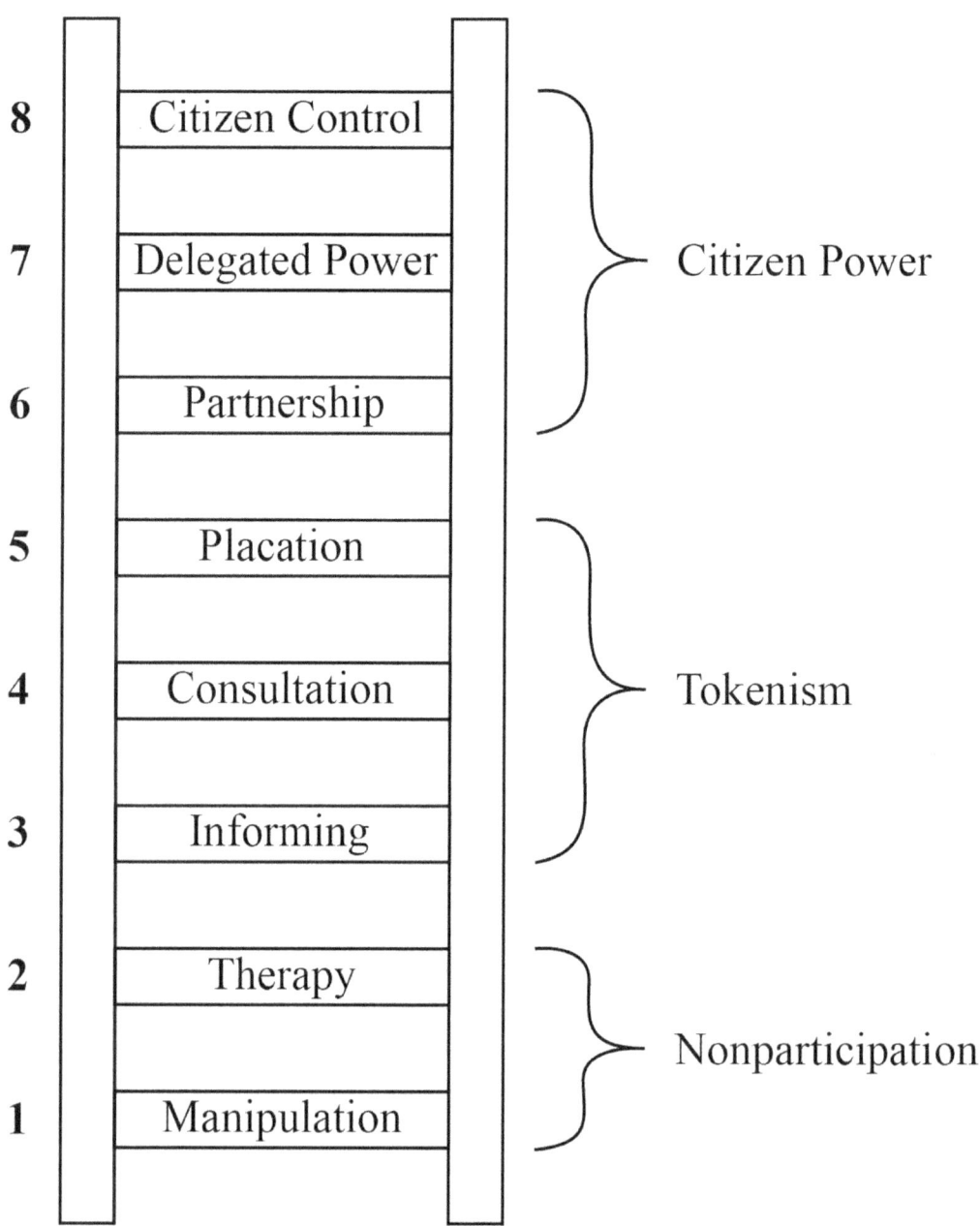

Figure 9.1 Sherry Arnstein's Ladder of Citizen Participation.

powerless in order to move their participation from lower to higher rungs of her conceptual ladder. Arnstein pulled no punches in exposing the hypocrisy of local governments that ignore or only grudgingly accept citizen participation in order to meet government requirements and receive federal money. She concludes that in America while virtually everyone vigorously applauds participation of the governed in their government as the cornerstone of democracy, that "when the have-nots define participation as redistribution of power, the American consensus on the fundamental principle explodes into many shades of outright racial, ethnic, ideological, and political opposition" (Arnstein, 1969: 216).

Arnstein call the lowest rungs of her ladder nonparticipation because they are really aimed at getting citizens to accept a course of action predetermined by the local government (manipulation) or as a way to cure citizens of beliefs that they want to eliminate (therapy). She calls the middle rungs—informing, consultation, and placation—tokenism. She considers them legitimate, but inadequate forms of participation. Arnstein feels that informing citizens of the facts about government programs and their rights, responsibilities, and options is a good first step, particularly if it is designed to go beyond a one-way flow of information. She places consultation—soliciting citizens' opinions—a rung above just informing them, so long as the process is honest and citizens' opinions are considered. Placation is higher up Arnstein's ladder of citizen participation. Government gives in to a few citizen demands. However, having government merely throw citizens some crumbs to placate them is not satisfactory participation.

The highest rungs on Arnstein's ladder—partnership, two rungs from the top, delegated power, one rung below the top, and citizen control at the very top—represent what Arnstein considers serious and legitimate forms of citizen participation. They grant citizens differing degree of power. Like partnerships in business and international relations, participation at the partnership level in neighborhood programs may be uncomfortable and tense, but if partners are able to work together, engage in political horse trading, and respect each other's core interests, they can produce good outcomes for all parties. Arnstein considers delegated power to be better—citizens have the power to make many decisions. At the highest rung of Arnstein's ladder—citizen control—neighborhood residents make fundamental plan decisions and control program implementation, including personnel and budget decisions.

By April, 2019—50 years after it was published—Arnstein's article had been cited more than 17,000 times. Few local governments have ceded control of urban programs to citizens.[1] However, many have delegated power to neighborhood groups or formed partnerships with them.

COMMUNITY PLANNING

A community plan—also called a neighborhood plan—covers an area larger than a site and smaller than a comprehensive plan for a city or county. In most cities and counties, neighborhoods are informally named, and their boundaries may be fuzzy or conflicting. Some local planning departments name, map, and describe neighborhoods and prepare separate neighborhood or community plans for them as part of their general plan or as separate plans. Chapter 8 describes Nashville, Tennessee's community plans for 14 neighborhoods.

Box 9.1 describes one notable community planning effort—the Dudley Street Neighborhood Initiative (DSNI). The DSNI allowed residents of the Roxbury neighborhood in Boston, Massachusetts to plan and implement a variety of successful neighborhood programs.

LOCALLY UNWANTED LAND USES (LULUS) AND THE NOT-IN-MY-BACK-YARD (NIMBY) SYNDROME

Neighborhood residents often want to radically scale down or stop a proposed development that they believe will negatively impact their neighborhood. They may try to push unwanted developments somewhere else. A NIMBY is someone who says "not in

BOX 9.1 THE DUDLEY STREET NEIGHBORHOOD INITIATIVE

The Dudley Street neighborhood is an ethnically mixed lower-income neighborhood in Roxbury—a neighborhood in Boston, Massachusetts. Roxbury had been a White working-class neighborhood before World War II, with a largely Irish and Italian population. During World War II many military-age White men left Roxbury to serve in the military. Many Black men and some Black women migrated from the rural South to the Boston area to work in wartime jobs, and some moved into Roxbury, including the Dudley Street neighborhood. After the war, the Black migration continued, along with immigration of Spanish-speaking Blacks from the Caribbean, and Portuguese-speaking Blacks from the Cape Verde Islands off the west coast of Africa. Many of the young Irish and Italian men who had been in the military moved out of Roxbury with their families to predominantly White Boston suburbs where they were able to buy modest homes with their wartime savings and zero-down payment, zero-interest Veterans (VA) Administration mortgages. Racial discrimination kept Blacks—including Black veterans—from buying houses in the suburbs. Redlining and racially restrictive covenants made it legally impossible for Black households to purchase many houses they were financially qualified to buy. Blacks were not eligible for VA loans. However, many Blacks had enough savings and income to afford to buy a housing unit in Roxbury, even if they had to pay a very high down payments or all cash and even if the interest rates were higher than for White households. They were attracted by the prospect of homeownership in an ethnically mixed neighborhood.

As the wartime boom turned into a bust, wages declined, and low–moderate-income homeowners had less money to spend on home maintenance. The physical condition of housing in the Dudley Street neighborhood deteriorated. Unscrupulous landlords committed arson—burning their buildings for the insurance proceeds. Illegal drug use and trafficking increased, and other crimes also became serious problems. Even owners with resources would not maintain their homes when resale values were plummeting.

Nonprofit foundations sometimes fund neighborhood regeneration projects. They may stimulate public–private partnerships (PPPs) to bring together federal, state, local, and private capital. Some philanthropic foundations provide "seed money" to pay for planning consultants and technical assistance, cover costs of staff for largely volunteer neighborhood organizations, and/or pay part of the costs of improving parks, playgrounds, and community centers. They may fund youth, job training, and other social service programs. Private businesses may support projects like these, and local politicians see political advantage in associating their regimes with successful projects.

A local Boston foundation—the Riley Foundation—decided to invest in the Dudley Street Neighborhood Initiative (DSNI) in the Dudley Street neighborhood in Roxbury. None of the (largely White) Riley Foundation staff lived in or knew much about Roxbury or the DSNI neighborhood firsthand. When Riley Foundation staff announced the Dudley Street Initiative at a public meeting in the neighborhood, residents showed up in large numbers—not to thank them, offer their support, or even ask questions, but to excoriate the outsiders for their arrogance in creating a top-down plan without consulting neighborhood residents.

Things got better. The Riley Foundation went back to the drawing board and initiated a long, thoughtful, sometimes conflictual community planning process. Rather than emphasizing problems in the neighborhood, it used an asset-based community development perspective. They drew on existing community strengths, such as the skills of local residents, the power of local churches and neighborhood associations, and the supportive functions of local institutions, to design a plan to build a stronger, more sustainable community for the future. The Riley Foundation funded a full-time project director selected by and accountable to the residents (initially a White community organizer; later a Black former mayor of Berkeley, California). They paid for a planning consultant that the residents selected (who was Black) to provide technical assistance. They provided funding for neighborhood youth to survey their neighbors.

The DSNI held bottom-up planning meetings in Spanish and Portuguese as well as English. Community organizers started with a campaign to close down illegal trash transfer stations in the neighborhood because that issue had universal support. Nobody likes garbage in their neighborhood, and all Dudley Street residents were eager to get rid of illegal activity by outsiders. The (White Irish) Boston mayor enforced the law forbidding illegal trash transfer stations. When the transfer stations were padlocked, the initiative gained enough credibility to move on to more ambitious projects, including renovating a park that had been taken over by drug dealers, creating a community center, economic development projects, and eventually a highly unusual community land trust with the power of eminent domain to assemble land for affordable housing. The land trust acquired parcels in a triangle (the Dudley Street Triangle) for a development of affordable new single-family homes. Eventually the DSNI, Riley Foundation, local banks, the Ford Foundation, the U.S. Department of Housing and Urban Development, and other investors collaborated to achieve development without displacement. Today the DSNI is alive and well. It is implementing a 2018 vision plan for neighborhood control and resident power, fostering local leadership, and ensuring equitable access to resources and opportunities. Current focus areas are development without displacement, neighborhood development, and empowering youth.

my back yard" to a locally unwanted land use (LULU). A LULU may be a problematic development such as a halfway house, homeless shelter, or sewage treatment plant that people feel is inappropriate in their neighborhood, even if they agree that is necessary if it is located somewhere else. NIMBYs can always generate a long list of reasons why a particular site is inappropriate. They assert that it will increase crime, lower property values, destroy critical habitat, endanger salamanders, or whatever. People even oppose developments they agree will benefit their neighborhood such as libraries, fitness centers, dog parks, and jogging paths if they feel that they are near enough to their own property to arguably affect parking, block views, create noise or traffic congestion, or otherwise inconvenience them. The vociferous participation of NIMBYs often torpedoes needed projects, drags out approvals, and imposes costs on public and private entities that are trying to get needed things done. NIMBYs show up at public hearings to object to programs; supporters often do not show up at hearings.

The closer a controversial development is to a local elected official's election year, the more eager the official is likely to be to avoid making decisions which will alienate voters. NIMEYs (not-in-my-election-year) are elected officials facing an upcoming election who try to avoid making controversial decisions until the election is over. NIMEYs may try to delay planning and land use decisions that will anger voters until after the election is over, or they will side with NIMBY voters if they feel that NIMBYs outnumber voters who support a project or plan.

The most common reason project opponents give for opposition to a project is that it will negatively impact the environment. NIMBYs' vehicles of choice are the National Environmental Policy Act (NEPA) and similar state little NEPAs. Massachusetts Institute of Technology professor Bernard Frieden called using environmental impact assessment as an excuse to block a LULU "the environmental protection hustle".

COMMUNITY PLANNING AND SOCIAL JUSTICE

Since demographics is so important to building community, people of the same race, religion, country of origin, language or sexual orientation frequently cluster in neighborhood communities. Social justice for all communities is a critical aspect of community planning.

There is no escaping the ugly fact that racism is pervasive in the United States today. People of color have different life experiences than White Americans. Their life experiences are often far less positive. Tensions between Black residents, the police, and local government are often high in communities of color. Unjustified police shootings of unarmed Blacks continue to provoke both peaceful protests and occasional riots. The Black Lives Matter movement is a visible manifestation of injustice and racial tensions. City and regional planners cannot reverse three centuries of inequality, but they can make significant contributions to social justice.

DISCRIMINATION AND SOCIAL JUSTICE 1607–1933

Both city and regional planning and the absence of planning have contributed to the serious structural equity and social justice problems the United States faces today. Planners can help cure inherited racial and equity injustices and proactively plan to prevent their recurrence in the future.

The first slaves arrived at Jamestown, Virginia in 1607. Black slaves who had been imported, or whose ancestors had been imported directly from Africa or via the Caribbean islands remained property in the slave and border states until emancipation in 1865. They were treated as a commodity to be bought, sold, used, and abused by White owners.

The first U.S. census (1790) enumerated half a million Blacks—60,000 of whom were classified as free. In 1860, the southern states that seceded from the union had 3,754,304 enslaved people, 250,787 of whom were nominally "free".[2] Border states that stayed with the union had 317,655 slaves.[3] There were 226,961 African Americans who lived in the northern states in 1860—all of whom were free. Vibrant communities of free Blacks formed in Boston, Philadelphia, and other cities. However, even nominally free Blacks were segregated and discriminated against in

Figure 9.2 Black Lives Matter (Albany, New York, 2020).

education, employment, property ownership, and countless other ways in both the North and the South.

Abolition of slavery in 1865 did not lead to equality for Blacks. "Jim Crow" laws perpetuated Blacks' inferior status both in the North and the South. Criminal laws sentenced Blacks to years of hard labor on chain gangs for minor offenses. Early studies by Black sociologist W.E.B. Du Bois documented the crushing discrimination Blacks faced in Philadelphia in 1899. Black sociologists St. Clair Drake and Horace Cayton's monumental 1945 study—*Black Metropolis*—documented discrimination against Blacks in Chicago's "Black Belt" in the 1930s.

A variety of discredited philosophical, religious, pseudo-scientific biological, and other writings have proposed standards by which to classify people by race. In the early 16th century, the Spanish—citing Aristotle and the Bible—concluded that American Indians were an inferior order of humans whose role was to serve their Spanish masters.

By the mid-16th century, the Spanish had concluded that American Indians were human, had souls, could be converted to the Catholic faith, and might attain salvation. However, they continued to believe that God had created Indians with natures particularly suitable for working as slaves.

Early biologists sought to classify people by race based on Swedish botanist, biologist, and physician Carl Linnaeus's (1707–1778) approach to classifying plant and animal species into rigid categories. The concept of hypodescent—legally enforced in some states well into the 20th century—classified anyone with a drop of Negro blood in their ancestry as Black in states where it was applied.

Anyone classified as Black was assumed to have distinct intelligence (inferior), sexuality (strong and uncontrolled), physique (suited for manual labor), and cultural preferences (unrefined). This provided a justification for the dominant society—including government—to segregate Blacks geographically in schools, hotels, hospitals, and restaurants and even require them to use separate (inferior) toilets and drinking fountains.

Modern approaches to understanding race reject all rigid classifications. Race is now generally conceptualized as a fluid socio-historical construct given concrete meaning by a specific set of social relations at a given time and place.

There is a long tradition of discrimination against women in the United States and many other countries. Until recently biologists defined gender as binary. Women were assigned domestic roles—childrearing, cooking, cleaning, and domestic chores at home, while men were expected to do most farm labor or work outside the home for wages. Women who did work often had low-status jobs like house cleaning or washing laundry. The few women who did the same work as men received lower wages for the same work. Women were denied the right to vote in national elections until the nineteenth amendment was ratified in 1920. In most states they had very limited property rights.

Until recently homosexuality was a crime in most of the United States, sometimes punishable by death. Gay neighborhoods were ignored in general plans and other plans.

Until the civil rights and women's liberation movements of the 1960s, planners and policy makers were largely indifferent to issues of race and gender. There were almost no Black planners and very few women city and regional planners until the 1960s.

Gender and sexual orientation are increasingly seen as falling along a continuum. The new science of sex and gender rejects rigid biological categories of male and female. Forty-five percent of the American Planning Association's members are now women. Still, few plans take an explicit gender perspective. Most plans still simply ignore LGBTQ individuals and neighborhoods as categories that merit analysis and planning.

RECENT SCHOLARSHIP ON MINORITY COMMUNITIES

Geographers, sociologists, ethnic studies scholars, and journalists as well as planners have produced a rich literature on racial, ethnic, religious, and other communities. There are classic and contemporary studies of

Irish, Italian, Black, Latinx, Indigenous, and Asian-American and Pacific Islander (AAPI) communities.[4] Both the American Planning Association (APA) and the Association of Collegiate Schools of Planning (ACSP) have special interest groups for women, Black, Latinx, Indigenous, and LGBT planners. There are no equivalent ACSP or APA interest groups for AAPI.

June Thomas (Box 9.2) and other pioneering planning faculty of color began to write about minority communities in the 1980s. However, most scholarly writing about city planning for communities of color has been written by Black, Latinx, and

---

BOX 9.2 JUNE THOMAS

June Thomas is a pioneering Black planning scholar who was among the first Black professors to teach at major city and regional planning programs. She was the first Black woman to hold a number of important positions and receive awards for planning education. Thomas is currently the Mary Frances Berry Distinguished Professor of Urban and Regional Planning at the University of Michigan. She is in the process of a phased retirement after many years teaching undergraduate, master's, and PhD students; authoring pioneering books on race, planning, redevelopment and other topics; and national service in the Association of Collegiate Schools of Planning (ACSP); and as a consultant to state and local government in Michigan. Thomas was a founding co-chair of ACSP's Planners of Color Interest Group (POCIG). She served as President of ACSP in 2015–2016.

In addition to teaching at the University of Michigan, Thomas taught urban and regional planning at Michigan State University (MSU) and urban studies at Cleveland State University. At MSU Thomas served as director of the Urban and Regional Planning Program from 1996 to 2000.

In 2017 the Society for American City Regional Planning History (SCARPH) awarded Thomas the Laurence Gerckens Prize for sustained excellence in the teaching of planning history. In 1999 she won the Association of Collegiate Schools of Planning's Paul Davidoff Award for her book *Redevelopment and Race* (1997; 2013). The ACSP awarded her the Jay Chatterjee Award for distinguished service to ACSP in 2016. She received the University of Michigan's Harold R. Johnson diversity service award in 2014. In 2003 she was inducted as a fellow of the American Institute of Certified Planners—AICP's highest honor.

Race and planning are common threads in Thomas's writing. She has written extensively about planning history, redevelopment, abandonment, community organizing, and other topics such as health and cool roofs.

Thomas tells the story of redevelopment in Detroit from the perspective of a Black planner—a story she describes as one of hope, vision, heartbreak, and frustration characterized by heroic acts and villainous deeds, but mostly good intentions. Thomas's primary purposes in studying the history of planning in Detroit was to discover why one city suffered decline and abandonment, what city and regional planners had to do with the situation, and what Detroit's experience can teach planners and local elected officials in other cities. It is a deeply personal story. Thomas, her husband, and many family members live in Detroit.

Between the time Henry Ford's factories began producing large numbers of Model T Fords in 1908 and the 1950s, Detroit was America's premier industrial city. In 1940, nearly half of the employment in metropolitan Detroit was in manufacturing. The auto industry provided stable employment for both White and Black blue-collar auto workers. During the period that is the main focus of *Redevelopment and Race*, Detroit

Figure 9.3 June Thomas.

suffered massive de-industrialization and racial conflict. In 1950 its population was 1.8 million; today it is about 673,000.

Thomas documents White flight—movement of Whites to the Detroit suburbs or other communities before rioting by Blacks in 1967—and how it accelerated as a result of the riots. After 2000 large numbers of middle- and upper-income Black households were also moving out of Detroit to the suburbs or other communities.

Detroit embraced planning. The city went through periods of post-war optimism, enthusiastic boosterism by the local growth machine, infatuation, and then disenchantment with urban renewal from 1949—when the Urban Renewal Program began—to 1974 when it ended. Massive corporate investment and efforts to stem the tide of decline with federal model cities funding, urban development action grants (UDAGs), and a federal empowerment zone were not enough to reverse Detroit's decline. Despite the best efforts of Detroit's talented and charismatic Black mayor, Coleman Young, between 1974 and 1994 Detroit continued to experience decline. Figure 16.1 shows Detroit's abandoned Packard automobile factory that closed in 1957 when Packard went out of business. Figure 16.2 shows the Renaissance Center that opened in 1967—a massive new corporate, living, and entertainment complex built by Detroit's leadership, led by Henry Ford II.

AAPI city and regional planning professors since 1990.

June Thomas provides an overarching framework within which to understand the role of planners of color and how they can contribute to the just city. Thomas begins by reiterating that race is a social construct—not a biological one. Race doesn't work well for classifying populations in countries like the United States with a population of diverse origins, many of whom who have intermarried over generations. Planners still often use the distinction between 'Blacks' or African Americans and 'Whites' or Caucasians even though both of these categories include extensive mixed-race variations. The same is true of Latinx, AAPI, and other groups. The U.S. census permits people who choose to respond to either identify themselves as members of one of five racial categories, self-report their race, or self-identify as of two or more races. Antiracism

Professor Thomas concludes that planners of color make a contribution to the planning profession both in the planning process and—more importantly—plan outcomes. She identifies powerful rationales for increasing the number of planners of color in the planning profession. Thomas concludes that planners of color impact the way in which city and regional plans are prepared in two main ways—by acting as advocates for communities of color within the agencies where they work, and by acting as bridges to communities of color. Members of communities of color often find it easier to communicate with a planner of their race. Planners of color tend to value social justice because of their own life experiences. They often encourage their co-workers to include social justice goals in plans.

CULTURAL COMPETENCY, INCLUSION, AND WHITE PRIVILEGE

Cultural competency is the ability to work effectively with difference, in cross-cultural situations. Dictionary definitions of the verb "include" are: "The practice of providing everyone with equal access to opportunities and resources" and "to consider as part of or allow into a group". Definition of "inclusion" as a noun are "an organizational effort and practices in which different groups or individuals having different backgrounds are culturally and socially accepted" and "the practice or policy of including and integrating all people and groups in activities, organizations, and political processes … especially those who are disadvantaged, have suffered discrimination, or are living with disabilities".

The Association of Collegiate Schools of Planning (ACSP)'s values statement states that graduate planning programs should provide planning students an education that supports inclusion and cultural competence as one of their five core values.

The concept of cultural competency was developed by Georgetown University professor Terry Cross and other mental health professionals based on their experience with severely emotionally disabled Black children and their families. While it is often invoked as a value that Whites need to embrace, developing cultural competency applies to people of every race and culture.

Julian Agyeman—a professor of urban and environmental policy and planning at Tufts University—and Jennifer Erickson at the Metropolitan Area Planning Council in Boston, Massachusetts describe five elements of cultural competency: (1) valuing diversity, (2) the capacity for cultural self-assessment, (3) consciousness of the dynamics of cultural interaction, (4) the institutionalization of cultural knowledge, and (5) the development of adaptations to service delivery based on understanding inter- and intra-cultural diversity.

White privilege refers to the fact that the entire social structure of some societies—including the United States—privileges White people over Blacks and other people of color. Wellesley College professor Peggy McIntosh—a White senior research scientist and former associate director of Wellesley's Center for Women—formulated the concept of White privilege in 1989. McIntosh recognized that Blacks and other minorities did not have the same privileges that she and the great majority of Whites take for granted. In her classic article describing White privilege, McIntosh discussed 26 examples of how she was privileged as a White person. These include being confident that if she needed to move, she could be pretty sure of renting or purchasing housing in an area she could afford, in which she wanted to live, and that her neighbors would be neutral or pleasant to her. If she needed legal or medical help, McIntosh knew that her race would not work against her. If a she was pulled over by a policeman for speeding, she could be sure she hadn't been singled out because of her race. McIntosh realized that invisible systems conferring dominance on Whites can be as damaging as individual racist acts. White privilege is more subtle than overt racism. Many people are unaware that it exists—simply accepting unfair and unequal systems as the normal and inevitable nature of things. Efforts have fallen short of meeting the challenge of transforming the culture of White privilege in U.S. society and in the planning profession.

ANTI-RACISM AND LEGAL PROTECTIONS FOR MINORITIES

Anti-racism is a current concern in city and regional planning, other professions, and all of U.S. society. Racism takes multiple forms that often occur in tandem to reinforce racist ideas, behavior, and policy. Restorative justice, affirmative action, and the possibility of reparations are approaches to overcoming the impact of centuries of racism.

The National Museum of African American History identifies four main types of racism:

- **Individual racism:** beliefs, attitudes, and actions of individuals that support or perpetuate racism in conscious and unconscious ways;
- **Interpersonal racism:** public expressions of racism, often involving slurs, biases, or hateful words or actions exchanged between individuals;
- **Institutional racism:** discriminatory treatments, unfair policies, or biased practices based on race in an organization that produce more favorable outcomes for Whites than for people of color;
- **Structural racism:** the overarching system of racial bias across institutions and society that gives privileges to White people and disadvantages people of color.

Being anti-racist is different for White people than it is for people of color. For White people, anti-racism is a distinctive form of reflective practice. Agyeman and Erickson argue that to overcome internalized racism, Whites must acknowledge and understand their privilege, take daily actions to eliminate racism, and interrupt racism when they see it. For people of color, anti-racism means recognizing how race and racism have been internalized, and whether or not they unconsciously apply it to other people of color. All planners need to be conscious of and work to eliminate racism.

There is a growing body of material on anti-racist practice. The Annie E. Casey Foundation's 2015 *Race Equity Inclusion and Action Guide* provides a seven-step model of how to advance and embed racial equity based on the rational planning model.[5] The International City Management Association's 2021 *Equity and Inclusion Toolkit* provides guidance on the experience of their member local governments in implementing equity and inclusion policies.[6] ACSP's Planners of Color Interest Group (POCIG)'s research and activities provide guidance on anti-racist practice for planners.

WOMEN IN PLANNING

Changing family and gender relations and the massive increase of women in the U.S. workforce have altered the relationship between home and work and created new needs for city and regional planners to address. The number of women working as planners and teaching and studying city and regional planning has increased rapidly. Forty-five percent of APA members are now women—up from just 10% in 1980.

The American Planning Association has had a "Planning and Women Division" that provides a national network for female planners since 1979. The division promotes the analysis and examination of issues of women and planning at every level of government, in colleges and universities, and in the teaching profession. It promotes professional growth of women in planning, and advocates for equitable treatment and advancement of female planners at all stages of their careers.

The ACSP's Faculty Women's Interest Group (FWIG) is an ACSP special interest group that provides a network for women planning professors, students, and others interested in women in planning, regardless of their gender identity. FWIG meets at the annual ACSP conference.

There are books and articles by women planning professors on theory and practice to make planning more responsive to contemporary women's needs. Yale University Professor of Architecture and American Studies Dolores Hayden has described her vision of what a non-sexist city might be like. University of Virginia Professor Emerita of Planning Daphne Spain has described how planners can adopt a gender perspective in all of their work.

Fewer than 20% of U.S. households now consist of a nuclear family with a husband, wife, and one or more children compared to 45% in 1960. Women are no longer only staying at home raising children and doing unpaid household work rather than participating in the labor force. This creates planning issues around land uses for daycare centers, density and sprawl, telecommuting, home offices and the location of work, and various other facilities in relation to housing. These issues affect men as well as women.

As the number of female-headed households has grown there has been a pressing need for more affordable housing suitable for them. Forty-four percent of Black children, 22% of Latinx children, 12% of White children, and 7% of AAPI children live in single-parent female-headed households. Alternative designs such as apartment units with safe shared play areas visible from multiple apartments occupied by single women (and men) with children make it easier for them to juggle work at home while they look after their children, cook, and do household chores.

PLANNING IN ETHNIC COMMUNITIES

The U.S. census estimates that as of July, 2019, 76% of the U.S. population was White, 19% Latinx, 13% Black/African American, 6% Asian alone, 1.3% American Indian and Alaska Native alone, 0.2% American Indian or Native Hawaiian/Pacific Islander, and 2.8% two or more races. The totals are greater than 100% because some people fall into two or more categories. The census estimates are extremely problematic for five main reasons: (1) race is a social—not a biological—construct, (2) many people are mixed-race and how they define themselves is not standardized, (3) the census relies on respondents' reporting of race, (4) many illegal residents do not respond for fear of deportation, (5) low-income, poorly educated, and non-English-speakers often refuse to respond to the census or provide false information.

Communities of color have faced a long history of racially discriminatory practices affecting all aspects of their residents' lives. Among the most pernicious planning practices was—and in disguised form still is—redlining. Until it was declared illegal, lending institutions drew an actual red line on a map delimiting Black and racially mixed or transitioning areas they considered financially risky. They would not approve mortgage loans within the redlined areas. Figure 9.4 is a map of the Boston Area in 1934. In this map redlined areas are colored in solid red. The U.S. Federal Housing Administration—the federal agency established to provide mortgage insurance to lower-income homebuyers to help them purchase homes—encouraged redlining and would not insure mortgages in redlined areas on the same terms for Blacks as for Whites, often not insure any mortgages for Blacks in redlined areas, or any mortgages for people of any race in redlined areas until the 1960s. As a result, Black households needed to borrow money to purchase a home from relatives, had to finance their homes with installment contracts—a type of housing financing that is more expensive and offers fewer protections than a mortgage—or remained renters.

A second practice that institutionalized racial discrimination in planning was legally enforceable restrictive covenants. Restrictive covenants were provisions in deeds prohibiting a homeowner from selling the house to a proscribed racial or religious minority—typically Blacks and Jews. Many restrictive covenants stated categorically that the house could never be occupied by anyone not of the Caucasian race. The U.S. Supreme

Figure 9.4 1934 Map of Boston Area Showing Redlined Neighborhoods.

Court declared racially restrictive covenants unconstitutional in 1948.

There are many different kinds of Black and mixed-race communities in the United States. In metropolitan areas, 10 percent of neighborhoods housing 14.4 million non-Hispanic Blacks (37 percent of the U.S. non-Hispanic Black population) are majority

Black. Approximately 5 million Americans from other racial and ethnic backgrounds live in these majority Black neighborhoods.

Some public housing projects are overwhelmingly composed of low-income, Black, female-headed households. Plans and policies for the poorest, most segregated Black communities justifiably receive the most attention from planners, but the full spectrum of Black and mixed-race communities require culturally sensitive planning.

Planning issues that are particularly acute for Black communities include the elimination of discrimination in mortgage lending, enforcement of fair housing laws, and deconcentration of tenants in large public housing projects where almost all tenants are Black. A major objective of the U.S. Department of Housing and Urban Development (HUD) is to create opportunities for Blacks and public housing tenants to have greater choice to secure housing that they can afford in neighborhoods of their choice. Chapter 17 describes HUD's Choice Neighborhoods Program that provides support and subsidies to accomplish that goal.

In 2019 the U.S. Census Bureau estimated that there were a little over 53 million people who self-identified as Hispanic or Latino (the census terms) in the United States, constituting 16% of the total population. This book uses the term Latinx unless it is referring to census data or terminology that the American Planning Association, Association of Collegiate Schools of Planning, or Planning Accreditation Board use. Whatever the terminology, the number of Latinx in the United States is large and growing rapidly. Planners need to be aware of the difficulty in defining the Latinx community and the need to be sensitive to the terminology preferences of members of Latinx communities themselves. These vary depending on age, country of origin, and other variables. There are large concentrations of Latinx from specific regions in some U.S. cities, such as Puerto Ricans in New York City, Mexican Americans in Houston, Texas, and Cuban Americans in Miami, Florida. These neighborhoods need culturally sensitive planning, including planners of Puerto Rican, Mexican American, and Cuban American heritage.

Historically, large parts of what is now the United States were predominantly Latinx.[7] Preserving the tangible and intangible Latinx heritage of historically Latinx regions is an important task for planners in these region.

Planning for the U.S. Latinx population along the border with Mexico and the states closest to Mexico poses special challenges. Key issues include accommodating the needs of undocumented migrants being held in U.S. Immigration and Customs Enforcement (ICE) and U.S. Customs and Border Protection (CPB) facilities, the uncertainty of future migration from Mexico and Central and South America, anti-immigrant bias, labor issues in *maquiladoras*—plants in Mexico just across the border where poorly paid Mexican workers assemble components into finished products for export and consumption in the United States—and planning for *colonias*, a distinct type of low-income informal community.[8]

Asian Americans and Pacific Islanders are usually grouped together as Asian American Pacific Islanders (AAPI). Census categories have changed, and recent reports sometimes use the categories "Asian Alone", "Asian American", and "Native Hawaiian and other Pacific Islanders". The census term "Native Hawaiian and other Pacific Islander" includes Native Hawaiians, Samoans, and Chamorros. Chamorros are indigenous people of the Mariana Islands (including Guam).

In addition to the categorization issue, it is difficult to determine the size or characteristics of the AAPI population for many of the same reasons as with the Black and Latinx populations. This is compounded by the fact that AAPI are the least likely ethnic group to provide information to the census. The Census Bureau estimates that there are 20 million AAPI in the USA. Most are concentrated in California, Hawaii, Texas, and New York. Honolulu, San Francisco, and New York City have the largest Asian American populations of U.S. cities.

AAPI communities have their own culture and planning needs. Historic Chinatowns often have historically significant buildings.

Monterey Park, California—an affluent, largely Chinese community—incorporates the ancient Chinese practice of feng shui—arranging living space harmoniously—in their planning!

University of Maryland urban studies and planning professor Willow Lung Aman has identified distinct planning challenges for Asian American communities that include opposition to large houses that are suitable for multi-generational household, resentment that their children may raise public school academic standards so that other students can't compete, and opposition to culturally specific shopping centers.

INDIGENOUS COMMUNITY PLANNING

Because of their history and culture, planning by and for Native American and other indigenous communities involves cultural sensitivity and unique practices. A growing number of planning professors have studied and written about planning for indigenous communities. These professors often hold faculty positions in parts of the United States and Canada where indigenous people constitute a significant percentage of the population.[9] The American Planning Association and the Association of Collegiate Schools of Planning each have a tribal planning and indigenous interest group.

Estimates of the pre-Columbian Native American population in what is now the United States range from several million to as many as 18 million. Genocide, war, disease, and oppression reduced the number of people who described themselves as Native Americans to the U.S. Census Bureau to a low of 240,000 in the 1890 census. The census now reports that over 5 million people in the United States self-report as Native Americans.

The census term "American Indian" refers to members of 574 federally recognized tribes living within the USA. The great majority (78%) live outside reservations. However, about half maintain an association with a reservation. Over 70% of Native Americans live in urban areas—up from 45% in 1970 and 8% in 1940. There are significant American Indian communities in New York City, Los Angeles, Chicago, Houston, Denver, Albuquerque, Phoenix, and Oklahoma City as well as other cities, towns, and rural areas within and outside of reservations. There are many mixed-race people who are partly of Native American ancestry. American Indian reservations range from the huge, largely rural Navajo Nation covering over 27,000 square miles in parts of Arizona, New Mexico, and Utah to reservations of fewer than a dozen members. Some reservations have extremely high poverty rates. Others have very high average incomes as a result of gambling revenue; the presence of oil, gas, coal, or mineral deposits on reservation land; or other circumstances.

On Native American reservations, critical planning issues include: how to determine tribal membership and rights; what extraction of oil, gas, and minerals to permit and with what protection of the environment and sacred sites; authorization to own and run gambling casinos; social planning to deal with poverty and alcoholism, as well as conventional land use, zoning, and other issues common to all communities.

One way in which American Indian communities are indirectly subsidized is by being authorized to legally allow gambling. Settlements with Indian casinos raise conventional planning issues such as traffic, parking, and provision of utilities. They also present unique political/cultural issues about the impact of gambling on tribal culture.

Nicholas Zaferatos—a scholar-practitioner and member of the Swinomish Indian tribe—has developed and describes what he calls "an adaptive and contingent model of tribal planning" to describe how to address planning issues common to many reservations.[10] In addition to making plans for the Swinomish reservation itself, the Swinomish Indians engaged in regional planning and worked with local governments that were often initially hostile. The tribe managed relations with the federal government—which is frequently a major challenge in tribal planning—and strengthened ties to state government agencies. They persuaded the U.S.

Environmental Protection Agency (EPA) to clean up oil-refinery waste on the reservation. They were able to get the tribes' fishing and water rights extended outside the reservation. The Swinomish implemented a climate change initiative. The tribe came to terms amicably with rights and obligations of non-Indians living on the reservation.

Zaferatos counsels that the effectiveness of tribal planning depends upon a tribe's capacity to exercise its political resolve while simultaneously assessing its planning environment. His narrative emphasizes the complexity of tribal planning. Navigating a strategic course through changing circumstances required a great deal of patience.

PLANNING WITH AND FOR LESBIAN, GAY, BISEXUAL, TRANSGENDER, AND QUEER (LGBTQ) COMMUNITIES

The Stonewall Rebellion in 1969 during which bar patrons forcibly clashed with police after the police raided the Stonewall Inn—a gay bar in Brooklyn, New York—signaled the beginning of the gay rights movement. Since the Stonewall Rebellion, the lesbian, gay, bisexual, transgender, and queer population has created queer spaces in many cities designed specifically to welcome and serve the needs of the gay population. Many formerly derelict neighborhoods in American cities have been transformed with capital and leadership from gays.

In 2017 a Gallup polling organization survey found that 4.5% of American adults surveyed identified themselves as lesbian, gay, bisexual, or transgender. That suggests that at least 11 million people in the United States are openly gay. The actual gay population of the United States is likely much higher, because some respondents—particularly older respondents—choose not to report their sexual orientation. The size of the openly LGBTQ population is growing—particularly among younger people. The American Planning Association and Association of Collegiate Schools of Planning both have LGBTQ special interest groups for LGBTQ members and their allies.

Demographers, sociologists, geographers, and city and regional planners have produced a rapidly growing body of scholarly work describing and analyzing LGBTQ communities in sociological and geographical terms. Studies have documented that LGBTQ communities are heterogeneous in income as well as sexual orientation and other demographics.

While gay neighborhoods with concentrations of middle- and upper-income men have been visible in New York and San Francisco since at least the 1950s, research shows that the LGBTQ community is now very diverse. Planner/sociologist/communications professor Manuel Castells concluded that in San Francisco in 1984 a majority of gays were middle-class professionals. They had often improved the quality of housing and urban space through renovation and maintenance of housing in neighborhoods such as San Francisco's Castro District.

While most gay neighborhoods are in cities, there are increasing numbers of gay neighborhoods in suburbs. There are housing complexes designed specifically for elderly gays. Planning issues in LGBTQ neighborhoods include zoning standards permitting occupancy by same-sex couples, zoning conditional use permits for gay bars and other gay venues, gay gentrification, privacy and surveillance by security cameras, and design standards that the gay community values.

There are fewer distinctly lesbian neighborhoods. The lesbian population of LGBTQ neighborhoods tends to be smaller, on average, than the population of gay neighborhoods where most residents classify themselves as male. Lesbian neighborhoods generally have fewer businesses catering to lesbians than the number of businesses catering to gay males in neighborhoods with concentrations of gay males.

Urban planning professor Petra Doan has documented how LGBTQ homebuyers often play a role in gentrifying neighborhoods. The "stage model of gay gentrification" argues that gentrification often starts with a pioneering group of gay men (and sometimes gay women) who move into an economically marginal older neighborhood with an attractive housing stock that needs to be renovated—particularly if it has an emerging gay culture. The in-movers are likely to have two wage earners, usually do not have the expense of childrearing, and sometimes form collective households to share housing costs. Because they are not very visibly different from existing neighborhood residents and many have more disposable income to spend in the neighborhood than long-time residents, there is often less opposition to gay households than Black and Latinx households experience.

The first-stage in-movers often purchase architecturally high-quality houses in need of rehabilitation and invest money and sweat equity—their own labor—to improve them. Professor Doan describes a second stage of "resurgent" or "super" gentrification by upper-middle- and upper-income gay investors once the pioneers have made the neighborhoods a desirable place to live. The second-stage gay gentrifiers are able to afford architects and urban designers and to invest heavily in rehabilitation and improvements. Lower-income gay renters are forced out as a new wave of wealthy homebuyers and apartment owners—both gay and straight—bid up the value of the housing stock in now fashionable largely gay neighborhoods.

There have been many studies of gentrification and displacement and recommendations about how planners can temper its harmful effects. Strategies to preserve affordable housing in second-stage gay gentrifying neighborhoods can draw on strategies such as inclusionary zoning and housing subsidy programs developed for other neighborhoods. Washington, D.C. created a Tenant Opportunity to Purchase Assistance (TOPA) program in 1980 that provides financial, organizational, and technical assistance to help tenants acquire ownership of buildings. San Francisco and Oakland, California have similar renters' "right to own" laws. Proponents credit these programs with preserving thousands of units of affordable housing in gentrifying neighborhoods.

The University of California, Berkeley's Urban Displacement Project (UDP) is a research and action initiative that conducts community-centered, data-driven, applied research on the nature of gentrification, displacement, and exclusion. The stated goal of the UDP is to produce rigorous research and create tools to empower advocates and policy makers, to reframe conversations, and to train and inspire the next generation of leaders in equitable development.

Since the 1990s the number and size of gay and lesbian business districts have grown. Many gay neighborhoods have gay small business associations. In addition to creating new small businesses that help revitalize neighborhoods, some gay neighborhoods have become tourist destinations.

Sites important to gay history are beginning to be designated as historic sites. The Stonewall Inn on Christopher Street in New York; the home of Harry Hays, the founding site of the first U.S. homophile political association—the Mattachine Society in Los Angeles; the Boston home of prominent 19th-century architect Henry Hobson Richardson; poet Walt Whitman's house in Camden, New Jersey; and author Willa Cather's childhood home in Red Cloud, Nebraska are examples.

Gay Freedom parades and other events bring money into the cities where they take place. In 2019 over 4 million people attended the 12-hour "Stonewall 50 – WorldPride NYC" parade celebrating the 50th anniversary of the Stonewall riot that marked the beginning of the gay rights movement.

DIVERSIFYING PLANNING EDUCATION AND THE PLANNING PROFESSION

The American Planning Association, Association of Collegiate Schools of Planning, and the Planning Accreditation Board have been working to increase the number of city and regional planning students, faculty, and practitioners of color for decades. However, city and regional planning still lags behind social work, public health, public administration, and other public-serving professions in the percentage of practitioners of color. The number of students and faculty of color in planning programs has increased, and the climate in planning schools, planning departments, and other places where planners work has improved, but the proportions have increased only marginally during the last decade. Nearly 80% of APA members currently self-identify as White, 5% as Black, 5% as Latinx, and 4% as AAPI. Planners of color and their allies are continuing to push the APA, ACSP, and PAB to do more to diversify the planning profession.

The American Planning Association (APA) established a Women and Planning Division in 1979, a Planning and the Black Community Division in 1980, a Latinos and Planning Division in 2007, and an LGBTQ Planning Division in 2017. There is no APA tribal and indigenous planning division, but there is an APA tribal and indigenous interest group. There is no APA Asian American and Pacific Islander division or special interest group. The APA interest groups for planners of color have produced many plans to improve diversity, including a diversity/inclusion (D/I) strategy that the APA adopted in 2018.

The Association of Collegiate Schools of Planning has produced 69 different official documents related to diversity, inclusion, and social justice since 2011. These include studies, reports, recommendations, and goal statements. They have adopted a values statement that includes teaching cultural competence, and a policy to promote anti-racism within ACSP. An ACSP Presidential Task Force on Anti-Racism within ACSP, the ACSP Planners of Color Interest Group, the ACSP Faculty Women's Interest Group, and the ACSP committee on diversity have all operationalized strategies to increase the proportion of planners of color in planning schools and the profession. ACSP encourages its member schools to recruit students and faculty of color, provide them support and training, and include more material on diversity in planning curricula. They have hosted workshops for PhD students and junior planning faculty of color to help them obtain teaching positions in college and university city and regional planning departments, secure tenure and promotions, and assume important administrative positions.

The Planning Accreditation Board (PAB)'s *2017–2022 Strategic Plan* includes a goal of promoting and encouraging a systemic approach to diversity and multi-cultural understanding in planning programs.

Planning students of color report that they feel their departments are generally responsive to them, but still report instances of racism, differential treatment, and discomfort. A significant thrust of their concern is for ideas about anti-racism, White privilege, and cultural competence to become integral to planning education.

THEORY FOR PLANNING WITH DIVERSE COMMUNITIES

Planning professors of color, women, and planners who are members of different religions or grew up in low-income households have been at the forefront of developing theory and practice to understand race, diversity, equity, and social justice. Among the most important concepts being developed are concepts about individual and systemic racism, cultural competency, White privilege, equity, and inclusion. The Black Lives Matter movement and conflicts between police and social justice activists have made these concepts more pressing than ever. Advocacy planning and equity planning are two important approaches to improving diversity and achieving social justice.

ADVOCACY PLANNING

Advocacy planning is an alternative model of the planning process. It takes the position that city and regional planners should act more like lawyers, planning hearings should be more like trials, and city planning commissions should act more like judges. Lawyer, planning practitioner, and academic Paul Davidoff (1930–1984) developed the theory and practice of advocacy planning. Davidoff led an informal network of (mostly White) progressive planning professors and activists named Planners for Equal Opportunity. He created and headed the

Suburban Action Institute that worked to integrate White suburbs.

Davidoff was contemptuous of value-neutral planning technocrats who never took a stand against racial discrimination in housing or land use. He did not believe there was a unitary public interest. Davidoff argued that the way planning commissions decided on plans was deeply flawed, precisely because it did not recognize conflicting values.

Davidoff argued that in democracies planning should be pluralistic—explicitly designed to incorporate the views of different groups. Since low-income and minority groups are not on an equal footing with the rich and powerful, he advocated for publicly funded "advocacy planners" to assist low-income communities to develop plans, by acting in a capacity similar to the way in which public defenders and poverty lawyers assist clients to develop their legal cases in civil and criminal court cases.

Advocacy planning has been attacked from the right as a radical and unworkable approach. On the left, social work professor Francis Fox Piven argued that well-intentioned, but naïve, advocacy planners unwittingly serve establishment interests by undercutting the political power of angry and threatening groups by channeling their clients into planning processes for which they are ill equipped.

A robust system of advocacy planning for low-income groups and communities of color with funding for advocacy planners has not developed in the United States or any other country. U.S. federal, state, and local governments and the APA did not embrace it. There is little public support for spending public money for advocacy planning. Lawsuits take a long time. Planning as slow and procedurally complex as litigation would be a cumbersome way to resolve planning disputes. Litigation is generally a last resort to be pursued only after other efforts to resolve a dispute have been exhausted.

Despite these criticisms and obstacles, Davidoff's view of how urban planning should be practiced has profoundly influenced activist planners. It encouraged planners to bring normative values front and center in planning. Each year at the annual meeting of the Association of Collegiate Schools of Planning, a city planning scholar whose work exemplifies the practice and ideals of Paul Davidoff receives the Paul Davidoff Award.

Chester Hartman—a White scholar-activist—led a group of progressive planners called the Planners Network in the 1970s and 1980s. After 1989 Hartman oversaw progressive planning research that provided factual information for advocacy planners at the Washington, D.C.-based Poverty and Race and Research Action Council (PRAAC).

EQUITY PLANNING

Equity Planning is a normative theory of planning closely related to advocacy planning. It was developed by Norman Krumholz (1927–2019), while he was the Cleveland, Ohio City Planning Director from 1969 until 1979 and later as a professor of urban planning at Cleveland State University.

In the 1970s, Cleveland was an economically distressed rustbelt city with a large and rapidly increasing poor population and many people of color—principally Black. Cleveland suffered from a high crime rate and declining assessed property values. In contrast to Davidoff—who envisioned outside advocate planners who might find sympathetic allies in local government—Krumholz was a local government insider who sought allies outside of government. He directed the Cleveland city planning department to work to mitigate impacts of the U.S. political and economic system on low-income and minority communities. Krumholz succeeded in getting the Cleveland Planning Commission to proclaim that its goal was to increase equity.

While Krumholz was the planning director, the Cleveland planning department's approach was based on five principles: (1) to provide individuals as wide a range of alternatives and opportunities as possible, leaving them free to define their own needs and priorities, (2) to create a more equitable society, (3) to reform legal, political, social, and economic institutions to reduce inequality, (4) to have commission staff ask "who benefits and who pays?" in all their work, and (5) to keep the consequences of inequitable decisions before decision-makers rather than seeking consensus.

Krumholz had a large impact on equity in Cleveland. Cleveland's equity planners pushed through thousands of new public housing units, restructured regional transit to improve public transportation for low-income households, supported Cleveland's municipally owned electric power company against privatization, and helped get progressive state legislation passed. The department helped build nine neighborhood-based advocacy groups and provided them with data, analyses, and suggested strategies. Many of these advocacy groups became community development corporations (CDCs) headed by planners. Later, as a Cleveland State University urban planning professor, Krumholz continued to develop equity planning theory and publish books and articles on the theory and practice of equity planning.

Like Davidoff and Hartman, Krumholz has remained an inspiration to many city and regional planners. His writings continue to motivate planners. Equity planning was always an exception, but there have been continuing experiments with equity planning in a number of cities.

SUMMARY

Citizen participation in planning is a cherished ideal—sometimes achieved, but often imperfect, and sometimes ignored. Since the mid-1960s the United States federal government has required some form of citizen participation in planning for virtually every urban program. Almost all state and local government programs now also require citizen participation in their urban programs.

Some neighborhood residents, such as the residents of Boston's Dudley Street neighborhood, demand to participate in programs they care about. Citizens at every level who are passionate about social justice, the environment, climate change, bicycles, property rights, fracking, disability rights, or other issues demand that their voices be heard. NIMBYs, NIMEYs, CAVE people, and BANANAs ferociously resist planning local unwanted land uses (LULUs).

Theories of citizen participation developed by Sherry Arnstein; communicative action planning developed by Jürgen Habermas, Patsy Healey, and Judith Innes; advocacy planning developed by Paul Davidoff; equity planning developed by Norman Krumholz; anti-racism in the planning profession and planning education developed by the ACSP's Planners of Color Interest Group (POCIG) and ACSP, APA, and PAB committees, Julian Agyeman, and Jennifer Ericksen; approaches to cultural competence developed by Terry Cross; eliminating White privilege based on ideas developed by Peggy McIntosh; inclusion of women developed by Dolores Hayden, Daphne Spain, and the ACSP Faculty Women's Interest Group; and inclusion of concerns of lesbian, gay, bisexual, transgender, and queer communities in planning developed by Petra Doan and other members of the ACSP's INCLUSION + Allies special interest group are changing the theory and practice of planning for low-income communities, communities of color, women, and LGBTQ individuals and communities.

CONCEPTS

Advocacy Planning
Anti-Racism
Arnstein's Ladder of Citizen Participation
Citizen Participation
Collaborative Planning
Communicative Action Planning
Community Design Center
Cultural Competence
Equity Planning
Local Unwanted Land Use (LULU)
Maximum Feasible Participation of the Poor
NIMBY (Not-in-My-Back-Yard)
Planners of Color Interest Group (POCIG)
Redlining

PEOPLE

Sherry Arnstein
Paul Davidoff
John Forester

Norman Krumholz
June Thomas

NOTES

1. The only time grassroots organizations in low-income communities came close to controlling large amounts of federal money was in the mid-1960s during President Lyndon Johnson's "War on Poverty". The Economic Opportunity Act of 1964 provided billions of dollars to low-income communities with a mandate for "maximum feasible participation of the poor" (Levitan, 1969; Orleck & Hazirjian, 2011). The model cities program required "widespread", but not "maximum feasible" participation and gave mayors ultimate authority over model cities programs. The community action program was phased out within a few years and Johnson's War on Poverty ended after President Nixon assumed office in 1969. U.S. Senator Daniel Patrick Moynihan—a former Harvard professor and expert on ethnic and racial communities—became President Nixon's chief domestic advisor. Moynihan urged Nixon to pursue a policy of "benign neglect"—simply ignoring low-income communities. Some neoliberals label the War on Poverty, Model Cities Program, and subsequent liberal urban programs failures (Rector, 2014).
2. The slave states were Alabama, Arkansas, Delaware, Florida, Georgia, Kentucky, Louisiana, Maryland (which included Washington, D.C. in 1860), Mississippi, Missouri, North Carolina, South Carolina, Tennessee, Texas, and Virginia.
3. The border states that had slaves, but did not secede were Kentucky, Delaware, and Maryland (including Washington, D.C.).
4. Notable studies of Black communities by Black sociologists include W.E.B. Du Bois's *The Philadelphia Negro* (1899) and St. Clair Drake and Horace Cayton's study of Chicago's Black Belt *Black Metropolis* (1945). Gary Nash's *Forging Freedom* (1991) describes Philadelphia's Black community from 1720–1840. Ron Takaki's *A Different Mirror* (2008) and *Strangers from a Different Shore* (1998) describe the history of Asian American and Pacific Islander communities. Oscar Handlin's *The Uprooted* (1973) describes the experience of 19th-century Irish immigrants.
5. The Annie E. Casey Foundation's *Race Equity Inclusion and Action Guide* (2015) describes seven steps to advance and embed race equity. They are: (1) establish an understanding of race equity and inclusion principles, (2) engage affected populations and stakeholders, (3) gather and analyze disaggregated data, (4) conduct systems analysis of root causes of inequities, (5) identify strategies and target resources, to address root causes of inequities, (6) conduct race equity impact assessment for all policies and decision-making, (7) continuously evaluate effectiveness and adapt strategies.
6. The International City Management Association (ICMA)'s *Equity and Inclusion Toolkit* (2020) is a 62-page guide to increasing equity and inclusion in local government. It includes material on community relations around sensitive topics such as police shootings and detainment and deportation of immigrants, as well as service delivery and internal government practices such as recruitment and retention. It references specific examples of good practice and contains checklists of things to consider, a glossary, and list of engaged organizations.
7. Between 1513 and the early 19th century the area that is now the Southwestern states and California was under the dominion of New Spain. The population of this region was thinly settled and largely Latinx. After the annexation of Texas in 1845 and the treaty of Guadalupe-Hidalgo in 1848 ceding the American Southwest, California, and the Pacific Northwest to the United States, migration by non-Hispanic Whites rapidly increased the population of what is now the American Southwest. Migration shifted composition of the new territories to predominantly White non-Hispanic residents. Spanish settlements laid out under the Laws of the Indies assumed a distinct new more Anglo pattern (Crouch, Garr, and Mundigo, 1982).
8. In the United States the term *colonia* refers to largely Latinx settlements in Texas, New Mexico, Arizona, and California, within 150 miles of the U.S.–Mexico border, that lack potable water and sewage systems and decent housing (Cranston-Gonzalez NAHA, 1990). A more accurate term is border *colonia*. The border *colonias* are unincorporated, low-income, poorly planned or unplanned rural areas. The majority of residents are Latinx from Mexico and South and Central America. Many border *colonias*, lack basic infrastructure and decent housing. Most have acute public health and education problems. Some are prone to flooding. One 2010 study estimates that 1.6 millon people lived in 2,069 border *colonias* in 2010—mostly in Texas (Henderson, 2019).
9. Laura Harjo and Theodore Jojola at the University of New Mexico are planning professors of American Indian descent who write about communities they know well. At the University of British Columbia Department of Urban and Community Planning Wayne Beggs from the Musqueam tribe teaches a community planning studio course jointly with Leonie Sandercock.
10. Zaferatos is a scholar-practitioner who served as a tribal planner for 35 years before becoming Professor of Urban Planning and Sustainable Development at Western Washington State University. As planning director of the Swinomish Indian tribal council in LaConner, Washington, he gained practical experience in indigenous planning.

SUGGESTIONS FOR FURTHER LEARNING

Citizen Participation: Sherry Arnstein, A ladder of citizen participation (1965). Carissa Slotterback

& Mickey Laurie, Building a foundation for public engagement in planning (2019). **The Dudley Street Neighborhood Initiative (DSNI):** Peter Medoff & Holly Sklaar, *Streets of hope* (1999). Mark Lipman, *Holding ground: The rebirth of Dudley Street* [video] (1996). Dudley Street Neighborhood Initiative [website] (2021). **Black Slavery in the United States:** Erin Bradford, *Free African American population in the U.S. 1790–1860* (2008). Ira Berlin, *The long emancipation: The demise of slavery in the United States* (2018). U.S. Bureau of the Census (1909). *A century of population growth: From the first to the twelfth census of the United States.* Washington, D.C.: United States Bureau of the Census. **Early U.S. Black Communities:** William Edward Burghardt (W.E.B.) Du Bois, *The Philadelphia Negro* (1899). St. Clair Drake and Horace Cayton, *Black metropolis* (1945). Elliot Liebow, *Talley's corner* (1967). **Minority Race Planners:** June Thomas, The minority race planner in the quest for the just city (2008). Annie E. Casey Foundation, *Race equity inclusion and action guide* (2015). International City Management Association, *Equity and inclusion toolkit* (2021). **Racist Planning Laws:** Richard Rothstein, *The color of law* (2017). **Cultural Competence and Addressing White Privilege:** Michael Omi & Howard Winant, Racial formation in the United States (1994). Terry Cross, Barbara Bazron, Karl Dennis, & Mareasa Isaacs, *Towards a culturally competent system of care* (1989). Julian Agyeman & Jennifer Sien Erickson, Culture, recognition, and the negotiation of difference (2012). Peggy McIntosh, White privilege (1989). **Planning Black Communities:** June Thomas, *Redevelopment and race* (1987). Pam Sporn, *Detroit 48202* [video] (2018). **Planning Latino Communities:** Ivis Garcia, Cultural insights for planners: Understanding the terms Hispanic, Latino, and Latinx (2020). Adrian Donelson & Angela Esparza (eds), *The colonias reader*, 3rd ed (2010). **Planning Asian American Communities:** Willow Lung-Aman, *Trespassers: Asian Americans and the battle for suburbia* (2017). National Coalition for Asian Pacific Americans Community Development [website] (2021). **Women in Planning:** Daphne Spain, *Gender and urban space* (2014), What happened to gender relations on the way from Chicago to Los Angeles? (2002), and *Gendered Spaces* (1992). Dolores Hayden, What would a non-sexist city be like? (1980) and *Redesigning the American dream* (2002). ACSP Faculty Women's Interest Group (FWIG) [website] (2021). **Planning LGBT Communities:** Ann Forsyth, Nonconformist populations and planning sexuality and space (2001). Petra Doan, *Planning and LGBTQ communities* (2015), INCLUSION + Allies [website] (2021). **Planning Indigenous Communities:** Theodore Jojola, Indigenous planning: An emerging context (2008). Nicholas Zaferatos, Planning the American Indian reservation (2015). Ryan Walker, Theodore Jojola, & David Natcher (eds), *Reclaiming indigenous planning* (2013). **Collaborative Planning:** Patsy Healey, *Collaborative planning* (2002). Judith Innes & David Booher, *Planning with complexity* (2010). **Gentrification and Displacement:** University of California, Berkeley Anti-Displacement Project [website] (2021). **Advocacy Planning:** Paul Davidoff, Advocacy and pluralism in planning (1969). Barry Checkoway & Paul Davidoff, Advocacy planning in retrospect (1994). **Equity Planning:** Norman Krumholz, *Making equity planning work* (1990) and A retrospective view of equity planning (1982). Norman Krumholz & Kathryn Hexter, *Advancing equity planning now* (2019). **The War on Poverty:** Sar Levitan, *The great society's poor law* (1969). Annelise Orleck & Lisa Hazirjian, *The war on poverty* (2011). Daniel Moynihan, *Maximum feasible misunderstanding* (1969). **The Model Cities Program:** Bernard Frieden & Marshall Kaplan, *The politics of neglect* (1977).

CHAPTER 10

Regional and National Planning

INTRODUCTION

Urbanization does not respect political borders. Most planning challenges have a regional dimension. This chapter focuses on planning through the lens of regions, rather than cities, counties, and other places defined by their political borders.

Planners with different specialties define regions at different scales and in many different ways. A transportation planner considering widening a section of highway in Riverside, California can't just look at Riverside's census Transportation Analysis Zones (TAZs) and other data just for Riverside County. Traffic from Southern California's enormous and fast-changing Inland Empire where the highway is located will impact the highway. She will need to define an appropriate region for analysis. An environmental planner working on a habitat conservation plan to protect threatened California gnatcatchers—an endangered bird species—can't just look at coastal sage habitat in one place; he needs to plan for parts of the California coastal region where patches of habitat that can support the gnatcatchers exist. Planners working on plans to give low-income households in troubled Chicago public housing projects greater choice in where to live, climate change plans to reduce carbon emissions from coal-powered plants in Pennsylvania, and economic development planning in Northeast Ohio must also consider areas they are planning in their regional context. At the national and global scale planners need to think globally and act regionally.

This chapter describes blocks, census tracts, metropolitan areas, and other units of analysis for which the U.S. census provides data and how planners use this data to analyze and plan regions. It introduces theory about regions and regional planning developed by pioneering regionalists in the 19th and 20th centuries. Sections discuss planning natural regions, rural areas, and water-related regional planning.

Much regional planning in the United States is performed at the metropolitan level by councils of government (COGs) and metropolitan planning organizations (MPOs). The chapter describes what these regional planning institutions do.

Few cities and counties collaborate on regional plans. The chapter contains a case study of notable exceptions in the Portland, Oregon Metro region where the only elected regional government in the United States does serious regional planning and cities and counties in Northeast Ohio that worked together on the *Vibrant Northeast Ohio 2040 Plan*.

Some cities are morphing into megacities. The concluding section of the chapter describes planning for megacities and the even larger megacity regions of which they are a part.

REGIONAL PLANNING

Regional planning may be for a natural region like the land covered by the *New Jersey Pinelands Comprehensive Management Plan*—which covers a large region in New Jersey with both forest resources and urban development; a metropolitan region like the Seattle–Tacoma–Bellevue, Washington combined statistical area; or a region defined by the boundaries of a park district, air basin, highway corridor, or some other defining characteristic.

In the digital age, planners use remote sensing, geographical information systems (GIS) software, and other technologies to capture and analyze spatial data they can use to delimit and describe natural and politically defined regions. Rather than deploying an army of researchers to walk through wilderness area in the Western United States looking for individual trees affected by sudden oak death—caused by a fungus-like pathogen—planners can identify the location of affected trees by analyzing remotely sensed data from satellite images. Once detected, regional planners can work with biologists, hydrologists, climatologists and other natural scientists on plans to manage forests and other resources. In addition to its value in understanding and planning for natural resources like forests, remotely sensed data can show other physical features of interest to planners in great detail and for large areas at different resolutions.

Regional *development* planning involves planning for the economic, social, and environmental well-being of regions as well as their spatial structure. It can guide economic development as well as land use, infrastructure, and the physical structure of human settlements. Sometimes regional planning explicitly seeks to balance a combination of conservation and development. For example, the stated purpose of the San Francisco Bay Area Conservation and Development Commission's *San Francisco Bay Plan* is both conservation and development of the Bay and land around it.

Oregon has a state Conservation and Development Commission that oversees Oregon's land use planning. While Oregon has no statewide plan, LCDC approves and monitors city and county land use plans, as well as Metro's plan. Their mission is to make sure each local plan conforms with state planning goals.

Regional planning can be for urban or rural areas or areas that are both urban and rural. Regions may be as small as the boundaries of a tiny mosquito abatement district with fewer than 100 residents and less than a square mile of land or as large as the Appalachian region with 25 million residents in 12 states. World regions like the European Union (EU) or the Sahel region North Africa cover multiple countries.

A frequently stated purpose of regional planning at the metropolitan level is to reduce spatial mismatch—the disconnect between job locations and where people live. This can improve jobs–housing balance and make regions operate more efficiently. In addition to reducing spatial mismatch, regional planning can help equity and social justice for low-income communities and communities of color by increasing economic integration, separating low-income communities and communities of color from hazardous waste sites, and assuring that public transit is accessible to all communities.

There was little regional planning in the United States between the beginning of European colonization in the early 17th century and the beginning of the New Deal in 1933. Since then, the theory and practice of regional planning have developed rapidly.

Neither the United States nor most other countries have a national development plan. China is an exception. China had a five-year "national new style urbanization plan" between 2015 and 2020 that established goals and described a change in urbanization philosophy. The European Union (EU) has regional development plans and policies for different sectors and regions. Multiple EU development plans guide significant investments in regional development within the EU's 27 member states.[1]

University of California, Berkeley Professor Emeritus Michael Teitz, describes four eras in the evolution of regional planning: (a) the utopian era from the mid-19th century until the early 20th century, (b) the heroic era in response to the Great Depression (1930–1945), (c) the development era between 1945 and 1985, when the United States and other countries invested heavily in domestic spatial planning and provided foreign aid to developing countries, and (d) the global era beginning about 1986.

The heyday of regional planning occurred during the four decades after World War II—what Teitz calls "the development era". At that time, a majority of countries at different stages of development and located in different regions of the world had some kind of area-based regional development planning and/or sectoral regional economic development planning. The main rationales for regional development planning then were to recover from World War II, advance leading sectors of the national economy, aid economically underdeveloped areas, and to decentralize development. Countries invested in regions that appeared to have high development potential. Many developed "growth poles" where they sought to develop factories and new communities. They invested in underdeveloped regions to reduce poverty and increase national equity and social stability. They sometimes built new towns to house the growing population in populous regions or for the workforce moving into sparsely populated regions that the country wanted to develop.

Teitz argues that three important streams of ideas in regional economic development and planning shifted as they were carried over into the 21st century. The first shift is from a regional to a sectoral focus for development—looking at the performance of economic sectors like coal mining or banking, with economic development as the goal. The second shift was the rise of supranational regionalism, together with the reemergence of ethnic regionalism. The third shift Teitz identified is making the environment a key factor in development planning.

For ten years during the New Deal (1933–1940), that Teitz calls the "heroic era" of regional planning, the U.S. National Resources Planning Board (NRPB) did background studies and some planning at the national level. Congress eliminated the NRPB in 1943 with an express congressional policy to prohibit national planning in the future.[2] Congress considered planning to be unwanted federal meddling in state and local affairs.

During the heroic era construction of dams transformed portions of the American South that were included in the Tennessee Valley Authority (TVA)—an ambitious New Deal project to build dams and new communities in much of Tennessee and parts of adjoining states.

Construction of the massive Hoover dam in Nevada and Arizona, the Bonneville Dam on the Columbia River near Portland, and the Grand Coulee Dam in Washington state helped development of the Southwest and the Pacific Northwest. Figure 10.1 shows TVA dam construction workers in 1943.

The private nonprofit organization named Resources for the Future (RFF) has produced non-partisan national and regional studies of U.S. natural resource issues since 1952. Today RFF does research about environmental, energy, and natural resources research at the regional and national scale both on the United States and other countries.

Between the end of World War II in 1945 and the mid-1980s, the major U.S. regional planning and development effort was in Appalachia. Appalachia is an impoverished region that had weak infrastructure for exporting its primary product—coal—and importing goods manufactured elsewhere in the United States. The federal government invested in building roads and other infrastructure to better connect Appalachia to the national economy. It subsidized education and job training to help the region industrialize.

In what Teitz terms "the global era", nation states have invested less money in place-based regional development. The emphasis has been on sectoral planning—strategically targeting specific industries that national planners consider promising and sectors that will benefit regions with high poverty rates, few natural resources, and typically lacking water and arable land.

While the United States has never had an explicit written national urban plan, the federal government indirectly influences development and urban plans. They do this in fragmented and sometimes contradictory ways through infrastructure, tax, subsidy, interest rate, and other policies. Legislation and policies on the environment; federal disaster relief; multi-modal transportation that may combine walking, bicycling, driving, and taking public transit; and the federal home mortgage deduction are *de facto* plans. Together they collectively approximate a national U.S. urban policy.

Figure 10.1 Tennessee Valley Authority Dam Construction Workers (1943).

U.S. CENSUS DEFINITIONS OF REGIONS

The United States Census Bureau conducts decennial censuses of the entire population. Since 2005 they have also conducted the American Community Survey (ACS) annually. The ACS collects information from people in a random sample of 3.5 million housing units and group quarters.

The Census Bureau has developed sophisticated metrics to define statistical regions starting with confidential information on households and aggregating household information into blocks. They provide information combining blocks into block groups, census tracts, transportation analysis zones, cities, counties, census designated places, congressional districts, states, several different kinds of metropolitan and micropolitan regions, and the entire United States.

Planners can construct datasets for regions with different boundaries by combining smaller census units. For example, if a planner wants to analyze the population of a watershed that extends beyond the boundaries of Las Vegas, Nevada, she can create and analyze a dataset that includes all of the census tracts within Las Vegas itself, plus additional census tracts on the fringe that are within the watershed.

The precise way in which the U.S. census defines urban areas is complex and has changed over time. Longitudinal analysis of census data comparing urban and non-urban areas at different times needs to recognize that the definition of the units of analysis has likely changed and the data may not be parallel from one decade to another.

The decennial censuses and the ACS provide a wealth of data on demographic, social, economic, and housing characteristics of the U.S. population. Since the census depends on households and individuals to provide information, census numbers often undercount the true population of an area. They do not include large numbers of undocumented immigrants or people who choose not to respond. Since respondents self-report their race, census data on race is questionable. Respondents may misrepresent other information to the census.

The U.S. Census Bureau classifies an area as urban if it has a population of 50,000 or more and a population density of 1,000 persons per square mile (ppsm) or greater. It also classifies places of 2,500 or more located outside urbanized areas as urban if their density is 1,000 ppsm or greater.

Mastering quantitative analysis of decennial, ACS, and other census data, is an essential city and regional planning skill taught in city and regional planning, geography, sociology, and other courses.

REGIONAL PLANNING THEORY

Four pioneering scholars shaped contemporary planners' thinking about regions and regional planning. The key figures were French anarchist Elisée Reclus, Scottish polymath Patrick Geddes, German economic geographer Walter Christaller, and American regional scientist Walter Isard.

Elisée Reclus's Universal Geography

French anarchist geographer Elisée Reclus (1830–1905) pioneered systematic study of regions in a 19-volume *New Universal Geography of Mankind and the Earth,* published between 1875 and 1894. Reclus was a colorful figure—an anarchist, nudist, and practitioner of free sex whose contributions to regional analysis were only recognized late in his life.[3] Reclus combined physical and cultural geography. He applied his approach to natural regions—particularly river systems. His most important theoretical contribution was showing the variety of physical features within natural regions and how they affected human settlements—providing an empirical basis for regional planning.

Patrick Geddes's Physical/Social/Cultural Approach

Consistent with his emphasis on natural systems, empirical research, and diagnosis before prescription, Patrick Geddes argued that planning for a city should begin with a study of the physical characteristics of the region in which it is located. Given his biological training, Geddes insisted that regional planning required a study of regional and local ecosystems. Geddes argued that the natural and built environments should be considered together. As an artist, historian, sociologist, and pioneer in the field of culture studies, Geddes believed that the plan for a city-region should reflect the history and culture of the region. All of these strikingly original ideas were introduced to experts and the public in the Watchtower Planning Museum Geddes created in Edinburgh, Scotland, and the traveling city planning exhibits he took to different cities in Great Britain, Continental Europe, India, and Palestine (Box 2.2).

One of Geddes's most celebrated diagrams is of a "valley section" showing changes in the environment, folk culture, and economies of human settlements from an ocean coast to high on a mountain (Figure 10.2). Geddes's schema does not work well for developed countries today, but the concept of fitting uses to the natural environment is sound. For example, many regional plans locate manufacturing plants and transportation infrastructure near natural resources such as coal and iron ore to reduce transportation costs between the sources of the resources and where they are processed.

Today the availability of big data on cell phone communications and transit trips provides a rich source of information on systems of cities within regions and the world city system. Researchers can mine longitudinal data on the location from which every cell phone call was made at exactly what time, by every one of a phone company's

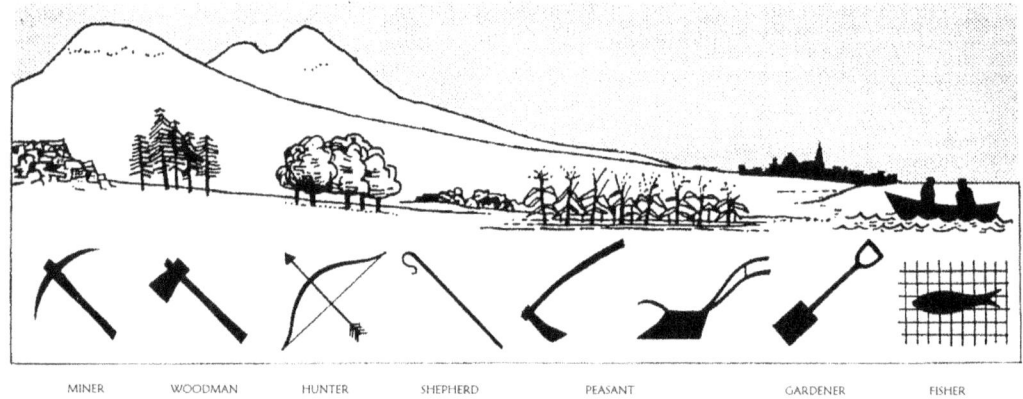

Figure 10.2 Patrick Geddes's Valley Section.

millions of customers. High-speed rail (HSR) and subway operators' passenger origin–destination data from electronic tickets provide big data on all the origins, destinations, and exact times of all ticketed passenger trips. Massive increases in data storage and improvements in software to mine and analyze big data make it possible to analyze big data in real time and produce summaries and visual representations of city systems. Michael Batty's visualizations of flows in the London tube system discussed in Chapter 1 are an excellent example of how big data and new analytics can reveal city and regional systems. Managers of transit systems, emergency response, flood control, and other vital urban systems can monitor urban systems from control rooms—rooms where they can view data from sensors in real time and respond to needs that they reveal. For example, a transportation planner in a city's transportation control room viewing congestion data captured by sensors at different locations in a city's subway system can request that additional subway cars head to a point where many people are waiting for a subway car. Transportation planners also use this kind of big data to make plans to alter or extend transportation systems.

Central Place Theory

Theory about regional systems began with German geographer Walter Christaller's central place theory in the 1930s. Central place theory is an approach to understanding regional space as a hierarchical network of nodes of economic activity. Christaller conceptualized city systems as networks with flows among hubs. He was the first person to recognize the importance of communications in understanding regions. Christaller derived central place theory from data on the volume of telephone calls among different places in Southern Germany. Based on differences in the volume of telephone calls, he argued that there is an underlying economic logic to the regional distribution of human settlements. Theoretically, on a uniform flat surface with evenly distributed population and resources and a free market, different-sized places with different populations and economic functions will be distributed in a systematic hierarchy. Christaller's work was highly theoretical. He was careful to point out that actual geographical features such as climate and topography, and political realities such as national borders, would produce different city-region spatial structures. Figure 10.3 is a diagram Christaller created in 1933 illustrating how a network of places with different levels of economic activity tends to cluster around a central place.

Walter Isard and the Birth of Regional Science

Economist and regional scientist Walter Isard (1919–2010) is the central figure in the field of regional science. Regional science is

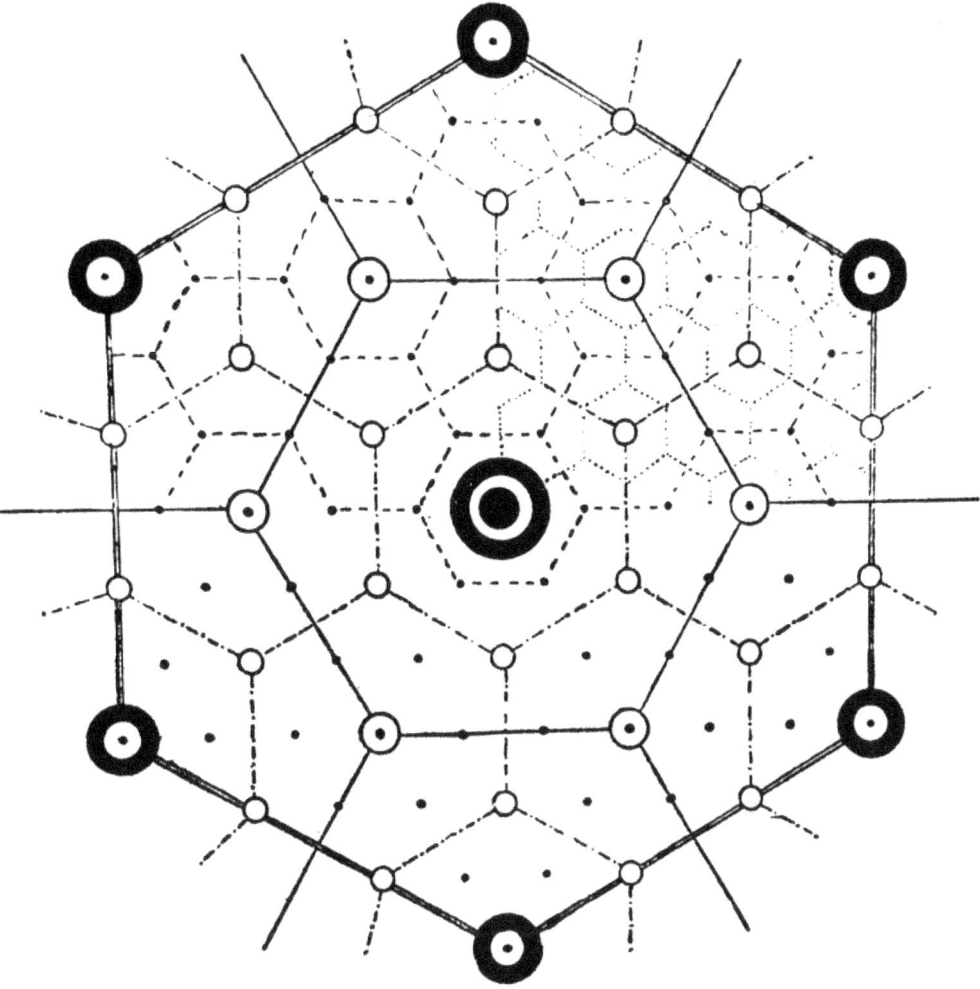

Figure 10.3 Illustration of Central Place Theory by Walter Christaller (1933).

an interdisciplinary field combining theory developed by economists, geographers, and planners to describe the way in which regions function economically and spatially. Isard taught at the University of Pennsylvania, Harvard, and the University of Chicago. In addition to creating regional science as a new applied social science field, he developed location theory—a body of quantitative theory that combines economics and geography. Isard also developed industrial location theory that helps explain why industries locate where they do and guides planners doing site suitability analysis to identify promising sites to develop.[4]

Isard was the prime mover in the creation of the Regional Science Association (RSA) in 1954. He was the RSA's first president. In 1956 the University of Pennsylvania hired him to head a new PhD-granting Department of Regional Science. Isard's books published in 1956, 1959, and 1960 laid the foundation for the field of regional science and immediately became the texts for regional science courses in the United States. Isard helped spread the study of regional science to Europe, Latin America, and Asia in the 1960s. In 1989, the Regional Science Association was re-named the Regional Science Association International (RSAI).

The writings of the regional planning pioneers are not easy reading. Geddes was a terrible writer, Reclus wrote voluminously, and Christaller and Isard were sophisticated quantitative theorists who employed advanced economic and statistical concepts. The regional planning pioneers' insights are distributed in lengthy books and multiple scholarly articles. Advanced students in city and regional planning, economics, or geography, and practitioners with a solid foundation in statistics who are interested in regional dynamics and regional planning will benefit from exploring the key primary sources. All city and regional planners can benefit from concepts developed by the pioneering regional theorists.

URBAN SPRAWL

Urban sprawl is a critical issue in regional planning. Managing sprawl is essentially a regional planning challenge. One helpful definition of sprawl by Oliver Gillham (2002), an architect and planner based in Cambridge, Massachusetts, is:

> a form of urbanization distinguished by leapfrog patterns of development, commercial strips, low density, separated land uses, automobile dominance, and a minimum of public space.

Yale University Professor Emerita of Architecture and American Studies, Dolores Hayden, and photographer Jim Wark have produced a provocative *Field Guide to Sprawl*. They combine descriptions and aerial photography of different types of sprawl that they label with colorful terms like tract mansions, greenfield development, and leapfrog development.

Figure 10.4 illustrates one example of urban sprawl. Low-density, primarily residential development and open space are jumbled together.

Not all low-density development is sprawl. Sprawl implies poorly planned and poorly regulated low-density growth on the fringe of existing urban areas. If it is well planned, low-density development may be appropriate in some places.

Much sprawl is residential, but sprawl may also include shopping centers, and commercial, industrial, and research and development firms. Sprawl is often discontinuous, with leapfrog development occurring in

Figure 10.4 Urban Sprawl.

patchy patterns beyond fully urban areas and commercial strip development along major arterial roads and highways. Sprawl may leave pockets of undeveloped land engulfed by cities. Fifty-four percent of the U.S. population live in suburbs and small metro areas—many of which are continuing to sprawl. Longitudinal research on the growth of urban areas by New York University professor Shlomo Angel (2010) shows that virtually every metropolitan region in the world has expanded greatly during the last seventy years.

Areas characterized by sprawl often have poor public transit service. Even if there are buses, the lines are limited and the wait times excessive. Ridership is too low to support subways or light rail systems in U.S. suburbs and most U.S. metropolitan areas.

Most city and regional planners criticize sprawl because of the high cost of infrastructure that is spread out to serve relatively few households, the long time it takes to commute between home and work, negative impacts on the natural environment, loss of agricultural land close to where people live, erosion of urban economies, and spatial segregation. Accordingly, most planners favor compact, city-centered, urban growth.

Free-market proponents called "smart growth contrarians" disagree with planners who advocate compact, city-centered growth. Professors Robert Bruegmann at the University of Illinois-Chicago, and Peter Gordon and Harry Richardson at the University of Southern California argue that low-density development is a natural market response that reflects what people in an affluent democratic society such as the United States want. Land costs are often lower in fringe areas. More large parcels that are appropriate for moderately-priced tract housing development and single-story factories are available there. Costs of building new infrastructure on raw land may be lower than replacing old urban infrastructure.

A few regions, such as the Portland, Oregon metropolitan region (Box 10.2) and the Northeast Ohio region (Box 10.3) plan core city, suburban, and rural development together and have made serious efforts to coordinate development and reduce sprawl on a regional basis.

PLANNING NATURAL REGIONS AND RURAL AREAS

Physical geographers, biologists, landscape architects, and environmental planners have long studied natural regions that are classified as functionally similar based on their landscape, physical characteristics, ecosystems, or other natural characteristics. They may define regions based on watersheds, air basins, coastal zones, riparian areas along river systems, alpine areas, tundra, or deserts.

Until about 1970, the built environment was planned with little regard to natural regions. Today, planning the natural and built environments of cities and regions together is accepted professional city and regional planning practice.

Many rural areas in the United States have some form of rural planning. Rural planning is critical in developing countries with much larger rural populations than the United States, many small villages, and many regional issues to resolve as development occurs. However, the theory and practice of rural development are not as well developed as theory about planning for cities.

In addition to resource-related planning and preservation of environmental and open space assets, rural planning can involve planning for the physical and economic development of small cities, towns, and sparsely populated areas. If population is moving out—as is often the case in rural areas—rural planning can involve planned shrinkage. Planned shrinkage strategies include planning to consolidate school districts and relocate elderly households to areas where they have greater access to medical care.

China gives high priority to planning for rural regions. In 2016 they changed the name of the Chinese Ministry of Housing and Urban Development to the Ministry of Housing and Urban-Rural Development. China renamed the profession of urban planning to urban-rural planning and elevated urban-rural planning from a subcategory of architecture to a professional field at the same level as architecture in China's education hierarchy. In 2018 China moved all planning under the direction of the Ministry of Resources. Every Chinese undergraduate and graduate urban-rural planning student studies rural as well as urban planning. Many take studio coursework where they engage directly with rural communities.

Some other countries with large rural areas also emphasize rural area planning. The EU's LEADER Liaison entre Actions de Développement de l'Économie Rurale (Connections among Rural Economic Development Actions) program is a European Union initiative to support rural development projects initiated and implemented at the local level by local action groups (LAGs). It links actions for development of the rural economy among rural settlements and between rural settlements and urban areas.

WATER-RELATED REGIONAL PLANNING

By their nature, water systems force planners to consider the relationship between natural regions and the built environment on a regional basis. Oceans, rivers, lakes, and streams often overlap jurisdictions, both within countries and among multiple countries.

Water problems occur when there is too much water, too little water, or water is polluted. Patchwork responses to floods, droughts, storm surges, erosion, and water pollution addressing water problems piecemeal is inadequate. Jurisdiction-by-jurisdiction, or agency-by-agency planning for water that crosses political boundaries is inefficient and rarely succeeds. Regional planning to address entire water systems is necessary. Integrated water resources management (IWRM) looks at all types of water in a region as one integrated system for planning and management. It draws heavily on systems theory—viewing rivers as essentially hydrological systems embedded in an economic and social context.

Rivers are arteries of commerce, essential to the economy of the regions through which they flow. They are essential to ecosystems and are critical for farming and fishing. Safe drinking water is essential to human life. Dams help provide electrical power, better navigation, safe transport of people and goods by water, and reliable supplies of water for agriculture and drinking. A factory discharging pollutants into a river, a dam altering the flow of water downstream, or a channel diverting water from a river can have existential consequences for safety, health, farming, navigation, recreation, and the quality of life along parts or all of an entire river system.

Historically, when the Nile, Mississippi, Yangtze, Amazon, or Congo rivers flooded, the impacts on human settlements along thousands of miles were catastrophic. Tens of thousands of smaller rivers, their tributaries, and the lakes, ponds, and marshes that they drain into were prone to periodic flooding. Dams and flood control systems have reduced these impacts in many areas—but by no means eliminated them. Climate change is stressing existing water control infrastructure. How governments plan and manage the segment of the river where they live impacts people downstream and sometimes upstream. Riparian areas—the areas along the banks of rivers—can be planned to support natural ecological systems and human settlements.

Before the 1970s the importance of flood plains—which are usually dry, but flood periodically—was widely ignored. Flood plains require special planning and regulation to reduce risk to people and property and protect plant and animal species. In China where monsoon flooding is a major problem, "sponge city" plans include hard and soft designs to retain, divert, and absorb flood water and reduce flooding damage. Sponge cities are described in Chapter 17.

Special areas require specialized water planning. Vernal pools—pockets that may fill up in spring but dry out in summer—support complex and fragile ecosystems. Wetlands—such as marshes, swamps, and bayous—have water on the surface or within the root zone. They often have unique soil conditions. Wetlands may be permanently or seasonally covered by water that is critical to ecosystems. They support plant and animal biota—tiny organisms that constitute important links in the food chain. Wetlands can act as sponges to protect coastal areas from flooding. Many wetlands were "reclaimed" (filled) for urban use. New Zealand and California have each lost 90% of their historic wetlands. Figure 13.6 in Chapter 13 illustrates the loss of wetlands as San Francisco Bay was filled between 1849 and 1960, and the U.S. Army Corps of Engineers designation of areas "susceptible to reclamation" in 1960 that would have reduced San Francisco Bay to a narrow channel by 2020. Plans can describe how to preserve, restore, and manage wetlands.

Underground water is important for irrigation and drinking water supplies. Management of aquifers—the natural areas where underground water accumulates—is critical. In many of the world's megacities, underground aquifers are being depleted rapidly, posing enormous challenges for hundreds of millions of people who depend on them. As water is pumped out of aquifers, many cities are sinking, causing soil subsidence, damaging buildings, and increasing damage from flooding. As water is diverted, agriculture is often harmed. Protecting aquifers is an important city and regional planning priority.

STATE-LEVEL REGIONAL PLANNING

States have the power to decide whether or not the state government and cities and counties within the state will do regional planning, and if so, what it will be like. Some states have established authorities to plan and manage sensitive areas, such as the Florida Everglades. California and Nevada have an interstate compact for planning and managing land use around the large, beautiful, and threatened Lake Tahoe. Georgia has a notable state-level transportation authority. Box 10.1 is a biography of Catherine Ross—a scholar-practitioner who did important regional transportation planning as Executive Director of the Georgia Regional Transportation Authority.

COUNCILS OF GOVERNMENTS (COGS) AND METROPOLITAN PLANNING ORGANIZATIONS (MPOS)

Metropolitan regions are politically fragmented, so regional planning for them is politically difficult. Political power and financial resources to address regional problems are divided among local governments, many of which are small. A fundamental task for planners is to help create effective region-wide mechanisms to address issues of regional significance.

Planners may plan for large-scale infrastructure such as ports, airports, bridges, and tunnels to make sure they are in the right places. They need to keep competing jurisdictions from duplicating functions within the same metropolitan area. They have a role to play in resolving issues that cross political borders, protecting regional environmental assets, and addressing other matters of significance to the metropolitan region as a whole in a coordinated way.

Metropolitan councils of governments (COGs)—also called areawide planning organizations (APOs)—are organizations of cities and counties in metropolitan areas that provide data, do research, assist their members, and plan on a regional basis to a limited extent. There is a COG in almost every U.S. metropolitan area. The National Association of Regional Councils (NARC) is the national organization representing COGs. COGs' predecessors were called regional councils (RCs). They were first created in the 1920s.[5] Some RCs still exist under that name.

To qualify as a COG, the National Association of Regional Councils (NARC) requires that at least 51% of the organization's board of directors be elected officials of constituent local governments. In practice, the percentage is higher. Most of the other members of COG boards of directors are political appointees from cities and counties. COGs are regional councils (RCs), but some regional councils do not qualify as COGs by NARC's standard.

The federal government encouraged metropolitan planning between 1968 and 1995 by requiring that COGs review

BOX 10.1 CATHERINE ROSS

Catherine Ross is an internationally recognized city and regional planning scholar who has made major contributions to understanding U.S. and world megacities and megaregions, transportation and infrastructure planning, resilience, healthy cities, and the role of women and people of color in the planning profession. She currently holds multiple professorships at Georgia Institute of Technology (Georgia Tech) including Regent's Professor, the Harry West Professor of City and Regional Planning, and an ADVANCE Professor position, assisting women and people of color with their academic careers. Professor Ross also has appointments in Georgia Tech's College of Design (COD) and Civil and Environmental Engineering Program (CEE).

Professor Ross's current research examines the impact of freight and passenger mobility options for cities and regions, e-commerce, and emerging technologies for managing freight and passenger movement. Her work uses a multidisciplinary focus on resilience, sustainability, analytics, and performance management.

Professor Ross served as the first female president of the Association of Collegiate Schools of Planning in 1993 and 1994. She has served on numerous National Academies' committees and as adviser to the Obama administration, where she helped create the first White House Office of Urban Affairs. She was a former visiting faculty member at the Transportation Research Board, and served on the boards of the ENO Transportation Foundation and the Metropolitan Atlanta Rapid Transit Authority. Ross was the first executive director of the Georgia Regional Transportation Authority from 1999 to 2003. She has conducted research for numerous governmental agencies, foundations, and the private sector.

Figure 10.5 Catherine Ross.

From 2012 to 2016, Professor Ross was deputy director of Georgia Tech's Center for Transportation System Productivity and Management—a $14 million Urban Transportation Center funded by the U.S. Department of Transportation's National Center for Transportation Systems Productivity and Management. The Center studied the U.S. National Moving Ahead for Progress in the 21st Century (MAP-21) program's implementation and monitoring. Other of the Center's research projects examined highway investment, "complete streets", pedestrian routes, smart pedestrian planning, congestion pricing, freight and passenger mobility options, and port facilities and economic competitiveness. Professor Ross has developed algorithms and modeling for human mobility and neighborhood change.

Professor Ross is the director of Georgia Tech's Center for Quality Growth and Regional Planning (CQGRD). The Center works to inspire individuals, organizations, and communities to create healthy and sustainable futures. CQGRD has formed a wide range of university, government, and organizational partnerships. The Center's Healthy Places Research Group (HPRG) works to improves public health through the design of the built environment by conducting research on sustainable development, health impact assessments, air quality modeling, the localized impact of hospitals, and how to make neighborhoods healthier. It serves as a model for similar organizations throughout the United States

Professor Ross's research extends to a wide range of other city and regional planning topics as varied as aging, disaster recovery, art and culture strategic planning, and crowdsourced social media monitoring. Her current research focuses on freight and passenger mobility options for cities and regions, e-commerce, and emerging technologies.

Professor Ross is the author of *Health Impact Assessment in the United States* (2014), editor of *Megaregions: Planning for Global Competitiveness* (2009), and the co-author with Thomas Boston of *The Inner City: Urban Poverty and Economic Development in the Next Century* (1997). She has authored numerous journal articles and currently serves on the editorial boards of the *Journal of Planning Education and Research* (*JPER*) and the *Journal of Planning Literature*.

Professor Ross founded Catherine Ross and Associates, a consulting firm in Atlanta and served as its director from 1980 to 1999. She is co-founder of Euquant, Inc.—an Atlanta-based economic and planning consulting firm.

Professor Ross received a master's of regional planning degree and a PhD degree in city and regional planning from Cornell University. She completed postdoctorate work in city and regional planning at the University of California, Berkeley.

applications for federal grants—so-called A-95 reviews, required by U.S. Office of Management and Budget (OMB) circular A-95. COGs generate data and facilitate communication among local governments on issues that involve multiple jurisdictions. Some COGs prepare metropolitan regional plans. Most conduct reviews that improve regional coordination of plans. The weakest COGs perform *pro forma* reviews, rubber-stamp proposals, and do little or no real regional planning.

Regional planning entities named metropolitan planning organizations (MPOs) are federally funded transportation planning and policy-making organizations mandated by the Federal Aid Highway Act of 1962. There is an MPO in all 408 urbanized areas in the United States with populations greater than 50,000. MPOs gained importance with passage of the Intermodal Surface Transportation Act of 1991 (ISTEA) which provided federal funding for transportation projects and decentralized transportation planning so that MPOs do much of the actual planning for transportation projects. Because transportation is such a critical regional issue and MPOs have substantial federal funding, many COGs and regional councils (RCs) have been blended into MPOs. This history explains why regional planning is often done by an MPO, sometimes by a COG, sometimes by a joint COG–MPO and occasionally by an RC.

Of the 39,000 local, general purpose governments in the United States (counties, cities, townships, towns, villages, boroughs, and parishes), more than 35,000 are served by COGs, MPOs, or RCs.

COGs', MPOs', and RCs' ability to plan or to enforce their plans is limited. There are three main reasons why they do not have greater power to do regional planning.

First, local governments and regional entities insist on making their own decisions without interference from neighboring jurisdictions. This is particularly true in Cooley doctrine (pro-home rule) states and among charter cities. Special purpose regional entities like regional Air Quality Boards and regional park districts believe they have the best personnel and skills to do planning in their domain and resist encroachment from COGs, MPOs, and RCs.

Second, COGs have little money. Most of their funding comes from member jurisdictions. Cities and counties pay for COG staff and may fund small projects with contributions from their limited own-source revenue or federal or state grants, but they are not able or willing to contribute significant own-source revenue for regional projects. COGs, themselves, don't have money to acquire open space land, build infrastructure, develop publicly owned enterprises, clean up polluted sites, build housing, or perform other functions of regional significance. They don't have the clout to plan or coordinate local government activities other than transportation projects. Highway, port, airport, and other authorities plan and operate many big infrastructure projects. MPOs generally have more money than COGs—primarily from federal transportation funds earmarked specifically for transportation projects.

Third, a COG's ability to plan is limited by the voluntary nature of COGs. If one or more members of a COG succeed in getting the COG to press a collective decision on a member government that disagrees, the city or county may retaliate or even withdraw from the COG. This promotes a culture of mutual backscratching in which COGs avoid making hard decisions dictating what individual jurisdictions should do for fear that the COG will disintegrate, or that in the future the COG will require them to do things that they do not want to do. Most COGs don't prepare a regional plan. Those that do tend to gloss over issues that will cause conflict among members.

The Portland, Oregon Metro Region has a metropolitan government—called Metro—with a governing body elected region-wide. It does more effective regional planning and decision-making than COGs, MPOs, and RCs in other U.S. metropolitan areas. Box 10.2 describes Metro and Metro's 2040 growth concept plan.

Two other metropolitan regions in the United States—the Minneapolis–Saint Paul region, and the region covered by the New York and New Jersey Port Authority—illustrate what more effective metropolitan regional planning might be like.

The Minneapolis–Saint Paul, Minnesota region has some measure of metropolitan tax sharing. New York and New Jersey have a joint Port Authority to coordinate rail and bus transit and plan and implement large transportation infrastructure projects, including construction and management of the George Washington Bridge and the Lincoln Tunnel linking the island of Manhattan where the core of New York City is located to the mainland. Many other cities have established similar port authorities on smaller scales.

REGIONAL TRANSPORTATION PLANNING

The U.S. Department of Transportation (DOT) requires three-year regional level metropolitan transportation action plans called Transportation improvement programs (TIPs) as a condition of federal funding. TIPs are developed by MPOs. They shape the form of regions and are critical to a region's economy. Regional transportation planning is described in Chapter 14.

Big transportation projects are expensive and provoke a lot of debate. Both macro-level

BOX 10.2 THE *METRO 2040 CONCEPT PLAN* (PORTLAND, OREGON)

The *Metro 2040 Concept Plan* for the Portland metropolitan area reflects the most advanced regional planning in the United States. It illustrates Metro's 50-year vision for how the region will develop.

The 492-square-mile Metro region includes the city of Portland (population 584,000), portions of Clackamas, Multnomah, and Washington counties, and 23 additional cities. Together there are more than 1.5 million people in the Metro region.

Metro is run by a regionally elected council with legal authority to plan and regulate land use throughout the region. The Metro council consists of a president, elected regionwide, and six councilors elected by district every four years in nonpartisan elections. Metro has developed and maintains a regional land information system (RLIS) with more than a hundred layers of spatial data in a consistent format that can be used by any of the cities and counties in the Metro region as well as Metro itself.

Metro developed and is implementing a 50-year growth concept using GIS analysis from its RLIS and extensive citizen participation (Figure 10.6). The concept envisages Portland remaining the region's center, with a series of secondary and tertiary centers separated by greenbelts and large linear areas of open space linked by green corridors—undeveloped land along highways and the region's light rail lines. Portland's 50-year urban growth concept emphasizes development of station communities along rail lines and mixed mode transit including free bus service in the core, and extensive bicycle routes and pedestrian paths. Metro adopted a regional urban growth boundary in 1979. While cities and counties within other metropolitan regions have urban growth boundaries (UGBs) and urban limit lines (ULLs) Metro's was the first regional urban growth boundary. Development outside the urban growth boundary is strictly limited—particularly on prime agricultural and environmentally sensitive land. Many cities have urban growth boundaries, but no other U.S. metropolitan region has established a regional urban growth boundary.

Metro's regional growth boundary has been controversial. Limiting where development can occur reduces the value of land that cannot be developed until the future. Land owners claim their losses may run into billions of dollars. Three initiatives, state legislation, and numerous lawsuits have dealt with compensation for losses in land value as a result of Portland's regional urban growth boundary.[6]

The Metro urban growth boundary can be changed through a transparent and orderly process. Every six years, the Metro Council reviews and reports on the land supply in an urban growth report. As of 2018, the UGB had been expanded by about 14% (31,000 acres) from the time it was established in 1979. During the same time period, the population inside the UGB increased by over half a million people—a 61% increase. Overall, Portland's regional growth concept and urban growth boundary have succeeded in increasing average density within the urban growth boundary, preserving a regional greenbelt around the core of the urbanized Portland region, maintaining green corridors along transportation routes, and directing growth away from agricultural and environmentally sensitive land.

Metro performs more government functions than metropolitan councils of governments (COGs) and metropolitan planning organizations (MPOs) in other U.S. metropolitan regions. It manages 17,000 acres of parks, trails, and natural areas throughout the region. Metro is improving water quality and restoring wildlife habitat within these areas. Metro operates the Portland convention center, the Portland Zoo, and performing arts venues. It owns some natural areas and is acquiring others on a regional basis with voter-approved bond funds.

Metro has more funding per capita than most COGs or MPOs. In addition to federal transportation funds and other federal and state grants, Metro gets revenue from

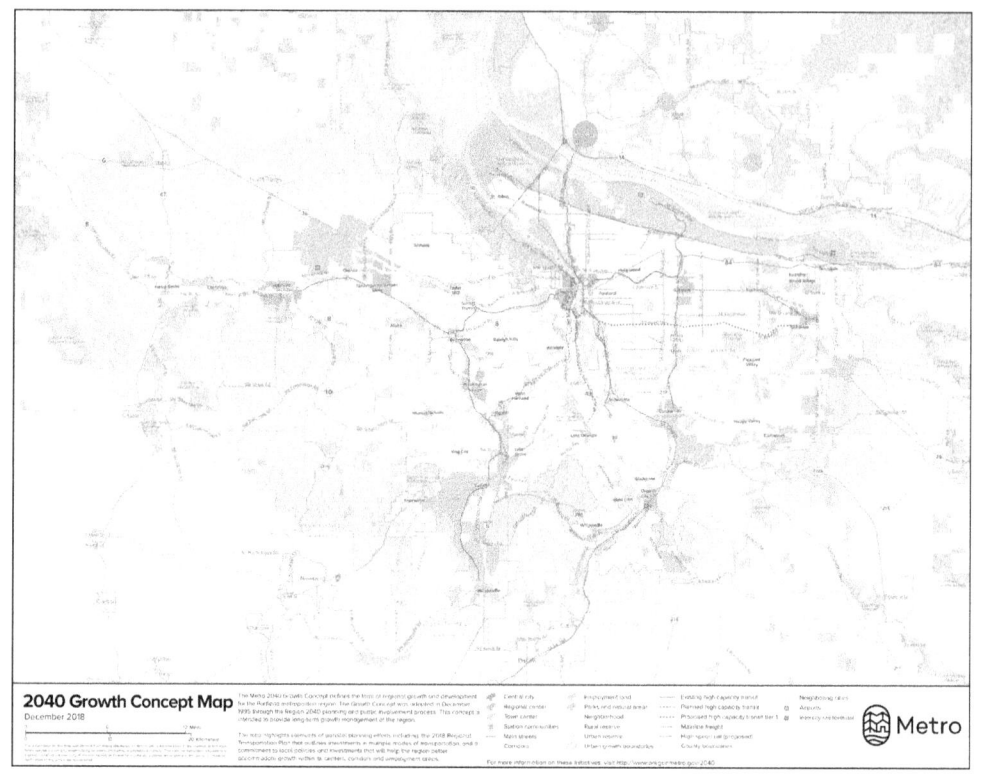

Figure 10.6 Metro's 2040 Growth Concept Map (Portland, Oregon, 1980).

a property tax, regional open space acquisition bonds, excise taxes paid by users of Metro facilities, general non-dedicated interest earnings, and enterprise activities.

While some Metro funds are earmarked for specific purposes, Metro is in the enviable position of having some discretionary general revenue. Metro's general fund revenue supports general government activities such as the council office, election costs, public information, advocacy, and land use planning as well as operations of the Portland Zoo, parks, and the arts venues.

systems decisions such as which communities they will pass through and micro-level decisions about the exact property they will use (and take by eminent domain if necessary) are critical for property owners and neighbors. Where freeway on- and off-ramps, transit stops, or other transportation access and exit points are located can provide economic windfalls for landowners whose land suddenly gains access and economic wipeouts for landowners whose access or views are blocked.

Transportation corridors are often planned regionally. Highways, roads, railroads, heavy and light rail systems, subways, bicycle lanes and paths, pedestrian paths, and walking, jogging, and equestrian trails are all typically built on publicly owned land, but sometimes on rights of way on private land. Land for transportation infrastructure must be identified and purchased or rights of way established during the planning phase, before land or easements are acquired and construction begins. This is a sensitive issue. If land is identified as possibly necessary for transportation infrastructure before the precise location is determined, this may cause "planners' blight"—depressing property values—or, conversely, inflate land prices in anticipation of infrastructure that will increase the land's value. An ethical issue planners face is transparency and timing for the release of information about transportation infrastructure.

State highway departments, other state-level authorities, cities, counties, and special districts may be authorized to condemn land for transportation rights of way, and take it by eminent domain so long as they pay just compensation to the landowners. They try to avoid using this power and are usually able to purchase most land voluntarily, but sometimes they exercise their power of eminent domain.

The land in the corridor close to major transportation infrastructure like a highway will typically generate much of the demand for travel on the system. Streets, sidewalks, parking, and other land uses within a quarter mile are sometimes planned in relation to the transportation infrastructure. A transportation corridor will often pass through multiple cities and counties, so planners in multiple jurisdictions are often called upon to consider transportation rights of way in their general and other plans.

COLLABORATIVE PLANNING BY CITIES AND COUNTIES

There are a few notable positive examples where cities and counties have collaborated successfully on regional plans. Counties and cities in Northeastern Ohio provide an important positive case study. Twelve counties, seven cities, and numerous towns and villages in the region collaborated on a regional plan to benefit each separate jurisdiction and the region as a whole. Box 10.3 describes the *Vibrant Northeast Ohio 2040 Plan*.

BOX 10.3 THE *VIBRANT NORTHEAST OHIO 2040 PLAN*

In 2015, a consortium of 12 counties and 7 cities in Northeast Ohio received the American Planning Association (APA)'s Burnham Award for excellent comprehensive planning, for the *Vibrant Northeast Ohio 2040 Plan* 2013–2040. The plan was created by the Northeast Ohio Sustainable Communities Consortium (NEOSCC)—a nonprofit corporation. The planning process and plan provide one model of how counties, cities, towns, and rural areas in older industrial regions can cooperate to produce a regional plan even when they have strikingly different conditions and interests.

Historic cities in the Northeast Ohio (NEO) region have lost population, while suburbs and rural areas have gained population. Between 1960 and 2010 the region's overall net population growth was virtually flat. Wages grew slowly. Every county lost tax revenue. The populations of Cleveland, Akron, Youngstown and four other legacy industrial cities collectively shrank by 44.7%. In the older industrial cities 174,900 homes were abandoned.

The *Vibrant Northeast Ohio 2040 Plan* defines its mission as: "to create conditions for a more vibrant, resilient, and sustainable Northeast Ohio that is full of vitality, a good steward of its built and natural resources, and adaptable and responsive to change". It describes eight vision objectives to operationalize this mission.

NEOSCC established a comprehensive outreach and communications system, a collaborative planning process that involved many different stakeholders and citizens, strong technical input, and a clear division of responsibility among working groups and caucuses to complete different streams of work on the plan. They made good use of local university talent and volunteers.

The *Vibrant NEO 2040 Plan* citizen participation process involved: input from a two-tiered "network of networks" of regional leaders and engaged stakeholders, phone and online surveys, 27 large public events to present updates and solicit feedback on the scenario planning process, and seven small caucuses of 100 regional leaders and technical experts who provided guidance on the regional vision. Figure 10.7 shows one of the scenario planning workshops.

The *Vibrant NEO 2040 Plan* provides an example for other city and regional planners of how to use historical material to contextualize and add interest to a plan. The plan includes early maps and town plans to illustrate the region's origin and growth and place the region's transformation and recent industrial decline in context. These are similar to the maps and town plans that Cornell planning historian John Reps collected (Reps, 1965).[7] From the air, many of the cities and towns in Northeast Ohio have the characteristic Northwest Ordinance grid pattern illustrated by the 1860 lithograph of nearby Geneva, Illinois—Figure 2.4 in Chapter 2.

Rather than selecting a "best" alternative, the *Vibrant NEO 2040 Plan* presents three alternative scenarios describing projections to 2040 if the region were to grow at the same rate as the rest of the United States is expected to grow, if the participating jurisdictions follow *Vibrant NEO 2040 Plan* policies and funding priorities, or if population and jobs grow at the same rate as the USA and the consortium pursues a "do things differently" scenario.

The plan includes an interactive online tool named imagineMyNEO with "digital dashboards" illustrating projected futures. Figure 10.8 illustrates the transportation investment dial. The arrow on the left shows that the current trend is towards building more auto-oriented infrastructure. The arrow on the right show that a majority of 156 participants at a NEO visioning workshop favored a significant shift to more investment on walking, biking, and transit infrastructure.

The *Vibrant NEO 2040 Plan* includes a similar fiscal tool. Users can see for themselves the projected economic consequences of different courses of action. The economic development dial shows that under the "growth the same scenario", the region-wide revenue-to-cost ratio is projected to fall 33.7% by 2040. All counties would experience declining revenues compared to costs if the region pursues this course of action. Users can see how this decline might be altered for different parts of the region using the fiscal tool.

The plan presents detailed site-specific recommendations about the planned location of strategic investments. In addition to investment strategies at the community level, the vision includes an inventory and map of strategic regional sites such as innovation zones.[8] The plan identifies and describes strategies for emerging cultural districts, the region's industrial waterfront, and other new industrial opportunity sites.

The plan describes nine recommendations for development in detail with easy-to-understand visuals including digital dashboards showing trends, current conditions, and alternative futures. It recommends nine specific initiatives to implement the recommendations including: remediation, assembly, marketing, and redevelopment of abandoned properties; enhancing and coordinating the region's rail and bus services; and supporting sustainable agriculture. The plan links the nine general recommendations to detailed site-specific recommendations. It articulates development strategies for different types of places such as university/college town districts, medical/institutional centers, senior living communities, corporate campuses, light industrial business parks, neighborhood main streets, and heavy industrial development districts. The plan describes each type of district with photographs of current conditions and illustrations of what might replace them; gives examples of local success stories; and describes principles for good development. The detailed, concrete, and specific suggestions for different areas are a great strength of the plan.

REGIONAL AND NATIONAL PLANNING | 223

Figure 10.7 *Vibrant Northeast Ohio 2040 Plan* Workshop.

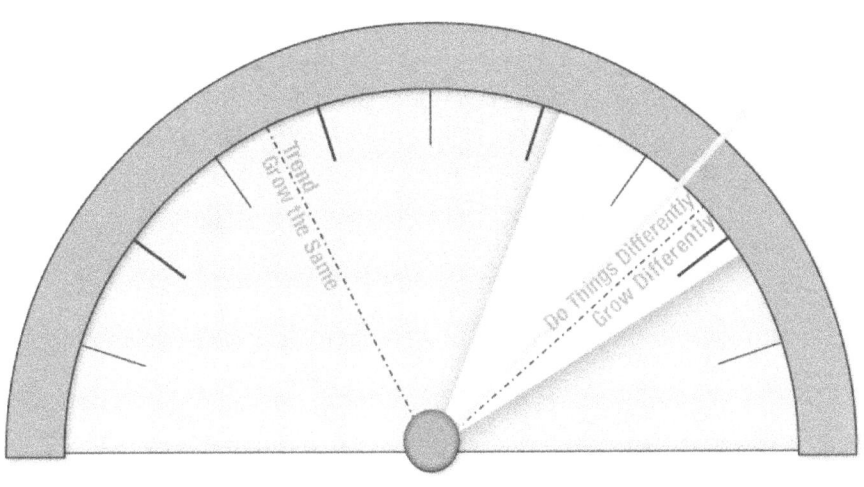

auto-oriented
infrastructure

walk, bike, transit
infrastructure

Figure 10.8 *Vibrant Northeast Ohio 2040 Plan* Digital Dashboard Dial.

U.S. MEGACITIES AND MEGACITY REGIONS

Very large cities—usually defined as cities with 10 million or more residents—are called megacities. Even larger regions consisting of one or more megacities, other large cities, smaller cities, towns, and the space between them are called megaregions, megacity regions, megalopolises, polycentric metropolises or poly-centric megacity networks. The United Nations (UN) uses the term urban agglomeration which includes an entire urban area rather than a region defined by the political boundaries of cities as their unit of analysis for very large city regions. By the UN definition New York City and Los Angeles are the only U.S. cities among the 31 megacities they identified in 2016, and also among the 41 they project will be in existence in 2030.

The New York-based Regional Plan Association (RPA)—a nonprofit organization that has promoted planning for the New York City region since the 1920s—has described and preliminarily mapped 11 megaregions in the United States. Figure 10.9 shows the RPA's projections of where U.S. megaregions will be in 2050. A number of scholars have created similar inventories and maps of U.S. megaregions.[9]

SUMMARY

Regional planning is an important specialty area within city and regional planning. Urban challenges like air and water pollution do not respect political boundaries. They need to be addressed on a regional basis.

In the United States Councils of Governments and Metropolitan Planning Organizations do some regional planning and coordinate local government programs to some extent—particularly with respect to transportation. However, they do not have the political power or resources to implement regional plans themselves. Basic economic forces and decisions by private sector actors drive most regional development.

Some planners work exclusively at the regional scale. Their plans ripple downwards to impact conditions at the neighborhood and site scale and upwards to impact

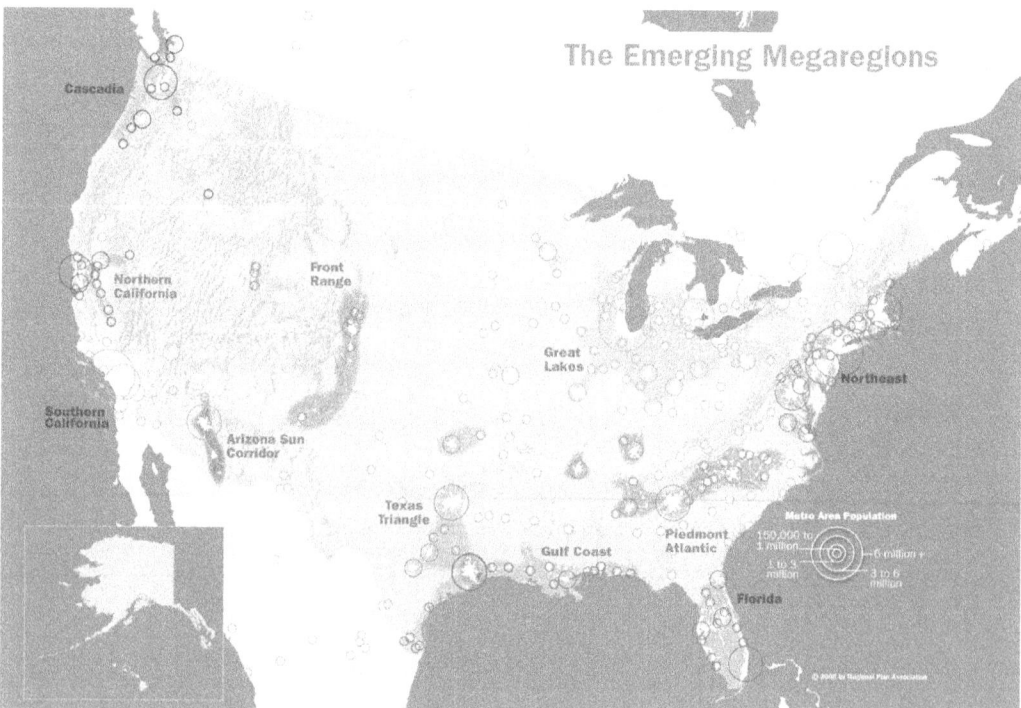

Figure 10.9 Regional Plan Association Projected U.S. Megaregions 2050.

urbanization at the state, national, and international scales. Planners working in specialized planning areas and at other levels need to consider the regional implications of their plans.

Regional planning may be for natural regions defined by features like river basins or for politically defined regions such as metropolitan areas. The regions may be very small or enormous. The difference between urban and rural areas and the boundaries of natural regions is generally a continuum with fuzzy boundaries.

As the population of the urban areas of the United States and other countries has grown and the number of jurisdictions has proliferated, the need to coordinate planning for land use, transportation, the environment, economic development, housing, parks and open space. and other matters on a regional basis has grown. As urban areas sprawl, strategies to manage growth regionally have become more critical.

There are already 41 megacities with population of ten million or more people. The number of megacities, their size, and the number of their residents is projected to increase rapidly. Some megacities have already become even larger megacity regions containing one or more megacity, other cities, and land between the components of the region.

Many planners, geographers, and regional scientists have built on region planning theory originated by regional planning pioneers Elisée Reclus, Patrick Geddes, Walter Christaller, and Walter Isard. New ideas and new technology continue to improve the quality of regional planning.

In the United States only a few areas like the Metro region around Portland, Oregon and a group of cities and counties in Northeast Ohio have succeed in getting local governments to work together to create and implement regional plans. The United States does not have a national urbanization plan. Except for two large historic multi-state regional planning efforts—by the Tennessee Valley Authority (TVA) in the 1930s and 1940s and the Appalachian Planning Commission, beginning in the mid 1960s—the United States has not had large-scale regional planning and regional development comparable to some other countries. The nonprofit organization Resources for the Future does regional research, but has no authority to prepare regional plans.

Despite the political and financial limitation on regional planning in the United States, city and regional planners play an important role in shaping regions. They can and should be empowered to do much more.

CONCEPTS

Central Place Theory
Council of Governments (COG)
Integrated Water Resources Management (IWRM)
Location Theory
Megaregion
Metropolitan Planning Organization (MPO)
Natural Region
U.S. Office of Management and Budget (OMB) Circular #A-95
Portland Metro 2040 Concept Plan
Public Use Microdata Area (PUMA)
Regional Science
Regional Plan Association (RPA)
Spatial Mismatch
Tennessee Valley Authority (TVA)
Vibrant Northeast Ohio 2040 Plan

PEOPLE

Walter Christaller
Patrick Geddes
Walter Isard
Elisée Reclus

NOTES

1 The European Union spent €348 billion between 2007 and 2013 for structural funds, a cohesion fund, the European Solidarity Fund, and projects funded by the European Investment Bank to "reduce structural disparities between EU regions and promote real equal opportunities for all" (Teitz, 2012: 144).
2 Franklin Roosevelt established the National Resources Planning Board (NRPB) in 1933 to study the nation's natural resources and propose policies to use mineral, forest, agricultural, and other resources

more efficiently. The board reported directly to him. There was virulent political opposition to the NRPB. Its critics depicted the NRPB as socialistic (Clawson, 1981).
3. Elisée Reclus left France in 1851 at age 21 when the conservative French President Louis-Napoléon Bonaparte staged a coup d'état and declared himself Emperor Napoleon III. Reclus spent six years traveling in Great Britain, the United States, and South and Central America observing the natural environment and the cultures of different regions. On his return to France, Reclus began producing brilliant articles and books on the relationship between physical and human geography. In 1871 he was banished from France for life for participating in a failed coup d'état. He settled in Switzerland where he produced his 19-volume *New Universal Geography of Mankind and the Earth* published in French and English between 1875 and 1894. Reclus led the international anarchist movement together with Russian anarchist Pëtr Kropotkin. In 1894 Reclus won the UK Royal Geographical Society's prestigious patron's gold medal. He was appointed Chair of Comparative Geography at the University of Brussels in 1894.
4. Nineteenth-century agricultural economist Johann Heinrich von Thünen (1783–1850), German economic geographer Alfred Weber (1868–1958), and 20th-century German economist August Lösch had developed theoretical models of the relations between economics and geography in agricultural, manufacturing, and spatial interactions that informed Isard's work.
5. A few weak voluntary nonprofit metropolitan organizations of governments that were called regional councils (RCs) were created beginning in the 1920s. COGs in their modern form began in 1947, when the Atlanta Regional Metropolitan Planning Commission and the Northern Virginia Regional Planning Commission were formed (NLC, 2021). By 1950, there were 18 COGs or similar regional planning organizations in the USA. By 1967, when the National Association of Regional Councils was created, there were 350 COGs or similar regional planning organizations (NARC, 2021). Beginning in 1969, the U.S. Office of Management and Budget (OMB) circular A-95 required local government applications for federal urban aid to be reviewed by a state, regional, or metropolitan clearing house (OMB, 1968; DRC, 1971; Myhra, 1973). Since virtually every eligible jurisdiction wants to compete for federal urban aid, states authorized COGs, and cities quickly established clearinghouses. Regional-level COGs were the vehicle of choice for the clearinghouses. OMB A-95 review ended in 1985. Currently virtually all local government in the South and Southwest are members of COGs and the great majority of local governments in other parts of the United States are as well.
6. Voters passed measure 7 in 2000—a statewide measure requiring government to reimburse landowners when regulations reduce the value of their property (Oregon DLCD, 2011). Measure 7 was overturned by the Oregon supreme court. A less extreme initiative that also required compensation—measure 37—passed in 2004. It was essentially replaced by a third initiative—measure 49—in 2007. Political and legal challenges to Metro continue.
7. The Northeast Ohio region was part of the Northwest Territories established in 1785. Between 1801 and 1807 General Moses Cleaveland (with an "a") surveyed the area and divided it into 36 square mile townships as required by the Northwest Ordinance. Cleveland was selected as the hub for the region. (A printer dropped the "a" in Cleaveland's name on an original document to save space!). The *NEO Plan* enlivens background on the subsequent eras of canal and railroad construction, industrialization, migration, suburbanization and industrial decline with visual historical material.
8. The *Vibrant NEO 2040 Plan* describes innovation zones such as universities and adjacent mixed-use commercial districts that have the potential to catalyze new business investment in the innovation economy.
9. University of Toronto business professor Richard Florida has identified 12 U.S. megaregions, one of which includes land in Mexico and one land in Canada (Florida, 2008). Florida provides colorful terms for U.S. megaregions including Cascadia for the megaregion in the Pacific Northwest, Nor-Cal and So-Cal for the San Francisco Bay Area and Los Angeles megaregions, and So-Flo for the Southern Florida megaregion. Virginia Polytechnic Institute Department of Urban Affairs and Planning professors Robert Lang and Dawn Dhavale have described and mapped 10 U.S. megaregions (Lang & Dhavale, 2007).

SUGGESTIONS FOR FURTHER LEARNING

Regional Planning Textbook: Peter Hall & Mark Tewdwr-Jones, *Urban and regional planning*, 5th ed (2010). **U.S. Census Definitions of Regions:** U.S. Office of Management and Budget (OMB), *Standards for delineating metropolitan and micropolitan statistical areas* (2010) and *Revised delineations of metropolitan statistical areas, micropolitan statistical areas, and combined statistical areas and guidance on uses of the delineations of these areas* (2015). **Pioneering Works in Regional Analysis and Planning:** Elisée Reclus, *The earth and its inhabitants* (1876–1894). Brian Berry, *Economic geography* (1987). Walter Christaller, *Central places in southern Germany (1933)*. Walter Isard, *Introduction to regional science* (1975). David Boyce, Walter Isard (1919–2010): Founding father of regional science (2020). **Regional and National Economic Development Planning:** Resources for the Future, *Resources* [magazine]. **Metropolitan Planning:** Bruce Katz & Jennifer Bradley, *The metropolitan revolution* (2007). Robert Lang & Dawn Dhuvale, *Beyond megalopolis: Exploring*

America's new megapolitan geography (2007). **Metro (Portland, Oregon):** Christina Rosan, *Governing the fragmented metropolis* (2016). Cam Owens, Portland's urban growth boundaries: Problem or solution? (2016). Metro [website] (2021). **Sprawl:** Robert Burchell, Anthony Downs, Barbara McCann, & Sahan Mukherji, *Sprawl costs* (2005). Robert Bruegmann, *Sprawl: A compact history* (2005). Robert Bruegmann, *Sprawl* (2016). Dolores Hayden & Jim Wark, *A field guide to sprawl* (2006). **Planning natural regions:** Ian McHarg, *Design with nature* (1969). **Rural planning:** Kathryn Frank & Michael Hibbard, Rural planning in the twenty-first century (2017). **Councils of Governments (COGs):** National League of Cities, *Metropolitan councils* (2019). **Collaborative City-County Planning:** Northeast Ohio Sustainable Communities Consortium, *Vibrant Northeast Ohio 2040 Plan* (2015). **Journals:** *Journal of Regional Science. Regional Studies. Area Development and Policy. Regional Science and Urban Economics.*

CHAPTER 11

Planning for an Urban Planet

INTRODUCTION

Apple labels most of its devices "Made in China" because that is where they are assembled. However, Apple sources materials and components for their devices from more than 200 suppliers throughout the globe. The iPhone chassis assembly comes from Chinese manufacturers; the Corning Glass Company in the United States supplies the iPhone's "gorilla glass" display cover; and Sony in Japan manufactures the iPhone camera.

Modern transportation technology has shrunk the time it takes for people and goods to move from one location to another by air, land, and sea. Raw materials, components, and finished products flow through worldwide supply chains to be transformed, assembled, exported, and consumed. Information and capital flow around the world.

Some planners work full-time on issues like climate change and world trade at the planetary scale. However, globalization and the world city network affect city and regional planners working at every scale, even planners working in a small towns and rural areas.

This chapter summarizes information on current world population and population projections. It begins by describing the distribution of the world population. Sections describe globalization, world cities, and the world city network. A section of the chapter discusses megacities—cities with populations of over 10 million people—and even larger megacity regions. The chapter closes with a review of the role international organizations like the United Nations, the World Bank, and the World Trade Organization play at the planetary level and bi- and multi-lateral agreements for planning the planet.

WORLD POPULATION AND POPULATION PROJECTIONS

Today 56% of the world's 7.9 billion inhabitants live in urban areas. The growth of the world's population and urbanization are both steeply increasing power curves growing at faster than exponential rates.[1] The population of earth has more than tripled since 1950. At the global level, demographer Kingsley Davis's S curves of urbanization in England, the United States, China, and Cambodia (Figure 2.1 in Chapter 2) illustrate the pattern of urbanization over time. They are similar S-shaped curves with a long left tail, an inflection point where the countries begin to urbanize rapidly, and then a flattening right tail as they approach full urbanization. However, the inflection point when urbanization starts to rise rapidly occurs at different times in these countries, and the S shape can be distorted by events like war, droughts, and economic crises, as dramatically illustrated by Cambodia's S curve during the last fifty years.

The world is now at the steep part of a global urbanization curve. World population and urbanization will likely continue to grow, but at a slower rate as more countries approach full urbanization. The United Nations projects that the world's population growth rate will progressively decline between 2022 and 2050, but that the percentage of the world's population living in cities will continue to increase. By 2050 the United Nations projects that the world's population will have increased to 9.8 billion and that two-thirds of all people on earth will live in urban areas. By 2100 the UN projects that the world's population will be 11.2 billion. It may stabilize at that level, but projections beyond 2100 are very uncertain. Global climate change, pandemics, war, medical advances, famines, new technology, and unanticipated changes may lead to different totals and radically different distributions of the world's population.

Most of the urban population growth in the next three decades will be in the developing countries of Asia, Africa, and Latin America. Urban population growth will occur both as a result of natural increase and as people migrate from rural to urban areas. Figure 11.1 shows the United Nations' estimate of the population and the percentage of the population living in urban areas for more developed regions, less developed regions, and the entire world in 1950, 1970, 1990, and 2020 and their projections to 2050.

The UN projects that world population will increase by more than 1.21 billion people by 2050. Only one out of every 18 of the net new urban residents in 2050 will live in a developed country. The UN expects that the fastest growing regions will be sub-Saharan Africa and the India–Bangladesh–Pakistan region.[2] The population of China—which in 2021 has the world's largest population at 1.4 billon—is projected to shrink slightly, but the percentage of Chinese living in cities will continue to increase dramatically as a result of rural-to-urban migration.

The United States is growing more rapidly than other developed countries. Of the 130 million projected new urban residents in North America and Western Europe by 2030, 80 million (62%) are projected to be in the United States. Some countries—notably Italy, Romania, and South Korea—will experience significant net population shrinkage, mostly as a result of declining birth rates.

There is an inverse relationship between a country's wealth—measured by per capita gross domestic product (GDP)—and family size. Generally, the wealthier the country, the fewer children there are per capita. Oil-rich Middle Eastern countries are an exception. They have both high per capita income and many more live births than the world average.

These demographic realities have profound implications for city and regional planners. In most of the developed world there will be little net overall population growth. Therefore, there will be little need for a net increase in the housing stock, though some new housing will be needed in growing regions. U.S. City and Regional Planners will have to shift to restructuring of the existing urban fabric; revitalization; changes in industrial, commercial, and retail areas; and new residential development—mostly on the fringe of existing urban areas. Global climate change will require every country—including the United States—to alter its settlement pattern. Existing infrastructure will need to be modernized and extended, new forms of energy production and distribution planned and built, and economies expanded. In sub-Saharan Africa, the India/Pakistan/Bangladesh region, Nigeria, and other populous and fast-growing countries,

World		More developed regions		Less developed regions	
Population (billions)	% urban	Population (billions)	% urban	Population (billions)	% urban
2.5	29.6	0.8	54.8	1.7	17.7
3.7	36.6	1.0	66.8	2.7	25.3
5.3	43.0	1.2	72.4	4.2	34.9
8.6	56.2	1.3	79.1	7.3	51.7
9.8	65.6	1.3	86.6	8.5	65.6

Figure 11.1 United Nations World Population Estimate 2020 and Projections to 2050.

Note: The 2000% urban is a 2018 estimate.

Source: United Nations World Population Prospects, the 2018 Revise.

planners will need to plan for massive population growth, continuing urbanization, and rapid peri-urban development—urbanization occurring on the urban fringe. "Climate change refugees"—forced to move because of climate change—will be a significant global problem. Climate change refugees could overwhelm populous and low-lying countries and their neighbors and provoke conflict as desperate people flee and nation states seek to keep them out. Chinese planners accustomed to planning for growth will have to change course as population stabilizes and shrinks slightly and migration patterns change.

THE DISTRIBUTION OF THE WORLD POPULATION

The world population is concentrated in the third of the earth's land area closest to the equator. More than three-quarters of the world's population still live in settlements of under one million people, and 44% still live in rural areas.[3]

Earth's population distribution is strongly related to the climate in different regions. For much of the year, sparsely populated polar regions in the far north and far south are so cold that permanent settlements are economically impossible. Freezing temperatures, snow, and ice make it too expensive to build and maintain infrastructure and support human life in all but the most hospitable coastal areas of the polar regions. Large distances and severe weather conditions make transportation of goods and people difficult and costly. Antarctica is surrounded by water and sea ice, and has no buildable land. There is land around the North Pole—primarily in Russia, the Scandinavian countries and Alaska. City and regional planners, civil engineers, architects, and others have developed the technology to build settlements in these regions and have been able to create some substantial cities there. However, they are expensive to build and service.[4]

Within the relatively temperate zone extending north and south of the equator, much of the human population is concentrated in coastal areas, along rivers, or in relatively flat and well-watered regions. Mountainous areas such as the Himalayas in Asia and the Andes in South America, and deserts such as the Sahara Desert in North Africa and Gobi Desert in China and Mongolia, are sparsely settled and have large areas that are essentially uninhabited. Desert areas in the American Southwest have few inhabitants.

A good way to understand the extreme differences in urban settlement around the world is to look at the U.S. National Aeronautics and Space Administration (NASA)'s satellite images of earth. NASA's "black marble" images of the night sky, showing light from human settlements, reveal the relationships between oceans and land, variations in human settlements depending on latitude, clustering of human settlements along coasts and rivers, and how deserts and mountains affect settlement patterns. They also illustrate the differing ability of countries to afford electric power to illuminate urban areas at night. Figure 11.2 is a NASA black marble image of Europe and North Africa. The area on the left is empty because it is part of the 70% of earth covered by oceans. Western Europe is largely illuminated—particularly along the coasts where population is concentrated. The bright patch on the upper right of Figure 11.2 is Moscow. The rest of European Russia is much darker than wealthier, more energy-consuming regions of Europe. Saint Petersburg—the large splotch of light to the northwest—and some mid-sized Russian cities are exceptions. The interior of the Scandinavian countries approaching the North Pole have only scattered light from cities like Stockholm, Helsinki, and Oslo. The satellite image shows Anchorage, Alaska—the U.S. city closest to the North Pole. The Nile River delta—the brightly illuminated splotch at the lower right of the image—illustrates the important relationship between infrastructure and urban development. Power from the Aswan Dam—completed in 1970—provides enough electrical power to illuminate the area of Egypt near the Nile River. Before the Aswan Dam was completed in 1970 much of this area would have been dark. Most of North Africa is dark because it is sparsely inhabited desert or has only small settlements that are

Figure 11.2 NASA "Black Marble" Night Sky in Western Europe and Northwest Africa.

too poor to produce enough light to be visible from space.

GLOBALIZATION, WORLD CITIES, AND THE WORLD CITY NETWORK

There is a large and sophisticated body of theory about globalization, the world city network, and world cities.[5] Globalization refers to the integration of the world economy. World cities—cities that are highly connected to other cities and where the most important, economic and cultural activities occur—are the dominant hubs in the world city network. The world city network connects firms within cities—particularly multi-national corporations—with other businesses throughout the world.

Networks of cities have existed for millennia, and a world city network has arguably existed for 500 years.[6] However, the world city network as we know it today is largely the product of digital technology and global political and economic integration in the last 40 years.

There is broad consensus among city and regional planners that:

1) the term "world city" is a useful category;
2) a network of world cities exists;
3) there is a hierarchy in the degree to which cities are connected;
4) connectivity is overwhelmingly among headquarters and branch offices of multi-national corporations and law, accounting, and other advanced producer services firms—not city governments or public sector entities;
5) many different indicators and indices are valid ways to describe global connectivity;
6) linkages in the world city network are in constant flux;
7) the world city network is significant for planning at every scale.

Columbia University sociology professor Saskia Sassen proposed the term "global city" in 1991. Sassen considers global cities a special category of the most important world cities. Other scholars often use the terms world and global cities interchangeably.

Cities provide agglomeration economies—cost savings achieved because businesses are close to each other. A traditional explanation of why businesses cluster in large cities is so that businesspeople can be in personal touch with each other and advanced service providers they need. Agglomeration also makes it easier to move raw materials, components, and finished products from place to place. Even though digital technology is reducing this advantage, face-to-face communication is still a reason why agglomeration in cities occurs.

The global digital network is uneven. There are information centers and information deserts. Business professionals can e-mail, skype, phone, fax, Zoom, or use other forms of video conferencing to remote locations. However, communications infrastructure in global cities facilitates transmission of huge quantities of information at lightning speed that may not be possible elsewhere.

Globalization is simultaneously both concentrating and dispersing activity at the global, national, and metropolitan levels—what University of Chicago sociology professor Neil Brenner calls urban implosions and explosions. Despite predictions that geographical space would become irrelevant and cities would wither away, cities—particularly world cities—have grown in population and importance in the digital age. Hundreds of millions of people have imploded into megacities and megacity regions. Features once found only in urban areas have exploded to locations everywhere in the world. Figures 11.3 and 11.4 illustrate the explosion of cities worldwide. They show the main business district in Hyderabad, India. The number of domestic and international firms with offices in Hyderabad—like many cities in developing countries—has exploded. At the same time hundreds of thousands of migrants from rural areas of Hyderabad have moved to the city in search of employment and a better life. The open-air market of the Charminar Bazaar is crowded from early morning until late at night.

Pundits speculated that corporate policies allowing employees to work and live anywhere during the COVID pandemic would change the continuing concentration of population in cities and the growth of world cities. There have been changes in migration and settlement patterns during the COVID-19 pandemic, but it is too early to tell how this will play out in the long run.

At the global scale, management of the world economy is concentrated in top-tier cities like New York and London. Manufacturing is becoming increasingly dispersed around the globe and decentralized to different regions within countries. Less retail occurs in brick-and-mortar stores and more through ordering and delivery of orders directly to homes and businesses.

Figure 11.3 Hyderabad, India (2012).

Figure 11.4 Charminar Bazaar, Hyderabad, India.

Traditional land use planning assumptions about the amount of space needed for retail are changing fast.

Like Apple, many corporations design products at one or more locations—perhaps (but not necessarily) in a world city. They contract with firms worldwide to produce components for the products they have designed, assemble them, and market the finished products worldwide. This kind of production process requires sophisticated support to manage dispersed and rapidly changing global supply chains—the pathways through which raw materials and components flow to city hubs for final assembly and distribution as finished products all over the world. Global connectivity may require lawyers familiar with British law, accountants who understand accounting practices in Bangladesh, and advertising executives sensitive to the cultural preferences of German consumers for products that may have been designed in London and produced in Bangladesh for consumption in Germany. Corporations rarely have the internal capacity to do all that. They turn to networks of specialized firms located in world cities to provide the services they need.

Globalization also affects the internal structure of cities. Saskia Sassen argues that three different models of global city structure are emerging. (1) In some cities, something close to a classic central business district (CBD) like the CBD in Chicago at the time that Chicago School sociologist Ernest W. Burgess developed his concentric zone theory in the 1920s still exists. New York City's Wall Street area is an example. (2) In other world cities there is a new pseudo-CBD just outside the historic city center. La Défense—a massive, planned office complex just outside the center of Paris (Figure 11.5) illustrates this pattern. (3) In other world cities, Sassen sees nodes of intense business activity emerging along "cyber routes" or "digital highways" such as Highway I-95 around the core of the Boston, Massachusetts metropolitan region. Information flows may follow historic infrastructure for highways, telecommunication cables, high-speed rail lines, and airports. Sassen argues that economic activity within the metropolitan areas of global cities manifests a dynamic of both concentration and dispersion just as is occurring in the world city system.

University of North Carolina business professor and airport business consultant John Kasarda named regions adjacent to international airports whose land use and economic function are dictated by the airport aerotropoli (singular aerotropolis) from the classical Greek words "city" and "of the air". Kasarda is a quantitative sociologist. His understanding of aerotropoli is based on research that began when he realized early in his career that international airports were rapidly expanding and generating economic change near them. Aerotropoli contain the airport itself and supporting airport facilities. They often have logistics centers, and facilities to store and transship time-critical goods traveling by air. They have facilities for business travelers such as hotels, restaurants, and conference, trade, and exhibition centers. They may include warehouses. They have

Figure 11.5 La Défense Business District (Paris, France).

transportation connections to move goods traveling by air to and from the aerotropolis. They may have residential areas. Notable U.S. aerotropoli are Aerotropolis Atlanta adjacent to the Hartsfield-Jackson Atlanta International Airport and two airports run by the Wayne County Airport Authority—the Detroit Metropolitan Airport and nearby Willow Run Airport. Figure 11.6 shows Ekurhuleni Aerotropolis in Ekurhuleni, South Africa.

There is currently a debate about how to conceptualize "urban" at the planetary scale. University of Chicago sociology professor Neil Brenner (2019: 14) acknowledges "the *implosion* of sociospatial processes into dense centers of population, infrastructure, and economic activity", but considers "the *explosion* of sociospatial relations across vast territories, landscapes, and ecologies" to be even more important. For Brenner, the whole world is urban. He argues that urban analysis should be vertical—examining issues at the global, national, and other scales rather than thinking in terms of a rural–urban dichotomy.

In contrast to Brenner, Shlomo Angel—a professor of city and regional planning at New York University—argues that we now live on a "planet of cities" on less than half of one percent of the earth's surface, surrounded by oceans, uninhabited regions, and rural areas. Angel argues that the movement of people into cities cannot be stopped or reversed and that the expansion of cities that it entails cannot be contained.

City and regional planners, geographers, economists, and sociologists have conducted empirical research and developed modern theory about the world city network since the 1980s. They been joined by scholars from architecture, law, communications, culture studies, and the arts and humanities.

Spanish-born, French-educated, U.S.-based Manuel Castells—a professor of communication and technology at the University of Southern California's Annenberg School for Communication and Journalism—is one of the world's most influential contemporary city and regional planning, communications, and urban sociology scholars. Castells argues that we now live in the information age in

Figure 11.6 Ekurhuleni Aerotropolis, Ekurhuleni, South Africa.

a network society. The leading world cities are no longer primarily industrial or post-industrial. They are informational—thriving or declining as nodes in the world city network. Castells distinguishes the "space of flows"—flows of information, people, goods, capital, and authority into and out of cities—from the "space of places"—physical sites in the real world. He concludes that a city's relationship to the space of flows is often as important as or more important than its relationship to the space of places it occupies.

The Globalization and World Cities Research Network—GaWC (pronounced gawk)—is a loose network of scholars doing world cities research. GaWC is led by Peter Taylor, a British geographer at Northumbria University, and Benjamin Derudder, a Belgian professor of city science at the Catholic University of Belgium's Public Governance Institute.

Taylor, Derudder, and other members of GaWC conduct empirical research on the location of multi-national corporations' headquarters and branches, flows of cargo containers among cities, international airport arrivals and departures, the volume of phone and internet activity among cities, and other indicators of connectivity in order to understand the world city network and the world city hierarchy. Their empirical research supports other theorists' views about the importance of information technology and economic globalization. They have found that the growth of world cities has not led to a dispersal of locations, but a new centralization into places of concentrated information flows and knowledge hubs.

Figure 11.7 is Taylor and Derudder's list of world cities with the greatest network connectivity as of 2012 and how their rank had changed since 2000. Cities in Figure 11.7 are ranked in a hierarchy with a global network connectivity (GNC) index score. London is at the top with a GNC score of 100. The GNC score of other cities in the table is expressed as a percentage of London's score. London is followed by New York with a GNC score of 93. Other rankings of cities in the world city hierarchy using different measures of connectivity also conclude that New York and London—referred to by the

2012 GNC	City	2012 Rank	20009 Rank
100.00	London	1	1
92.66	New York	2	2
78.31	Hong Kong	3	3
71.62	Paris	4	4
65.62	Singapore	5	6
63.66	Shanghai	6	31
63.63	Tokyo	7	5
62.09	Beijing	8	36
62.06	Sydney	9	13
61.33	Dubai	10	54
58.81	Chicago	11	7
58.81	Mumbai	12	21
58.58	Milan	13	8
57.20	Moscow	14	34
57.19	Sao Paoulo	15	16
56.88	Frankfurt	16	14
55.06	Toronto	17	10
54.90	Los Angeles	18	9
54.44	Madrid	19	11
53.20	Mexico City	20	18
52.68	Amsterdam	21	12
52.10	Kuala Lumpur	22	26
51.98	Brussels	23	15
50.05	Seoul	24	43
49.18	Johannesburg	25	45

Figure 11.7 Global Network Connectivity according to the Global and World Cities Network.

acronym NYLON—have been at the top of the world city hierarchy for a long time. There is a large gap between New York and London and the next highest-scoring world city—Hong Kong—which had a GNC index score of 78 in 2012. The rank order of Hong Kong and other cities in Figure 11.7 is constantly changing. The order is undoubtedly different now than it was in 2012. Other cities move up and down the hierarchy. For example, between 2000 and 2012 Shanghai's and Dubai's GNC ranks in Figure 11.7 changed rapidly as these cities became much more interconnected according to Taylor and Derudder's metrics.

Rich countries and rich cities—places central to the world economy—are very economically privileged compared to those that exist at the margin. The opportunity for hyper-profits in international finance is creating extraordinary wealth for Wall Street and London bankers. Extracting raw materials, and manufacturing basic goods like shoes and clothing in factories in developing countries like India, Bangladesh, and Vietnam is much less profitable.

Rich cities are themselves very economically unequal. In São Paulo, Brazil wealthy Brazilian nationals and expatriates earn high salaries and participate in lifestyles comparable to those of wealthy New York and London professionals, while poorly paid service workers in neighborhoods in São Paulo struggle to survive, as do service workers in London, New York, and other world cities. World cities have wealthy enclaves for transnational elites working in multi-national corporations and advanced producer services firms. Low-income neighborhoods house poor people (often migrants) who do the low-paid unskilled work necessary to keep world cities and high-powered multi-national firms functioning, such as maintaining city infrastructure, cleaning the streets, disposing of garbage, working as janitors in high-rise office buildings, doing low-skilled restaurant work or working at low-wage factory or retail jobs.

World cities generate costs for health, education, and welfare for low-income workers that exceed the fiscal capacity of the state—the government resources to pay for them—leaving working-class people—particularly low-income migrants—in need. An important public policy question facing city and regional planners all over the world is how to promote greater economic equity and help more people reap benefits from the new world economic order.

The COVID-19 pandemic re-invigorated a long-standing debate about whether cities will wither away as physical space and distance become irrelevant. The debate was first raised in 1964 by University of California, Berkeley professor of city and regional planning Melvin Webber. Webber predicted that communications technology would produce a "post-city age". While Webber was prescient to predict more than fifty years ago that communications technology would be the most important force altering cities, his prediction that large cities would become less relevant and decline as information could be shared has not proven to be true.

During the COVID-19 pandemic, Apple, Jet Blue Airlines, Facebook, American Express, and other large multi-national corporations adopted policies to allow employees to work from locations remote from physical corporate offices. Popular media reported outmigration from high-cost centers like San Francisco and New York City to cities like Austin, Texas and Ogden, Utah with a high quality of life and where house prices and the cost of living are much lower. There are many new predictions of a coming post-city age. Early empirical research suggests that the COVID pandemic did indeed cause some employees to move and some restructuring of the U.S. city system. However, restructuring appears to have occurred in more complex ways than reported in the media. It is too early to tell what the long-term impacts of the pandemic on world cities will be.

City and regional planners need to understand where a city or region they are planning for fits in the world city network in order to make sense of, and forecast, the demographic and economic forces that will likely shape, its future. A city transportation plan, for example, needs to be cognizant of global flows of people and goods into and out of the city as a hub in the world city network. Forecasting the city's economy and developing an economic development strategy require an understanding of the connectivity of headquarters and branch firms in the city to other firms worldwide. Decisions about land use planning and urban design are shaped by the world city network as cities shift from traditional to industrial to post-industrial to informational economies. Planners working in developing countries—where 90% of the world's population growth and most urbanization will occur in the next 30 plus years—need to be particularly aware of global forces. All planners need to consider global and country-specific impacts of climate change.

CONNECTIVITY, HEALTH, CRIME, AND TERRORISM

The COVID-19 pandemic emphasized one of the downsides of globalization and growing city connectivity—the speed with which pandemics can spread. One person infected with COVID-19 flying from China to San Francisco or from Italy to New York in spring, 2020 could be a super-spreader infecting dozens of people who could then each infect dozens more through community spread. Early in the pandemic, the United States banned travel from the China and Italy. As the pandemic came under greater control in China and Italy, but became worse in the United States, China and Italy banned travel from the United States. Planners and policy makers faced a classic wicked problem—any policy to help combat the pandemic in one area created new problems elsewhere. Requirements to wear a face mask, socially distance, or minimize travel helped, but these in turn wrought economic havoc and disrupted the life plans of businesspeople, students, and households with family members in different countries.

Digital connectivity creates other new problems. Computer viruses can spread globally even more quickly than disease. State, corporate, and individual computers have been hacked and billions of dollars' worth of intellectual property and personal information stolen and money extorted in ransomware attacks.

Another consequence of globalization and flows among world cities is heightened risk of terrorism. Some architects and planners incorporate features to protect against terrorism into airports, government buildings, and other potential terrorist targets. Efforts to respond to terrorism are producing an increase in security and surveillance. Planners are confronting the issue of how many surveillance cameras to place in public and private outdoor and indoor spaces. They have to face troubling ethical issues of invasion of privacy.

MEGACITIES AND MEGACITY REGIONS

Enormous "megacities" are emerging worldwide. The United Nations estimated that there were 31 megacities with populations of over 10 million inhabitants in 2016. Only two cities in the United States qualified as megacities by the UN definition—New York City with a population of 8.5 million people within New York City itself and Los Angeles City, with a population of 4 million people. The UN projects that New York and Los Angeles will still be the only U.S. megacities in 2030 when they project that there will be 41 megacities in the world.

There is a lively debate among planners worldwide about how to define megacities, what population threshold constitutes a megacity, and how much megacities contribute to the world economy, innovation, and global warming. The United Nations uses "agglomeration"—functionally related urban areas—rather than political borders to define megacities. Other sources use different units of analysis, thresholds and other metrics. All sources agree that there are now many megacities and that the number will almost certainly increase rapidly in the future.

Four terms seek to describe urban areas that may be even larger than megacities—megaregions, megacity regions, polycentric urban networks, and, in China, Large City Clusters (LCCs). Giant city regions are sometimes called megalopolises. Patrick Geddes invented the term megalopolis in 1915. French geographer Jean Gottman popularized it in 1961 by calling the entire eastern seaboard of the United States Megalopolis.[7] Catherine Ross, a professor of urban planning at Georgia Institute of Technology, describes a megaregion as a grouping of several urban areas, linked by social, economic, demographic, environmental, and cultural ties, interconnected through information exchanges, movements of capital and labor, new technologies, and shared natural resources joining together to make infrastructure and planning decisions. Box 11.1 describes the Jabodetabek megaregion around Indonesia's capital—Jakarta—and challenges it faces. Many other megaregions face similar challenges.

BOX 11.1 JABODETABEK: THE JAKARTA, INDONESIA MEGAREGION

Jakarta, Indonesia's metropolitan megacity region includes the surrounding administrative regions of Bogor, Depok, Tangerang and Bekasi, so the region is called Jabodetabek (JA-BO-DE-TA-BEK). The population within Jakarta's borders—9.6 million people—is larger than the population of New York City. The Jabodetabek region has over 30 million people and is predicted to grow to 35.6 million people by 2030.

Many of Jakarta's and Jabodetabek's problems stem from the inability of the physical setting to support the region's population size. Jabodetabek has grown from a small colonial settlement (Dutch Batavia) founded in 1833 with no thought to whether the location could support a population as large as it has become. Most megacities began small, and were never planned to accommodate their current population.

Jakarta lies in a low and flat alluvial plain, with an average elevation of only 26 feet above sea level. Large parts of Jakarta lie below sea level. Thirteen rivers flow through

Figure 11.8 Flooding in Jakarta, Indonesia (2013).

the city from highlands to the south. During monsoon season each year, low-lying impoverished areas adjacent to rivers are flooded (Figure 11.8). Many other megacities are located on or near coasts with much of their land area close to or even below sea level. Global climate change is increasing the number and severity of floods.

Many megacities—including New York, London, and Tokyo—are sinking as well as smaller cities such as Miami, Florida; Venice, Italy; and Rotterdam in the Netherlands. Pressure from the weight of buildings is causing Jakarta to sink between 2 and 4 inches each year, and nearly 8 inches a year in the northern coastal areas. Depletion of aquifers contributes to the problem, as soil compacts into what was previously underground water. This is happening in other megacities worldwide.

Like other coastal cities, Jakarta is turning to technology to alleviate flooding and sinking. Jakarta has built a dyke, dams, and water tunnels. A giant sea wall is under construction.[8] These may help, but it is unlikely that technological fixes can stop Jakarta's flooding and sinking problems.

Planning solutions to prohibit building on floodplains, protect aquifers, and restrain flooding from rivers could all help in Jakarta and the Jabodetabek region. However, like many megacity regions, governmental fragmentation keeps the Jabodetabek region from addressing their problems regionally. The different provinces and cities that comprise the region compete for foreign direct investment by allowing developers to disregard environmental hazards and to build in areas that are vulnerable to floods; deplete aquifers; and contribute to land subsidence. The key issue is lack of political will—not lack of understanding of problems or lack of expertise.

Jakarta is considering a radical response to the flooding and sinking problem. In August 2019, President Joko Widodo announced plans to move the capital to the province of East Kalimantan on the island of Borneo.

Every country wants economic development of their cities and regions to succeed. To do that, they make development plans and decide development policy in relation to the world city network. That requires deciding what posture to take in world trade and deciding on how to measure progress. Developing countries have to decide how dependent on more developed countries to be and on what conditions to accept foreign investment.

The standard macroeconomic measure of a country's level of economic development is its gross domestic product (GDP)—the total market value of all the finished goods and services produced within the country's borders in a specific time period, such as one year. Since the cost of living is generally much lower in developing countries, economists and planners sometimes use purchasing power parity (PPP) in their analyses. They calculate purchasing power parity by comparing a basket of goods and services that can be purchased with the currency of a country or region to a similar basket in other countries and regions. With one notable exception, every country's main measure of success is how much its GDP has increased. The little Buddhist kingdom of Bhutan measures its success based on indicators of human happiness!

IDEOLOGY AND DEVELOPMENT

Debates about regional development planning are politically charged. Left-leaning planning scholars and activists criticize globalization as a form of neo-imperialism leading to uneven development and an international division of labor that exploits developing countries, distorts their economies, and makes them dependent on global capitalism. Protesters converge to condemn the World Trade Organization (WTO)—the international organization that promotes world trade—as a group of self-serving rich nations engaged in neo-colonial exploitation of the developing world. Riots occur when the WTO meets. Neoliberals take the opposite position. They argue that capital investment from wealthier nations helps less developed nations grow their economies. Neoliberals believe that capitalism is the best approach to international development. Marxist, neo-Marxist, dependency, and new industrial division of labor theory question that assumption.

Marxist theory was developed by Karl Marx (1818 – 1883) and Friedrich Engels (1820–1895) in the latter half of the 19th century. Marx and Engels depicted relations between 19th-century capitalist countries and their colonies as an aspect of ruling class oppression. European colonies in Africa, Asia, and Latin America were mostly pre-industrial societies at the time they were acquired by European powers beginning in the 16th century and were still colonies when Marx and Engels developed their theories. Colonial cities facilitated exports of primary sector commodities like minerals, agricultural produce, lumber, fish, and grain from the colonies at low prices, and the import of more expensive finished goods from the colonial powers. Marx argued that colonial development harmed developing countries by making their workers produce goods for their colonial masters. In 1917, on the eve of the Russian Revolution, Marxist Russian revolutionary Vladimir Lenin described late 19th- and early 20th-century imperialism as "the highest stage of capitalism." Like Marx and Engels, Lenin predicted that the extreme inequality between rich European colonial powers and their poor and exploited colonies would cause the workers of the world in both the exploited colonial countries and the colonial powers to unite in class struggle, violently overthrow the capitalist system, and establish world communism.

By the late 1940s most former European colonies had achieved independence. Marxist theory continued to influence later theories about how former colonies should develop after they achieved independence and policies of the newly-independent governments of the former colonies.

Dependency theory was developed by Argentinian economist and stateman Raúl Prebisch. It was popular among U.S. and other planners during the Marxist ascendency in planning theory during the 1960s and 1970s. Dependency theory views the world economy as consisting of a core of developed countries that exploit the periphery of less developed countries.

New international division of labor (NIDL) theory was developed by Folker Fröbel, Jürgen Heinrichs, and Otto Kreye in the late 1960s. NIDL theory is concerned with the shift in much of the world's manufacturing to the "global south" from the "global north".

Planners frequently use the term "global south" as a proxy to describe the less developed and poorer countries of the world. This is not geographically accurate. Some countries in the northern hemisphere such as Haiti, Mongolia, Yemen, Sudan, and Albania are poor, underdeveloped countries. The countries of Brunei and New Zealand in the Southern Hemisphere and many cities within them are well developed and wealthy. So is the country of Singapore which is essentially a single city. Brazil and Colombia have GDP close to the global median and have territory on both sides of the equator.

INTERNATIONAL ORGANIZATIONS AND PLANETARY PLANNING

While world city network theorists agree that connectivity in the world city network is largely through firms and other non-state actors, a number of important international organizations engage in planning at the planetary scale. Nation states also have many bi- and multi- lateral agreements related to city and regional planning. Most of these agreements deal with economic matters and trade. International organizations and international agreements of particular interest to planners seek to address climate change; protect the natural environment; save endangered species; and address health, crime, human trafficking, and other issues.

The United Nations is the most important international organization that impacts city and regional planning at the global scale. The UN's *New Urban Agenda* (2017)[9] and *Agenda 2030* (2015) express goals developed by member countries to guide national governments' urban policies. The *New Urban Agenda* has been translated into over 30 languages and is available in audio versions and braille. UN divisions of particular importance to city and regional planners provide world urbanization data, work to improve human settlements, and address global climate change.[10]

The World Bank is the principal organization that finances international development projects. The World Trade Organization is the leading international organization concerned with world trade. The International Monetary Fund monitors the international monetary system and global economic development to identify risks and recommend policies for growth. It makes emergency loans to countries. The Organization for Economic Co-operation and Development, Group of 7 (G7) and Group of 20 (G20) are organizations of the countries that dominate the world economy. They perform important functions that impact city and regional planning at the global scale.[11] The Global Planning Education Association Network (GPEAN) connects city and regional planning faculty and students from North America, Europe, Asia, and other regions of the world. The Regional Science Association International brings together economists, geographers, city and regional planners and other scholars and practitioners interested in regional science. The International City Management Association is an organization of professionals involved in urban management.

Box 11.2 is a biography of University of Pennsylvania city and regional planning professor Eugenie Birch. It illustrates how city and regional planners can engage in planning at the international scale.

BOX 11.2 EUGENIE BIRCH

Eugenie Birch is a city and regional planning scholar-practitioner who is deeply engaged in global planning policy and education. She illustrates what international city planning can be like.

Birch is the Lawrence C. Nussdorf Chair of Urban Research and Education at the University of Pennsylvania, Co-Director of the Penn Institute for Research, and co-editor of the University of Pennsylvania's *The City in the 21st Century* e-journal series. She leads several of the United Nations' most important committees related to city and regional planning and policy. These include serving as President of the General Assembly of Partners (GAP)—the engagement platform for the implementation of the United Nations' *New Urban Agenda* (2017) and associated global agreements; and co-chair of the UN's Sustainable Development Solutions Network (SDSN) Thematic Group on Cities. Birch also chairs UN-Habitat's World Urban Campaign. UN-Habitat is the United Nations Human Settlements Organization, with headquarters in Nairobi, Kenya.

At the university of Pennsylvania's Department of City and Regional Planning Professor Birch teaches courses on global urbanization and the doctoral seminar and serves as chair of the graduate group in city and regional planning. She has held teaching appointments at Rutgers University, the State University of New York Purchase, the City University of New York Graduate Center, and Hunter College. Birch has been a visiting professor at Yale University, Queen's University in Ontario, Canada, the University of Hong Kong, and the University of the Witwatersrand in Johannesburg, South Africa.

Professor Birch is a member of the editorial board of the *Journal of the American Planning Association (JAPA)* where she previously served as co-editor. She has served on the editorial boards of the *Journal of Planning History* and *Planning Perspectives*.

Professor Birch received the American Planning Association's journalism prize in 1994, the Association of Collegiate Schools of Planning (ACSP)'s Margarita McCoy

Figure 11.9 Eugenie Birch.

award for outstanding contribution to furthering women in the planning academy (1994), ACSP's Jay Chatterjee Award for distinguished service to ACSP (2006), the ACSP Distinguished Educator Award (2009), and the American Planning Association's President's Award (2013). The Society of American City and Regional Planning History awarded her its Lawrence C. Gerckens prize in 2009 in recognition of her contributions to planning history. She was elected to the College of Fellows of the American Institute of Certified Planners and made an honorary member of the UK's Royal Town Planning Institute.

In the early 1990s, Birch was a member of the New York City Planning Commission. In 2002, she served on the jury to select the designers for the World Trade Center site. She has chaired the board of trustees of the Municipal Art Society of New York. She is currently a member of the board of trustees of the Regional Plan Association of New York. In the past, Professor Birch served as President of the Association of Collegiate Schools of Planning, President of the Society of American City and Regional Planning History, and President of the International Planning History Society. She chaired the planning accreditation board from 2004 to 2006.

Birch has written widely about urban history, women in planning, global urban policy, and other topics. She received a bachelor's degree in history cum laude from Brynn Mawr College and a master's and PhD in urban planning from Columbia University.

SUMMARY

Globalization has connected cities and regions everywhere on planet earth. Modern transportation technology has shrunk the time it takes for people and goods to move from one location to another by air, land, and sea. Raw materials, components, and finished products from one location flow to other locations worldwide to be transformed, assembled, and consumed. Information and capital flow around the world. All of these great structural changes affect cities and city planning.

Planners are confronting both an explosion of the world's population and an implosion of population into cities. The world's population will likely continue to grow. By 2100 most parts of the world other than sub-Saharan Africa and some poor regions in other countries will likely be nearly fully urbanized.

It appears inevitable that the population of cities and the land area that they cover will continue to increase. An essential planning role is to anticipate and structure this growth. This is particularly important for megacities and megacity regions as rural migrants migrate into cities. Today 56% of the 7.6 billion people on earth live on the half of one percent of the surface of the Earth that is classified as urban.

Planners need to understand and make plans based on the world city network. As people, goods, capital, information, and command and control move through the space of flows, planners need to consider global networks in their transportation, economic development, land use, and other plans.

Globalization, connectivity and foreign direct investment (FDI) from developed countries to developing countries have helped modernize developing countries and greatly increasing the standard of living for some of their residents, as neoliberals assert, but has not improved the lives of many other of their residents. Neo-Marxists, dependency theorists, and new international division of labor theorists argue that the capitalist system favors rich countries and distorts the economies of developing countries. Planners need to address economic inequality, environmental damage, destruction of traditional culture, and other negative aspects of globalization.

There are downsides of globalization. Massive international flows of people and goods can spread disease, including pandemics. Connectivity facilitates internet-related crime, terrorism, and drug and human trafficking. Planners need to address the prospect of tens of millions of climate refugees as climate change forces people to move.

The world city network affects large-scale regional planning and development planning at the nation state and subnational level. Planners need to incorporate an understanding of planetary forces in planning at every level in every type of plan.

CONCEPTS

Advanced Producer Services
Agglomeration
Agropolitan Development
Corporate Services Complex
Foreign Direct Investment (FDI)
Globalization
Global and World Cities Network (GaWC)
Global City
Global North
Global South
Gross Domestic Product (GDP)
Informational City
Making Room Paradigm
Megacity
Network Society
New International Division of Labor (NIDL) Theory
Purchasing Power Parity
Space of Flows
Stages of Growth Theory
World City Network
World Trade Organization (WTO)

PEOPLE

Shlomo Angel
Manuel Castells
Arthur O. Lewis
Walt Whitman Rostow

Saskia Sassen
Peter Taylor

NOTES

1   According to the U.S. Census, the population of the world was no greater than 20 million in both 10,000 BCE and 5,000 BCE, 400 million in 1 CE, 345 million in 1000 CE and 2.54 billion in 1950 (U.S. Census, 2018). Today earth has about 7.8 billion inhabitants (UN, 2019). About 7% of all humans who have ever been born are alive today (Biraben & Langeney, 1980; Population Reference Bureau, 2020; Haub, 2011).
2   Currently the world population is 7.9 million people (World Population Clock, 2022). The United Nations projects that 35% of urban population growth between 2020 and 2050 will occur in just three countries—India, China, and Nigeria (UN, 2019). They project that by 2050 India will add 416 million more urban dwellers, China 255 million and Nigeria 189 million (ibid). China's population is expected to decline slightly as a result of the one-child (now two-child) policy, availability of contraceptives, and the propensity for middle- and upper-income households to have fewer children.
3   The United Nations estimates that only 23% of the world's population lived in a city with at least 1 million inhabitants in 2016 (UN, 2019: 3). They estimate that in 2016 there were 31 megacities with populations of 10 million or more inhabitants, 45 cities with populations between 5 and 10 million, 436 cities with populations between 1 and 5 million, and 551 cities with populations between 500,000 and 1 million (UN, 2016: 4). There are tens of thousands of cities with fewer than 500,000 people and hundreds of thousands of towns and villages in the long left tail of the world population curve. The UN projects that there will be 41 megacities by 2030 (ibid: 4). The distribution will remain lopsided as the much larger number of small cities, towns, and villages will also continue to grow.
4   Murmansk, Russia (population 307,000) and Tromsø, Norway (population 71,500) lie within the Arctic Circle. St Petersburg, Russia (5,323,300) is only 7° south of the Arctic Circle. Helsinki, Finland (1.2 million), Stockholm, Sweden (949,000), Reykjavik, Iceland (202,000), Anchorage, Alaska (291,000), Oslo, Norway (673,000), Bergen, Norway (280,000), Trondheim, Norway (182,000), and Arkhangelsk, Russia (348,000) are close to the Arctic Circle.
5   Patrick Geddes (Box 2.1) coined the term "world cities" in 1915 (Geddes, 1915). Lewis Mumford spread Geddes's world city idea to a world audience. Chicago School sociologist Roderick McKenzie described power relations in the world city network in the 1920s (McKenzie, 1927). Walter Christaller's central place theory describes places as hubs in networks (Christaller, 1966 [1933]). Walter Isard, Brian Berry, and other regional scientists and quantitative economists developed quantitative models to explain location at the world scale during the systems revolution of the 1960s and 1970s (Isard 1956, 1959, and 1960; Berry, 1964, 1987; Berry & Horton, 1970; Teitz, 2012). Dependency and international division of labor theorists Friedrich Fröbel, Jürgen Heinrichs, Otto Kreye, and Doreen Massey described economic and power inequality in the world city system beginning in the 1960s (Fröbel, Heinrichs, & Kreye, 1977; Massey, 1984). Peter Hall breathed new life into Geddes's world cities idea in *The world cities* (1966). Hall's work stimulated a host of world city studies in the late 1960s, 1970s, and 1980s. U.S. planning theorist John Friedmann summarized the world city hypothesis as it had crystalized by the mid-1980s (Friedmann, 1986). In 1991 Columbia University sociology professor Saskia Sassen proposed the term "global city" to distinguish the modern form of world cities from cities that have existed for millennia as trade centers (Sassen, 1991: 126).
6   At various times London, Rome, Damascus, Baghdad, Tenochtitlan (Mexico City), Constantinople (Istanbul), Samarkand, Madrid, Lisbon, Babylon, Xi'an, Nanjing, Hangzhou, and Beijing dominated systems of cities in the territory they controlled. During the era of European colonies from the 15th through second half of the 20th century, London, Seville, Lisbon, Amsterdam, Brussels, Paris, and other European cities were world cities, but on a much smaller scale than today's world cities. Between 1913 and 1945, the British empire's colonies, dominions, protectorates, mandates, and other territorial units covered more than 20% of the world's land area and population. The Belgian Congo, owned by the King—not the nation state of Belgium—had 77 times as much land area as Belgium! Connectivity in pre-digital-era cities was frequently based on family firms that were at least nominally independent of the government such as the Medici family in Florence, Italy and the Fugger family in Augsburg, Germany.
7   By the early 20th century London had expanded and merged with smaller adjacent cities. Patrick Geddes was the first person to formulate the idea that this represented a new type of human settlement. He coined the terms conurbation from the Latin *con* (together) and *urb* (city)—literally cities together and megalopolis from the Latin *mega* (big) and *polis* (human settlement) to describe the new phenomenon (Geddes, 1915). Forty-six years later, in 1961, French geographer Jean Gottmann (1915–1994) labeled the entire eastern seaboard of the United States "Megalopolis". Megalopolis, as Gottmann described it, ran from north of Boston, Massachusetts to south of Washington, D.C. and extended inland more than fifty miles over the Piedmont region—the 600-mile region from New Jersey to Alabama between the Atlantic Ocean and the Appalachian Mountains. Gottmann predicted, correctly, that similar megalopoli (plural) would

become the dominant human settlement pattern of the future.

8   In January 2014, the central government agreed to build two dams in Ciawi, Bogor and a 1.2-kilometre (.75-mile) tunnel from Ciliwung River to Cisadane River to ease flooding in the city. The tunnel between the Ciliwung River and the East Flood Canal has a capacity 60 cubic meters (2,100 cubic feet) per second to ease the Ciliwung River overflows. A ring dyke is under construction around Jakarta Bay to help cope with the threat from the sea. The dyke will be equipped with a pumping system and retention areas to defend against seawater. The project, known as "Giant Sea Wall Jakarta", is expected to be completed by 2025.

9   The UN's *New Urban Agenda* (2017) seeks to promote inclusivity and ensure that all inhabitants of earth "are able to inhabit and produce just, safe, healthy, accessible, affordable, resilient, and sustainable cities and human settlements to foster prosperity and quality of life for all." Among 175 principles in the agenda are civic engagement; gender equality; resilience; mitigation of and adaptation to climate change; minimizing environmental impacts of growth; and changing to sustainable consumption and production patterns. The stated overarching vision of *The New Urban Agenda* includes 17 aspirational principles including ending poverty, protecting the planet from degradation, and using the oceans sustainably. The UN resolution adopting *Agenda 2030* includes 17 similar sustainable development goals.

10 The UN Division of Economic and Social Affairs (DESA) has produced population and urbanization data since 1950. DESA's population division prepares updated estimates and projections of the total and urban population for all countries or areas in the world. DESA's *World Urbanization Prospects* reports are the authoritative source of information on world urbanization. The most recent is the 2019 revision (UN, 2019). UN Habitat undertakes research, convenes conferences, and coordinates demonstration projects to help improve human settlements, but lacks funding and authority. The UN's International Panel on Climate Change (IPCC) addresses global climate change.

11 The World Bank uses funding from national governments to assist world development. Their World Development Indicators are an important source of world-scale urban data. The World Trade Organization (WTO) develops standards for world trade. The Group of Seven (G7) and Group of Twenty (G20) countries are organizations of the wealthiest and most powerful 7 and 20 countries in the world respectively. In 2014 Russia was suspended indefinitely from what had previously been the G8 following the annexation of Crimea. In 2017, Russia announced its permanent withdrawal from the G8. As this book goes to press pressure is building to suspend Russia from the G20. World leaders meet annually for high-level meetings, and G7 and G20 staff prepare background studies and work to implement formal and informal agreements that heads of state make at the annual G7 and G20 meetings. The Organization for Economic Co-operation and Development (OECD) is a consortium of 37 countries that works to foster prosperity, equality, opportunity and well-being. Their bi- and multi-lateral trade agreements impact many planning issues.

SUGGESTIONS FOR FURTHER LEARNING

Overview of Global Urban Conditions: Shlomo Angel, *Planet of cities* (2012). Shlomo Angel, Jason Parent, Daniel Civco, & Alexander Blei, *Atlas of urban expansion* (2012). Shlomo Angel, *The anatomy of density* [video] (2020). John Palen, *The urban world*, 10th ed (2014). **World Population and Urbanization Data:** United Nations, *World urbanization prospects: The 2019 revision* (2019). World Bank, *World development indicators* (2021). United Nations *The world's cities* (2016). **Urbanization:** Kingsley Davis, The urbanization of the human population (1965). **Globalization:** Xuefie Ren & Roger Keil (eds), *The globalizing cities reader*, 2nd ed (2017). Neil Brenner & Roger Keil, From global cities to globalized urbanization (2015). **Informational Cities:** Manuel Castells, *The Information Age*, 3 vols (1996–1997). Saskia Sassen, The impact of new technologies and globalization on cities (2011). **World and Global Cities:** Patrick Geddes, *The world cities* (1915). John Friedmann, The world city hypothesis (1986). Peter Taylor & Ben Derudder, *World city network* (2015). Peter Taylor, Global city network (2015). Global and World Cities (GaWC) [website] (2021). Saskia Sassen, *The global city* (2007) and *Cities in a world economy*, 5th ed (2018). Peter Hall, *The world cities* (1966). Doreen Massey, *World city* (1966). **Aerotropoli:** John Kasarda & Greg Lindsay *Aerotropolis: The way we'll live next* (2011). **Global Inequality:** Roderick McKenzie, The concept of dominance and world-organization (1927). Hollis Chenery & Moises Syrqin, *Patterns of development 1950 – 1970* (1975). Folker Fröbel, *The new international division of labor* (1977). Greg Charnock & Guido Starosta (eds), *The new international division of labor* (2016). François Bourguignon & Christian Morrisson, *Inequality among world citizens 1820 – 1992*. Joseph Stiglitz, *The price of inequality* (2013) and *The great divide* (2015). Thomas Piketty, *Capital in the early 21st century* (2017). **Neil Brenner's Theory of Urbanization:** Neil Brenner, *Implosions /explosions* (2013) and *New urban spaces* (2019). **Megacities and Megaregions:** Deden Rukmana, *The Routledge handbook of planning megacities in the global south* (2020). Jonathan Barnett, *Designing the megaregion* (2020). Catherine Ross (ed), *Megaregions* (2009). John Harrison &

Michael Hoyler, *Megaregions* (2017). **International Development Planning:** Michael Spence, Patricia Annez, & Robert Buckley, *Urbanization and growth* (2009). Arthur O. Lewis, Economic development with unlimited supplies of labor (1954). Douglas Gollin, The Lewis model: A 60-year retrospective (2014). Walt Whitman Rostow, *Stages of economic growth* (1960). Raul Prebisch, *Change and development* (1971). Michael Teitz, Regional development planning (2012). United Nations, *The new urban agenda* (2017). Judith Ryser & Teresa Franchini, *International manual of planning practice*, 6th ed (2015). International Society of City and Regional Planning Professionals (ISOCARP) [website]. **Jabodetabek:** Chris Silver, *Planning the megacity: Jakarta in the twentieth century* (2007). **Journal:** *International Journal of Urban and Regional Research*.

CHAPTER 12

The Evolution of Cities and City and Regional Planning, 1933–Present

INTRODUCTION

Just before President Franklin Roosevelt was inaugurated in March 1933 Detroit, Michigan mayor Frank Murphy took the unprecedented step of going to Washington, D.C. to beg for federal assistance for Detroit and other big cities. Until the Great Depression began in 1929, American cities, large and small, had worked to expand the powers granted to them by their states, resented intervention in their affairs by the federal government and would never consider asking for money or policy direction from the federal government.

After four catastrophic years of the Great Depression, Detroit could no longer pay for even basic municipal services or provide relief to its desperate citizens. One third of Detroit's industrial workforce was unemployed. Property values had plummeted. Many homeowners had defaulted on their mortgages and stopped paying property taxes. Debt service was consuming 70% of Detroit's municipal budget. Big banks holding Detroit's bonds had required Mayor Murphy to cut relief that had been supporting 40,000 families in half. Murphy had been forced to eliminate all public works projects and deeply cut Detroit's police and fire departments, and public health, recreation, and cultural activities. Virtually all funding for city planning was gone. Detroit had defaulted on its bonds. Local banks closed in February 1933. Scrip replaced currency as the medium of exchange. Conditions in other big U.S. cities were equally dire.

Every crisis creates opportunities. The Great Depression forced the United States to reinvent federalism from the way it had operated since ratification of the U.S. Constitution in 1787.

The New Deal is the umbrella term for the public works projects, federal laws and regulations, and financial reforms created from 1933 to the early 1940s during Franklin Roosevelt's presidency in response to the Great Depression. By the time the United States entered World War II in 1941, planning in the United States operated in a fundamentally different context than it had before the New Deal. City and regional planning in the United States still takes place within the federal–state–local political and economic framework created during the New Deal as modified by successive Republican and Democratic administrations.

This chapter picks up the story of how U.S. cities and city planning have evolved since the beginning of the New Deal in 1933. In addition to describing the Great Depression and New Deal urban reforms, it describes other significant structural changes that have occurred in planning in the United States since 1933.

The first section of this chapter reviews growth in the number and size of U.S. cities and the number and percentage of the population living in urban areas since 1933. It describes changes as the United States continued to shift from an agricultural to an industrial society in the first half of the 20th century, to an increasingly post-industrial society after World War II, and more recently to a predominantly informational society. It continues the history of the evolution of the planning profession and planning education.

The chapter discusses how the Great Depression led to the federal public housing program and today's pattern of federal–state–local relations. It discusses advances and retreats in federal urban policy under successive Republican and Democratic administrations after Roosevelt's death in 1945. A discussion of the Tennessee Valley Authority and pushback against the National Resources Planning Board illustrate the possibilities and political difficulty of implementing large-scale regional spatial or sectoral planning in the United States.

The chapter describes how local planning departments and local comprehensive plans have matured and the environmental turn that began in 1970. Sections describe legacy housing programs; the failure of the federal urban renewal program; and the emergence of community development and urban revitalization as alternatives. A section of the chapter describes how America's electric streetcar system was dismantled; the massive federal aid highway program and the freeway revolt opposing it; and the growth of public transit and multi-modal transportation planning. The early history of climate change and energy planning and policy provide background for Chapter 17 on climate change and energy planning.

Box 12.1 is a biography of Harvard urban planning professor Ann Forsyth, whose work reflects many recent themes in U.S. cities and city planning.

THE EVOLUTION OF URBAN AMERICA, 1933–PRESENT

The population of the United States has nearly tripled since 1933. The urban population has quadrupled.[1] The U.S. Census Bureau projects that the absolute population of the United States will increase by 79 million people by 2060—more rapidly than the population of most other developed countries. However, the percentage of the U.S. population living in urban areas is likely to remain about the same. Because the U.S. population is aging, the Census Bureau projects that immigration will overtake natural increase—the excess of births over deaths—as the primary driver of U.S. population growth. The U.S. population is projected to age considerably, and become more racially and ethnically diverse.

In 1933 the U.S. economy was still mostly a mixture of primary sector economic activities, like agriculture, mining, fishing, lumbering, and secondary sector industrial production. Today city- and suburb-based post-industrial services and information-related activities drive the U.S. economy.

A great boom in suburban development occurred after World War II. There was a post-war baby boom, low unemployment, and a rapid increase in real wages. Economic prosperity gave more households enough disposable income to purchase single-family detached suburban homes. Thirty-year mortgage terms and lower down payments allowed more households to become homeowners. The GI Bill of Rights provided millions of veterans zero-interest loans with no down payments to purchase starter homes. The Federal Aid Highway Program helped link suburbs to core cities, and suburbs grew rapidly after the mid-1950s. Greatly increased automobile ownership made the United States even more auto dependent than before the war. The number of automobiles in the United States has grown six-fold since 1933.[2]

As the population of U.S. suburbs has grown, the populations of many older industrial cities in America's frostbelt—the Northeast, North Central, and Northwestern United States—have declined. Rustbelt cities—old industrial cities where many former factories have closed—have been hard hit. The population of Detroit has decreased by more than 50% since 1950, and is continuing to decline. In contrast, many cities and suburbs in the sunbelt—the American South, Southwest, and Southern California—have grown. Between 1950 and 2010 the population of the South grew 14.4%, the West 14.2%, but the Northeast just 2.3%. The main reasons the growth of the sunbelt are better climates, more retirees, more federal government defense spending, and Mexican immigration.

The number of housing units in the United States has quadrupled since 1933—growing faster than new household formation. The average size of owned units has doubled.

BOX 12.1 ANN FORSYTH

Ann Forsyth is a professor of urban planning at the Harvard Graduate School of Planning. She is the current editor of the *Journal of the American Planning Association* (*JAPA*) as of 2021. She is the director of Harvard's Master of Urban Planning program, the Healthy Places Design Laboratory, and the New Towns Initiative. She is affiliated with Harvard's Joint Center for Housing Studies, Center for Population and Development Studies, University Center for the Environment, Harvard's Weatherhead Center for International Affairs, the Harvard–China Project, and the Harvard Global Health Institute.

From 2007–2012 Professor Forsyth was a professor of city and regional planning at Cornell University. Before that she taught at the University of Minnesota (from 2002 to 2007) where she directed the Metropolitan Design Center; Harvard (from 1999 to 2002); and the University of Massachusetts (from 1993 to 1999). At the University of Massachusetts she was co-director of a community design center called the Urban Places Project. She has held short-term positions at Columbia, Macquarie, and Sydney universities.

Professor Forsyth's teaching, research, and writing focus mainly on the social aspects of physical planning and urban development—particularly how to make cities more sustainable and healthier. Her scholarly output falls into three main categories—academic and professional publications; manuals, methods, and planning "tools"; and other media such as videos, websites, and blogs. She is the author or co-author of five books and over 200 articles. She has been active in developing and evaluating new instruments and measures using GIS, fieldwork, surveys, impact assessments, public participation processes, and evidence-based practice guidelines.

Figure 12.1 Ann Forsyth.

In her research and professional work as a planner and urban designer, Professor Forsyth has studied and and participated in plans, developed tools, and reflected on practices in projects in three areas.

- *Innovative and high-density planning and design projects*: in this research she asks whether high-density planning and design projects achieve the benefits proponents claim for them—particularly related to sustainability, health, and well-being. Much of this work has been in suburbs, analyzing the actual and potential success of planned alternatives to sprawl in new towns on or beyond the urban fringe of metropolitan areas and new suburban and ex-urban neighborhoods. She has done research and written about how to achieve walkability, plan higher-density affordable housing, design for aging, increase social diversity, develop appropriate green space, and balance social and ecological values in these areas.
- *Using physical places to improve health*: Professor Forsyth's research and writing examine the wide range of intersections between health and environments. Her interdisciplinary and holistic approach broadens understanding of health and place beyond a focus on food and physical activity—particularly in suburban sites. This line of research involves assessing healthy environments in a suburbanizing world—particularly at the neighborhood scale. She has conducted research on physical activity and food environments, the interplay between densification and green space, and healthier new towns. She has developed GIS protocols, surveys, audits, health assessment tools, participatory process tools, and two books of guidelines about how to use physical places to improve health.
- Finally, Professor Forsyth has investigated how to connect research and practice in her areas of interest. This research builds on the literature on reflective professional practice by Donald Schön and John Forester described in Chapter 5. It includes analyzing and describing different forms of research and investigation and how research can inform the process and substance of planning.

Professor Forsyth organized and participated in a week-long seminar for planning professors of color sponsored by the Association of Collegiate Schools of Planning (ACSP) and ACSP's Planners of Color Interest Group (POCIG). Her writings on planning for women, the LGBTQ community, and other nonconformist communities are widely used in planning courses.

Forsyth's current research focuses on developing healthier places in a suburbanizing world, with overlapping emphases on aging and planned communities. Her recent research involves new towns, neighborhood urban form, planning and design in a pandemic, healthy cities, Chinese urban communities, walkability, reflective practice, feminism, gender, and planning.

Professor Forsyth received a BSc in architecture from the University of Sydney, Australia, a MA in urban planning from the University of California, Los Angeles (UCLA), and a PhD in city and regional planning from Cornell University.

Virtually all U.S. housing units now have indoor running water and toilets. The number of dilapidated units has shrunk to a small fraction of the housing stock. Affordability is now the major U.S. housing problem—particularly in desirable places to live and work. The divide in housing adequacy between rich and poor; owners and renters; and the White population and people of color has widened. A majority of extremely and very low-income households are severely cost-burdened—paying 50% or more of their income for shelter. Homelessness has grown substantially.

Low-income households and households of color have become increasingly concentrated in central cities and older suburbs. By 1980, central cities had more than twice their proportionate share of low-income households. The numbers of Black, Hispanic, Latinx, AAPI, and other people of color in suburbs have greatly increased. Black migration to cities from the rural South, immigration from Mexico, in-migration of low-skilled people from rural areas of the USA and other countries, and higher fertility rates and live births among Latinx, Blacks, and other people of color than among Whites are the main causes for the change in the ethnic mix of cities and suburbs.

The decline of many U.S. central cities generated a politically charged debate about triage, benign neglect, and planned shrinkage. In the 1970s New York City housing and planning official Roger Starr (1918–2001) applied the medical term triage to urban neighborhoods. After a battle, medics devote scarce resources to treating wounded soldiers they believe will survive, leaving the severely wounded to die. Starr argued that local governments should practice triage with urban neighborhoods—reserving limited funds for neighborhoods that stood a reasonable chance of recovery and ignoring the needs of those in greatest distress. At the same time, New York Senator Daniel Patrick Moynihan—President Nixon's chief domestic policy advisor—urged Nixon to adopt a policy of "benign neglect" towards troubled urban neighborhoods—also essentially ignoring their problems.

Planned shrinkage accepts the inevitability of neighborhood decline, but in contrast to triage and benign neglect, it seeks creative, low-cost ways to cushion the impact of shrinkage and to revitalize neighborhoods. New York and other cities have implemented innovative plans to help revitalize some of their most troubled neighborhoods. Urban homesteading, for example—inspired by the 1862 Homestead Act—involves essentially giving deteriorated housing units that a city has repossessed to people willing to live in and invest in them. (The term urban homesteading is also used to describe backyard farming.)

The declining population in older U.S. core cities may be ending. Between 2000 and 2010 only three of the largest U.S. cities shrank—all in the North Central rustbelt. In contrast New York City's population grew by more than 400,000 between 2000 and 2010 and the population of Phoenix, Arizona; Austin, Texas; Jacksonville, Florida; San Diego, California; Las Vegas, Nevada; and other sunbelt cities also grew substantially.

During the pandemic, Apple, Google, Twitter, Facebook, and other large U.S. corporations allowed many or all employees to work remotely. Some employees moved out of high-cost cities like New York and San Francisco to attractive communities like Austin, Texas and Park City, Utah where housing costs are much lower. Whether or not this trend will continue in the post-COVID-19 era remains to be seen.

The back-to-the-city movement raises the issue of how city and regional planners should respond to gentrification—the movement of higher-income households back into some old city neighborhoods. The term gentrification was first used in England as young, upper-class people—what the British call the gentry—began buying and rehabilitating deteriorated housing units in formerly elite urban neighborhoods. Long-time renters in gentrifying neighborhoods resent the rent increases gentrification brings. They don't like expensive new restaurants and coffee shops which they do not frequent that push out community-serving restaurants and bars that cannot afford higher rents. Homeowners and apartment owners in gentrifying neighborhoods are conflicted. Their property taxes go up because assessors calculate the value of their homes based on the sale price of comparable homes. As a result, it is more expensive for homeowners to continue to live in their homes and apartment owners to cover costs of rental units they own. On the other hand, both homeowners and owners of rental property stand to make substantial gains when they sell their properties. Owners of rental property can usually increase rents more than enough to pay their higher property taxes and still often make additional income. Some homeowners in gentrifying neighborhoods—called incumbent upgraders—remain in their houses and fix them up. Other households in gentrifying neighborhoods cannot afford to maintain or improve their houses. They remain in their houses as they deteriorate or move to less expensive housing elsewhere. Planners working in gentrifying neighborhoods can help with policies and programs to help protect renters and low-income (often elderly) homeowners, encourage incumbent upgraders, help financially pressed homeowners maintain their properties, and discourage speculators.

Modernist planning—dominant in 1933—has been largely supplanted by post-modernist approaches. Citizen participation—rare in 1933—is now nearly universal, at least to some degree. Site planning as a field did not exist until Kevin Lynch invented it in the early 1960s. Many current planning concepts and practices such as sustainability, resilience, collaborative planning, privately owned public open space (POPOS), landscape urbanism, design with nature and transit-oriented development did not exist in 1933. Neither did concepts such as 3Cs—continuing, cooperative, and comprehensive—transportation planning, environmental impact analysis, and inclusionary zoning. Until the U.S. Green Building Council was created in 2002 there was little systematic attention to energy-efficient building or neighborhood design.

THE EVOLUTION OF THE PLANNING PROFESSION, 1933–PRESENT

In 1933 there were only a few hundred practicing city and regional planners in the United States. The American Planning Association (APA) did not exist, though predecessor U.S. planners' associations had existed since 1917.[3] There are more than 40,000 practicing city and regional planners in the United States today.

Curricula in planning schools in 1933 were limited largely to civic design. Planning specializations were not available. Faculty were almost all architects. Students had little contact with the people they were planning for. They learned little quantitative or qualitative research methodology. They did not use computers.

The Association of Collegiate Schools of Planning was not established until 1969 and only began holding meetings separately from the APA in 1981. The Planning Accreditation Board did not begin accrediting city and regional planning programs until 1984. The leading U.S. planning journals—the *Journal of the American Planning Association* and the *Journal of Planning Education and Research*—did not exist.[4]

THE NEW DEAL, FEDERALISM, AND CITY AND REGIONAL PLANNING

Roosevelt's New Deal profoundly altered federal–state–local relationships. Patterns established between 1933 and 1941 modernized the federal system that had been established by the U.S. Constitution in 1791. As further adapted by subsequent Republican and Democratic administrations, it is the system that city and regional planners navigate today.

Before the New Deal, the federal government had a very limited role in city and regional planning and urban programs. Urban issues were considered matters for the private sector or state and local government.

The three small organizations of cities that existed in 1933—the National Municipal League, now named the National Civic League, the International City Management Association, and the American Municipal League—were weak and ineffective in lobbying for the interests of cities. Their main interest was in keeping the federal government from meddling in local affairs, not encouraging federal programs or seeking federal funds.

In February 1933, a month before Franklin Roosevelt was inaugurated for his first term, the largest cities created the U.S. League of Cities. Under the leadership of Detroit mayor Frank Murphy, the League became an effective lobbying organization. It remains the principal lobbying organization for U.S. cities today. Two years later U.S. counties founded the National Association of Counties (NACo) which remains the national organization representing counties.

Initially, Roosevelt—a wealthy patrician who had grown up in the countryside—focused on recovery from the stock market crash, collapse of the U.S. banking system, mass unemployment, and agricultural problems—not urban problems. During his first term Roosevelt quickly ramped up public works projects, which employed 3,000,000 people—many of whom lived in cities. He secured greater federal funding to ease the cost burden of municipal relief for indigent households that was bankrupting Detroit and other cities. In 1934 Roosevelt helped secure passage of the Municipal Debt Adjustment Act—a bailout for cities on the brink of bankruptcy, but it was never used by any city with a population over 30,000.

During his first term, Roosevelt backed, but then abandoned, a tiny program to resettle city dwellers in rural subsistence homesteads in small communities. The program was led by Rexford Tugwell—the furthest left of Roosevelt's top officials. Tugwell's critics called him "Rex the red". Tugwell oversaw construction of three small "greenbelt towns" inspired by Ebenezer Howard's ideas and Letchworth, England described in Chapter 6. The greenbelt towns were small. Greenbelt, Maryland had 885 housing units, Greenhills, Ohio had 676 and Greendale, Wisconsin only 572. The program was expensive. It aroused a firestorm of criticism from conservatives, who considered it socialistic. Roosevelt dismantled the Resettlement Administration in 1937 and closed the program. A different New Deal agency—the Farm Security Administration—oversaw remaining work closing out work on the greenbelt towns.

Three New Deal events had a profound long-term impact on city and regional planning: 1) the precedent set by Roosevelt's 1935 decision for the federal government not to directly acquire land for a federal housing project in Louisville, Kentucky by eminent domain, 2) the authorization of the Tennessee Valley Authority (TVA) in 1933, and 3) creation of the public housing program by the 1937 Housing Act.

In the *U.S. vs Louisville* case in 1935, Roosevelt avoided having the conservative U.S. Supreme Court decide a fundamental constitutional question. He kept the Supreme Court from deciding whether or not the federal government had the constitutional authority to take land by eminent domain to carry out development programs at the local level.[5]

The federal public housing program—created in 1937 during Roosevelt's second term— established the basic structure of federal–state–local relations that continues today. The federal government provides funding and program direction for urban programs, but state governments have to pass state enabling legislation authorizing cities and counties to accept the funding. The local governments must in turn set up local agencies to apply for funding and run the programs in order to receive the federal aid. The idea that there should be a strong federal role in urban affairs with many federal regulations and agencies that provide guidance and funding for programs implemented at the state and local level was novel. Other New Deal programs followed the pattern of a newly created federal program providing policy direction and funding, and states enabling entities to receive the funding and plan and implement programs.

The Tennessee Valley Authority (TVA) was the most ambitious New Deal regional planning and development program. The TVA is a federal corporation created to plan and implement programs for a huge region in the Tennessee River basin in Tennessee and nearby states—a very low-income area that was severely underdeveloped in 1933.

The TVA plan involved constructing dams to provide hydroelectric power, control flooding, improve agriculture, and develop the economy of the region. The TVA also had ambitious plans for a new towns program. The TVA succeeded in reducing unemployment and increased the economic viability of the Tennessee River basin region. However, its bold new towns and urban planning programs were not implemented. During World War II, power from the TVA for wartime industries was considered a national defense priority, and the federal government

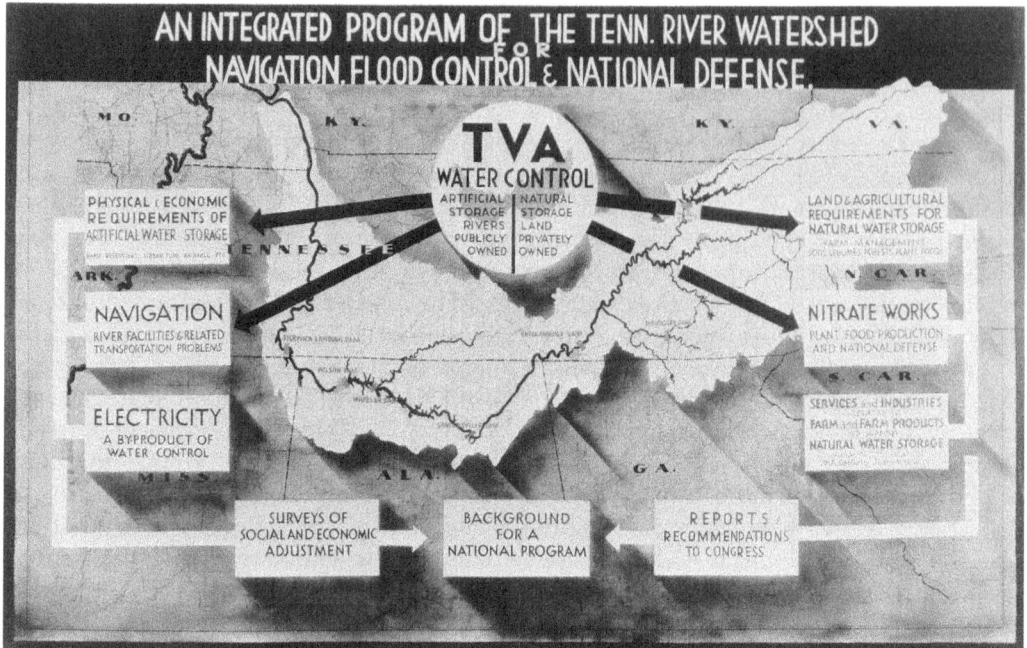

Figure 12.2 Tennessee Valley Authority Programs.

continued to invest in the TVA. Figure 12.2 is a 1943 poster describing the TVA's programs.

The TVA is still owned by the federal government, but receives no taxpayer funding. It now provides electric power to approximately 10 million people. TVA energy comes from the original New Deal hydroelectric facilities and coal-, oil-, natural gas-, and nuclear power-fueled plants that were built later.

The only other large multi-state regional planning entity in the United States is the Appalachian Regional Commission (ARC), which was established in 1965. ARC operates in a 205,000-square-mile region in parts of 13 states from southern New York to northern Mississippi. Appalachia is characterized by lack of development, poverty, and high unemployment. Most ARC funding has been used for highways to make it easier to export coal and other natural resources and to import goods into the Appalachia region. The ARC also provides funds for workforce training and to subsidize industrial parks in order to make Appalachia more economically competitive. The results have been mixed.

During the Great Depression the federal government invested in other large dam projects. Congress authorized Boulder (subsequently named Hoover) Dam in 1928. It was built between 1931 and 1936. Hoover Dam is 726 feet high, contains 66 million tons of concrete, and is almost one-quarter mile across the crest. The Grand Coulee, Bonneville, and other Depression-era dams are equally large. After World War II the federal government funded even larger dams.

THE NATIONAL RESOURCES PLANNING BOARD (NRPB)

The closest thing to national planning for the United States occurred between 1933 and 1943, when the National Resources Planning Board (NRPB) existed. The NRPB reported directly to Roosevelt. A small staff of natural and social scientists and field branch workers conducted studies of land use, multi-use water planning, natural resources, population, industrial structure, transportation, science, and technology. The NRPB was highly interdisciplinary, bringing together natural and social scientists, executive and legislative branch officials, planners and private and public institutions. The NRPB created the first national inventories of significant U.S. resources like timber and mineral deposits. It provided empirical information to serve as the basis for new policy in reaction to the Great Depression and industrial site location studies at the beginning of World War II. Until its termination in 1943 the NRPB engaged in planning for economic readjustment after World War II. Most states established planning agencies that used NRPB data. Regional planning groups in New England and the Pacific Northwest and planning boards in many cities used NRPB data and studies for plans and programs. Congress abolished the NRPB in 1943. It expressly prohibited any other agency in the federal government from assuming the board's national planning functions in the future. Congress did not want to give any president the authority and staff to engage in even basic research and exploration of alternatives as the NRPB did.

FEDERAL URBAN POLICY AFTER THE NEW DEAL

At the national level, control of the presidency and Congress continued to impact federal urban policy after the New Deal. Efforts both to continue and to dismantle federal programs that had originated during the New Deal and continued disputes over the relationship between federal, state, and local power continue to this day.

Democratic president Harry Truman continued variations of Roosevelt's New Deal programs from 1944 to 1953 as the Fair Deal. The Fair Deal's centerpiece was the 1949 Housing Act, which provided for a large increase in the public housing program to subsidize housing for low-income households and created the federal urban renewal program to clear slums and eliminate blight in economically distressed neighborhoods.

Conservative, market-oriented Republican president Dwight Eisenhower (1953–1961) cut back the New Deal/Fair Deal programs. Eisenhower sought a return to "normalcy" guided by "dynamic conservatism". He cut the 135,000 public housing units per year authorized by the 1949 Housing Act to 35,000 per year ostensibly in order to increase funding for the Korean war effort. National defense was Eisenhower's principal justification for the interstate highway system (1956–1992)—the largest infrastructure funding project in history. The 1954 Housing Act attempted unsuccessfully to get local governments to better coordinate federal, state, and local programs by requiring every local government receiving federal aid to prepare a "workable program for community improvement" that was supposed to coordinate urban renewal, public housing, and other federal programs with state and local programs. The workable program was a flop. Cities simply described what they were doing as their workable program, and the federal government accepted what they said.

Democratic president John Fitzgerald Kennedy (1961–1963) was a vigorous, progressive liberal from a Boston political family. Urban voters—particularly Irish Americans—were an important part of Kennedy's political base. Kennedy pledged to make cities the "New Frontier". He prohibited racial discrimination in public housing, and created the first below market interest rate (BMIR) housing program—in which the federal government paid part of the interest on mortgages for owners of moderate-income rental projects in exchange for limits on their rental profits and income limits on the tenants. Kennedy was working to create a cabinet-level federal agency for urban affairs when he was assassinated just 1,000 days into his presidency.

Lyndon Johnson (president from 1963–1967)—Kennedy's successor and also a liberal Democrat—created the U.S. Department of Housing and Urban Development (HUD) in 1965. Johnson re-invented, morphed, and expanded federal involvement in cities in "Great Society" programs—federal anti-poverty and social programs—and the "War on Poverty"—programs intended to eliminate poverty in the United States. He created the U.S. Office of Economic Opportunity (OEO) to fund local community action programs (CAPs); greatly expanded BMIR programs and deepened their subsidy so they served very low-income households; and created the model cities program to provide flexible funding for projects in low-income neighborhoods in 150 cities and urban counties.

The Nixon administration's urban policy between 1969 and 1974 had three main threads "benign neglect"—cutting back the Kennedy–Johnson urban programs; the "New Federalism" to decentralize power from Washington to lower levels of government; and a turn towards environmental protection. In the New Federalism, Nixon sought to combine many federal categorical grant programs into block grants—giving lower levels of government funding based on objective measures of need. This was a major change from categorical grant programs that had been created by the Kennedy and Johnson administrations, which required detailed applications and politics. He worked to devolve program planning and implementation authority to state and local government, and to greatly simplify federal review and oversight. Nixon succeeded in ending the urban renewal program in 1974 and consolidating its remains and other physical development categorical programs into the Community Development Block Grant (CDBG) program. The prospect of Nixon's imminent impeachment stopped the creation of other federal block grant programs. While Kennedy and Johnson created the below market interest rate (BMIR) housing program, most of the BMIR housing ever built in the United States was built during Nixon's first term. However, Nixon terminated funding for all BMIR programs early in his second term and froze virtually all new federal urban aid. Nixon succeeded in getting the National Environmental Policy Act (NEPA) and amendments to greatly strengthen the Clean Air Act enacted into law.

During his two terms (1981–1989) President Ronald Reagan ended new public housing construction in 1984 and the United States Department of Housing and Urban Development began to demolish the most distressed big city public housing projects with little opposition from Congress or the public. No new public housing projects were built until the 1990s. Ideologically, Reagan favored "enterprise zones" to give large corporations tax breaks and regulatory relief if they provided jobs in inner-city neighborhoods. The idea of enterprise zones was modeled on Conservative British prime minister Margaret Thatcher's enterprise zone program in the United Kingdom. However, no federal enterprise zone legislation was passed during Reagan's eight years in office.

The Democratic Carter, Clinton, and Obama administrations resuscitated and extended some of the earlier Democratic urban programs. The two Bush administrations and particularly the Trump administration have cut them back.

FROM MASTER PLANS TO GENERAL PLANS

The number of U.S. cities and counties that established planning commissions and prepared master plans grew rapidly during the 1920s and early 1930s. During the Great Depression some local planning departments were strengthened, because the communities where they were located saw planning as essential to coping with the Depression. Other local planning departments were gutted or eliminated altogether to save money.

Most U.S. cities and counties did not have comprehensive plans in 1933. Master plans at that time were long-range physical plans that addressed land use, transportation, and other elements that Edward Bassett and the Commerce Department's 1926 Standard State Planning Act Enabling Act (SSPEA) recommended. They typically included civic design, land use, and transportation elements, but did not include modern elements dealing with issues such as sustainability, resilience, transit-oriented development, equity, and climate change. Since the 1960s, T.J. Kent's concept of a flexible, bottom-up general plan to guide local elected officials, citizens, and other stakeholders has largely supplanted Bassett's concept of a top-down master plan serving an independent city planning commission and local elites.

In 1933 there were only a small number of zoning ordinances in the United States. Some states passed enabling legislation permitting their cities and counties to create zoning ordinances based on the Commerce Department's 1922 Standard State Zoning

Enabling Act (SSZEA) even before they had a city or county plan. In 1926 the U.S. Supreme Court held that zoning was constitutional in the *Euclid vs Ambler Realty Company*. Many additional local governments then adopted zoning ordinances. Still, most counties and smaller cities had no planning commission, master plan, or zoning in 1933.

THE LEGACY FEDERAL HOUSING PROGRAMS

Between 1937 and 1972 the federal government implemented a series of housing programs that are still important for city and regional planners. Millions of existing legacy affordable housing units still require continued planning and policy decisions. The legacy federal housing programs provide lessons about housing politics and housing program design.

At the beginning of the New Deal in 1933 there was very little federal, state, or local government funding for or regulation of housing. Beginning in 1937 the federal government began two types of housing programs to assist households who could not afford decent, safe and sanitary housing in the private market. Supply-side programs pay developers and/or owners part of their costs to build and operate housing if they agree to rent to people who meet specified income criteria. Demand-side housing programs pay tenants whose incomes are below a specified threshold a subsidy to cover the difference between what they are deemed able to pay and a fair market rent. The primary intent of both types of housing programs is to reduce the housing cost burden on as many households as funding permits. Eligibility, the depth of the subsidy, and the amount different types of households must pay in both supply- and demand-side programs are complex and have changed over time. U.S. housing subsidy programs are not entitlement programs in which every eligible household receives the benefit. They serve only a fraction of households in need of housing assistance. The following sections discuss the history of the major legacy federal housing programs left over from the New Deal, Fair Deal, New Frontier, and Great Society eras (1933–1968).

PUBLIC HOUSING

President Franklin Roosevelt created the first small federal affordable housing program in 1933. It was administered by the Public Works Administration (PWA)—the initial New Deal agency charged with providing federally funded jobs for people who were unemployed as a result of the Great Depression. The PWA acquired land and built 25,000 housing units. Roosevelt stopped the program because it proved costly, unpopular, and he feared that the conservative Supreme Court would use a lawsuit challenging it to establish precedent overturning much larger New Deal programs.

The U.S. Housing Act of 1937 created the federal public housing program. The act authorized local public housing authorities (PHAs) to issue bonds to finance the development costs of public housing for low-income households. The federal government paid principal and interest on the bonds. Tenant rental payments only needed to cover the cost of operating and maintaining the public housing projects. The 1937 Housing Act—also called the Wagner–Steagall Act after Senator Robert Wagner and Congressman Henry Steagall who introduced the legislation—authorized the federal government to provide funding to public housing authorities (PHAs). States needed to pass enabling legislation to allow cities and counties to create PHAs. Once a city or county created a PHA, and it successfully applied for the funding, they could proceed with a project largely paid for by the federal government.

The public housing program was a supply-side program. It provided federal subsidies to increase the stock of housing affordable to low-income households. To qualify, a household had to have income in the bottom 20% of income in their area and almost no assets. They could not be indigent—with no income. The public housing admission standards have changed over the years, but have always provided public housing to households with very limited income and assets.

The 1937 act was a triumph for modernist housing crusader Catherine Bauer (Box 12.3). However, there was furious conservative opposition to the legislation. As passed, it was riddled with compromises with the real estate industry and fell short of Bauer's vision. Public housing units had to be designed not to compete with even low-end private housing.

Some first-generation public housing projects in New York City, Chicago, and Boston were sources of pride to the cities, tenants and sometimes local politicians and other residents of the neighborhoods where they were located—at least at first. Other early public housing units were poorly designed, ugly, physically inferior, located on problematic sites, poorly constructed, lacked amenities, and were clearly distinguishable from private market housing. Many units produced during World War II were inferior barracks-like low-rise projects.

The federal–state–local structure established by the 1937 Housing Act was a result of the 1935 *U.S. vs Certain Lands in Louisville* case that established the pattern of federal funding, state enabling, and local implementation. After the *Louisville* case the federal government no longer used eminent domain to acquire land for public housing, but could fund public housing projects on land local governments had acquired in states that permitted them to do so. Public housing qualified as a public purpose as required by the fifth amendment of the U.S. Constitution, so PHAs, as units of local government, could condemn properties and take land by eminent domain, so long as they provided just compensation. Since taking private land by eminent domain is unpopular, virtually all PHAs only purchased land that the owners were willing to sell voluntarily, and did not use the eminent domain power they possessed.

PHAs made a payment in lieu of property tax (PILOT) payment lower than the local property tax. Tenants' rents only had to cover operations and 10% of maintenance costs. Initially maintenance costs were very low, but became much higher as the projects aged.

Initially PHAs had strict tenant selection policies. With a limited supply of units and great demand, public housing project managers could carefully screen for tenants. The target population was initially the middle third of the income spectrum—the "submerged middle class"—but the public housing program subsequently targeted somewhat lower-income households. Most households accepted were the so-called "deserving" or "worthy" poor—unemployed because of the Depression, widows, orphans, and the blind—not the so-called "unworthy poor"—physically and mentally healthy working-age men and women who were not working. Households had to have enough income that they could afford to pay 20% of their income for rent. Many of the initial tenant households included an able-bodied husband, wife, and one or more children. Some units housed single-parent households headed by women. Investigators from the PHAs visited applicants in their homes and interviewed landlords to confirm that the households applying for public housing kept their apartments clean and paid rent regularly. The early public housing projects were racially segregated. Public housing was not desegregated until 1962.

Congress passed legislation providing for a massive increase in public housing for war workers in 1940—the National Defense Housing Act (Lanham Act). In 1942 a new National Housing Agency was created to administer the program. By the end of World War II the United States had spent over $2 billion and constructed 700,000 additional public housing units for military households and workers in war industries. Many of the Lanham Act public housing units were quickly and poorly built barracks-like emergency units intended to be demolished after the war. Communities patriotically accepted Lanham Act public housing projects because almost all the tenants were members of the armed forces, military dependents, or war workers. Many Lanham Act units remained in operation long after the war. A few still exist today.

A third round of public housing construction occurred as a result of the 1949 Housing Act which authorized construction of 810,000 additional public housing units by 1955—an average of 135,000 units a year. President Eisenhower cut funding for the program by more than 80% to 35,000 housing units per year to redirect funding to the Korean War effort.

As the U.S. economy improved after World War II, many able-bodied White public housing tenants were able to find stable employment and used military savings and benefits to move out of public housing projects. Black tenants faced discrimination in the job and housing markets—including from the Federal Housing Administration (FHA) itself. Black GIs were denied federal housing subsidies that their White peers received. As a result many Blacks who otherwise might have moved out of public housing remained in public housing.

The Supreme Court held racially restrictive mortgage covenants illegal in 1948. President Kennedy banned racial discrimination in public housing tenant selection in 1962. *De facto* segregation of public housing continued after it was legally prohibited. Illegal racial discrimination in private sales and rental markets decreased, but still occurs.

In the 1960s, PHAs became much less strict in screening tenants. Many public housing projects filled up with very low-income, predominantly Black, female-headed households. Many unemployed males lived illegally in, or drifted in and out of, large urban public housing projects. The number of teenagers in the projects increased, and gangs formed. Crime and drug problems in public housing grew, particularly in the large urban projects. The Cabrini–Green public project in Chicago, Illinois and the Pruitt–Igoe public housing project in St. Louis, Missouri began with enthusiasm for their prospects, but became iconic symbols of the failure of big city public housing projects (Box 12.2).

BOX 12.2 THE CABRINI–GREEN HOMES AND PRUITT–IGOE PUBLIC HOUSING PROJECTS

Cabrini–Green Homes in Chicago, Illinois and the Wendell O. Pruitt Homes and William Igoe Apartments (the Pruitt–Igoe Project) in St. Louis, Missouri illustrate the trajectory of many large big-city public housing projects. However, they are extreme cases and are not representative of all public housing.

The first units at Cabrini–Green Homes were two- and three-story row houses opened by the Chicago Housing Authority (CHA) in 1942, followed by extensions in 1958 and 1972, so there were 55 buildings in all. The project was named for Frances Xavier Cabrini—an Italian American Catholic nun. It was known as Little Sicily and most of the original tenants were Italian American Catholics. William Green Homes—a 1,096-unit project at the same site was completed in 1962. It consisted of 1,096 housing units in eight 15- or 16-story concrete buildings. The project was named for William Green—the (White) leader of the American Federation of Labor from 1924 to 1952. During the 1960s Cabrini–Green's tenants became nearly entirely low-income female-headed Black households. The project developed serious physical and social problems.[6] By 2011 all the high-rise buildings had been demolished.

The Pruitt–Igoe Project was a modernist public housing project with 2,870 apartments in 33 11-story buildings. It was racially segregated. Blacks lived in units named for Black World War II fighter pilot Wendell O. Pruitt and Whites lived in units named for Italian American congressman William Igoe. The project was designed by architect Minoru Yamasaki, who later designed the New York World Trade Center. When it opened in 1956, *Architectural Forum* magazine named the Pruitt–Igoe project the best apartment project of the year. Pruitt–Igoe is generally depicted as an unmitigated disaster, but recent research challenges that stereotype. The entire project was demolished between 1972 and 1976 (Figure 12.4).[7]

Figure 12.3 Community Leaders Reviewing a Model of the Pruitt–Igoe Public Housing Project (St. Louis, Missouri, circa 1953).

By the early 1970s, the terrible problems of vandalism, illegal occupancy, drugs, and crime in the Cabrini–Green, Pruitt–Igoe, and other large public housing projects caused The U.S. Department of Housing and Urban Development (HUD) to stop building new large public housing projects that concentrated poverty in favor of smaller scattered site affordable projects and housing vouchers. Community resistance and the reluctance of landlords to rent to public housing households—particularly if they were Black or other people of color—made it difficult to get even small well-designed public housing projects built on suitable sites.

A lawsuit filed by the American Civil Liberties Union against the Chicago Housing Authority and HUD in 1966 on behalf of Dorothy Gautreaux and other Cabrini–Green tenants—*Gautreaux vs Chicago Housing Authority*—has been central to the struggle to allow households receiving federal housing assistance to move to units in communities they feel will provide better education, work, or other opportunities for themselves and their children.[8] The *Gautreaux* case alleged that the Chicago Housing Authority (CHA) had violated U.S. Department of Housing and Urban Development regulations, the 1964 Civil Rights Act, and the U.S. Constitution by locating public housing whose tenants were almost entirely Black in areas of concentrated poverty. Even though it was a defendant, HUD—then headed by Carla Hills, the first Black woman to head HUD—joined the tenants as a party and in 1976 and participated in an appeal to the U.S. Supreme Court. The Supreme Court found in favor of the tenants and HUD. The CHA agreed to give thousands of CHA tenants housing vouchers to allow them to move to less isolated public and private housing in neighborhoods of their choosing.

Figure 12.4 Demolition of the Pruitt–Igoe Project (1972).

The *Gautreaux* decision required the parties to formulate a comprehensive plan to remedy the past effects of the CHA's unconstitutional site selection and tenant assignment procedures and prohibited such practices in the future. In a notable 1981 decree the Chicago Housing Authority (CHA) agreed to remedy past discrimination by providing housing vouchers that permitted some CHA tenants to move to private market housing. In 2019, the U.S. district court where the *Gautreaux* case had been filed, 53 years earlier, signed an order approving what parties hope will be the final settlement order in the case.

Devising and implementing the remedy in the *Gautreaux* case has been a painful 50 plus-year process by tenants, HUD, the CHA, and federal trial and appellate courts. The remedy in the *Gautreaux* case has provided thousands of former tenants of Chicago public housing greater choice in deciding where to live and helped make housing in many neighborhoods they could not previously afford financially available to them.

HUD implemented an experiment called the Moving to Opportunity (MTO) program between 1994 and 1998 inspired by the Gautreaux case remedy. The MTO program provided tenants of large, troubled, racially segregated public housing projects flexible vouchers and greater funding to enable them to move to neighborhoods with better schools or closer to work opportunities or other features they wanted and still pay no more than 30% of income for rent. Tenants were not required to use the vouchers to move into neighborhoods that were less racially segregated, but the MTO program made that financially possible. The results of the MTO program, described in

Chapter 15, were mixed. HUD is currently operating and expanding a program called Choice Neighborhoods with similar goals.

The *Gautreaux* case has been settled. However, a number of smaller *Gautreaux*-like projects based on legal settlements are still underway. New programs—notable HUD's Rental Assistance Demonstration program (RAD)—entitle public housing tenants to remain in public housing projects (and former public housing projects financed by project or tenant-based vouchers) even if their incomes are above public housing limits. This is intended to increase the income mix in remaining public housing.

President Reagan ended new public housing construction in 1984 and instituted a program to demolish the most distressed projects with little opposition from Congress or the public. No new public housing projects were built until the 1990s when a program called HOPE VI began to build some replacement units as it demolished units in old public housing projects.

Critics of public housing have promoted an image of public housing projects as physical and social disasters, unfairly using the examples of Pruitt–Igoe, Cabrini–Green, and other large housing projects as representative of all public housing. The disaster narrative was never true of the great majority of public housing projects.

Today there are 1.2 million public housing units managed by some 3,300 PHAs located in every state. Public housing include lowrise and highrise units in small and large projects. Public housing provides units for low-income families—particularly female-headed households, the elderly, and people with special needs. Most are well maintained and financially viable. City and regional planners confront questions of what of the public housing stock to preserve or rehabilitate and how to preserve affordability for existing tenants. Chapter 15 picks up the story of legacy public housing today.

FEDERAL PROGRAMS TO SUBSIDIZE PRIVATE AND NONPROFIT RENTAL HOUSING

The second major type of federal supply-side housing subsidy programs provides federal subsidies to housing that is mostly privately owned or owned by nonprofit housing development corporations. Most are below market interest rate (BMIR) programs in which the federal government pays a portion of monthly mortgage payments. Private developers, private apartment owners, banks, the real estate industry, and conservatives generally favor the more private market approach of BMIR housing, compared to what they consider more socialistic public housing.

Many federal housing programs are known by the section of the housing act that created them. The BMIR housing programs began with the Section 221(d)(3) program in 1961 that provided subsidies for moderate-income rental units and the Section 515 program in 1963 that subsidizes rural housing. These were two of the Kennedy administration's New Frontier programs. BMIR subsidies were greatly expanded in 1968 with the Section 236 rental housing and Section 235 home purchase programs—two of President Lyndon Johnson's Great Society programs.[9] Since they began in 1961, federal demand-side housing programs have been started and stopped, the subsidies have changed, and programs have morphed and been combined with other housing subsidy programs.

The Section 221(d)(3) program provided below market interest rate (BMIR) loans to developers who built and managed housing for moderate-income households whose income typically came from one or more household member(s) working full-time in a low-paying job, part-time work, social security, pensions, or from other limited sources of income. Income limits were too high for the lowest-income households without sufficient income to pay even their (modest) share of rent. The program provided developers who built 221(d)(3) projects with 3% mortgages.

The Section 236 program provided a subsidy similar to, but deeper than, the Section 221(d)(3) program. It paid the difference between a mortgage with a 1% interest rate and the market interest rate. The deeper subsidy allowed the Section 236 program to reach very low-income households such as households with one or more members serving fast food, mowing lawns, or working as a part-time security guard. Some households living in Section 236 units also received rent supplement payments that paid the difference between 30% (later 25%) of their income and the rent, so there was considerable income mix in Section 236 projects. Rents were set by formula based on comparable rents in the neighborhood. The Section 236 program produced more than 544,000 units before President Ronald Reagan terminated it in 1984.

Initially many small faith-based nonprofit organizations (churches), with little or no housing or financial expertise, and other well-intentioned but unsophisticated nonprofit organizations formed nonprofit housing development corporations (HDCs) to take advantage of the section 221(d)(3) and section 236 BMIR programs. Over time the weakest HDCs failed. The remaining nonprofit HDCs have matured and are an important part of the U.S. subsidized housing system.

The Section 221(d)(3) and Section 236 programs have had serious problems. No new Section 236 units have been produced since 1984. Since the late 1990s more than 80% of the older assisted stock of Section 221(d)(3) and Section 236 units has been converted to other forms of housing assistance, moved into the private market, or demolished. The remaining stock of Section 221(d)(3) and Section 236 units has dwindled to about 41,000 units. HUD's Office of Affordable Housing Preservation (OAHP) Office of Recapitalization (Recap) administers programs to close out and restructure the remaining Section 221(d)(3) and 236 units.

The Section 235 Program—created in 1968 at the same time as the Section 236 program—was a BMIR program that provided funding to build or substantially rehabilitate housing for low–moderate-income homeowners. Income-qualified buyers of modest homes selling below a HUD-established threshold received subsidies of the difference between a market rate mortgage and a mortgage at 1% interest for the life of the mortgage—an exceptionally deep subsidy. The homebuyers kept any appreciation. The Section 235 program was costly and widely abused. The substantial rehabilitation part of the program was plagued by corruption. In *Cities Destroyed for Cash* (1973) muckraking journalist Brian Boyer describes how unscrupulous developers bribed local housing inspectors to approve shoddy work and pocketed exorbitant profits for houses in Detroit rehabilitated under the Section 235 program. Naïve first-time buyers (mostly Black) purchased inferior houses that they could not afford to repair when defects became apparent. Many Detroit households that purchased rehabilitated Section 235 units abandoned their homes, leaving the federal government with a costly inventory of unlivable vacant homes.

Section 235 subsidized 400,000 units between 1968 and 1973. Lessons for planners from the Section 235 program are that low-income homeownership programs must be very carefully structured, buyers screened and counselled, and programs carefully monitored for corruption. Planners need to weigh the use of scarce resources for deep low-income homeownership subsidies compared to shallower subsidies that will benefit a larger number of needy renter households.

In addition to subsidizing private owners of existing rental housing, the Section 8 program provided funding for new construction and substantial rehabilitation—the NCSR program. Between the time President Nixon created the Section 8 NCSR program in 1974 and President Reagan terminated it in 1984, the program subsidized 850,000 new or substantially rehabilitated housing units. The NCSR program typically provided either 20-year or 40-year contracts. Since the units were in high demand, developers and owners could expect close to zero vacancies and a steady income stream. Owners could accelerate depreciation—receiving a large tax subsidy in the early years. They could generally terminate the mortgages after 20 years and return the units to the private market. Section 8 subsidies were also available to owners of properties subsidized under other programs or even without subsidies to bolster their finances and prevent them from defaulting.

As market conditions changed, rents in some desirable BMIR units rose higher than rents in comparable units in the neighborhood. Rents in undesirable BMIR projects fell. Since tenants paid 30% of their income for rent, these market changes did not change how much rent they paid. However, expensive rents were bankrupting the BMIR programs. Owners had an incentive to terminate mortgages of desirable projects as early as possible because they could make more money in the private market. They opted out of projects where they were not making the profit they expected, if possible, because the rents were lower than what they could earn in the private market. Congress launched the "mark to market" program in 1997 to adjust high rents downward and the "mark up to market" program in 1999 to adjust low rents upward. Owners were permitted to restructure debt in ways intended to give them the incentive to remain in the programs without making excessive profits.

THE SECTION 515 RURAL HOUSING PROGRAM

The Section 515 rural rental housing program is a BMIR program that was created in 1962. It is administered by the U.S. Department of Agriculture (DOA)—not HUD. Section 515 has financed more than 533,000 units. About 80% of all projects with Section 515 loans also receive rent subsidies to ensure that low-income tenants pay no more than 30% of their adjusted income on rent. The Section 515 program has not supported the development of new units since 2011. Congress has cut funding for the preservation of existing Section 515 developments far below previous funding levels.[10]

Section 515 loans are similar to Section 236 loans. They pay the difference between market rate and a 1% interest rate for rental projects for low-income tenants in rural areas. Section 515 mortgages have a 50-year amortization period—longer than other conventional or BMIR program mortgage terms—so tenants' rents can be very low. About 75% of Section 515 loans also receive rent subsidies, so the Section 515 program reaches very low- and even extremely low-income rural households as well as low-income households. It is a more vertically efficient subsidy than the other federal BMIR programs—all the money goes to people in need. It is a large enough program to reach a significant number of low-income rural households.

As of 2008 there were about 445,000 Section 515 units still in existence. Since Section 515 is a rural program, many Section 515 units are located in unincorporated land. County planners and planners in rural states are more likely to work with Section 515 units than city planners.

None of the BMIR programs worked as intended for the intended duration of the program. All were fundamentally changed—often many times. There has not been new funding for any of the legacy BMIR programs since 2011. Some legacy BMIR housing units have been demolished; many have been converted to funding by housing vouchers and are no longer classified as BMIR housing; some have moved into the private market. The remaining BMIR units still have some form of subsidy, though the source and amount are different from what they were at the time the housing was built and first financed. Today they constitute an important, but threatened, tangle of programs.

City and regional planners working with the legacy BMIR programs face two challenges—to physically maintain the units and to keep them affordable to low-income tenants. Where it is impossible to maintain the net number of BMIR units, planners work to assure that displaced tenants get alternative affordable project-based units or vouchers. Flexible state and local funding and dedicated city and regional planners can make the legacy housing programs work despite their troubled history, funding shortages, deferred maintenance, and constant threats from political opponents.

HOUSING VOUCHERS

Housing Choice Vouchers (HCVs) are now the major U.S. demand-side housing assistance program. Legacy voucher programs were folded into the HCV program.

The first housing voucher program was created by section 8 of the 1974 Housing Act as "section 8 certificates". In 1998, section 8 certificates were combined with a much smaller housing voucher program created by President Reagan and are now a category of housing choice vouchers.

Housing choice vouchers (HCVs) provide tenants the difference between a percentage of their income (now 30%) and a payment standard that public housing authorities can set at 90% to 100% of a fair market rent (FMR) for housing units in the housing market area. HUD sets the FMR based on the costs of a minimal decent, safe, and sanitary housing unit in the area adjusted for household size. The federal government pays private or public landlords the subsidy each month.

NEW DEAL HOUSING FINANCE REFORM

The New Deal had a major impact on the way in which private housing in the United States—95% of the housing stock—is financed. The current U.S. system of mortgage finance and the secondary mortgage market invented by the federal government during the New Deal have grown into a gigantic and complex system.

By 1933 hundreds of state-chartered savings and loan associations (S&Ls) throughout the U.S. lent money to homebuyers by pooling individual local savings account deposits. S&Ls generally operated independently and made home loans in their community without much connection to each other. There was no federal oversight of their operations, and states also failed to oversee their operations.

In 1933 few homebuyers borrowed more than 50% of the house purchase price. Home mortgages were generally short-term, principal-only, balloon payment mortgages. They required monthly interest payments with a single "balloon" payment at the end of the mortgage term to repay the principal. For an $8,000 house a household might pay 50% of their own money down ($4,000) and borrow the balance ($4,000) for 5 years (60 months) at a 7% interest rate. Each month the borrower would pay $26.61 in interest (7% of $4,000). At the end of the mortgage term he or she would make a one-time balloon payment of the $4,000 principal. The cost of borrowing the $4,000 for the five years would be $1,362.

When the Great Depression occurred, huge numbers of mortgagees did not have the money to make mortgage payments, leaving the banks without enough money to pay depositors. Depositors panicked and withdrew their savings for fear the bank would go bankrupt. President Roosevelt was forced to declare a "bank holiday" temporarily closing virtually all banks in the United States soon after he assumed office.

The New Deal solution to this death spiral was to charter new federal banks which lent money only to stable, relatively low-risk borrowers who made large enough down payments to cushion lenders if the house value did go down. Much stricter standards for chartering banks and greater federal oversight created a much safer home loan banking system. A new Federal Deposit Insurance Corporation (FDIC) guaranteed depositors that the federal government would pay any shortfall if the bank failed and was unable to pay them 100% of their savings. Federally chartered banks required new mortgagees to purchase mortgage insurance from a newly created Federal Housing Administration (FHA) to insure mortgages on low- and moderate- priced housing units so that lending institutions would be protected if the owners defaulted. Backed by the FDIC, the FHA insurance pool, and ultimately the full faith and credit of the United States, depositors had essentially no risk of losing their saving and began putting money back into the federally chartered banks.

The new mortgages federally chartered banks made were much longer term—often 30 years or more, rather than 5 years as was common with balloon payment mortgages. They were self-amortizing mortgages, with principal and interest paid in equal installments over the life of the mortgage. They were structured so that the mortgage was fully paid off at the end of the mortgage term, with no balloon payment. Each monthly payment paid off a portion of the principal as well as interest. Most of the initial mortgage payments were interest, which the borrower could deduct from his or her federal income tax, making owning rather than renting financially advantageous for most people who could afford it.

Another important New Deal housing finance innovation was creation of a national secondary mortgage market. The Federal National Mortgage Corporation (FNMA)—nicknamed "Fannie Mae"—created liquidity in national mortgage markets. Fannie Mae buys and sells blocks of mortgages that meet federal standards so that capital is more available when and where needed. If FNMA bought a block of 1,000 mortgages from a distressed little S&L in Bismark, North Dakota, the S&L would get a large infusion of capital with which to pay off creditors and make new mortgage loans. This could save the S&L from bankruptcy, increase local homeownership, and stimulate the Bismark economy by providing construction jobs, sales of building materials, and income for realtors. Fannie Mae would assume the risk that some of the mortgages would not be paid back. Fannie Mae was well enough capitalized to hold risky loans for a long time and could sustain loss in some part of their portfolio so long as overall, they broke even.

Congress created a second national secondary mortgage entity—the Government National Mortgage Association (GNMA)—nicknamed Ginnie Mae—in 1968 to purchase troubled mortgages. They created a third—the Federal Home Loan Mortgage Corporation (FHLMC)—nicknamed Freddie Mac—in 1970. The secondary mortgage market entities are an important part of the public/private housing finance system city planners work within today. Complex packaging and selling of blocks of mortgages worked well when housing was appreciating, but proved to be a huge problem during the 2008 financial crisis.

TRANSPORTATION PLANNING

By 1933 the series of disruptive transportation technologies that began about 1800 had produced in roughly chronological—but overlapping—order steamboats, railroad trains, cable cars, electric street cars, subways, automobiles, trucks, and first-generation airplanes. The United States had a national network of ports and airports and a national telephone system. Many local zoning ordinances and master plans had transportation elements. There was no interstate highway system. Transportation planning was almost entirely about mobility.

Civil engineers dominated (and still dominate) transportation planning. Engineers do most of the nuts and bolts planning in local public works departments and for large transportation systems. Engineers and other transportation planners ignored the environmental impacts of wood- and coal-burning trains and steamboats. Virtually none were aware of global climate change until very recently. Transportation engineering designs—particularly highway designs—often disrupted the physical and social fabric of neighborhoods. Without computers and before well-thought-out quantitative models, the empirical basis for transportation planning was weak.

The biggest change in transportation since the beginning of the twentieth century is the rise of gasoline-powered motor vehicles. By 1933 about 40% of U.S. households owned an automobile. The U.S. Federal Highway Administration (FHWA) estimates that there were 20,657,257 commercial, private, and publicly owned automobiles in the United States in 1933. Between 1929 and 1940 the number of registered automobiles in the United States increased by 4.5 million despite the Great Depression. During World War II Almost all non-military production of motor vehicles was suspended, and gasoline was rationed. With postwar prosperity and improved roads and highways, auto ownership massively increased. Today there is about one automobile, sports utility vehicle (SUV), or light truck per U.S. household. Five other big changes in transportation planning have occurred since 1933.

First, is the loss of urban and interurban electric streetcar systems that had been constructed since the 1880s. These included streetcar lines within cities, between cities and streetcar suburbs, and interurban streetcar lines. The U.S. streetcar system had been largely destroyed and replaced by automobiles and bus systems by the mid-1960s.

Second is improvements in automotive technology. The great breakthrough came with the Model T Ford, beginning in 1908. Since then, new technologies have made automobiles, SUVs, and light trucks more efficient, cleaner, safer, and smarter. Motorized vehicles are now able to interact digitally with other motorized vehicles (vehicle-to-vehicle communication), traffic controls (vehicle-to-infrastructure communication), and remote "control rooms". Clean hybrid and zero-emission vehicle (ZEV) sales are still a small percentage of all motorized vehicle sales, but increasingly rapidly. However, it will likely take at least several decades before gasoline-powered motor vehicles are phased out.

The third big change in transportation planning and policy was construction of the U.S. national highway system. President Eisenhower justified federal investment in highways as a matter of national defense, and made investment in highways a national priority. The Federal Aid Highway Act of 1956—the National Interstate and Defense Highways Act—authorized construction of a 41,000-mile interstate highway system over the following 13 years. The federal government paid 90% of highway construction costs from a highway trust fund that receives revenue mostly from an excise tax on gasoline. Between 1956 and 1992 when the system was completed, the federal government spent $114 billion (equivalent to $521 billion after adjusting for inflation) to construct the national federal aid highway system. The federal highway system opened access to cheap suburban land and drove suburbanization. Construction of segments of the system within cities disrupted neighborhoods and led to anti-highway revolts in many cities.

The fourth big change in transportation planning involves a shift to multi-modal transit systems. Since 1991 federal transportation legislation has sought to create systems integrating highways and other modes of transportation such as travel by subways, heavy and light rail systems, boats, airplanes, bicycle, and walking.

The fifth big change in federal transportation policy since 1933 has been growing recognition by planners and policy makers that transportation-related planning should involve much more than mobility. City and regional planners now recognize that highway construction should minimize impacts on the natural environment—particularly air pollution and greenhouse gas emissions that contribute to global warming. Transportation planners now try to minimize highway construction within cities that disrupt neighborhoods. Current transportation planning practice has drawn on ideas described in Chapter 14, including Alan Jacobs's ideas about street and boulevard design, Jane Jacobs's ideas about how "eyes on the street" can deter crime, Donald Appleyard and Kevin Lynch's ideas about designing to optimize the view from the road, Jan Gehl's ideas about pedestrianizing streets, and Robert Cervero's ideas about the transit metropolis and functions of streets beyond mobility.

The federal government passed a federal road act in 1916. President Hoover increased funding for road construction to provide jobs for unemployed men during the first years of the Great Depression. New York City and other large cities had begun building freeways. However, construction of a federal highway system did not begin until 1955. Federal legislation mandating continuing, cooperative, and comprehensive ("3Cs") planning did not begin until 1962. The U.S. Department of Transportation was created in 1967. The federal government began setting corporate average fuel efficiency (CAFE) standards requiring automakers to improve fuel efficiency in 1975.

Federal legislation establishing the current system of multi-modal transportation planning began with the Intermodal Surface Transportation Efficiency Act (ISTEA) in 1991, followed by the Moving Ahead for Progress in the 21st Century (MAP-21) program in 2012, and the Fixing America's Surface Transportation (FAST) Act in 2015. Copenhagen, Denmark pioneered pedestrianized streets in the early 1970s.

"Complete streets" planning that considers sidewalks, streetscaping, street furniture and other non-mobility aspects of planning, and the needs of bicyclists and pedestrians as well as car, truck, and motorcycle drivers has mostly developed within the last 20 years. So has the practice of congestion management. Serious analysis and planning for parking began after 1997, largely because of University of California, Los Angeles planning professor Donald Shoup's research and writing, described in Chapter 14. The movement to eliminate traffic fatalities—the Vision Zero movement—began in Sweden in 1997. Most of the growth in the Vision Zero network has occurred within the last ten years.

The first mass produced hybrid vehicle—the Toyota Prius—became available only in 1997. The first Defense Advanced Research Projects Agency (DARPA) Grand Challenge for experimental autonomous (self-driving) cars occurred in 2004. The first mass produced all-electric vehicle—the Nissan Leaf—became available only in 2010.

ENVIRONMENTAL AND CLIMATE CHANGE PLANNING

Before 1970 environmental planning in the United States barely existed. Planners' awareness of fundamental biological, ecological, and environmental processes was primitive. Except for the work of a few pioneering landscape architects, there was almost no effort to relate planning for the built and the natural environment. There were few federal or state environmental laws, and those that existed were very weak. There were no "adequate public facilities" ordinances assuring that infrastructure needed to protect the natural environment, such as landfills and wastewater treatment plants, kept pace with development. Environmental impact assessment, air and water quality planning and regulation, protection of endangered and threatened plant and animal species, and other aspects of modern environmental planning did not exist. Most planning schools did not have faculty qualified to teach environmental planning, did not teach a course on it, and did not include much about the natural environment in land use planning and other coursework.

Since 1970 state and local environmental plans and individual and community actions have produced a huge range of changes benefitting the environment such as habitat conservation plans, green roofs, reforestation projects, and reduction of corporate and household carbon footprints. Every graduate U.S. city and regional planning program has courses that deal with environmental planning and sustainable urban development. Many more planning faculty are well educated in environmental planning.

City planning programs, the planning profession, and policy makers only began to engage seriously with climate change education and planning after the United Nations' Intergovernmental Panel on Climate Change (IPCC)'s *Third Assessment Report* in 2001 stated unequivocally that anthropogenic climate change was real and posed a significant imminent threat to planet earth. State and local governments, neighborhoods, and individual households have become much more conscious of their carbon footprints. They have planned and implemented a range of policies to mitigate the impacts of global warming that have already occurred, reduce carbon and other greenhouse gas (GHG) emissions, and make themselves more resilient to respond to climate change shocks. Many state and local governments have adopted policies to reduce future global warming, such as carbon cap-and-trade policies, green roofs, reforestation, and incentives to accelerate the shift to solar, wind, and other clean renewable energy sources. Still, action to address climate change has been much too little too late.

URBAN RENEWAL, REGENERATION, AND COMMUNITY DEVELOPMENT

Programs to develop, redevelop, renew, or regenerate parts of cities have waxed and waned since 1933. In the United States the term urban renewal usually refers to federally funded projects undertaken between 1949 and 1972 pursuant to the 1949 U.S. Housing Act. The term urban renewal is also used to refer to some state-funded redevelopment projects and loosely to refer to any new construction or rehabilitation of older areas. Community development, urban revitalization, and urban regeneration are more recent terms for approaches to upgrading older neighborhoods.

In 1972 President Nixon suspended the urban renewal program. Congress formally ended it in 1973. In 1974 the federal Community Development Block Grant (CDBG) program became the major successor to the federal urban renewal program.

The U.S. federal urban renewal program involved federal direction and funding for projects planned and administered by local governments. States had to pass enabling legislation permitting local entities to use the federal funds. If they wanted to apply for federal urban renewal funding individual local governments had to set up local redevelopment agencies. This follows the pattern established in public housing. Almost all states passed legislation enabling local governments to establish redevelopment agencies shortly after 1949. Local governments that chose to participate in the federal urban renewal program usually set up redevelopment commissions overseeing local redevelopment agencies to implement urban renewal projects. In a few cities and counties, the city council or county board of supervisors also acts as the redevelopment commission. Some conservative jurisdictions considered the program socialistic and never participated as a matter of principle.

Most urban renewal funding went to core cities. Some went to suburbs and occasionally urban counties and small towns. The largest and best funded redevelopment agencies were in New York, San Francisco, and other solidly Democratic cities.

Planners working for redevelopment agencies—not planners in local city planning departments—did redevelopment planning, prepared urban renewal funding applications, and helped administer redevelopment programs. Planning department staff often worked with the redevelopment agencies' planning staff.

By the time of its demise in 1974, the federal urban renewal program was excoriated by conservatives as intrusive, bureaucratic, and wasteful; by Blacks as "Negro removal"; and by neighborhood activists like Jane Jacobs for replacing lively human-scale neighborhood communities with soulless, over-scaled modernist developments. Urban renewal's most vocal critic was Martin Anderson—a conservative Columbia University business professor. Anderson concluded in 1964 that urban renewal "was not logical, practical, or moral" and had been a "thundering failure and should be repealed".

No new federal urban renewal projects were funded after 1972, when President Nixon put a freeze on urban renewal funding. The program ended in 1974. Federal urban renewal projects that were started before 1972 were completed later or have been blended into other federal, state, and local programs.

Most of what was built in areas redeveloped between 1949 and 1972 by the federal urban renewal program is still in existence. City and regional planners may still be involved in planning new construction of affordable housing or other development or rehabilitating older buildings in some redevelopment project areas.

Some states have state redevelopment programs. State redevelopment projects tend to be much smaller-scale and more sensitive to local conditions than projects undertaken during the height of the federal urban renewal era. Most are funded by tax increment financing (TIF) in which the redevelopment agency borrows money to clear and prepare land using the anticipated value of the cleared land as collateral and then pays off the debt with tax revenue from the project.

The idea of the federal urban renewal program was that when "blighted" land in an urban renewal project area had been acquired, buildings demolished, and new infrastructure had been installed so that the site was ready for development, most land would be sold to private developers for its market value to develop for its "highest and best use". Land sales were projected to provide local governments enough money to repay the federal government for the urban renewal loan.

Urban renewal was a categorical grant program. Initially cities applied for a federal planning advance—a relatively small loan to pay for planners to survey and delineate a "slum and blighted" project area and prepare a plan to redevelop the area. Applicants who received a planning advance then developed a budget for acquiring land; relocating people and businesses; demolishing old structures; clearing and rezoning land; building new roads, sewer, water, and electrical lines; and landscaping public spaces. The cleared land was often rezoned. When the plan was complete, the redevelopment agency would then submit an application for a much larger combination federal urban renewal loan and grant to carry out the project. The city or county was obligated to repay the loan, but not the grant.

This looked good on paper. A slum and blighted area would be replaced with functional new uses at almost no cost to local government and very little cost to the federal government once the loan had been paid back. The redeveloped area would be attractive, economically productive, and with little or no crime. It would generate much more municipal revenue. Residents would be relocated to better housing and businesses relocated or fairly compensated for their losses.

In reality few federal urban renewal projects succeeded as envisioned. Every stage of the urban renewal process was filled with conflict. Optimistic timelines stretched for years. There were massive cost overruns. Land and building owners fought acquisition of their land in lengthy and costly eminent domain lawsuits. Neighborhood residents fought displacement. On the right, neoliberal critics like Martin Anderson. attacked urban renewal as a heavy handed, wrong-headed, incompetently run, socialistic government program. Progressive planners like Charles Abrams and Chester Hartman attacked the program as a pro-business boondoggle that destroyed low-income communities and communities of color. Individual and class action lawsuits proliferated. There were charges of pork barreling and improper contracting where local elites gave inflated contracts to perform redevelopment tasks to their friends and self-serving local businesspeople used redevelopment to help their own businesses. Cleared land often remained vacant for years. Inflated estimates of revenue from land sales to cover payback of the federal loan were seldom realized. Even when land was successfully cleared and resold, pie-in-the-sky market projections did not materialize. The federal government stretched definitions of "in-kind" contributions so that cities generally paid back most or all of the urban renewal loans with funny money from capital improvement projects they would have funded anyway.

Defenders of urban renewal argue that the federal urban renewal program made areas with obsolete lots and streets usable; permitted central cities to compete with their surrounding suburbs; provided revenue essential for public services; produced some excellent parks and public buildings; and retained or attracted businesses that provided local jobs.

When President Nixon terminated the urban renewal program in 1973, the federal government had spent approximately $ 13 billion dollars on urban renewal. They had funded 2,000 urban renewal projects on 1,000 square miles of land. Approximately 120 million square feet of public floor space and 224 million square feet of commercial floor space had been built on renewal land.

The pioneering proponent of modern housing, Catherine Bauer, labor leaders, and other progressives had envisaged urban renewal providing land for low–moderate-income housing. That did not happen. By 1973 urban renewal had demolished some

BOX 12.3 CATHERINE BAUER

Catherine Bauer (1905–1964) is a towering figure in American housing policy. A Vassar College-educated woman, she became a dominant voice in male-dominated intellectual circles in Europe and America (Oberlander & Newbrun, 1999).

By the time she was 32, Bauer had become an influential member of two of the most important urban planning movements in Europe and America—the modernist movement and the regional planning movement that was led by the Regional Plan Association of America. She had written the planning classic *Modern Housing* (1934), was leader of the American labor movement's advocacy for government-assisted low-cost housing, and was the originator and helped draft the 1937 Housing Act that created the U.S. public housing program.

After graduating from Vassar in 1926 at age 21, Bauer traveled to Paris as a freelance journalist and quickly began working with Le Corbusier and the small circle of avant-garde European modernist architects and planners that was later to dominate European architecture and planning theory and practice in the 1930s, 1940s, and beyond.

Traveling throughout Europe, Bauer saw large, modern, government-supported housing developments for the working class such as the Bauhaus-inspired Römerstadt in Frankfurt, Germany and a large modernist housing complex named Karl-Marx-Hof built by Vienna's Marxist government to replace working-class housing that had been destroyed during World War I. During the Weimar Republic, beginning in 1919 after the end of World War II, and ending after 1933, when Adolf Hitler became the Chancellor of Germany, Berlin, Frankfurt, and other German cities had socialist governments. They owned much of the land, and by the mid-1930s had built more than 1.5 million modern dwelling units in multi-family housing projects that also contained stores, recreational facilities, and other uses. A million of the German modernist projects provided low and moderate-income housing occupied by factory workers and other working-class households. Bauer was impressed with public housing being built as an employment program by workers in Kassel, Germany who would live in them after they were completed. She realized that a mass housing program was possible even during depression times. She recognized the political importance German and Austrian labor unions had in mass social housing programs

Bauer became convinced that housing should be treated as a public utility and that the U.S. government should subsidize projects in the United States along the lines Le Corbusier and the European modernists proposed, and which were being built in England, the Netherlands, and the Scandinavian countries as well as Germany.

Back in New York, Bauer immediately fell in with the small anti-establishment group of regional planning intellectuals named the Regional Plan Association of America (RPAA) headed by Lewis Mumford and Clarence Stein. Mumford expanded Bauer's understanding of Ebenezer Howard's garden cities and Patrick Geddes's regional planning ideas.

In 1934 Bauer completed her masterpiece titled *Modern Housing*. In it she described the failure of the private market in the United States to provide decent affordable housing for the working class, the impressive strides European countries had made in building modern state-subsidized housing, and a vision for a modern housing program for America.

Bauer's timing was just right. What would have been dismissed as un-American or ignored as just an academic fantasy resonated during the Great Depression. American labor unions saw the crisis as an opportunity to push for new federal housing programs and progressive politicians in Washington were desperate for bold, well-thought-out new policy prescriptions. Bauer swept into this maelstrom at age 29 as the improbable Executive Secretary of the Labor Housing Conference—a housing initiative by Pennsylvania labor organizations. She toured union halls and helped organize almost all-male working-class union members. At the same time she argued the case for modern housing as described in *Modern Housing* to politicians and academics. Bauer played a major role in crafting the 1937 Housing Act which created the U.S. Low Rent Public Housing program. The Act was passed over the furious opposition of the U.S. Chamber of Commerce, National Association of Real Estate Boards, and U.S. Savings and Loan League, only after Roosevelt convinced Bauer to compromise with more conservative House and Senate sponsors of the legislation. The public housing program created by the 1937 Act reflects many of Bauer's ideas, but on a smaller scale than she hoped, and with fewer amenities. It established the modern role of the federal government in urban programs.

In 1940 Bauer married architect William Wurster, who became the founding Dean of the University of California, Berkeley's College of Environmental Design. After she was married, she sometimes went under the name of Catherine Bauer Wurster. She became the first female professor at the University of California, Berkeley. She taught courses about cities and housing—initially in the Department of Architecture and later in Berkeley's Department of City and Regional Planning.

American housing legislation never came close to achieving what Bauer had hoped it would. Federal affordable housing never received funding on the scale of European public housing projects. By 1957 Bauer described public housing as caught in a "dreary deadlock". Nonetheless, Bauer's progressive, humane, activist vision has had a profound and positive impact on American urban planning and housing policy.

Robert Weaver (Box 15.1 in Chapter 15)—the first Secretary of the U.S. Department of Housing and Urban Development (HUD), and a lifelong friend of Bauer—commissioned a bronze sculpture of Bauer which is just inside the entrance to the Department of Housing and Urban Development (HUD) in Washington, D.C. A second identical statue is at the entrance to the University of California, Berkeley's College of Environmental Design library. In both Bauer, depicted in mid-career, leans slightly forward, resolute, looking far into the future.

600,000 units housing approximately two million people. Only 250,000 new housing units had been built on project land. Most of the new housing units were for households with much higher incomes than the displacees. Many of the displacees were Black. Large numbers of Puerto Ricans were displaced by urban renewal projects in New York City. New residents of housing built in redevelopment areas were disproportionately White and had much higher incomes than the displacees. Displacees were rarely satisfied with their replacement housing. Studies found that the units they moved to were often of better physical quality, but smaller and much more expensive per square foot. Many were located on the fringe of urban renewal projects that were later expanded so that some households were displaced multiple times. Bauer had envisioned redevelopment projects producing entire working-class communities similar to ones she saw in Europe in the 1920s and 1930s with workplaces, stores, and public building. That did not happen. Projects completed by the federal urban renewal program usually served a limited purpose such as providing land for new business development.

HISTORIC PRESERVATION PLANNING

Preservation of tangible and intangible cultural heritage is an important aspect of city and regional planning. According to the United Nations Educational, Scientific, and Cultural Organization (UNESCO), "tangible cultural heritage" refers to physical artifacts produced, maintained, and transmitted intergenerationally in a society. In addition to built heritage such as buildings and monuments, it includes artistic creations, and other physical or tangible products of human creativity that are invested with cultural significance in a society. Historic preservation also involves preserving "intangible cultural heritage" such as music, dance, folklore, oral traditions, customs, beliefs, knowledge, and language.

Historic preservation initially focused on saving particular buildings—especially ones that were associated with patriotic figures. Later, historic districts with multiple historic buildings and sites—such as the early industrial districts in Paterson, New Jersey and Lowell, Massachusetts—were established to illustrate important periods in American history. Still more recently patriotism and a desire to preserve period buildings merged with romantic tradition, science (particularly archeology), and economic motivations—tourism and economic development.

Buildings and artifacts may be simply saved from destruction. Minor repairs and refurbishing may protect and restore deteriorating structures. Some buildings may be moved. Historic buildings and sites are often clustered in districts. The Vieux Carré (Old Quarter) in New Orleans; the historic core of Savannah, Georgia; Deerfield, Massachusetts; Galena, Ohio; and Williamsburg, Virginia are rich historical sites where almost all the buildings are several centuries old. Sometimes parts, or even entire sites, are rebuilt as copies of the original. There are museum villages in the United States such as Old Sturbridge Village near Boston which shows what an early 19th- century New England town was like. Many cities have walking tours of historic districts and architecturally significant buildings like Boston's Freedom, Black Heritage, and Women's history trails and Chicago's tour of historic downtown Chicago architecture.

Architectural historians play a particularly important role in historic preservation planning as they are educated to understand the historic significance of buildings and districts and how they were built. Box 12.4 describes historic preservation planning for Pike Place Market in Seattle, Washington—a very successful effort to preserve a historic market area to serve needs of Seattle residents, a variety of communities that exist in the area, and to create a tourist destination to bring revenue to the city.

BOX 12.4 PIKE PLACE MARKET (SEATTLE, WASHINGTON)

Pike Place Market is unique in the extent to which a historic market area has been preserved and re-purposed to retain historic architectural features, upgrade essential building components, serve neighborhood residents, generate economic opportunity for family businesses, and serve the city population as well as tourists. A combination of a clear vision, political savvy, economic strategy, and good design made it possible to preserve Pike Place Market.

Pike Place Market climbs a steep hillside near the Seattle, Washington waterfront. It began in 1907 as a populist protest against a wholesaler's cartel that kept food prices high. The local government set aside vacant land at the site of the present market where producers could sell directly to consumers, cutting out the middlemen and lowering food prices. This proved a great success. Soon entrepreneurs built a covered shed for the rainy season—extensive in Seattle! Later the area was paved and permanent restaurants, butcher shops, a creamery, and other stores were constructed. By 1917 many of the market buildings that still exist were complete. The Japanese–American internment during World War II crippled the market because many of the original tenants and vendors were Japanese–Americans. Post-war suburbanization and the impact of trucking, refrigeration, and supermarkets further threatened the market. As early as 1950 there were plans to demolish it and replace it with a parking garage. In

Figure 12.5 Pike Place Market (Seattle, Washington, 2019).

the 1950s and 1960s physical deterioration, traffic congestion, parking shortages, low tax revenues, and social problems continually threatened the market's existence.

Victor Steinbrueck, a University of Washington architecture professor, organized a volunteer organization named the Friends of the Market in 1964 and led a grassroots effort to save the market. The group succeeded in getting the Washington state legislature to designate the market and surrounding area a National Register Historic District.

Eventually Seattle agreed to pursue a radically different approach—to preserve and renovate the area. They incorporated this new vision in a 1963 plan for Seattle's downtown, and obtained a million dollars in federal urban renewal funds to preserve and improve the market.

In 1971, the Friends of the Market won a referendum to establish a 7+-acre historic district supervised by a newly created Market Historical Commission for the preservation, restoration and improvement of Pike Place Market buildings and the continuance of uses deemed to have architectural, cultural, economic, and historical value. Individuals and groups with different approaches banded together to form the Market Foundation in 1982. Merchants, preservationists, downtown interests, farmers, nonprofit social service agencies, craftspeople and city officials (many of whom had tried to reduce or get rid of the market) finally came to terms. The result has been an economically viable market that has retained as many historic buildings as possible.

Bringing the old nine-story wood-frame central market building up to building code standards required many changes including a new concrete frame for earthquake safety, construction of elevators and exit stairs, a sprinkler system, and street redesign. The concept of making Pike Place Market meet various needs of neighborhood and city residents as well as tourists is different from the concept of festival markets like Harborplace in Baltimore and South Street Seaport in New York designed to maximize revenue and primarily to serve tourists and wealthy visitors.

Design played a large role in the Pike Place restoration. Many different architects and designers were included to avoid uniformity. The old "rabbit warren" interior was retained, challenging newcomers to find what they are looking for but adding to the charm of the market. Wood has been retained, brick restored, simple old arches and cornices, and "market green" walls exposed.

The rent structure makes it possible for small farmers to make a living wage. Much of the produce is sold by the growers themselves. There are no chain stores. The market works to assure that there will be fresh produce affordable to low- and moderate-income residents despite the fact that the entire market could have much higher-priced specialty foods as is the case with some festival markets. An Indochinese food project supports Indochinese immigrants who raise specialty Asian produce and market it. Tables for small craftspeople enliven the market and provide craftspeople and artists a modest living. There is cheap rent for a bread shop and used goods store. Pike Place Market won a Rudy Bruner award for design excellence in 1987.

In addition to shopping and eating, locals and tourists can drink coffee at the original Starbucks coffee shop, see workers in the fish market toss 3-foot salmon from boats to stores, watch jugglers and flame throwers, listen to Howlin' Hobbit play retro-jazz on his ukulele, and get herbal medicine and advice from the Tenzing Momo ("Divine Dumpling") Tibetan herbal apothecary. Rachel, the market's life-sized bronze piggy bank generates $6,000–$9,000 a year in donations for Market Foundation social service projects.

The Pike Place Market Foundation has been able to provide some affordable housing. In the urban renewal area, new or renovated buildings provide about 450 subsidized low-income units.

Pike Place is close to Seattle's historic skid row (named because logs were skidded down the hill where the market is located). There is a substantial homeless population in the area, including runaway youth and people suffering from drug and alcohol addiction. Rather than allowing market forces to push these populations out, the local government, Market Foundation, and private charities use some proceeds from the market to help meet their needs.

Other cities can learn from Seattle's preservation of Pike Place Market. Its goals include preserving a diverse social ecology, as well as buildings that impart a sense of the city's history. The market is economically viable but pursues many objectives other than maximizing profits or municipal revenue. It provides fresh, healthy, reasonably priced food for low- and moderate-income city residents as well as high-end food for wealthier residents and tourists. The historic district seeks to provide employment for low- and moderate-income family farmers (including immigrants) and craftspeople as well as more established businesses. It seeks to provide some affordable housing and pursues policies to protect very low-income neighborhood residents, including "undesirables" such as homeless people with drug and alcohol addiction. Because of—not in spite of—this remarkable vision Pike Place Market is an enormously successful economic development project. In 2014 *Forbes* magazine listed it as the 33rd most-visited tourist destination in the world with 10 million annual visitors—more than the Eiffel Tower, Great Pyramid, or Stonehenge! Visitors contribute hundreds of millions of dollars a year to Seattle's economy.

Most city planning departments lack funding to include even one full-time historic preservation planner. One or more planning department staff may be assigned to work on historic preservation planning part-time. A staff member with a degree or particular interest in history is a natural choice for this role. Some planners work or volunteer for public, nonprofit, and private historic preservation organizations.

There is growing recognition of the importance of including the tangible and intangible cultural contribution of diverse racial, ethnic and religious groups, women and in a few cases LGBTQ communities.

While expertise can provide clarity about candidates for historic preservation, agreeing that something is sufficiently historically significant to merit special attention and treatment is a subjective and normative planning decision. Some individual buildings such as Thomas Jefferson's home are easy choices because of their historic importance or outstanding building quality.[11] Other buildings, districts, artifacts, and intangible heritage that are less significant or less architecturally outstanding are less clear.[12] Cultural historian John Brinkerhoff (J.B.) Jackson—a great student of the American landscape— forcefully argued for the preservation of representative examples of vernacular architecture—created without professional architects—to remind succeeding generations of folk traditions.

Main streets of smaller cities and towns may be good candidates for designation as historic districts. The National Trust for Historic Preservation—a fund held in trust by the federal government to pay for historic preservation—oversees a Main Street America program that provides support to help small towns, mid-sized communities, and urban commercial districts revitalize historic main streets, downtowns, and commercial districts. In 2015 there were more than 1,500 Main Street programs in the United States.

Once there is a consensus that a building or district qualifies as historic, an important step in historic preservation is listing it is on a register of historic places. The National Register of Historic Places lists districts, sites, buildings, structures, and objects that are deemed significant on a national, state, or local level in American history, architecture, archeology, engineering, or culture. State and local registers are similar inventories at the state level. Once a property is listed it gets a certain degree of protection, such as special review by the planning commission or a landmark preservation board before it can be altered or demolished.

The U.S. National Historic Preservation Act of 1966 is the principal federal law for historic preservation planning. The federal government provides policy direction and funding. States must pass legislation authorizing federal historic preservation funds to be spent in the state before projects can be funded by the act. Local governments carry out historic preservation projects. To receive the benefits of the act, states must have a State Historic Preservation Office (SHPO) to oversee the state program. SHPOs develop the state's rules for certifying local governments to do historic preservation planning and oversee historic preservation projects. A certified local government (CLG)—certified by the state—develops a preservation plan. Approved sites are then eligible to apply for federal matching grants for surveys, planning, property acquisition, and other preservation activities consistent with the plan. They may be eligible for historic preservation tax credits administered by the U.S. Department of the Interior's National Parks Service. Historic preservation tax credits allow owners of historic buildings to reduce their federal income tax liability. Being on the federal or a state list as a historic building may also help sites receive state or local funding and private contributions. Owners of listed properties are regulated and cannot alter their buildings in ways that change their historic character. Some property owners do not want their properties listed because they consider the disadvantage of regulation to outweigh the prestige and other advantages of listing.

SUMMARY

The demographics, economy, spatial structure, transportation technology, housing, and environment of the United States today are vastly different from what they were in 1933. The U.S. population has nearly tripled and the urban population has nearly quadrupled. The number of cars, trucks and other motorized vehicles has grown ten-fold. Most of the existing U.S. built environment has been constructed since 1933.

From a predominantly agricultural and industrial country in 1933, U.S. cities have become the world's leading post-industrial and informational cities. America's land, water, plants, animals, and natural resources have been badly depleted and damaged in the process.

Since 1933, in the United States there has been a population shift from the frostbelt to the sunbelt; rapid suburban growth; the economic decline of cities in the frost- and rust belts and economic growth of cities in the sunbelt; growing racial and income disparity between core cities and suburbs; the rise of edge cities and boomburgs; and a back to the city movement.

The number of accredited North American city and regional planning programs has increased ten-fold since 1933. Instead of faculty who were almost all architects, planning professors now have PhDs from planning programs and many social science and public policy disciplines. Still, few planning faculty have degrees in the natural sciences. Neither the Planning Accreditation Board (PAB) nor the Association of Collegiate Schools of Planning (ACSP) existed in 1933. Now the PAB sets standards for planning education and ACSP provides a network that keeps planning faculty, students, and practitioners in touch with each other and aware of emerging best practices.

The New Deal fundamentally altered federal–state–local relations. As a result, the federal government provides policy guidance and funding, but states largely define how urban planning and programs are to be developed and implemented. States in turn delegate responsibility for most planning and program implementation to cities and counties.

Except for the ten-year period from 1933 to 1943 when the National Resources Planning Board existed, there has been no formal national sectoral or spatial planning in the United States. Congress terminated the NRPB and specified that there should be no national planning in the future.

The Tennessee Valley Authority, federal dam construction projects, and the Appalachian Regional Commission (ARC) illustrate the possibility and limitations of large-scale regional planning in the United States. The results were impressive but mixed and have not been replicated since the ARC was created in 1965.

Since 1974, T.J. Kent's ideas about the urban general plan as a bottom-up, practical, political document have increasingly replaced Edward Basset and the 1926 Standard State Planning Enabling Act (SSPEA)'s conception of the master plan as a top-down plan for use by an independent planning commission.

In 1933 few planners had any scientific knowledge of, or paid much attention, to the relationship between the built and natural environment. The rise of environmental consciousness and Ian McHarg's principles of design with nature revolutionized environmental planning starting in the early 1970s. Initially, environmental planners' main environmental concerns were with air and water pollution and depletion of non-renewable resources. They now focus increasingly on responding to global climate change and clean energy policy.

Innovations in information technology now widely used in city and regional planning did not exist in 1933. GIS, CAD, Illustration and modeling software have revolutionized planning and urban design practice during the last half century. Big data and the new urban analytics are even more recent and promise more scientific planning in the future.

The number of practicing planners in the United States has grown fifty-fold since 1933. Nearly half of U.S. planners are now women. People of color are still underrepresented among planning students and in the planning profession.

We live in an extraordinary time. Cities have changed more since 1933 than all of prior human history. The future is rich in opportunity and rife with danger. There has never been a greater need for professional, evidence-driven city and regional planning. City and regional planners can be inspired and take pride in how rapidly their new profession has grown and matured. There have been many mistakes and plenty of room for improvement, but the recent history of city and regional planning is cause for optimism that the profession will grow, flourish, and continue to improve in the future. It is badly needed.

CONCEPTS

Balloon Payment Mortgage
Below Market Interest Rate (BMIR) Housing
Benign Neglect
Cabrini –Green Public Housing Project
Categorical Grant
Certified Local Government
Demand-Side Housing Subsidy
Fair Deal
Fair Market Rent (FMR)
Federal Housing Administration (FHA)
Frostbelt
Gentrification
Great Society
Highway Trust Fund
Historic District
Historic Preservation Tax Credit
Housing Voucher
National Defense Housing Act (Lanham Act)
National Interstate and Defense Highways Act
National Trust for Historic Preservation
New Deal
New Federalism
New Frontier
Pruitt–Igoe Public Housing Project
Public Housing
Public Housing Authority (PHA)
Public Works Administration (PWA)
Rustbelt
Section 221(d)(3) Housing
Section 236 BMIR Housing Program
Section 515 Rural Housing Program
Section 8 Certificate
Self-Amortizing Mortgage
State Historic Preservation Office
Sunbelt
Supply-Side Housing Subsidy
U.S. Housing Act of 1937
U.S. League of Cities
United States v. Certain Lands In City of Louisville
War on Poverty
Workable Program for Community Improvement
Works Progress Administration

PEOPLE

Catherine Bauer
Franklin Roosevelt
Robert Weaver

NOTES

1   In 1930 the U.S. Bureau of the Census estimated the population of the United States to be 125 million people (U.S. Census, 1933). Seventy-one million—57%—were classified as urban (ibid). Today the U.S. population is 329 million, of which 266 million—(81%)—are classified as urban (U.S. Census, 2020).

2   There were 23 million automobiles in the United States in 1933, 40 million in 1950, 61 million in 1960, and 89 million in 1970. Today there are about 130 million household motor vehicles including sports utility vehicles (SUVs) and light trucks.

3   The American City Planning Institute (ACPI) was created at the ninth national conference on city planning in Kansas City in 1917. Local planning commissioners and planning directors created the American Society of Planning Officials (ASPO) in 1934. The ACPI was renamed the American Institute of Planners (AIP) in 1939. In 1978 AIP and ASPO were consolidated into the American Planning Association (APA).

4   *JAPA* was started in 1935 as *The Planner's Journal*. It was renamed in 1971. ACSP started the *Journal of Planning Education and Research* (JPER) in 1981.

5   *U.S. vs Louisville* involved a small federal housing program run by the Federal Emergency Relief Administration (FERA). In 1935 the U.S. circuit court of appeals for the 6th circuit upheld the constitutionality of FERA's power to take land by eminent domain (*U.S. vs Louisville*). Roosevelt feared that on appeal the conservative U.S. Supreme Court would reverse the decision and invalidate the entire Public Works Administration (PWA)—a much larger public works agency that was fundamental for the New Deal. To avoid that result he ordered FERA and the PWA to stop taking land by eminent domain. The case became moot, so the U.S. Supreme Court did not decide the constitutionality of direct federal taking of local land by eminent domain. Today, as a result of the Louisville case it is almost always states or local governments—not the federal government itself—that take land by eminent domain even if the taking is for federally funded projects. Local governments can only take land by eminent domain after states pass enabling legislation.

6   By 1970 almost all of Cabrini–Green's 20,000 legal tenants were Black single-parent households (Vale, 2007: 233). An estimated 6,000 unregistered tenants lived illegally in Cabrini–Green, almost all young unemployed adult males (ibid: 246). Drugs, robbery, and violent crime proliferated. Galleries

designed as an attractive alternative to hallways were wrecked, elevators were vandalized, tenants feared to use stairwells where they could be mugged. Units and grounds deteriorated. Efforts to rehabilitate Cabrini–Green units failed.

7 Skip-stop elevators stopped only at the first, fourth, seventh, and tenth floors (Von Hoffman, 2000). Tenants on other floors had to walk up or down stairwells where they could easily be assaulted. The Pruitt–Igoe project was never fully occupied. It soon became plagued with illegal drugs and violent crime. Public spaces were routinely vandalized, and maintenance became very expensive. Positive features of the project are described in Unicorn Stencil Films' *The Pruitt–Igoe Myth* (Friedrichs, 2011) which argues the project's problems were largely a result of larger economic forces—particularly the decline of the St. Louis economy. It includes interviews with tenants who appreciated new functional housing units and worked hard to keep the project viable.

8 In 1969 the federal district court for the Northern District of Illinois held that the CHA's racially motivated site selection and tenant assignment policies violated the equal protection clause of the fourteenth amendment of the U.S. Constitution which forbids states from making or enforcing any law that denies any person within its jurisdiction the equal protection of the laws. The court held that tenants have the right to have sites selected and to be assigned to units without regard to the racial composition of either the surrounding neighborhood or of the projects themselves.

9 Most Section 221(d)(3) mortgages were originated by private lenders or state housing finance agencies (HFAs) with a fixed low interest rate and Federal Housing Administration (FHA) mortgage insurance. The originators usually sold them to the Federal National Mortgage Association (FNMA). Some 221(d)(3) mortgages had higher interest rates, but HUD reimbursed owners for the costs of debt service exceeding a fixed 3%. Developer-owners had to agree to limit the dividend they get for a specified period of time—typically either 20 or 40 years. BMIR mortgages reduced financing costs substantially. For example, if the market interest rate is 6.5%, a 3% interest rate section BMIR loan would save 3.5% of the interest a borrower must pay each month. This would allow the owner to earn a limited dividend of 6% and make a 27% reduction in tenants' rent possible for 20 years (Aaron, 1972: 129). In 1968 the Government National Mortgage Association (GNMA) was created to purchase high-risk and troubled federally insured mortgages.

10 Congress appropriated $40 million for the Section 515 program annually from 2018 through 2020—less than half the amount appropriated for the program in the early 2000s, and a fraction of the $885 million average annual appropriation during the program's peak years from 1979 to 1985.

11 Important historic buildings in the United States include Independence Hall in Philadelphia where the Declaration of Independence was drafted and announced, George Washington's home Mount Vernon, the Spanish governor's palace in Santa Fe, New Mexico, and Boston's Old North Church where lanterns in the church steeple signaled Paul Revere from which direction British troops were beginning to march towards the outlying communities of Lexington and Concord at the beginning of the Revolutionary War—"one if by land; two if by sea".

12 The first McDonald's restaurant building (1937), Alcatraz Prison (1934–1963), the garage where Steve Jobs and Steve Wozniak assembled Apple 1 computers (1976), and the last remaining Blockbuster Video store (now available for rent by Airbnb) have all been preserved.

SUGGESTIONS FOR FURTHER LEARNING

U.S. Urban History: Howard Chudakoff, Judith Smith, & Peter Baldwin, *The evolution of American urban society*, 8th ed (2014). Raymond Mohl & Roger Biles, *The making of urban America*, 3rd ed (2012). Charles Glaab & Andrew Brown, *A history of urban America*, 3rd ed (1983). Steven Corey & Lisa Boehm, *The American urban reader* (2010). John Brinkerhoff Jackson, *A sense of place, a sense of time* (1994). **Histories of Urban Policy since 1933:** Mark Gelfand, *A nation of cities* (1975). Roger Biles, *The fate of cities* (2011). **U.S. Urban Planning History:** Donald Krueckeberg (ed), *Introduction to planning history in the United States* (1982). Mellior Scott, *American city planning since 1890* (1995). **Pike Place Market:** Phillip Langdon, The market as organizer of an urban community (1990). Alice Shorett & Murray Morgan, *The Pike Place Market* (1982). Alice Shorett, *Soul of the city*. **New Deal Planning History:** Marion Clawson, *New Deal planning: The National Resources Planning Board* (1981). **The Sunbelt and the Frostbelt:** Janet Pack, *Sunbelt / frostbelt* (2015). **History of U.S. Suburbs:** Kenneth Jackson, *The crabgrass frontier* (1985). Becky Nicolaides & Andrew Wiese (eds), *The suburb reader*, 2nd ed (2016). Herbert Gans, *The Levittowners* (1967). **U.S. Environmental History:** William Cronin, *Nature's metropolis* (1997). **U.S. Black Urban History:** W.E.B. DuBois, *The Philadelphia Negro* (1899), St. Clair Drake & Horace Cayton, *Black metropolis* (1933). Nicholas LeMann, *The promised land* (1991). Richard Rothstein, *The color of law* (2017). **The Federal Public Housing Program:** John Bauman, Roger Biles, & Kristin Sylvain, *Tenements to the Taylor Homes* (2000). Lawrence Vale, *From the puritans to the projects* (2007). Edward Goetz, *New Deal ruins* (2013). Alex Polikoff, *Waiting for Gautreaux* (2005). Chad Freidrichs, *The Pruitt–Igoe myth* [video] (2011). Alexander Van Hoffman, *A study in contradictions: The origins and legacy of the housing act of 1949*. Alexander Van Hoffman, Why they built Pruitt–Igoe (2000). **Other Legacy Federal**

Housing Programs: Alex Schwartz, *Housing Policy in the United States*, 4th ed (2021). **The Federal Urban Renewal Program:** James Q. Wilson, *Urban renewal: The record and the controversy* (1966). Martin Anderson, *The federal bulldozer* (1964). June Thomas, *Redevelopment and race* (1987). Charles Abrams, *The city is the frontier* (1966). **The War on Poverty:** Sar Levitan, *The Great Society's poor law* (1969). **Progressive Planning in the 1960s:** June Thomas, *Socially responsible practice* (2019). Norman Krumholz, A retrospective view of equity planning (1982), *Making equity planning work* (1990), *Reinventing cities* (1994), and Advocacy planning (1994). **The Model Cities Program Community Development Block Grant Programs:** Bernard Frieden & Marshall Kaplan, *The politics of neglect* (1997). **Gentrification and Displacement:** Karen Chapple, Gentrification, displacement, and the role of public investment (2017). **Historic Preservation:** U.S. National Historic Preservation Act (1966). Kevin Lynch, *What time is this place?* (1972). Andrew Hurley, *Beyond preservation* (2010). John Brinkerhoff Jackson, *The necessity of ruins* (1980). Max Page, *Why preservation matters* (2016). Thompson Mayes, *Why old places matter* (2018). Hayden Swanke, *Historic preservation* (2001). Main Street America [website] (2021). National register of historic places [website] (2021). **Journals:** *Journal of Planning History. Urban History.*

CHAPTER 13

Environmental Planning

INTRODUCTION

The speed with which the environmental movement arose and the breadth of its appeal are unprecedented. In 1969, a 26-year-old student named Denis Hayes dropped out of Harvard's Kennedy School of Government to organize an event called Earth Day. A year later, 20 million people worldwide participated in the first Earth Day—celebrating planet earth and protesting how humans were abusing it. Hayes still chairs the Earth Day Network. A billion people participated in Earth Day 2019.

With the rise of environmental consciousness, environmental planning has developed rapidly. The U.S. National Environmental Policy Act (NEPA) and amendments greatly strengthening the federal Clean Air Act were passed the same year as the first Earth Day. These were followed by new programs at every level of government to protect air and water quality, save endangered plant and animal species, better manage public land, increase wilderness areas, safely dispose of household and toxic waste, clean up toxic sites, and protect the environment in other ways.

Environmental planning is now taught in a variety of academic departments, and is a well-developed planning specialization area within city and regional planning. It is a planning specialization recognized by the Planning Accreditation Board—the organization that accredits city and regional planning programs in the United States and currently one program (The University of British Columbia) in Canada.

There has been plenty of pushback, many failures, and widespread opposition to environmental plans and policies that impinge on unlimited private property rights and cost private and public landowners and goverments money. Population growth; urbanization; a massive increase in oil, gas, and coal extraction and consumption; more vehicle miles driven; urban sprawl; and practices that disregard science continue to stress the environment. Low-income communities and communities of color face the worst environmental problems. Global climate change poses an imminent existential threat.

Environmental planning and regulation is not for the faint of heart. However, it is essential to keep earth livable, and pass on to our children land, air, water, habitat, and species that exist today and keep existing human settlements good places to live.

This chapter begins by describing land use-, air quality-, and water-related planning. Sections describe planning to protect endangered and threatened plant and animal species and the habitat necessary for them to survive.

The National Environmental Policy Act (NEPA) is the fundamental federal environmental law. Sections describe environmental impact analysis based on NEPA and similar state "little NEPAs".

Sustainable urban development, design with nature, biophilic design, and other theoretical approaches to environmental planning guide environmental planning practice. Sections discuss this body of theory. The chapter includes a biography of Ian McHarg—a landscape architect who developed theory about design with nature.

The U.S. Green Building Council has promulgated "Leadership in Energy and Environmental Design" (LEED) standards. A section describes how LEED standards help architects and planners create more energy efficient and environment-friendly buildings and neighborhoods.

Sections of this chapter address public land and natural resources planning and management, waste management, and cleanup of brownfields and toxic sites.

The concluding sections address environmental justice and coastal zone planning and management.

LAND

Environmental planning is closely related to land use planning. Land use plans should consider the impact of land use on the environment, including air and water quality. Natural hazards, soil compaction, the hydrology of surface and subsurface water, and toxic contamination of soil are major land use planning concerns. Recently landscape urbanism—the theory of how to plan and manage landscapes in urban areas in harmony with the natural environment—has become an important field within landscape architecture. Landscape architects, planners, and urban designers have developed the theory and practice of design with nature and eco-design to build sustainably in harmony with nature. Physical geographers and civil engineers bring special tools, concepts, and expertise from their respective academic disciplines and professional fields to land use and environmental planning.

Historically the United States and other countries exploited forests, mineral deposits, wildlife, and other natural resources—clear-cutting old-growth forests; mining coal, iron ore, gold, silver, copper, and other minerals in ways that ruined landscapes; and drilling for oil and natural gas with little regard for the impact of the drilling operations on land, air, water, and human settlements. Many species of mammals and fish were decimated. An important planning task now is to revisit scenes of environmental destruction to make them safe and restore them to the extent possible.

Much of the undeveloped land in metropolitan areas in the United States is in unincorporated areas of counties. Massive and rapid urbanization is having an enormous impact on the natural environment there. Accordingly, county planners play an important role in protecting the natural environment on county land. Rural planning can remediate past damage done by extracting coal, oil, and natural gas, harvesting timber, failing to control pollution from fertilizer and animal waste, diverting rivers and streams, and other destructive practices. It can mitigate future damage of this kind.

Shifting soil—particularly soil subsidence from the weight of buildings and swelling as a result of heat or water—is the most widespread and costliest geological hazard in the United States. A 3% increase in soil volume can damage building foundations. Some soils swell by as much as 50%. Mining coal, gravel, and other substances, pumping oil and natural gas, fracking—hydraulic fracturing of oil shale to release oil and gas by injecting water, sand, and chemicals under high pressure—and extracting groundwater can all lead to soil subsidence that may damage buildings or other parts of the built and natural environment. Soil subsidence is particularly problematic in low-lying coastal cities. Land is sinking below sea level in parts of Miami, New York, Houston, New Orleans, and other U.S. cities because the combined weight of so many more buildings is compacting soil, cities are pumping water out of underground aquifers, and because of rising sea levels. Venice, Tokyo, Manila, Bangkok, Lagos, Dhaka, and other cities worldwide are also sinking at alarming rates.

Geological hazards such as earthquakes, volcanos, landslides, avalanches, flooding, and mudflows present risks to human life and property. City and regional planners work with physical geographers, geologists, and other experts to understand and map these geological hazards and protect people and property on them in site, neighborhood, city, and regional plans.

Geological events are probabilistic. The precise areas at risk and the extent of risk are often uncertain. However, the likelihood of damage from geological phenomena can be scientifically assessed and greatly reduced by implementation tools. Zoning laws can prohibit construction of schools, hospitals, housing, commercial buildings, and public utilities on or near earthquake faults; on land prone to landslides; and in other geological hazard zones. Building codes can require building foundations that reduce or eliminate damage from earthquakes, floods, hurricanes, and tornadoes. The U.S. Federal Emergency Management Agency (FEMA) has mapped floodplains. Local governments may prohibit building in high-risk parts of floodplains. Landowners who are permitted to build and choose to build in floodplains may be required to purchase special flood insurance so that they have some economic protection and will be less of a burden on society if their homes are damaged or destroyed.

AIR QUALITY

Air quality is essential to human health and livability. Worldwide the combined effects of outdoor ambient air pollution emitted by industries, households, cars, and trucks and indoor air pollution in homes, workplaces, and stores cause about 7 million premature deaths every year—mostly in low- and middle-income countries. Particulate emissions and other types of air pollution contribute to lung disease—a leading cause of death worldwide. Particulate emissions also harm or kill animals and plants. Release of carbon and other greenhouse gases (GHGs) from oil, coal, and natural gas is the principal cause of anthropogenic—human-caused—climate change described in Chapter 17.

City and regional planners are involved in air quality planning and regulation governed by federal, state, regional, and local clean air laws. The 1963 federal Clean Air Act defines the federal–state–regional clean air planning and management system in the United States. Amendments to the Clean Air Act in 1970 require comprehensive federal and state regulation of both point sources of air pollution, such as factories, and mobile sources of pollution, such as cars, trucks, and motorcycles.

Regulation of factories has reduced air pollution from industry in the United States. However, the enormous recent expansion of industry in developing countries with lower air quality standards has counterbalanced the improvement worldwide.

Federal legislation has led to much more efficient engines for motorized vehicles and less pollution per vehicle mile traveled. However, population growth, increased automobile ownership, and the number of trips and total vehicle miles traveled have all greatly increased, leading to more air pollution from motorized vehicles.

Greater attention to pollution from the time oil is extracted through the refining process and as motorized vehicles are operated is called well-to-wheel analysis. Well-to-wheel analysis and steps to reduce air pollution at every stage in the production and consumption process are making some improvement in reducing air pollution caused by gasoline-powered vehicles.

The United States Environmental Protection Agency (EPA) sets air quality standards and oversees air quality planning. However, plans and programs to reduce air pollution are largely prepared and carried out by state, regional, and local entities.

Regional Air Quality Districts (AQDs) within states oversee the implementation of federal air quality policies and programs. The 1970 Clean Air Act Amendments require the EPA to promulgate National Ambient Air Quality Standards (NAAQS) for carbon dioxide (CO_2), nitrogen dioxide (NO_2), 2.5-milligram particulate matter—tiny particles less than the width of a human hair that can damage human lungs—and other pollutants. Amendments to the Clean Air Act in 1990 addressed acid rain, ozone depletion, and toxic air pollution; established a national permit program for stationary sources; and increased the Environmental Protection

Agency (EPA)'s enforcement authority to regulate air quality.

The Clean Air Act requires states to establish Air Quality Control Regions (AQCRs). These are designated as either (a) attainment regions in which the ambient air quality standards must be met quickly, or (b) nonattainment regions where states are required to submit a plan to reach attainment status somewhat later. The EPA requires states to develop state implementation plans (SIPs) to meet the NAAQ standards. State-level regional air quality boards assist in developing and implementing air quality plans. The EPA continues to strengthen NAAQs and ratchet up air quality standards. Metropolitan planning organizations (MPOs) play a key role in formulating plans to address air pollution from mobile sources.

The EPA has adopted National Emissions Standards for Hazardous Air Pollutants (NESHAPs) and New Source Performance Standards (NSPS) for new and modified stationary sources. The federal government requires New Source Review (NSR) permits for development in areas that meet air quality standards and unclassified areas. The EPA requires a Prevention of Significant Deterioration (PSD) permit for building or making a major modification to a new major source in an attainment area. Building or adding to a major stationary air pollution source in a nonattainment or unclassified area requires a Non-Attainment Area (NAA) permit.

The Clean Air Act prohibits states from adopting air quality standards stronger than the federal standards. A very important exception—implemented in 1978—is for California, which was permitted to develop tougher air quality standards. California continually strengthened its own state Corporate Average Fuel Economy (CAFE) standards—standards that require automakers to meet an average number of miles per gallon for each year's vehicle fleet—beyond federal standards. It has led the United States in fuel economy standards and reduction of air pollution from mobile sources. California has 40 million residents and an economy larger than Germany's. Accordingly, many of the large automobile manufacturers have adopted California's fuel economy standards in order to do business in California. In 2019, the Trump administration revoked California's CAFE exemption. California challenged the Trump administration's authority to do this in court. President Biden reversed Trump's order.

The Clean Air Act has improved overall air quality in the United States, despite population growth, growth in industry, greater car ownership, and many more vehicle miles driven. Automobiles, trucks, and motorcycles have become much more efficient, with greatly reduced emissions from individual vehicles. Some air pollutants—notably atmospheric lead pollution and ground level ozone pollution—have been dramatically reduced. However, greenhouse gas (GHG) emissions from transportation sources have grown and will almost certainly continue to grow for at least a decade.

Cities are heat islands with temperatures higher than surrounding forests and fields. Ordinarily cooler air is above warmer air closer to the surface of the earth. Carbon dioxide (CO_2), sulfur dioxide (SO_2), nitrogen oxide (NO) and other air pollutants are borne up and away as heat rises. When heat inversions occur, warmer air moves above cooler air, trapping air pollution in cooler air below. Heat inversions are common in Los Angeles, Tucson, and cities in valleys like Cincinnati and St. Louis. City and regional planning can reduce heat island and inversion effects. Urban form and density influence the intensity of heat islands more than city size. The amount of air pollutants trapped by buildings lining streets depends significantly on planning and urban design decisions about street width, the height and shapes of buildings, street orientation in relation to wind, and design of individual buildings to produce up and down drafts of air. Residential and other setbacks, and distancing sitting areas from streets prone to high levels of air pollution can reduce health effects from polluted air. Trees absorb and buffer air pollutants, so planting trees that absorb large amounts of air pollutants along streets and around point sources of pollution will reduce air pollution. Parks and plazas can create green oases with clean air in cities.

WATER-RELATED PLANNING

Water is another natural element that provides opportunities and creates challenges in cities and regions. City and regional planners frequently address problems of too little water, too much water, and polluted water. Global climate change is altering earth's oceans, polar ice, glaciers, rivers, and lakes. This is leading to sea-level rise, flooding, desertification, and other challenges described in Chapter 17.

Lack of water is an important city and regional planning issue. Many big cities struggle to keep an adequate supply of water in aquifers and city reservoirs for tap water and other domestic and commercial uses.

Desertification has already occurred on a large scale and threatens to increase large areas that are nearly uninhabitable. Huge amounts of sand and dust may blow hundreds of miles from deserts, causing enormous damage to urban and rural areas. A combination of higher average temperatures and less precipitation is increasing the risk of wildfires in many regions. Australia, Northern California, and Greece experienced more and larger wildfires during the 2020 and 2021 fire seasons than they had ever experienced in the past, with an enormous toll in lost lives, property, habitat, animals, and forest cover.

Flooding is the costliest and most common natural disaster in the United States, claiming lives, inflicting financial losses on households and businesses, and straining the government agencies that provide flood response and relief. City and regional planners and geographers play a major role in mapping and regulating areas susceptible to flooding.

A 100-year flood is a flood that has a 1% probability of occurring in any given year. The National Flood Insurance Act of 1968 requires the Federal Emergency Management Agency to map all 100-year floodplains in the United States. Landowners in floodplains are required to purchase special flood insurance.

Architects and urban designers can design buildings and sites to be less flood-prone or to sustain less damage in the event flooding does occur. Natural drainage systems can absorb, store, and drain floodwater from major storms.

City general plans and other city and regional plans can include hard protect or soft protect solutions to flooding or a mix of both. After Hurricane Katrina planners and policy makers in New Orleans made plans to build and built massive and costly dams, levees, pumping stations, and other flood prevention infrastructure—a hard protect solution to flooding. In contrast, Woodlands, Texas—a new town 19 miles from Dallas—has pursued mostly soft protect solutions to flooding. Woodlands was carefully designed with nature, with input from Ian McHarg's landscape architecture firm—Wallace McHarg Roberts & Todd (WMRT). Woodlands preserved and enhanced ponds and swales that retain and absorb water. Land was graded to direct natural runoff in ways that prevent damage to buildings. Even though it is built on flat land that is prone to flooding, Woodlands' natural water collection and drainage systems have kept Woodlands from sustaining as much damage as Dallas and other cities in the region. However, Woodlands' flood prevention system was not sufficient to prevent water damage from Hurricane Harvey in 2017—a 500-year flood—a flood with a probability of occurring once in 500 years.

Turenscape—one of the largest urban design firms in the world—is designing and building "sponge cities" in China. Sponge cities are designed to absorb floodwater from monsoons and other flooding events using natural features and processes. Sponge cities enhance natural systems to quickly absorb water and prevent flooding. They use soft protect strategies to retain floodwaters in ponds and swales until the floodwaters subside. Sponge cities are described in Chapter 17.

Water pollution is the third major water-related challenge that city and regional planners confront. Pathogenic organisms—bacteria, protozoa, worms, viruses, and fungi are responsible for outbreaks of waterborne disease. Most pathogens enter surface water via human and animal feces. Lead in drinking water flaking off of old lead pipes is extremely dangerous. Runoff containing toxic pollutants from chemicals and fertilizer also contribute to water pollution. Planners can incorporate policies to protect against water-borne disease, eliminate lead water pipes, and minimize or eliminate runoff carrying pollutants in their plans.

The U.S. Clean Water Act (CWA) is the primary federal law governing water pollution. It was enacted in 1948 as the Federal Water Pollution Control Act, and significantly reorganized and expanded in 1972. The amended Clean Water Act is modeled on the Clean Air Act. The Environmental Protection Agency sets water quality standards (WQS) for point and non-point sources that can pollute water. Point sources are at fixed, identifiable locations such as a factory that is discharging chemical waste into a river. Non-point sources of water pollution combine pollutants from a large area, such as fertilizer runoff from agricultural land in rural areas and lawns in urban areas. The Clean Water Act seeks to control pollutants from percolating into underground aquifers as well as contaminating surface water. States develop water quality plans and programs based on the federal standards. Local water districts and local governments implement the plans.

The Clean Water Act requires developers to get permits for significant new developments and modifications of existing developments that might contribute to water pollution under permitting procedures similar to Clean Air Act procedures. The Environmental Protection Agency (EPA) manages a National Pollutant Discharge Elimination System (NPDES) to track permits controlling discharges into water. Regional and local planners use NPDES data in their plans.

Federal legislation to protect safe drinking water—the Safe Drinking Water Act (SDWA)—was passed in 1974. The Act authorizes the EPA to establish and enforce minimum health-related National Primary Drinking Water Regulations (NPDWRs) to protect drinking water. The act also requires the EPA to develop non-binding National Secondary Drinking Water Regulations (NSDWRs) for contaminants that may cause cosmetic effects such as skin or tooth discoloration or aesthetic effects such as taste, odor, or color in drinking water. State governments can be authorized to implement SDWA rules for the EPA.

Storm drainage, flood control, water supply, water conservation, waste disposal, and sewage treatment are all related. Integrated water resource management (IWRM) involves treating them together comprehensively.

HABITAT, PLANTS, AND ANIMALS

Massachusetts Institute of Technology professor of landscape architecture and planning Anne Whiston Spirn calls cities granite gardens composed of many smaller gardens set in a garden world. She argues that: "Nature in the city must be cultivated, like a garden, rather than ignored or subdued" (Spirn, 1984). Cities are teeming with plant and animal life, despite the massive human alteration of habitat and natural communities within them.

Of particular concern are species determined by the federal government to be endangered—near extinction—or threatened species—species determined to be at risk of becoming endangered. The 1973 federal Endangered Species Act uses a top-down approach to protect endangered and threatened species.

Forty-six states have state endangered species acts modeled on the federal Endangered Species Act. They may define endangered and threatened species more broadly than the federal law and may offer additional protections to endangered and threatened species within the state. State agencies, like the New Mexico Department of Game and Fish, are authorized by state law to list endangered and threatened species within the state using their own criteria and protect them using regulations that may be stricter than the federal regulations. Staff of federal and state agencies charged with protecting endangered and threatened species often include city and regional planners as well as biologists and other natural scientists qualified to conduct the necessary research to list and delist species.

The most important feature of the Endangered Species Act is listing—placing a plant or animal species on either a list officially classifying it as endangered or a separate list classifying it as threatened. The U.S. Fish and Wildlife Service is responsible for listing terrestrial plant and animal species on land and in fresh water. The National Marine Fisheries Services is responsible for listing marine plant and animal species living in oceans. If either agency determines that a species is endangered, the agency is required to add it to the official national list of endangered species. As soon as it is on the endangered species list, the species is covered by very important legal protections. If the agency determines that a species is threatened, they must place it on a separate list where it is immediately covered by important, but lesser protections. The agency designated to list the species monitors the status of all endangered and threatened species that they are responsible for. If a threatened species declines to the point that it is endangered, the agency must move it to the endangered species list. If the agency determines that a listed endangered species has sufficiently recovered, they are required to move it to the threatened species list or delist it. If they determine that a species on the threatened species is no longer threatened, they must delist it.

Under the Endangered Species Act, killing or harming an endangered plant or animal is called a taking. (Taking under the Endangered Species Act should not be confused with taking of private land by eminent domain under the fifth amendment of the U.S. Constitution.) After a species is listed as endangered, the ESA forbids taking it, with a few exceptions. Economic hardship may be sufficient to permit a taking, and plant and animal species may be taken if the EPA approves a Habitat Conservation Plan conserving sufficient habitat to assure that the species will survive even if some individual members are taken (killed).

The federal government designates critical habitat essential for survival of each of the endangered species it lists. A special review is required before development can take place in these areas. Altering critical habitat in ways that is likely to kill or injure the species is considered a taking.

Listing and delisting species as endangered or threatened and drawing the boundaries of critical habit are controversial. Large amounts of money can be at stake to save a small number of remaining animals or plants. Lumber companies that stand to lose millions of dollars oppose a ban on cutting redwood trees to prevent taking of spotted owl habitat. Factories that are counting on a dam to provide power to hundreds of thousands of people oppose halting construction because it would threaten a few endangered snail darter fish with extinction.

Listing under the Endangered Species Act is a mixture of science and politics. President George H.W. Bush's administration listed 145 species, Obama's administration listed 71, George W. Bush's 25, and the Trump administration 21. Over furious opposition from environmentalists, the Trump administration issued new rules that would have eliminated virtually all protection of threatened species and otherwise crippled the Endangered Species Act if they had been implemented. However, they were not implemented before Trump left office.

Survival of a species depends on adequate habitat—an environment containing food, shelter, water, nutrients, and everything else a plant or animal needs to survive. Since the 1980s, planners have been involved in preparing Habitat Conservation Plans (HCPs). The idea of a Habitat Conservation Plan is to conserve or expand enough critical habitat for an endangered or threatened species to assure that there is virtual certainty that it will survive—indeed likely increase. A habitat conservation plan may involve destroying some critical habitat and taking (killing) some members of the endangered species contrary to the prohibition in the Endangered Species Act. This was first done experimentally to protect an endangered butterfly that was known to exist only on a part of a mountain near San Francisco.[1] The plan worked and the Endangered Species Act was subsequently amended to allow HCPs as an option. The U.S. Fish and Wildlife Service has subsequently approved over 400 HCPs.

A broader and more recent concept for protecting species by protecting their habitat is to adopt Natural Communities

Conservation Plans (NCCPs). NCCPs can cover multiple species in much larger areas.[2] Only a few NCCPs have been created.

Conservation banking is a U.S. Fish and Wildlife Service (FWS) program that planners may use to protect habitat for endangered and threatened species. Conservation banking is similar to transfer of development rights (TDRs) and carbon cap-and-trade programs. Developers of land whose development could damage or eliminate endangered species habitat may enter into a conservation banking agreement with the FWS. The agreement may grant a conservation easement precluding future development of the property and restricting land uses that would endanger the species. Conservation banking agreements typically require the owner to develop a long-term management plan for the banked land and provide funding for monitoring management of the land. In return, the FWS authorizes landowners to sell a specified number of credits to project proponents seeking mitigation for listed endangered and threatened species. The FWS designates a service area for the conservation bank within which the landowner/bank sponsor may sell credits. The FWS can require developers of other projects that would reduce critical habitat to purchase credits as a condition of development. The property owner gets the proceeds as compensation for partial use of their property.

LAND USE, TRANSPORTATION, AIR QUALITY, INFRASTRUCTURE, AND ENVIRONMENTAL PLANNING LINKAGES

Environmental planning is closely related to land use, transportation, infrastructure and other kinds of planning. Land use plans should consider the impact of land use on the environment, including air quality and water quality.

The "comprehensive" and "coordinated" aspects of metropolitan planning organizations' continuing, comprehensive, and coordinated (3Cs) transportation planning address the impact transportation projects will have on the environment and air quality if they are done properly. Chapter 14 discusses 3Cs planning. Residential zoning, housing and building codes, discussed in chapter 16 should be closely coordinated with environmental planning.

A variety of developments in transportation planning have helped to protect the environment and can be further extended. Incentives for shared mobility such as carpooling and high-occupancy vehicle (HOV) lanes can reduce the number of vehicles on the road. Transit-oriented development promotes density around transit stops and transit corridors, which in turn can reduce the use of automobiles and benefit the environment. More compact city development around transit hubs permits lower-density development and more open space elsewhere. The U.S. Department of Transportation's Corporate Average Fuel Economy (CAFE) standard and California's tougher CAFE standard are pushing auto manufacturers to produce more fuel-efficient cars and trucks and to move more rapidly to replace the existing motorized vehicle fleet with hybrid and zero emissions vehicles that are reducing and can eventually eliminate all air pollution and greenhouse gas emissions from cars, trucks, and other motorized vehicles.

Local capital improvement programs (CIPs), and other infrastructure plans discussed in chapter 16 should be closely coordinated with environmental planning. Local "adequate facilities" ordinances that specify minimum public facilities can contribute to environmental planning. They may require that local capital improvement programs (CIPs) provide adequate storm drain capacity, sewers, reservoirs, water storage facilities, landfills, wastewater treatment facilities, and other infrastructure that help protect the environment.

THE NATIONAL ENVIRONMENTAL PROTECTION ACT (NEPA)

The most pervasive environmental planning activity in the United States is environmental impact analysis pursuant to the 1970 U.S.

National Environmental Policy Act (NEPA). NEPA is a procedural law requiring that an environmental impact statement (EIS) be approved before any federal or federally funded development that will have a significant environmental impact begins. EISs provide a detailed statement of: (i) the environmental impact of a proposed action, (ii) adverse environmental effects which cannot be avoided if the proposal is implemented, (iii) alternatives to the proposed action, (iv) the relationship between local short-term uses of the environment and the maintenance and enhancement of long-term productivity, and (v) irreversible and irretrievable commitments of resources if the proposed action is implemented.

NEPA established the president's Council on Environmental Quality (CEQ) to advise the president on environmental issues. The CEQ promulgates regulations to implement NEPA. Federal agencies like the U.S. Department of Housing and Urban Development and the Department of Transportation develop procedures and standards for how NEPA is to be applied to projects they administer, consistent with CEQ standards. EISs are public documents that must be filed with the CEQ. EISs must accompany reports and recommendations for congressional funding.

NEPA is not a substantive law. It does not *prohibit* development that will damage the environment. Rather, it requires developers to think before they act, fully describe the environmental impacts a project will have, explain alternatives, justify their choices, and put in writing proposals to mitigate (minimize) damaging impacts on the environment as much as feasible. Requiring a clear process, serious analysis, and transparency about the environmental impacts developments will have has greatly reduced negative impacts of development on the environment in the United States. State "little NEPAs"—state equivalents of NEPA—apply review requirements similar to NEPA to state-funded development. About half of the world's 195 countries have legislation modeled on NEPA.

Planners in local planning departments, private environmental consulting firms, and specified government departments and agencies help prepare thousands of federal EISs and their state equivalents under state little NEPAs each year. Some pundits call NEPA "the urban planner's relief act of 1970" because of the enormous demand for professional environmental planning and planners to prepare them that it created.

NEPA applies if a project is funded at least in part by the federal government, whether it is carried out by a federal government entity like the U.S. Army Corps of Engineers, a state agency such as the Colorado Department of Transportation, or a city or county government. It does not apply to projects that receive only state support or purely private development.

NEPA only applies to projects that may have a significant impact on the environment. Policy makers and courts generally consider even small impacts such as loss of a few trees during the development of a small subdivision significant. Some actions are exempt from NEPA—for example where compliance with another environmental law such as the Clean Air Act serves the same purpose. A few actions are categorically excluded. For example, the U.S. Department of Transportation categorically excludes emergency repair of essential rail facilities damaged by a natural disaster from NEPA review. The Council on Environmental Quality permits this because it has determined that essential rail facilities must be repaired as quickly as possible without taking the time to prepare an EIS and since they are repairs of a facility that already existed there is almost no risk of a significant negative environmental impact in rebuilding them.

Much environmental impact analysis is overseen by local planning departments. Some state agencies and some city or county departments and agencies other than planning departments oversee environmental impact analysis. If multiple agencies are involved, one will act as the lead agency. Many EISs are prepared by consultants paid for by the developer.

Consulting firms that specialize in environmental impact assessment develop data and methodologies that can be reused or replicated, and efficient procedures for repeating parts of environmental analyses. They have checklists of possible impacts that different types of projects might cause and can reuse material. For example, a firm that has completed dozens of analyses of impacts on hydrology in a region can cut, paste, update, and modify material on significant hydrological issues and how to mitigate their impact from analyses of hydrological issues they prepared in prior EISs. They will not waste time analyzing impacts that they are sure do not apply. For example, if they know from prior experience that there are no endangered red-legged frogs where a development will take place, they will not spend time analyzing potential impacts on red-legged frogs. Firms that prepare EISs and the planning staff that monitor the EIS as it is prepared usually err on the side of caution. If there is even a remote possibility of an impact, they will generally investigate it. Delay costs money. Developers have learned that it is generally better to spend time and money to be thorough and complete a "bulletproof" EIS that anticipates and describes every environmental impact, than to risk having the draft or final EIS sent back by a planning commission or city council for additional time-consuming and costly studies.

City and regional planners can do all the necessary research to prepare routine EISs. Large, complex, or unusual projects may require input from natural scientists or other experts. An environmental planning firm reviewing a major project may have full-time staff with degrees in biology, climatology, or other natural sciences or a roster of experts they can turn to for specialized analyses.

The first step in NEPA review is to determine if the action is categorically excluded. If the agency concludes that the proposed action is among a small number of actions that are legally excluded, they prepare a categorical exclusion (CatEx) and no EIS is required. If an initial environmental assessment (EA) indicates that the proposed project will not have a significant impact on the environment, they prepare a Finding Of No Significant Impact (FONSI) explaining the basis for their determination and indicating that it is not necessary to prepare an EIS. If the EA shows that the project may have significant environmental impacts, the lead agency will require preparation of an EIS.

EISs must discuss a range of alternatives. Agencies are not supposed to approve a project if there is a feasible alternative with lesser environmental impacts than the proposed project. One alternative is the "no project" alternative.

EISs are the vehicle of choice for anyone or any organization that wants to stop or scale back a proposed development for any reasons, whether or not they are legitimate. Opponents will analyze the EIS looking for significant impacts that were omitted or minimized or if there was any procedural irregularity in preparation of the EIS. If so, they are likely to challenge it before it is finalized. After they have exhausted their administrative remedies, they may challenge the adequacy of the EIS in the courts after it is approved.

EISs move through a draft and final stage. Public parties, outside parties, and other federal agencies are legally entitled to provide input to the EIS as it is being prepared. A draft EIS is released as a public document. Pro- and anti-development individuals, officials, and neighborhood groups may express their views on the draft EIS in private meetings with the planning staff, in writing, and orally at public hearings before the planning commission and city council or county board of supervisors or another department or agency overseeing the EIS.

Once a planning commission or other entity with the authority to approve an EIS has approved a final EIS, it goes to the city council or county board of supervisors for final approval. A final EIS is a revised version of the draft EIS re-written to respond to comments raised during the review process. The planning director and the senior planners involved in preparing the EIS will respond to questions and answer objections by the local elected officials conducting the hearing. Supporters and opponents of the project have the opportunity to provide input at the mandatory public hearing.

In addition to weighing the merits of the EIS, elected officials' own normative values come into play. A commissioner whose electoral base is among environmentalists will likely play to her base by taking a tough pro-environmental stance on an EIS. A developer on the commission will likely be more lenient. Elected officials are reluctant to offend major campaign donors. Decision-makers also consider how voters will judge their EIS decision. NIMEYs—local elected officials facing an election—say "not in my election year" and may not approve a politically controversial project in their election year. Once the local government has approved an EIS, the EIS review process is over, unless an aggrieved party sues.

Project opponents have the right to sue in federal courts for alleged NEPA violations and to sue in state court for alleged little NEPA violations. Only a small percentage of NEPA and little NEPA cases go to court and only a tiny percentage of those that do go to court go to trial. An even smaller percentage reach federal or state appellate courts, which may then write an opinion interpreting the law.[3] In controversial cases, city and regional planners often work with lawyers who specialize in NEPA law. Some attorney-planners, with both planning and law degrees work for city or county attorneys' offices or in private firms that specialize in land use law, environmental law, or both.

The most common type of EIS is a development-specific EIS for a single project. A typical development-specific EIS contains a table of contents, executive summary, description of the project, lists of significant and unavoidable environmental impacts, and descriptions of proposed mitigation measures. It will identify alternatives to the proposed project and the extent to which they will mitigate environmental damage. An EIR for a subdivision or new office building may be 150 to 300 pages long or longer.

A master EIS covers a series of actions for a large development, such as a major revitalization project that will first clear land, build infrastructure, and then develop different areas for industrial, retail, or residential use. A program EIS describes a project that may involve many different developments, such as a 20-year project to upgrade power transmission lines. Projects with cumulative impacts may have a master or program EIS followed by focused or tiered EISs for each phase. A ten-year project to install thousands of small rooftop communications antennae—none of which may be significant alone, but which together will have a significant impact—is an example of cumulative impact from a project.

There may be additions, supplements, or technical corrections to completed EISs. Significant changes in the project or local conditions may require a supplemental EIS. If the nature of a project changes enough, an entirely new EIS may be necessary.

The environmental impact assessment process is expensive. The EIS for even a small project like a twenty-unit subdivision can cost several hundred thousand dollars. The EIS process is time-consuming. It will likely take at least a year to complete an EIS for even a relatively small project.

Legally, an EIS that identifies significant, unmitigated environmental impacts can be approved, with a statement of overriding considerations. Statements of overriding consideration describe economic or social benefits that arguably outweigh the harm to the environment. This is rare. More common is for local governments to approve an EIS that identifies negative environmental impacts, only if it commits to serious mitigation measures that will greatly minimize their effect or even improve the environment. It is not unusual for EISs to include a hundred or more mitigation measures.

As well as checking for completeness and compliance with legal procedures, local elected officials evaluating the sufficiency of an EIS may look to see that it includes timelines, monitoring and reporting plans, and that it identifies who will be responsible to assure compliance. Local governments rarely follow up to see if mitigation measures promised in an EIS were fully met unless serious problems or complaints are brought to their attention.

Despite their lack of substantive standards, NEPA and little NEPAs have greatly reduced negative environmental impacts of development in the United States during the last fifty years. Despite grumbling about the time and cost involved, and continuing attempts to water them down, NEPA and little NEPAs have strong enough bi-partisan support to have survived for fifty years.

LITTLE NEPAS

Sixteen states and four other government entities have enacted "little NEPAs" modeled on NEPA.[4] Little NEPAs extend NEPA-like environmental impact assessment requirements to state development, even if the development involved receives no federal funding and is, therefore, exempt from NEPA. Most of the population in the United States lives in these 20 states, and most of the potentially environment-damaging development occurs within them. Each state's little NEPA varies with regard to which projects must be reviewed and what kind of environmental review is required.

Since counties are political subdivisions of the state, and cities are state municipal corporations, state little NEPAs require essentially the same environmental impact assessments for city- and county-funded projects that they do for state-funded projects. Between NEPAs and little NEPAs, most federal, state, city, and county development in the United States that significantly impacts the environment is now subject to environmental review.

Private development does not require an environmental impact assessment in most states. California's Little NEPA—the California Environmental Quality Act (CEQA)—requires an environmental impact report (EIR)—which is essentially the same as an EIS—for private development that may significantly impact the environment if it is determined to be a "legislative act" similar to decisions made by local elected officials, or a "quasi-judicial" act similar to decision made by a court that require a discretionary government approval.[5] For example if a city is reviewing a proposal for a planned unit development (PUD) and the city council has the discretionary authority to require the PUD to be changed or deny it all altogether, this qualifies as a quasi-judicial act that would be covered by CEQA and would require an EIR. Merely approving a plan to build a new house under a municipal building code that grants the landowner the right to build, so long as he or she complies with the code would not be covered. The local government has no discretion to deny the permit if it complies with the law. The legal term granting a permit like this is a ministerial act.

SUSTAINABLE URBAN DEVELOPMENT

The concept of sustainable development was central to a 1987 report by the United Nations-sponsored World Commission on the Environment and Development. The WCED was chaired by former Norwegian Prime Minister Gro Harlem Brundtland—the only prime minister of a major country to have previously served as an environmental minister. Accordingly, the WCED's report is commonly referred to as the Brundtland Report. The Brundtland Commission defined sustainable development as "development that meets the needs of the present without compromising the ability of future generations to meet their own needs".

City and regional planning professors like Steven Wheeler at the University of California, Davis and Timothy Beatley at the University of Virginia immediately began to apply the concept of sustainable development to urban areas. Sustainable urban development theory and practice are now well developed. Sustainable urban development seeks to meet the needs of present residents of urban areas without compromising the ability of future city residents to meet their own needs. Substitution of renewable for non-renewable resources, recycling, attaining net-zero carbon emissions, controlling sprawl, conserving habitat, protecting aquifers, restoring streams and native plants, and providing infrastructure that is adequate to protect the natural environment are all examples of sustainable urban development.

DESIGN WITH NATURE

Design with nature is an influential approach to integrating the natural, social, and policy sciences to jointly plan the built environment in relation to the natural environment. It was developed by University of Pennsylvania Landscape Architecture Professor Ian McHarg (1920–2001). Design with nature begins planning at any scale with analysis of the natural environment and makes preservation of environmentally important features of the natural landscape a paramount goal. Box 13.1 is a biography of Ian McHarg and a description of his method for designing with nature.

BOX 13.1 IAN MCHARG

Ian McHarg (1920–2001) was the founder of the University of Pennsylvania's Department of Landscape Architecture, and the author of *Design with Nature* (1961)—one of the most influential books in landscape architecture and city and regional planning of all time. He was a principal in Wallace McHarg Roberts & Todd (WMRT)—the world's premier landscape architecture firm. As a public intellectual he was powerful spokesperson for the environmental movement.

McHarg grew up in Edinburgh, Scotland in a house from which he could see the spectacularly beautiful Scottish countryside in one direction and smokestacks and pollution from factories on the River Clyde in the other. After serving in Italy during World War II, he received landscape architecture and planning degrees from Harvard in 1949. He was hired as an assistant professor of landscape architecture at the University of Pennsylvania in 1954—charged with creating the department, devising the curriculum, hiring faculty, and attracting students. McHarg created a graduate program and became the new department's first chair. The University of Pennsylvania's landscape architecture program received major funding from the Ford Foundation beginning in 1966, which allowed McHarg to hire a geologist, hydrologist, soils scientist, biometeorolgist, computer scientist, remote-sensing expert, and ecologists to join the faculty.

By the time McHarg wrote his autobiography in 1996 the University of Pennsylvania Landscape Architecture Department had graduated 1,000 students, 11 of whom had become deans, 31 department chairs, and 140 professors. McHarg's approach at the University of Pennsylvania was replicated on a smaller scale by many landscape architecture and environmental science programs and by some physical geographers.

McHarg began teaching a course titled "Man and Environment" and hosting a television program titled *The House We Live In* in 1959. He invited philosophers, psychologists, and theologians as well as landscape architects, planners, and natural scientists to lecture in his course and discuss their ideas on his television program. Both his course and the television show explored the science of matter, life, plants, animals, and humans; views of God, humans and nature; physiological and psychological relationships of humans and nature; and natural and human ecology. It became one of the University of Pennsylvania's most popular courses.

McHarg created environmental plans for many projects and for Minneapolis, Denver, Miami, New Orleans, and Washington, D.C. He prepared notable environmentally based master plans for Sanibel Island and Amelia Island Plantation in Florida, Woodlands, Texas, and the Potomac River basin in the Washington, D.C. region.

With a grant from the Conservation Foundation during a sabbatical leave in 1966 and 1967, McHarg wrote *Design with Nature* (1969). This was the right book at the right time: published on the cusp of the 1970s environmental decade. It made McHarg famous. He became a public intellectual lecturing at universities and other venues all over the world, appearing on television talk shows, making films, and writing newspaper op ed pieces. By 1996, 350,000 copies of *Design with Nature* had been published in French, Italian, and Japanese as well as English. Many more copies have been sold since that time, including multiple Chinese editions.

Design with nature as McHarg proposed it has three main dimensions: (1) it is a theoretical-philosophical approach to planning the built and natural environments in harmony with each other, (2) a methodology for relating different important environmental resources in order to decide where and what kind of development or preservation is appropriate, and (3) a range of specific policies such as planting dune grass to stop coastal erosion.

McHarg taught his students and employees to draw grayscale maps by hand on transparent plastic Mylar sheets at the same scale for each environmental or other value in an area he was planning. Placing a layer with areas where flamingos congregate for example—light for areas where there are just a few and darker where there are many—on top of the Mylar sheet showing suitable flamingo marsh habitat will produce a composite map. The areas that are least suitable for development because of the damage

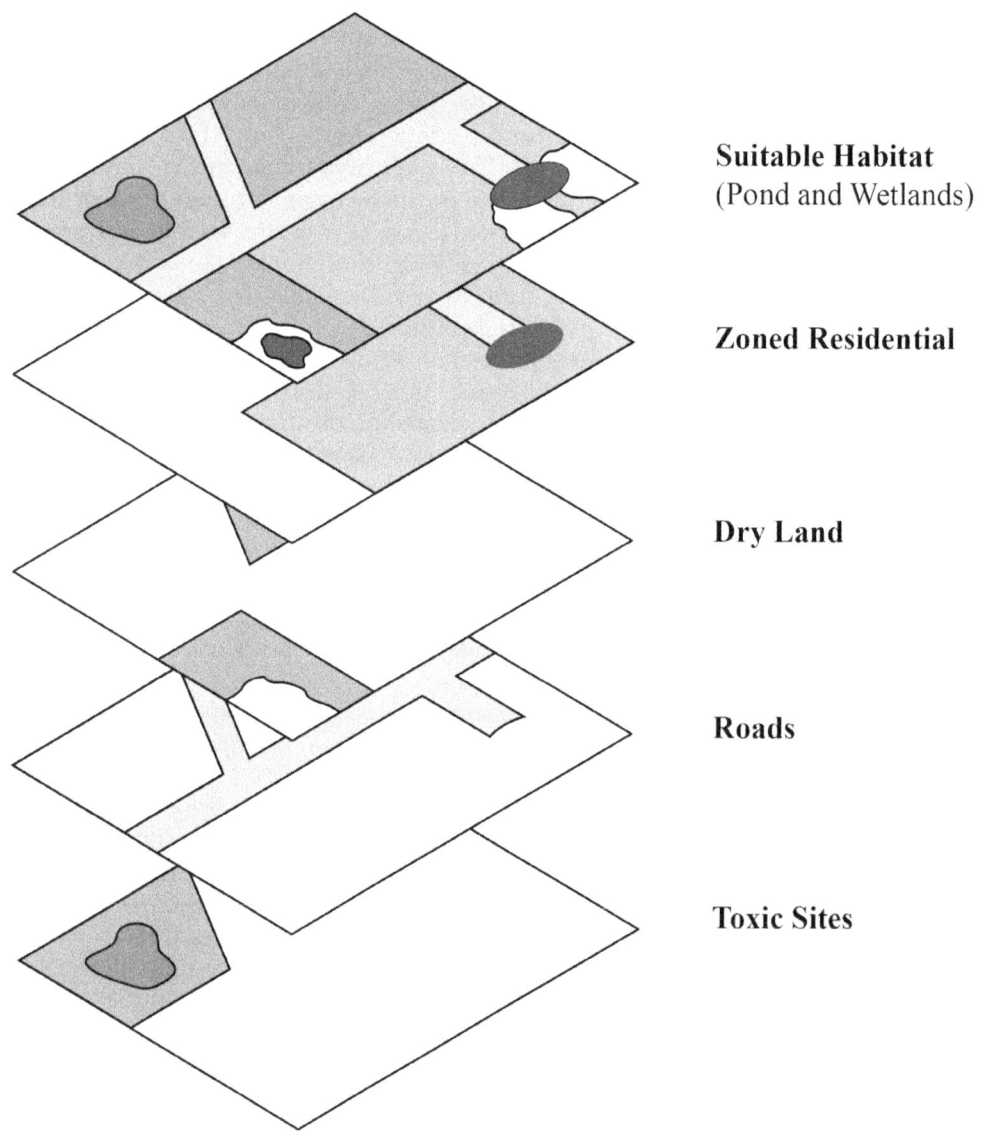

Figure 13.1 Map Layers Illustrating Ian McHarg's Design with Nature Method.

they would do to flamingo habitat appear dark gray and the most suitable areas are light gray or even transparent—appearing white on the map. As many layers representing as many more environmental resources as the analyst-mapmakers consider useful and the budget permits will produce more complex and precise maps. Figure 13.1 is based on a triptych from *Design with Nature* showing grayscale McHargian map layers. It illustrates a toxic site (very dark gray), two floodplains (medium gray), and prime agricultural land (light gray). Figure 13.1 shows layers for a site suitability analysis of habitat for roseate spoonbills who live in wetlands, fed by streams that have small fish to eat, and are away from roads.

Planners armed with McHargian maps testifying to exactly what environmental impacts will occur under different planning scenarios could outgun avaricious developers arguing for environment-damaging development only from self-interest and emotion. Environmentally sensitive developers who had commissioned McHargian analyses could outgun NIMBYs and convince local government decision-makers using precise, evidence-based, easy to understand McHargian maps.

Many of the most advanced ecological design projects in the world today grew out of McHarg's approach. It remains an inspiration for city and regional planners worldwide today.

Flora and fauna live in geographically defined habitats in interdependent ecosystems. McHarg developed the theory and practice of how landscape architects, planners, and policy makers can use ecological information to plan areas to conserve and where to locate development in order to preserve critical habitat that in turn protects species. McHargian analysis recognizes that natural scientists can identify and geographers can map rivers, lakes, streams, wetlands, forests, grasslands, scrub brush, fields, and other features that define different ecosystems and habitat suitable for different species.

Technology makes is possible to capture data digitally from satellites, airplanes, and drones rather than time-consuming and expensive field investigations. Geographical information systems (GIS) software makes it possible to analyze layers of environmental data together with demographic, physical, and cultural features without the tedium of drawing them on Mylar transparencies by hand as McHarg's students and firm did. Digital layers can be created with great precision and then overlaid with others at the same scale and analyzed. Figure 13.2 illustrates GIS map layers for a McHargian analysis.

LEED STANDARDS

Leadership in Energy and Environmental Design (LEED) standards created by the independent nonprofit U.S. Green Building Council provide a rating system that architects, planners, landscape architects, and urban designers can use to improve energy efficiency in buildings and neighborhoods. LEED building and neighborhood standards can greatly reduce use of energy, which in turn reduces demand for energy production and consumption that may both harm the environment. There are similar green rating systems in other countries. The World Building Council—similar to the U.S. Green Building Council—provides green rating standards countries worldwide can use or adapt.

BIOPHILIC PLANNING AND DESIGN

Harvard biologist Edward O. Wilson developed theory about biophilia—from the Latin "love of living things". Wilson argues that that human beings have an innate emotional affiliation for other living organisms. University of Virginia Professor Of Sustainable Communities Timothy Beatley

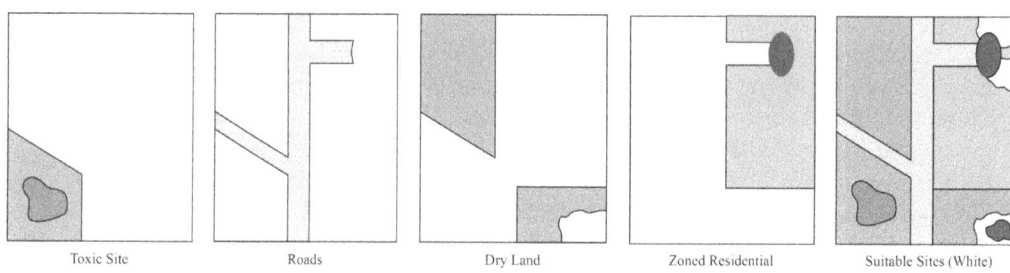

Figure 13.2 Geographical Information System Map Layers.

Figure 13.3 Biophilic Design, Eindhoven, the Netherlands (2021).

has applied Wilson's biophilic concepts to city and regional planning. Beatley argues that biophilic urbanism can improve mental health, reduce stress, help humans heal from disease, even increase birth rates and reduce crime. Biophilic urban planning and design practices include preserving and restoring natural areas; protecting parks, trails, wetlands, rivers, and lakes; creating green roofs and gardens; building vertical living exterior building facades; designing interior spaces that use green walls and natural ventilation and light; and even creating interior forest atria to bring nature into workplaces and individual homes. Figure 13.3 shows a street in Eindhoven, the Netherlands illustrating biophilic design

Ecological design, ecodesign, and green city design are terms for approaches that also make respect for nature and natural processes the central feature of planning. Like design with nature and landscape urbanism, these approaches all utilize natural features in city and regional planning and design.

PUBLIC LAND AND NATURAL RESOURCE PLANNING AND MANAGEMENT

Only 3.5% of U.S. land is within incorporated places. Nearly 40% of the land in the United States is publicly owned. Accordingly, management of natural resources on public and private land that is not in cities is critical. Regional planning includes planning for large areas of sparsely populated and uninhabited land in private as well as public ownership.

The great majority of public land in the United States is in the Western United States—generally in very large undeveloped areas.[6] Between 1781 and 1867 the federal government acquired more than 75% of the land in the United States. By 2019 it had disposed of nearly 1.3 billion acres—mostly as homestead land and grants to railroads. The federal government still owns a majority of the land west of the Mississippi River—mostly in partnerships with states. Some planners—particularly in the Western United States and Alaska—work for federal agencies such as the Bureau of Land Management (BLM) within the U.S. Department of the Interior (DOI) that control public land, for state agencies that make plans and implement policy for public land, or for local governments that make use of public land. Extraction of oil and natural gas, mining, ranching, and other use of public lands is most done under contract by private corporations who employ planners and interact with federal and state planners and regulating bodies. Planners may make plans for large undeveloped swaths of public lands for recreation and preservation as wilderness. They oversee national monuments and plan capital improvements on federal public land. All city and regional planners need to be aware of the distribution of rural and urban land, public and private land ownership, and what natural resources exist where, in order to prepare many of the different kinds of plans described throughout this book.

Federal public trust lands were generally disposed of in units of 640 acres called sections. As a condition to acceptance into the Union, each western state received federal public land to manage in trust consisting of two sections of 640 acres of land—1,280 acres per township. This land was originally used primarily for grazing or mining to provide revenue for public schools and this is still often the case.

Management of federal public land is dispersed among a number of federal agencies within different U.S. cabinet-level departments. Eleven bureaus that managed federal public land are within the Bureau of the Interior—the Bureau of Land Management (BLM), National Park Service, Bureau of Reclamation, U.S. Fish and Wildlife Service, and seven other bureaus. The U.S. Departments of Housing and Urban Development, Transportation, and other federal departments own and manage some land. Among the most important are the Forest Service (within the Department of Agriculture); the National Oceanic and Atmospheric Administration (within the Department of Commerce); and the Army Corps of Engineers (within the Department of Defense).

Authority cascades down from the different federal agencies to the states. States assign some of this authority to manage public land to state government entities and grant the rest of the authority to manage public land to cities and counties. All states plan and manage state-owned land such as state parks, state wildlife management areas, and state forests.

Wilderness areas are a special designation for some federal public lands, established by the 1964 Wilderness Act. Wilderness areas are completely undeveloped. They are managed by many different federal agencies, often in partnership with state, local, or private entities. Some federal parks and refuges are entirely, or almost entirely, designated wilderness areas. A "wilderness study area" is a tract of land that has wilderness area characteristics and is managed as a wilderness area, but has not received a wilderness designation from Congress.

There is fierce political conflict around federal, state, and private property rights and control of public land. The "sagebrush rebellion" emerged in Western states in the mid-1970s in opposition to a large increase in designated national wilderness areas and an increase in the federal government's authority over them. The Sagebrush Rebellion includes or is supported by anti-environmentalist neo-liberal groups, many companies in resource extraction industries, land development companies, and other parties that have a financial stake in exploitation of natural resources. Beginning in 1988 the terminology and optics changed. The so-called "wise use" movement in the Western United States began pushing for increased extraction of oil, gas, and minerals; protection of private property rights against environmental regulations; and reducing the amount of federal wilderness land and federal regulation of it. The wise use movement appropriated and distorted the term "wise use" that had been coined by President Theodore Roosevelt's secretary of the interior Gifford Pinchot (1865–1945)—an early advocate of stewardship of national resources. President Ronald Reagan, and secretaries of the interior and the Environmental Protection Agency who he appointed, supported the new wise use movement and ideology. Coalitions that favor increased exploitation of natural resources received a boost from the Trump administration. They have strong support in Western states and other states whose economies are highly dependent on extracting or refining oil, gas, and other natural resources. This creates conflict with planners and policy makers trying to quickly change the way in which energy is produced to rely much less on oil, coal, and natural gas. There are enormous differences in self-interest and values between people in Western states and other states whose economies are highly dependent on extracting and refining natural resources and planners and policy makers working to address global climate change. The latter are working to facilitate a massive shift away from use of oil, coal, and natural gas to solar, wind, and other clean energy sources as quickly as possible. Chapter 17 picks up discussion of this issue—perhaps the most important planning issue of this generation.

WASTE MANAGEMENT, BROWNFIELDS, AND TOXIC CLEANUP

In the United States, municipal governments have primary responsibility for disposal of household solid waste. Industries have primary responsibility for storage of hazardous waste they generate onsite and for transporting it to offsite treatment, storage, or disposal facilities (TSDFs). City and regional planners are involved in planning and management of both day-to-day household waste and hazardous waste from factories, power plants, hospitals, and other sites that produce hazardous waste.

U.S. municipalities generate about 292 million tons of municipal solid waste (MSW)—daily—approximately 4.8 pounds per capita. City and regional planners help local governments determine the location of different types of waste-generating activities; set onsite waste storage policy; and determine where landfills and waste storage facilities will be located. They may be involved in plans to reduce the amount of locally generated waste and promote recycling.

Industries generate an enormous amount of industrial waste, some of which is classified as hazardous. The United States Environmental Protection Agency defines hazardous waste as solid waste with a chemical composition or other property that makes it capable of causing illness, death, or some other harm to humans, plants, animals, and ecosystems when mismanaged in the environment.

Before enactment of the Resource Conservation and Recovery Act (RCRA) in 1976, uncontrolled dumping of wastes, including hazardous wastes, was common. Some hazardous waste was co-disposed with municipal solid waste or other nonhazardous waste. Former manufacturing sites such as the wasteland at a former industrial site in New Jersey illustrated in Figure 13.4 have become unusable wastelands containing only the remains of old industrial buildings and vacant land known to contain toxic substances or which is unusable because there are no records or adequate studies of what substances they might contain.

Landfills and surface impoundments containing hazardous materials were usually unlined and uncovered, resulting in contaminated soil, air, surface water, and underground water in aquifers. Contaminated sites range from small sites that are relatively easy to clean up to enormous mines, steel

Figure 13.4 Industrial Wasteland.

plants, and military sites with unexploded ordinance.

The Resource Conservation and Recovery Act covers facilities whose industrial processes and other actions are significant hazardous waste hazards. Initially hazardous waste is usually stored onsite or sent to transfer sites. Transfer and storage of toxic waste is now regulated and monitored by federal and state agencies, so the danger from new toxic waste dumping has been greatly diminished. The great majority of non-hazardous wastes are ultimately disposed of on land in landfills, surface impoundments, or land application units—areas where wastes are applied onto or incorporated into the soil surface. Most hazardous solid wastes are eventually disposed of underground. Hazardous wastewater is often permanently stored in deep wells.

Sites contaminated by hazardous waste are called brownfields in contrast to greenfield sites that remain in their uncontaminated natural state. There are about 450,000 brownfield sites in the United States. Some like the Cornell Dubilier site in South Plainfield, New Jersey illustrated in Figure 13.5 are fenced off and unusable while cleanup is going on.

The U.S. Environmental Protection Agency (EPA) defines a brownfield as idle real property, the development or improvement of which is impaired by documented contamination and by the uncertainty about what more contamination might exist. The EPA's Toxic Release Inventory (TRI) reports that large U.S. manufacturers generate more than 3 billion pounds of hazardous waste each year. The TRI provides details on the location and characteristics of the toxic sites and the types of toxic substances in them. The TRI is based on voluntary reporting and does not cover all hazardous waste generated by large manufacturers; hazardous waste produced by small companies; or hazardous waste accumulated before the first TRI was released in 1988. Not all industry sectors are covered by the TRI, and not all facilities in covered sectors are required to report to the TRI. Despite these limitations, the TRI provides essential information for planners.

Analyzing brownfields and developing strategies to clean them up is a specialized planning activity. Assessing the true extent

Figure 13.5 Cornell Dubilier Superfund Site (South Plainfield, New Jersey).

of toxic waste hazards is technical work appropriate for natural science experts and environmental engineers. Many states license environmental site experts for this kind of work.

In 1980, the federal government passed the Comprehensive Environmental Response, Compensation, and Liability Act (CERCLA), to establish a process to identify the largest, most dangerous brownfield sites in the United States—so-called superfund sites—and get them cleaned up. The Environmental Protection Agency oversees brownfield cleanup under CERCLA. CERCLA requires the original polluters or their successors in interest—subsequent buyers, heirs, or others legally responsible for the site—to pay the costs of cleanup to the extent possible if the original polluter(s) still exist, can be found, and have money to pay for some or all of the cleanup. Hazardous manufacturing facilities go in and out of business and sometimes move. Most states have published directories of manufacturing since the 1950s. From these directories it is often possible to determine when, where, and how industrial land became industrialized, reused, and hidden. If the original polluters no longer exist, their identities are so changed that it is impossible to successfully prosecute them, or they lack funds to clean up the dangerous sites, federal and state funds may be used to clean up superfund sites. Since 1980 the EPA has spent about $32 billion to clean up superfund sites. Much of this cleanup work is undertaken by the states working with local government. Some states have passed state legislation similar to CERCLA.

Cleaning up brownfields presents interesting and challenging work for qualified city and regional planners. Planners with natural science expertise important to understanding toxic sites and lawyer-planners with the skill to prosecute polluters who created the superfund sites are in demand.

ENVIRONMENTAL JUSTICE

Brownfields and polluting industrial sites are much more likely to be located near communities of color and low-income and immigrant communities than White communities and middle- and upper-income communities. Companies usually locate their dirtiest businesses in low-income areas near communities of color because these areas usually offer the path of least political resistance. Some planners work to increase environmental justice. The federal Environmental Justice Act—introduced in the House and Senate unsuccessfully in 2017 defines environmental justice as:

> the fair treatment and meaningful involvement of all people regardless of race, color, culture, national origin, or income, with respect to the development, implementation, and enforcement of environmental laws, regulations, and policies to ensure that each person enjoys (1) the same degree of protection from environmental and health hazards; and (2) equal access to any federal agency action on environmental justice issues in order to have a healthy environment in which to live, learn, work, and recreate.

The Environmental Justice Act—renamed the Environmental Justice for All Act—was reintroduced in 2020. It was under consideration by Congress as this book went to press in spring, 2022.

A study of toxic water treatment, storage, and disposal facilities (TSDFs) led by University of Southern California urban planning professor Manuel Pastor, and a study of Exide—a battery recycling facility located in the heavily industrial city of Vernon, California by University of Southern California (USC) geography professor Laura Pulido are notable recent studies of environmental racism.[7]

Since the 1990s, across Democratic and Republican presidential administrations, federal engagement with environmental justice has waxed and waned. President Clinton created the Environmental Protection Agency's Office of Environmental Justice and a National Environmental Justice Advisory Council in 1992. Clinton directed federal agencies to ensure that communities of color are not disproportionately impacted by environmental burdens. In 2016 the Obama administration developed an Environmental Justice Action Agenda—EJ 2020—to integrate environmental justice into the EPA's federal and regional operations and to target low-income communities for clean energy investment. President George Bush's administration was less sympathetic to environmental justice. The Trump administration reversed course on environmental justice— rolling back rules, approving controversial projects, ignoring scientific evidence, and cutting enforcement funding and qualified EPA staff.[8]

Expectations are high that the USA will see improvements in the federal response to environmental justice under President Joe Biden. It will take time to rebuild the EPA, undo damage done under the Trump administration, wrap up pending lawsuits, and devise and implement new federal environmental justice policies.

COASTAL ZONE PLANNING AND MANAGEMENT

Coasts present challenges for planning both the natural and built environment in the shallow water near coastlines that can be filled and on the land just inland from them. Coastal zones and the bays, estuaries, rivers, streams, lagoons, swamps, and marshes connected to them have complex ecosystems that can be damaged by development and climate change. They provide important habitat for fish and waterfowl, and for plants and animals' food chains. Sand dunes help buffer built up urban areas. Developable land on coasts is limited and expensive. Political decisions about how to use precious coastal zone resource are often heated.

The continental USA, Alaska, and Hawaii have nearly 100,000 miles of coastline. More than a third of the U.S. population lives within a coastal zone. There is no agreed-upon legal definition of what constitutes the U.S. shoreline. Numbers for the length of the U.S. shoreline vary depending on how the shoreline is defined. The National Oceanic and Atmospheric Administration (NOAA) estimates the shoreline as 95,471 miles along the Atlantic and Pacific Oceans, the Gulf of Mexico, Alaska, Hawaii, and the Great Lakes. There are over 124 million people and 53.6 million jobs in U.S. coastal communities. They contribute 7.6 trillion dollars—46% of the nation's GDP—to the U.S. economy. How to protect coastal areas from sea-level rise, storm surges, and extreme weather events is increasingly essential because of global climate change.

The 1972 U.S. Coastal Zone Management Act provides for the federal government and 35 states that have coasts on the Pacific or Atlantic Oceans or the Great Lakes to work jointly on coastal zone planning and management. All 35 eligible states participate, with the exception of Alaska. The National Aeronautics and Atmospheric Administration (NOAA)'s Office of Coastal Management administers the National Coastal Zone Management Program.

NOAA provides funding, oversight, implementation, and technical assistance to lower levels of government. Local governments are involved in coastal planning and projects. Goals, objectives, and program strategies include helping coastal communities plan for, and prepare to minimize risk from changing coastal conditions; fostering integration of social and economic information into coastal management; protecting and restoring coastal and ocean ecosystems; and strengthening coastal management. Many states also have supplemental state-level coastal zone management programs. Box 13.2 describes the San Francisco Bay Conservation and Development Commission—one of the most successful coastal zone planning and management agencies in the United States.

BOX 13.2 THE SAN FRANCISCO BAY CONSERVATION AND DEVELOPMENT COMMISSION

The San Francisco Bay Conservation and Development Commission (BCDC) was the first and remains one of the most successful state coastal zone management programs. San Francisco Bay lies between San Francisco and adjacent cities and counties to the north, south, and east of San Francisco. The west coast of San Francisco is on the Pacific Ocean. The Bay is the jewel in the San Francisco Bay Area crown—beautiful and central to the economy, environment, recreation, and livability of the region. It is essential for maintaining the Bay Area's temperate climate. Wetlands along the shore of the bay are critical habitat for fish to spawn and for migrating birds along the Pacific flyway traveling from Siberia to the tip of South America. Maintaining water quality and the safety of fill that has been dumped in the bay are important issues.

San Francisco Bay is very shallow. About two-thirds of the bay is less than 18 feet deep. Water two or three miles into the bay may be less than five feet deep at low tide.

Political control of the bay is fragmented. Fifty per cent of San Francisco Bay is owned by the state, 23% by cities and counties, 22% is in private ownership, and 5% is owned by the federal government. Most of the shallowest areas of the bay closest to shore, and thus easiest to fill and develop, are owned privately or by local governments—both of whom are motivated to fill and develop it. One acre of land on the bay may be worth millions of dollars.

In 1849, as California's Gold Rush was beginning, the Bay was 787 square miles in size. By 1965 about 237 square miles of the bay had been filled. Plans developed by the U.S. Army Corps of Engineers and promoted by the U.S. Department of Commerce in the late 1950s, would have resulted in about 325 additional square miles of fill by 2020. The Bay would have become little more than a broad river as illustrated in Figure 13.6.

Concerned Bay Area activists formed a grassroots organization named Save the Bay. In 1965 Save the Bay successfully used the initiative process to force the California state legislature to create the San Francisco Bay Conservation and Development Commission (BCDC) as a temporary agency charged with preparing a San Francisco Bay plan. The

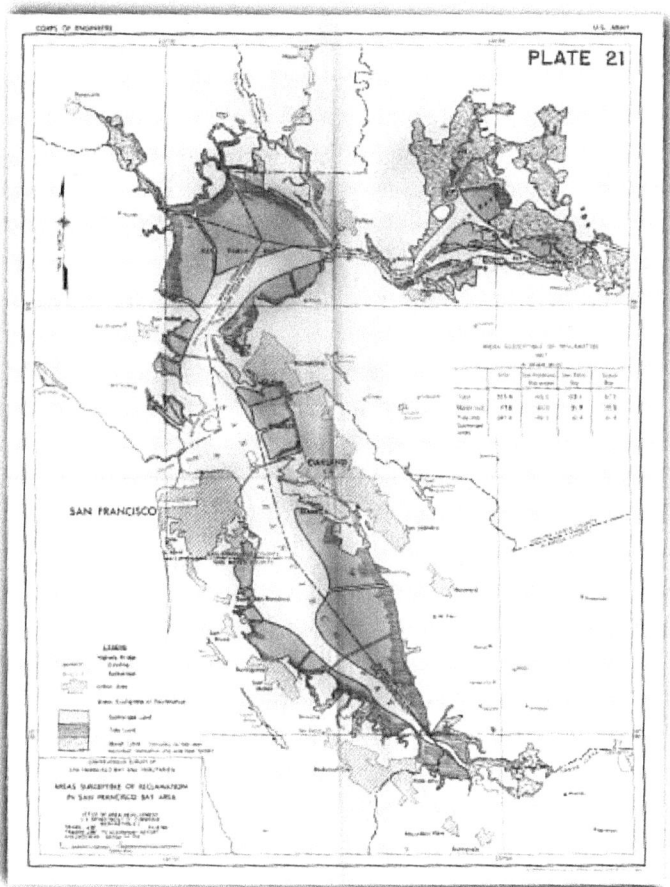

Figure 13.6 U.S. Army Corps of Engineers Map Showing Areas of San Francisco Bay "Susceptible to Reclamation" (1960).

California state legislature made BCDC permanent and adopted the *Bay Plan* in 1969. BCDC has periodically updated the plan since then. The plan and BCDC enforcement have preserved the Bay at close to its 1965 size—about 550 square miles.

BCDC is the federally designated state coastal management agency for the San Francisco Bay segment of the California coastal zone. Its 27-member commission controls Bay filling and dredging and bay-related shoreline development. BCDC follows the national Coastal Zone Management Act and National Aeronautics and Oceanographic Administration guidelines to ensure that federal projects and activities are consistent with the policies of the *Bay Plan* and state law.

The *Bay Plan* maps the entire bay and designates areas of the bay and shoreline for different water-related purposes. The plan treats the bay as a regional resource—a single body of water rather than real estate. Shoreline areas suitable for priority uses—ports, water-related industry, airports, wildlife refuges, and water-related recreation—are clearly specified. The plan reserves them for these purposes.

BCDC has jurisdiction over filling and dredging in the Bay itself (all areas that are subject to tidal action), managed wetlands, specified marshlands, salt ponds, and former bay lands. It controls development on land 100 feet landward of shorelines. Any development in the bay itself or on the shoreline requires a BCDC permit.[9] As a result of BCDC oversight, the water area of San Francisco Bay has increased slightly since 1969.

> In sharp contrast an average of four square miles of the Bay had been filled, on average, during each of the previous 110 years.
>
> Dire predictions by BCDC's opponents that stopping bay fill and regulating shoreline development would wreck the Bay Area economy have not come to pass. The San Francisco Bay shoreline is now fringed by hundreds of miles of trails, parks, beaches, promenades and restoration projects—even in heavily urbanized and industrial locales. The Bay has the largest urban wildlife refuge in the United States and thousands of acres of permanently protected diked areas.

SUMMARY

Environmental planning is one of the most important and most rapidly changing fields of city and regional planning. It is critical for the survival of plant and animal species and the human race. Cities are granite gardens with a great variety of flora and fauna, set in regions with agriculture, forest, and watershed uses. Planning and urban design should be based on scientific understanding of ecosystems. Respect for natural processes is essential.

Until 1970 most development in the United States and elsewhere in the world paid little attention to the natural environment. City and regional plans rarely reflected even rudimentary understanding of natural systems or addressed consequences of environment-destructive practices for the generation living at the time, let alone future generations. Ian McHarg, Anne Whiston Spirn, Timothy Beatley, Steven Wheeler, and hundreds of other planning academics and practitioners have developed a robust body of theory and practice on how planners can integrate understanding of natural systems into planning practices.

The bottom-up revolution in environmental consciousness that became evident on Earth Day 1970 inaugurated rapid and continuing federal, state, and local environmental legislative action. This produced the National Environmental Policy Act, strengthened Clean Air and Water Acts, and legislation to protect endangered and threatened species, clean up toxic sites, and address many other environmental issues.

Most of the plans and projects that environmental planners work on are concerned with issues and use approaches that were not even imagined only a short time ago. Federal- and state-mandated environmental impact assessment, clean air and water planning, protection of endangered species, clean up of toxic sites, and preparation of habitat conservation plans are all relatively new and quickly evolving city and regional planning activities. Remote sensing, GIS, and other technologies have revolutionized environmental planning and made it much more scientific.

There has been plenty of pushback against environmental planning and regulation that impacts private property, reduces private profits, or costs government money. Neoliberals in areas whose economies are dependent on natural resources define "wise use" of natural resources to include large-scale exploitation of natural resources and lead opposition to environmental regulation.

Nearly sixty years ago Rachel Carson—the great marine biologist and environmentalist who alerted the world to the dangers chemical fertilizers and educated citizens and policy makers to ocean and coastal zone processes—declared that "the human race is challenged more than ever before to demonstrate our mastery, not over nature but of ourselves" (Carson, 1962). The human race still has a long way to go to demonstrate mastery of humans' relationship to nature. City and regional planners, as evidence-based professionals, play an important role in environmental planning.

CONCEPTS

100-Year Flood
Air Quality Control Region (AQCR)

Brownfield
Clean Air Act (1970)
Clean Water Act (1972)
Critical Habitat
Cumulative Impact (NEPA)
Design with Nature
Endangered Species
Environmental Impact Statement (EIS)
Finding Of No Significant Impact (FONSI)
Habitat Conservation Plan
Hard Protect Solution to Flooding
Heat Island
LEED Standards
Little NEPA
Mobile Source of Pollution
National Ambient Air Quality Standards
National Environmental Policy Act (NEPA)
Point Source (Air Pollution)
Sagebrush Rebellion
Section
Significant Environmental Impact
Soft Protect Solution to Flooding
Sponge City
Sustainable Urban Development
Taking (Endangered Species Act)
Trust for Public Lands (TPL)
U.S. Green Building Council
Wise Use

PEOPLE

Timothy Beatley
Gro Harlem Brundtland
Ian McHarg
Anne Whiston Spirn
Edward O. Wilson

NOTES

1 Habitat Conservation Planning (HCP) originated with efforts to protect the endangered Mission blue butterfly known to exist only on part of San Bruno Mountain in the small town of Brisbane, California near San Francisco. In 1981 the developers, environmentalists, and the Brisbane city council agreed on a plan to dedicate most of the land on the top of San Bruno Mountain in private ownership for habitat suitable for Mission blue butterflies, increase the amount of habitat, and maintain it in perpetuity in order to increase the species in the long run. In exchange, developers were permitted to build a subdivision that would take (kill) some Mission blue butterflies.

2 Only 13 NCCPs have been created in 25 years (Fulton & Shigley, 2018: 392). The first NCCP was created to protect the California gnatcatcher—an endangered bird that lives only in patches of sage scrub on a small part of the California coast. Environmentalists, landowners, and local governments agreed to create an NCCP preserving 95% of California's remaining coastal scrub land in 11 different locations. The Coachella Valley Multiple Species Habitat Conservation Plan, created in 2008 is a 75-year plan, covering 1.2 million acres inhabited by 10 endangered or threatened plant or animal species and 17 other species (ibid: 393). The plan includes desert and mountain land in one county, eight cities, and four special districts. The Eastern Contra Costa County HCP/NCCP, created in 2012, is a 50-year plan involving eight listed and nine non-listed species (ibid).

3 Trial court judges are reluctant to substitute their judgment for the conclusions of the experts who prepared the EIS or the decision of local elected officials about its adequacy, so long as they are convinced that a complete, procedurally correct environmental assessment was conducted. If a judge finds that there was a procedural irregularity or serious omission, he or she may enjoin the start of construction until the EIS is revised or a satisfactory new one is prepared. Appellate court decisions have interpreted when judicial review of agency actions is appropriate, what parties have standing to sue (bring the case), what the obligation to comply with NEPA to the "fullest extent possible" means, what constitute "significant" acts, "major" federal actions, and "reasonable" alternatives to a proposed action, and how to assess cumulative impacts.

4 The sixteen states that have enacted little NEPAs are California, Connecticut, Georgia, Hawaii, Indiana, Maryland, Massachusetts, Minnesota, Montana, New Jersey, New York, North Carolina, South Dakota, Virginia, Washington, and Wisconsin (Ballotpedia, 2018). The District of Columbia, Puerto Rico, the Tahoe Regional Planning Compact—an interstate compact between California and Nevada to protect Lake Tahoe, and New York City also have little NEPAs.

5 Lawyers distinguish legislative acts, in cases where a local government has discretion to similar to a city council or board of supervisors from a quasi-judicial decision, where the court resolves a dispute between parties much like a court of law would do. They distinguish both kinds of decisions from ministerial acts, in which local governments only review a proposed private action to confirm that it complies with the law. The most important California Supreme Court decision interpreting CEQA—*Friends of Mammoth vs Mono County* (1972)—held that even a discretionary quasi-judicial act as minor as approving a small development at a ski resort area was covered by The California Environmental Quality Act (CEQA). The court held that the discretionary action constituted government action sufficient to trigger CEQA. Since the great majority of private developments of any

significance require discretionary reviews, the *Friends of Mammoth* case has had an enormous impact.

6 As of 1989 the federal government owned 662,158,000 acres (1.035 million square miles) of land in the United States (U.S. Bureau of Land Management, 2019: 382). Two-hundred thirty-one million acres (about 361,000 square miles) are national forest land (ibid). The national park system includes 119,000 square miles of land (ibid). In Alaska, 96% of the land is publicly owned (U.S. Census, 2010).

7 Pastor's study of waste treatment, storage, and disposal facilities (TDSFs) concluded that the presence of minority residents—not just low-income people— tended to attract TDSFs (Pastor, Sadd, & Hipp, 2001). Exide used lead and arsenic in their manufacturing. The South Coast Air Quality Management District (SCAQMD) had issued 44 citations and sought to close Exide at the time of Pulido's study. Rather than complying, Exide sued the SCAQMD. Pulido concluded that Exide was motivated by White supremacist values (Pulido, 2015).

8 Within his first week in office, President Trump issued an executive memorandum directing the Secretary of the Army to approve permits for completion of the Dakota Access Pipeline to bring oil from Canada to the United States across land in the Sioux Indian reservation watershed. Indigenous people and environmentalists strongly opposed the plan. Trump repealed President Obama's 2015 Clean Power Plan to reduce pollution in vulnerable communities created by the electric power sector. Trump's budgets proposed deep cuts to the EPA, including a proposed 69% reduction in the EPA's budget for environmental justice activities (Outka & Warner, 2019: 110). It proposed deep cuts to funding for environmental programs on Indian reservations, native Alaskan villages, and mostly-Latinx and indigenous communities along the USA–Mexico border (ibid). The Trump EPA weakened rules regulating animal waste emissions, pesticides, and toxic coal ash. During the Trump administration, the EPA brought many fewer civil enforcement actions for violations of environmental laws than during the Obama administration. Environmental justice advocates and their allies fought back, and many Trump rules were defeated, delayed, or remain in litigation. The final Trump administration EPA report to Congress on environmental justice claims that under the Trump administration the environment became cleaner and healthier, partnerships more effective, and there was greater certainty, compliance, and effectiveness (EPA, 2019).

9 BCDC grants permits for projects they consider justifiable including filling for port terminals, land for industries that require access to shipping channels, recreational uses such as shoreline parks, marinas, fishing piers, beaches, hiking and bicycling paths, and scenic drives, airport terminals and runways, new freeway routes, some types of housing, and public access to the Bay.

SUGGESTIONS FOR FURTHER LEARNING

The Fate of the Earth: British Broadcasting Company, *Planet earth: the future* (2006). World Wildlife Federation (WWF), How to save our planet (2019). **Environmental Planning:** Forster Ndubisi, *Ecological design and planning reader*, 3rd ed (2014). Tom Daniels, *Environmental planning handbook* (2014). John Randolph, *Environmental land use planning*, 2nd ed (2011). Anne Whiston Spirn, *The granite garden* (1984). **Biophilia and Biophilic Urbanism:** Edward O. Wilson, *Biophilia* (1984). Timothy Beatley, *Biophilic cities* (2010), *Blue urbanism* (2014), *Blue biophilic cities* (2017), and *Handbook of biophilic city planning and design* (2017). **Urban Environments and Landscape Urbanism:** David Owen, Green Manhattan (2004). Charles Waldheim, *Landscape as urbanism* (2016) and *The landscape urbanism reader* (2006). Frederick Steiner, *The living landscape*, 2nd ed (2008). Lisa Benton Short & John Short, *Cities and nature*, 2nd ed (2013) **U.S. National Environmental Laws:** U.S. Environmental Protection Agency, *Laws and regulations* (2021). Wilderness Act (1964). Clean Air Act Amendments (1970). Clean Water Act (1972). U.S. Environmental Protection Agency EPA, *Summary of the Clean Water Act* (2021). Safe Drinking Water Act (1974). United States Environmental Protection Agency, *Summary of the Safe Drinking Water Act* (2021). U.S. Endangered Species Act (1973). U.S. Resource Recovery Act (1976). U.S. Comprehensive Environmental Response, Compensation, and Liability Act (1980). **The National Environmental Policy Act (NEPA):** National Environmental Policy Act (1970). United States Environmental Protection Agency, *A citizen's guide to the NEPA* (2007). Charles Eccleston & J. Peyton Doub, *Preparing NEPA environmental assessments* (2012). **Little NEPAs:** Ballotopedia, *State environmental policy acts* (2018). Patrick Marchman, 'Little NEPAs': State equivalents to the National Environmental Policy Act in Indiana, Minnesota and Wisconsin (2012). **Air Quality:** World Health Organization (WHO), *Air pollution* (2021). U.S. Clean Air Act Amendments (1970). United States Environmental Protection Agency (EPA), *Overview of the Clean Air Act* (2021) and *Plain English guide to the Clean Air Act* (2007). **Water Quality:** Cecilia Tortajada, *Integrated water resources management* (2018). Robert Olshansky & Laurie Johnson, *Clear as mud: Planning for the rebuilding of New Orleans* (2010). Public Broadcasting System (PBS), Sinking cities series: London, Tokyo, New York, Venice, Miami, Jakarta and other cities [videos] (2018). Mona Hanna-Attish, *What the eyes don't see.* (2018). **Coastal Management:** U.S. Coastal Zone Management Act (1972). Timothy Beatley, *An introduction to coastal zone management* (2002) and *Planning for coastal resilience* (2009).

San Francisco Bay Conservation and Development Commission [website] (2021), and *San Francisco Bay Plan* (2021). **Sea Level Rise and Sinking Cities:** Stefan Al, *Adapting to sea level rise* (2018). World Economic Forum, *These 11 sinking cities could disappear by 2100* (2019). Public Broadcasting System (PBS), Sinking cities [videos] (2018–2019). **Sustainable Urban Development:** Steven Wheeler & Timothy Beatley, *The sustainable urban development reader*, 3rd ed (2014). Stephen Wheeler, *Planning for sustainability* (2013). Jeffrey Sachs, *The age of sustainable development* (2015). Joan Fitzgerald, *Emerald cities* (2012). Douglas Farr, *Sustainable urbanism* (2007). Peter Newman & Isabella Jennings, *Cities as sustainable ecosystems* (2008). Mark Roseland, *Toward sustainable communities* (2012). **Design with Nature:** Ian McHarg, *Design with nature* (1969). Frederick Steiner, Richard Weller, & Karen McKloskey, *Design with nature now* (2019). Ian McHarg, *Quest for life* (1996). **Ecodesign:** Jonathan Barnett & Larry Beasley, *Ecodesign for cities and suburbs*, 2nd ed (2015). Richard Register, *EcoCities* (2006). **Green Politics:** Andrew Dobson, *Green political thought*, 4th ed (2007). Andrew Dobson & Robyn Eckersley (eds), *Political theory and the ecological challenge* (2006). David Downes, Christian Hunold, David Schlosberg, & Hans-Kristian Hernes (eds), *Green states and social movements* (2002). Green Party USA [website] (2021). **Earth Day:** Earth Day [website] (2020). Robert Stone, Earth Days [video] (2009). **Environmental Justice:** Julian Agyeman, Robert Bullard, & Bob Evans, *Just Sustainabilities* (2003) and Exploring the nexus: Bringing together sustainability, environmental justice and equity. Laura Pulido, White supremacy vs White privilege in environmental racism (2015). Manuel Pastor, Jim Sadd, & John Hipp Which came first? Toxic facilities, minority move-in, and environmental justice (2001). Presidential Executive Order (EO) 12898, *Federal actions to address environmental justice in minority populations and low-income populations* (1994). Uma Outka and Elizabeth Warner, Reversing course on environmental justice under the Trump administration (2019). United States Environmental Protection Agency *EPA annual environmental justice progress report FY 2020* (2021). **Coastal Zone Management:** Timothy Beatley, David Brower, & Anna Schwab, *An introduction to coastal zone management* (2002). John Clark, *Coastal zone management handbook* (2019). Rachelle Alterman & Cygal Pellach (eds), *Regulating coastal zones: International perspectives on land management instruments* (2021). National Oceanographic and Atmospheric Administration, *National coastal zone management program strategic plan 2018–2023* (2018). **Brownfields:** United States Environmental Protection Agency, *National overview: Facts and figures on materials, wastes, and recycling* (2021). Todd Davis (ed), *Brownfields* (2011). Justin Hollander, Niall Kirkwood, & Julia Gold, *Principles of brownfield regeneration* (2010). Scott Frickel & James Elliott, *Sites unseen: Uncovering hidden hazards in American cities* (2018). United States Environmental Protection Agency, EPA's brownfields and land revitalization program (2021). United States Environmental Protection Agency, Toxic release inventory [website] (2021). **Natural Resources Management:** John Loomis, *Integrated public lands management*, 2nd ed (2002). Char Miller, *Public lands, public debates* (2012). **Endangered Species:** Josh Donlan (ed), *Proactive strategies for protecting species* (2015). Dale Goble, J. Michael Scott,& Frank Davis (eds), *The Endangered Species Act at thirty* (2005). Joe Roman, *Listed: Dispatches from America's Endangered Species Act* (2011). **State Endangered Species Acts:** Susan George & William J. Snape III, State endangered species acts (2010). Ryan Pellerito, State endangered species chart (2002). **Journals:** *Environment and Urbanization. International Journal of Sustainable Built Environment. Environmental Impact Assessment Review.*

CHAPTER 14

Transportation Planning

INTRODUCTION

Transportation planning is a robust professional field within city and regional planning and civil engineering. Transportation infrastructure is expensive, complex, and integral to other major infrastructure systems. It shapes the way entire cities and regions function. Transportation, land use, and air quality need to be planned together.

The amount of public funding available for planning and managing transportation is much greater than for most other types of city and regional planning. Accordingly, there is demand for a large number of transportation planners with all manner of interests, skills, and levels of education. Transportation planners work in local planning departments; in metropolitan planning organizations (MPOs); at the state and national levels; in consulting firms; and in the private sector. Planners and civil engineers with quantitative skills who have completed advanced courses in transportation planning and modeling are in high demand and command high salaries.

Streets, sidewalks, parking spaces, and other transportation-related uses cover a large percentage of city land. Streets have a large impact on a community's livability, and profoundly affect human interactions. Urban designers' and architects' aesthetic and livability concerns augment transportation planners' and civil engineers' concerns for mobility and accessibility. Street and sidewalk designs can permit or deny safe play space for children. They can facilitate "eyes on the street", which can in turn, reduce criminal activity. Improving walkability and bikeability can reduce obesity, diabetes, and heart disease. Good street and sidewalk design can improve mobility and the quality of life. Streetscaping can protect and enhance ecosystems and make a critical difference to plants, birds, and other animals as well as the quality of life for people. Adequate transportation infrastructure and public transportation in low-income communities and communities of color and improving jobs–housing balance to reduce the spatial mismatch between housing and jobs are important social justice issues.

TRANSPORTATION PLANS

Systems planning theory is more highly developed in transportation planning than in most other areas of city and regional planning. Planners and civil engineers who are planning new transportation systems or how to manage and modify existing ones model the impacts of changing one part of a transportation system, such as closing a street or extending a light rail line, throughout the system. Location theory and principles of regional science developed by Walter Isard, discussed in Chapter 8, are important theoretical contributions to transportation planning.

Planners analyze how much travel demand there is within an area, how many trips a residential, commercial, or industrial land use is likely to generate, and trip origins and destinations. They use trip generation studies to gather data on places like office buildings and sports arenas that generate trips. Origin–destination studies reveal patterns in flows of people and goods from one place to another. These help planners plan the location and modes of transportation that will best meet travel demand. For a single system like a subway, a plan might calculate that 20% of a million city residents will use the system during peak morning hours, so the system should be able to accommodate 200,000 riders overall. Lines from dense residential areas to major employment centers will need to accommodate more riders than lines where travel demand is lower. Empirical studies using big data and advanced analytics permit transportation planners to shift capacity where it is most needed and to calibrate their models as they are planning new transportation systems or adapting existing ones.

TRANSPORTATION PLANNING AT DIFFERENT SCALES

At the global and international scales, planners and policy makers set policy on what transportation infrastructure to build, how to manage transportation systems, and how to incorporate new transportation technology to make the world city network function. They develop criteria for governments in order to connect airports, ports, and other hubs to the world city network.

At the national level, the United States Department of Transportation (DOT) oversees transportation policy, planning, and management. Much of the funding for national, regional and local transportation projects comes from DOT. The U.S. Federal Highway administration—the division of DOT that specializes in highways—monitors and regulates the national highway system.

The federal government provides funding and policy guidance for transportation planning and programs. State Departments of Transportation perform a variety of planning, funding, and other roles. Planners and engineers in metropolitan planning organizations (MPOs) and at the local government level—cities and counties—do much of the detailed local transportation planning.

There have been four major federal transportation acts in the United States. The 1956 Federal Aid Highway Act paid 90% of the cost of constructing 41,000 miles of interstate highways. It was the largest public works project in history at that time. Another large round of federal transportation funding came with the Intermodal Surface Transportation Efficiency Act (ISTEA)—pronounced "ice tea"—in 1991. ISTEA shifted priorities away from just highway and road construction to more multi-modal approaches, including support for buses, subways, and heavy- and light rail public transportation systems. More recent federal transportation funding has come from the Moving Ahead for Progress in the 21st century (MAP-21) Act in 2012, and the Fixing America's Surface Transportation (FAST) Act in 2018.

As early as 1962, the federal government began to encourage Continuing, Comprehensive transportation plans in Cooperation with state and local government transportation providers—the 3 Cs transportation planning process. The federal transportation acts and the 3Cs process also apply to planning for bridges—many of which are in need of repair or replacement.[1] Transportation planning that receives any federal funding must meet standards of the National Environmental Policy Act, federal Clean Air and Water Acts, the Americans with Disabilities Act (ADA), and other federal legislation.

At the regional scale, metropolitan planning organizations (MPOs) develop three-year Transportation Improvement Programs (TIPs) for metropolitan areas. Regional transportation programs shape the distribution of activities and population in entire regions and are critical to a region's economy.

States play a variety of roles in transportation planning and construction—empowering state transportation departments to plan and implement highway construction projects and enabling and overseeing transportation projects by cities, counties, and transportation districts. State Transportation Improvement Programs (STIPS) implement federal policy at the state level. State Departments of Transportation often have responsibility for preparing State Transportation Improvement Programs (STIPs), but that varies from state to state. Local governments in some states prepare TIPs. States typically have five-year work programs for transportation, and short-term plans with transportation funding allocations. They allocate funding to Metropolitan Transportation Organizations (MPOs) and local governments to implement transportation projects. States sometimes plan and manage transportation projects of statewide significance in addition to highways. They also conduct standard and compliance reviews, develop policies for transportation with statewide significance, and support transportation research and innovations.

At the local level, city and county public works departments do most of the planning for roads, light rail, and other local transportation infrastructure. Public works departments develop and manage local capital improvement plans (CIPs) that operationalize plans and set budgets for local transportation infrastructure construction and maintenance. General plans prepared by city and county planning departments include transportation elements.

Transit districts and authorities that are independent of city and county government often plan and manage bus, port, ferry, and heavy and light rail systems. Other local government departments plan and regulate parking and may manage local traffic congestion or do other kinds of transportation planning.

Effective citizen participation in transportation planning is usually more difficult than for smaller projects that can be built more quickly. People directly affected by small-scale transportation planning decisions, such as discontinuing a bus route or adding speed bumps are often passionate about them and turn out to participate in decision-making. Since it often takes years to plan a street, subway, or light rail system, few citizens are likely to turn out if a government agency invites them to give input on a proposed transportation plan for these large, multi-year projects at an early stage. Years later, after plans have solidified and land has been acquired at great expense, it is hard to change the plans. At that point citizens may turn out to oppose the plan. The famous confrontation between Jane Jacobs and Robert Moses in New York City that forced highway engineers to abandon plans for a highway through Washington Square described in Chapter 1 is a case in point. Moses never made much of an effort to involve neighborhood residents in his highway planning and was taken to task for his arrogance. Other transportation planners made the same mistake and paid a price during the "highway revolt" in the 1960s and 1970s when angry neighborhood residents fought plans to build highways that they felt would ruin their neighborhoods. Collaborative planning and complexity in city (CIC) planning, described in Chapter 5, generally lead to better outcomes today.

MOBILITY AND ACCESSIBILITY

What matters most to users is how quickly and easily they can get from an origin to a destination—not the time it takes to travel from point to point using any one link in a multi-modal transportation system. Transportation planners differentiate "modes" of transportation like cars, buses, trains, and airplanes. Transit system design requires multi-modal analysis. Travelers weigh comfort, safety, and the quality of the travel experience in their mode choice as well as the time it will take. To get from Boston, Massachusetts to Denver, Colorado, a traveler will likely drive or take a taxi to Logan Airport in Boston, fly to Denver International Airport, take transit, a taxi, or pay for a ride by a transportation network company (TNC) like Uber, or rent a car to get from the airport into downtown Denver. If she drives from the Denver Airport she must park and walk or rent a bike or scooter to get to her ultimate destination.

Transportation planners often face a tradeoff between mobility and accessibility. Local streets with mostly local traffic and little or no access control provide ready access to houses, stores, schools, and other destinations from local streets. However, local streets may limit mobility because traffic moves relatively slowly along them. In contrast, highways with speed limits of 60 or more miles per hour provide high mobility. Drivers can get from one place to another on the highway quickly. However, vehicles can only enter or exit highways via on- and off-ramps. Drivers need to exit at the highway ramp closest to their intended destination and proceed on local streets. On- and off-ramps may be miles from the driver's intended final destination, so accessibility is much lower than for local streets. Transportation planners have to strike a balance between mobility and accessibility.

Travel demand models typically follow a four-step process:

1) analyzing trip generation from an origin to a destination—an O–D study;
2) determining trip distribution based on the O–D study using a gravity model that incorporates measures of how strongly travelers are pulled towards different destinations;
3) estimating mode split that predicts the number of travelers that will use each available mode for origin–destination pairs; and
4) analyzing trip assignment (route choice).

Traditionally transportation planners have focused on the "journey to work"—the numbers of people commuting from home to and from work. New transportation models consider journeys among multiple destinations.

Transportation planners measure travel characteristics and demand using traffic volume counts collected by observation and sensors for different times of the day, week, and year. They typically use traffic volume, speed and density to describe traffic characteristics. The standard measures of vehicular transportation system use is vehicle miles traveled (VMT)—how many total miles people travel in a given area. VMT studies often disaggregate VMT by mode and time of day. Transportation planners measure congestion by constructing indices such as a Travel Time Index (TTI) or Roadway Congestion Index (RCI).[2] Transportation planners may compute an average daily traffic (ADT) summary statistic for an entire area or calculate more fine-grained traffic statistics broken down by location, time, mode, or in other ways.

Travel demand is derived demand. It is determined by demand for something else, such as the desire to attend a baseball game, go to work, or attend school. It occurs for a trip purpose. Travelers "purchase" travel as a good. Flows or equilibrium within a transportation system can be analyzed using conventional deterministic supply and demand models in which the outcome of the model is determined by the initial conditions and parameter values. Alternatively, transportation planners use stochastic models that predict the probability of different outcomes. Stochastic models do not necessarily assume rational behavior. They try to account for unpredictability and the possibility of random events.

For systems that have fixed stops, one way to conceptualize where stops should be located is as a circle with a start point, multiple destinations, and a return to the point of origin. Another way to conceptualize a transportation system is as a network linking destination nodes. Potential users weigh the distance and time it takes to get from their origin to their destination by any combination of transportation modes—including wait times for necessary transfers.

Transit demand over time is not uniform. There are usually morning and evening peaks as commuters travel to and return from work and students go to and from school. Demand will likely be higher on weekdays than weekends, except for Saturday night. It may be higher or lower during different days in a holiday season. Transportation planners may need to choose between recommending that transit providers invest in systems that can best handle peak travel demand, but may require people on less-used lines to wait during peak demand periods, or invest in transportation systems that best address lower-volume basic demand that will reach more people with shorter wait times, but may require people on heavily-traveled routes to wait longer at some times.

Demands on transportation systems and networks change over time—generally imposing heavier demands on systems than when they were originally built as time passes.

Traffic congestion is a common problem as road networks and other systems that were built to accommodate demand when they were built, must handle much more traffic later in their life cycle.

Accessibility is determined by the spatial distribution of potential destinations, ease of reaching each destination, and the magnitude, quality, and character of the activities found there. It depends on both the physical fitness of individuals and their perceptions of what they believe will be the best transportation option for them. Elderly people or people with disabilities may not be able to use parts of a transportation network that lacks accessibility in the same way as younger or more fit people. People may choose to avoid a bumpy ride on a gravel road in favor of a longer ride on a paved one. They may avoid a street they perceive as dangerous, prefer to walk to get exercise over getting to a destination as quickly as possible, or choose a ride on a comfortable subway rather than riding on a less comfortable bus.

Accessibility is determined by a combination of land use patterns, the transportation system, and the way in which individuals evaluate their accessibility options based on their abilities and preferences. As the number of nodes in a trip proliferate, the nature of the network becomes more complex, and planners' ability to model behavior on the network becomes more challenging. Big data is producing much more information on complex transit systems. Planners are using information from big data to derive new metrics for measuring and improving accessibility.

Travel time studies look at portal-to-portal travel time; vehicle travel time; congestion; mobility; accessibility; travelers' characteristics and other variables. Travel demand models often use a zonal system reflecting the socio-geographical characteristics of households in concentric rings or sectors along transit corridors. Statistical packages and GIS allow them to analyze flows among the sectors. Activity-based modeling and microsimulation focus on individual travelers' transportation network use.

Transportation modeling is a specialized field that requires mathematical ability and advanced education. However, new software and analytics are revolutionizing transportation modeling and making it much easier for generalists to model travel behavior.

In addition to traditional transportation infrastructure planning, state and local transportation planners now take a broader perspective. Some develop performance measures and seek to identify alternative strategies to influence travel behavior and system performance. Travel demand management (TDM) to influence how many people travel by which mode of transportation at what time of day is one approach. Travel demand may be managed to some extent by policies such as charging tolls, changing the number of lanes going in a direction during the morning and evening peak commute hours, creating bicycle and high-occupancy vehicle (HOV) lanes, or carpooling. Intelligent transportation systems (ITS) use wireless digital technology to inform drivers of congestion, so they can choose less congested routes. Planners and managers can use ITS to allocate buses, subway trains, and other public transit in real time in response to travel demand.

TRANSPORTATION PLANNING DATA

Transportation planners use data from many different sources. A fundamental source is the Federal Highway Administration (FHWA). The FHWA's National Household Travel Survey (NHTS) is an important source of national transportation data. It allows users to analyze trends in personal and household travel. The U.S. Bureau of Transportation Statistics website lists and contains links to the main sources of federal transportation data. Transportation planners also use transportation data from state and local government, nonprofit, academic and other sources.

The United States Census Bureau collects demographic, income, employment, vehicle ownership, and other data useful for transportation planning in the decennial census and annual American Community Surveys. Individual and household data is available at the block, block group, and census tract levels, and aggregated into transportation analysis zones (TAZs)—groups of blocks where transportation is functionally interconnected. The U.S. census collects and makes available data on the number of motor vehicles per household, trips, and other data in each TAZ. The area and number of people in a TAZ vary depending on population density and other factors. In very dense areas, like Midtown Manhattan, a TAZ may consist of a single block, while in a low-density part of New York City it may include many blocks.

Planners can aggregate data from small units like blocks and TAZs into spatial units that meet their analytic needs such as a highway corridor—the land on either side of a highway—or the commute shed of a core city—the entire part of the metropolitan area and beyond within which most commuting occurs. State, regional, and local data supplement NHTS and census data.[3]

Mobile phones capture location data that private companies own and use. In the United States, laws prohibit private companies from selling data that can reveal information about individuals, including data on their location and travel behavior. However private companies may sell transportation data that is aggregated so that information on individuals cannot be determined. AirSage is the largest of several private companies in the United States that purchase cell phone data from major phone companies, such as AT&T, T-Mobile, Sprint, and Verizon, that show the exact departure and arrival time of millions of trips from different locations. AirSage sells summaries and visualizations of the data that do not reveal personal data to governments and organizations that do transportation planning.

Data from smart cards used in subways, toll-collection stations, and elsewhere is the property of transit agencies. The transit agencies can use it to model travel patterns and help with transit management and planning. Some transit agencies and phone companies sell data that has been cleaned so that it does not reveal individual data to third parties or transportation providers who use the data for planning, marketing, and other purposes. As more and more systems collect very precise data about trips and analytic tools become more sophisticated, this is making transportation planning much more scientific. Where people go and when can be determined very precisely from big data sources. However, determining who they are and why they are traveling cannot. Many transportation planners produce estimates of travelers' demographics, and of the likely reason for their trips based on multivariate analysis and probability theory. For example, the exact number of people who travel from a residential area to a downtown between 7:00 AM and 9:00 AM may be considered a reasonable proxy for commuters going to work, even though some are traveling for other reasons.

OTHER CONSIDERATIONS IN TRANSPORTATION PLANNING

Good transportation planning considers externalities—positive and negative impacts—that any transportation project will have. Transportation systems affect individuals, businesses, areas around transportation infrastructure, and the natural environment. Businesses in the neighborhood immediately around a new subway station, for example, almost always get a financial windfall (a positive externality of the project) when the station becomes operational. Land prices jump, store owners' sales increase, and restaurants get new customers—with little or no effort or cost to the owners. Residential properties adjacent to a noisy new elevated highway may experience a wipeout—losing much of the value of their property. Residents' satisfaction and land and house values will decline. Construction of a high-speed rail line may disrupt the natural environment and harm plant and animal species unless environmental impacts of the project are analyzed and adequately mitigated.

Land value capture—capturing some portion of windfall profits to pay for the cost of transportation infrastructure—is an important planning concept. Hong Kong, Singapore, and other cities use land value capture to fund subways and other transportation infrastructure. Value can be captured by permit fees, taxes, or in other ways.

During construction of transportation infrastructure, city and regional planners need to anticipate and plan for impacts that the construction project will have on residents and businesses such as noise, street closures, and other inconveniences. Even a modest month-long street improvement project can drive away enough customers from a café to have a serious economic impact. Big transportation projects like construction of a highway extension or subway stop can disrupt neighborhoods for years. How well negative impacts are anticipated during the planning phase, and mitigated during construction and in the final project, will make a big difference in support for or opposition to the project.

Timing matters in transportation planning. Concurrency is a central concept. Transportation infrastructure needs to be planned and built so that it is available concurrently with completion of new residential, commercial, or industrial buildings that depend on it.

TRANSPORTATION TECHNOLOGY PAST, PRESENT, AND FUTURE

In the 19th century a series of revolutionary changes in transportation technology discussed in Chapter 2 occurred. The steamboat, horse-drawn streetcar, cable car, electric streetcar, and subway were fundamental paradigm shifts in how to move people and goods. A second revolution occurred with the invention of the internal combustion engine to power gasoline-powered cars and other motor vehicles. Mass production of Model T Ford automobiles (and Model TT trucks) beginning in 1908 changed transportation in the United States more than anything that had come before.

Between the beginning of the New Deal in 1933 and today the number of automobiles in the United States has quintupled. There are now nearly two cars, light trucks, or SUVs per household in the United States. The average number of trips people take and the average number of vehicle miles traveled (VMT) per capita have both greatly increased.

There is growing dissatisfaction with conventional gasoline-powered automobiles and increasing interest in other modes of transportation. Longer commute times and the difficulty and cost of parking in cities contribute to disaffection with automobiles. The U.S. population is aging, and elderly people tend to drive less. Millennials—people born between the early 1980s and early 2000s—are less interested in owning automobiles than previous generations. Many prefer walking, bicycling, and public transportation to driving. Availability of car sharing and services provided by transportation network companies like Uber and Lyft make automobile ownership less necessary. E-commerce—conducted electronically via the internet—is reducing the need for shopping trips. Wireless internet connectivity and videoconferencing software like Zoom have reduced the need to travel for face-to-face meetings. The COVID-19 pandemic accelerated these trends. Some people—particularly young and well-educated people—choose not to own automobiles because of concern for the environment.

The urban planning literature criticizes many aspects of the existing U.S. mobility architecture. Critics blame dependence on automobiles for producing low-density, land-consuming, sprawl development. They don't like the fact that an enormous amount of precious urban land is devoted to streets and parking. They point out that reliance on gasoline-driven motorized transportation is unsustainable because it is depleting non-renewable fossil fuels. They criticize use of cars, trucks, and motorcycles for contributing to serious health risks from air pollution, exacerbating global climate change, and fatalities, injuries, and property damage.

Changes in automobile design are reducing these problems, but are still far from eliminating them. There have been major advances in motorized vehicle fuel efficiency, reduction of emissions, and safety. Private industry and governments in the United States, Europe, China, Japan, Korea, Sweden, and other countries are investing in research and development to reduce or eliminate motorized vehicle emissions and make motorized vehicles more efficient and safer. Significant incremental improvements have become standard in the last decade. Automakers in the United States invest $19 billion per year on research and development (R&D)—an average of $1,700 for each new vehicle produced. The European Council for Automotive Research and Development (EUCAR) spends about US$38.5 billion a year on automotive research and development.

We are on the cusp of a third great wave of innovation that will rapidly make zero-emission, autonomous vehicles controlled by digital technology commonplace in developed countries and eventually universal everywhere in the world. This will fundamentally alter cities, regions, and society itself.

COMPLETE STREETS PLANNING

The "complete streets" movement envisions planning, designing, and operating roads, sidewalks, bicycle lanes, and other transportation infrastructure holistically. Complete streets plans integrate plans for bus lanes, bike lanes, conventional and high-occupancy vehicle (HOV) lanes, and sidewalks, as well as plans for automobiles, trucks, and motorcycles. They include consideration of public transportation stops, road crossings, median islands, pedestrian signals, curb extensions, streetscapes, street furniture, and landscaping. Complete streets plans are intended to improve livability as well as make the transportation network safer and more efficient for motorized vehicles, bicycles, and pedestrians. Major organizations including the American Planning Association, American Society of Landscape Architects, and the National Association of Realtors joined bicycle advocacy groups to form the National Complete Streets Coalition (NCSC) in 2005. Over 1,600 complete streets policies have been passed in the United States, including policies adopted by 35 state governments, the Commonwealth of Puerto Rico, and the District of Columbia. These range from simple aspirational statements to detailed policy plans. Figure 14.1 is a rendering created by DPW Associates urban designer Nelson Peng illustrating features common to many complete streets plans.

The National Complete Streets Coalition updates an inventory of all complete streets policies quarterly and releases an annual report on best complete streets practices. San Francisco, New York, Boston, and

Figure 14.1 Complete Streets Design.

many university towns have produced detailed complete streets manuals. New York City became a leader in complete streets policy implementation under the leadership of Janette Sadik-Khan. Box 14.1 is a biography of Sadik-Khan and a discussion of transportation plans and policies in New York City.

> ### BOX 14.1 JANETTE SADIK-KHAN
>
> Janette Sadik-Khan is a global transportation planning consultant who served as New York City's Transportation Commissioner from 2007 until 2013 under Mayor Michael Bloomberg. Sadik-Khan's account of her epic battles—*Streetfight: Handbook for an Urban Revolution* (Sadik-Khan & Solomonow, 2017) co-authored with her former press secretary Seth Solomonow, describes protests, lawsuits, and media controversy as she pushed through ambitious plans to transform many of New York City streets.
>
> Sadik-Khan succeeded in converting one of the world's most used street intersections—Broadway at 34th Street in New York City—into pedestrian areas combined with bicycle lanes. She oversaw the building of nearly 400 miles of bike lanes and more than 60 pedestrian plazas citywide, started seven rapid bus routes across all five of New York City's boroughs—the New York equivalent of counties. She created the largest bike share network in the United States—Citi Bike. During her six and a half years in office, approximately 180 acres of former New York City road space for motor vehicles was converted to use by bicycles and pedestrians, and another 44 acres designated as bus-only lanes. Sadik-Khan was convinced that most major streets are wider than they need to be. She eliminated lanes for automobiles to provide bicycle lanes and reduced crossing distances for pedestrians on streets.
>
> European-style rapid-transit buses in exclusive camera-enforced lanes reduced average bus travel time on New York City's crowded streets. Sadik-Khan oversaw planning and policy for New York City's bridges, roads, and ferry terminals. Other of her projects included a pedestrian wayfinding project that put signs on sidewalks to give pedestrians directions and distances to nearby landmarks; a "park smart" program for dynamic parking pricing following principles proposed by Donald Shoup described below; a freight trucking pilot program; and the "midtown in motion" project that allows traffic engineers to adjust stoplights remotely as traffic conditions change. Fewer people were killed in traffic crashes on New York's streets annually during Kahn's tenure as New York City Planning Commissioner than at any time in the past century.
>
> Sadik-Khan made data analysis fundamental to all her decisions under the famously data-oriented Mayor Bloomberg, and used modern quantitative transportation planning methods. She was a good observer. She learned from desire lines—naturally occurring travel patterns that reflect where people want to travel. For example, she and the New York City Department of Transportation created 6½ Avenue, a Harry Potter-inspired midblock crossing between Sixth and Seventh Avenues because that is where people wanted to go.
>
> Sadik-Khan learned from the famous street fights of the 1950s and 1960s between Robert Moses and Jane Jacobs, among others. She calls Moses "a public works tyrant who answered to no authority but his own as he force-engineered a car-based future onto New York" while Jacobs "envisioned a future built to a human scale instead of one designed to move as many cars as possible" (Sadik-Khan & Solomonow, 2017).
>
> As chair of the National Association of City Transportation Officials (NACTO)—an organization of transportation commissioners and directors in 86 cities—Sadik-Khan led the development and publication of guides to street and urban bikeway design that

Figure 14.2 Janette Sadik-Kahn.

Figure 14.3 New York City Pedestrianized Street at Broadway and 34th Street.

have been recognized by the U.S. Department of Transportation and adopted by more than 100 cities worldwide.

Prior to her appointment as New York City's Transportation Commissioner, Sadik-Khan worked under former New York City mayor David Dinkins, first in the New York City Department of Transportation as special counsel for state and federal affairs, and then as director of the Mayor's Office of Transportation, where she attracted attention by cracking down on diplomats with unpaid parking tickets that they received for parking illegally around the United Nations headquarters building. She moved to Washington as a deputy administrator at the U.S. Department of Transportation and then returned to New York City as a senior vice president of Parsons Brinckerhoff—a leading international engineering firm. In that role she consulted on the rebuilding of the World Trade Center among other important projects.

Sadik-Khan currently advises mayors of cities around the world as a principal at Bloomberg Associates, a philanthropic consultancy established by former New York City mayor Michael Bloomberg to help cities around the world improve the quality of life of their citizens. She has assisted mayors and their teams in developing street redesigns in Los Angeles, Detroit, Mexico City, Rio de Janeiro, Athens, and other cities.

Sadik-Khan holds a JD from Columbia University School of Law. She received a BA in political science from Occidental College.

CONGESTION MANAGEMENT PLANNING

Implementing programs to reduce traffic congestion is called traffic management. It involves congestion management planning. Traffic congestion is inconvenient and annoying. It is costly for individuals and the U.S. economy. Congestion management recognizes that there are too many vehicles for many existing streets and roads, and too little money to build enough new transportation infrastructure to make congestion disappear any time soon. Accordingly, congestion management seeks to manage traffic congestion—to reduce congestion and its impacts as much as possible. Plans and programs to address this problem are called congestion management programs (CMPs). The process is called Active Transportation Management (ATM). In addition to working to improve mobility, DOT now has a program to reduce the impact of congestion on air quality.

A recent study of congestion in the entire United States by researchers at Texas A&M University and the research and consulting firm INRIX found that in 2017:

a) trucks accounted for $20 billion (11%) of the total U.S. congestion cost;
b) the average auto commuter spent 54 hours in congestion and wasted 21 gallons of fuel due to congestion at an average cost of $1,080 in wasted time and fuel per year;
c) to reliably arrive on time for important highway trips, U.S. drivers had to allow an average of 34 minutes to make a trip that takes 20 minutes in light traffic;
d) congestion is bad in areas of the United States of every size; it is not just a big city problem;
e) congestion is much worse in evenings; and
f) approximately 54% of travel delay in large regions is on highways.

In the United States the accepted measure for rating traffic at intersections is the level of service (LOS). Standard transportation reference manuals rate congestion from LOS level A (no problem) to level F (serious delays). LOS level A permits free flows of traffic at or above the posted speed limit with complete mobility between lanes and delays no greater than ten seconds. Level F is a breakdown in the flow of traffic in which every vehicle moves slowly in lockstep with the vehicle in front of it, or stop-and-go traffic making travel time unpredictable. A common transportation planning goal in city and county general plans and congestion management plans is to achieve the LOS closest to A everywhere in the city given local conditions and budget constraints. Realistically this may be level B or C in parts of some cities. Congestion management plans based on the rational planning model generally prioritize use of funds available to improve the most congested and highest-volume choke points soonest.

A congestion management process (CMP) is a systematic and regionally accepted approach for managing congestion that provides accurate, up-to-date information on transportation system performance and assesses alternative strategies for congestion management to meet state and local standards. CMPs use an objectives-driven, performance-based approach to planning for congestion management based on system performance data, analysis, and evaluation.

The U.S. Department of Transportation requires a CMP in metropolitan areas with population exceeding 200,000, known as transportation management areas (TMAs). The CMP must be developed and implemented as an integrated part of the metropolitan transportation planning process. Federal regulations do not prescribe the methods and approaches that must be used to implement a CMP. However, the Federal Highway Administration recommends active traffic management (ATM) and provides guidance about how transportation agencies can make informed investment decisions regarding ATM by determining the feasibility of ATM strategies before committing significant resources towards any subsequent project development and design activities. Congestion management may rely on hard or soft strategies. Hard strategies include building new roads, subways, or light rail systems; increasing road widths; and physically modifying traffic lanes. Soft strategies include promoting carpooling; changing traffic lanes; and implementing better systems to inform motorists of congestion in real time, so that they can alter their routes. Many congestion management plans combine hard and soft strategies.

Congestion management planning and active transportation management are frequently combined with other transportation planning in metropolitan regions. CMP strategies are often metropolitan planning organization (MPO) strategies.

PARKING

Planning for parking is often a weak link in comprehensive city plans and even weaker in plans for metropolitan and other regions. Parking planning is one of few areas in which planners rarely use the rational planning model or think holistically about relationships among different areas and land uses.

A monumental 2005 study by University of California, Los Angeles urban planning professor Donald Shoup titled *The High Cost of Free Parking* has revolutionized planners' thinking about parking and encouraged more cities to think seriously about parking planning and policy.

Planning for parking is reflected in standards and regulations for two main types of parking—(a) public parking on streets and (b) requirements for parking availability in private residential and commercial buildings. Detailed parking standards are common. However, the basis on which the parking standards were determined is rarely clear and seldom reflects a comprehensive top-down vision of what will work best for an entire city or region.

Municipal zoning ordinances typically specify minimum parking requirements for private residential and other buildings based on their density, location, and use. Zoning ordinances usually call for one parking space for each car expected to be parked at a building. For example, if a proposed apartment building will have six one-bedroom units designed for households with two adults, and local research has shown that half the households will own one car and half will own two cars, a standard requiring that the building must contain an average of 1.5 parking spaces per unit would require the developer to provide a total of nine spaces. The ordinance will reduce the demand for on-street parking, but add to building construction costs and, accordingly, the cost of houses, condominiums, and rental units to which they apply—exacerbating housing affordability problems. San Francisco and some other cities deliberately limit the number of parking spaces in new residential buildings to fewer than the number of cars they anticipate owners will have, fully aware that this will increase on-street parking and make it more difficult to find on-street parking. Their reasoning is that if it is difficult and time-consuming to find on-street parking, some households will choose to have fewer cars or no car at all and more residents will choose public transportation, such as buses or light or heavy rail. Increasing ridership can help public transportation systems get enough more riders to warrant continuing them, and more farebox revenue to help keep them financially viable. Reducing parking spaces may also be justified by concern for the environment, since many public transit systems reduce greenhouse gas emissions compared to gasoline-burning cars and trucks. This strategy creates a dual market. A renter or condo owner pays more if they also get a parking space with their unit. Critics question whether designing inadequate parking, deliberately making on-street parking difficult, and relying on market failure to increase public transit is good policy.

Most public parking is curbside parking on streets where parking may be controlled by parking meters or signage specifying time limits. Planners help set different rates for different locations—higher for parking near restaurants, for example, than on residential streets.

Zoning ordinances may include private parking lots as a permitted use and rely on the private market to help provide parking. Some cities build municipal parking structures. Separate parking lots or structures serving commercial buildings are common in the United States, but separate parking lots or structures for vehicles from residential buildings are not.

Shoup found that the standards for the number of parking spaces for different kinds of land uses were often arbitrary or questionable. The rates charged were almost always much lower than the real cost of parking. Parking on public streets is often free. When metered, the revenue collected almost never covers the full costs of providing the parking. Shoup argues that "free" parking is not costless in economic terms. If parking is left unpriced or is improperly priced, distortions in resource allocation occur.

Shoup concludes that off-street parking requirements appear arbitrary and excessive even when planners have data that purport to predict parking demand. Land for parking is land lost for other uses. Providing free parking or parking which is effectively deeply subsidized reduces drivers' costs relative to other modes of travel and leads to more vehicle ownership and more trips by car—arguably many more than there should be. If parking was not subsidized and was more expensive, there would be fewer parking places. In Shoup's opinion, excessive parking supply generates more vehicle trips and higher road capacity than are necessary. It contributes to high utility costs and other negative impacts of urban sprawl. Shoup also argues that parking requirements tied to land use can inhibit the redevelopment of old buildings for new uses because their sites may not be able to accommodate the required number of parking spaces for the new use. Encouraging car trips by underpricing parking creates a self-reinforcing vicious cycle. Municipal governments come under pressure to provide more parking spaces to accommodate the growing number of cars, and urban planners respond by setting aside more space for parking, which in turn encourages more car trips. In sum, Shoup states that parking requirements often "subsidize cars, distort transportation choices, warp urban form, increase housing costs, burden low-income households, debase urban design, damage the economy, and degrade the environment" (Shoup, 2005).

Shoup proposes policy options that municipal governments can adopt to address parking more rationally. Most important is to reduce parking demand by lowering the cost of travel by alternatives to cars. For example, cities could allow developers to pay a fee in lieu of providing the normally required parking space for a particular land use. The fees collected could then be used either to provide for public parking spaces (priced realistically based on market demand) or improve bus service or other public transportation.

Another strategy Shoup recommends is to implement plans and policies to reduce the time drivers spend cruising to look for a parking space. Drivers search for free curb space (cruise) because it can reduce or eliminate the cost of paying for parking, even as it increases drivers' time, congestion, and fuel costs. Shoup argues that charging the market price for curbside parking—a price at least equal to the price of adjacent off-street parking—removes the economic incentive to cruise. He suggests setting curbside parking prices that vary over the course of a day, so as to achieve an average parking space occupancy rate of 85%.

Shoup's clear thinking has begun to change parking planning. But parking planning still has much room for improvement.

PUBLIC TRANSIT PLANNING

Public transit consists of regularly scheduled vehicle trips, with the capacity to carry multiple passengers and open to all paying passengers. It may be by bus, subway, heavy rail, light rail, streetcar, ferryboat or other public modes of transportation. Transportation planners usually do not consider travel by carpools, school buses, or taxis public transportation.

Public transportation represents a small percentage of all trips in the low-density, auto-oriented United States. The percentages of trips by public transportation is much higher in Western Europe and some Asian cities and city regions.

Statistics on public transportation are available in the annual American Public Transportation Association (APTA) *Fact Book*. APTA reports that in 2018, there were over 2,000 public transit systems in the United States—928 in urban areas and 1,279 in suburban and rural areas. There were over 4,500 nonprofit transit systems in the United States in 2018. Forty-eight percent of public transit in the United States was by rail, 47% by bus, and 5% by other modes.

The number of trips on public transportation by fare-paying passengers in the United

States peaked in 1945 at the end of World War II when the big auto manufacturers had been mostly producing jeeps and other military vehicles for several years, and gasoline was rationed. It reached a post-war low in 1975. The number of trips on public transportation in the United States is now increasing. The American Transportation Association reports that there was a 28% increase in public transit ridership between 1995 and 2009—faster than the 23% growth in the American population during the same period.[4] In 2009 almost one-third of all public transportation occurred within the New York City metropolitan area—3.2 billion trips—followed by Chicago and Los Angeles.[5]

Based on hundreds of hours of interviews Jarrett Walker—an independent transportation consultant—concluded that, to be useful, public transit must meet seven demands including taking people where they want to go and respecting riders' safety and comfort.[6] Public transit must be economically viable. Operating costs are a key consideration in public transit finance. Farebox revenue almost never covers 100% of public transit's cost.

Bus systems are essential—particularly for lower-income people. In the United States, more affluent riders often choose other travel options. In some other countries bus systems (or parts of them) are much higher-quality than in the United States and attract a broad ridership. Curitiba, Brazil, and Bogotá, Colombia, have notably successful bus systems that are widely used by different types of riders.

The visionary mayor of Curitiba, Brazil, Jaime Lerner—an architect—made the decision in the early 1970s to construct a bus rapid transit system rather than a subway to serve the rapidly growing city. Lerner's plan involved building broad highways from the center of Curitiba out to rapidly urbanizing peri-urban land, and locating specially designed boarding platforms where passengers could pre-pay fare and stand on a platform that opened into specially designed articulated buses so that a large number of passengers could all board at once. Lerner's projections showed that if systems met riders' needs a large enough number would use them that buses could be very frequent and move large numbers of people quickly to destinations along the highway. This was a huge gamble, but Lerner's design worked, making Curitiba an icon for transportation planners. Curitiba's BRT system has been imitated all over the world. Figure 14.4 shows Curitiba's BRT system.

While many cities accommodate bicycles on special bicycle lanes, more or less successfully, Bogotá, Columbia is well-known to transportation planners for its ciclovias ("bicycle roads") where there are lanes that

Figure 14.4 Bus Rapid Transit, Curitiba, Brazil (2006).

Figure 14.5 Ciclovia, Bogotá, Columbia (2015).

can accommodate large numbers of bicyclists. Figure 14.5 shows one of Bogotá's ciclovias. In addition to bicycles, lanes accommodate pedestrians.

Many countries in Western Europe have high-quality bus routes with new, high-quality, and well-maintained buses that middle- and upper-income riders use. There are some bus systems like this in the United States. In New York City, the Transportation Commissioner—Janette Sadik-Khan—successfully implemented comfortable European-style rapid transit buses that could travel quickly in exclusive camera-enforced lanes. The combination of comfort and speed attracted middle- and upper-income riders (Box 14.1).

Private buses transporting workers from San Francisco to Google and other high-tech firms in Silicon Valley are called "Google buses". Google buses provide a comfortable interior where tech workers can work during the long commute from home to work and back. Less affluent neighborhood residents in San Francisco object to Google buses for competing for curb space, adding to traffic congestion, and making it easier for highly paid tech workers from Silicon Valley to live in San Francisco and bid up rents and the price of homeownership.

A recurring debate in congestion management involves latent demand. If more people want to travel from the residential suburb of Fremont, California, to clusters of high-tech industry in nearby Palo Alto than choose to go because of congestion during the morning and evening rush hours, adding a lane to the highway connecting Fremont and Palo Alto will meet some of the latent demand. However, it may not relieve congestion. Enough additional commuters may choose to use the highway that conditions stay essentially the same. Lewis Mumford famously observed that "trying to fix congestion by adding lanes is like trying to prevent obesity by loosening your belt".

Transportation planners often manage congestion through pricing. Theoretically if users pay the true costs of transportation—including internalizing externalities—the system will be optimally efficient. However other values are involved. Planners often recommend discounts for frequent riders, school-age children, people with disabilities, and seniors. Congestion pricing can shift demand to make traffic flow more smoothly and provide revenue that can be used to subsidize public transit. High-occupancy vehicle (HOV) lanes encourage carpooling because they dramatically reduce traffic congestion in the HOV lanes. High-occupancy toll (HOT) lanes that allow vehicles to travel in HOV lanes if they pay tolls that reflect the number of passengers and time of day are becoming more common.

A recurring urban design issue in transportation planning involves the interface between transit systems and large destinations like shopping centers. Transportation to shopping centers is often time-consuming at the destination because it involves a many-to-one location flow on the way to the shopping center and a one-to-many flow as shoppers return home. Many shopping centers set stores back from access roads, requiring shoppers to walk long distances to and from parking lots and public transit stops. Portland, Oregon, is notable for planning direct local bus access to shopping centers designed so that buses arrive and depart directly adjacent to mall stores.

Transit systems require adequate ridership to at least offset some of the costs of construction and operating expenses. Ridership equals the number of potential riders times the ridership rate—the percentage of people who will choose to ride on the system. Side effects from transit systems like emissions, noise, vibration, and the impact on the environment affect ridership and, in turn, the system's viability. There is a relationship between density and ridership. In the United States, the auto-centered urban form and low-density development of single-family homes, make it difficult to get enough ridership to support public transit. This is different from the enormous densities in the core of Asian megacities where hundreds of thousands of riders live near transit, do not have cars, and can afford to take public transit. The enormous volume of ridership makes it possible for public transit systems in high-density areas to provide frequent trips and generate enough revenue that fares can be kept low. Shanghai—the largest city in the world—operates the largest bus system in the world. Shanghai's new subway system is now more extensive than the subway systems in London, New York, and Paris.

The key to getting enough ridership to make a public transportation system financially viable is not just high ridership from a large area. It also involves adequate density around transit stops. Transit villages—high-density residential clusters with other amenities around transit stops—are a common planning recommendation. More and more are being built in the United States.

PLANNING FOR THE COMING TRANSPORTATION REVOLUTION

Transportation planning requires planners to consider technologies and needs in the next few decades that will be fundamentally different from what they are today. The growth in travel demand and new technologies will require two kinds of creative transportation planning. The first is to extend and adapt existing transportation infrastructure to accommodate carbon-neutral autonomous and zero-emission vehicles (ZEVs). The second is to develop and implement strategies to address new paradigm-changing transportation technologies.

CONNECTED AUTONOMOUS VEHICLES (CAVS)

Cars that drive themselves without human intervention are called connected autonomous vehicles (CAVs). They are also known as connected automated cars and driverless cars, or simply autonomous vehicles. The Society of Automotive Engineers (SAE) International—a worldwide group of engineers that establishes transportation standards—divides CAVs into 5 levels. Level 0 means the car is always under human control. Level 4 CAV software can slow or stop a car when the car in front slows down, move a car back into its proper lane if it begins to drift out of its lane, and move a car to avoid a collision if a car in an adjacent lane gets too close. At level 5 a CAV is fully self-driving.

In 2004, the U.S. Defense Advanced Research Projects Agency (DARPA)—an

Figure 14.6 Autonomous Rapid Transit System Design (2021).

agency that supports basic research on technologies that may have military applications—began a competition for experimental autonomous—self driving—vehicles called the DARPA Grand Challenge. To encourage automakers and faculty–student university teams working on prototypes for autonomous vehicles, DARPA offered a $1 million prize to the team that built an autonomous vehicle best able to successfully navigate a relatively simple course in the Mojave Desert. None of the 15 autonomous vehicles that competed in the first DARPA Grand Challenge completed the course. DARPA doubled the prize amount in 2005. One hundred ninety-five autonomous vehicle prototypes competed, and five completed the course. The Stanford University racing team won. In 2007, DARPA's Grand Challenge required vehicles to obey traffic regulations and deal with intersections, merging traffic, parking, and other challenges on a 60-mile course that simulated urban conditions. Carnegie-Mellon University working with General Motors, Continental AG, and Caterpillar won the 2007 DARPA competition.

By spring, 2013 many new vehicles being sold were level 3 CAVs that could take over all driving controls in select conditions. In 2016 General Motors, Mercedes, Tesla, Toyota, Honda, and Google all announced that they would be making self-driving cars by 2020. They have all had to push back that target date. Once autonomous vehicle technology works safely it will take time for regulators to phase in permission to use CAVs on existing streets. However, the change is coming fast.

CAV technology can be applied to public transportation systems as an alternative to conventional buses or subways. Designs could include passenger vehicles very similar to buses or light rail cars, but without a driver or pods that could accommodate a few passengers or even a single passenger. The new term for systems like this is automated rapid transit (ART) systems. Figure 14.6 is a rendering by HDR Partners urban designer Nelson Peng illustrating what an ART system replacing a bus or light transit system might be like.

SMART VEHICLE TECHNOLOGY

A second revolution is that transportation is becoming smarter. Planners need to respond to the way in which information technology has already transformed mobility and will continue to do so. Developments in information systems related to transportation are proceeding apace. Big data, cloud storage, and other changes in the digital technology environment promise ever greater connectivity. In 2003 a group of the largest European, American, and Japanese automakers formed the Automotive Open System Architecture (AUTOSAR) consortium to establish an open and standardized software architecture for automotive electronic control units (ECUs). AUTOSAR ECU standards provide a set of specifications that describe basic software modules, define application interfaces, and provide a common development methodology for designing transportation-related technology based on a standardized exchange format. This has helped digital technology for motorized vehicles, sensors, and humans at remote locations to interact.

As smartcard technology and transit management systems have improved, analyzing passenger flows has become more precise. Commercial mapping and route guidance software, such as Google Maps and WAZE, already offer drivers the ability to plan trips and check traffic conditions in real time. Mobility tools that intelligently sort information and present only user-relevant options are already well developed and are improving rapidly. The ability to capture and filter transportation information in real time and deliver personalized mobility solutions to cell phones and screens on vehicle dashboards in text, maps, and voice already works well and is becoming increasingly accurate.

"Smart cities" innovations already embed sensors capable of capturing transportation (and other) data in real time and delivering it to physical or digital control rooms where it can be analyzed. User-friendly information can be sent back in real time to people making travel decisions. Push technology can send information to cell phones or other devices to alert travelers of traffic choke points, accidents, stalled vehicles, and objects in the road. The internet of things (IOT) promises to link people, cars, public transit, and traffic management to a much greater extent in the near future.

Vehicles are becoming smarter in many ways in addition to CAV technology for individual vehicles. Vehicle-to-vehicle communication holds the promise of making much more efficient use of existing infrastructure by reducing the distance needed between moving vehicles. Traffic signals with embedded sensors monitoring conditions in real time can adjust to traffic flows and alter start and stop times to improve mobility.

Innovations to facilitate shared mobility are changing rapidly. The average U.S. car is idle 96% of the time. Programs to improve carpooling and car sharing can reduce the cost of mobility. Since Uber began operation in 2009, private transportation network companies (TNCs) like Uber and Lyft have revolutionized paying for individual or pooled rides. Car sharing is reducing the need for multiple vehicle ownership or ownership of any automobile. Transport for London has integrated bus, subway (tube), local rail, light rail, river services, taxi, private hire cars, buses, bicycle rental, and road and traffic management. London's Oyster card can be used to pay for travel on any part of this system throughout Greater London.

AUTOMOBILE SAFETY

In the United States about 39,000 people are killed in automobile accidents each year. Automobile accidents are the ninth leading cause of death worldwide with more than 1.25 million fatalities annually.[7]

Traffic calming is a common approach to increasing automotive safety. It is intended to slow down traffic and smooth out speeds so that drivers are less stressed and there are fewer accidents. Physical design features can slow traffic and protect pedestrians and bicyclists. Speed bumps, diverters, street closures, roundabouts, chokers, bump outs, extending sidewalks to reduce the crossing distance, and chicanes (serpentine curves in a road) are common traffic-calming designs. Traffic calming can also involve changes such as adding or widening sidewalks, using part of a road for landscaping or bicycle lanes, reserving land for light rail tracks in the middle of a road, and providing reversible center lanes. Road diet techniques reduce the number of lanes on a roadway to improve safety or provide space for bicycles and other modes of travel. The Netherlands developed *woonerfs*—streets designed for cars, bicycles, and pedestrians to share space. In the right context and if they are properly designed, woonerfs have proven safe and effective. Other countries are now experimenting with woonerfs. Figure 14.7 illustrates a woonerf in Lodz, Poland.

The Vision Zero auto safety program is a worldwide movement to eliminate traffic fatalities. Sweden has become a world leader in automotive safety. In 1997 the Swedish parliament resolved to work to eliminate all traffic fatalities in Sweden. Since then, the Swedish government has coordinated public and private sector plans and policies to eliminate traffic fatalities. The Swedish government collaborated with the two largest Swedish automakers—Volvo and Saab—on the Vision Zero program. Their combined efforts reduced per capita traffic fatalities in Sweden by more than 70% between 1980 and 2013 compared to a 36% reduction in the United States during the same period. In 2013, 27 people per million were killed in traffic fatalities in Sweden compared to 104 in the United States. Sweden's approach is an example of collaborative planning between private industry and government, attacking the problem of traffic fatalities, injuries, and property damage by a combination of safer vehicle design, driver education, better road design, lower speed limits, better signage, and other hard and soft strategies. The Vision Zero idea—modeled on Swedish practice—has spread to other countries, including the United States. Some states and some local U.S. governments are adopting policies to implement Vision Zero plans.

While these advances in vehicle safety have been occurring in affluent developed countries, the exponential growth in the number of automobiles and other two- and three-wheeled gasoline-driven vehicles on roads in India, China, Indonesia, Nigeria, and other developing countries is rapidly increasing the worldwide number of auto-related accidents, fatalities, injuries, and property damage. The combination of bad roads, new drivers, congestion, weak traffic enforcement, and vehicles that do not meet modern Western safety standards is creating

Figure 14.7 Woonerf (Lodz, Poland, 2014).

serious safety problems. The World Health Organization (WHO) estimates that there were 261,367 road traffic fatalities in China in 2013—18.8 per 100,000 people—and 207,551 in India—16.6 per 100,000. In the United States there were 34,064 traffic fatalities in 2013—10.6 per 100,000.

PARADIGM-CHANGING TECHNOLOGIES

The most important changes in technology involve paradigm changes. In the 19th and early 20th centuries, steamboats, horse-drawn streetcars, cable cars, electric streetcars, subways, automobiles, and airplanes operationalized entirely new ways of moving people and goods that only their inventors and a small group of others even imagined. Those who knew about the emerging technologies were often convinced that they would fail. Many prototypes of new paradigm-changing transportation technologies now exist. We can expect some of them to become operational and others to be invented in the near future. In addition to travel by CAVs and ZEVs, in coming decades people and goods may move quickly, comfortably, and safely in vehicles that glide on magnetic fields, soar in the air, or are propelled by puffs of air. Box 14.2 describes hyperloops and magnetic levitation trains—two of the most debated of the new transportation technologies.

BOX 14.2 MAGNETIC LEVITATION AND HYPERLOOPS

Transportation planners have long sought alternatives to rail systems running on steel rails. If their proponents prove correct, improvements in two emerging technologies may realize that dream. Magnetic levitation systems might transform heavy train transportation within metropolitan areas and among major population centers. Theoretically, hyperloops could transport people and goods for hundreds of miles between major concentrations of population in minutes.

Figure 14.8 Magnetic Levitation Train (Shanghai, China, 2006).

Figure 14.9 Proposed Sydney to Melbourne, Australia Hyperloop (2020).

Magnetic levitation (mag lev) involves suspending passenger or freight cars using a magnetic field. Mag lev systems are powered by electricity. Trains glide frictionlessly on a cushion of air. A mag lev train has been transporting passengers at over 430 kilometers per hour (a little under 270 miles per hour) on a silent and vibrationless line between Shanghai's main airport (Pudong) half way to the Shanghai's older Hongqiao Airport since 2004. Shanghai's mag lev system works, but proved so expensive, controversial, and electric-power-consuming that the other half of the line has not been built. If magnetic levitation technology improves and costs decrease sufficiently, magnetic levitation trains could become a very fast and comfortable alternative to trains, heavy rail systems, and subways.

Could people and freight be propelled by compressed air at Mach 5—hypersonic speed that is five times the speed of sound—in pods suspended on a cushion of air in an elevated tube that looks like a circular hamster Habitrail or in underground subway tunnels? Figure 14.9 is a rendering of what a hyperloop between Sydney and Melbourne, Australia might be like by Zac McClelland, the co-founder of VicHyper—an Australian transportation technology startup firm McClelland created while he was a graduate student in aeronautics and aerospace engineering at the Royal Melbourne Institute of Technology.

Half of the people that Elon Musk—a flamboyant technology entrepreneur, investor, and engineer who has built prototype sections of hyperloops—pitched this idea to said the answer was an obvious "yes". The other half said it was impossible. The jury is still out, but SpaceX—a company Musk started and still runs—has built an above-ground section of a hyperloop and bored a prototype hyperloop tunnel at their headquarters in Hawthorne, California.

In 2012 Musk unveiled his idea for a hyperloop that could transport people and freight for distances close to 1,000 miles at a speed above Mach 1 (767 miles per hour). People took notice, because Musk is a serial entrepreneur who has started other bold, high-risk transportation and energy ventures. Musk created Tesla which is a leader in zero-emission vehicles, SpaceX—a company that builds and operates rockets traveling to space and returning intact at fractions of the costs of other space vehicles—and SolarCity—the second-largest manufacturer of solar panels in the United States. As of January 2022, by some measures Musk was the wealthiest person in the world with plenty of his own money to invest and credibility to interest talented scientists and other heavy hitters in his ideas.

Musk assigned engineers from SpaceX to elaborate on his idea for a hyperloop and design a prototype. In 2013, armed with their design, he unveiled a proposal for a hyperloop that could travel the 350 miles between Los Angeles and San Francisco at 760 miles per hour—bringing passengers door to door in less than half an hour, compared to five or more hours of annoying and unpredictable freeway driving. The pod designs for the passenger version look like French, Japanese, or Chinese bullet train cars. Instead of riding on steel rails, the pods would ride on a cushion of air. Rather than getting electrical power from the rails, they would be propelled pneumatically by linear induction motors and air compressors.

One of the best ways to interest investors and potential users skeptical of a new technology is to build a proof-of-concept prototype. Musk and another wealthy entrepreneur—Richard Branson, the founder of the Virgin Group—have built above-ground and underground hyperloop demonstration projects.

Musk created The Boring Company (TBC) to design technology to bore under-ground tunnels at what he hopes will be about 8% of the cost of boring tunnels with existing tunneling technology. The Boring Company opened their first mile-long test tunnel at SpaceX headquarters at the end of 2018. Musk's third-generation boring system—named Prufrock—claims to be able to support a 15-fold improvement in tunneling speed compared to other state-of-the-art technologies without disturbing the land surface. The Boring Company has a product line of five different tunneling systems.

Musk has made his hyperloop designs open source and inaugurated competitions to encourage other companies and faculty–student university teams to create their own variants of hyperloops. Virgin Hyperloop—a Virgin Group company—is testing their own hyperloop designs in Las Vegas. Virgin Hyperloop's prototype vehicles seat about 28 passengers. However, convoys of the vehicles might be able to transport thousands of passengers per hour. A three-station hyperloop is operating in Las Vegas. Other companies and student teams are working on hyperloop designs.

TRANSPORTATION AND CLIMATE CHANGE

Perhaps the most important issue facing city and regional planners is the existential problem of global climate change discussed in Chapter 17. Reducing greenhouse gas (GHG) emissions as quickly as possible must be a top global priority. Automobiles, trucks, buses, motorcycles, scooters, airplanes, and ships account for about one-third of GHG emissions. Planners and policy makers are increasingly considering transportation, global warming, and energy jointly.

A combination of technological advances, government regulations, and market forces, have produced rapid and major reduction of GHGs from individual automobiles, trucks, buses, and motorcycles both by reducing combustion inside internal combustion engines and treatment of gases at the tailpipe. The use of lead in gasoline was phased out by the mid-1990s in most of the Western world. Polluting fuel additives like sulfur have been reduced or eliminated. Catalytic converters fitted to autos' exhaust systems convert carbon dioxide CO_2 to carbon monoxide (CO) (which is less harmful to the atmosphere than CO), and water. However, the growth of ownership of automobiles and other forms of motorized transport and vehicle miles traveled (VMT) have increased

CO_2 emissions from motorized vehicles. Over 90% of the fuel used for transportation is petroleum-based gasoline and diesel fuel.

The percentage of zero-emission vehicles will increase rapidly in the next few years. California has announced that it will require all new vehicles sold in the state to be ZEVs by 2035. Experts agree that the connected and automated vehicle market share will increase rapidly as CAV technology improves, prices decrease, and CAVs become more cost effective. They disagree about how quickly CAVs and ZEVs will replace conventional motor vehicles. Planning new transportation infrastructure with a long useful life now needs to anticipate the impact of CAVs.

THE CORPORATE AVERAGE FUEL ECONOMY (CAFE) STANDARD

The most important U.S. federal regulation concerning fuel efficiency is the Corporate Average Fuel Economy (CAFE) standard. The engineering concept is complex, the law arcane, and conflict over the power of the federal government to preempt state CAFE standards that are higher than the federal standard is intense. The basic concept, however, is clear and logical. If government requires automakers to attain an *average* fuel efficiency (measured in miles per gallon) for all of the vehicles in the entire fleet they produce for each successive model year that is lower than what would occur in the free market, that will improve fuel efficiency.[8] Enforcing the standard will reduce gasoline consumption, which in turn will reduce automobile emissions. Automakers are free to make many very fuel-efficient vehicles and just a few gas guzzlers; almost all vehicles close to the average; or any mix of gasoline-powered, hybrid, and all electric vehicles so long as they meet the corporate average standard. Chapter 17 describes the CAFE standard.

SUMMARY

Mobility is fundamental to well-functioning cities and regions. Transportation systems, sidewalks, parking and other transportation-related parts of the built environment have impacts well beyond the movement of people and goods from place to place. They dramatically impact the natural environment.

At the neighborhood and site scale, transportation and transportation-related systems affect the quality of urban life and are one of the most important determinants of livability. Transportation planning at different scales requires planners with a variety of skills and the imagination and technical ability to combine transportation with land use, environmental, housing, and other plans.

Transportation infrastructure occupies much of the built environment and is costly to build and maintain. As a result, transportation planning has developed its own advanced techniques and special features. Transportation planning provides opportunities for many people with a great range of skills. Because transportation is so important, costly, and durable, skilled transportation planners with the ability and education to model transportation systems and networks play a particularly important role. Beyond the mobility and accessibility functions of transportation systems, urban planners and urban designers consider impacts on the natural environment and society.

From a pure mobility perspective, transportation planning is about moving people and goods from place to place within a neighborhood, city, region, or larger area. Planners use micro-level data on population, income, employment, vehicle ownership and trip origins and destinations to prepare trip generation and origin–destination studies. They determine travelers' mode split and mode choice. These analytics help policy makers decide where to locate different types of transportation infrastructure, manage travel demand, and adapt and extend existing transportation infrastructure.

Individuals more-or-less consciously evaluate trip alternatives in terms of time, cost, comfort, privacy, speed, convenience, ambience, and perhaps carbon emissions or other environmental concerns. Urban and regional planners planning mobility architecture at any scale can help design systems that will allow users flexibility to satisfy these concerns.

Since most trips are multi-modal and the nature of trips change at different times of the day, week, or season, multi-modal analysis at different times is essential. Speed and distance are important, but the most critical issue transportation planners face is to make places accessible.

Information is important to mobility. Digital technology is making vehicles "smart". Smart systems are connecting vehicles to each other, digital data sources, and humans at remote locations in real time. Transportation planning should take place within a connected, heterogeneous, intelligent, and personalized (CHIP) mobility framework along the lines developed by Massachusetts Institute of Technology professors Venkat Sumantran, Charles Fine, and David Gonsalvez. A CHIP mobility framework responds to digital technology connecting motorized vehicles. It takes advantage of increasingly heterogeneous modes of travel as new travel modes join older modes, and intelligent systems replace much human thinking with guidance by computers.

Motor vehicles are the largest sources of air pollution in the United States. Planning to create more compact city-region form, public transportation that minimizes or eliminates pollution, and transportation infrastructure that reduces the negative impacts of vehicle-generated air pollution are important aspects of transportation planning. Transportation-related GHG emissions account for a third of all GHG emissions, so transportation planning to reduce them is critical to climate change planning.

Livability is a critical aspect of transportation planning. Planners and urban designers know how to create great streets with complete streets designs that will improve the experience of driving, bicycling, or walking along (or even in) streets or *woonerfs*—streets that permit walking, bicycling, and motor vehicles.

Disruptive new transportation technologies like the steamboat, electric streetcars, and the Model T Ford altered mobility and changed city and regional form during the last 200 years. New technologies promising zero-energy autonomous vehicles (ZEVs) connected to big data with smart technologies and new transportation paradigms such as magnetic levitation and hyperloops, promise to alter cities more than anything that has come before. Transportation planners will play a critical role in the coming transportation revolution.

CONCEPTS

3Cs Planning Process
Active Transportation Management (ATM)
Adequate Public Facilities Ordinance
Autonomous Vehicle
Complete Streets Program
Congestion Management
Connected, Heterogeneous, Intelligent, and Personalized (CHIP) Mobility Framework
Corporate Average Fuel Economy (CAFE) Standard
Federal Transit Administration (FTA)
Fixing America's Surface Transportation (FAST) Act
Gravity Model
Highway Performance Monitoring System (HPMS)
Hybrid Vehicle
Intelligent Transportation System (ITS)
Intermodal Surface Transportation Efficiency Act (ISTEA)
Journey to Work
Level of Service (LOS)
Mode Split
Moving Ahead for Progress in the 21st Century (MAP 21)
Origin–Destination Study
Road Diet
State Transportation Improvement Program (STIP)
Traffic Calming
Transportation Analysis Zone (TAZ)
Travel Demand Management (TDM)
Trip Generation Study
Vehicle Miles Traveled (VMT)
Vision Zero Program
Zero-Emission Vehicle (ZEV)

PEOPLE

Donald Appleyard
Donald Shoup
Venkat Sumantran

NOTES

1 Of 607,000 bridges in the USA, 67,000 were classified as structurally deficient in 2012 (ITE & Meyer, 2016). Between 2005 and 2015 15% of state capital spending on highways went to bridge rehabilitation and replacement (U.S. DOT, 2015).
2 A travel time index (TTI) is the ratio of actual motor vehicle trip travel time to travel time under free flow conditions. A TTI of 1.18 means that travelers took 18% more travel time than a similar trip with no delays. Travel time reliability is measured by a Travel Planning Time index (PTI) that reflects the probability of delays. For example, a PTI value of 3.0 means a person needs to plan 60 minutes for a 20-minute trip in order to arrive on time 19 out of 20 times.
3 Regional, state, and local data include primary data that metropolitan planning organizations, cities, counties, and transit providers collect for proposed projects, state finance office data, and academic studies. State bureaus of transportation generate additional statistics available on the Bureau of Transportation Statistics (BTS) website (BTS, 2021). Transit mobility data collected by transit agencies are pooled in the National Transit Database (NTD) managed by the U.S. Federal Transit Administration (FTA).
4 There were 19 billion trips on buses, subways, trains, and other forms of public transportation by fare-paying passengers in the United States in 1945 (Levy, 2017: 238). The total declined to a postwar low of 5.6 billion trips in 1975 and rose to 10.4 billion in 2009 (ibid: 238).
5 Of the 10.4 billion public transit trips in the United States in 2009, 3.2 billion were provided by the New York City Metropolitan Transportation Authority. There were a little over half a billion trips by public transportation in Chicago, and just under half a billion in Los Angeles. Over two-thirds of all subway trips in the United States are on the New York City subway system, which has 36 subway lines, 472 stations, and 6,418 vehicles (Levy, 2017: 238).
6 Walker's list of seven demands transit must meet to be useful are: (1) It takes me where I want to go. (2) It takes me when I want to go. (3) It is a good use of my time. (4) It is a good use of my money. (5) It respects me in the level of safety, comfort, and amenity it provides. (6) I can trust it. And (7) It give me freedom to change my plans (Walker, 2007: 31).
7 The United States National Safety Council estimated that 38,800 people were killed in U.S. automobile accidents in 2018 (NSC, 2019). There is about one traffic fatality in the United States for every 100 million miles traveled. The U.S. Bureau of Transportation Statistics Fatality Reporting System (FARS) reports that there were 33,654 fatal motor vehicle crashes in the United States in 2018 in which 36,560 people were killed—11.2 deaths per 100,000 people and 1.13 deaths per 100 million miles traveled. The FARS fatality rate per 100,000 people ranged from 4.4 in the District of Columbia to 22.2 in Mississippi.
8 The CAFE standard applies to passenger cars or light trucks with a gross vehicle weight rating (GVWR) of 8,500 pounds (3,856 kg) or less, and medium-duty passenger vehicles, such as large sports utility vehicles and passenger vans, with GVWR up to 10,000 pounds, produced for sale in the United States. The standard is set at the maximum feasible levels DOT determines in each model year.

SUGGESTIONS FOR FURTHER LEARNING

Overviews: Robert Cervero, Erick Guera, & Stefan Al, *Beyond mobility* (2017). Institute of Transportation Engineers (ITE) & Michael Meyer, *Transportation planning handbook*, 4th ed (2016). Carlos Daganzo & Yanfeng Ouyang, *Public transportation systems* (2019). Jarrett Walker, *Human transit* (2007). Genevieve Giuliano & Susan Hanson, *The geography of urban transportation*, 4th ed (2017). **Transportation Data:** American Public Transportation Association (APTA), *Fact book* (2020). National Transit Database [website] (2021). Transportation Research Board (TRB) [website] (2021). Bureau of Transportation Statistics Statistical Products and Data [website] (2021). Bureau of Transportation Statistics website (2022). **Short Transportation Planning Videos (Many Topics):** City beautiful, YouTube channel. **Metropolitan Transportation Planning:** Robert Cervero, *The transit metropolis* (1998). **Street Design:** Allan Jacobs, *Great streets* (1995). NACTO, *Urban street design guide* (2013). Michael Southworth & Eran Ben Joseph, *Streets and the shaping of towns and cities* (2003). **Boulevards:** Allan Jacobs, Elizabeth MacDonald, & Yodan Rofe, *The boulevard book* (2003). **Street Livability:** Donald Appleyard, *Livable streets* (1981). Bruce Appleyard, *Livable streets 2.0* (2020). Jane Jacobs, *Death and life of great American cities* (1961). NACTO, *Urban street design guide* (2013). **Walking and Bicycling:** John Pucher & Ralph Buehler, *City cycling* (2012). Melody Hoffman, *Bike lanes are white lanes* (2016). Janette Sadik-Khan & Seth Solomonow, *Streetfight* (2017). Janette Sadik-Khan, New York's streets? Not so mean any more [video] (2013). **New Transportation Technologies:** Venkat Sumantran, Charles Fine, & David Gonsalvez, *Faster, smarter, greener: The future of the car and urban mobility* (2017). Richard Gilbert &

Anthony Perl, *Transport revolutions* (2010). Daniel Sperling, *Three revolutions: Steering automated, shared, and electric vehicles to a better future* (2018). *Transportation Planning and Technology*, Part C: *Emerging Technologies*. [journal]. **Active Transportation Management:** U.S. Federal Highway Administration, *Active traffic management feasibility and screening guide* (2020). **Automobile Safety:** Vision Zero Network [website] (2021). World Health Organization (WHO), *Global status report on road safety (2015)*. **Parking:** Donald Shoup, *The high cost of free parking* (2005) and The high cost of free parking [video] (2018). **Bus Rapid Transit:** Robert Lindahl, *The smart city: Learning from Curitiba* (2013). **Transportation Journals:** *ACCESS. Transportation Research Record (TRR).* Institute of Electrical and Electronics Engineers (IEEE), *Access Journal. Transportation Research*, Part A: *Policy and Practice*, Part D: *Transport and Environment. Transportation Quarterly. Transportation. Transport Reviews. Transport Policy.*

CHAPTER 15

Housing Planning and Policy

INTRODUCTION

Decent, safe, and sanitary housing is essential to households' quality of life. It is the stated goal of U.S. housing policy. In the words of New York University sociologist Matthew Desmond (2016), housing is "the wellspring of personhood" and "without stable shelter, everything else falls apart." Berkeley landscape architecture and architecture professor Claire Marcus calls housing a "mirror of self"—fundamental to psychological well-being and human dignity (1995).

Housing occupies a large part of the land area of cities. Residential property taxes are the main source of local government revenue. For homeowners, housing equity provides security to cover medical or other emergencies and for old age. The two-thirds of U.S. households who own their homes are better housed than their counterparts in most other developed countries, but some are hard pressed financially to pay for their homes. Nearly half of all renters are cost-burdened and the great majority of low-income households are severely cost-burdened. Homelessness in the United States is a national disgrace.

City and regional planners play a critical role in all aspects of housing. At the local level they formulate housing elements of general plans—the part of a city or county comprehensive plan that describes plans for housing—and prepare plans required for federal and state housing programs. Planners often work as staff for local nonprofit housing development corporations (HDCs) that plan, build and manage affordable housing and public housing authorities (PHAs) that manage public housing for low-income households subsidized by the federal government. Some planners plan or manage homeless shelters that provide emergency overnight shelter. Planners also plan and manage transitional housing for people in recovery from drug and alcohol issues on a continuum from being homeless to having permanent housing. Since much new residential construction takes place in unincorporated county land on the urban fringe, county planners can play a significant role in inducing private developers to produce more housing with a mix better able to meet local needs.

At the state level, planners help state housing finance agencies make plans for distribution of federal and state funds. At the U.S. Department of Housing and Urban Development (HUD)—the federal government department that oversees federal housing programs—planners manage subsidy programs, monitor and evaluate programs, and develop new housing and urban development policy.

This chapter covers housing and housing planning and policy in the United States. It begins with a description of the U.S. housing stock, the conventional homebuilding industry and exceptions to conventional homebuilding such as mobile homes and other manufactured housing. A section reviews mortgage finance and the secondary mortgage market in the United States. It describes the cyclic nature of homebuilding and lessons from the subprime mortgage crisis in 2007, 2008, 2009, and beyond. Housing performs important social, economic, and psychological functions and must mesh with transportation and infrastructure, so a section of the chapter describes these non-shelter aspects of housing. Material on housing theory reviews filtering, targeting, and the post-shelter society. Most of the chapter deals with federal, state, and local housing subsidies. This part of the chapter distinguishes supply-side from demand-side subsidies. It includes a description of the federal mortgage interest and other tax subsidies, and an update on the status of the legacy federal housing programs described in Chapter 12. Sections provide material on federal Low-Income Housing Tax Credits, Housing Choice Vouchers, the Home Investment Partnership (HOME) program, and other current federal housing subsidy programs. There is a section on state and local housing subsidy programs. Concluding sections discuss the right to housing, fair housing, and landlord tenant law.

THE U.S. HOUSING STOCK

Housing planners use housing units and households as defined by the U.S. Census Bureau as their basic units of analysis.[1] The supply of single- and multi- family housing units should ideally match housing demand measured by the number of households of different sizes, types, income levels, and with special needs. Ideally, there should be one appropriate decent, safe, and sanitary housing unit, at a rent or price each household can afford, available to them. Vacancy rates—the percentage of units vacant in a given market—should be in the range of 5% for rental and 1% for owned housing to allow choice and mobility. Since it is almost never possible to meet these ideals, planners analyze the need for different types of units and propose realistic strategies to encourage new construction and preservation of as many of the right kinds of units as the context requires.

There are about 140 million housing units in the United States. About two-thirds of the U.S. housing stock is owner-occupied. Fewer than 2% of U.S. households live in rental units that they reported to the U.S. Census Bureau that in their opinion have severe physical problems. Less than 1% live in owner-occupied units that they consider to have severe physical problems. Housing in the United States is not like housing in developing countries where a large percentage of the housing stock consists of informal self-built vernacular housing lacking indoor water and toilets, adequate insulation against cold, and protection from the elements.

In recent decades, America's housing conditions have improved for most moderate- and above moderate-income U.S. households. Twenty-one million new housing units have been built since 2000, and 51 million since 1980. The average size of homes in the United States has increased dramatically to over 2,300 square feet. This is very large by world standards. Most newer dwelling units are higher-quality and have more and better amenities than housing in most other countries. There is little overcrowding (more than one person per room) except in the lowest-priced rental housing.

Housing in the United States is problematic for extremely low-income households with incomes below 30% of area median income, very low-income households with incomes between 30% and 50% of area median income, and low-income households whose income does not exceed 80% of the area median income. Their situation has worsened during the last three decades. The numbers and percentages of cost-burdened households paying more than 30% of their adjusted gross income for rent and severely cost-burdened households paying more than 50% have increased.

The homeless population includes households as well as individuals and people of every gender, race, and age. Over half a million Americans are homeless at any given time. Some homelessness is episodic, but nearly 100,000 homeless people in the United States are chronically homeless. About 1.5 million experience homelessness some time during the course of a year. Homelessness is particularly prevalent in high-cost metropolitan areas and for Blacks (40% of all homeless people), recent immigrants, the mentally ill, people with drug and alcohol addiction, and people with limited education and job skills.

Figure 15.1 Homeless and Hungry.

Nearly two-thirds of U.S. households own their homes. The U.S. homeownership rate has been between 63% and 69% since the mid-1960s. A small number of households—particularly young adults without children—prefer not to own housing even if they can afford to do so. High housing costs make homeownership impossible for most of the remaining third of U.S. households.

THE U.S. HOMEBUILDING INDUSTRY

The U.S. homebuilding industry is essentially private. Almost all U.S. housing—including government-assisted housing—is built by the private building industry. Homebuilding is a complex industry. General contractors, subcontractors, realtors, banks, and title companies are essential actors. The homebuilding industry is fragmented. Most single-family homes are built by homebuilders who complete only a few houses a year—all in one small geographic area. The U.S. Small Business Administration (SBA) classifies 96% of homebuilders as small businesses. In 2019 the largest U.S. homebuilding company built less than 4% of the housing units constructed.

Housing construction is cyclic, with booms and busts. During the height of the subprime mortgage crisis, between 2007 and 2009, more than half of U.S. small homebuilders went out of business. Within a few years most were back in business along with many new builders. Housing demand is highly elastic. During recessions people defer housing consumption, and homebuilders cut production. Because so much of the cost of purchasing housing is borrowed, homebuilding is sensitive to changing interest rates.

The U.S. homebuilding industry is efficient. Small local builders know their local market niches and adjust production to building cycles. Large builders achieve economies of scale and employ expert construction managers.

Housing is context-sensitive. It reflects regional variations in weather, heat, rain, land costs, union practices, and environmental hazards like hurricanes, tornadoes, and earthquakes. It serves diverse populations including seniors, students, people with disabilities, elderly households, and single households. Housing also includes on- or off-base military housing, group homes, halfway houses, and homeless shelters.

Housing is essentially immovable. The average single-family U.S. home weighs 233 tons and is attached to a foundation and utility lines. Virtually all U.S. housing is built onsite and never moved. Even most mobile homes stay on a single site. U.S. housing is durable. The U.S. housing stock only grows by about 1% a year. The number and demographics of occupants may change rapidly, but the housing stock in most areas almost always changes slowly. Most housing units last for many decades.

A common neoliberal proposal for reducing new construction housing costs is to ease the regulatory burden on developers by simplifying review processes and cutting red tape. Devices like one-stop permitting—where a builder can get all building-related permits in one place (perhaps at the same time)—and reducing the paperwork and fees required for building permits can reduce costs to developers. These cost savings may be passed on to buyers or go into the developer's pocket, depending on the elasticity of demand. City and regional planners play an important role alerting policy makers to the tradeoffs between building quality and cost.

Studies and environmental impact statements (EISs) for new construction take time and add to up-front legal, architectural, and construction costs. However, most planners feel that EISs and other studies are necessary and contribute to better-quality housing. Adequate sewers, schools, and other infrastructure also contribute to up-front costs, but produce superior development that will usually reduce long-term costs.

EXCEPTIONS TO CONVENTIONAL HOMEBUILDING

Manufactured housing, including mobile homes and kit homes built in factories and transported to a mobile home park or other site, are important exceptions to conventional U.S. homebuilding. About 10% of annual U.S. new single-family home starts are manufactured housing. Twenty million people live on over four million sites for manufactured housing in approximately 40,000 communities. There is manufactured housing in every state.

Mobile Homes

Most manufactured housing units are mobile homes—housing units built in a factory and transported to a site. Planners in the American Southwest, Southern California, Florida, and other areas with hospitable climates are engaged in more planning related to mobile homes than planners in other states.

Long, double-wide, and double-high mobile homes may provide as much space as a moderate-sized single-family detached house. The price per square foot of mobile homes is almost always much lower than the cost of ownership of a single-family home or condominium. It is often even lower than local rental alternatives. Many mobile home parks have a stable population consisting mostly of retirees.

Most people living in mobile homes own their units. Some mobile home owners own the land where their unit is located. Others rent land in a mobile home park and pay rent and sewer, water, electricity, and other charges for use of a space. The top-rated parks have large lots, landscaping, and amenities such as swimming pools, gyms, tennis courts, and clubhouses. In a noted eviction study, sociologist Matthew Desmond (2016) described one of the lowest-rated mobile home parks where he lived while he was doing field research. The mobile home park where Desmond lived had small lots, virtually no landscaping, few amenities, dysfunctional infrastructure, and many tenants with drug problems and criminal records.

The Secretary of the United States Department of Housing and Urban Development (HUD) oversees a national building code with standards for new construction of manufactured housing, including mobile homes. Mobile homes built in the United States since the act became effective in 1976 are required to meet Federal Housing Administration (FHA) certification requirements. The FHA makes mortgage insurance available to qualifying mobile home owners to protect lenders from losing money in the event that the homeowner defaults on their mortgage. Once a homeowner has mortgage insurance, the home is mortgageable through the Veterans Administration

(VA) and the Federal National Mortgage Association (Fannie Mae) as well as private lenders. Local mobile home building and housing code enforcement is largely up to local governments.

On the positive side, mobile homes offer affordable housing that their owners—often low- or moderate-income retirees—value. On the negative side they contribute to low-density sprawl that most planners and environmentalists oppose. Many mobile home parks are in rural areas where they may disrupt the natural environment. Pre-1974 mobile homes, built before federal manufactured housing code standards went into effect, present safety issues. Unlike most housing, mobile homes usually do not appreciate very much; most depreciate.

A majority of middle- and upper-income voters do not want mobile homes in their community—particularly ones that will provide housing for low-income and low–moderate-income residents. Planning conflicts arise around regulating mobile home parks or closing them down. In metropolitan areas, mobile home parks that were built on or just beyond the urban fringe, when land was cheap, are under pressure as the urban fringe expands and land values increase. Developers seeking large sites acquire the land, close the parks, displace the residents, and build office parks or other more lucrative developments.

Factory-Built, Modular, and Kit Homes

Factories can build housing modules, such as a complete kitchen or bathroom with all the plumbing, wiring, and appliances in place. Several modules can fit together to form an entire apartment unit or a single-family home. Modules or entire factory-built units built in a factory may be transported to a site. The prospect of providing affordable factory-built housing has always appealed to some policy makers. The most ambitious attempt to promote modular and factory-built housing in the United States was a failed federal program named Operation Breakthrough from 1968 to 1972.

Factory housing kits include all the lumber, plumbing, wiring, and other components that can be transported to a site as a single kit. They do not include cement and other heavy foundation materials that can be acquired locally with lower transportation costs. Between 1908 and 1933 Sears, Roebuck and Company—then America's closest equivalent to Amazon.com—had an extensive line of home kits. Before the internet, the Sears catalogues were the most widely used source of information about products. Sears shipped all manner of items throughout the United States. Figure 15.2 is an advertisement from the 1926 Sears, Roebuck catalogue for "The Magnolia", a kit that provided components for a five-bedroom mansion that sold for $6,488 (in 1926 dollars). Amazon.com ships housing kits to build tiny homes for prices starting under $10,000.

Manufactured and kit homes are more likely to be accepted in rural areas than cities. Construction trade unions and their supporters in city government where construction trades unions are strongest often resist non-traditional building that does not require union labor.

HOUSING FINANCE

Housing is most U.S. homeowners' largest lifetime expenditure. Most owners take out a mortgage—a loan using the housing unit as collateral—when they purchase a home. They make an initial down payment and borrow the balance for a specified term at a specified interest rate. They may refinance their home multiple times.

The costs of owning a house that is financed involve four major components: payment of mortgage principal, mortgage interest, local property taxes, and homeowners' hazard insurance. Hazard insurance pays for repairs if the home is damaged by a fire or in other ways. These four types of payment together are called PITI payments. Principal and interest are usually paid monthly to the mortgage holder, property taxes annually or semi-annually to the city or county where the house is located, and homeowners' insurance monthly to a private insurance

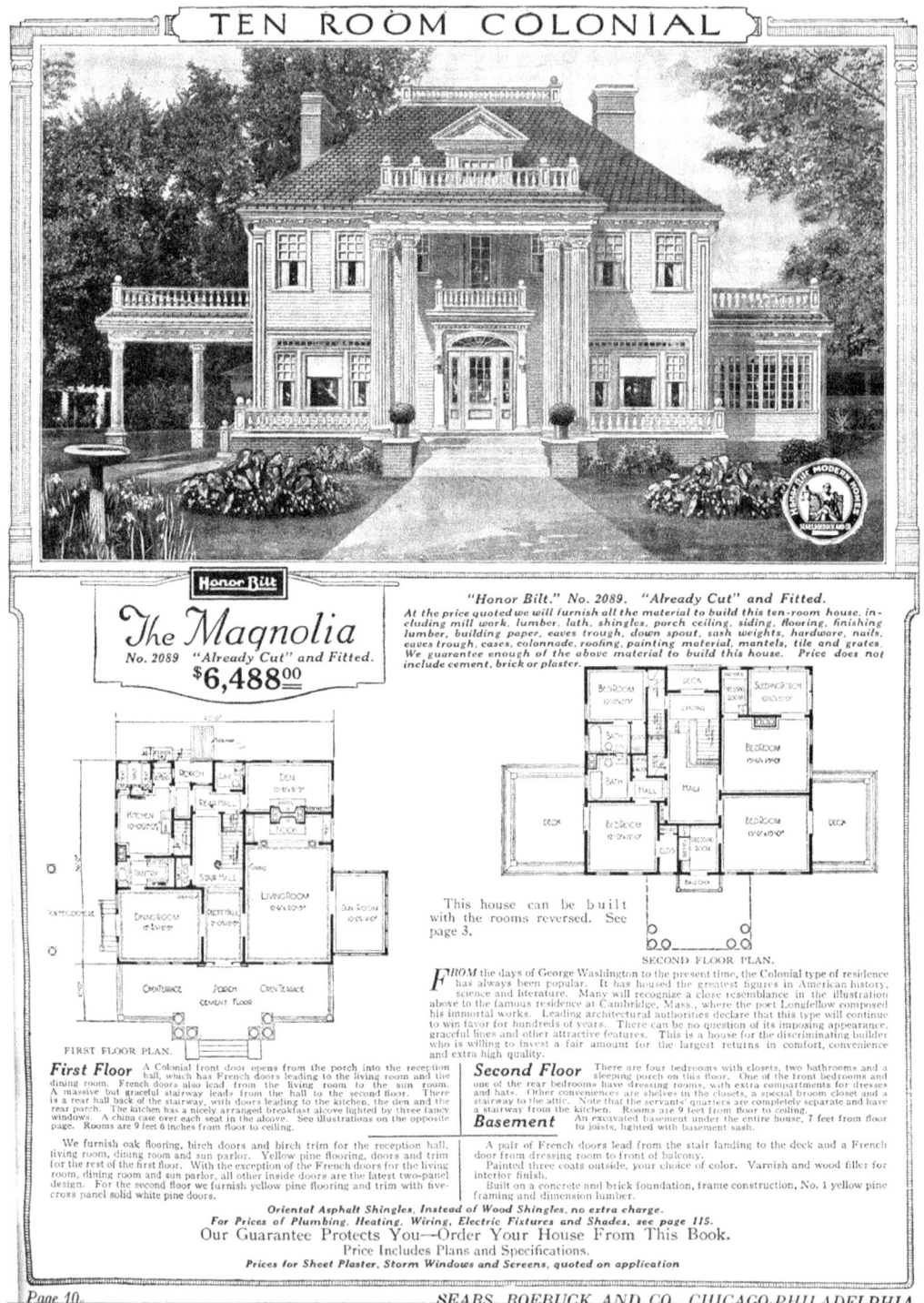

Figure 15.2 Sears, Roebuck and Co. Mail Order House "The Magnolia" (1926).

company, Fannie MAE, or Freddie MAC. Lenders require homeowners with low down payments and limited income and assets to purchase mortgage insurance from the Federal Housing Administration (FHA).

There are many different kinds of mortgages involving different down payment requirements, mortgage terms, and interest rates. They may have interest rates that are fixed for the term of the mortgage or which adjust up or down in relation to the consumer price index (CPI) or some other index.

In the United States almost all home mortgages are now level-payment, self-amortizing mortgages. Borrowers pay the same amount each month. By the end of the mortgage term the entire mortgage has been paid. Payments consist mostly of interest at the beginning and mostly of principal towards the end of the mortgage term. This is important, because the federal home mortgage interest tax deduction allows borrowers to deduct the interest paid on up to $750,000 in mortgage debt from their federal income taxes—providing significant savings, particularly in the early years.

Banks and other institutions that originate mortgages usually sell most individual mortgages in large bundles to federal intermediaries. The intermediaries hold some in their own portfolios and issue securities (bonds) backed by the mortgages to private investors worldwide.

Jumbo mortgages are home loans for an amount that exceeds the conforming loan limit on mortgages set by lenders, or do not conform with conventional lending standards in some other way. The institutions that originate jumbo loans may keep some in their portfolios, but bundle and sell most jumbo mortgagtes to Fannie MAE or Freddie MAC—secondary mortgage market entities described in Chapter 12.

While the United States does not engage in macro-level sectoral planning like some national governments, federal monetary and fiscal policy decisions impact housing. The U.S. Federal Reserve Board and the Department of the Treasury establish monetary policy that affects interest rates. Even a small change in a mortgage's interest rate will significantly affect housing costs during the life of a mortgage. A lower mortgage rate on an owned home reduces monthly mortgage payments, saving homeowners money. When mortgage interest rates increase the number of new housing starts usually declines and when they drop new housing starts usually increase. A lower mortgage interest rate on an apartment building saves the owners of the building money on debt service that they can use to reduce rents, improve maintenance, make improvements, and still make a profit. Monetary policy affects inflation which may benefit or harm owners and renters depending on the policy.

THE SUBPRIME MORTGAGE CRISIS

Housing is prone to booms and busts. An economic crisis during which house prices plunged and many homeowners defaulted on their mortgages—generally referred to as the subprime mortgage crisis—began in the United States in late 2007 and mushroomed into the most severe global financial crisis since the Great Depression. In the years immediately preceding the subprime mortgage crisis, mortgage lenders made millions of risky mortgage loans. While most subprime loans went to moderate- and middle-income households, millions went to high-risk low-income households. Because house prices had risen sharply since the early 2000s, homebuyers assumed that their homes would appreciate rapidly and they would soon have a large enough equity cushion to survive any financial shock. Many of the subprime mortgages were fraudulent. Households of color, immigrant, and elderly households did not receive adequate information or counseling on the risks homeownership entailed from the lenders. Federal and state banking regulators went along—reducing underwriting standards to allow down payments as low as 0% and high loan-to-income ratios. Regulators were often aware of fraudulent information on loan applications, but looked the other way. By 2007 there were millions of risky "liar's loans" where lenders and mortgage brokers helped applicants make up whatever income, credit, and other information was necessary to get a mortgage loan. Lending institutions and federal regulators frequently did not verify the information.

Some applicants with no income, no job, and no assets got "NINJA" loans.

In late 2007 and 2008 the housing bubble burst. Mortgage defaults skyrocketed as overburdened households failed to make their mortgage payments. A panic ensued and the crisis spiraled downward. Millions of at-risk new homeowners defaulted, and lost their homes. Because house prices had plunged, many lost their home equity and sometimes their life savings. The impact spread to other sectors of the U.S. economy and worldwide.

Massive federal bailouts and changes in monetary policy during the Bush and Obama administrations saved most private mortgage lending institutions from bankruptcy. The Troubled Assets Relief Program (TARP), Making Home Affordable (MHA) Program, Home Affordable Modification Program (HAMP), and Hardest Hit Fund (HHF) provided homeowners some relief by extending their mortgage terms, reducing or temporarily suspending interest payments, or paying a portion of their mortgage costs.

Most bailout money the federal government loaned to keep lending institutions solvent and provide relief to homeowners during the height of the home mortgage crisis in 2007, 2008, and 2009 has been paid back. Federal legislation to restructure the financial regulatory system and prevent another crisis from occurring—The Dodd–Frank Act—was enacted in 2010, but pushback from the mortgage industry limited its scope.

There are important lessons for city and regional planners in the global financial crisis. There is a tradeoff between making it possible for marginal households and developers of rental housing for low-income households to get mortgage financing versus creating greater risk that they will default on their mortgages if the economy or their personal situations change. Plans and policies to extend mortgage credit to the most marginal, highest-risk households must be realistic. Congress needs to enact and enforce regulations along the lines of the Dodd–Frank Act (before it was watered down) and monitor the federal agencies charged with regulating banks and other mortgage lenders to make sure they do not issue overly risky loans or engage in the kind of rampant fraud that precipitated the meltdown that occurred during the mortgage crisis. Educating potential first-time homebuyers to their obligations and the risk they are assuming is critical.

SOCIAL, ECONOMIC, AND PSYCHOLOGICAL ASPECTS OF HOUSING

There is much more to meeting the stated U.S. national goal of an affordable, decent, safe, and sanitary housing unit for every American household than providing adequate physical housing units. Housing planning also involves how a housing unit fits into a neighborhood and how well infrastructure will serve the unit. Physically adequate housing in high-crime neighborhoods where there is substantial illegal drug dealing does not meet the "decent, safe, and sanitary" standard. Jobs–housing balance—having residential housing units reasonably close to jobs—is important. Spatial mismatch requiring workers to either pay more than they can afford for housing near their work or commute long distances for housing in lower-cost areas needs to be minimized. Income, class, and racial segregation of housing is unacceptable, as is mortgage discrimination by government and private lenders.

University of California, Berkeley professor of architecture and landscape architecture Clare Cooper Marcus has written eloquently about how where one lives affects the human psyche from early childhood throughout a person's life cycle. Marcus discusses the psychological damage to the self-esteem of a child or adult living in a public housing project that is visibly different from and inferior to surrounding housing. She urges planners to consider the impact of moving, forming a new household with a partner, and the psychological damage forced moves such as displacement can have.

HOUSING CONCEPTS AND THEORY

Planners, housers, economists, and other scholars have developed theory about housing markets and housing planning and policy. Theory about housing affordability, filtering, horizontal and vertical efficiency, and targeting housing subsidies are particularly helpful for city and regional planners.

Affordability

HUD provides precise definitions of low-, moderate-, and other income categories. Households paying between 30% and 50% of their income on rent or PITI payments are considered cost-burdened and households paying more than 50% are considered severely cost-burdened. Rents in the United States have risen more rapidly than inflation or real wages—contributing to the persistent and worsening shortage of low-cost rental housing. In 2019, 30% of all U.S. households were cost-burdened—16% moderately and 14% severely. Over half of renter households (54%) were moderately or severely cost-burdened. About 570,000 people were homeless on average, each night in 2019. About three times as many were homeless for one or more nights during the year. Higher percentages of Black, Latinx, Native American and Alaskan Native households are cost-burdened, severely cost-burdened, and homeless than average. The percentage of cost-burdened renters has declined since 2001, but the absolute number has increased.

HUD calculates the median income of a four-person household in a geographical area and uses percentages of that amount, adjusted for family size, to designate income categories. Planners can then identify shortfalls in the number of existing units affordable by different income groups in an area they are planning for, and estimate how many of what type should be built and preserved for each category during the time period covered by a plan.

HUD classifies households with adjusted income less than 30% of the area median income as extremely low-income households, with less than 50% as very low-income households, between 50% and 80% as low-income households, and with incomes between 80% and 125% as moderate-income households. They classify households with incomes over 125% of area median income as above moderate-income households. Most federal, state, and local housing subsidy programs are targeted to households that fall into the low-, very low-, and extremely low-income categories.

The great exception to targeting federal housing subsidies to lower-income households is the very large federal home mortgage interest deduction. The federal home mortgage interest deduction allows homeowners to deduct mortgage interest from the income they report to the Internal Revenue Service so that they do not have to pay federal income tax on it. The home mortgage interest deduction is enormous, and overwhelmingly benefits above moderate-income households. It is described below.

HUD assumes that households can afford to pay 30% of gross income for housing. Gross income is the amount of income a household receives from wages and other sources before taxes and other deductions. Many city and regional planners use that assumption in housing plans. The 30% rule, or any single rigid percentage rule for what constitutes affordable housing, is a very bad measure. Very low-income households must pay more than 30% of their income on shelter to have enough money for food and other essentials. Above moderate-income households can afford to pay much less than 30% of their income on housing and still have money left over for a high quality of life. Households earning the same income need to spend different amounts on basic necessities such as medical bills. Percentage of income measures do not reflect cost-of-living differences among different regions unless they are adjusted. Households in the military and some other occupations may receive relatively inexpensive housing. Some households can draw on savings to pay for monthly housing costs. Housing affordability is closely related to geography. Housing in rural and economically depressed areas which have experienced out-migration is much less expensive than housing in economic hot spots. The longer the commute time between housing and jobs, the less expensive similar housing will be.

There are two basic ways to define and measure home value. Local tax assessors look at the sale of comparable properties (abbreviated in assessor-speak as comps)—adjusting for factors such as distance, size, quality, amenities, lot size, and how recently the sale occurred—to come up with an assessed value. The more recent a sale, the more accurate. Standard and Poor's (S&P) Case–Shiller index provides quarterly information on house price trends based on repeat sales of the same home. The Federal Housing Finance Agency (FHFA) calculates another widely used weighted, repeat-sales index of single-family properties. The FHFA website provides links to other housing indexes. Housing planners use assessors' information and information from housing price indices in their plans.

To understand rental housing costs and affordability, housing planners and policy makers analyze gross rent that includes the rental payment itself, plus water and waste disposal. Tenants usually pay for electricity, phone, cable television, and internet usage separately.

For public housing projects, HUD calculates a fair market rent (FMR) that estimates what a household can expect to pay for a modestly priced rental unit in either the metropolitan area or nonmetropolitan county where the housing unit is located. FMRs are adjusted for unit size in all metropolitan areas and nonmetro counties. HUD requires public housing authorities in 24 metro areas to use small area FMRs (SAFMRs) based on ZIP codes to determine maximum allowable rents for units in their projects. Housing authorities in other metro areas have the option of using SAFMRs.

Filtering

One of the most important contributions to housing theory is the concept of filtering. Land economist Richard Ratcliff—who first developed filtering theory—described filtering as the change in occupancy when a housing unit occupied by one income group becomes available to the next lower income group as its sales price or rent decreases. That does not mean that members of the lower income group always get the unit. Ratcliff assumed that most housing would filter down. In reality filtering works both ways. A household moving into a house or apartment may have an income as high as or higher than the household moving out—particularly in gentrifying neighborhoods where higher-income homebuyers and renters are moving in.

University of Pennsylvania city and regional planning professor William Grigsby developed a more elegant filtering theory. Grigsby described housing markets as consisting of many interdependent submarkets serving different groups such as owners and renters, with different income levels, linked directly or indirectly more or less strongly. According to Grigsby, the effect of a price or rent change within one submarket is diffused among other submarkets based on how similar they are.

Horizonal and Vertical Efficiency

In the United States housing assistance is not an entitlement. Housing is not like cash or food stamps that are easy to distribute in different amounts. About one-quarter of households that are eligible to receive a housing subsidy get a deep housing subsidy such as the right to rent a public housing unit, receive a housing choice voucher (HCV), or receive project-based rental housing assistance that may cover half or more of their housing expenses. Other eligible households may receive a shallow subsidy such as the right to live in a unit subsidized by the federal Low-Income Housing Tax Credit (LIHTC) program that may cover less than 10% of their housing expenses. Many eligible households get no subsidy. Some housing subsidies last for as long as the recipient remains eligible; others are for terms as short as a year or less. Since there is almost never enough funding or subsidized housing units to meet all of the housing need for low-income households in an eligible category, planners often face a wicked problem—whether to provide fully adequate housing for some needy households and little or nothing for others that are equally needy or to distribute available resources to all households more equitably, but thinly.

The concept of targeting housing subsidies is helpful. Imagine a target with a bullseye representing a group of households in greatest need of a specific type of housing subsidy surrounded by rings showing less needy households. A volley of arrows that all hit the bullseye represents a well-targeted subsidy. One in which some arrows hit the bullseye, others are off center, and some miss the target altogether would show less good targeting. Ideally, once a universe of people in need of a housing subsidy has been identified, enough housing would be perfectly targeted to fully close the gap between what each household can afford to pay and the cost of appropriate decent, safe, and sanitary shelter without spending money on any household that does not need the subsidy.

If the goal of a housing subsidy is to distribute available funding equitably, horizontal and vertical efficiency are useful concepts. Horizontal efficiency refers to how much of the group in need of a subsidy receives it. The principle is that similarly situated people should receive the same treatment. Vertical efficiency refers to what percentage of funding goes to people who need it. Ideally that should be 100%. Figure 15.3 illustrates horizontal and vertical efficiency in housing subsidies. Figure 15.3a illustrates the best possible case; need and supply of the subsidy exactly overlap. Every household in need gets the subsidy; no household that is not in need gets it. In reality, perfect targeting like this rarely happens. There is not enough money, defining levels of housing need is difficult and subjective, and household housing need changes frequently. Figures 15.3b and 15.3c illustrate housing subsidies that are somewhat horizontally and somewhat vertically inefficient. Figure 15.3d shows the worst case in which all the subsidy goes to people who do not need it.

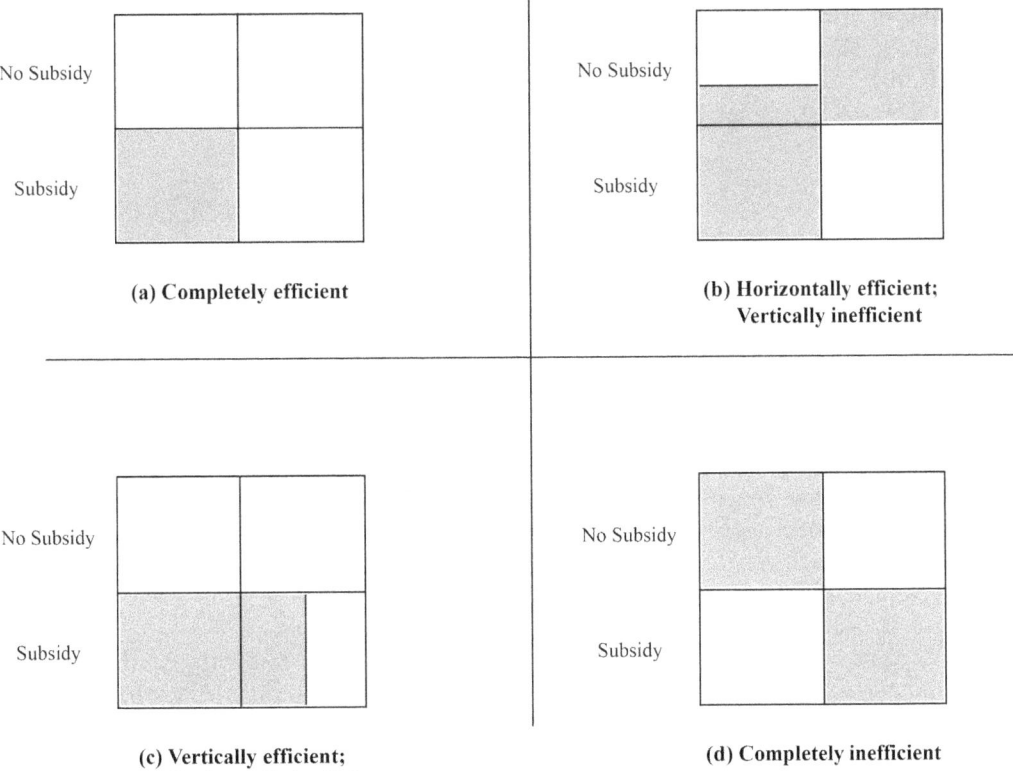

Figure 15.3 Housing Efficiency.

THE POST-SHELTER SOCIETY

Rutgers urban planning professors George Sternlieb and James Hughes advanced a provocative view that by the late 1970s, the United States had become a "post-shelter society" in which housing is as important as a form of investment and savings and a refuge from inflation as it is a refuge from the elements.

Concern for the future—particularly worries about inflation and the stability of the U.S. currency was undermining confidence in the stock market and other investments at the time Sternlieb and Hughes invented the concept of the post shelter society. They observed that American households tend to purchase more expensive housing than they would choose just for their own shelter needs because they consider it an investment and a hedge against inflation. Homeownership is far more widespread in the U.S. than ownership of stocks. Almost half of U.S. households in the bottom half of the U.S. income distribution own a home, but less than one-quarter own stocks. Historically stock prices have almost always increased faster than home values. However, homeownership has tax and other advantages that can make it a better investment choice depending on a household's situation.

LAND USE REGULATION AND HOUSING

Land is a critical component of housing cost. The cost of raw land can amount to a third of the cost of a single-family home or more. The local buildable land supply is essentially fixed. Land costs are partly a physical matter determined by how much buildable land there is given the local geography, how much infrastructure capacity there is to accommodate development of the land, where the land is located, and characteristics of the site such as views and proximity to services and amenities. Land costs are also determined by what types of housing policy makers permit to be built where, at what densities, and to what construction standards. City and regional planners play a large role in defining what housing can be built using general plan housing elements, subdivision and zoning ordinances, growth management plans, and other implementation tools described in Chapter 8. Laying out more smaller lots in a subdivision can help increase the housing supply and assure that some smaller, less expensive single-family housing is built. This can contribute to spatial equity and likely more ethnic and racial diversity. Subdivisions with more lots for multi-family housing will make it possible for the private market to produce more affordable rental housing than subdivisions where all, or almost all, of the housing is for single family homes. New Urbanist plans—following the Congress of New Urbanism's principles—can assure that new communities are denser than they would otherwise be, and include at least some low- and moderate-income units. Reducing exactions and building fees can reduce the cost of housing and increase the supply of affordable housing. So can lowering building standards—but at a cost in amenities for residents and the risk of shoddy construction that will prove dangerous or costly to fix later.

FEDERAL, STATE, AND LOCAL U.S. HOUSING PROGRAMS

The multi-level U.S system of federal, state, and local government housing programs that originated during the New Deal, described in Chapter 12, has evolved and become much larger and more complex. There are many new housing programs. Many legacy programs have disappeared. Remaining legacy housing programs have morphed and now involve private and nonprofit developers, owners, and managers. The federal government, state and local governments, and nonprofit organizations provide housing subsidies either to eligible housing units or eligible households.

Housing subsidies can be divided into two categories—supply-side programs that provide funding to increase the supply of affordable housing units and demand-side programs that provide low-income households financial assistance in the form of vouchers to increase their ability to pay for housing so that it does not cost more than a specified percentage of their adjusted household income—currently generally 30% of adjusted household income. Subsidies may be household-based subsidies that subsidize households or project-based subsidies that subsidize housing units.

Federal Tax Subsidies for Homeowners

The federal mortgage interest deduction allows homeowners to deduct mortgage interest up to specified amounts from their gross income and pay federal income tax only on the reduced amount. The amount of tax savings the federal government grants homeowners via the home mortgage interest deduction totals much more than all the federal housing programs for low-income households combined. It is a perverse subsidy. The higher the household's tax bracket, the greater the subsidy. Homeowners can deduct home mortgage interest from their adjusted gross income on mortgage amounts up to $750,000. Most U.S. homeowners have less mortgage debt than that, so they can deduct all of the mortgage interest they pay. However, in areas where house prices are high, the $750,000 limit on the federal home mortgage deduction is important, because it caps the deduction for people with expensive homes and large mortgages. Rationales advanced for the home mortgage deduction are that homeownership is a merit good—a valued part of the American dream, builds pride, provides for security and social stability, and incentivizes Americans to work hard in order to become and remain homeowners. Critics of the home mortgage deduction feel that the money could be much better spent to assist people with much greater housing needs than the beneficiaries of this enormous tax subsidy.

Homeowners may also deduct property taxes from their gross income for federal tax reporting. Ex-president Trump's 2017 Tax Cuts and Jobs Act capped the combined deduction for property taxes, state and local income taxes, and sales taxes at $10,000.

The Low-Income Housing Tax Credit (LIHTC)

The Federal Low-Income Housing Tax Credit (LIHTC) program—created in 1986 and made permanent in 1993—is currently the largest source of subsidies for affordable housing in the United States. It provides an indirect subsidy to developers to finance part of the cost of construction or substantial rehabilitation of affordable rental housing. LIHTCs are part of the U.S. tax code—not a HUD program.

In exchange for paying part of the costs to develop affordable rental housing, investors who get LIHTCs receive tax credits that provide a dollar-for-dollar reduction in their federal tax liability for ten years.

There are two main categories of LIHTCs. About half are non-competitive LIHTCs, which must be used together with bond financing. Non-competitive LIHTCs are called four percent LIHTCs. They pay 30% of the project cost over ten years. Four percent LIHTCs are available to any qualifying project. The rest are competitive LIHTCs. They are called nine percent LIHTCs. Nine percent LIHTCs pay 70% of the project cost over ten years. LIHTCs can be combined with other housing subsidies. Nine percent LIHTCs are allocated to states based on population. In 2020 states received $2.81 in nine percent LIHTCs times the number of residents in the state.

There are over 3.2 million LIHTC units in 50,000 projects throughout the United States. Over 60% of LIHTCs have been for new construction projects. The great majority of LIHTCs (81%) are in suburbs or central cities. Most are in mixed-income and mixed-race census tracts.

A recent study by University of Kansas planning professor Kirk McClure concluded that the LIHTC serves households with very little need for additional units—not needy ones; that it is increasing the rental housing stock in soft markets rather than tight ones; that it is not promoting mixed-income housing; and that it contributes to spatial and racial concentration.

State and local housing finance agencies (HFAs) implement the LIHTC program.

They receive annual budget authority to issue tax credits for the acquisition, rehabilitation, or new construction of rental housing targeted to lower-income households. They then distribute LIHTCs to individual projects in accordance with a state qualified allocation plan (QAP). States have great discretion in developing the criteria for what types of LIHTC projects to fund where. They rate and rank nine percent LIHTC applications they receive each year and fund the highest-scoring ones based on their QAP criteria. Applicants may receive points for criteria such as good design, energy efficiency, the percentage of multi-bedroom units, and locations that deconcentrate poverty. City and regional planners in state HFAs are often involved in preparing QAPs.

Properties that receive LIHTCs must remain affordable to households earning up to 60% of area median income for 15 years—5 years longer than the tax years during which the credits are given to the owner. After 10 years, the property owner is free to rent units at whatever amount the market will bear to any mix of tenants, so long as the project continues to meet overall LIHTC affordability standards, which vary from state to state and year to year.

Most LIHTCs are held by limited partnerships. A developer, such as a nonprofit housing development corporation (HDC)—a nonprofit corporation established to build affordable housing—builds or rehabilitates the units. The developer sells interests in the property to investors, who receive the tax credits. Investors may benefit from the cash flow derived from unit rentals and from appreciation if the development is sold for a profit. Investors receive other tax benefits, including a depreciation allowance to account for obsolescence.

Most tax credits are bundled and sold directly to banks. Owners of the tax credits leave responsibility for managing the units and meeting IRS rules to the syndicators. Syndicators are individuals or a group of individuals who find potential investment opportunities, put together a deal to offer to investors, raise money to close the deal, and upon closing, make sure the deal is run effectively and profitably. Investors are not involved in day-to-day operations like building maintenance or collecting rents. The project is just a number in a portfolio. They usually never see the units.

LIHTC project units are in high demand. They usually have long waiting lists, rent quickly, and have continuing high occupancy rates. If the projects are well managed, investors get a reasonable return. Tax-credit housing projects are spread throughout the United States, in cities, suburbs, and nonmetropolitan areas. They average 63 units. Most residents of LIHTC units earn between 40 and 60% of the area median income.

The maximum allowable rent in LIHTC units is based on 30% of area median income (AMI) for households earning up to 60% of AMI. Tenants earning less than 60% of AMI pay the same rent and therefore may spend more than 30% of their income on rent. Unlike public housing and housing choice vouchers (HCVs), rents in LIHTC properties are not adjusted in response to tenant incomes.

Housing Choice Vouchers

The second largest federal housing program is the Housing Choice Voucher (HCV) program. HCVs are a type of tenant-based subsidy, where the subsidy goes to a household rather than a housing unit. They increase the demand for low-income housing by providing low-income households additional money to spend on rent by paying the difference between 30% of a household's adjusted income and a fair market rent (FMR) that HUD establishes.[2] The HCV program:

- Authorizes public housing authorities (PHAs) to set payment standards from 90% to 110% of FMR and higher under certain circumstances;
- Allows housing authorities to establish higher and lower payment standards within the same metropolitan area reflecting market differences;
- Allows participants to spend more than 30% of their income on housing, but no more than 40%;

- Permits voucher holders to take their vouchers anywhere in the United States;
- Requires that extremely low-income households (earning less than 30% of the area's median family income adjusted for family size) receive at least 75% of all vouchers issued annually;
- Requires assisted units to meet physical quality and space standards to assure they are decent, safe, sanitary, and not overcrowded.

Over 2.5 million U.S. households have received HCVs. The great majority are low-income households. The recipients' demographics vary.[3] Over 600,000 landlords participate in the program.

HUD establishes FMRs annually for more than 2,600 housing markets. How many vouchers Congress authorizes in a given year depends on political and economic realities.

In 24 metropolitan areas where prices vary widely from neighborhood to neighborhood, HUD calculates small area fair market rents (SAFMRs) by ZIP code. Public housing authorities (PHAs) in other areas have the option of using SAFMRs. SAFMRs give recipients greater flexibility to select a unit in a higher rental cost area that may have better schools, be close to their work, or have other features they value. Since recipients pay a percentage of their income, it costs them no more to rent a high-cost unit in an SAFMR where costs are high than a lower-cost unit elsewhere. Nevertheless, few HCV recipients have chosen to reside in higher-cost neighborhoods.

Most FMR ceilings are low, but they vary greatly. In 2021 FMRs in San Francisco for a four-bedroom unit were $4,970 while in some municipalities in Puerto Rico they were $571.

Not all HCVs allocated are actually used. In many areas landlords are not required to accept HCVs and may choose not to rent to a voucher holder. In many markets, one-third or more of tenants who receive an HCV fail to find a qualifying unit. In that case the PHA assigns the voucher to another eligible household. Large families typically have a harder time finding a qualifying unit than smaller households, and greater difficulty in being accepted once they do find a qualifying unit. Providing information, counseling, and support to households who receive HCVs may increase utilization rates. Elderly tenants with mobility or cognitive challenges may need special help in finding HCV units.

The voucher program has succeeded in providing low-income households with greater residential choices. Compared to public housing, voucher recipients generally live in neighborhoods with lower poverty rates and—to a lesser degree—lower levels of racial segregation. However, the HCV program has not been as effective as expected (or hoped) in helping recipients avoid neighborhoods with high levels of poverty or high levels of racial segregation compared to LIHTC units and other project-based subsidies.

The presence of voucher recipients rarely if ever changes the socioeconomic or racial character of neighborhoods they move into significantly. HCV recipients seldom make up more than a small proportion of the residents in communities they move into or account for more than a small percentage of a census tract's households in poverty. HCVs do not appear to be reconcentrating low-income minority communities in areas where HOPE VI projects are located. HOPE VI projects are HUD projects that may demolish most of the original public housing units in an old project and replace them with fewer units some of which are for moderate-income households and some that rent at market rates. HOPE VI is described below.

Other Federal Housing Subsidy Programs

Congress created the federal HOME Investment Partnership (HOME) program in 1990 to provide federal grants to states and units of general local government to implement local housing strategies. The HOME program is a project-based subsidy program that is designed to increase affordable rental housing and homeownership. It has an annual budget of about $2 billion. The HOME program has provided subsidies to nearly 1.7 million households. About 50% of HOME funds have been used to support development of low- and moderate-income housing for households with incomes no higher than 80% of area median incomes. Sixty-five percent is reserved for renters. A little more than half of HOME funds have gone to low-income renters. The other 35% have gone to moderate-income homeowners.[4]

The National Housing Trust Fund, funded by Fannie Mae and Freddie Mac and managed by HUD, mostly subsidizes low-income rental housing and also provides some housing subsidies for homeowners.[5] It provides funding to nonprofit housing development corporations (HDCs) and other developers to build and maintain affordable rental housing and subsidize home purchases and improvement for low- and low–moderate-income homeowners. The federal Housing Trust Fund program was not used until 2016, because no money was available during and in the aftermath of the financial crisis. In 2021 the National Housing Trust Fund disbursed $689 million to states and local governments for low- and very low-income housing assistance.

STATE, LOCAL, AND NONPROFIT HOUSING PROGRAMS

Since the 1980s, state and local governments have taken more initiative for subsidizing housing, the numbers and size of nonprofit housing development corporations (HDCs) have grown, and the private sector has become more engaged in public–private affordable housing partnerships.

State, local, and quasi-governmental housing trust funds and private funding are a growing source of funding for low-income renters. Some housing trust funds also fund homeownership for low/moderate-income homebuyers. Local housing trust funds receive money from multiple sources and fund a variety of affordable housing activities. Every state has a state housing finance agency (HFA) that administers at least one state housing trust fund, as well as mortgage revenue bond and other state housing programs. As of 2020 there were 556 city and 155 county-level housing trust funds with about $1.5 billion in funding annually.

State Mortgage Revenue Bonds—MRBs—finance low-cost mortgages for lower-income first-time homebuyers and subsidize production of affordable multi-family housing for lower-income families. They have assisted over 3.25 million lower-income homeowners and provided financing for 1.2 million apartments that are affordable to lower-income families. HUD determines how many housing bonds each state may issue and specifies eligibility rules and how many of the units financed by them must go to renters and how many to low-income households. State housing finance agencies may also use their MRB authority to issue mortgage credit certificates, which provide a federal income tax credit for part of the mortgage interest that qualified home buyers pay each year.

Most affordable housing funding is still federal, in the form both of direct payments and tax expenditures—tax revenue that the federal government does not collect. Funding for housing still constitutes a tiny fraction of state and local budgets.

Legacy Federal Housing Subsidy Programs

Chapter 12 described the legacy federal housing subsidy programs. Few new units have been built or rehabilitated by these programs since 1980. Many legacy units have moved into the private market. Some have been demolished. Remaining units are often funded in different ways. The 2 million remaining legacy housing units are a critical housing resource that presents planning challenges. The main legacy federal housing programs are the public housing program and the Section 236 Below Market Interest Rate (BMIR) program.

Public Housing since 1980

President Reagan stopped new public housing construction in 1984. Since then the public housing program has been transformed. Over one-third of all public housing units have been sold off; transferred to other subsidy programs; or demolished—including almost all the units in troubled high-rise projects. Some units originally built as public housing have been transferred to the project-based Section 8 program, making them eligible for bank loans, tax-exempt bonds, and LIHTCs to cover essential rehabilitation costs under the Rental Assistance Demonstration (RAD) program.

There are about 950,000 remaining public housing units—down from a peak of 1.4 million units in 1994. There are 2,900 public housing authorities. Half of the PHAs manage fewer than 100 units. The ten largest PHAs operate 30% of all public housing. The New York City Housing Authority alone accounts for nearly 17% of all the public housing in the United States. Current public housing tenants represent a range of incomes, income sources, ages, genders, races, and disability statuses.[6]

Since 1990 almost all public housing funding has gone to operations, maintenance, preservation and rehabilitation of public housing units. Congressional authorizations to maintain public housing from the public housing capital fund have been erratic and inadequate. After adjusting for inflation, federal operating support for public housing declined by nearly 11% from 2010 to 2020. City and regional planners face the challenge of how to maintain, preserve, and rehabilitate public housing in the face of these cuts.

One-fifth of all remaining public housing in the United States is at least 60 years old. Only 17% of the remaining units have been built after 1989. Nearly all of the post-1989 units replaced older public housing that have been torn down. The post-1989 units are almost always better quality than the older units. Most are in mixed-use projects built under the HOPE VI, Choice Neighborhoods, and Rental Assistance Demonstration (RAD) programs.

HOPE VI, the Rental Assistance Demonstration (RAD) Program, and the Choice Neighborhoods Program

The U.S. Department of Housing and Urban Development considers concentration of very low-income households—particularly very low-income households of color—in public housing in low-income neighborhoods to be a source of many of public housing's most dire problems. Congress has been verbally committed to deconcentrating poverty and racial concentration in public housing since 1974, but has flip-flopped on policy to implement that goal. Beginning in 1993 the Moving to Opportunity (MTO) program was replaced by the Moving to Work (MTW) program that provided tenants of public housing vouchers allowing them to move into other public or private housing. The MTO program was followed by HUD's HOPE VI, Moving to Opportunity, and Choice Neighborhoods programs. All of these programs were intended to reduce poverty and racial concentration in public housing and to grant public housing tenants greater flexibility and additional subsidies to allow them to live in more economically and racially mixed neighborhoods.

The Housing Opportunity for People Everywhere VI (HOPE VI)—program began in 1992 as one of a series of housing experiments, was institutionalized and expanded in 1993, and implemented until the late 2000s. The program distributed about $6 billion to over 450 cities. Congress has not appropriated funding for HOPE VI since fiscal year (FY) 2011.

The HOPE VI strategy was to demolish or substantially rehabilitate all or almost all of the units in old, high maintenance cost, high-rise public housing projects tenanted almost entirely by low-income households. It then replaced the units that had been demolished with new units in new low-rise complexes with a mix of tenants in households that meet public housing standards, low–moderate-income households, and market rate housing. Job training and other support services intended to equip tenants with skills to enter the workforce are associated with the projects. HOPE VI demolished about 100,000 public housing units net between 1993 and 2010.

Physically, HOPE VI projects may consist of townhouses, small apartment buildings, and even some single-family housing. Their designs often incorporate Oscar Newman's defensible space and crime prevention through environmental design (CPTED) principles for creating defensible space discussed in Chapter 3. Many HOPE VI planners embraced New Urbanist principles and designed projects to be environmentally friendly, with porches, front yards, and other amenities. This made them attractive, but expensive. Some critics consider the New Urbanist HOPE VI project designs excessively costly and feel the money could have been better spent on providing a greater number of less expensive units.

HOPE VI projects provide much better housing and social environments for tenants fortunate enough to live in the new or substantially rehabilitated units. However, since they replaced dense high-rise housing with much lower-density housing with fewer units—only some of which are affordable by low-income tenants—many of the original tenants did not return. An estimated 80% of the HOPE VI displacees were Black. A fifth of the displacees did not receive relocation assistance or new subsidies. The rest received Housing Choice Vouchers, were relocated to other public housing developments, were evicted, or can no longer be found. Massachusetts Institute of Technology professor Lawrence Vale terms this "purging the poorest" (2013). The cost to build or rehabilitate HOPE VI units was high—draining money that might have been used in other ways to reach a larger number of people in the greatest need.

The Obama administration replaced HOPE VI with the Choice Neighborhoods Program. Unlike HOPE VI, the Choice Neighborhoods Program requires one-for-one replacement of all public housing units that are torn down. It requires communities to develop a transformation plan for the revitalization of the distressed public housing units, other subsidized housing, and the surrounding neighborhood. Few units planned under the Choice Neighborhoods Program have been completed to date, but many are in the pipeline. Through 2020, HUD had awarded nearly $1 billion to the Choice Neighborhoods Program. HUD plans to expand the program to 100 cities by 2022.

In 2013, HUD Secretary Julian Castro (Box 4.1) launched a Rental Assistance Demonstration (RAD) program that allows owners of public housing projects to obtain long-term 30–40-year mortgages and have access to Low-Income Housing Tax Credits to finance capital improvements. A RAD development can be owned by a public housing authority, a PHA affiliate, another public agency, or—if they receive a federal tax credit and are subject to federal LIHTC regulation—a for-profit entity. Participating developments are removed from the public housing program inventory and instead receive a long-term project-based contract providing the owner of the development with a subsidy that covers the difference between 30% of tenant income and total operating costs (including debt service). The RAD program allows up to 80% or more of the capital and operating funds allocated to a public housing development to be applied towards debt service. PHAs can rehabilitate or demolish and replace units under the RAD program. However, if they demolish units, they are required to replace the demolished units so there is no net reduction. RAD makes the development eligible for low-income housing tax credits. Congress has approved converting up to 455,000 public housing units to Section 8 units under the program. As of July, 2020 they had converted 136,000 units and most of the rest were in the pipeline.

The Moving to Work (MTW) Program is a related HUD program that provides PHAs the opportunity to design and test innovative, locally designed strategies to help residents find employment and become self-sufficient.[7] Currently, 70 public housing authorities (PHAs) nationwide have MTW programs. HUD plans to expand the program to an additional 69 PHAs by 2022. Figure 15.4 shows Jackson Gardens in Boston—an MTW Rental Assistance Demonstration (RAD) project.

The One-Strike Eviction Policy

A final element in the transformation of public housing since the 1990s consists of the "one-strike you're out" eviction policy

Figure 15.4 Jackson Gardens Public Housing Project (Boston, Massachusetts).

adopted by the Clinton administration in 1996 to combat violent crime and drug dealing in public housing. Under the one-strike policy, just one criminal charge against any one household member requires a public housing authority to evict the entire household from public housing. The one-strike policy bans convicted sex offenders and persons convicted of certain other crimes such as manufacturing methamphetamines in public housing from living in public housing. It gives PHAs broad discretion not to admit other people who they consider likely to commit crimes.

Legacy Federal Private Market Rental Housing Subsidies

Less than one-fifth of the 728,000 Section 221(d)3 and Section 236 private market rental housing units built between 1963 and 1975 still receive subsidies under those programs.[8] The mortgages on some units matured and were not renewed. Some mortgages were prepaid and owners opted out of the program. Others projects were foreclosed. Many of the remaining units now receive project- or tenant-based HCVs and are counted as HCV units. HUD's Office of Affordable Housing Preservation and Office of Recapitalization oversee preservation and conversion of the remaining Section 221(d)3 and Section 236 units.

The Saint Francis Square Cooperatives in San Francisco illustrate how imaginative local leadership could make use of the Section 221(d)(3) program. Saint Francis Square was one of the first Section 221(d)(3) projects in the United States. It was a housing cooperative that opened in 1964. The project was built by the International Longshore and Warehouse Union using capital from the ILWU's pension fund. The principal architect had been a longshoreman, and a longshoreman who was on the San Francisco board of supervisors helped push the project through. Many of the units were for active and retired union members, but the ILWU made units available to any applicant as a matter of principle. Saint Francis Square proudly offered units to people of every race and religion long before that was common in other government-assisted housing. Saint Francis Square still provides attractive ownership units at prices that are well below San Francisco's very high market rates.

The principal challenge that city and regional planners face for the legacy BMIR units is how to keep them available to low-income tenants rather than losing them to the private market as owners opt out of the programs when their mortgage terms expire. Most of the mortgages on remaining units will end by 2024. As federal maintenance support money decreases, a second big challenge is maintenance. Planners use all of the new programs described in this chapter and the implementation tools discussed in Chapter 11 to assist these legacy units.

FAIR HOUSING AND SOCIAL JUSTICE

Advocates for low-income individuals and communities have played an important role in U.S. housing policy. Box 15.1 profiles Robert Weaver, the first Secretary of the Department of Housing and Urban Development. Weaver helped shape U.S. housing policy from the first New Deal public housing program in 1933 through the Kennedy and Johnson administrations between 1961 and 1969. He made a major contribution to social justice in federal housing and urban development programs.

The Fair Housing Act—the Civil Rights Act of 1968—was passed a week after the assassination of Dr. Martin Luther King Jr. It followed landmark civil rights laws that

---

BOX 15.1 ROBERT WEAVER

Robert Clifton Weaver (1907–1997) was a pioneering housing scholar and practitioner who played a key role in state, local, and national housing and urban development and civil rights policies from the New Deal until the late 1990s. He was the first United States Secretary of Housing and Urban Development (HUD) from 1966 to 1968 and the first Black person to be appointed to a U.S. cabinet-level position. Weaver was a politically astute moderate progressive scholar-activist who worked tirelessly to improve housing and living conditions for low-income and minority individuals and communities.

Weaver received BS, MA, and PhD degrees in economics from Harvard. At Harvard he developed an academic knowledge of housing economics and policy.

Figure 15.5 Robert Weaver.

He was appointed as an aide to United States Secretary of the Interior Harold L. Ickes in 1933, a year before he completed his doctorate. He was one of 45 prominent Blacks who Roosevelt appointed to executive agencies and called upon for advice—Roosevelt's "Black Cabinet". Weaver informally advised Roosevelt on housing issues, particularly as they related to Blacks.

Weaver alternated numerous public policy positions between stints in academia. He was appointed New York State Rent Commissioner (1955–1959)—the first Black state cabinet member in New York state. He served as the Vice Chairman of the New York City Housing and Redevelopment Board in 1960.

Weaver was recruited by newly elected President John F. Kennedy to serve in his administration as head of the Housing and Home Finance Agency (HHFA)—an umbrella organization that had consolidated federal housing programs that existed at that time. Appointing a Black person to head of the HHFA cost Kennedy political capital in the South and among Democrats from small cities and rural areas who assumed (correctly) that federal involvement in housing would disproportionately benefit New York City and other large cities. Weaver maintained a low profile in Kennedy's efforts to create HUD because of conservative opposition to a potential Black cabinet secretary. Kennedy—eager to get enough political support to create HUD—was careful not to suggest he might appoint Weaver secretary of the new agency.

Kennedy's assassination left the creation of HUD and selection of its first secretary to his successor, Lyndon Johnson. How the federal government enforced civil rights and the provisions of the Voting Rights Act of 1965 were sensitive topics. Johnson knew that a politically influential White secretary would be more palatable to conservatives and politicians in the South than a Black secretary who had worked primarily in New York. Johnson wanted a strong proponent for the new department and seriously considered powerful and politically connected White candidates, including Richard Daley, the powerful mayor of Chicago—a master of old-fashioned machine politics who could reliably deliver enough Chicago votes to assure Democrats would win presidential elections. Johnson also considered offering the position of Secretary of Housing and Urban Development to Laurence Rockefeller—a wealthy New York City financier, venture capitalist, developer, conservationist, and philanthropist. Rockefeller was a prominent third-generation member of one of America's wealthiest families. Nonetheless, Johnson appointed Weaver despite opposition from racists, anti-city forces, and conservatives.

Weaver succeeded in organizing HUD and reducing racist and anti-poor features of the Federal Housing Administration (FHA) that had long redlined Black and racially mixed neighborhoods and the federal urban renewal program that was disrupting low-income, predominantly Black communities. After serving under Johnson, Weaver became President of Baruch College in 1969. The following year, he became a professor of urban affairs at Hunter College in New York where he taught until 1978.

Weaver was a close friend of the great New Deal housing reformer Catherine Bauer (Box 12.3). He had a bronze statue of Bauer erected at the entrance to HUD.

---

prohibited discrimination in public facilities and voting. The federal Fair Housing Act prohibits discrimination in the sale, rental, and financing of housing based on race, color, religion or national origin. Congress added sex as a protected category in 1974 and familial status and disability status as protected categories in 1988. The Fair Housing Act does not expressly include sexual orientation as a protected category. The Fair Housing Act has two main purposes—to prevent discrimination and reverse the effects of housing discrimination and segregation. It provides clear, enforceable legal entitlements and requires proof only of racially discriminatory *impact*—not *intent*. The Fair Housing Act requires HUD to affirmatively further fair housing. HUD's Office of Fair Housing and Equal Opportunity (FHEO) is responsible for enforcing the act.

The U.S. Supreme Court has held that plaintiffs—tenants of government-assisted housing and their allies—must prove that the defendant(s)—housing authorities and other entities that finance or own government-assisted housing—intended to discriminate against members of one or more protected categories to win a lawsuit based on the equal protection clause of the U.S. Constitution. This is almost impossible to do unless there is a clear written record, as was the case with the Chicago Housing Authority at the time they selected sites for the Cabrini–Green and Robert Taylor homes.

The Fair Housing Act applies to the rental or sale of dwelling units with the exception of single-family homes. States and localities may have fair housing laws with broader protections than those encompassed in the federal Fair Housing Act, including protection of classes defined by age, sexual orientation, and source of income.

FHEO receives, investigates, and makes determinations regarding complaints of Fair Housing Act violations and may obtain settlements and relief for victims of racial discrimination in housing.[9] FHEO attempts to resolve disputes without going to court. If that it is not possible, it makes a determination of whether there is reasonable cause to believe discrimination has occurred or is about to occur. If FHEO finds reasonable cause to believe that discrimination occurred or is about to occur, it issues a charge—a written statement of facts on which the determination was based. Either party may then request that the case be heard in court.

HUD funds state, local, and nonprofit organizations that investigate fair housing complaints based on federal, state, or local laws through the Fair Housing Assistance Program (FHAP) and Fair Housing Initiatives Program. If a state or local FHAP agency exists, HUD must refer complaints to them. If a complaint alleges a challenge to a zoning or land use law HUD refers the complaint to the United States Department of Justice. State and local fair housing agencies and nonprofit fair housing organizations do most of the work of investigating and enforcing the Fair Housing Act and other fair housing laws. About 30,000 fair housing complaints are filed each year—mostly by state and local private and nonprofit fair housing organizations. About a third are settled as a result of conciliation, 40% result in a finding of no reasonable cause. The remainder are either dropped, withdrawn, or referred to the Department of Justice. Most complaints involve disability status, not race. Fewer involve religion and very few color unrelated to race. FHEO also conducts outreach and education activities to increase public awareness of fair housing rights and responsibilities and ensures civil rights in HUD programs.

Gated communities—which only allow access to residents, their invited guests, and delivery people—pose important social issues. They provide the feeling, if not the reality, of safety from crime for their residents. Gated communities are legal, but liberal planners and policy makers criticize them for physically and symbolically dividing communities by income and race.

Social justice advocates also press for greater economic equity in housing and less economic segregation at every scale. The wealth gap in the United States is large and growing. Rapid appreciation of owned housing advantages the two-thirds of U.S. households who own their homes compared to the third of the population who are renters and get none of the appreciation in rental housing. General plans and zoning can exacerbate or ameliorate housing inequality. All of the programs described in this chapter can at least make a dent in low-income renters' housing cost burdens.

Many local governments have adopted inclusionary zoning provisions that require some percentage (typically 15%) of units in new condominium or apartment projects to be set aside for low- and moderate-income households. Inclusionary housing programs have produced approximately 150,000 affordable housing units in more than 500 cities and counties in 28 states—helpful, but a tiny contribution given that there are nearly 140 million housing units in the United States. Inclusionary housing units increase income diversity and may indirectly increase racial diversity in housing. However, most inclusionary housing units go to moderate-income households earning up to 120% of the metropolitan area income. Inclusionary housing programs are horizontally and vertically inefficient housing subsidies—meeting a tiny fraction of need and mostly going to households with less need than households with lower incomes. The burden of inclusionary housing subsidies falls initially on developers. Since most inclusionary housing is built in areas where there is high housing demand and housing elasticity is low, developers can usually pass the increased cost on to people purchasing other units. This is less equitable than a subsidy system that would spread the burden more widely and more in relation to ability to pay.

Minneapolis, Minnesota and Portland, Oregon have recently eliminated single-family zoning for new housing altogether. Many other cities are considering a similar change. This should produce more affordable multi-family units in these cities. Many cities are changing their zoning laws to permit additional units called in-law units, granny flats, and casitas ("little houses" in Spanish) to be added as units within existing houses or separate dwelling units to be built on the same lot as another house.

LANDLORD–TENANT LAW

State landlord–tenant law governs landlord–tenant relations in private housing. Landlord–tenant law in public housing—including the one-strike eviction rule—is national, but individual public housing authorities (PHAs) have some discretion in applying it.

Most tenants in private rental housing have one-year written leases that specify the parties' rights and responsibilities. Tenants without leases rent month-to-month, protected only by state law. If a tenant fails to pay rent or violates another lease provision he or she can be evicted. State eviction law specifies requirements for notice, the right to appear in court, and how evictions take place. Most eviction cases are heard in low-level courts that handle a large volume of eviction cases. In most cases, judges grant landlords default judgments—judgments granted without a trial—one after another, because tenants fail to appear in court. Once a court has issued an eviction judgment most tenants leave voluntarily. After a specified period and with proper notice, those who do not move are forcibly evicted. Typically a county sheriff moves their possessions out to the curbside and changes the lock. State landlord–tenant law is overwhelmingly pro-landlord. New Jersey is an exception with protections of tenant rights that are much stronger than other states.

Many states have adopted a legal doctrine in landlord tenant law called the implied warranty of habitability that holds that by renting a unit, a landlord represents that it is habitable—livable and not dangerous—even if the lease does not say so explicitly in writing. The implied warranty of habitability is usually invoked as a defense to stop an eviction and relieve the tenant of the obligation to pay some or all of the rent during the time when the unit was uninhabitable. Tenants can also sue landlords affirmatively for violating the implied warranty of habitability. Precise definitions of what habitable means vary from state to state. Gross violations like lack of electricity or heat, faulty plumbing, leaky roofs, or dangerous structural deficiencies almost always qualify as violations. Most states also accept a legal doctrine called the retaliatory eviction defense protecting tenant union organizers from eviction if a court finds that an attempt to evict them is in retaliation for their organizing activities.

RENT REGULATION

Rent regulation—also called rent stabilization and sometimes rent control—is a conflictual housing policy. In states that permit local government to regulate rents, cities and counties may adopt ordinances regulating rents in private market housing. HUD regulates rents in public housing and other federally assisted housing.

The only times in American history when strict rent control was overwhelmingly accepted were during World Wars I and II when rent gouging in areas facing an influx of war workers was deemed unpatriotic. Ordinances freezing rents during the duration of both wars were repealed after the wars ended. Strict rent control has also been politically acceptable in unusual circumstances such as construction of the pipeline from Point Barrow to Valdez, Alaska when policy makers (and oil companies) considered it unfair to allow private owners to wildly inflate rents for oil workers.

Rent regulations vary enormously from state to state. California and Oregon have statewide rent stabilization programs. The federal government and some states temporarily prohibited evictions during the COVID pandemic even if tenants were behind on their rent payments. Some jurisdictions regulate rents so long as the same tenant occupies a unit, but allow landlords to increase rents to market rates when they are vacated (vacancy decontrol). Other jurisdictions preserve the regulated rent from tenancy to tenancy (vacancy control). Some rent stabilization ordinances apply only to new rental units. Many exempt rented single-family houses and small apartments. How much rents can rise may be pegged to an indicator such as the consumer price index or determined in some other way.

As of 2021 some local governments in five states—California, New York, New Jersey, Maryland, and Oregon and in Washington, D.C.—had some form of rent regulation. Eight states allow their cities to regulate rents, but have no cities that had done so. Thirty-seven states either prohibit or preempt rent regulation. Rent regulation is most common in large cities and in politically liberal jurisdictions such as university towns. A few jurisdictions regulate rents in mobile home parks.

Proponents of rent regulation see it as a necessary measure to protect low-income tenants from rent gouging. Critics see rent regulation as top-down meddling that distorts markets. They assert that it will hurt new construction and may provide windfalls to long-term tenants who can afford market rents and do not need rent regulation to permit them to pay for housing. Some studies have shown that many rent-controlled units are occupied by middle- and upper-income households or students who are only temporarily low-income rather than long-term low-income households.

THE RIGHT TO HOUSING

A long-term aspirational housing goal is the right of every person to housing. The right to housing was first declared by the United Nations in 1948 and has since been restated in many international human rights declarations, laws, pronouncements, and treaties. It is a stated goal of the UN's *2030 Agenda for Sustainable Development* (2015) and *New Urban Agenda* (2017). U.S. theorists have fleshed out and operationalized the concept. A United Nations fact sheet lists features the UN considers essential to the right to housing.[10] Many UN member countries do not want to be legally bound by these goals, and they remain far from realized.

In the United States providing housing for the homeless, transitional housing, and decent, safe, and sanitary subsidized housing that is affordable to low-, very low-, and extremely low-income households and cost-burdened renters and homeowners are still aspirational goals. The right to housing is critical in developing countries where large informal housing settlements called *favelas, callampas, bidonvilles, taudis, barrios marginales, tugurios, peri-urban slums* and by other names are often occupied illegally by rural migrants who build whatever shelter than can from waste wood, tin, carboard, cloth, and other materials. Many lack safe drinking water and sanitary facilities. Social critic Mike Davis envisages a planet of slums with only little pockets for the rich sealed off from the misery surrounding them (Davis, 2007). Studies by anthropologists, sociologists, planners, and others paint a more nuanced picture. Empirical research has found that the residents of informal settlements are remarkably creative, and

Figure 15.6 Paraisópolis, São Paulo, Brazil.

many of the settlements develop a complex social structure that helps people survive. Even poor settlements are rarely marginal. Their residents find niche specialties in the local economy. Canadian journalist Douglas Saunders conducted interviews in what he called "arrival cities"—informal settlements in developing countries where many rural migrants had settled. Saunders found that the residents were nearly always glad that they had moved to the city and optimistic about their future. Over time informal settlements like the *favela* of Paraisópolis ("Paradise") in São Paulo, Brazil may develop to become better built and more adequate settlements.

SUMMARY

Because the great majority of housing units in the United States are privately built and owned, planners mostly shape how much housing there will be in an area indirectly through subdivision, zoning, growth management, and other regulations. Policy makers impact housing indirectly through tax, fiscal, and monetary policy and programs to subsidize mortgage interest. City and regional planners appropriately devote much of their attention to subsidy programs for low-income housing, but also plan for the great majority of housing that is not subsidized.

Housing involves a bundle of goods and services. It requires adequate supporting infrastructure and access to transportation, schools, and public services. It should be free of air and water pollution, away from toxic waste sites, and without too much noise.

The U.S. homebuilding industry is efficient, despite being fragmented, complex, small-scale, localized, and cyclic. Most U.S. housing is built by small builders. Mobile homes and other manufactured housing and a small number of large residential builders are exceptions.

Ideally there should be a decent, safe, and sanitary housing unit affordable to every U.S. household at every income level. Moderate and above moderate income U.S. households that own their homes are relatively well off. In contrast, about one-quarter of homeowners and nearly half of all renters in the United States are cost-burdened—paying more than 30% of their income for housing. Cost-burdened renter households are disproportionately low-income households and households of color.

Most new affordable housing programs rely on the Federal Low-Income Housing Tax Credit, HOME Investment Partnership (HOME) Program, Mortgage Revenue Bonds, or Housing Trust Funds. The legacy federal Public Housing and Below Market Interest Rate Programs are being phased out in favor of housing choice vouchers.

U.S. housing subsidies are both vertically and horizontally inefficient. Planners can help policy makers better target housing subsidies.

Rent regulation in the United States is controversial. California and Oregon have statewide rent regulation programs. Only a few states permit their cities and counties to regulate rent, and in most of these states no city or county has chosen to regulate rents. The U.S. Department of Housing and Urban Development regulates rents in federally subsidized housing.

Landlord–tenant relations in the United States are governed by state law. State landlord–tenant laws overwhelmingly favor landlords. The implied warranty of habitability and retaliatory eviction defense offer tenants and tenant union organizers some protections and rights.

The "right to housing" is an aspirational goal the United Nations advocates that has been included in many international treaties and policy statements since 1948. The United States has aspired to provide a decent, safe, and sanitary housing unit and a rent or purchase price every household can afford since 1948. Both the international and U.S. versions of the right to housing goal are far from being realized.

CONCEPTS

Building Code
Case–Shiller Index
Demand-Side Housing Program
Exclusionary Housing
Fair Housing Act
Fair Market Rent
Federal Home Mortgage Interest Deduction
Federal Housing Administration (FHA)
Filtering
HOME Program
Horizonal Efficiency
Household-Based Subsidy
Housing Code
Housing Development Corporation (HDC)
Housing Element
Housing Finance Agency (HFA)
Housing Opportunity for People Everywhere VI (HOPE VI) Program
Inclusionary Land Use Policy
Jobs–Housing Balance
Landlord–Tenant Law
Liar's Loan
Low-Income Household
Low-Income Housing Tax Credit (LIHTC)
Mobile Home
Moving to Opportunity Program (MTO)
Principal, Interest, Taxes, and Insurance (PITI) Payment
Post-Shelter Society
Project-Based Subsidy
Public Housing
Rent Regulation
Rental Assistance Demonstration (RAD) Program
Right To Housing
Section 8 Certificate
Self-Amortizing Mortgage
Subprime Mortgage Crisis
Supply-Side Housing Program
U.S. Department of Housing and Urban Development (HUD)
Vertical Efficiency

PEOPLE

Julian Castro
Robert Weaver

NOTES

1   The U.S. census defines a *housing unit* as a house, apartment, group of rooms, or a single room occupied or intended for occupancy as separate living quarters. The census defines a *household* as consisting of all the people who occupy a housing unit when the occupants do not live with any other persons in the structure and there is direct

access from the outside or through a common hall. Households may include a single individual, related family members, and any lodgers, foster children, wards, employees and other unrelated people who share a housing unit. Households do not include people living in group quarters (U.S. Census, 2019).

2 Adjusted income is a household's gross (total) income minus deductions for dependents under 18 years of age, full-time students, disabled persons, elderly households, households with certain disability assistance and medical expenses. It allows a deduction for households where a single person, the head of a household, or the spouse of the head of a household is older than 62. An individual over 62 living with a live-in aide and the aide are also an elderly household.

3 In 2019 Housing Choice Voucher recipients' income distribution was:
Forty-three per cent of HCV recipients had children; almost all were headed by a single mother. Forty-five percent of HCV recipients were elderly households. Black and White households with

Income ($)	%
0	4
1–5,000	9
5,000–10,000	25
10,000–15,000	25
15,000–20,000	14
20,000–25,000	8
25,000+	14

HCVs each account for 47% of the total. Eighteen percent of the recipients were Latinx (both Black and White) (HUD, 2020).

4 The HOME Program assisted 1,696,244 low- and moderate-income units for low-income households between 1992 and 2020 at a cost of over $35 billion (HUD, 2021). Thirty-one percent of HOME funding during that period went to development of rental housing and 22% to tenant-based rental assistance. About one-third assisted homebuyers. Fifteen percent went to owner-occupied rehabilitation. Almost all the homeowners assisted had incomes over 60% of area median income. Sixty percent of HOME funding goes to cities and 40% to states based on need. The HOME program provides a 15% set aside for non-profit community housing development organizations (CHDOs) to build and/or acquire affordable housing. The HOME program requires local matching funds. To qualify for funding, units must remain affordable for between 5 and 20 years depending on the type of project.

5 Ninety percent of National Housing Trust Fund money must be used to support activities that build, preserve, repair, or operate rental housing for low-income and very low-income households. Up to 10% of funds can support homeownership for first-time home buyers such as down payment and closing cost assistance and funding to reduce interest rates. No disbursements from the fund occurred until 2016, when $174 million was dispersed with each state receiving at least $3 million (Gramlich, 2018). In 2021 HUD allocated $689,565,492 from the Housing Trust Fund (HUD, 2021).

6 Ninety-five percent of public housing tenants earn 80% of median income or less. Seventy percent are women. One-third are elderly. Thirty-six percent are children. Most able-bodied adult public housing tenants work. Fifty-six percent receive social security, retirement benefits, or pension income. Twenty-nine percent receive welfare. Seven percent have no income. Fifty-one percent describe themselves as White only, 44% percent Black/African American only, and 2% Asian only. Twenty-six percent self-report their race as Hispanic or Latino, divided between White Hispanic (82%) and Black Hispanic (18%) (HUD, 2021).

7 The Moving to Work (MTW) program grew out of the Experimental Housing Allowance Program (EHAP)—a 15-year HUD research and demonstration program. It was designed to test the choices households from distressed public housing projects in big cities would make if they were given vouchers that allowed them to choose where to live, including the option to move into private market rental housing. Between 1994 and 2009 four large PHAs randomly selected 4,608 households with children. Two-thirds of the sample were offered vouchers. Some voucher recipients did not move. Most moved—often to low-income neighborhoods and neighborhoods of color. HUD evaluated the long-term effects on adult and child well-being (U.S. HUD, 2011; Comey, Popkin, & Franks, 2012). The EHAP program evaluation concluded that MTO had sizable positive impacts on housing and neighborhood conditions and social networks, but mixed results regarding employment, income, education, health, and social well-being of family members at the end of 7, 10, and 15 years (Kling et al, 2004).

8 The Section 221(d)(3) program produced 184,000 units between 1960 and 1964 (Aaron, 1972). The Section 236 program produced 544,000 units between 1965 and 1973 (Olsen, 2001). As of 2020, 41,655 of these 728,000 units still received either Section 221(d)(3) or Section 236 subsidies (HUD, 2020).

9 In fiscal year (FY) 2019 HUD reported working on the following types of fair housing complaints: disability (4,767), race (2,002), retaliation (979), sex (853), national origin (743), family status (756), color (313), and religion (202). In FYs 2018 and 2019, FHEO and its partners, in cooperation with HUD's Office of General Counsel (OGC) and the Department of Justice (DOJ), launched a coordinated nationwide initiative to address and prevent sexual harassment in housing.

10 A United Nations fact sheet on the right to housing takes the position that to be adequate housing must include legal security of tenure, physical safety, adequate space, infrastructure for safe drinking

water and sanitation, protection against the elements, access to employment opportunities, healthcare services, schools, childcare centers, and other social facilities, and not be located in polluted or dangerous areas (UN, 2009).

SUGGESTIONS FOR FURTHER LEARNING

Overviews: Alex Schwartz, *Housing policy in the United States*, 4th ed (2021). Katrin Anaker, *Introduction to housing* (2018). National Low-Income Housing Coalition (ed), *2020 Advocates' guide: A primer on federal housing and community development policy* (2020). Harvard Joint Center for Housing Studies (JCHS), *The state of the nation's housing* (2021), *State of the nation's housing* (2020), and *State of the nation's housing* [video] (2020). Andrew Carswell, *The encyclopedia of housing*, 2nd ed (2012). **Homebuilding:** Tracy Kidder, *House* (1985). **Mobile Homes:** Esther Sullivan, *Manufactured insecurity: Mobile home parks and Americans' tenuous right to place* (2018). **Sears, Roebuck and Company Mail Order Homes:** Rebecca Hunter, *Mail-order homes* (2012). Katherine Stevenson & H. Ward Jandi, *Houses by mail* (1995). Sears, Roebuck and Company, *Sears, Roebuck and Company home builder's catalogue* (1926). **Housing Markets:** William Grigsby, *Housing markets and public policy* (1963). **Psychological Aspects of Housing:** Claire Cooper Marcus, *House as a mirror of self* (2010). **Housing Demography:** Dowall Myers, *Housing demography* (1991). **Public Housing:** Lawrence Vale, *From the Puritans to the projects* (2007) and *Purging the poorest* (2007). Alexander Polikoff, *Waiting for Gautreaux* (2005). **The Right to Housing:** Rachel Bratt, Michael Stone, & Chester Hartman, *A right to housing* (2006). United Nations Right to Housing Fact Sheet (2009). **Federal Housing Programs:** Allen Hayes, *The federal government and urban housing*, 2nd ed (1998). Henry Aaron, *Shelter and subsidies* (1964). **Exclusionary Land Use:** David Kirp, John Dwyer, & Larry Rosenthal, *Our town: Race, housing, and the soul of America* (1997). **Inclusionary Housing:** Nico Calavita & Alan Mallach, *Inclusionary housing in international perspective* (2010). Rick Jacobus, *Inclusionary housing* (2015). **Jobs–Housing Balance:** Robert Cervero, Jobs–housing balancing and regional mobility (1989) and Jobs–housing balance revisited (1996). **Homelessness:** Mary-Beth Shinn & Jill Khadduri, *In the midst of plenty: Homelessness and what to do about it* (2020). Eliot Liebow, *Tell them who I am: The lives of homeless women* (1993). U.S. Department of Housing and Urban Development, *The annual HOMES Assessment Report (AHAR) to Congress* (2021). **Rent Regulation:** Dennis Keating, Michael Teitz, & Anjdrejs Skaburskis, *Rent control* (1998). **Landlord–Tenant Relations:** Matthew Desmond, *Evicted: Poverty and profit in the American city* (2017). **Journals:** *Housing Policy Debate. Housing Studies. Housing Theory and Society. Journal of Housing and the Built Environment.*

CHAPTER 16

Economic Development and Revitalization Planning

INTRODUCTION

Every country wants to have economically healthy cities and regions that can produce goods and services the society needs, employ their residents, pay for maintenance and modernization of the built environment, and generate revenue for public purposes. Development and revitalization planning helps achieve these goals. Development refers to both new development and modernization of existing residential, commercial, industrial, public, and other areas. Revitalization refers to improvement of older buildings, infrastructure, and other neighborhood features. It may include job training and economic development and health, education, and other welfare programs.

The boundary between revitalization and development is fuzzy. The terms development and economic development overlap. Much of the planning literature on development and revitalization focuses on neighborhoods or communities. "Community development" and "community economic development" are subfields of development.

At the national and international scale, economic development planning involves the theory and practice of planning to totally transform societies. In traditional "underdeveloped" societies most human settlements have little connection to the world city network. Modes of production and human relations may have changed little in millennia. The goal of economic development planning at this scale is to transform the societies into modern, dynamic industrial, post-industrial or information economies. Planners seek to connect the re-invented economy to the world city network in ways that will provide well-paying jobs and generate wealth that can provide people a high quality of life. How well the new wealth actually does that depends on how well a society distributes it.

Within the social science discipline of economics, the field of urban economics provides a theoretical framework for understanding economic aspects of development and revitalization. "Welfare economics" applies macro- and microeconomic concepts to the public sector.

This chapter begins by describing the relevance of key concepts in urban economics and the application of welfare economics concepts to land use, transportation, environmental, and other types of city and regional planning discussed throughout this book.

The next section describes development planning. It describes the theory and practice of planning for development at different scales from communities to countries. Since much development planning is for economic development, that is a main focus of this section.

A section on revitalization planning follows the development section. It distinguishes the modern theory and practice of revitalization from urban renewal as it was practiced in the United States between 1949 and 1974. In the United States many revitalization activities are called community development. The principal source of funding for revitalization in the United States is the federal Community Development Block Grant (CDBG) program. Community development generally refers to activities authorized and funded by the CDBG program, so the chapter describes the CDBG program in detail. Sometimes the term community development is used loosely to refer to any plans or programs to develop communities physically, economically, or socially.

Ideology shapes approaches to development and revitalization planning. Liberals favor an expansive role for government in development and revitalization. They favor programs that

DOI: 10.4324/9781003195818-16

provide funding and significant government regulation to support development and revitalization. Many liberals favor bottom-up economic development and revitalization planning and programs. They often encourage local community development corporations (CDCs) as the vehicle to develop and revitalize neighborhoods. In contrast, the most important neoliberal strategy for neighborhood revitalization is to attract private sector investment from large companies to create jobs in low-income, high-unemployment zones. They encourage use of private sector companies to achieve development and revitalization. A section of this chapter explains the ideology behind liberal and neoliberal development and programs and describes British and U.S. programs that take one or the other of the two approaches.

Infrastructure includes physical structures and facilities needed for development and revitalization to help a society function. It includes roads, schools, reservoirs, dams, libraries, courthouses, electrical and gas lines, sewers, storm drains, wastewater treatment plants, landfills, and other physical constructs necessary for development and revitalization. By some definitions, infrastructure includes technological, economic, and social improvements. The chapter closes with a discussion of planning and programs to provide, alter, and extend infrastructure.

ECONOMIC CONCEPTS FOR URBAN DEVELOPMENT AND REVITALIZATION

Many graduate city and regional planning programs in the United States require or recommend that planning students take at least one course in urban economics. Urban economics is a field within the social science discipline of economics. Urban economics courses may be taught by faculty in the city and regional planning department itself, or the university's economics, public administration, or business administration departments. Urban economics courses assure that all planning graduates have a basic knowledge of how to apply micro- and macroeconomic concepts to city and regional planning issues. The leading U.S. textbook on urban economics by Arthur O'Sullivan (2018) defines urban economics as follows:

> The discipline of urban economics is defined by the intersection of geography and economics. Economics explores the choices people make when resources are limited. Households make choices to maximize their utility, while firms maximize their profit. Geographers study how things are arranged across space, answering the question, "Where does human activity occur?" Urban economics puts economics and geography together, exploring the geographical or locational choices of utility-maximizing households and profit-maximizing firms. Urban economics also identifies inefficiencies in location choices and examines alternative policies to promote efficient choices.

Welfare economics provides theory about the extent to which government can and should intervene to improve human welfare. It applies economic concepts to evaluate welfare at the individual and aggregate (economy-wide) level. "Welfare" in this context means well-being; it does not mean public assistance. Three concepts from welfare economics are fundamental in urban economics—public goods, merit goods, and payments to redistribute income. City and regional planners frequently base decisions about what infrastructure and public sector services should be provided on these concepts.

Governments provide public goods, such as streets and libraries at no cost to the user, for everyone to use. Unlike the cost of goods or services in the private market, the price of public goods is often implicit. Consumers do not think how much it will cost society—and indirectly them as taxpayers—to drive from home to a local library on a public street. They consider both the trip and use of the library free goods. The failure to think through the actual economic cost of public goods and to price them accordingly may lead to muddled and sometimes irrational policy. Donald Shoup's critique of "free" parking in Chapter 14 is an excellent analysis of market failure to consider the real costs of providing parking as a public good.

Merit goods are a category of public goods that governments provide for free because they believe that everyone should have them regardless of whether they would voluntarily choose to pay for them and without regard to ability to pay. Free primary school education is an example. Governments want every child to master basic reading, math, and other skills and to be socialized with other children regardless of their families' ability to pay, because they consider this essential for the society to function. In the United States, neoliberals—who favor market solutions—generally take the position that only a few critical goods should be classified as merit goods. This is quite different from the view in welfare states like the Scandinavian countries, where there is a consensus that many goods such as universal health care and college education should be provided free by the state rather than purchased by individuals from the private sector.

Payments to redistribute income are a third key concept in welfare economics. The classic example is a welfare payment to an indigent person, such as a payment to a severely disabled person with no assets or income. One group (taxpayers) pays and another group—indigent severely disabled people—receives the payment. The recipient benefits directly. The payment may save society costs associated with emergency response, medical care, and homelessness. It assures other members of society that they will receive at least a minimal level of care if they become unable to pay for their own needs. All societies redistribute income both explicitly through programs that target specific groups of people and implicitly through tax policy and the location of publicly funded infrastructure that benefit some people more than others. City and regional planners' decisions have redistributive implications.

The United States has fewer public and merit goods and less income redistribution than most developed countries. Americans distrust government's ability to manage welfare and merit goods and resent redistributive policies that take money from working taxpayers and give it to people they feel do not pay their own way for what they receive. Americans accept free universal education through 12th grade, police and fire services, Supplemental Security Income (SSI) for the indigent, free public parks, libraries, and other programs that do not charge a user fee. However, Americans rely primarily on private market solutions to meet other human needs and desires.

Analyses of the implicit redistributive impacts of tax and other policies show that U.S. government policies often increase, rather than decrease, inequality. The federal home mortgage interest deduction, which subsidizes primarily upper-income homeowners, is a prime example. The federal home mortgage deduction was discussed in Chapter 15. City and regional planners involved in macro-level policy can sometimes impact implicit or explicit redistributive policies. At the regional, city, and neighborhood level, advocacy and equity planners seek to redistribute public goods to better serve low-income communities and individuals.

User fees and congestion pricing are important tools for planners. They indirectly encourage or discourage the way in which the built environment is constructed and used. User fees, such as fees for admission to a public park or zoo, seek to cover at least some of the costs of constructing and operating the facility.

Congestion pricing involves charging more for the use of public transportation or other publicly provided goods and services during periods of peak demand. People who value their mobility highly at certain times of the day and are able to pay—such as affluent commuters rushing to drive to work on time—are willing to pay a high toll to use a public highway. People for whom mobility at that time is less important—such as friends planning to get together to work out at an exercise studio—may choose to travel to and from the exercise studio between the morning and evening rush hour when congestion prices are lower in order to save money. Congestion pricing has had a dramatic impact on commuting patterns in the entire London region, Singapore, Stockholm, and other cities where it has been used. It is being successfully implemented in some U.S. cities.

PUBLIC PLANNING AND PRIVATE DEVELOPMENT

In modern society the idea that society should continue to "develop" is nearly universal. Citizens of every political persuasion want, and governments support, development to improve the societies efficiency, productivity, and standard of living, though they often disagree on how to accomplish these goals. This is true both for cities and regions that are prospering and modernizing independent of government intervention and for ones that are distressed and declining.

The term development implies economic development—continual modernization and improvement of the economy. However, development extends to change that improves an area's quality of life, such as more attractive public spaces or parks, preservation of historic buildings, and public art, which have only an indirect economic impact or no economic impact at all.

In the United States and most other countries, the private sector drives development. Increasingly public–private partnerships (PPPs) combine public and private funding and share the return on their investment. Accordingly, the planning literature discusses ways in which government can encourage and support largely private development. Yale University architecture professor and planning consultant Alexander Garvin has studied public and private development in the United States and other countries. Garvin's principal message to planners is to consider the context in which private or public–private partnership development occurs. In Garvin's opinion what will make an individual development succeed or fail is how it fits into the fabric of the place where it is built. If there is sufficient demand and the project concept is realistic, a project will succeed. The best designed project in a place that cannot support it will fail. Planners can learn from Garvin's analysis and his detailed description of successful and unsuccessful private sector developments in the United States. Garvin's measure of successful economic development extends beyond an individual new project. If a project generates more positive economic change nearby, he considers it a model of economic development success.

Massachusetts Institute of Technology professors Bernard Frieden and Lynn Sagalyn reach similar conclusions about the way in which largely private downtown developments, not supported by government, succeed or fail. They have described successful and unsuccessful development of shopping malls, festival markets, big box stores, convention centers, and even pornography districts. Frieden and Sagalyn's (1991) case studies of private risk-taking, entrepreneurial cities, deal making, and joint ventures are full of insights for city and regional planners.

At the international scale many developing countries rely on a mix of public and private sector development and public–private partnerships. Fulong Wu, a Bartlett Professor of Planning at University College London, has provided a detailed description of how cities in China plan for development that is relevant for planners in other developing countries and in the United States (Wu, 2018).

THE THEORY AND PRACTICE OF ECONOMIC DEVELOPMENT PLANNING

The International Economic Development Council (IEDC) defines economic development as a program, group of policies, or activity that seeks to improve the economic well-being and quality of life for a community, by creating and/or retaining jobs that facilitate growth and provide a stable tax base.

City and regional planners draw on a large theoretical literature on economic development planning. These include economic base and location theory, and input–output analysis.

Economic base theory involves conceptualizing an area's economy as consisting of two sectors: a basic sector and a nonbasic sector. The basic sector of an economy produces goods and services for export outside the area (domestically or internationally). For example a large cell phone assembly plant in a small city will sell virtually all of the finished cell phones it assembles outside the city where it is located. In contrast the non-basic sector provides goods and services for local consumption. For example, a local bakery will sell almost all of the muffins it produces each day to residents of the city where it is located. Many economic development plans emphasize growing the basic sector. This is because each new basic sector job generates some number of non-basic sector jobs. If an auto plant adds 100 new basic jobs on an assembly line it will generate many more than 100 non-basic jobs at the local bakery, supermarkets, restaurants, and institutions such as schools and hospitals that serve the additional workers. Economists have determined how many non-basic jobs different kinds of basic jobs generate on average. The number of non-basic jobs that one basic sector job of a specific type generates depends on an employment multiplier. For example, if empirical research has found that a basic job like a factory assembly worker usually generates one and one half non-basic jobs, the employment multiplier is 1.5. If research shows that the director of an insurance claim unit generates three non-basic jobs, the employment multiplier will be 3. Local economic development planners can empirically estimate how many non-basic jobs every basic job will create by using employment multipliers adjusted to local conditions. If policy makers feel that the benefit of the new jobs outweighs the cost of development for an economic activity, they are likely to proceed with the plan.

Location theory—developed by Walter Isard and other regional scientists—was introduced in Chapter 10. Location theory attempts to explain why economic activities locate where they do, and to guide planners and policy makers in where to locate future activities. City and regional planners and regional scientists draw on location theory to recommend where firms, transportation infrastructure, housing, and economic activities should optimally locate. Planners working for large private sector companies like McDonald's, Amazon.com, Starbucks, and Walmart, which have operations in thousands of locations, draw on location theory to decide where to locate stores and facilities. Planners for these companies use site selection theory—also called site suitability analysis—to decide where individual stores and facilities should be located. Bid rent curves visually show how much purchasers will pay ("bid") for land in locations at different distances from a central business district (CBD) or other area where land values are highest. Planners in the public sector draw on location theory and use bid rent curves to help decide where to locate public facilities.

Input–output analysis examines arrays of inputs to an economic activity in a business or area and outputs that result from combining them. For example, grapes, glass, cork, and paper are inputs into a wine making and bottling plant. Cases of wine—in corked and labeled glass bottles—are outputs.

Similar industries or industries that produce products used by other industries tend to cluster. Cluster analysis and other multivariate statistical analysis methods can help economic development planners understand and plan the location of industry clusters. Spatial statistics and GIS visualizations are good ways to illustrate patterns in industrial location, industry clusters, and economic development opportunity sites.

ECONOMIC DEVELOPMENT PLANNING IN THE UNITED STATES

A productive economy that produces goods and services needed for domestic consumption, and for export to provide revenue, is essential to cities and regions. Governments promote economic development both because good paying jobs are essential for their residents to support themselves and their families, and because the governments want to increase their own revenue. A strong property tax base and other revenue from local businesses will help cities and counties pay for police and fire services, education, health, welfare, parks, recreation, and other services and amenities from property tax revenue and other revenue the development generates. Sales and other local taxes may also augment local governments' own-source revenue.

Economic development planning is one of the most common specializations in U.S. city and regional planning. It is one of the largest and best-paid city and regional planning specializations.[1] Economic development planning is concerned with making plans and devising programs to improve local, regional, and national economies. Approaches include supporting existing economic activities and using bundles of carrots and sticks to attract new ones. Community economic development involves economic planning for neighborhoods or communities defined by race, ethnicity, religion, occupation, or some other group characteristic. It is intended to improve the economy of a targeted geographic area at the site, neighborhood, city, regional, or national level or of a specified group. Economic development planning often takes the form of strategic planning in which planners look beyond physical land use issues to everything that might make an economic development plan succeed or fail. Strategic planning is rooted in the academic disciplines of economics, city and regional planning, geography, business administration, and public finance.

There are no national or state licensing requirements for economic development planners. Individuals from any academic background with any level of education can call themselves economic development planners and work in economic development planning.

The International Economic Development Council (IEDC) performs a role for economic development planners similar to the role the American Planning Association and American Institute of City and Regional Planning (AICP) perform for city and regional planners described in Chapter 1. The IEDC has more than 5,000 members—mostly in the United States. If they meet IEDC work and educational requirements, individuals can become Certified Economic Developers (CEDs). This is similar to the process by which the AICP certifies Fellows of the American Institute of Certified Planners (FAICP). The end result is similar—a certification and a title that may help economic developers be better professionals, advance more rapidly, and earn higher salaries. The IECD website reports that in 2019, CEDs earned, on average, $24,000 per year more than economic development professionals without an IEDC certification.

GROWTH MACHINES AND THE CREATIVE CLASS

Civic leaders promote private economic development of their cities. Urban growth machines—pro-growth coalitions dominated by business interests—are powerful actors in most local governments in the United States. Many other interest groups support pro-growth regimes.

University of Toronto business professor Richard Florida argues that a key to economic development is for cities to attract "creative class" individuals. Florida emphasizes that artists, chefs, musicians, and actors help create a milieu that will attract inventors and entrepreneurs who can help develop the local economy. Chefs in Mountain View, California and musicians in Memphis, Tennessee help make these cities magnets for high-tech industries and knowledge workers.

INDUSTRIAL DECLINE AND PLANNED SHRINKAGE

Between 1960 and 2000 the population in many older cities in the East, Midwest, and North Central region around the Great Lakes shrank. Jobs and people moved from the core cities in these areas to suburbs, other regions, or overseas. Planners in St. Louis, Missouri; Cleveland, Ohio; Detroit, Michigan; and other distressed cities that lost jobs and population proposed "planned shrinkage" as declining "sunset" industries withered or disappeared altogether. Planned shrinkage strategies include demolishing abandoned houses and factories, turning vacant lots into community gardens, consolidating schools, repurposing old industrial sites as arts and culture venues, and downsizing local government operations. Shrinking cities also try to attract or incubate new software, pharmaceutical, and other high-tech and emerging "sunrise" industries that appear likely to grow. Box 16.1 describes how Bethlehem, Pennsylvania used these and other approaches to economic development.

Figures 16.1 and 16.2 illustrate the decline of Detroit's auto-based economy and the effort to reinvent Detroit. Figure 16.1 shows the abandoned remains of Detroit's once-thriving Packard automobile assembly plant that was closed in 1956. Figure 16.2 shows Renaissance Center—a massive redevelopment project led by Henry Ford II that provides office, hotel, retail, and residential space in a modern building complex. The Renaissance Center opened in 1997.

After about 2000, central city decline in the United States appeared to be over in most of the country. Of the fifty largest U.S. cities, only Detroit, Chicago, and Cleveland lost population between 2000 and 2010. Cities in high-tech areas like Silicon Valley in the San Francisco Bay Area, Austin, Texas, and the beltway around Boston, Massachusetts gained jobs and population.

Economic development planning is particularly important in America's rustbelt—declining industrial areas located primarily in the Northeastern and Midwestern USA. In these locations uncompetitive older factories are closing and jobs are moving elsewhere. However, virtually every local government is working to attract desirable economic activity—including growing cities and counties in the sunbelt in the American South and Southwest.

Local governments and private sector urban growth machines have tried many different ways to promote economic development. There are two broad approaches: (a) government planning and investment in low-income areas, favored by liberals who support greater government to foster social change and (b) support for private sector companies that are willing to invest in low-income zones, favored by neoliberals who favor free-market solutions to economic problems and minimal intrusion by government.

Some economic development policies are spatially targeted—planned for specific

Figure 16.1 Abandoned Packard Automobile Assembly Plant (Detroit, Michigan, 1955).

Figure 16.2 Renaissance Center (Detroit, Michigan, 2014).

neighborhoods, economic zones, cities, or regions. These geographically targeted economic development programs require government planning at the appropriate scale. Other economic development policies are aimed at different sectors of the economy. While they may have greater impacts in some geographic areas, they are not explicitly spatial policies.

DATA FOR ECONOMIC DEVELOPMENT PLANNING

Data for economic development planning comes from the U.S. Census Bureau within the U.S. Department of Commerce (DOC), state finance offices, primary data generated by local governments and academics, and other sources. The U.S. Decennial Census and American Community Survey (ACS) include data on population, income, and employment and characteristics of goods-producing and service-providing industries based on the U.S. Bureau of Labor Statistics (BLS) Standard Occupational Classification System (SOCS). The SOCS classifies all workers into 867 detailed occupations grouped into 459 broad occupation categories, 98 minor occupation groups, and 23 major occupation groups.

Economic development planning draws on location theory and regional science concepts and analytic techniques such as input–output analysis. It uses methods unique to economic development planning such as shift-share analysis that tracks how a local economy is performing over time in relation to a regional or national economy. Decisions about what kind of economy a community should have are normative—involving questions of equity and social justice, work–life balance, racial and gender relations, and other value questions as well as economic efficiency and revenue generation.

Location quotients compare the number of people in an occupation in an area—usually a U.S. Bureau of Labor Statistics-defined area—to the number in a larger region. They allow economic development planners and policy makers to compare the local employment situation and trends in an area they are planning for to the larger region and national averages. Longitudinal analysis of the changing occupational structure of the community is helpful in formulating plans and policies to retain or attract industry, define appropriate skills training to help the local labor force adapt, facilitate economic adjustment, and improve economic integration.

Box 16.1 describes how an adaptive reuse program transformed the abandoned site of what was once America's largest steel factory into an arts and culture venue, multi-use complex, open space, and a historic preservation site. The site has a hotel, restaurants, casino, and other amenities that draw people to Bethlehem, Pennsylvania.

BOX 16.1 STEELSTACKS ARTS AND CULTURAL CENTER (BETHLEHEM, PENNSYLVANIA)

The SteelStacks Arts and Cultural Center in Bethlehem, Pennsylvania, in the Lehigh Valley about 90 miles from New York City, is an economic revitalization project that illustrates four different types of adaptive reuse of an old industrial site. Most of the site was cleaned of toxic contamination and adapted as sustainable park and open space land. The remains of the steel factory became a historic site. Under the direction of the city, a nonprofit arts organization turned the core of the site where the remains of a massive steel factory still exist into a new arts and culture venue. A public–private partnership between the city and local businesses turned another part of the site into a multi-use business park.

For decades in the late 19th and early 20th century, Bethlehem was an industrial city. The Bethlehem Steel Corporation was Bethlehem's largest employer. It provided steel for many New York City skyscrapers. At one time it was the largest steel plant in the world. At its peak in 1943, the Bethlehem Steel Factory employed 31,000 people.

As the United States shifted to a post-industrial and then an informational economy, demand for steel waned. Foreign competition undercut domestic steel companies. Bethlehem Steel Corporation filed for bankruptcy in 2001 and was dissolved in 2003. The city had to confront what to do with a 1,760-acre site with many derelict buildings that were no longer contributing to the city economy. They had to address massive unemployment as a result of the plant closure. Removing the buildings would be enormously costly. No single reuse seemed economically feasible.

Before it was dissolved, the Bethlehem Steel Corporation worked with the city on a plan to redevelop the site. The original concept evolved through many changes, but eventually succeeded.

The master plan for revitalization of the 1,760-acre site—now largely realized—divided the site into two development zones: a 150-acre education and entertainment zone where the plant's most historic structures are located and a 1,610-acre parcel named the Bethlehem Commerce Center—part of which was developed as an industrial park.

One of the most common adaptive reuses for abandoned industrial buildings is to convert them into cultural and arts venues. In Bethlehem, a local nonprofit organization named ArtsQuest was created and succeeded in developing a 9.5-acre arts and cultural campus within the education and entertainment zone. The performance venue provides employment for actors and musicians; access to art, culture and educational programs; revenue for local hotels, restaurants, and other businesses; and musical, art, and cultural enrichment for people in the Bethlehem region and beyond. Figure 16.3 shows a concert at Levitt Pavilion in the SteelStacks Arts and Cultural Center.

Figure 16.3 Concert at Levitt Pavilion, SteelStacks Arts and Cultural Center (Bethlehem, Pennsylvania, 2020).

A second common revitalization strategy for old industrial sites is for a city and private sector businesses to form a public–private partnership to develop new industrial or commercial uses—often in a mixed-use area. Private capital can redevelop the area if land is prepared and government supports the infrastructure costs. The city may make a profit from a publicly owned convention center or other income-producing businesses. Local investors purchased a 126-acre district within the Bethlehem Steel site and entered into a development partnership with the Las Vegas-based Sands Corporation to form BethWorks Casino Gaming LLC and the BethWorks Retail shopping complex. The casino provides employment, entertainment, and revenue. The complex has flexible outdoor public spaces, and additional performance venues in a mix of new and historic buildings. In addition to a casino, the site includes a hotel, convention center, restaurants, bars, luxury housing, retail stores, and parking structures.

A third common use for old industrial sites is park and open space land. Bethlehem developed a program to restore and sustainably maintain open space in the site. They received support from the U.S. Environmental Protection Agency to clean up toxic waste. Three hundred seventy-five tons of soil contaminated with heavy metals and toxic compounds were excavated and transported to a landfill, then backfilled with clean fill. Bioswales were created to manage flooding and purify water in the local aquifers.

The fourth common reuse of old industrial buildings is to designate them as historic sites. The Bethlehem Steel site now houses the Smithsonian Institution's National Museum of Industrial History. An elevated pedestrian walkway and park provide close-up views of Bethlehem's historic blast furnaces and offer a cultural, historical, and industrial interpretation of the site. Five 20-story blast furnaces form part of the northern border of the district and serve as an iconic backdrop for performance venues, arts and cultural activities, and public programming.

Economists and planners sometimes distinguish what they call the new economy from the old economy. Edward Blakeley and Nancy Greene Leigh—the authors of the leading economic development planning textbook define the new economy as "a global entrepreneurial and knowledge-based economy in which the keys to success lie in the extent to which knowledge, technology, and innovation are embedded in products and services" (Leigh & Blakeley, 2016). The old economy is based largely on industrial manufacturing.

Many former and current industrial cities are intent on reindustrialization to bring back outsourced jobs. Economic development plans often take the position that it is important to retain a middle class—defined loosely as individuals who fall between the working class and the upper class—rather than to become polarized between rich and poor residents. The visions of economic development plans like this often include goals such as creating good jobs with job security and a living wage—particularly for young people and racial minorities. Sometimes economic development plans are also directed specifically to provide job opportunities for migrants, ex-convicts, and members of the working poor.[2]

Most local governments measure how successful their economic development plans have been by the number of jobs created by new businesses. In the words of public administration professor Herbert Rubin (1988), planners in depressed communities are under pressure to "shoot anything that flies, claim anything that falls" by taking credit for any new business or positive change in the economy. Blakeley and Leigh suggest that a better approach is to consider a range of indicators such as whether or not local jobs provide good salaries, benefits, job security, and the opportunity for workers to advance; are inclusive of racial, religious, and ethnic minorities, women, and people with disabilities; and provide for racial and gender equity.

Sometimes governments form explicit public–private partnerships (PPPs). Occasionally, local governments run their own profit-making municipal enterprises. The most common municipal enterprises in the United States are public utilities that provide electric power, and waste management companies that charge for their services. Municipally owned, for-profit enterprises may generate revenue to pay part or all of their costs or even a surplus for the local government. Cash grants from government to assist a private business or public–private partnership are rare. Most government support takes the form of indirect assistance that will reduce the cost of doing business, subsidize borrowing, provide infrastructure, pay for labor force development, or reduce taxes. Here are some examples:

- A state government reduces business taxes by providing a tax credit for every previously unemployed person hired or a new hire in an empowerment zone;
- A city rezones land to an industrial classification suitable for a type of business they want to attract, such as pharmaceuticals;
- A city builds a municipal parking garage next to a department store that is struggling to compete with suburban shopping centers, making it more competitive;
- A water district replaces old lead water pipes to make drinking water safer, so that it will be possible for more development to occur;
- A county establishes a one-stop center to facilitate processing of business permits quickly at little cost to applicants;
- A city locates a new police station near a business and increases police protection, reducing their risk of crime and saving the business the cost of private security;
- A county changes its subdivision ordinance to make it easier to get approvals to develop new manufacturing plants on raw land;
- A city creates a small business incubator offering free or subsidized office space and supporting services to startup companies;
- A city reduces environmental standards so a business can avoid costly environmental reviews and mitigation measures.

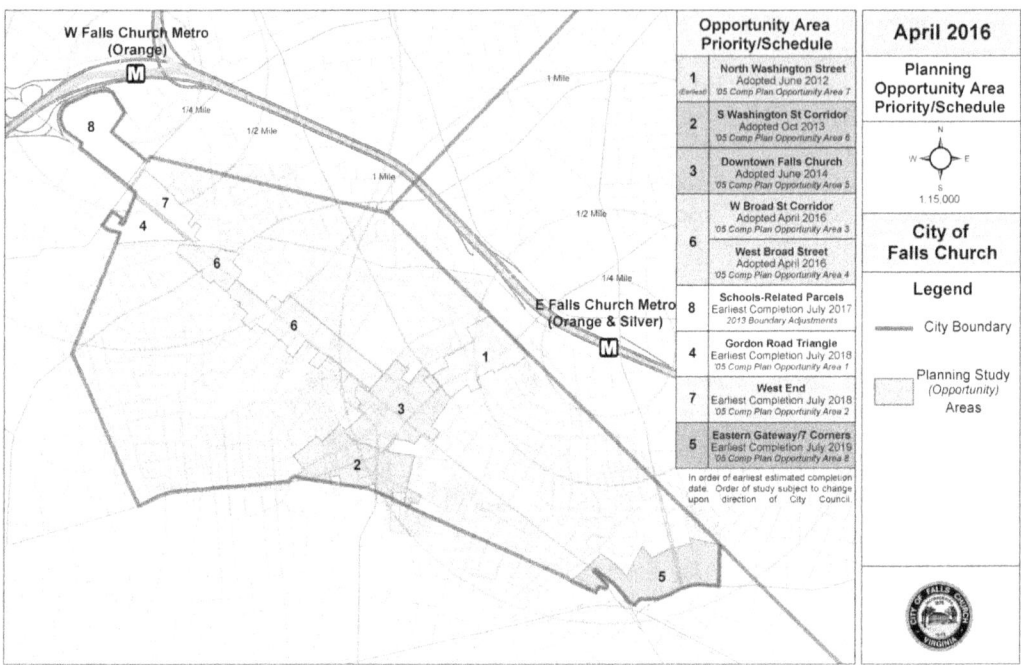

Figure 16.4 Falls Creek, Virginia Comprehensive Planning Opportunity Area Priority Schedule (2021).

Some cities systematically look for sites that present revitalization opportunities. The site may be vacant or underutilized. Some may have particular locational advantage such as being adjacent to a university or in an industrial park. Lists and maps of "opportunity sites" may appear in general plans or they may be free-standing documents. Figure 16.4—the Falls Creek, Virginia Comprehensive Planning Opportunity Area Priority Schedule—illustrates this approach.

The American Planning Association (APA) has an economic development division. The division supports the APA's stated mission to "advance the practice and state of the art of economic development".[3]

Most states have a state development office and some type of state development plan. States offer a variety of policies to aid economic development, including statewide tax incentive plans, targeted incentives for specific industries, information dissemination through electronic bulletin boards, and providing information on sites that are available for economic development.[4] Many state offices of economic development are engaged in public relations to market the state to potential investors.

The University Economic Development Association (UEDA) is a national association of universities that have economic development programs. UEDA members assist local governments and nonprofit organizations to plan and implement local and regional economic development strategies and projects. The U.S. Economic Development Administration and the UEDA have over 60 long-term partnerships with universities located in regions of chronic and acute economic distress. UEDA maintains a website where more than 160 colleges and universities, private industries, local governments, economic development organizations, federal agencies, manufacturing partnerships, workforce development organizations, and financial institutions share information.

Five Historically Black Colleges and Universities (HBCUs) provide economic development support services to their communities. These include economic research, workforce development, and business counseling services. HBCUs help local organizations with feasibility studies, analyze data, and convene seminars and workshops on topics such as regional strategic planning and capital budgeting.

There is no cabinet-level equivalent for economic development to the U.S. Department of Housing and Urban Development. The closest is the U.S. Department of Commerce (DOC). The DOC defines its mission as promoting job creation and economic growth by ensuring fair and reciprocal trade, providing data necessary to support commerce, setting standards, and doing research. The federal government agency most directly focused exclusively on economic development is the U.S. Economic Development Administration (EDA) within the DOC. The EDA defines its mission as "to lead the federal economic development agenda by promoting innovation and competitiveness and preparing American regions for growth and success in the worldwide economy". The EDA has five stated priorities:

1) recovery and resilience;
2) critical infrastructure;
3) workforce development and manufacturing;
4) exports; and
5) foreign direct investment (FDI) and opportunity zones.

The EDA serves as a clearinghouse for other federal government economic development programs. It is sometimes able to provide significant funding to assist businesses and individuals recover from hurricanes, tornadoes, floods, and other natural disasters. The EDA has a variety of grant programs for state and local organizations.

COMMUNITY ECONOMIC DEVELOPMENT

Community economic development is directed specifically at communities rather than economic sectors, entire cities, or regions. Its focus is specifically on economic development rather than physical or social development of the communities. Community economic development projects are usually located in lower-income, working-class neighborhoods. They have a narrower focus than programs funded by the federal community development (CDBG) program, which may include projects to improve housing, infrastructure, health, education, and other physical and social aspects of a community as well as economic development.

Communities may be defined geographically, such as a neighborhood, or based on race, ethnicity, religion or some other group characteristic. Nonprofit community development corporations (CDCs) are the main organizations that undertake community economic development. Nonprofit organizations—including CDCs—cannot legally make a profit. However, they may legally earn enough money to cover their costs—including employee salaries. Nonprofit organizations may have profit-making subsidiaries. The Jewish kosher and Islamic halal food industries and the Christian Broadcasting Network are examples.

The term community development is generally used to describe programs that focus on physical and social development as well as, or rather than, just the economic development of communities. It is intended to make physical improvements, improve health, education, and other social services, and build local social capital, civil society institutions, and political capacity at the neighborhood level.[5]

Sociologists, geographers, and planners have developed a variety of ways to define a community. Depending on the context, a community may be based on geography, such as New York City's Greenwich Village neighborhood; race, such as Falcon, Mississippi—which is 98% Black; ethnicity like Little Italy in San Diego, California which once had 6,000 Italian Americans; religion such as the Hasidic Jewish neighborhood in New York City's Williamsburg neighborhood; sexual orientation, like San Francisco's Castro District with a substantial gay population; or economic characteristics such as Hershey, Pennsylvania, a factory town where many employees work at a large chocolate manufacturing plant.

REVITALIZATION PLANNING

The term revitalization comes from the Latin prefix *re*-"again" combined with the Latin noun *vitalitas*—literally "creating the capacity to live, grow, or develop again". Revitalization refers to any program to upgrade the infrastructure, economy, housing, and/or quality of life in older neighborhoods. Revitalization programs often include programs to improve health, education, and employment and to combat illegal drugs and crime as well as to provide physical improvements.

Revitalization is a preferred term for any program to renew older buildings or neighborhoods. It is very different from urban renewal—described in chapter 12—which refers to the discredited federal urban renewal program that existed from 1949 to 1973. The federal urban renewal program was a heavy-handed top-down federal program that lost the support of both progressives and neoliberals because of its inability to accomplish program goals, enormous cost, and the damage it did to neighborhoods and communities of color. Planners are careful to distance themselves from the term "urban renewal" and not to repeat the program's approach.

THE COMMUNITY DEVELOPMENT BLOCK GRANT PROGRAM

In the United States community development usually refers to programs funded by the federal Community Development Block Grant (CDBG) program. In 1974 the CDBG program became the principal successor to the federal urban renewal program that existed between 1949 and 1973. Urban renewal projects that were in the pipeline in 1973 were eventually either completed—sometimes with CDBG funding—abandoned, became state-supported, or morphed into other forms.

The CDBG program was President Richard Nixon's major "New Federalism" program. It consolidated funding that had previously gone to categorical urban programs for narrowly defined activities such as improving old sewers or funding senior centers into a single block grant that could be used for a variety of locally-selected community development activities. This approach is different from the categorical urban programs, which each required a separate application. CDBG grants could fund existing urban renewal projects and new community development activities. The block grant gave local governments much more discretion about what community development activities to undertake.

CDBG decentralized control over the program from the federal government to local governments. The CDBG program distributes an annual amount of federal funding based on dual allocation formulas, rather than requiring a detailed application and compliance with voluminous federal requirements. CDBG funds in cities are controlled by the mayor.

CDBG funds are supposed to principally benefit low- and moderate-income people. However, the funds do not have to be spent within low-income areas.

Communities have great discretion in the kind of community development projects to fund. Conservative suburbs often spend their CDBG grant money on uncontroversial public works projects, such as maintenance and improvement of curbs, gutters, and sewers that would otherwise have to be paid for from their own-source revenue. Liberal core cities often choose to spend their CDBG funds on projects that directly benefit low-income people, such as improving homeless shelters or supporting transitional housing.

Congress appropriates CDBG funding each year. The appropriated funds are distributed by the U.S. Department of Housing and Urban Development by formula. Seventy percent of the funding goes to principal cities of metropolitan statistical areas (MSAs), other metropolitan cities with populations of at least 50,000, and qualified urban counties with populations of at least 200,000 (excluding the population of entitled cities). A small amount of CDBG funding is set aside for Indian tribes. HUD distributes the other 30% of CDBG funds that are available in a given year to states, which in turn distribute the CDBG funds to smaller cities and other recipients. The funding each community receives each year is based on the total amount of CDBG funding Congress has authorized, how much Congress appropriates in a given year, and the jurisdiction's share, based on dual allocation formulas that consider population, poverty, housing built before 1950, and the extent to which growth in the community lags the national average.[6] This is different from urban renewal grants, where, while the program existed, politically adept cities that aggressively pursued urban renewal funds got large amounts of urban renewal funding and less nimble or less politically connected cities got little or no urban renewal funding. One-third of all urban renewal funding went to New York City.

There is a requirement that HUD monitor CDBG expenditures. However, funding is nearly automatic. CDBG provides a steady stream of quite flexible funding that local governments welcome.

In years when the U.S. economy is prospering and when Democrats control Congress, the total amount of CDBG funding that Congress authorizes is higher than during periods when Republicans control Congress and/or the national economy is weak. Conservative presidents Ronald Reagan and Donald Trump proposed zero funding for CDBG in budgets they sent to Congress. However, the CDBG program proved popular enough with both political parties that Congress restored substantial CDBG funding each year.

CDBG funds go to the mayor's office—not to a city authority like a redevelopment agency or public housing authority or directly to a CDC or other nonprofit corporation that implements CDBG programs. Each jurisdiction establishes a process for allocating CDBG funds to government agencies or nonprofits that carry out the CDBG program.

CDBG primarily funds brick-and-mortar activities. Eligible CDBG activities include acquisition of real property; relocation of households and businesses; demolition of buildings and other structures; rehabilitation of residential and non-residential structures; construction of water and sewer facilities; streets; and neighborhood centers. CDBG funds can also be used for the conversion of school buildings; activities relating to energy conservation and renewable energy resources; and to assist profit-motivated businesses to carry out economic development and job creation/retention activities. Some CDBG funds can be spent on social services related to CDBG projects. About one-third of CDBG funding in recent years has gone towards housing.

CDBG recipients are required to prepare a five-year consolidated plan (con plan) specifying their community development needs, a five-year CDBG strategy, and an annually updated one-year CDBG plan. City and regional planners play an important role in preparing these plans.

CDBG has proven a popular program. As of 2022, It has survived for 48 years. Local elected officials like it because it provides flexible funds. Neighborhood residents and activists like it because it provides funding for projects that benefit low-income communities.

REDEVELOPMENT AND TAX INCREMENT FINANCING

Some cities and counties still have redevelopment agencies despite the fact that the federal urban renewal program ended in 1973. The agencies that carry out redevelopment may have been renamed or combined with other local agencies or departments. Remaining redevelopment agencies carry out state redevelopment programs similar to the discontinued federal urban renewal program, but generally smaller, involving less residential displacement, and more sensitive to low-income neighborhoods and communities of color.

An important vehicle for funding state redevelopment projects is tax increment financing (TIF). TIF pays the public share of redevelopment through bonds secured by the increment (additional funds) an area will eventually generate from increased property taxes (and in some states sales taxes) after it is redeveloped. Banks and other investors with deep pockets, who are able to take a long view, purchase municipal bonds backed by the anticipated new revenue, calculating that the bonds will eventually yield a return that justifies the risk.

Imagine a blighted neighborhood in San Jose, California with a mix of vacant lots, empty commercial buildings, old housing, and small businesses that generate little property tax. The area drains more in police, fire, and public school funding from the city and county than it contributes in property and other taxes. The neighborhood is prime real estate in booming high-tech Silicon Valley, where San Jose is located. If the land can be assembled, cleared, and prepared, high-tech industries like Google, Hewlett-Packard, Facebook, Adobe, Twitter, and hundreds of other high-tech companies in Silicon Valley might purchase the land and build large new buildings that will generate an enormous increase in property tax and perhaps other municipal revenue. Some well-paid employees of the new companies will settle in San Jose, increasing residential property values and residential property tax revenue. Affluent new residents will spend money locally, which will benefit local businesses. Since there will be little or no residential development, the redeveloped area will not cost the San Jose municipal government much for education, public health, or other social services. The buildings will meet modern fire codes, so that the city will not need to spend much for fire protection for the redeveloped area. Big corporations will provide most of their own security, so municipal police costs will be low. After a period when the project will generate even less revenue as land is cleared and prepared, the area will start to provide more revenue than it did before the project began—a "tax increment". For a specified time—generally 20 or 30 years. Property tax revenue up to the amount that existed before redevelopment began will be distributed in the same way it was distributed before the project began. The new money—the increment—will be used to pay off the development costs that were incurred early on, funded by the bonds. After the bonds are paid off, the money generated by the tax increment will become a major new source of local revenue. From a city's perspective, tax increment financing often appears to be a good way to renew themselves and generate revenue at no cost to the city. Critics argue that TIFs may rob other neighborhoods of potential development and displace residents who do not want to move. Some empirical studies have found that there was little or no net gain from tax increment financing. California abolished a very large statewide tax increment program in 2011, even though a portion of the revenue from the tax increment was allocated to affordable housing and the TIF program had support from both urban growth machines and housing advocates. Local officials, big banks, and community activists formed an unusual coalition to save TIF in California, but were unsuccessful.

ENTERPRISE ZONES, EMPOWERMENT ZONES, ENTERPRISE COMMUNITIES, AND THE RENEWAL CITY (RC) PROGRAM

An alternative approach to revitalization and development is to incentivize private companies to invest in special zones in economically depressed neighborhoods that have high poverty and unemployment rates. Governments try to provide sufficient tax breaks, regulatory relief, concentrated support redirected from existing urban programs, and other incentives to the zones to induce private companies to locate new activities and increase employment in the zones. This approach assumes that creating new jobs will ameliorate social ills and reduce crime as residents of the assisted zones are able to find work and support themselves legally.

The idea of creating special economic development zones called enterprise zones in low-income areas in the developed world was originally proposed by Anglo-American geographer/planning professor Peter Hall (Box 16.2). Hall got the idea from the experience of export processing zones in Asia that governments in Singapore, Korea, Taiwan, and Hong Kong had created. The Asian export processing zones were free of the regulations that applied elsewhere in

BOX 16.2 PETER HALL

Sir Peter Geoffrey Hall (1932–2014) was an eminent city and regional planning academic and practitioner and a public intellectual whose scholarship and professional service have had an enormous impact worldwide. Hall was educated as a geographer. He taught both geography and city and regional planning in England and America. His ideas catalyzed urban policy and shaped important planning decisions—particularly in England. Hall's books and articles synthesized and advanced the art and science of city and regional planning worldwide. Hall was a polymath with an extraordinary command of the social and policy science literature on cities, city planning, and geography.

Hall received a doctorate in geography from Cambridge University in 1957. He held multiple, often overlapping positions as a professor of both city and regional planning and geography in England and the United States while regularly advising governments at the highest levels. Hall's main teaching positions were at the University of London (1957–1967) and the University of Reading (1968–1989) where he taught and chaired both the geography and planning departments, overlapping with teaching and research appointments at the University of California, Berkeley (1980–1992). He returned to England as a professor of planning and regeneration at University College London from 1992 to 2014.

Hall authored or co-authored fifty books and more than 2,000 articles and shorter pieces. His books are lively and highly readable as well as written clearly and with meticulous documentation. Hall's first book—*London 2000* (1963)—imagined a rebuilt London at the turn of the millennium, then 37 years in the future. *The World Cities* (1966) launched modern world city network research. *Cities of Tomorrow* (1988) is the definitive intellectual history of Anglo-American city and regional planning in the late 19th and 20th centuries. *Sociable Cities* (1998) (co-authored with Colin Ward) is an exhaustive account of Ebenezer Howard and the garden cities movement. *Cities in Civilization* (1998) is a wide-ranging study of the creative role of cities in the production of culture and scientific discovery. Hall's final book, *Good Cities, Better Lives* (2014) urges a wide audience to embrace the humanistic principles he had always loved. Other of Hall's books and articles examine high-speed rail; regeneration; planning disasters; motorways; airports; the future of capital cities; information technology and technopoles (science cities); polycentric European city-regions; and many other topics.

Ideologically, Hall is difficult to classify. Throughout his life he argued for centrally coordinated planning, garden cities along the lines Ebenezer Howard proposed, new towns, and high-speed rail systems. As a young man he was an active Fabian socialist—a moderate form of socialism that rejected violence—and a founding member of Britain's Social Democratic Party. He served as an adviser to the Labour prime minister, Harold Wilson, in 1966, working on new towns policy. He worked on urban regeneration with Michael Heseltine, Britain's conservative secretary of the environment under Margaret Thatcher and with Andrew Adonis, the secretary of state for transport during the Labour government of Gordon Brown.

Hall is credited with inventing the enterprise zone concept which was embraced (and distorted) by the Conservative Thatcher government (1979–1990) and conservative U.S. presidents Ronald Reagan (1981–1989) and George Herbert Walker Bush (1989–1993). Hall championed centralized planning, but also cautioned about the disasters that overly ambitious planning could cause. He played a major role in Britain's new town, airport, and motorway planning; London docklands redevelopment; the Chunnel under the English Channel connecting England to the Continent; and high-speed rail programs in England and other countries.

Hall received top awards from the Royal Town Planning Institute and the British Royal Geographic Society and the prestigious Baltzan Prize for *Cities in Civilization*. He was knighted in 1998—joining only Ebenezer Howard and Patrick Abercrombie as British urban planners to receive that honor. Transport of London—London's transportation agency—has dedicated a train named for him in recognition of his contribution to London's transport infrastructure.

Hall never lost touch with the role cities played in the lives of ordinary people. He grew up in a family of modest means in the seaside resort town of Blackpool, England. At age 72—the most celebrated urban planner of his generation—Hall accepted a position to chair Blackpool's Regeneration Agency (2004–2008). In 2007, at age 75, he wrote *London Voices, London Lives* (2007) based on interviews with residents of the city he loved and had re-envisaged in his first book.

Hall died in 2014 at the age of 82. His books in many languages continue to shape urban planning education and policy, and his students and research colleagues continue his legacy.

---

the country that created them, and received preferential tax treatment, infrastructure investment, and other kinds of support. They generated revenue for private sector investors and the national governments of the countries that created them.

The British government created an enterprise zone to redevelop London's derelict docklands along the Thames River in 1981. Conservative prime minister Margaret Thatcher, who served as prime minister between 1979 and 1990, made the enterprise zone concept a centerpiece of her revitalization strategy for the UK. Thatcher succeeded in creating an enterprise zone program for the UK that provided tax breaks for large corporate developers and reduced environmental, occupational health and safety, and other regulations. By the mid-1980s more than two dozen enterprise zones had been established in the UK. There was massive clearance and new building in the flagship Docklands enterprise zone. The developer—Canadian development corporation Olympia and York—went bankrupt. However, eventually the portion of the zone called Canary Wharf was redeveloped into London's major financial center. Figure 16.5 shows Canary Wharf.

Overall, the UK enterprise zone program had mixed results. Most scholars now consider the first-generation UK enterprise zones a failure. Without large capital expenditures on infrastructure, the regulatory relief and tax incentives that they offered usually proved insufficient.

Since 2012, the UK government has announced plans to extend some existing enterprise zones and build new ones, but changes in the government, Brexit (the UK's withdrawal from the European Union), and the COVID-19 pandemic have prevented the proposed new enterprise zones from being funded as planned. Their future is unclear.

President Reagan admired Margaret Thatcher and embraced the enterprise zone concept. A Republican-controlled Congress passed enterprise zone legislation in 1987, but never appropriated funding for enterprise zones, so no federal enterprise zones were ever created in the United States.[7]

Many states passed state-level enterprise zone legislation in the 1980s and 1990s. Thirty-seven states currently have some type of state enterprise zones. Most have had little impact for five reasons:

1) states generally provided no outright grant funding;
2) tax incentives and regulatory relief were too little to entice companies to create jobs in the zones;
3) states did not fund necessary infrastructure for the zones;
4) the state governments were not able to

Figure 16.5 Canary Wharf (London, England).

redirect enough aid from other federal and state programs to the zones to make them work as intended; and

5) many of the zones were so large that any advantages were too diluted to attract businesses.

National legislation to create empowerment zones and enterprise communities in the United States (the EZ/EC program) was passed and funded in 1993 during the Clinton administration. The EZ/EC concept is similar to the enterprise zone concept, but promotes bottom-up development by small businesses rather than top-down development by large corporations. There have been three rounds of EZ/EC funding. A first round of 9 empowerment zones and 95 enterprise communities (65 urban and 30 rural) began in 1993. Two subsequent rounds of funding were authorized in 1987 and 2001.[8] The Renewal Community (RC) program was started in 2000. Like the EZ/EC program it provides tax incentives for businesses to locate and hire residents in specified urban and rural areas. The program includes areas that have not experienced recent economic expansion, rather than only areas that have declined economically.[9]

EZs and ECs had to meet specified criteria to establish their need, based on poverty, unemployment, and economic distress. Applicants submitted bottom-up strategic plans with:

1) a vision for change that identified what the community would be like in the future and how it would achieve its goals;
2) a description of community-based partnerships that would encourage all stakeholders to participate in achieving economic revitalization;
3) expanded economic opportunity through increased capital and credit for businesses and assistance with job training and placement for residents; and
4) sustainable community development, so that economic, physical, and environmental factors are aligned as the community is revitalized.

Currently U.S. empowerment zones and enterprise communities funded during the three rounds of funding, and renewal communities (RCs), continue to receive support. Their future is uncertain.

INTERNATIONAL DEVELOPMENT PLANNING

Two Nobel prize-winning neoliberal economists developed theory justifying capitalist development of developing countries—Arthur O. Lewis and Walt Whitman Rostow. Lewis developed a "dual development" model of development with unlimited supplies of labor and absorption of the surplus agricultural labor force into the capitalist economy. Rostow developed a "stages of growth" model of economic development describing how countries could proceed from a traditional society to a high mass consumption society. Chapter 11 described critiques of the neoliberal development paradigm by Marxists, neo-Marxists, and academics who developed dual development theory. Some socialist countries and developmental states do not accept the neoliberal paradigm. However, since the "Washington consensus" of the 1980s, most countries and most international development planners subscribe to development theory developed by Arthur O. Lewis and Walt Whitman Rostow.

Arthur O. Lewis (1915–1991) taught at the University of Manchester, England and Princeton University. He advanced his dual development model of development in 1954. Lewis was Black and grew up in the British Commonwealth island of Santa Lucia. At the time Lewis was growing up, Santa Lucia's economy was largely based on producing sugar cane and bananas for export. Drawing on his own life experience, Lewis described within-country income and productivity gaps between what he termed the subsistence and capitalist sectors of the economy. Lewis concluded that the large surplus agricultural labor force in developing countries—able-bodied people in rural areas whose labor is not needed in the economy—have a negligible, zero, or even negative marginal productivity, and that without capital accumulation, rural areas cannot develop. In contrast, he argued that the small capitalist sector generates wealth and makes development possible. Accordingly, Lewis believed that modernization of developing countries depended on a shift of surplus rural labor to the modern (largely urban) sector. Since foreign capital helps grow the capitalist sector, Lewis believed capitalism would help developing countries. While he believed that market forces would promote development, Lewis was sympathetic to government programs that bolster naturally occurring private market development. Lewis's most important policy prescription was for government to adopt policies to speed up absorption of surplus rural labor into the capitalist sector to help traditional societies develop. City and regional planners in China, India, Indonesia, and other developing countries experiencing massive rural–urban migration today draw heavily on Lewis's dual economy theory.

Harvard professor Walt Whitman Rostow (1916–2003) developed a "stages of growth" model of urban development in 1960. Rostow argued that countries pass through five stages of economic development—traditional society, pre-conditions for takeoff, takeoff, drive to maturity, and the age of high mass consumption. Rostow's model views development as a process that produces a continuum of different economic, spatial, and social relations as the economy develops and the proportion of the population living in urban areas increases. Accordingly, Rostow argued that developing countries should develop the infrastructure to exploit natural resources, export the resources to accumulate capital, and then initially invest some of the social surplus strategically in relatively simple export-oriented industries like textiles or shoe manufacturing. As these industries generated wealth, Rostow argued that the industries could and should reinvest, expand, and diversify into more complex (and lucrative) enterprises. He believed that development would snowball, leading to modernization. Rostow's theory assumes development is linear, and that all countries progress through stages similar to developed Western European and North American countries. Rostow was a neoliberal. He favored market solutions and fundamentally disagreed with Marxist, neo-Marxist, dependency, and NIDL theorists. He opposed the economic development policies of developmental states like Singapore where the central government steers the private sector. He subtitled his book "a non-communist manifesto". In the 62 years since Rostow's classic statement, many countries have followed his prescriptions. Not all countries have experienced the uniform linear progression Rostow envisioned. Rostow's model does not consider post-industrial and informational activities that were just emerging or did not exist in 1960; how globalization has fundamentally changed world spatial patterns; the impact of digital technologies; or how non-Western social structures produce quite different development patterns.

In the last 30 years, China has experienced the most rapid and massive migration of rural labor to urban areas in human history. Employers in the capitalist sector in China often pay more than a modest premium for workers at every skill level—including unskilled workers—compared to what they can earn in rural areas. Rural–urban migration of what Lewis termed surplus rural labor has occurred, but Chinese urbanization has not followed Rostow's model in other ways.[10]

Beginning in the late 1980s, the "Washington Consensus" that globalization should be encouraged dominated thinking. President Bill Clinton (1993–2001) and most international organizations and other countries adopted this policy beginning in the 1990s. The United States government, International Monetary Fund (IMF), World Bank, and countries with neoliberal governments agreed with the Washington consensus and practiced neoliberal economic policies.

Agropolitan development offers a different model of regional and national development. Proponents of agropolitan development argue that countries should invest directly in agricultural modernization first. As the agricultural sector becomes more efficient, they argue that it will generate capital that can be re-invested either in further agropolitan development or in industrial development. Fewer people will be needed to produce food for the entire population—freeing up people to join the industrial labor force and later the post-industrial and informational labor force.

An important question in international development planning is the relationship between urbanization and a country's level of development. In 1977 economists Hollis Chenery and Moise Syrqin analyzed world patterns of development and concluded that there was a strong correlation between a country's urbanization level—the ratio of the urban population to the total population—and a country's gross domestic product (GDP) and other indicators of its development level. The higher the urbanization rate, the higher the country's GDP. Based on Chenery and Syrqin's findings, some scholars and policy makers concluded that countries should try to urbanize as quickly as possible. However, there is evidence that if countries urbanize too fast, cities cannot absorb the rural migrants into their urban economies. Many scholars believe that Latin America countries tend to be "over-urbanized". The percentage of their population living in urban areas is above the regression line that Chenery and Syrqin created predicting how high it should be based on the country's GDP, and updates and variations of it. Many Latin American cities have high unemployment and underemployment in low-wage jobs that contribute little to the economy. What was previously the country's surplus rural labor force has become a surplus urban labor force. Given these findings, some scholars and policy makers aim to help cities to develop the capacity to absorb surplus rural labor rather than making urbanization itself their primary goal.

SAN ANTONIO TEXAS'S RIVERWALK REVITALIZATION PROJECT

Planning, maintaining, and adapting infrastructure are critical for economic development and revitalization. Infrastructure planning is a Planning Accreditation Board specialty in graduate city and regional planning programs in the United States (and one program in Canada at the University of British Columbia).

Infrastructure is often thought of as roads and bridges, but there are many additional different types of infrastructure. Public infrastructure can be conceived of as a public good—collectively provided because it cannot be privately purchased by individuals in a market economy.

A revitalization project in San Antonio, Texas illustrates how re-imagining infrastructure can revitalize an area. In the 1920s a bend in the San Antonio River in the downtown of San Antonio, Texas known as the Great Bend was a dirty and unused channel. Open storm drains poured storm water and sewage into the river. The river banks were lined with derelict buildings. The entire area was an unattractive and little-used part of the city. In 1921 water from a category one hurricane flooded the area. There were plans to cut off the Great Bend and pave over the storm drains.

A young architect named Robert Hugman, inspired by New Orleans' preservation of the French quarter and his studies of Spanish architecture, imagined revitalization of the area as a Spanish-themed riverfront park and tourist venue with a river-level walk, shops, cafes, and apartments. Hugman designed attractive cobbled streets, landscaping, and bridges to provide an interesting experience for pedestrians and take advantage of curves in the river to provide vistas and views. He proposed shops, cafes, and parks at river level. The Hugman plan highlighted the areas heritage. The urban design enhanced view corridors and vistas.

Hugman's brilliant designs inspired some San Antonio residents and helped prevent paving over the storm drains. However, Hugman and his supporters were not able to get the political support or raise enough money for the project. Finally, in 1936 the New Deal Works Progress Administration agreed to provide $380,000 for most of the project if the city would provide a $75,000 match. Jack White, the owner of the largest hotel in the area—the Plaza Hotel—helped convince the city to "clean up that dirty little river" next to his hotel, voters approved a $75,000 bond, and construction of the River Walk began.

The essential elements of Hugman's design were completed in 1940—just before the outbreak of World War II put a halt to private development and tourism. After the war some restaurants, cafes, stores, and apartments were built, and modest numbers of local residents began to use and enjoy the River Walk. However, it was not until 1968—when San Antonio hosted a World's Fair—that the River Walk really took off. Hugman lived until 1980 and saw his vision realized. By 2014 the River Walk was drawing over 9 million non-resident visitors a year and generating over $2 billion in revenue. Figure 16.6 shows the River Walk.

There is currently a national political debate in the United States about what the category called infrastructure should include.[11] Six main types of public infrastructure are:

1) transportation systems such as highways, streets, roads, subways, and heavy and light rail systems;
2) bridges;
3) ancillary transportation infrastructure such as sidewalks, curbs, gutters, and street lighting;
4) environmental systems such as reservoirs, water supply systems, sewage treatment plants, landfills (dumps), and sewers;
5) energy and telecommunications infrastructure such as telecommunications towers and electrical power transmission lines; and
6) community facilities such as police and fire stations, public schools, and libraries.

As this book went to press in May 2022 Democrats and Republicans were debating a massive "Build Back Better" infrastructure investment plan proposed by President Biden. The debate illustrates a division between Democrats who propose much more spending on an expansive range of infrastructure, climate change, and social programs and Republicans who want to spend much less and limit spending to conventional infrastructure projects such as roads, bridges, rail, transit, ports, and

Figure 16.6 River Walk (San Antonio, Texas).

airports. Both political parties favor some funding to improve internet bandwidth and the U.S. information infrastructure. The debate also illustrates the ideological division between the progressive wing of the Democratic Party who are seeking to tie infrastructure legislation to broader legislation that would provide funding to address climate change, provide for daycare and early childhood education, support low income households, and fund "social safety net" programs. Exactly what the legislation will cover and how much money will be authorized and appropriated for its components will depend on the balance of power between the political parties in upcoming congressional and presidential elections. Whatever the outcome of the current debate, these ideological divisions will shape infrastructure planning and programs in the future.

In addition to offsite public infrastructure, local governments require individual homeowners to provide onsite infrastructure such as driveways; sewer and storm-drain laterals; and water and gas lines at the owners' expense. Property owners also pay for cable television and internet connectivity if they choose to have them.

Some public infrastructure is built and maintained by public–private partnerships (PPPs). Some transportation infrastructure such as highways, airports, railroads, bridges, and tunnels, and some environmental infrastructure such as water and wastewater facilities are financed in this way. "Design–Build–Finance–Operate–Maintain" (DBFOM) toll concessions provide PPP funding for some highways. For example, a $1 billion-plus Texas state highway DBFOM project for Texas State Highway 288 between Houston and the Gulf of Mexico will provide four new toll lanes plus maintenance and reconstruction of existing highway lanes and interchanges. About two-thirds of the project is being funded by private activity bonds, a loan, and other funds. The other third is being financed by private equity. PPPs have also been used to finance and build school buildings, prisons, student dormitories, and entertainment and sports facilities.

Government organization and funding are often inadequate to meet infrastructure needs. This is partly the result of the Balkanized U.S. local government structure and patchwork system of local public finance described in Chapter 4. It reflects the U.S. neoliberal emphasis on relying on the private market.

At the regional and higher levels, infrastructure planning involves airports, power plants, the electrical grid, water distribution systems, ports, and conventional and high-speed transportation systems. In developing countries infrastructure planning is a critical aspect of national development planning.

CAPITAL IMPROVEMENTS PROGRAMS

At the city scale, most public infrastructure is part of local capital improvements programs (CIPs). Projects to build or maintain public infrastructure are called public works projects. CIPs typically present a 20-year strategy for infrastructure construction and maintenance, with five-year action plans and annual budgets. They address and prioritize needs for investment in streets, sidewalks, curbs, gutters, sewers, storm drainage systems, and other types of local public infrastructure. Because infrastructure has a spatial dimension, CIPs often present spatial aspects of their strategy in map form. CIPs are usually backed up by engineering studies.

Infrastructure is capital intensive. Costs are "lumpy"—most fall in a short time period while the infrastructure is being built. Costs are generally amortized (paid back) over a long period of time. New capital projects are costly. It may be difficult to pay for them from annual local general revenue. As a result, capital improvements are often funded by bonds that are paid back (with interest) over 20, 30, or more years.

Capital improvements must be planned. Ongoing planning is necessary to maintain and adapt existing infrastructure Some cities have defined standards for maintaining, augmenting, and replacing capital improvements in "adequate public facilities" ordinances.

At the local level in the United States, most capital improvement construction and maintenance is performed by municipal public works departments. However, capital improvement planning may be done by the city or county planning department or jointly by the planning department and the public works department. Sometimes, other government entities such as parks and recreation departments, transit agencies, or private entities such as private power or telecommunications companies are involved directly or indirectly in infrastructure planning. Sometimes cities or counties contract with neighboring jurisdictions to supply water, electricity, sewer, or other services rather than build the necessary infrastructure themselves. Even though onsite infrastructure on private property is privately built and owned, it requires government planning and regulation.

There is a large difference in the size, funding, staffing, and culture of local public works departments, compared to city planning departments. Many of the professional staff of public works departments are civil engineers. They may have technical skills that most city and regional planners lack, that equip them to solve engineering problems. However, their education as engineers may not give them an adequate planning or policy background. Public works departments have substantial budgets and many employees to build and maintain infrastructure. This contrasts with planning departments which typically have few or no engineers, smaller budgets, much smaller staffs, and are not involved in constructing or operating infrastructure.

City and regional infrastructure planning is a special niche of particular interest to three kinds of planners—planners with civil engineering backgrounds, planners with a passion for a specific type of infrastructure such as recycling centers or solar power plants, and planners working in regional or higher-level planning in developing countries.

SUMMARY

Every country seeks to have economically healthy cities and regions that can produce goods and services the society needs, employ their residents, and generate revenue for public purposes. Development and revitalization planning are critical to accomplish these goals. The blurred professional activities of economic development, urban economic development, urban revitalization, community development, and capital improvement planning can all help both declining cities and regions and thriving cities and regions whose economies are growing.

Approaches to urban development and revitalization reflect ideology. Liberals favor a larger role for the state in planning and steering the economy of cities and regions. Liberals support higher levels of taxation and more government funding and regulation than neoliberals. They generally favor increasing investment in conventional public infrastructure like roads and bridges, but also infrastructure that would address climate change, daycare and early childhood education, and social safety net programs.

In the United States the former urban renewal program and the current Community Development Block Grant program exemplify the liberal approach to economic development and revitalization. In contrast, neoliberals believe that, for the most part, the free hand of the market will produce the best economic and social outcomes. With limited exceptions for market failure, neoliberals would leave provision of goods and services to the private sector. Their vehicles of choice for economic development and revitalization are programs that augment the private sector such as enterprise zones.

CONCEPTS

Basic Sector
Bid Rent Curve
Capital Improvement Program (CIP)
Certified Economic Developer
Community Development Block Grant (CDBG)
Community Economic Development
Congestion Pricing
Consolidated Plan (Con Plan)
Creative Class
Developmental State
Economic Development Administration (EDA)
Employment Multiplier
Empowerment Zone
Enterprise Community
Enterprise Zone
Foreign Direct Investment (FDI)
Industry Cluster
Non-Basic Sector
Planned Shrinkage
Primary Sector
Property Tax
Public Works Department
Renewal Community (RC) Program
Secondary Sector
Standard Occupational Classification System (SOCS)
Tax Increment Financing (TIF)
Tertiary Sector
University Economic Development Association (UEDA)
Urban Regeneration
Urban Revitalization

PEOPLE

Arthur O'Sullivan
Peter Hall
Arthur O. Lewis
Walt Whitman Rostow

NOTES

1. Economic development is the fifth most frequent specialization that planners mentioned in the American Planning Association's 2018 salary survey (APA, 2018). The APA found that the average salary for planners working in public economic development agencies in 2018 was $85,000 a year. It was $95,000 in private economic development firms (ibid).

2. In 2018 the U.S. Department of Labor's Bureau of Labor Statistics identified 7.6 million individuals among the working poor—persons who spent at least 27 weeks in the previous year in the labor force either working or looking for work, but whose incomes still fell below the federal poverty level (FPL) (BLS, 2018). The 2018 FPL was $12,140 for a single individual, $14,460 for a two-person household, and $20,780 for a three-person household.

3. The APA's Economic Development Division proposes to advance economic development practice in five ways: (1) increasing understanding of economic development at all levels of government, (2) promoting economic development as a critical element of neighborhood, community, regional, and national planning processes, (3) disseminating

materials and information about current economic development theory and practice to members, (4) assisting APA in positively influencing economic development policy, and (5) promoting professional communication among members of the division.

4. Other state economic development programs and policies include activities such as, promoting business councils and industry associations; workers compensation and tort reform; lotteries to raise revenue for the state; building community attraction and retention capacity; university outreach programs; electronic bulletin boards; providing information on building sites; supporting business incubators to nurture startups, micro finance support, and one-stop permit shops (Leigh & Blakeley, 2013: 280).

5. Community development projects may include physical upgrading of infrastructure such as new sewer and water mains, roads, curbs, gutters, and signage. Some include support for public and private housing rehabilitation and business revitalization. They may include social welfare programs for education, health, welfare, and culture such as reducing average primary school class sizes, increasing the number of doctors at neighborhood clinics, job training programs, free meals delivered to the indigent elderly, and supporting neighborhood art projects.

6. The two CDBG allocation formulas are based on population, poverty, and overcrowded housing (formula A), and population "growth lag", poverty, and pre-1950 housing (formula B). "Growth lag" is the shortfall in population that a community has, compared to the population it would have had if it had grown at the average rate for all metro cities in the United States from 1960 to 2000.

7. Legislation to create a national enterprise zone program for the United States was eventually passed as Title VII of the 1987 Housing and Community Development Act. Congress authorized funding for enterprise zones during George Herbert Walker Bush's presidency. Bush's Secretary of HUD—Jack Kemp—encouraged cities, counties, and Indian tribes to apply, and 270 distressed communities applied for enterprise zone designation and funding. Congress never appropriated the funds, so no federal enterprise zones were ever created in the United States. Six years later funding was finally available under the Clinton-era empowerment zone/enterprise community legislation.

8. The first round of empowerment zones and enterprise communities was authorized by the Omnibus Budget Reconciliation Act of 1993 (OBRA, 1993). OBRA authorized the Secretary of Housing and Urban Development (HUD) to designate 9 empowerment zones (EZs) and 95 enterprise communities (ECs) (65 urban and 30 rural). The nine first-round EZs each received tax incentives and grants of $100 million (urban) and $40 million (rural). The 95 first-round ECs received tax benefits and grants of $2.95 million each. The Taxpayer Relief Act of 1997 authorized the designation of two additional first-round urban EZs and 20 additional EZs—15 urban and 5 rural. The Consolidated Appropriations Act of 2001, authorized nine additional new EZs (seven urban and two rural). Tax credits for businesses operating in EZs and ECs include a tax credit of up to $3,000 per year for each of the businesses employees who resides in the EZ, a work opportunity tax credit for hiring 18–39-year-old EZ area residents, a deduction of $35,000 for the cost of eligible equipment purchases, and tax exempt EZ facility bonds for commercial development.

9. The Renewal Communities (RC) program was created by the Community Renewal Tax Relief Act of 2000. The act authorized the secretary of HUD to select 40 RC areas, 12 of which had to be in rural areas. The areas had to have populations under 200,000 and have a high poverty rate. Recipients were eligible for (1) a renewal community employment credit for new full-time employees and summer workers, (2) a commercial revitalization deduction for tangible assets, (3) increased expensing for renewal community business assets, (4) a 100% exclusion for capital gains on the sale of specified renewal community business interests or tangible assets, (5) a work opportunity credit for hiring youth residing in renewal communities, (6) a "new markets" tax deduction for industries opening new markets, and (7) other benefits. Later RCs received wage credits, and tax investment incentives, but no grant funding.

10. In 2010, 260 million members of China's "floating population" were living somewhere other than their official residence (*hukou*) address for six or more months of the year (PRC, 2014). Average wages in urban China are now nearly triple average wages in rural areas. Rural areas in China have generated savings and have been able to productively use them for rural development (Chen, LeGates, & Fang, 2018). Wages in most of rural China are well above the subsistence level. Remittances from migrants to family members left behind in the countryside have greatly improved the quality of life in rural China. Peri-urban areas adjacent to core cities or county seats blur the physical and economic distinction between urban areas and their rural hinterlands.

11. Conventional infrastructure includes highways, roads, bridges, ports, airports, and transit systems. It is usually considered to includes environmental improvements to water and wastewater treatment and distribution systems, stormwater systems, and solid waste management facilities such as dumps, landfills, and recycling centers. Community facilities such as government buildings, police and fire stations, courthouses, public colleges and universities, civic centers, senior centers, marinas, and public parking structures are often considered infrastructure. So are recreation facilities such as playgrounds, swimming pools, tennis courts, parks, and open space. Most definitions include energy and telecommunications infrastructure such as power stations, telecommunications towers, and electrical transmission lines.

SUGGESTIONS FOR FURTHER LEARNING

Urban Economics: Arthur O'Sullivan, *Urban economics*, 9th ed (2018). **Urban Poverty:** William Julius Wilson, *The truly disadvantaged* (1987). **Local Economic Development Planning:** Nancey Green Leigh & Edward Blakeley, *Planning local economic development* (2016). Lincoln Land Institute, *Cleveland: Confronting decline in an American city* [video] (2012). Herbert Rubin, Shoot anything that flies, claim anything that falls (1988). **Urban Growth Machines:** Harvey Molotch, The city as a growth machine (1976). Harvey Molotch & John Logan, *The political economy of place* (1987). Harvey Molotch & John Logan, *Urban fortunes* (1987). **Private Sector Development and Public–Private Partnerships:** Alexander Garvin, *The American city: What works and what doesn't*, 3rd ed (2013). Bernard Frieden & Lynn Sagalyn, *Downtown, Inc.* (1991). Fulong Wu, Planning for growth (2015). **Competitive Strategy:** Michael Porter, *Competitive strategy* (2008). **Urban Renewal:** James Q. Wilson, *Urban renewal: The record and the controversy* (1966). Martin Anderson, *The federal bulldozer* (1964). Derick Hyra, Conceptualizing the new urban renewal (2012). **River Walk, San Antonio, Texas:** River Walk [website] (2021). River Walk: Our history [video] (2021). **Tax Increment Financing:** Richard Brooks, Catherine Plante, & Denise Hayes Something for nothing? Understanding tax increment financing (2017). Phuong Nguyen-Hoang, Is tax increment financing a fiscal bane or boon? (2021). **Community:** John Bruhn, *The sociology of community connections* (2011). **Community Development:** James DeFilippis & Susan Saegert (eds), *The community development reader*, 2nd ed (2012). Bernard Frieden & Lynn Sagalyn, *Downtown, Inc.* (1991). Rhonda Phillips & Robert Pittman (eds), *An introduction to community development*, 2nd ed (2014). Gary Green & Anna Haines, *Asset building and community development*, 4th ed (2015). **Enterprise Zones:** Peter Hall, Enterprise zones: British origins, American adaptations (1981). Matthew Ward, Enterprise zones (2020). Colin Jones, Verdict on the British enterprise zone experiment (2006). **Community Development Block Grants:** Marshall Kaplan & Bernard Frieden, *The politics of neglect* (1975). **Shrinking Cities and Abandonment:** Margaret Dewar & June Thomas, *The city after abandonment* (2013). John Metzger, Planned abandonment (2000). Philipp Oswalt, *Shrinking cities*, 2 vols (2005/2006). Philipp Oswalt, Tim Rieniets, & Henning Schirmel, *Atlas of shrinking cities* (2006). Brent Ryan, *Design after decline: How America rebuilds shrinking cities* (2012). Karina Pallagst et al. (eds), *The future of shrinking cities* (2009). **Russian and Chinese Economic Planning:** Mark Harrison, *Soviet planning in peace and war, 1938–1945* (1985). Jieming Zhu, *The transition of China's urban development: From plan-controlled to market-led* (1999). Dorothy Solinger, *China's transition from socialism* (1993). Fulong Wu, *Planning for growth* (2016). **Planned Shrinkage:** Jill Desimini, From planned shrinkage to formerly urban (2014). **The Creative Class:** Richard Florida, *The rise of the creative class* (2003). Shannan Clark, *The Making of the American creative class* (2021). **Infrastructure Planning:** Vickie Elmer & Adam Leighland, *Infrastructure planning and finance* (2013). Alvin Goodman & Makaran Hastak, *Infrastructure planning, engineering and economics*, 2nd ed (2015). **U.S. Federal Agency Websites:** Department of Commerce (DOC). Economic Development Administration (EDA). Bureau of Labor Statistics (BLS). **Journals:** *Journal of Urban Planning and Development. Community Development Journal. Revitalization. Regeneration and Renewal.*

CHAPTER 17

Climate Change and Energy Planning

INTRODUCTION

In 2012, Superstorm Sandy destroyed entire communities on the New Jersey Shore, flooded parts of the New York City subway system, killed 285 people and cost $70 billion in damages. In 2020 more than half of Bangladesh was flooded, four percent of California burned, and Australians spent weeks blanketed in smoke from wildfires with huge losses to wildlife and destruction of precious ecosystems. Thirty million acres of land are affected by desertification each year. The amount of carbon suspended in the atmosphere has reached the equivalent of 300 billion billion tons (gigatons). All of these events are linked to anthropogenic (human-caused) climate change. For more than two decades the United Nations has taken the position that it is unequivocal that human influence has warmed the atmosphere, ocean, and land. The scale of recent changes across the climate system as a whole and the present state of many aspects of the climate system are unprecedented. Changes in the last few decades have been greater than the change that occurred over many centuries to many thousands of years.

The United States has only 4% of the world's population but emits 10% of the world's Greenhouse Gases (GHGs). A disproportionate share of the carbon already in the atmosphere, oceans, and sequestered underground came from the United States.

This chapter begins by reviewing information and disinformation on the science of climate change.[1] It describes how much land surface temperatures and oceans have warmed and sea levels risen. Since The United Nations Intergovernmental Panel on Climate Change (IPCC) is the authoritative world source on climate change, much of this discussion is based on the most recent IPCC reports. The chapter draws on information from the U.S. Global Change Research Project, UN Environmental Programme, American Institute of Physics, National Oceanographic and Aeronautics Administration, U.S. Energy Information Administration, and other reputable sources of information about global climate change.

The chapter discusses how much carbon and other Greenhouse Gases have been released into the atmosphere. It describes the severe impacts that rising land temperatures have already had on droughts, floods, wildfires, desertification, and altered ecosystems. A section describes the catastrophic impacts of ocean warming on fish and other marine life, ocean currents, coral bleaching, melting Arctic and Antarctic snow and ice, wetlands, and the release of sequestered methane and carbon into the atmosphere from oceans and seabeds.

Since change in any part of the complex global climate system affects other parts of the system, this chapter discusses how tipping points and feedback loops from one part of the system may reinforce change in other parts. It evaluates prospects that passing local, regional, or global tipping points could result in rapid, catastrophic, unpredictable, and uncontrollable change.

A major section of the chapter is devoted to planning for both conventional energy production and consumption and planning how to shift to solar, wind, and, other clean and renewable energy sources. Since energy extraction and consumption are the main source of anthropogenic climate change, the chapter contains a section on energy planning at different levels, including global energy planning and policy. Parts of the chapter describe the Paris Climate Agreement—the main international climate change agreement and its shortcomings.

DOI: 10.4324/9781003195818-17

Since much climate change planning takes place at the state and local levels, the chapter describes how city and regional planners are preparing state and local government plans to reduce GHG emissions, and help communities to adapt to and mitigate damage from climate change. The chapter describes efforts to reduce carbon footprints at every level from individual households to nation states.

GLOBAL WARMING

Increasing temperatures at and near the surface of the earth are the most visible evidence of global warming. Since 1880 global warming has been a little less than 1°C (1.8°F). Most of the increase is recent and anthropogenic. This seemingly small increase is already having major impacts.

Anthropogenic surface temperature increase comes from point sources such as factories and mobile sources such as cars, trucks, and other motorized vehicles. Impacts of global warming include significantly accelerating desertification; sea-level rise; impacts on the life cycles of plants and animals; extreme heat events; melting polar ice, mountain snow, ice packs, and permafrost; increasing coastal flooding; reduced water for agriculture and to sustain human and animal life; economic disruption; and security threats.

A change in air temperature of even a fraction of a degree can have a large impact. The United Nations Intergovernmental Panel on Climate Change has concluded that global surface temperature will continue to increase until at least the mid-century. They project that global warming will exceed 2°C during the 21st century unless deep reductions in CO_2 and other greenhouse gas emissions occur in the coming decades. The IPCC's best estimate is that compared to 1850–1900, global surface temperatures at the end of this century—averaged over 2018–2100—are very likely to be 1.4°C higher, but could increase by as much as 5.7°C.

City and regional planners should be aware of eight key facts about land surface temperature increase: (1) the absolute increase is small, (2) even a small increase can have catastrophic effects, (3) the increase has been greater in some regions than others, (4) increases can vary greatly even within microregions, (5) the impact of the rise is context specific, (6) the rate of increase has been increasing rapidly, (6) surface air temperatures will continue to rise through at least 2050, (7) by 2050 global average surface temperature will be dangerously high, (8) how much surface temperatures will change depends on implementation of plans and policies now, (9) international treaties and national plans to address global warming are inadequate, and (10) countries are not meeting commitments to slow global warming that they have made.

Global warming is highest at the equator and lower at the poles. Climate zones have shifted towards the North and South Poles. Some parts of earth are becoming colder. For example, the U.S. National Aeronautics and Oceanographic Administration (NOAA) is studying a "cold blob" in the North Atlantic that is apparently caused by changing ocean currents.

There are large differences in the change in surface air temperature within the continental United States. The changes are even greater if Alaska, Hawaii, and U.S. Caribbean and Pacific Ocean possessions are included.

The Paris Climate Accord—the principal international climate change agreement—took the position in 2015 that global warming should be held "well below" 2°C (3.6°F). In 2019 the IPCC concluded that holding the rise to below 1.5°C (2.7°F) is critical. Many scientists and policy makers feel that standard is too high.

The most recent IPCC report on the physical science basis of climate change—*Climate Change 2021*—states that it is unequivocal that human influence has warmed the atmosphere, ocean and land; that widespread and rapid changes in the

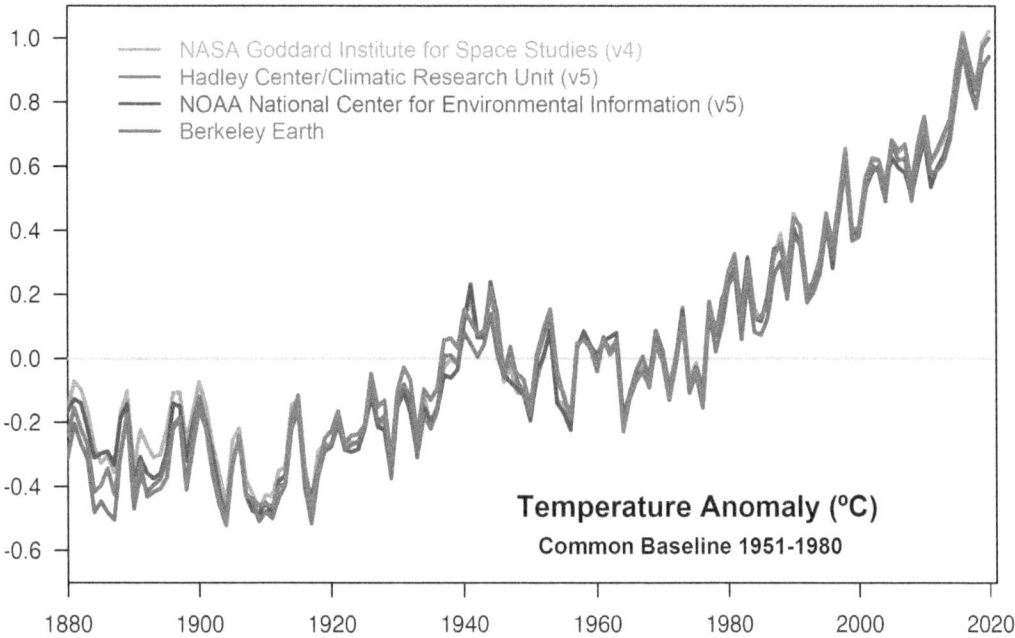

Figure 17.1 Global Mean Atmospheric Temperature 1880 to 2020 Relative to 1951–1980 Mean.

atmosphere, ocean, biosphere (the regions of the surface, atmosphere, and hydrosphere of the earth occupied by living organisms), and cryosphere (the part of the earth's surface characterized by the presence of frozen water) have occurred. The IPCC concluded that global surface temperature will continue to increase until at least the mid-century and that many changes due to past and future greenhouse gas emissions are irreversible for centuries to millennia—especially changes in the ocean, ice sheets, and global sea level.

Virtually no government is meeting their own nationally determined commitments (NDCs) to reduce carbon emissions that they entered into as part of the Paris agreement. The emissions gap is now so large that it will be impossible to hold global warming below 1.5°C without a dramatic and immediate change from current practices that is virtually impossible.[2] The "emissions gap" is a critical indicator of global progress towards reducing GHG emissions, or the lack thereof. It is the difference between the level of GHG emissions countries need to achieve in order to limit global warming to 2°C or lower and what they are actually achieving (EIA, 2020). The IPCC takes the position that multiple shared socioeconomic pathways may limit warming to below 2°C relative to pre-industrial levels. However, all pathways will require dramatic emissions reductions over the next few decades and near-zero emissions of CO_2 and other GHGs by the end of the century. Figure 17.1 shows the change in global mean average temperature between 1880 and 2020. Until about 1940 the average was below the 1951–1980 average, but since about 1980 it has risen rapidly and has been well above the 1951–1980 mean each year.

The IPCC, U.S. Global Change Research Project (USGCRP), and the UN Environmental Programme (UNEP) conclusions with respect to global warming between 2050 and 2100 are less certain, but even more alarming than their projections through 2050. The IPCC's best estimate of the human-caused global temperature increase from 1850–1900 to 2010–2019 is 1.07°C (1.9°F). The IPCC concludes that the increase in annual average global temperature relative to preindustrial times could reach 9°F or more by the end of this century. That would cause much more devastating catastrophic change than anything earth has experienced for millions of years.

CLIMATE CHANGE IMPACTS

Until about 1970, the handful of scientists and policy makers who were even aware of global climate change mostly believed its impacts were too remote to merit any current response. Most believed that if climate change did occur, the results would likely be beneficial—saving heating costs, increasing arable land, opening Arctic shipping channels, and improving life in cold regions. Measurements of increasing carbon dioxide (CO_2) in the atmosphere began in the 1950s, but the IPCC did not take the position that anthropogenic climate change was having a significant impact until their third assessment report in 2001.

A critical aspect of climate change impact studies is the attribution question—to what extent the impacts of a specific climate-related event may be attributed to anthropogenic, rather than natural, causes. Rapid advances in climate change science allow experts to better disentangle anthropogenic from natural causes, and link causes and effects.

CARBON AND OTHER GREENHOUSE GASES (GHGS)

Carbon in the atmosphere limits the amount of energy from sunlight that is reflected back into space. Earth's atmosphere extends only about 300 miles, and the part of the atmosphere that most affects life on earth lies within 10 miles of the earth's surface. This critical lower level is warming rapidly in complex ways that differ in different regions.

Humans release carbon dioxide (CO_2), methane (CH_4), and nitrous oxide (N_2O) into the atmosphere both during energy production—extracting fossil fuels (coal, natural gas, and oil)—and energy consumption—primarily by burning fossil fuels to produce energy for transportation, to power factories and office buildings, and heat homes. Other leading sources of anthropogenic GHG emissions are ranching, which produces methane from animal manure (and belches!), and agriculture, which releases sequestered carbon. CO_2 accounts for over 80% of GHG emissions. Methane and nitrous oxide (N_2O) account for all but 5% of the rest.

Since more than 80% of GHG emissions consist of CO_2, planners and policy makers average equivalent amounts of carbon from all sources with (CO_2) to produce summary measures expressed in gigatons (billion billion tons) of CO_2 equivalents ($GtCO_2e$). Currently the USA. produces about 12% of the world total of 56 $GtCO_2e$.

Carbon particles are tiny. Once they have diffused, GHGs become well mixed, so the amount of carbon in the atmosphere becomes roughly the same everywhere, regardless of the source of the emissions.

Only about 0.04% of the atmosphere now consists of carbon—416 parts per million. However, the amount of carbon in the atmosphere is already more than enough to cause catastrophic impacts. It is growing rapidly. There is about 60% more carbon in the atmosphere now than there was in 1990. The IPPC has concluded with a high degree of confidence that in 2019 atmospheric CO_2 concentrations were higher than at any time in at least two million years.

About half of CO_2 that enters the atmosphere is removed naturally within 30 years and 30% more within a few centuries—mostly through precipitation. The remaining 40% may stay in the atmosphere for many thousands of years.

Carbon that returns to earth may be sequestered for millions of years within ocean water, and in other carbon "sinks". Oceans are by far the largest carbon sink. They cover 71% of the earth's surface and hold 97% of the world's water. Oceans absorb about 31% of the CO_2 humans emit annually. Carbon has also accumulated below the ocean floor, in soil, forests, permafrost (land that remains permanently frozen for two or more years), and peatlands. Planning to protect carbon sinks is critical.

Forests—particularly the vast Arctic boreal forests in Scandinavia and Russia and rainforests in the Amazon and Indonesia—currently offset about 11% of GHG emissions. Deforestation in order to increase agricultural land—particularly by burning huge areas of rainforest in Brazil and Indonesia—increases GHG emissions and reduces the amount of carbon that the former forest land can sequester. Mitigation strategies planners propose include stopping the burning of forests, reducing the use of wood as a building material, and planting trees—particularly fast-growing trees that absorb and sequester large amounts of carbon.

A main source of carbon and methane now entering the atmosphere is from peatlands that are melting much more rapidly than in the past as a result of global warming. Peat consists of deposits resembling soil, formed by the partial decomposition of vegetable matter in the wet acidic conditions of bogs and fens. Peatlands sequester more than twice as much carbon as all forests on earth and also sequester large amounts of methane. Peat is very deep in enormous areas in the northern parts of the Scandinavian countries, Russia, northern China, Canada, Ireland, and Alaska. Methane also enters the atmosphere from swamps, bogs, rice paddies, animal dung, and other sources that can be better planned and managed to protect carbon sinks.

Group of Twenty (G20) countries—the 20 countries with the largest economies—account for 78% of global GHG emissions. Group of Seven (G7) countries—including the USA and China—emit about one-third. China and the United States are by far the largest CO_2 emitters.[3] Accordingly, planners in the U.S., China, and other big emitting countries have a particularly important role to play in reducing carbon emissions.

Production of beef and dairy products, soybeans, and palm oil contribute significantly to global warming. A shift to production and consumption to less meat and dairy products, regenerative agriculture that improves soil, and greater reliance on crops that require limited water or sequester carbon can reduce global warming. Figure 17.2 shows sheep grazing under solar panels on the Cabriejo Ranch—a solar farm in Millington, Tennessee. Cabriejo Ranch is one of more than 150 solar ranches licensed by the Silicon Ranch Corporation. Cabriejo and other Silicon Ranch Corporation ranches are engaged in regenerative agriculture that provides additional grassland as well as producing solar energy. When there is enough grass, the ranch introduces sheep which graze on the grass. Sheep manure fertilizes the grass. The grass sequesters carbon. Over time Silicon Ranch intends to convert all of the farms they license to regenerative agriculture.

Transportation—cars, trucks, ships, trains, and planes—account for about a third of CO_2 emissions. Over 90% of the fuel used for transportation is petroleum-based gasoline and diesel fuel. A combination of technological advances, government regulations, and use of ethanol—refined from corn—are producing

Figure 17.2 Silicon Ranch Farm Combining Solar Energy Generation and Regenerative Agriculture (Millington, Tennessee, 2020).

rapid and major reduction of GHGs from motorized vehicles. Most important are plans to accelerate the shift to hybrid vehicles and zero emission vehicles (ZEVs). U.S. planners are making plans for electric vehicle-charging stations, more public transit, fewer parking spaces, more high-occupancy vehicle (HOV) lanes, and street corridors with carbon-absorbing trees and other vegetation.

Emissions from ethanol or ethanol blends release much less carbon into the atmosphere than gasoline alone. Production of ethanol is the largest source of energy from biomass (plant and animal waste) in the United States. However, automobile ownership and increases in vehicle miles driven (VMD) in the United States and worldwide have largely negated the reduction in GHGs. Transportation-related plans and policies to reduce global warming include increasing fuel efficiency, reducing driving, increasing carpooling, and increasing bicycling.

Phasing out existing gasoline-powered cars, trucks, and other motorized vehicles as quickly as possible and replacing them with ZEVs is critical. There are about 275 million motor vehicles in the United States, and over 1.4 billion worldwide. California has announced that it will require all new vehicles sold in the state to be ZEVs by 2035, but other states have no such requirement. There is a huge market in developing countries for gasoline-powered vehicles that can no longer be legally operated in developed countries. Plans to change public vehicle fleets to ZEVs, get rid of old motor vehicles that pollute, and stop exporting polluting vehicles to other countries can all help reduce global warming. These strategies are often part of state and local climate action plans. Over a quarter of U.S. GHG emissions come from generation of electricity by burning coal, oil, and natural gas. The demand for electric power is increasing rapidly in the United States and worldwide. The most important way to reduce GHG emissions from electricity production is to shift to solar, wind, and other non-polluting sources of electric power. Planning and designing more energy-efficient buildings will reduce energy consumption.

Industrial processes contribute about 22% of CO_2 emissions—mostly from burning fossil fuels to produce energy for industry. More energy-efficient production and greater use of non-polluting energy sources to produce steel, cement, and other industrial goods will reduce GHG emissions. Planners working for air quality boards or other regulators are making plans requiring industries to be more energy-efficient and cleaner. Planners working for industry are making clean energy production a priority to meet the law or because it is in the industries' long-term self-interest.

GHG emissions from commercial and residential uses account for about 22% of CO_2 emissions, primarily from fossil fuels burned for heat, use of products like leaf blowers, and the handling of waste. Programs to encourage or require households to reduce household carbon footprints from these uses can contribute to reducing GHG emissions.

RISING SEA TEMPERATURES AND LEVELS

Sea temperatures are increasing. The pattern of sea temperature increase is similar to land temperature change. Oceans are rising. The UN has concluded with a high level of confidence that sea levels will rise for centuries to millennia due to continuing deep ocean warming and ice sheet melt, and will remain elevated for thousands of years.

Oceans occupy 71% of the earth's surface. They average 2.3 miles deep. Since the mid-20th century, oceans have absorbed over 90% of the excess heat caused by GHG emissions. Currently they absorb more than a quarter of anthropogenic CO_2 emissions.

The surface of the ocean is warmer than the ocean depths. Most fish and marine animals and plants live within 2,000 feet of the surface. Accordingly, the most common measure of ocean temperature that planners use is ocean surface temperature. Planners devote more effort to strategies to mitigate and adapt to surface temperature rise in areas which are important for fishing than in areas deep in the ocean which are less important for fish—at least in the short run. However, massive, catastrophic, long-term change is also occurring deep in oceans and in ocean currents.

The absolute amount of ocean warming, and sea-level rise are both small—only about 1.5°F (0.85°C) and 8 inches (20 centimeters) since 1900. Sea temperatures and sea-level rise are increasing rapidly.[4] Processes that have already occurred will continue to warm the oceans even if no new GHGs are added. This will continue to alter ocean and atmospheric currents and land temperatures. Temporary solutions are not enough—humanity must adapt to ocean warming and sea-level rise that will last for millennia.

Planning to slow, stop, adapt to and mitigate the impacts of ocean temperature increase and sea-level rise depends on locations and the local context. A habitat conservation plan for a coastal settlement in Alaska must be based on different facts and projections than one in Florida or the U.S. Virgin Islands. A general plan for a coastal city on the East Coast of the United States must anticipate more extensive sea-level rise than one at the same latitude on the West Coast. Planners need to keep abreast of the most up-to-date information and policy changes concerning global warming because understanding of the problem and responses to it are evolving so quickly.

Nearly two-thirds of the world's major cities are on coasts. Much of the U.S. population lives within fifty miles of an ocean. Ports, naval bases, power plants, fisheries, farmlands, rice paddies, beaches, and other recreational areas are on coasts. So are wetlands critical to ecosystems and which buffer flooding from storm surges.

A major impact of climate change is melting ice sheets in Antarctica, Greenland, near the North Pole, and in glaciers around the world. This increases sea levels as snow and ice melt, and as edges of ice sheets break off and slide into oceans. Sea ice reduces ocean temperatures, but not nearly enough to offset the net increase from other changes. The IPCC considers the likelihood of ice sheet collapse low, but that it cannot be ruled out.

The majority of mountain glaciers and icecaps are retreating. Snow cover in the Himalayas, Andes, Alps, and other alpine regions is decreasing.

Warming in Arctic regions near the North and South Pole is a serious global threat. Even though they are remote and sparsely populated, melting ice from Arctic regions is already impacting earth and has the potential for great harm.[5]

Major consequences of ocean warming include ocean acidification and coral bleaching; increasing atmospheric water vapor (hence more clouds and heavy precipitation); loss of oxygen in ocean water needed to support plant, fish, and animal species; changing ocean and atmospheric currents; and extreme weather events such as tropical cyclones, ocean storm surges, hurricanes, and monsoons. All these phenomena have recently become worse and are projected to increase rapidly.

The ocean depths, ocean floor, and the layer below the ocean floor are important sinks that sequester carbon and methane. Reducing carbon in the ocean and preserving and enhancing ocean sinks are planning problems best addressed at the international scale.

Flooding is a major problem in the United States and other countries. Hurricanes and storm surges regularly flood the Atlantic and Gulf coasts of the United States, causing billions of dollars damage in a single event. Heavy rain causes flooding in many other parts of the United States.

Bangladesh, Pacific Island countries, and low-lying parts of many other countries already suffer from much more severe flooding than in the recent past, and some face imminent existential peril. Even a three-foot sea level rise will submerge the Maldives in the Indian Ocean—the lowest-lying country in the world. Twenty percent of Bangladesh—where tens of millions of very low-income people live—flooded in fall, 2020. Bangladesh will periodically flood catastrophically, even if Paris Accord goals are met.

Many large cities—including London, New York, Jakarta, and Miami are sinking. London, New York City, Leningrad, Rotterdam, and other cities have built enormous surge barriers to protect themselves from flooding from storm surges. Most of Rotterdam is below sea level. Rotterdam's

Figure 17.3 Storm Surge Barrier (Rotterdam, Netherlands).

harbor—the largest in Europe—directly faces the North Sea, where very large storms have become much more frequent. Figure 17.3 shows Rotterdam's storm surge barrier.

Protecting against sea-level rise has become an important goal in planning for resilient cities. Planning resilient cities involves two main activities—making and implementing plans to protect cities from damage before it occurs and planning for and implementing plans to help cities recover from climate shocks. The Rockefeller Foundation has supported resilient city planning, including helping cities become more resilient in the face of sea-level rise.[6]

One of the most innovative responses to flooding has been developed by Kongjian Yu, a Beijing-based landscape architect who received his PhD from the Harvard Graduate School of Design. Yu has developed the idea of "sponge cities" that use features of the natural landscape to absorb water during monsoons. Box 17.1 is a biography of Yu.

INTERACTION EFFECTS AND TIPPING POINTS

Unanticipated changes, interaction effects, feedback loops, and possible tipping points make climate change planning different from other types of planning. Not only do planners not know what effects identified phenomena will have, they do not know what effects that they have not identified may emerge. How multiple known and unknown phenomena will impact each other is impossible to predict with certainty.

GHG emissions, rising surface temperatures, warming oceans, rising ocean levels, extreme weather events, and other causes and consequences of global climate change do not occur in isolation from each other. Many changes are compound events. Feedback loops may exacerbate an effect once it has started. Impacts can cascade from one type of change to others.

The U.S. Global Change Research Project identifies two types of unanticipated climate change events: compound events, where multiple extreme climate events that occur either simultaneously or sequentially create greater overall impacts together than they would create separately, and critical threshold or tipping point events, which may lead to rapid and unexpected change if they are exceeded. Some scientists fear earth may reach a global tipping point in climate change, triggering large, rapid, cascading, and unpredictable changes in the state of earth's entire climate

BOX 17.1 KONGJIAN YU

Kongjian Yu is a Chinese city and regional planner, landscape architect, and urban design scholar-practitioner who specializes in ecological design. He is best known for developing the sponge city concept—the idea of using soft protect strategies using natural features of the landscape to prevent or reduce the impacts of flooding—and for implementing sponge city projects in China. Sixty-two percent of Chinese cities flooded between 2011 and 2014, imposing $100 billion in economic losses. Sponge cities are a kind of reverse-engineering to lessen flooding—giving water space to expand and contract and letting it soak into the ground.

Yu received a PhD in design from the Harvard Graduate School of Design in 1995. At Harvard he conducted field work on flood-prone areas in South China. Yu's work builds on Ian McHarg's design with nature ideas—described in Chapter 13—and low-impact flood management and stormwater systems and green infrastructure in the United States, UK, the Netherlands, China, and other countries.

Yu's main goal has been to learn how to control surface runoff during flood peaks. He has also studied how to use natural processes to protect water quality, replenish groundwater, recharge aquifers, and provide wildlife habitat and recreation spaces in urban areas by making use of rainwater resources as an organic part of the landscape. Yu seeks to do this using as little traditional civil engineering hardscaping as possible. His design approaches include developing tree and plant root systems to capture and retain water, unearthing buried creeks, making parking lots and driveways permeable, and adjusting slopes to make water drain naturally into bioswales, retention ponds, and sunken parks. Sponge city designs can preserve or restore floodplains and wetlands, clean water, re-create habitat for wildlife, and provide sites for recreation. Designs like the Puyang River Ecological Corridor (Figure 17.5) give urbanites access to nature.

Figure 17.4 Kongjian Yu.

Figure 17.5 Puyang River Ecological Corridor (Zhejiang Province, China).

Yu has been a professor of urban and regional planning at Peking University (PKU) since 1997. He is the founder and dean of the PKU's College of Architecture and Landscape Architecture. He founded a planning, landscape architecture, and urban design firm in Beijing named Turenscape in 1998 that specializes in environmental planning and sponge city design. Turenscape has a staff of about 600 professionals. The firm has planned and designed over 300 ecological cities and 1,000 landscape projects in China. They have built more than 600 projects. Turenscape's projects have won 13 consecutive American Society of Landscape Architects (ASLA) awards in the past ten years, five World's Best Landscape Awards at the World Architecture Festival, and many other awards. Yu's Puyang River Ecological Corridor in his native Zhejiang Province (Figure 17.5) won the 2019 APA International Planning Excellence Award and the Ian McHarg Environmental Planning Award.

Yu has published over 20 books and 300 articles in English and Chinese. He is the founder and chief editor of a leading international landscape architecture magazine, *Landscape Architecture Frontier*.

The United Nations has endorsed nature-based solutions for water and the sponge city concept (UN, 2018). Even the U.S. Army Corps of Engineers—staffed by engineers long committed to hardscape solutions to manage rivers and wetlands—now has an engineering with nature initiative.

system. Efforts to address climate change once a tipping point is passed could spin out of control. Global or regional tipping points may occur over a period of a few years if there is a large enough increase in emissions from a huge source such as methane clathrate in ocean sea beds, melting permafrost near the North Pole, or burning or clear-cutting forest land in Brazil or Indonesia. A global tipping point might occur suddenly if an enormous ice sheet from Antarctica or Greenland detaches from the continental ice shelf—an event that the IPCC considers unlikely, but does not rule out.

OTHER GLOBAL WARMING IMPACTS

By the beginning of the 21st century impact studies of climate change moved beyond geophysical impacts. Planners and policy makers began to consider economic, security, health, food, and other impacts of global warming.

Economic impacts

Nicholas Stern, a former chief economist of the World Bank, calculated that if global warming in the 21st century reaches the upper range of what scientists believe likely, the direct effects will cut the world's annual global gross domestic product (GDP) by about 5% and that ripple effects might raise the loss as high as 20%. The IPCC's fourth assessment report (2007) and later analyses reference Stern's (2006) conclusions.

Security Impacts

In 2019 the nonpartisan Center for Climate and Security (CCS) concluded that climate change poses a serious security threat because "megadroughts, famine and widespread rioting [could] erupt across the world [bringing] the planet to the edge of anarchy as countries develop a nuclear threat to defend and secure dwindling food, water and energy supplies". The Obama administration reached a similar conclusion in 2015. Except during the Trump administration, United States Department of Defense (DOD) reports have also consistently found that climate change poses serious security risks. Climate change-related drought in Syria contributed to the violence that precipitated 5.6 million foreign refugees and over 6 million internally displaced people. A nuclear war would likely so damage the global climate that a "nuclear fall" would kill many more people than the bomb blast and a "nuclear winter" could extinguish human life on earth.

Health Impacts

Tropical diseases like malaria, yellow fever, and dengue fever that thrive in warm environments will likely increase as global warming expands the zones where they can thrive. Insects like the mosquitos that transmit malaria and the Zika and West Nile viruses will be able to live in regions further from the equator, including parts of the Southern United States. The number of disease cases in the United States from mosquitos, ticks, and fleas has tripled in the last 13 years.

Food Impacts

Growing, transporting, and storing food requires energy that produces carbon and other GHGs. In the short term, global warming may make it possible to raise more food in areas like Siberia and Alaska, but it will reduce net food security quite rapidly. Half a billion people live in areas at risk of desertification—particularly in the enormous Sahel region of North Africa. Destruction of the Amazonian rainforest, to plant soybeans and raise cattle for beef, and of rainforests in Indonesia, to plant palm trees for palm oil, are major contributors to GHG emissions. Increased reliance on beef and dairy products reduces land cover that sequesters carbon and increases animal dung and other by-products that release methane into the atmosphere. Shifting diets to use less meat and dairy produce, farming in more intensive ways, and locating farms close to consumers to reduce transportation and storage can help reduce climate change.

Energy Planning

Energy planning is a city and regional planning specialization recognized by the Association of Collegiate Schools of Planning. It is concerned with analyzing sources and uses of energy, planning to meet future energy needs, and developing energy plans, policy, and programs. It is closely related to climate change planning, environmental planning, and transportation planning.

World consumption of all forms of primary energy increased more than tenfold during the 20th century and is projected to continue to increase even more rapidly. The massive increase in energy production in developing countries began only in the 1980s and is rapidly accelerating.

City and regional planners are concerned with both energy production and energy consumption. Some planners do energy planning work at the federal level for the U.S. Department of Energy, Department of Transportation, Environmental Protection Agency, or other federal agencies. Other planners work in state or local government offices that do energy planning, oversee construction and maintenance of energy infrastructure, or regulate energy producers and distributors. Some do energy planning for international organizations, nonprofits, or in the private sector.

The 1973 oil embargo by the Organization of Petroleum Exporting Countries created an oil shortage in the United States and dramatic gasoline price increases.[7] Between October 1973 and March 1974, world crude oil prices quadrupled. In the United States, there were gasoline shortages, and the price of gasoline skyrocketed. The oil crisis forced U.S. government officials and policy makers to focus on energy independence and make plans to greatly increase domestic production of energy. At that time, they looked to coal, oil, and nuclear sources rather than solar, wind, or other renewable and clean energy sources. The war in Ukraine is making energy independence a priority for Europe, the United States and other countries. It may accelerate the shift to clean and renewable energy sources.

The amount of energy at a source where it is produced diminishes as it is distributed and used, so the total primary energy supply (TPES)—how much total energy equivalent is produced at the source—is the standard indicator of how much energy each country produces overall and in different sectors and regions. About 80% of U.S. TPES comes from non-renewable sources—petroleum (37%), natural gas (32%), and coal (11%). Eight per cent comes from nuclear sources. Solar, wind, hydro, and other clean and renewable energy sources and biomass (which is renewable, but not clean) supply the other 14% of TPES.

CONVENTIONAL ENERGY PLANNING

While there is an abundance of oil that has already been extracted or is in proven oil reserves that can be extracted in the future, the massive disruption of global oil and gas supply chains by the COVID pandemic and the war in Ukraine has created shortages and a spike in oil and gas prices as this book goes to press in spring, 2022. The United States exports oil and natural gas, and may need to export more to Europe and other countries to make up for a shortfall in supplies from Russia.

The big oil and coal companies have plans to continue to extract and refine oil, natural gas and coal for decades. They are still exploring and drilling for new oil and gas reserves.

Coal is becoming less economically viable. However, as of spring, 2022 some coal companies that had closed had re-started operations as the cost of oil and natural gas increased, largely because of disruption in global supply chains caused by the COVID pandemic and the war in Ukraine. Depending on the international situation coal production may stop because of market realities. That will require regional economic development planning to help regions that are economically dependent on coal to adjust. Some planners work for oil and coal companies in order to help them wind down conventional operations as quickly and economically as possible or in the clean and renewable energy divisions of these companies to help plan the companies' shift to clean energy production. The phasing out of coal will require regional economic development planning to help regions that are economically dependent on coal to adjust. However, oil and coal companies have enormous political power to protect their ability to continue conventional energy production as long as it is economically feasible and to bend the economy to favor themselves. Some planners work for oil and coal companies in order to help them wind down conventional operations as quickly and economically as possible or in the clean and renewable energy divisions of these companies to help plan the companies' shift to clean energy production.

Hydroelectric power in the United States was mostly developed between the early 1930s and mid-1980s. It is a clean and renewable energy source, but poses safety risks to life and property if dams overflow or fail. Dams disrupt natural water flows and may harm fish and agriculture. Few new dams are planned for the U.S., but planners continue to work on plans to upgrade or replace older dams. Small low-head hydro dams—where the water drops less than 65 feet—may make a modest addition to the U.S. energy supply. More than half of the world's projected increase in hydroelectric power in the next few decades will likely be in China.

Nuclear power was mostly developed between 1970 and 1990. Nuclear energy is nearly carbon-neutral, but poses catastrophic risks in the event of a nuclear accident. The partial meltdown of a nuclear reactor at Three Mile Island in Middletown, Pennsylvania in 1979, the melting of part of the core of the Chernobyl nuclear reactor near Kiev, in what was then the Soviet Union in 1986, and the disabling of the power supply and cooling systems of three nuclear reactors at the Fukushima Daiichi nuclear power plant near Tokyo after a tsunami in 2011, illustrate the risk of nuclear reactor accidents killing millions of people and making large areas uninhabitable for millennia.[8] Prospects of new nuclear plants in the United States now appear remote. Energy planners confront continuing safety issues as existing nuclear plants age, and need to make long-term plans if they are to be closed.

PLANNING FOR CLEAN AND RENEWABLE ENERGY

Given the global climate crisis and the need to slow, stop, and reverse GHG emissions where possible, planning for clean and renewable energy is a city and regional planning priority.

Fourteen per cent of U.S. total primary energy supply (TPES) in 2019 came from renewable energy sources—mostly wind (24%), hydroelectric (22%), wood (20%), and biofuels (20%). Solar contributed 9% and geothermal 2% of the total. In the United States, solar works best in the sunbelt—particularly desert areas in Nevada, Arizona, Texas, Utah, and California. Use of solar and wind power is growing very rapidly worldwide. The United States, Germany, and China are leaders in developing solar and wind technology. China is a major exporter of solar panels to other countries. Germany leads Europe in solar power use.

Countries like Morocco with abundant sunlight and deserts are in a position to make the most of their geographical advantage. The Noor III solar energy complex in Ouarzazate, Morocco supplies most of Morocco's energy. Energy from North Africa holds the prospect of contributing substantially to Europe's energy supply. Arizona, Utah, Nevada, and other Southwestern states with a large amount of desert land and strong sunlight may become major domestic U.S. sources of energy from very large solar installations.

Currently the largest source of renewable energy in the world is biomass. Old biomass from burning agricultural waste, dung, wood, straw, and other plant material is an important heating and cooking source in developing countries. It contributes to air pollution and GHGs. In contrast, new biomass from compressed sawdust and ethanol (from corn) is the main kind of biomass used in the United States and other developed countries. New biomass produces a small share of renewable energy, but with almost no GHG emissions or air pollution.

Between now and 2050, production and consumption of energy will continue to grow rapidly in the United States and worldwide. Initially, energy will continue to come predominantly from conventional sources—oil, natural gas, and coal. The amount of energy produced from solar and other clean and renewable energy sources will increase very rapidly. Renewables may account for 50% or more of all energy use by 2050. Before the end of the 21st century it is possible that virtually all the world's energy will come from clean renewable sources. However, this can only happen if planners and policy makers make bold plans very soon and have the courage to implement them.

City and regional planners face unprecedented challenges and exciting opportunities in energy planning in the coming decades. Assuring enough energy to meet human needs without catastrophic climate change will be a delicate balancing act. Major changes must occur in the G20 countries which produce and consume most of the world's energy and create most GHG emissions. More and cleaner energy is critical to developing countries where most of world urbanization will occur. It is short-sighted for developing countries to destroy forests or endanger the heath of their citizens from dirty energy sources. Planners can help them produce energy with as few GHG emissions as possible. It is equally short-sighted for developed countries to continue to consume as much energy as they do from sources that release carbon into the atmosphere and invest so little in implementing alternatives. The United States needs to play a leadership role in energy innovation and planning. City and regional planners at every level in the public, private, and nonprofit sectors can contribute to better energy planning.

INTERNATIONAL CLIMATE CHANGE AND ENERGY PLANNING

The principal international agreement to reduce global climate change is the 2015 Paris Climate Agreement—the latest and most important of a series of failed international agreements within the United Nations Framework Convention on Climate Change (UNFCCC) which took effect in 1992. All 197 UN sovereign states are parties to the UNFCCC. World energy ministers meet annually in a UN-sponsored "Conference of the Parties" (COP) to assess progress in dealing with climate change. The most recent meeting of the COP—the 26th—took place in Glasgow, Scotland in November, 2021. Working group contributions to the IPPC's *Sixth Assessment Report* that is scheduled to be released in 2022 are the fundamental sources of information on the science of climate change and policy to slow or stop it, mitigate its effects, and adapt to changes that have occurred and will inevitably occur.[9]

The United States, China, and other signatories to the Paris Climate Agreement agreed to significantly reduce GHG emissions, but to different extents, in different ways, and on different timelines—virtually none of which have been met.[10] The Trump administration withdrew the United States from the agreement in November 2020. President Biden issued an executive order for the United States to re-enter the accord on his first day in office in January, 2021.

The stated goal of the Paris Climate Agreement is to decrease global warming by:

1) Holding the increase in the global average temperature to well below 2°C above pre-industrial levels and to pursue efforts to limit the temperature increase to 1.5°C above pre-industrial levels;
2) Increasing the ability to adapt to the adverse impacts of climate change and foster climate resilience and low GHG emissions development, in a manner that does not threaten food production; and
3) Making finance flows consistent with a pathway towards low GHG emissions and climate-resilient development.

Each signatory country stated a nationally determined contribution (NDC) to reducing GHG emissions they intended to make. The Paris Climate Agreement is non-binding. There are no mechanisms to enforce compliance with country NDC goals.

The Paris Agreement is based on the principle of "common but differentiated responsibility" reflecting countries different past emissions and present and projected future capabilities. It does not provide a specific division of responsibility. Per capita emissions is a preferred measure for assigning responsibility, given the large disparity in populations in different countries. How much each country is expected to contribute to reducing GHG emissions, and when, is largely based on a combination of their population, the amount of carbon they emit, past carbon emissions, and their economic capacity and potential. A very poor country like Burkina Faso that contributes little to GHG emissions should pay much less than Qatar with a per capita income 100 times greater that Burkina

Faso's that is emitting almost 2,000% more carbon per capita.

A major issue in global climate change planning is what financial assistance, if anything, developed countries should provide to less developed countries to help them pay for climate change adaptation and mitigation projects. The UN has established a Green Climate Fund (GCF) to do this, but made little progress in collecting and disbursing funds.[11]

Critiques and early evaluations of the Paris Climate Agreement generally conclude that its goals are inadequate, the mechanisms to achieve its targets and goals are too weak, and that almost no country is taking necessary actions they agreed to. It is very unlikely that 2030, 2035, or 2050 NDC goals will be met.

There are many other international treaties, agreements and declarations related to climate change. In 2009 the European Union passed legislation to reduce CO_2 emissions by 20%, increase the market share of renewable energy to 20%, and increase energy efficiency by 20% by 2020—the EU 20/20/20 Targets. The EU essentially met its first two goals—reducing CO_2 emissions by 20% and increasing the share of renewable energy to 20%, but fell short of increasing energy efficiency by 20%. The current EU climate targets call for a 55% reduction in CO_2 emissions by 2030 and carbon neutrality by 2050.

The nonprofit International Council on Local Environmental Initiatives (ICLEI), with its main office in Toronto, Canada, has built a network to help cities achieve more sustainable low-carbon development. ICLEI's Cities for Climate Protection (CCP) program helps over 700 local governments formulate and implement local action programs to reduce their carbon footprints. The Under2 Coalition is a global climate pact among governments and other organizations that have committed to reducing GHGs to under the 2°C target that the Paris Climate Agreement set. More than 200 jurisdictions from 38 countries (not including the United States government) have signed or endorsed the agreement. Nonprofit organizations like the Environmental Defense Fund (EDF), National Resources Defense Council (NRDC), Union of Concerned Scientists (UCS), CoolClimate Network, Sierra Club, Greenpeace, Earth Justice, Center for Climate and Energy Solutions (C2ES) Solutions Project, and Nature Conservancy promote progressive climate change planning and policies.

The Montreal Protocol, banning the use of extremely damaging chlorofluorocarbons (CFCs)—high global warming potential gases that come mostly from aerosol sprays—demonstrates that it is possible to get virtually all countries to agree upon and implement an important policy to essentially eliminate a serious climate change problem. A ban on above-ground nuclear testing to eliminate release of extremely dangerous strontium-90 into the atmosphere, shows that countries can agree to stop fundamental damage to the atmosphere if they perceive the threat to be serious enough. The United States, the UK, the Soviet Union, and China succeeded in negotiating a partial ban on above-ground nuclear testing in 1963. In 1996, 71 nations signed a multi-lateral Comprehensive Nuclear Test Ban Treaty (CTBT), which bans all nuclear tests for both civilian and military purposes in all environments. Neither treaty is perfect, but they are beacons of hope for how countries might cooperate on climate change policy.

NATIONAL CLIMATE CHANGE AND ENERGY PLANNING

The United States has flip-flopped in the seriousness with which it has addressed global warming and the need for shifting to clean and renewable energy. Joe Biden's election as the 46th president of the United States, his appointment of John Kerry as the United States "Energy Czar", and the Democratic Party's control of the House of Representatives and the Senate (barely) hold the promise that the United States will aggressively reassert leadership in climate change planning at the national and international levels. France, Germany, and China have been leaders in taking action within their borders and pressing for more effective international action. The Russian invasion of Ukraine has greatly complicated international efforts to address climate change.

STATE CLIMATE CHANGE PLANNING

Twenty-four states plus the District of Columbia either have some form of written climate change plan or are considering one. Every state has policies that impact climate change, directly by altering activities such as state highway construction, and indirectly through policies that they set for their cities, counties, and special districts. Seven state policies are particularly important:

1) land use laws,
2) carbon cap-and-trade programs,
3) infrastructure projects,
4) environmental regulation,
5) public land management,
6) energy efficiency standards for motor vehicles and household appliances, and
7) shifting state energy portfolios to use more solar, wind, and other clean and renewable energy sources.

State planning, zoning, subdivision, growth management, and other land use laws and policies described in Chapter 8 impact urban form and density. More compact city-centered development and more sensitive land use can reduce anthropogenic climate change.

State carbon cap-and-trade programs cap GHG emissions for different industries and allow companies to sell credits if they are under their cap in a given year. Eleven states that are members of the Regional Greenhouse Gas Initiative have implemented energy-related cap-and-trade programs.

States fund much of the costs of constructing, operating, and maintaining infrastructure of state-level significance such as highways, bridges, dams, and water infrastructure. Designing new state infrastructure and retrofitting old infrastructure to release less GHGs can reduce carbon emissions.

State little NEPAs—state equivalents of the National Environmental Policy Act—can require environmental reviews that emphasize measures to mitigate climate change. State air and water quality, coastal zone management, habitat conservation, and other environmental laws and policies can also be applied to help mitigate climate change. Laws and regulations governing forest management can reduce carbon entering the atmosphere from wildfires.

States' policies for managing their public lands can reduce GHGs during energy production, help sequester carbon, and otherwise reduce global warming. State standards for extracting and refining oil and gas and minerals can reduce GHG emissions by regulating how much resources can be extracted and requiring oil companies to limit GHG emissions during the extraction and refining process. Some academics, governments, and private oil companies, are now doing well-to-wheel analysis that examines the entire process of extracting, refining, and distributing gas and diesel fuel—looking for ways to reduce GHG emissions at every point in the entire process.

The federal government has left responsibility for fracking (hydraulic fracturing) during the extraction of oil and gas to the states.[12] Fracking is a controversial process that has greatly increased extraction of oil and natural gas trapped in rock formations, but with considerable damage to the environment and earth's climate. Fracking requires pumping huge amounts of fracking fluid (water, sand, and chemicals—some of which are toxic) at great pressure into shale that contain pockets of oil and natural gas. Horizontal drilling can reach out to frack (fracture) a large area from a single bore hole. During the fracking process some natural gas escapes—releasing carbon and methane into the atmosphere.

New York state prohibits all fracking. The adjacent state of New Jersey permits fracking and has prohibited local governments from zoning that would interfere with it. Fracking is a major issue in electoral politics. President Trump enthusiastically supported fracking. The left wing of the Democratic Party and some Democratic candidates in the 2020 presidential primaries supported banning fracking altogether. President Biden supports fracking, so long as it can be done without releasing methane and carbon as oil and gas are extracted.

Transportation planning can increase vehicle efficiency and reduce carbon and other GHG emissions from vehicles. How well states implement the federal ISTEA, FAST, and MAP-21 acts and carry out federally mandated 3Cs planning, described in Chapter 14, can increase energy-efficient transportation. California and Oregon have low-carbon fuel standards aimed at reducing greenhouse gas emissions from motorized vehicles below the federal Corporate Average Fuel Economy (CAFE) standard. President Biden has reversed the Trump administration's effort to preempt their authority to do this.

State appliance efficiency standards for household and industrial products can reduce energy demand. Currently 15 states and the District of Columbia have appliance efficiency standards that exceed federal requirements.

Some state energy portfolio standards require state agencies that produce energy to shift to increasingly greater percentages of solar, wind, and other clean and renewable energy sources to replace energy production by dirty, environment- and climate-damaging non-renewable sources like coal, oil, and natural gas.

Air Quality Districts (AQDs) are logical units to reduce GHG emissions. While they are regional bodies that operate within a national policy framework overseen by the U.S. Environmental Protection Agency, their standards are largely controlled by states. California illustrates what states can do. California has a GDP larger than the United Kingdom's, advanced innovative technology companies, and liberal pro-climate management politics. California's Global Warming Solutions Act (2006) empowers the California Air Resources Board (CARB) to oversee comprehensive statewide planning to reduce GHGs, electrify the state's vehicle fleet, and improve the energy efficiency of state buildings. CARB's *2017 Scoping Plan* calls for California to reduce GHG emissions to 40% below 1990 levels, reduce petroleum use in vehicles by 50%, and achieve 50% renewable energy by 2030. By 2035 California will require that all new cars sold in the state be zero-emission vehicles (ZEVs). It is a leader in carbon cap-and-trade policy and building energy efficiency standards. California has made 90% of the total U.S. investment in clean transportation. Solar energy produces about 14% of California's energy. California provides leadership in climate change planning for the United States and other countries. It is a leader in the Under2 Coalition.

REGIONAL CLIMATE CHANGE PLANNING

Compact city-centered regions produce fewer carbon emissions than low-density sprawl. Suburbs account for approximately 50% of total U.S. GHG emissions. Compact metropolitan area development could arguably reduce vehicle miles traveled by 20 to 40% and reduce carbon dioxide (CO_2) emissions by 10% or more by 2050. Contrary to the popular perception, New York City is the greenest large city in the United States and the New York City metropolitan area one of the greenest large city regions in the world.

California has the most advanced regional climate change planning of any state. In 2008 California passed legislation requiring metropolitan planning organizations (MPOs) to plan land use, transportation, and air quality together—Senate Bill 375. The legislation requires every California MPO to develop a Sustainable Communities Strategy that integrates transportation, land use, and housing policies as part of their Regional Transportation Plan. Each of California's 18 MPOs must make plans to reduce per capita greenhouse gas emissions from passenger vehicles by 2035 to reach the target percentages set by CARB. These range as high as a 23% reduction.

LOCAL CLIMATE AND ENERGY PLANNING

Many U.S. cities and counties are working to reduce their carbon footprints, increase energy efficiency, and protect sequestered

BOX 17.2 DAVIS, CALIFORNIA'S *CLIMATE ACTION AND ADAPTATION PLAN*

University towns are often centers for innovation in environmental planning. The mix of "creative-class" residents, idealistic students, university experts, and progressive local governments sometimes produces innovations that are then diffused much more widely.

Davis, California—where the University of California, Davis is located—is an attractive university town of about 70,000 residents near the California state capital of Sacramento. It has been a pioneer in sustainable urban development and design with nature. In 2010 Davis became one of the first communities in the world to adopt a local climate action plan—the *Davis Climate Action and Adaptation Plan* (D-CAAP). D-CAAP illustrates local climate action planning and serves as a model for other communities. It illustrates concretely how local governments can "think globally and act locally".

Three years of effort preceded the adoption of D-CAAP in 2010. In 2007 the Davis City Council adopted *The Davis Climate Protection/Community Sustainability Strategy Framework* and created a 20-member Climate Action Team (CAT). Davis joined the International Council of Local Environmental Initiatives—Local Governments for Sustainability (ICLEI)—a global network of more than 2,500 local and regional governments committed to sustainable urban development and began following ICLEI's five-step program to reduce local GHG emissions:

1) establishing a baseline (inventory) (2007/2008);
2) setting reduction targets (2008);
3) identifying actions and adaptation strategies to achieve the targets (2009/2010);
4) ramping up environmental and energy programs they had pursued since 1958 after 2010; and
5) monitoring their activities to make sure the actions were effective and reexamining targets and actions based on results beginning as soon as the plan was adopted.

After three years of study, public hearings, and review of successive drafts the Davis City Council adopted the *Davis Climate Action and Adaptation Plan* in 2010.

D-CAAP adopted an ambitious greenhouse gas emission reduction target of reducing GHG emissions to their 1990 level by 2010 (well below California's state target, which was the toughest state standard). They planned to be carbon-neutral by 2050—then considered a wildly unrealistic goal, but now nearly universally acknowledged as necessary.

D-CAAP took the form of an amendment to Davis's general plan. It did not require an environmental impact report (EIR), because plans to reduce GHG emissions are categorically exempt under California's little NEPA—the California Environmental Quality Act (CEQA).

Vision statements express ambitious, often slightly utopian goals. D-CAAP's vision statement includes imagining:

- Alternative transportation as the "normal" way for Davis residents to travel;
- Fossil-fueled vehicles collectors' items, seen only in Davis's annual "sustainability days" parade;
- All residents living within walking/biking distance of essential services that allow them to meet their daily needs;
- Claiming the title "Healthiest City in America";
- A green business magnet, with green-collar jobs dominating the local economy;
- Ringed with community-based farms providing 25% of local food needs;

- A 50-megawatt community solar array on the outskirts of the city, fully meeting local electricity needs and exporting energy;
- Every household in Davis completing the Davis low-carbon diet challenge.

D-CAAP includes objectives and actions in nine areas:

1) mobility;
2) energy;
3) land use and buildings;
4) consumption and waste;
5) food and agriculture;
6) community engagement;
7) government operations;
8) advocacy; and
9) climate change preparation (adaptation).

The D-CAAP specifies five-year goals and objectives for each of the nine areas. For example, objectives for energy include: (1) reducing per household daily vehicle miles traveled (VMTs) by Davis residents by 10% from 2010 levels and increasing the overall efficiency of passenger vehicles operated by Davis residents by 5% over California's already-strict Corporate Average Fuel Efficiency (CAFE) standards. For each action D-CAAP provides estimates of the number of metric tons of GHG emissions the action is expected to eliminate.

Davis's self-study of sources of local GHG emissions found that 53% of Davis's GHGs were produced by transportation. Accordingly, the D-CAAP prioritizes bicycling, transit, walking, carpooling, and more efficient goods movement as strategies to reduce GHG emissions.

Each of the nine areas has five-year and long-term goals and objectives. These include reducing total energy use by 5%, achieving net zero energy use in all new buildings and homes, achieving zero waste, and increasing use of local food by 10%. Davis's general plan contains hundreds of policies to reduce GHG emissions that are consistent with the D-CAAP.

Davis has engaged citizens and the University of California, Davis in its plan implementation. The city manager's recommendation to the city council for adoption of a draft of the plan stated that the full value of the plan could only be achieved if the community buys in and develops a sense of ownership of the plan, so the plan places great importance on a well-designed, effectively executed community engagement program.

Since 2013 the University of California system—of which UC Davis is a part—has been committed to emitting net-zero GHGs from its buildings and vehicle fleet by 2025, something no other major university system is planning to do.

carbon. Dozens have adopted local climate action plans. Box 17.2 describes Davis, California's *Climate Action and Adaptation Plan*.

Following is a sampling of climate change reduction and adaptation strategies U.S. cities and counties have undertaken.

Urban Limit Lines and Compact City Form

City or county urban limit lines—also called urban growth boundaries—establish a limit within which all, or almost all, growth will be contained for a specified time. This encourages infill of vacant lots within the growth boundary and discourages sprawl on the urban fringe. More compact growth at higher average densities reduces commuting, pollution from automobiles and trucks, and GHG emissions.

Reducing and Mitigating the Impact of Sea-Level Rise

Many coastal cities have plans to mitigate the impacts of sea-level rise, require vulnerable buildings to be able to better withstand floods, and implement hard and soft land use and development strategies to reduce damage from flooding. New York City's 2013 post-Superstorm Sandy plan—*A Stronger, More Resilient New York*—details 250 potential hard and soft actions that will cost an estimated $19.5 billion to protect New York City from sea-level rise.

Municipal Energy Portfolio Efficiency Standards

Many cities with municipal power companies are changing their energy portfolios to reduce use of fossil fuels and increase use of solar, wind, and other clean and renewable energy technologies. They are doing this whether or not they are required to do so by the state where they are located.

Municipal Carbon Taxes

Boulder, Colorado levied a municipal Carbon Action Plan tax on residential, commercial, and industrial electricity consumption beginning in 2006. Boulder credits the CAP tax with reducing GHG emissions by 16%, reducing GHG emissions by between 250,000 and 750,000 metric tons, and raising over $17 million dollars between 2005 and 2019 to fund programs to address climate change.

Tree Planting

Living trees absorb and sequester carbon. Decomposing dead trees increase soil that sequesters carbon. New York, Chicago, Denver, and Los Angeles have undertaken "million tree" urban forestry programs, and many other cities, non-profit organizations—like San Francisco's Friends of the Urban Forest—and grassroots neighborhood organizations promote tree planting and urban forestry.

Reducing Heat-Absorbing Driveways, and Roads

Asphalt on streets and driveways is black and absorbs heat, contributing to urban heat islands, global warming, and heat inversions that can trap carbon close to the earth. Light-colored cement or asphalt streets and driveways or streets and driveways treated with a whitish surfacing agent can reflect heat and reduce these effects.

Cool Roofs and Green Roofs and Walls

White roofs reflect sunlight. Reflective roofs can reduce the amount of heat that roofs absorb. "Cool roofs" reduce how much heat roofs absorb, reduce the need for air conditioning, lower electricity consumption, and reduce GHG emissions. In 2013, Los Angeles amended their building code to require all new and refurbished homes to have cool roofs. California's Go Solar California project is investing $ 3.3 billion to subsidize a million solar roofs. New York City has an initiative to paint roofs with light-colored reflective paint—providing jobs as well as reducing global warming. Green roofs such as the roof of Chicago's City Hall (Figure 17.6) are layers of living vegetation installed on roofs, that can also absorb heat, sequester carbon, and provide other benefits.[13]

Building and Neighborhood Energy Efficiency Standards

Many cities and counties have adopted building codes based in whole or in part on Leadership in Energy and Environmental Design—(LEED)—model energy efficiency standards for buildings, issued by the United States Green Building Council (USGBC). Buildings meeting LEED standards save

Figure 17.6 Chicago City Hall Green Roof.

energy by being oriented towards the sun; requiring more effective insulation; requiring double-paned windows; and having heat-absorbing roofing materials to increase energy efficiency. Some jurisdictions build all public buildings to LEED silver, gold, or platinum standards. While most of the USGBC's efforts have focused on increasing energy efficiency in individual buildings, they also have created standards for neighborhood design to reduce energy consumption. LEED neighborhood planning standards can increase energy efficiency for entire neighborhoods.

Water Conservation

Municipal standards to conserve water include requirements for low-flow showerheads, faucets, and toilets in building codes for new construction. Older toilets typically use at least 3.6 gallons per flush, but low-flush toilets can use less than one gallon. Some jurisdictions require that existing water fixtures be retrofitted to current standards at the time a building is sold.

Minimizing paved surfaces, or requiring that surfaces be permeable, can reduce the volume of stormwater runoff. Vegetated swales—linear depressions in the earth beside roads, at the edges of parking lots and through neighborhoods—absorb stormwater. Onsite water retention ponds or pools can temporarily hold stormwater until it is absorbed into the ground or storm drains can handle it. The Village Homes neighborhood in Davis, California has experimented successfully with natural systems to hold and absorb water since the 1970s. The Netherlands has a large, planned system of polders—temporary or permanent water-retaining marshes and ponds.

Green Street Design

Green street designs include converting unneeded portions of street rights of ways into vegetated planting strips, road diets (reducing road widths) and bulb-outs (curb extensions where pedestrians cross at intersections) that can create land to support trees or other vegetation. Urban designers can improve street tree health by expanding permeable areas of soil and artificial surfaces below and around them. Complete streets designs often incorporate a green street component.

CORPORATE ENERGY PLANNING

Many private businesses are working to be more energy efficient and reduce GHG emissions. They do this either because they see this as in their long-term economic self-interest, for public relations purposes, or as a form a philanthropy. Some financial institutions encourage investment in clean energy. Morgan Stanley—a leading global financial services company—estimates that total investment in renewable energy will reach $5.1 trillion globally by 2030. They have created a climate change mitigation index and provide an online site with 125 individual metrics, grouped into 50 indicators to help investors assess potential climate change investment opportunities.

REDUCING HOUSEHOLD AND INDIVIDUAL ENERGY FOOTPRINTS

Even though they represent only 4% of the world's population, the 331 million residents of the United States can collectively significantly reduce global climate change. Each individual in the U.S. releases about 16 metric tons of carbon into the atmosphere annually—much more than the world average. Americans have greater economic wherewithal to reduce individual energy consumption than most of the 7.7 billion inhabitants of earth.

A carbon footprint is a measure of the total amount of carbon emissions that any population from a single individual, through the total population of earth produces. The size and composition of household carbon footprints vary dramatically depending on the number of people in the households; household income; geographic regions; and depending on the commitment of household members to reducing their carbon footprint. Carbon footprint calculators are tools that help individuals, governments, and companies calculate their carbon footprint and identify ways to reduce it. The online CoolClimate network carbon footprint calculator allows households to calculate the savings they can achieve by reducing the amount of carbon that the household uses through transportation, energy, water, waste, food, goods, and services the household uses. The UC Berkeley professors who created the CoolClimate footprint calculator—Christopher Jones and Daniel Kammen (2011)—conclude that large carbon footprint reduction that will save households money is possible across all household types, income brackets, and locations in the United States.

CLIMATE JUSTICE

Climate change disproportionately impacts vulnerable communities in which pollution and environmental damage have already exacerbated systemic racial, social, environmental, and economic injustices. Vulnerable communities often have greater exposure to floods, erosion, salinity, drought, heat waves, water scarcity, mudslides, and other climate-related hazards and extreme weather events than middle- and upper-income communities. They are less able to cope with and recover from damage than more affluent communities. Vulnerable communities have fewer resources to pay to protect themselves from climate damage. People and businesses in them are less likely to be adequately insured. Politically, vulnerable communities have less power to garner public resources for disaster recovery. Climate justice advocates are helping to reduce climate injustice by organizing communities to protect themselves from environmental racism, reporting to authorities on neighborhood environmental problems, protesting government neglect or bad decisions about protecting vulnerable communities from damage from climate change, suing polluters, and seeking change from responsible authorities.

Climate change impacts some countries much more than others. The poorest countries that have contributed the least to the climate crisis are among the most likely to be harmed. Almost three-quarters of global carbon emissions come from the G7 countries—just 7 of the 175 sovereign nations in the world. If emissions generated in developing countries from production of goods consumed in the G7 countries were attributed to the G7 countries (where they are consumed) rather than the country where they are produced, the imbalance would appear even greater.[14] Pacific Island nations and other low-lying countries are already suffering catastrophic impacts of climate change they did not cause. Planners working at the national and international level can help protect the interests of countries with low GDP in climate plans and policies.

SUMMARY

Anthropogenic climate change poses an imminent existential threat to planet earth. It is already too late to undo all the damage that failure to plan and take effective action to address climate change in the recent past has caused. Conditions will dramatically worsen during the lifetime of the current generation of planners. Mastering data and scientific climate change planning are necessary, but not sufficient. Action is necessary at every level.

Many more planners will need to work at very large scales—the level of regions, nation states, and the planet itself. Experts with skills in modeling complex systems and applying complexity in cities (CIC) theory to climate challenge are essential. However, climate change planning and policy making in the United States occurs mostly at the state and local level, so many more planners will work on climate change action planning at the subnational level. This is also true in other countries.

Climate change planning must be interdisciplinary. The ability to work in teams is essential. Even more than in other areas of planning, this will involve work with natural scientists—climatologists, biologists, oceanographers, glaciologists, and all manner of other natural science specialists and engineers. Some climate change planning will proceed under that name, but adapting to climate change needs to be an integral part of land use, transportation, environmental, infrastructure, energy and other kinds of planning.

Unless good ideas are translated into action, the best climate change planning will fail. The essence of the problem is political will. Mastering the politics of planning, advocacy, collaborative planning, mediation, and dispute resolution are all parts of the solution to the climate change puzzle.

So far, efforts at international cooperation to seriously address climate change at the global scale have failed. The Paris Climate Accord was too little, too late, and it is not being implemented. Whether the Biden administration in the USA and the leaders of the G7 and G20 countries will change course to seriously address climate change quickly enough is uncertain. It is possible to overcome the tragedy of the commons. Most countries will make reasonable contributions to reducing climate change if the USA, China, and other main contributors take action. Climate justice needs to happen from the level of nation states down to communities and individuals.

Uncertainty about climate change is not an excuse for inaction. There is plenty of reliable data on aspects of the climate change problem. The era of climate change denial is largely over, though many powerful corporations still oppose effective action to address climate change. What can be done to slow, mitigate, or adapt to climate change is well known. There are plenty of examples of exemplary national, state, and local plans and policies to reduce global warming, adapt to it, and mitigate its impacts. Planners at every level of government and in the non-profit and public sectors can play a significant role in addressing climate change.

CONCEPTS

20/20/20 Targets (European Union)
100-Year Floodplain

Anthropogenic Climate Change
Biomass
Cap-and-Trade Program
Climate Action Plan
Common but Differentiated Responsibility (for Reducing Carbon Emissions)
Emissions Gap
Energy Efficiency Standards
Green Roof
Greenhouse Gas (GHG) Emission
Hard Solution to Flooding
Intergovernmental Panel on Climate Change (IPCC)
Leadership In Energy and Environmental Design (LEED) Standards
National Determined Commitment (NDC)
Net Zero Carbon Emissions
Non-Renewable Energy Source
Organization of Petroleum Exporting Countries (OPEC)
Paris Climate Agreement
Renewable Energy Source
Resilient City
Soft Solution to Flooding
Sponge City
Under2 Coalition

PEOPLE

Senator James Imhof
Charles Keeling
Spencer Weart

NOTES

1   Reliable information on the science of climate change, and policies to address it, is synthesized by the United Nations Intergovernmental Panel on Climate Change (IPCC, 2021, 2019, 2014), U.S. Global Research Project (USGRP, 2017), and other reputable organizations such as the American Institute of Physics (AIP) (Weart, 2021), National Oceanographic and Aeronautics Administration (NOAA), and the U.S. Energy Information Administration (EIA). Online hubs of information on global climate change include sites maintained by NOAA (2021), RealClimate (2021), the Massachusetts Institute of Technology (2021), and the Climate Science Rapid Response Team (2021). Disinformation on global warming is in Imhofe (2012) and many other web-based and written sources. Climate change disinformation is described and critiqued in Oreskes & Conway (2011), Mann (2013), and Banerjee et al. (2015).

2   The UN Environmental Programme (UNEP) estimates that in 2018 about 55 $GtCO_2e$ of carbon were released into the atmosphere (UNEP, 2020). UNEP concluded that emissions in 2030 would need to be cut to approximately 41 $GtCO_2e$—a 26% gap between what will happen if current trends continue and what is necessary to hold global warming below 2°C and a 55% gap if the goal is to keep it below 1.5°C (ibid).

3   In 2017, China emitted 9.8 $GtCO_2e$ (9.8 billion billion tons equivalent of CO_2), and the USA emitted 5.3 $GtCO_2e$ of carbon. India was a distant third, emitting 2.5 $GtCO_2e$. All of the countries in Europe combined emit less CO_2 than either China or the United States.

4   Three inches of the total 8-inch rise in sea levels since 1900 has occurred since 1993 (USGCRP, 2017). The CSSR projects that sea levels will likely rise about 5 additional inches by 2030, 7 more inches by 2050, and 2½ feet by 2100. The most alarming CSSR finding is that gross mean sea-level rise (GMSLR) could be much higher than these projections—possibly exceeding 8 feet by 2100, which would alter life on earth beyond recognition.

5   Over four million people live in the Arctic. The average population density in the Arctic is low, and the its distribution is highly varied. Most human settlements are in coastal areas well below the North Pole. Greenland—a largely autonomous region of Denmark—has one-third the land area of the United States, but has only 50,000 residents. Antarctica is not a country. It has no government and no indigenous population. Fifty-four countries are parties to the 1961 Antarctic Treaty that declares the entire continent a scientific preserve. Planners working with sparse populations and scattered communities in the Arctic, Greenland, and alpine areas are trying to mitigate impacts, slow climate change, and help local communities adapt. However, these areas demand international climate change planning and concerted action that has not been forthcoming.

6   The Rockefeller Foundation's 100 Resilient Cities (100RC) project provided funds to 100 cities worldwide between 2013 and 2019, to pay the salary of a chief resilience officer and for resilience-related planning. Rotterdam, New York, New Orleans, and other cities with extensive experience of planning for and recovering from flooding and sea-level rise are part of the 100RC network. As of 2021, the Rockefeller Foundation is continuing to provide limited funding to 100RC network cities.

7   The Organization of Petroleum Exporting Countries (OPEC) is a global cartel composed largely of Arab countries. It was created in the 1960s, but became much more assertive in response to Israel's spectacular defeat of Egypt and allied Arab countries in the Arab–Israeli War of 1973 (the Yom Kippur War). OPEC embargoed much of the world's oil supply to punish the United States and its allies for aiding Israel. Federal, state, and local governments

responded with tough domestic measures to conserve oil and reduce U.S. dependency on imported foreign oil.
8 A combination of personnel error, design deficiencies, and component failures caused the Chernobyl nuclear disaster. For several months it appeared likely that the plume from Chernobyl could kill tens of millions of people in the Soviet Union and northwestern Europe and render millions of square miles uninhabitable for centuries. The USSR was able to keep the core of the Chernobyl reactor from melting only by dropping massive amounts of water from airplanes. Thousands of nearby inhabitants and the pilots sent to drop the water died of radiation from the disaster. Japanese planners made emergency plans to evacuate all of the Tokyo–Yokohama megacity region—the largest urban agglomeration in the world—but the meltdown was contained before they had to be implemented. The Fukushima Daiichi nuclear power plant disaster in Japan killed more than 18,000 people and cost the Japanese economy over US$187 billion dollars.
9 Three United Nations Intergovernmental Panel on Climate Change (IPCC) reports prepared by working groups that will form the basis for the 2022 *Sixth Assessment Report* are: *Climate Change 2021: The Physical Science Basis*; *Special Report on the Ocean and Cryosphere in a Changing Climate*; and *Climate Change and Land*. Together with the IPCC's 2019 report *Global Warming of 1.5°C*, they summarize the collective understanding of UN members and the experts they consulted through spring 2022. The IPCC's *Climate Change 2014: Synthesis Report* summarizes contributions of earlier working groups.
10 In 2015, during the Obama administration, the United States agreed to cut U.S. GHG emissions by 26% to 28% below their 2005 levels by 2025 and make best efforts to reduce U.S. emissions by 28% (NRDC, 2017). China agreed to have its carbon emissions peak no later than 2030, increase non-fossil fuels to 20% of their energy mix, and reduce carbon emissions per unit of gross domestic product (GDP) by 60 to 65 percent from 2005 levels by 2030 (ibid).
11 The Green Climate Fund's goal was to have a budget of $100 billion a year by 2020. The Paris Climate Accord extended the timeline to 2025. As of February 2020, 49 countries, regions, or cities had made some sort of pledge to the Green Climate Fund for a total of US$10.3 billion. Very little of the pledged money has actually been provided. Most is private sector investment, contributions that developed countries are already making in foreign aid, or in-kind (non-cash) contributions.
12 In 2005 Republican vice president Richard Cheney—the former CEO of Haliburton, the giant oil company that invented fracking and is the world's largest provider of fracking services—succeeded in getting Congress to pass what critics sarcastically call the "Haliburton Amendment" to the Safe Drinking Act, prohibiting the U.S. Environmental Protection Agency (EPA) from considering impacts of fracking when they review permits.
13 In addition to absorbing heat and sequestering carbon, green roofs can improve air quality, reduce urban heat islands, reduce energy use by insulating buildings, reduce stormwater runoff, extend the life of the roof, and provide rooftop gardens and areas from which to view other buildings. Green walls supporting vegetation such as ivy or edible plants have many of the same benefits.
14 IPCC, USGCRP, and national statistics on individual countries' carbon emissions look only at how much carbon the countries release by producing and consuming energy within their own borders. They do not include GHG emissions caused by goods consumed in the country that are produced in other countries. GHG emissions from a coal-powered Chinese factory to produce T-shirts exported to the USA appear as an addition to Chinese GHG emissions. If they were classified as a U.S. contribution to GHG emissions and subtracted from China's emissions, in national accounting, China's emissions would decrease, and the United States' emissions would increase. Since the G7 and G20 nations consume most of the world's goods, their contribution to GHG emissions and their responsibility would be much higher than national, IPCC, and USGCRP accounts now show if this method of accounting were used.

SUGGESTIONS FOR FURTHER LEARNING

Intergovernmental Panel on Climate Change (IPCC) and Other United Nations Reports: IPCC, *Climate change 2021* (2021). IPCC, *Climate change 2014* (2014). Ove Hoegh-Guldberg et al., *Impacts of 1.5°C global warming on natural and human systems* (2018). U.S. Energy Information Agency, *Emissions gap report 2020*. United Nations Environment Programme [website] (2021). United Nations Stockholm Convention [website] (2021). **U.S. Climate Change Reports:** U.S Global Change Research Program, *Fourth national climate assessment* (2018) and *Climate science special report (CSSR)* (2018). **Climate Change Skeptics and Deniers:** James Imhofe, *The greatest hoax* (2012). Naomi Oreskes, *Merchants of doubt* (2011). Michael Mann, *The hockey stick and the climate wars* (2013). Neela Banerjee et al. *Exxon: The road not taken* (2015). **Climate Change Overviews:** William McKibben, *Falter* (2020) and *The end of nature* (2006). Spencer Weart, *The discovery of global warming* (2008). Kerry Emanuel, *What we know about climate change* (2012). John Houghton, *Global warming* (2015). Joseph Romm, *Climate change* (2015). Elizabeth Kolbert, *The sixth extinction* (2014), *Field notes from a catastrophe* (2015), and *Under a white sky* (2021). Robert Henson, *The thinking person's guide to climate change* (2014).

Thomas Friedman, *Hot, flat, and crowded* (2009). Mark Lynas, *Six degrees: Our future on a hotter planet* (2008). David Wallace-Wells, *The uninhabitable earth* (2019). U.S. National Aeronautics and Space Administration (NASA), *Global warming from 1880 to 2020* (2021). **Climate Change Planning:** Al Gore, *An inconvenient truth*, *Our choice: A plan to solve the climate crisis* (2009), and *An inconvenient sequel* (2017). Paul Hawken, *Drawdown: The most comprehensive plan ever proposed to reverse global warming* (2017). Michael Boswell, *Climate action planning* (2019). **Sea-Level Rise:** Public Broadcasting System (PBS), *Sinking cities* series (London, New York, Tokyo, Jakarta, Miami, Venice, and other cities) [videos] (2021). British Broadcasting Corporation (BBC), *Sandy: Anatomy of a superstorm* [video] (2012). Arnold Armanafa, *Katrina: New Orleans' nightmare* [video] (2015). **Agriculture, Soil, and Climate Change:** *Kiss the Ground* [movie] (2020). **Climate Change Movies:** David Attenborough, *Climate crisis* (2019), *Planet earth* (2006), *Planet earth II* (2016), and *A life on our planet* (2020). **Resilient City Planning:** Lawrence Vale & Thomas Campanella, *The resilient city* (2005). Lawrence Vale, Resilient cities: Clarifying concept or catch-all cliché (2016). Peter Newman, Timothy Beatley, & Heather Boyer, *Resilient cities*, 2nd ed (2017). **Climate Justice:** Mary Robinson, *Climate justice* (2019). Michael Mendez, *Climate change from the streets* (2020). Mona Hanna-Attisha, *What the eyes don't see.* (2018). **Energy Planning:** John Randolph & Gilbert Masters, *Energy for sustainability* (2018). Stephen Peake (ed), *Renewable energy*, 4th ed (2018). Bent Sørensen, *Renewable energy* (2017). **Climate Change Websites:** The discovery of global warming [website created by Spencer Weart for the American Academy of Physics] (2021). NASA, NOAA, RealClimate.org, and ClimateRapidResponse websites have additional information on climate change.

BIBLIOGRAPHY

1000 Friends of Oregon (2008). *Blueprint for Oregon's future*. Portland, OR: 1000 Friends of Oregon.
1000 Friends of Oregon (2021). 1000 Friends of Oregon website. Retrieved 4/12/21 from https://friends.org/.
Aaron, H. (1972). *Shelter and subsidies: Who benefits from federal housing policies?* Washington, D.C.: Brookings Institution.
Abbott, C. (2016). *Imagining urban futures: Cities in science fiction and what we might learn from them*. Middletown, CN: Wesleyan University Press.
Abbott, C. (2018). Metro regional government. *The Oregon Encyclopedia*. Retrieved 2/8/21 from https://oregonencyclopedia.org/articles/metro/#.XgduItZKh0I.
Abercrombie, P. (1933). *Town and country planning*. London, GB: Thornton Butterworth.
Abrams, C. (1966). *The city is the frontier*. New York City, NY: Harper & Row.
Abu-Lughod, J. (1991). *Before European hegemony: The world system A.D. 1250–1350*. Oxford, GB: Oxford University Press.
Abu-Lughod, J. (2017 [1999]). Global city formation in New York, Chicago and Los Angeles: A historical perspective. In X. Ren & R. Keil (eds), *The globalizing city reader*, 2nd ed (pp. 53–59). Abingdon, GB and New York City, NY: Routledge.
Adams, T. (1935). *Outline of town and city planning*. New York City, NY: Russell Sage Foundation.
Adams, T. et al. (1929). *Regional plan of New York and its environs*. New York City, NY: Russell Sage Foundation.
Adley, P. (ed) (2017). *The Routledge handbook of mobilities*. Abingdon, GB and New York City, NY: Routledge.
Agyeman, J. & Erickson, J. (2012). Culture, recognition, and the negotiation of difference: Some thoughts on cultural competency in planning education. *Journal of Planning Education and Research*, 32(3), 358–366.
Agyeman, J., Bullard, R., & Evans, B. (2002). Exploring the nexus: Bringing together sustainability, environmental justice and equity. *Space & Polity*, 6(1), 77–90.
Agyeman, J., Bullard, R., & Evans, R. (2003). *Just sustainabilities*. Cambridge, MA: Massachusetts Institute of Technology Press.
Ahrentzen, S. & Steiner, R. (2019). *Housing models for aging in community*. Abingdon, GB and New York City, NY: Routledge.
Al, S. (2018). *Adapting cities to sea level rise*. Washington, D.C.: Island Press.
Alba, R. (2005). Bright and blurred boundaries: Second-generation assimilation and exclusion in France, Germany, and the United States. *Ethnic and Racial Studies*, 28(1), 20–49.
Allmendinger, P. (2017). *Planning theory*, 3rd ed. New York City, NY: Palgrave Macmillan.
Almy, D. & Benedikt, M. (2007). *Center 14: On landscape urbanism*. Austin, TX: University of Texas, Austin School of Architecture.
Alterman, R. (2017). From a minor to a major profession: Can planning and planning theory meet the challenges of globalization? *Transactions of the Association of European Schools of Planning*, 1, 1–17.
Alterman, R. & Cygal Pellach, C. (eds) (2021) *Regulating coastal zones: International perspectives on land management instruments*. Abingdon, GB and New York City, NY: Routledge.
Amazon.com (2021). Best sellers in tiny house kits. Retrieved 4/21/21 from www.amazon.com/Best-Sellers-Garden-Outdoor-Tiny-House-Kits/zgbs/lawn-garden/21424006011.
American Bar Association (ABA) (2016). *Model rules of professional conduct*, Rule 12. Chicago, IL: ABA.
American Institute of Architects (AIA) (2021). AIA website. Retrieved 1/14/21 from www.aia.org/.
American Institute of Certified Planners (AICP) (2016). *AICP code of ethics and professional conduct*. Chicago, IL: AICP.
American Institute of Certified Planners (AICP) (2021). AICP website. Retrieved 1/16/21 from www.planning.org/aicp/.
American Planning Association (APA) (2017). National Planning Pioneers. Retrieved 1/19/21 from www.planning.org/awards/pioneers/.
American Planning Association (APA) (2018). APA 2018 salary survey. Retrieved 2/23/21 from www.planning.org/salary/.
American Planning Association (APA) (2018). *APA diversity and inclusion strategy*. Chicago,

IL and Washington, D.C.: APA. Retrieved 2/20/21 from www.planning.org/ media/document/9149453/.
American Planning Association (APA) (2018). Diversity efforts. Chicago, IL and Washington, D.C.: APA. Retrieved 2/20/21 from www.planning.org/diversity/forum/.
American Planning Association (APA) (2019). *Annual Report*. Chicago: APA www.planning.org/annualreport/.
American Planning Association (APA) (2019). Equity diversity inclusion. Chicago, IL and Washington, D.C.: APA. Retrieved 2/20/21 from www.planning.org/diversity/.
American Planning Association (2021). A path to an enlightened planning future. Retrieved 1/12/21 from https://planning.org/blog/9209666/path-to-an-enlightened-planning-future/.
American Planning Association (APA) (2021). American planning history since 1900 [slideshow]. Retrieved 1/18/21 from www.planning.org/timeline/.
American Planning Association (APA) (2021). APA dashboard. Retrieved 1/12/21 from www.planning.org/dashboard/.
American Planning Association (APA) (2021). APA website. Retrieved 4/5/21 from www.planning.org/.
American Planning Association (2021) Divisions. Retrieved 1/12/21 from https://planning.org/divisions/.
American Planning Association (APA) (2021). Economic development division website. Retrieved 3/16/21 from www.planning.org/divisions/economic/.
American Planning Association (APA) (2021). Latinos and planning division. Retrieved 2/23/21 from www.planning.org/divisions/latinos/.
American Planning Association (APA) (2021). LGBTQ and planning. Retrieved 2/20/21 from www.planning.org/divisions/lgbtq/.
American Planning Association (APA) (2021). National Planning Awards. Retrieved 2/1/21 from www.planning.org/awards.
American Planning Association (APA) (2021). Planning and the Black community division. Retrieved 2/23/21 from https://blackcommunity.planning.org/.
American Planning Association (APA) (2021). Planning and women. Retrieved 2/22/21 from www.planning.org/divisions/planningandwomen/.
American Planning Association (APA) (2021). Research KnowledgeBase. Retrieved 1/29/21 from https://planning.org/ knowledgebase/.
American Planning Association (APA) (2021). Sustaining Places Initiative. Retrieved 2/10/21 from https://planning.org/sustainingplaces/.
American Planning Association (APA) (2021). Tribal planning and indigenous interest group. Retrieved 2/23/21 from www.planning.org/divisions/groups/tribal/.
American Planning Association (APA) (2021). Women and planning division. Retrieved 2/20/21 from https://women.planning.org/.
American Public Transportation Association (APTA) (2020). *APTA 2020 Public transportation fact book*. Washington, D.C.: APTA
American Society of Civil Engineers (ASCE). ASCE website. Retrieved 1/14/21 from www.asce.org/.
American Society of Landscape Architects (ASLA) (2021). ASLA website. Retrieved 1/14/21 from www.asla.org/.
Anacker, K. et al. (2018). *Introduction to housing* (pp. 255–272). Athens, GA: University of Georgia Press.
Anacker, K., Nguyen, M., & Varady, D. (2019). *Routledge handbook of housing policy and planning*. Abingdon, GB and New York City, NY: Routledge.
Anderson, M. (1964). *The federal bulldozer*. New York City, NY: McGraw-Hill.
Andrew, J, Greenlee, A, Jackson, A, Garcia Zambrana, I, Lee, A. & Chrisinger, B. (2018). *ACSP-POCIG Climate survey: Summary of findings*. Retrieved 1/16/21 from https://cdn. ymaws.com/www.acsp.org/resource/resmgr/docs/pocig/pocig_climate_survey_summary.pdf.
Angel, S. (2010). *Planet of cities*. Cambridge, MA and Washington, D.C.: Lincoln Land Institute and Brookings Institution Press.
Angel, S. (2020). *The anatomy of density* [video]. Retrieved 2/12/21 from www.youtube.com/watch?v=y99wA1JOOGg.
Angel, S., Parent, J., Civco, D., & Blei, A. (2012). *Atlas of urban expansion*. Cambridge, MA: Lincoln Land Institute.
Annie E. Casey Foundation. (2015). *Race equity and inclusion and action guide*. Baltimore, MD: Annie E. Casey Foundation.
Anthony, K. (1983). The major themes in the work of Donald Appleyard. *Environment and Behavior*, 15(4), 411–418.
Appalachian Regional Commission (ARC) (2015). *Investing in Appalachia's future*. Retrieved 4/18/21 from www.arc.gov.
Appleyard, B. (2020). *Livable streets 2.0*. Amsterdam, NL: Elsevier.
Appleyard, D. (1981). *Livable streets*. Berkeley, CA: University of California Press.
Appleyard, D., Lynch, K., & Mayer, J. (1965). *The view from the road*. Cambridge, MA: Massachusetts Institute of Technology Press.
Arefi, M. (2014). *Deconstructing placemaking: Needs, opportunities, and assets*. London, GB and New York City, NY: Routledge.
Argonne National Laboratory (ANL) (2010). *Well-to-wheels analysis of energy use and greenhouse gas emissions of plug-in hybrid electric vehicles*. Oak Ridge, TN: Argonne National Laboratory.

Argyris, C. (1982). *Reasoning, learning, and action: Individual and organizational.* San Francisco, CA: Jossey-Bass.

Argyris, C. & Schön, D.A. 1978. *Organizational learning: A theory of action perspective.* Reading, MA: Addison-Wesley.

Arlington County Virginia (2020). *The Columbia Pike Special Revitalization District form-based code.* Retrieved 6/11/21 from https://arlingtonva.s3.dualstack.us-east-1.amazonaws.com/wp-content/uploads/sites/31/2016/12/2016-FBC-Reprint-for-web.pdf

Armitage, R. & Ekblom, P. (eds) (2019). *Rebuilding crime prevention through environmental design.* Abingdon, GB and New York City, NY: Routledge

Arnold, J. (1971). *The New Deal in the suburbs: A history of the Greenbelt Town Program, 1935–1954.* Columbus, OH: Ohio State University Press.

Arnstein, S. (1969). A ladder of citizen participation. *Journal of the American Planning Association*, 35(4), 216–224.

Asset-Based Community Development Institute (abcd Institute) (2021). Chicago, IL: DePaul University. Retrieved 3/10/21 from https://resources.depaul.edu/abcd-institute/Pages/default.aspx

Association of Collegiate Schools of Planning (ACSP) (2017).Values statement. Retrieved 4/28/21 from www.acsp.org/page/ValueStatement.

Association of Collegiate Schools of Planning (ACSP) (2021). ACSP website. Retrieved 4/5/21 from http://acps.org.

Association of Collegiate Schools of Planning (ACSP) (2021). Anti-racism within ACSP. Retrieved 1/20/21 from https://www.acsp.org/page/AntiRacismWithinACSP.

Association of Collegiate Schools of Planning (ACSP) (2021). Faculty Women's Interest Group (FWIG) website. Retrieved 1/22/21 from acsp.org/page/FacultyWomen.

Association of Collegiate Schools of Planning (ACSP) (2021). Planners of Color Interest Group (POCIG). Retrieved 5/25/21 from www.acsp.org/page/POCIG_History.

Association of Collegiate Schools of Planning (ACSP) (2021). Tribal and Indigenous Planning Interest Group. Retrieved 4/29/21 from www.planning.org/divisions/groups/tribal/.

Association of European Schools of Planning (AESOP) (2021). AESOP website. Retrieved 4/5/21 from www.aesop-planning.eu/.

Atlas, R. (2013). *21st century security and CPTED: Designing for critical infrastructure protection and crime prevention*, 2nd ed. Boca Raton, FL: CRC Press.

Atwood, M. (2004). *Oryx and Crake.* New York City, NY: Anchor.

Austin, G. & Yu, K. (2016). *Constructed wetlands and sustainable development.* London, GB and New York City, NY: Routledge.

Auto Alliance (2020). Auto Alliance website. Retrieved 10/21/20 from https://autoalliance.org/innovation/.

Babcock, R. (1974). *Exclusionary zoning.* New York City, NY: Praeger.

Bachrach, P. & Baratz, M. (1962). Two faces of power. *American Political Science Review*, 56(4), 947–952.

Badger, E., Quealy, K. & Katz, J. (2021, March 17). Close-up picture of partisan segregation, among 180 million voters. *The New York Times*. Retrieved 4/16/21 from www.nytimes.com/interactive/2021/03/17/upshot/partisan-segregation-maps.html.

Ballard, J. (1962). *The drowned world.* New York City, NY: Doubleday.

Ballotopedia (2018). State environmental policy acts. Retrieved 3/14/21 from https://ballotpedia.org/State_environmental_policy_acts.

Banerjee, N. et al. (2015). Exxon: The road not taken. *Inside Climate News*. Retrieved 3/18/21 from https://insideclimatenews.org/book/exxon-the-road-not-taken/.

Banerjee, T. & Loukaitou-Sideris, A. (eds) (2011). *Companion to urban design.* London, GB and New York City, NY: Routledge.

Banerjee, T. & Southworth, M. (eds) (1995). *City sense and city design: Writings and projects of Kevin Lynch.* Cambridge, MA: Massachusetts Institute of Technology Press.

Banfield, E. & Meyerson, M. (1964). *Politics, planning, and the public interest.* Glencoe, IL: Free Press.

Barbaux, S. (2016). *Sponge city.* Mulgrave, AU: Images Publishing Distributors/AC.

Barclay, C. & Gray, M. (2020). *California land use and planning law*, 37th ed. Point Arena, CA: Solano Press.

Barnett, J. (1982). *Introduction to urban design.* New York City, NY: Harper & Row.

Barnett, J. (2008). *Redesigning cities: Principles, practices, implementation.* Abingdon, GB and New York City, NY: Routledge.

Barnett, J. (2016). *City design: Modernist, traditional, green, and systems perspectives*, 2nd ed. Abingdon, GB and New York City, NY: Routledge.

Barnett, J. (2020). *Designing the megaregion: Meeting urban challenges at a new scale.* Washington, D.C.: Island Press.

Barnett, J. & Beasley, L. (2015). *Ecodesign for cities and suburbs*, 2nd ed. Washington, D.C.: Island Press.

Barth, G. (1975). *Instant cities.* Oxford, GB: Oxford University Press.

Bassett, E. (1938). *The master plan.* New York City, NY: Russell Sage Foundation.

Batty, M. (2012). Smart cities, big data. *Environment and Planning B: Urban Analytics and City Science*, 39, 191–193.

Batty, M. (2013). A theory of city size. *Science*, 340(1639), 1418–1419.

Batty. M. (2015). Cities in a completely urbanized world. *Planning and design*, 42(3), 481–483.

Batty, M. (2017). *The new science of cities*. Cambridge, MA: Massachusetts Institute of Technology Press.

Batty, M. (2020). The smart city. In R. LeGates & F. Stout (eds), *The city reader*, 7th ed (pp. 503–515). Abingdon, GB and New York City, NY: Routledge.

Bauer, K. (2009). *City planning for civil engineers, environmental engineers, and surveyors*. Boca Raton, FL: CRC Press.

Bay Conservation and Development Commission (BCDC) (2021). *San Francisco Bay plan*. Retrieved 5/25/21 from www.bcdc.ca.gov/plans/sfbay_plan.html.

Beasley, L. (2020). *Vancouverism*. Vancouver, BC: University of British Columbia Press.

Beatley, T. (2002). *An introduction to coastal zone management*. Washington, D.C.: Island Press.

Beatley T. (2009). *Planning for coastal resilience: Best practices for calamitous times*. Washington, D.C.: Island Press.

Beatley, T. (2010) *Biophilic cities: Integrating nature into urban design and planning*. Washington, D.C.: Island Press.

Beatley, T. (2014). *Blue urbanism*. Washington, D.C.: Island Press.

Beatley, T. *Blue biophilic cities* (2017). London, GB and New York City, NY: Palgrave Macmillan.

Beauregard, R. (2018). *Cities in the urban age*. Chicago, IL: University of Chicago Press.

Beauregard, R. (2020). *Advanced introduction to planning theory*. Cheltenam, GB and Northhampton, MA: Edward Elgar Press.

Beevers, R. (1988). *The garden city utopia: A critical biography of Ebenezer Howard*. New York City, NY: St. Martin's.

Bellamy, E. (1888). *Looking backward*. Cambridge, MA: Harvard University Press.

Berkes, F. (2015). *Coasts for people*. London, GB and New York City, NY: Routledge

Berlin, I. (1992). *Slaves without masters: The free Negro in the antebellum South*. New York City, NY: Free Press.

Berlin, I. (2018). *The long emancipation: The demise of slavery in the United States*. Cambridge, MA: Harvard University Press.

Berry, B. (1964). Cities as systems within systems of cities. *Regional Science*, 13(1), 147–163.

Berry, B. (1987). *Economic geography: Resource use, locational choices*. Englewood Cliffs, NJ: Prentice-Hall.

Berry, B., Conkling., E, & Ray., M. (1992). *The global economy: Resource use, locational choice, and international trade*. New York City, NY: Pearson.

Berry, B. & Horton, F. (1970). *Geographic perspectives on urban systems: With integrated readings*. Englewood Cliffs, NJ: Prentice-Hall.

Berry, B. & Pred, A. (1965). *Central place studies: A bibliography of theory and applications*. Philadelphia: Regional Science Institute.

Bielo, D. (2009, December 8). Peat and repeat: Can major carbon sinks be restored by rewetting the world's drained bogs? *Scientific American*.

Biles, R. (2011). *The fate of cities: Urban America and the federal government 1945–2000*. Lawrence, KS: University of Kansas Press.

Biraben, J. & Langeney, A. (1980). An essay concerning mankind's evolution. Paris, FR: Institut National d'Études Demographiques.

Blakeley, E. & Snyder, M. (1997). *Fortress America*. Washington, D.C: Brookings Institution Press.

Bloomberg Finance L.P. & the Business Council for Sustainable Energy (2021). *Sustainable energy in America factbook* (2021). New York City, NY: Bloomberg Finance L.P. and the Business Council for Sustainable Energy. Retrieved 3/18/21 from https://bcse. org/factbook/.

Boardman, P. (2017). *Patrick Geddes: Maker of the future*. Chapel Hill, NC: University of North Carolina Press.

Boehm, L. & Corey, S. (2014). *America's urban history*. Abingdon, GB and New York, NY: Routledge.

Boeing, G. (2017). OSMnx: New methods for aquiring, constructing, analyzing, and visualizing complex street networks. *Computers, Environment and Urban Systems*, 65, 136–139. doi:10.1016/compenvurbsys.2017.05.004.

Bohl, C. & Cusumano, G. (2002). *Place making: Developing town centers, main streets, and urban villages*. Washington, D.C.: Urban Land Institute.

Boileau, I. (1959). La ciudad lineal: A critical study of the linear suburb of Madrid. *Journal of the Society of Architectural Historians*, 181(2), 230–238.

Bordoff, J., Linn, J., & Losz, A. (2018). *Making sense of the Trump administration's fuel economy standard rollback*. Washington, D.C.: Resources for the Future.

Bosselmann, P. (2008). *Urban transformation: Understanding city form and design*. Washington, D.C.: Island Press.

Boston, T. & Ross, C. (eds) (1997). *The inner city: Urban poverty and economic development in the next century*. Abingdon, GB and New York City, NY: Routledge.

Boswell, M., Greve, A., & Seale, T. (2019). *Climate action planning: Guide to creating low-carbon, resilient communities*. Washington, D.C.: Island Press.

Boulder, CO (2019). Cap tax. Retrieved 3/18/21 from https://bouldercolorado.gov/climate/climate-action-plan-cap-tax.

Bourguignon, F. & Morrisson, C. (2002). Inequality among world citizens: 1820–1992. *American Economic Review*, 92(54), 727–744.

Boyce, D. (2020). Walter Isard (1919–2010): Founding father of regional science. In P. Batey & E. Plane (eds), *Great minds in regional science*, vol 1 (pp. 15–24). Berlin, DE: Springer.

Boyd, I., Freer-Smith, P., Gilligan, C., & Godfray, H. (2013). The consequence of tree pests and diseases for ecosystem services, *Science*, 6160, 823–834.

Boyer, B. (1973). *Cities destroyed for cash*. Chicago: Follett.

Boyer, M.C. (1983). *Dreaming the rational city: The myth of American city planning*. Cambridge, MA: Massachusetts Institute of Technology Press.

Boyle, G. (ed) (2012). *Renewable energy for a sustainable future*, 3rd ed. Oxford, GB and New York City, NY: Oxford University Press.

Boyle, R. & Mohamed, R. (2007). State growth management, smart growth and urban containment: A review of the U.S. and a study of the heartland. *Journal of Environmental Planning and Management*, 50(5), 677–697.

Bracken, I. (2007). *City and regional planning methods: Research and policy analysis*. Abingdon, GB and New York, NY: Routledge.

Bradford, E. (2008). *Free African American population in the U.S. 1790–1860*. Charlottesville, VA: University of Virginia Library Retrieved 1/15/2021 from www.ncpedia.org/sites/default/files/census_stats_1790-1860.pdf.

Bradshaw, C. et al. (2021). Underestimating the challenges of avoiding a ghastly future. *Frontiers of Conservation Science*, 1, 1–10.

Bratt, R., Stone, M., & Hartman, C. (2006). *A right to housing*. Philadelphia, PA: Temple University Press.

Brenner, N. (2013). *Implosions/explosions: Towards a planetary urbanization*. Berlin, DE: Jovis.

Brenner, N. (2019). *New urban spaces: Urban theory and the scale question*. Oxford, GB: Oxford University Press.

Brenner, N. & Keil, R. (2006). *The global cities reader*. London, GB and New York City, NY: Routledge.

Brenner, N. & Keil, R. (2020 [2015]). From global cities to globalized urbanization. In R. LeGates & F. Stout (eds), *The city reader*, 7th ed (pp. 699–708). Abingdon, GB and New York City, NY: Routledge.

Bridenbaugh, C. (1938). *Cities in the wilderness: The first century of urban life in America 1625–1742*. New York City, NY: Knopf.

Brinkley, C. & Hoch, C. (2021). The ebb and flow of planning specializations. *Journal of Planning Education and Research*, 41(1), 79–93. Retrieved 3/16/21 from https://journals-sagepub-com.jpllnet.sfsu.edu/doi/pdf/10.1177/0739456X18774119.

Brooks, M. (1993). A plethora of paradigms? *Journal of the American Planning Association*, 59(2), 142–143.

Brooks, M. (2002). *Planning theory for practitioners*. Abingdon, GB and New York City, NY: Routledge.

Brooks, R., Plante, C., & Hayes, D. (2017). Something for nothing? *Journal of Government Financial Management*, 66(3), 48–54. Retrieved 3/16/21 from http://web.a.ebscohost.com.jpllnet.sfsu.edu/ehost/pdfviewer/pdfviewer?vid=1&sid=8229c177-4cc7-414c-8fab-ed978ef776c8%40sessionmgr4008.

Brouillard, C. & van Pelt, S. (2020). *A community takes charge: Boulder's carbon tax*. Retrieved 5/5/21 from www-static.bouldercolorado.gov/docs/community-takes-charge-boulders-carbon-tax-1-201305081136.pdf.

Brown, L., Dixon, D., & Gillham, O. (2009). *Urban design for an urban century: Placemaking for people*. Hoboken, NJ: Wiley.

Brugemann, R. (2008). *Sprawl: A compact history*. Chicago, IL: University of Chicago Press.

Bruegmann, R. (2016). Sprawl. *International Encyclopedia of the Social Sciences*, 2nd ed, vol. 24, 934–939.

Bruhn, J. (2011). *The sociology of community connections*. Berlin, DE and New York City, NY: Springer.

Bruner Foundation (2021). Rudy Bruner award for urban excellence. Retrieved 1/29/21 from Rudy Bruner Foundation awards website: www.rudybruneraward.org/.

Buder, S. (1990). *Visionaries and planners: The garden city movement and the modern community*. Oxford, GB: Oxford University Press.

Burchell, R., Downs, A., McCann, B., & Mukherji, S. (2005). *Sprawl costs: Economic impacts of unchecked development*. Washington, D.C.: Island Press.

Bureau of Labor Statistics (BLS) (2018). *Standard Occupational Classification System* (SOCS). Washington, D.C.: United States Department of Labor (DOL): Retrieved 3/17/21 from www.bls.gov/soc.

Bureau of Land Management (BLM) (2019). *Public land statistics*. Washington, D.C.: BLM. Retrieved 3/11/21 from www.blm.gov/sites/blm.gov/files/PublicLandStatistics2019.pdf.

Bureau of Transportation Statistics (BTS) (2018). *Highway fatalities by mode, 2018*. Washington, D.C. United States Department of Transportation (DOT). Retrieved 2/24/21 from www.bts.gov/content/transportation-fatalities-mode.

Bureau of Transportation Statistics (BTS) (2021). BTS website. Retrieved 2/28/21 from www.bts.gov.

Burnham, D. & Bennett, E. (1909). *Plan of Chicago*. Chicago, IL: Chicago Commercial Club.

Cabet, É. (1842). *Voyage en Icarie* [Voyage to Icarus]. Paris: Mallet.

Calavita, N. & Mallach, A. (2010). *Inclusionary housing in international perspective*. Cambridge, MA: Lincoln Institute of Land Policy.

California Air Resources Board (CARB) (2017). *Climate change scoping plan: A strategy for achieving California's 2030 greenhouse gas target*. Sacramento, CA: CARB. Retrieved 3/19/21 from https://ww2.arb.ca.gov/sites/default/files/classic//cc/scopingplan/scoping_plan_2017.

California Air Resources Board (CARB) (2021). California reformulated gasoline program. Retrieved 3/1/21 from https://ww2.arb.ca.gov/our-work/programs/gasoline/about.

California Building Energy Efficiency Standards (2019). *California code of regulations*. Sacramento, CA: State of California. Retrieved 3/18/21 from www.energy.ca.gov/programs-and-topics/programs/building-energy-efficiency-standards/2019-building-energy-efficiency.

California Constitution (1850). Retrieved 1/23/21 from https://archives.cdn.sos.ca.gov/pdf/1849-california-constitution-for-website-9-16-20.pdf.

California Constitution (1879). Chapter 490, California Statutes of 1877–78. Retrieved 1/23/21 from https://archives.cdn.sos.ca.gov/collections/1879/archive/1879-constitution.pdf.

California Government Code (2021). Authority for and scope of general plans. Title 7, Division 1, Chapter 3, Article 5, Sections 65300–65303.4. Retrieved 2/2/21 from https://law.justia.com/codes/california/2018/code-gov/title-7/division-1/chapter-3/article-5/.

California Governor's Office of Planning and Research (OPR) (2011). *Planning, zoning, and development laws*. Sacramento, CA: OPR. Retrieved 4/15/21 from https://opr.ca.gov/docs/complete_pzd_2011.pdf.

California Governor's Office of Planning and Research (OPR) (2017). General plan guidelines: 2017 update. Sacramento, CA: OPR. Retrieved 5/12/20 from http://www.opr.ca.gov/planning/general-plan/guidelines.html.

California Governor's Office of Planning and Research (OPR) (2021). OPR website. Retrieved 4/12/21 from www.opr.ca.gov/.

California League of Cities (CLC) (2020). CLC website. Retrieved 1/23/21 from www.cacities.org/.

California Planning and Zoning Law (2018). *California government code*, sections 65000–66035. Retrieved 4/11/21 from https://law.justia.com/codes/california/2011/gov/title-7/.

California Subdivision Map Act (2018). *California government code*. Title 7, Planning and land use, Division 2, Subdivisions 66410–66499. Retrieved 4/11/21 from https://law.justia.com/codes/california.

California's Global Warming Solutions Act (AB 32) (2006). *California health and safety code*, sections 38500 et seq. Retrieved 2/18/21 from https://leginfo.legislature.ca.gov/faces/codes_displaySection.xhtml?sectionNum=38500&lawCode=HSC.

Callenbach, E. (1975). *Ecotopia*. New York City, NY: Bantam.

Callenbach, E. (1979). *Ecotopia emerging*. New York City, NY: Bantam.

Callenbach, E. (1980). *The Ecotopian encyclopedia for the 1980s*. Berkeley, CA: And/Or Press.

Callies, D., Freilich, R., & Saxer, S. (2017). *Cases and materials on land use*, 7th ed. Eagen, MN: West Academic Publishing Company.

Calthorpe, P. (1993). *The next American metropolis: Ecology, community, and the American dream*. Hudson, NY: Princeton Architectural Press.

Calthorpe, P. (2013) *Urbanism in the age of climate change*. Washington D.C.: Island Press.

Calthorpe, P. (2017). *Seven principles for building better cities*. Retrieved 1/29/21 from www.ted.com/talks/peter_calthorpe_7_principles_for_building_better_cities.

Campbell, S. (2021). Planning history timeline: A chronology of events. Retrieved 1/19/21 from www-personal.umich.edu/~sdcamp/timeline.html.

canadianuniversities.net (2021). Canada urban and regional planning programs. Retrieved 1/17/21 from www.canadianuniversities.net/Universities/Programs/Urban_and_Regional_Planning.html.

Carmona, M. (2002). *Haussmann*. New York City, NY: Ivan R. Dee.

Carmona, M., Heath, T., Oc, T., & Tiesdell, S. (2010). *Public places urban spaces: The dimensions of urban design*, 2nd ed. Abingdon, GB and New York City, NY: Routledge.

Carmona, M. & Tiesdell, S. (eds) (2007). *The urban design reader*. Oxford, GB: Architectural Press.

Carson, R. (1962) *Silent spring*. New York City, NY: Houghton Mifflin.

Castells, M. (1977). *The urban question*. Translated by A. Sheridan. Cambridge: Massachusetts Institute of Technology Press. Originally published as *La question urbaine*. Paris, FR: François Maspero (1972).

Castells, M. (1983). *The city and the grassroots*. Berkeley, CA: University of California Press.

Castells, M. (1996). *The information age: Economy, society and culture*, vol I: *The rise of the network society*. Malden, MA: Blackwell.

Castells, M. (1997). *The information age: Economy, society and culture*, vol II: *The power of identity*. Malden, MA: Blackwell.

Castells, M. (1997). *The information age: Economy, society and culture*, vol III: *End of millennium*. Malden, MA: Blackwell.

Castro, J. (2017). Housing as a platform for opportunity. Washington, D.C: U.S. Department of Housing and Urban Development.

Castro, J. (2018). *An unlikely journey: Waking up from my American dream*. New York City, NY: Little, Brown.

Center for Applied Transect Studies (CATS) (2021). The transect. Retrieved 2/17/21 from https://transect.org/transect.html.

Center for Applied Transect Studies (CATS) (undated). *SmartCode Version 9.2*. Retrieved 1/29/21 from http://smartcodecentral.com.

Center for Biological Diversity (CBD) (2021). CBD website. Retrieved 3/14/21 from www.biologicaldiversity.org/.

Center for Climate and Security (CCS) (2019). *World climate and security report 2020*. Retrieved 3/19/21 from https://climateandsecurity.org/wp-content/uploads/2020/02/world-climate-security-report-2019_2_13.pdf.

Center for Climate Policy Resilience (CCR) (2021). State climate policy maps. www.c2es.org/content/state-climate-policy/.

Center for Community Change (CCC) (2016). *Opening doors to homes for all: The 2016 Housing Trust Fund survey report*. Washington, D.C.: CCC.

Cervero, R. (1989). Jobs–housing balancing and regional mobility. *Journal of the American Planning Association*, 55(2), 136–150.

Cervero, R. (1996). Jobs–housing balance revisited: Trends and impacts in the San Francisco Bay Area. *Journal of the American Planning Association*, 62(4), 492–511.

Cervero, R. (1998). *The transit metropolis*. Washington, D.C.: Island Press.

Cervero, R., Guerra, E., & Al, S. (2017). *Beyond mobility: Planning cities for people and places*. Washington, D.C.: Island Press.

Chadwick, G. (1971). *A system view of planning: Towards a theory of the urban and regional planning process*. Oxford, GB: Pergamon.

Chappell, M. (2020). The strange career of urban homesteading: Low-income homeownership and the transformation of American housing policy in the late 20th century. *Journal of Urban History*, 46(4), 747–774.

Chapple, K. (2017). Gentrification, displacement, and the role of public investment. *Journal of Planning Literature*, 33(1), 31–44.

Charnock, G. & Starosta, C. (eds) (2016). *The new international division of labour: Global transformation and uneven development*. Basingstoke, GB: Palgrave Macmillan.

Checkoway, B. & Davidoff, P. (1994). Advocacy planning in retrospect. *Journal of the American Planning Association*, 60(2), 139–234.

Chen, C., LeGates, R., & Fang, C. (2018). From coordinated to integrated urban and rural development in China's megacity regions. *Journal of Urban Affairs*, 41(2), 150–169.

Chenery, H. & Syrqin, M. (1975). *Patterns of development 1950–1970*. Oxford, GB: Oxford University Press.

Chicago Commercial Club (1909). *Plan of the city of Chicago 1909*. Chicago, Il: Chicago Commercial Club.

Chicago (2019). Green Roofs. Chicago, IL: City of Chicago. Retrieved 5/5/21 from www.chicago.gov/city/en/depts/dcd/supp_info/chicago_green_roofs.html.

Childe, V.G. (1950). The urban revolution. *Town Planning Review*, 21, 3–17.

Chinese Exclusion Act (1883). PL 47-126, 22 Stat. 58.

Christaller, W. (1966 [1933]). *Central places in Southern Germany*. Englewood Cliffs, NJ: Prentice-Hall. Originally published in German as *Die zentralen Orte in Süddeutschland: Eine ökonomisch-geographische Untersuchung über die Gesetzmäßigkeit der Verbreitung und Entwicklung der Siedlungen mit städtischen Funktionen*. Jena, DE: Gustav Fischer.

Christiansen, R. (2018). *City of light: The making of modern Paris*. New York City, NY: Basic Books.

Chudakoff, H., Smith, J., & Baldwin, P. (2014). *History of American urban society*, 8th ed. Abingdon, GB and New York City, NY: Routledge.

Citizens Planning Institute (CPI) (Philadelphia) (2021). CPI website. Retrieved 2/2/21 from https://citizensplanninginstitute.org.

Clark, C. (1958). Transport: Maker and breaker of cities. *Town Planning Review*, 28(4), 237–250.

Clawson, M. (1981). *New Deal planning: The National Resources Planning Board*. Washington, D.C.: Resources for the Future Press.

Cleveland City Planning Commission (1975). *Cleveland policy planning report*. Cleveland, OH: Cleveland City Planning Commission.

Climate Science Rapid Reponse Team (2021). Climate Science Rapid Response Team website. Retrieved 3/13/21 from www.realclimate.org/.

Clinton v Cedar Rapids and the Missouri River Railroad Company (1868). 24 *Iowa* 455.

Coastal Zone Management Act (CZMA) (1972). Retrieved 3/14/21 from https://coast.noaa.gov/data/czm/media/CZMA_10_11_06.pdf.

Cobb, R. et al. (2013). Biodiversity conservation in the face of dramatic forest disease: An integrated conservation strategy for tanoak (*Notholithocarpus densiflorus*) threatened by sudden oak death. *Madroño*, 60(2), 151–164.

Cohen, D. (2015). Population trends in incorporated places: 2000–2013. Washington, D.C.: U.S. Department of Commerce Economics and Statistics Administration, U.S. Census Bureau. Retrieved 6/11/21 from www.census.gov/library/publications/2015/demo/p25-1142.html.

Coleman, P., Deutsch, M., & Marcus, E. (eds) (2014). *The handbook of conflict resolution: Theory and practice*, 3rd ed. San Francisco, CA: Jossey-Bass.

Collins, G. (1959). The ciudad lineal of Madrid. *Journal of the Society of Architectural Historians*, 18(2), 38–52.

Collins, G. & Collins, C. (1981). *Camillo Sitte: The birth of modern city planning*. New York City, NY: Rizzoli.

Comey, J., Popkin, S., & Franks, K. (2012). MTO: A successful housing intervention. *Cityscape*, 14(2), 87–107.

Committee on the Regional Plan of New York and Its Environs (1929). *Regional plan of New York and its environs*. New York City, NY: Russell Sage Foundation.

Congress for the New Urbanism (CNU) (1999). *The charter of the new urbanism*, 1st ed. Washington, D.C.: CNU.

Congress for the New Urbanism (CNU) (2013). *The charter of the new urbanism*, 2nd ed. Washington, D.C.: CNU. Also cited as Talen, E. (ed), *The charter of the new urbanism*, 2nd ed.

Congress of the New Urbanism (2021). CNU website. Retrieved 1/28/2021 from www.cnu.org/.

Construction Industry Association vs City of Petaluma (Petaluma I) (1974). 375 F. Supp. 574, 576 (N.D. Cal.).

Construction Industry Association vs City of Petaluma (Petaluma II) (1976). 522 F.2d 897 (9th Cir. 1975), cert. denied, 96 S. Ct. 1148, 47 L. Ed. 2d 342.

CoolClimate Network (2021). CoolClimate website. Retrieved 3/20/21 from https://coolclimate.berkeley.edu/.

Cooper, C. & Sarkissian, W. (1988). *Housing as if people mattered*. Berkeley, CA: University of California Press.

Corburn, J. & Gottlieb, R. (2009). *Toward the healthy city: People, places, and the politics of urban planning*. Cambridge, MA: Massachusetts Institute of Technology Press.

Corey, S. & Boehm, L. (2010). *The American urban reader: History and theory*. Abingdon, GB and New York City, NY: Routledge.

Costonis, J. (1988). *Icons and aliens*. Urbana, IL: University of Illinois Press.

Council on Environmental Quality (CEQ) (2021). *International environmental impact assessment*. Washington, D.C.: CEQ. Retrieved 3/13/21 from https://ceq.doe.gov/get-involved/international_impact_assessment.html.

Cranston-Gonzalez National Affordable Housing Act (NAHA) (1990). 2 U.S. Code § 12703.

Cranz, G. (1982). *Politics of park design: A history of urban parks in America*. Cambridge, MA: Massachusetts Institute of Technology Press.

Cronin, W. (1991). *Nature's metropolis: Chicago and the great west*. New York City, NY: W.W. Norton.

Cross, T., Bazron, B., Dennis, K. and Isaacs, M. (1989). *Towards a culturally competent system of care: A monograph on effective services for minority children who are severely emotionally disturbed*. Rockville, MD: Georgetown University Child Development Center. Retrieved 2/18/21 from https://spu.edu/~/media/academics/school-of-education/Cultural%20Diversity/Towards%20a%20Culturally%20Competent%20System%20of%20Care%20Abridged.ashx.

Crouch, D., Garr, D. & Mundigo, A. (1982). *Spanish city planning in North America*. Cambridge, MA: Massachusetts Institute of Technology Press.

Crowe, T. (2000). *Crime prevention through environmental design*, 2nd ed. Singapore: National Crime Prevention Institute.

Cuff, D. (1984). The writings of Donald Appleyard. *Places*, 1(3), 75–84.

Daganzo, C. & Ouyang, Y. (2019). *Public transportation systems: Principles of system design, operations planning and real-time control*. Hackensack, NJ: World Scientific Publishing Company.

Dahl, R. (1961). *Who governs? Democracy and power in an American city*. New Haven, CT: Yale University Press.

Daniels, T. (2014). *Environmental planning handbook: For sustainable communities and regions*, 2nd ed. Abingdon, GB and New York City, NY: Routledge.

Danielson, M. & Doig, J. (1982). *New York: The politics of regional development*. Berkeley, CA: University of California Press.

Dastrup, S., Finkel, M., Burnett, K., & Sousa, T. (2018). *Small area fair market rent demonstration evaluation: Final report*. Washington, D.C.: HUD. Retrieved 1/20/21 from www.huduser.gov/portal/publications/Small-Area-FMR-Evaluation-Final-Report.html.

Davidoff, P. (1965). Advocacy and pluralism in planning. *Journal of the American Institute of Planners*, 31(4), 331–338.

Davidoff, P. (1974). *The politics of turmoil: Essays on poverty, race, and the urban crisis*. New York City, NY: Pantheon Books.

Davis, K. (1965). The urbanization of the human population. *Scientific American* 213(3), 40–53.

Davis, M. (1990). *City of quartz: Excavating the future in Los Angeles*. London: Verso.

Davis, M. (1990). Fortress LA. In M. Davis, *City of quartz: Excavating the future in Los Angeles*

(pp. 221–264). London, GB and New York City, NY: Verso.
Davis, M. (2007). *Planet of slums*. London: Verso.
Davis, T. (ed) (2011). *Brownfields: A comprehensive guide to redeveloping contaminated property*, 3rd ed. Washington, D.C.: American Bar Association.
de Roo, G. & Silva, E. (2010). *A planner's encounter with complexity*. Farnham, GB: Ashgate.
de Roo, G., Hillier, J., & Van Wezemael, J. (2012). *Complexity and planning: Systems, assemblages and simulations*. Abingdon, GB and New York City, NY.: Routledge.
de Roo, G., Yamu, C., & Zuidema, C. (eds) (2020). *Handbook on planning and complexity*. Cheltenham, GB and Northhampton, MA: Edward Elgar.
DeFilippis, J. & Saegert, S. (eds) (2012). *The community development reader*, 2nd ed. Abingdon, GB and New York City, NY: Routledge.
DeHaan, H. (2016). *Stalinist city planning*. Toronto, CA: University of Toronto Press.
DeLeon, R. (1992). *Left coast city*. Topeka, KS: University of Kansas Press.
Desimini, J. (2014). From planned shrinkage to formerly urban: Staking landscape architecture's claim in the shrinking city debate. *Landscape Journal*, 33(1), 17–35.
Desmond, M. (2016). *Evicted: Poverty and profit in the American city*. New York City, NY: Broadway Books.
DeVries, J. (1984). *European urbanization, 1500–1800*. Cambridge, MA: Harvard University Press.
Dewar, M. & Thomas, J. (2013). *The city after abandonment*. Philadelphia, PA: University of Pennsylvania Press.
Dilger, R. (1992). ISTEA: A new direction for transportation policy. *Publius*, 22, 67–78.
DiMento, J. & Graymer L. (eds) (1991). *Confronting regional challenges: Approaches to LULUs, growth, and other vexing governance problems*. Cambridge, MA: Lincoln Institute of Land Policy.
Dinnie, K. (2011). *City branding: Theory and cases*. New York City, NY: Palgrave Macmillan.
Dion, T. (2002). *Land development for civil engineers*. 2nd ed. San Francisco, CA: Wiley.
Discover Letchworth (2021). A brief history of Letchworth. Retrieved 1/28/21 from www.discover-letchworth.com/visiting/a-brief-history-of-letchworth.
Doan, P. (2010). The tyranny of gendered spaces: Living beyond the gender dichotomy. *Gender, Place, and Culture*, 17(5), 635–654.
Doan P. (2015). *Planning and LGBTQ communities: The need for inclusive queer spaces*. London, GB and New York City, NY: Routledge.
Doan, P. (2015). Beyond queer space: Planning for diverse and dispersed LGBTQ populations. In P. Doan (ed), *Planning and LGBTQ communities: The need for inclusive queer spaces* (pp. 251–259). Abingdon, GB and New York City, NY: Routledge.
Doan, P. (2015). Why plan for the LGBTQ community? In P. Doan (ed), *Planning and LGBTQ communities: The need for inclusive queer spaces* (pp. 1–15). London, GB and New York City, NY: Routledge.
Doan, P. (2016). *Queerying planning: Challenging heteronormative assumptions and reframing planning practice*. Abingdon, GB, and New York City, NY: Routledge.
Doan, P. & Higgins, H. (2011). The demise of queer space? Resurgent gentrification and the assimilation of LGBT neighborhoods. *Journal of Planning Education and Research*, 31(1), 6–25.
Dobson, A. (2007). *Green political thought*, 4th ed. London, GB and New York City, NY: Routledge.
Dobson, A. & Eckersley, R. (eds) (2006). *Political theory and the ecological challenge*. Cambridge, GB: Cambridge University Press.
Dodd–Frank Wall Street Reform and Consumer Protection Act (2010). Pub. L. No. 111-203, § 929-Z, 124 Stat. 1376, 1871. Codified at 15 U.S.C. § 780.
Donelson, A. & Esparza, A. (eds) (2010). *The colonias reader: Economy, housing and public health in U.S–Mexico border colonias*, 3rd ed. Tucson, AZ: University of Arizona Press.
Donlan, C. (ed) (2015). *Proactive strategies for protecting species: Pre-listing conservation and the endangered species act*. Berkeley, CA: University of California Press.
Drake, S, & Cayton, H. (1945). *Black metropolis*. Chicago, IL: University of Chicago Press.
Druhle, L. (undated) *Critical atlas of the internet*. Self-published. Retrieved 6/11/21 from https://louisedrulhe.fr/internet-atlas/.
Dryzek, J. (ed) (2002). *Green states and social movements: Environmentalism in the United States, United Kingdom, Germany and Norway*. Oxford, GB and New York City, NY: Oxford University Press.
Duany, A. [video] (2015). *Principles of New Urbanism*. Retrieved 1/29/21 from www.youtube.com/watch?v=G0SFiK4AvII.
Duany, A. & Plater-Zyberk, E. (1991). *Towns and town-making principles*. New York City, NY: Rizzoli.
Duany, A. & Plater-Zyberk, E. (2000). *Suburban nation*. Boston, MA: North Point Press.
Dubois, W.E.B. (1899). *The Philadelphia Negro*. Philadelphia, PA: University of Pennsylvania.
Dzurik, A., Kulkari, T., & Boland, B. (2018). *Water resources planning: Fundamentals for an integrated framework*, 4th ed. Lanham, MD: Rowman & Littlefield.

Eccleston, C. & Doub, P. (2012). *Preparing NEPA environmental assessments*. Boca Raton, FL: CRC Press.

Economist (2019). Global warming 101: The past, present, and future of climate change. Retrieved 3/12/21 from www.economist.com/briefing/2019/09/21/the-past-present-and-future-of-climate-change.

Ellen, I. (2020). Addressing affordability challenges: The role and scope of local housing plans. In K. Anacker, M. Nguyen, & D. Varady, *Routledge handbook on housing policy and planning* (pp. 375–389). Abingdon, GB and New York City, NY: Routledge.

Elmer, V. & Leighland, A. (2013). *Infrastructure planning and finance: A smart and sustainable guide*. Abingdon, GB and New York City, NY: Routledge.

Emlen, B. (2010). Adoption [of] *Davis climate action and adaptation plan*. Davis, CA: Office of the City Manager.

Encyclopedia Britannica (2021). Élisée Reclus. Retrieved 2/10/21 from www. britannica.com/biography/Elisee-Reclus.

Energy Information Administration (EIA) (2020). *International energy outlook 2020*. Washington, D.C.: EIA.

Engels, F. (1845). *The condition of the working class in England in 1844*. Leipzig, DE: O. Wigand.

Esnard, A. (2012). Visualizing information. In R. Crane & R. Weber (eds), *The Oxford handbook on urban planning* (pp. 306–322). Oxford, GB: Oxford University Press.

Etzioni, A. (1967). Mixed scanning: A 'third' approach to decision-making. *Public Administration Review*, 27(5), 385–392.

European Union (2019). Regulation (EU) 2019/631 of the European Parliament and of the Council of 17 April 2019 setting CO_2 emission performance standards for new passenger cars and for new light commercial vehicles and repealing Regulations (EC) No 443/2009 and (EU) No 510/2011.

Ewing, R., Bartholomew, K., Winkelman, J, Walters, J., & Chen, D. (2009). *Growing cooler: The evidence on urban development and climate change*. Washington, D.C.: Urban Land Institute.

Ewing, R., Meakins, G., & Parker, B. (2012). Planned unit development. In E. Carswell (ed), *The encyclopedia of housing*, 2nd ed (vol 2, pp. 545–547). Thousand Oaks, CA: Sage.

Fainstein, S. (2021). Urban planning. *Encyclopedia Britannica*. Chicago, IL: Encyclopedia Britannica.

Fainstein, S. & DeFilippis, J. (eds) (2016). *Readings in planning theory*, 4th ed. New York City, NY: Wiley Blackwell.

Fainstein, S. and Servon, L. (2005). The intersection of gender and planning. In S. Fainstein & L. Servon (eds), *Gender and planning: A reader* (pp. 1–15). New Brunswick, NJ: Rutgers University Press.

Farr, D. (2007). *Sustainable urbanism: Urban design with nature*. Hoboken, NJ: Wiley.

Farthing, S. (2016). *Research design in city and regional planning: A student's guide*. Thousand Oaks, CA: Sage.

Federal Housing Finance Agency (FHFA) (2021). FAFA house price index. Washington, D.C.: FHFA. Retrieved 3/3/21 from www.fhfa.gov/DataTools/Downloads/Pages/House-Price-Index.aspx.

Federal Housing Finance Agency (FHFA) (2021). FHFA website. Retrieved 3/3/21 from www.fhfa.gov/.

Federal Reserve Bank of St. Louis (FRED) (2021). *S&P Dow Jones Indices LLC, S&P/Case–Shiller U.S. national home price index* [CSUSHPINSA]. St. Louis, MO: FRED. Retrieved 3/2/21 from https://fred.stlouisfed.org/series/CSUSHPINSA.

Federal Transit Administration (FTA). (2021). National transit database. Retrieved 3/1/21 from www.transit.dot.gov/ntd.

Finkel, M. et al. (2010). *Capital needs in the public housing program*. Revised final report. Abt Associates, Inc. for U.S. Department of Housing. Retrieved 1/8/22 from http://portal.hud.gov/hudportal/documents/huddoc?id=PH_Capital_Needs.pdf.

First Evangelical Church of Glendale vs County of Los Angeles (1987). 482 U.S. 304.

Fischer, W. (2020). Moving to work demonstration & expansion. In National Low Income Housing Coalition, *Advocates' guide 2020: A primer on federal affordable housing and community development programs* (pp. 4-57–4-60). Retrieved 1/8/22 from https://nlihc.org/explore-issues/publications-research/advocates-guide.

Fisher, R. & Ury, W. (1981). *Getting to yes: Negotiating agreement without giving in*. Boston, MA: Houghton Mifflin.

Fishman, R. (1982). *Urban utopias in the Twentieth century*. Cambridge, MA: Massachusetts Institute of Technology Press.

Fitzgerald, J. (2012). *Emerald cities: Urban sustainability and economic development*. Oxford, GB: Oxford University Press.

Fleming, R. (2007). *The art of placemaking: Interpreting community through public art and urban design*. London, GB: Merrell.

Flint, A. (2011). *Wrestling with Moses: How Jane Jacobs took on New York's master builder and transformed the American city*. New York City, NY: Random House.

Florida, R. (2002). *The rise of the creative class: And how it's transforming work, leisure, community and everyday life*. New York City, NY: Basic Books.

Florida, R. (2008). The rise of the mega-region. *Cambridge Journal of Regions, Economy and Society*, 1(3), 459–476.

Ford, G.B. (1913). The city scientific. *Engineering Record*, 67, 551–552.

Forester, J. (1982). Planning in the face of power. *Journal of the American Planning Association*, 48(1), 67–80.

Forester, J. (1987). Planning in the face of conflict. *Journal of the American Planning Association*, 53(3), 303–314.

Forester, J. (1988). *Planning in the face of power*. Berkeley, CA: University of California Press.

Forester, J. (1993). *Critical theory, public policy, and planning practice*. Albany, NY: State University of New York Press.

Forester, J. (1999). *The deliberative practitioner*. Cambridge, MA: Massachusetts Institute of Technology Press.

Forester, J. (2007). Critical theory and planning practice. *Journal of the American Planning Association*, 46(3), 275–286.

Forester, J. (2009). *Dealing with differences: Dramas of mediating public disputes*. Oxford, GB: Oxford University Press.

Forester, J. (2013). *Planning in the face of conflict*. Abingdon, GB and New York City, NY: Routledge.

Form-Based Codes Institute (FBCI) (2021). Form-based codes defined. Retrieved 2/3/21 from https://formbasedcodes.org/definition/

Form-Based Codes Institute (FBCI) (2021). What are form-based codes? Retrieved 1/29/21 from https://formbasedcodes.org/.

Forsyth, A. (1999). *Constructing suburbs*. London, GB and New York City, NY: Routledge.

Forsyth, A. (2001). Nonconformist populations and planning sexuality and space: Nonconformist populations and planning practice. *Journal of Planning Literature*, 15(3), 339–358.

Forsyth, A. (2005). *Reforming suburbia: The planned communities of Irvine, California and the Woodlands*. Berkeley, CA: University of California Press..

Forsyth, A. (2016). *China's urban communities*. Basel, CH: Birkhäuser Verlag.

Forsyth, A. (2019). *Creating healthy neighborhoods: Evidence-based planning and design strategies*. London, GB and New York City, NY: Routledge.

Forsyth, A. (2020). *New towns for the twenty-first century*. Philadelphia, PA: Penn Press.

Forsyth, A. (2021). Ann Forsyth's personal website. Retrieved 2/20/21 from http://annforsyth.net.

Forsyth, A. (2021). Ann Forsyth's Harvard faculty website. Retrieved 2/18/21 from www.gsd.harvard.edu/person/ann-forsyth/.

Forsyth, A. (2021). Ann Fosyth's *Planetizen* blog. Retrieved 2/18/21 from www.planetizen.com/blog/10386

Forsyth, A. & Musacchio, L. (2005). *Designing small parks*. Hoboken, NJ: Wiley.

Forsyth, A., Salomon, E., & Smead., L (2017). Creating healthy neighborhoods: Evidence-based planning and design strategies. Chicago, IL: APA Planners Press/Routledge.

Fourier, C. (1841–1848). *Oeuvres complètes de Ch. Fourier*, 6 vols. Paris, FR: Librairie Sociétaire.

Frank, A. & Silver, C. (2018). *Global planning education: Beginnings, global movement and future prospects*. Abingdon, GB and New York City, NY: Routledge.

Frank, K. & Hibbard, M. (2017). Rural planning in the twenty-first century: Context-appropriate practices in a connected world. *Journal of the American Planning Association*, 37(3), 299–308.

Freidrichs, C. (2011). *The Pruitt–Igoe Myth* [video]. Columbia, MO: Unicorn Stencil Films. Retrieved 2/2/21 from www.pruitt-igoe.com/watch-now.html.

Freitag, B., Bolton, S., Westerlund, F., & Clark, J. (2009). *Floodplain management: A new approach for a new era*. Washington, D.C.: Island Press.

Frickel, S. & Elliott, J. (2018). *Sites unseen: Uncovering hidden hazards in American cities*. New York City, NY: Russell Sage Foundation.

Fried, M. & Gleicher, P. (1961). Some sources of residential satisfaction in an urban slum. *Journal of the American Institute of Planners*, 27(4), 305–315.

Frieden, B. (1979). *The environmental protection hustle*. Cambridge, MA. Massachusetts Institute of Technology Press.

Frieden, B. & Kaplan, M. (1997). *The politics of neglect: Urban aid from model cities to revenue sharing*. Cambridge, MA: Massachusetts Institute of Technology Press.

Frieden, B. & Sagalyn, L. (1991). *Downtown, Inc.* Cambridge, MA: Massachusetts Institute of Technology Press.

Friedman, T. (2009). *Hot, flat, and crowded: Why we need a green revolution—and how it can renew America*. New York City, NY: Farrar, Straus and Giroux.

Friedmann, J. (1986). The world city hypothesis. *Development and Change*, 17, 69–83.

Friedmann, J. (1987). *Planning in the public domain: From knowledge to action*. Princeton, NJ: Princeton University Press.

Friedmann, J. (2008). The uses of planning theory: A bibliographic essay, *Journal of Planning Education and Research*, 28, 247–257.

Friedmann, J. (2011). *Insurgencies: Essays in planning theory*. London, GB: Royal Town Planning Institute.

Friends of Mammoth et al. vs Board of Supervisors of Mono County et al. (1972). 8 Cal. 3d 247; 502 P.2d 1049; 104 Cal. Rptr. 761.

Fröbel, F. (1977). *The new international division of labour*. Cambridge, GB: Cambridge University Press.

Frug, G. & Barron, D. (2008). *City bound: How states stifle urban innovation*. Ithaca, NY: Cornell University Press.

Fulton, W. & Shigley, P. (2018). *Guide to California planning*, 5th ed. Point Arena, CA: Solano Press.

Gage, R. & McDowell, B. (1995). ISTEA and the role of MPOs in the new transportation environment: A midterm assessment. *Publius*, 25, 133–54.

Gallagher, M., Lo, L., & Pendall, R. (2019). An introduction to the national longitudinal land use survey and data. Washington, D.C.: Urban Institute.

Gans, H. (1967). *The Levittowners*. New York City, NY: Pantheon.

Garcia, I. (2020). Cultural insights for planners: Understanding the terms Hispanic, Latino, and Latinx. *Journal of the American Planning Association*, 86(4), 393–402. Retrieved 2/24/21 from www.tandfonline.com/doi/abs/10.1080/01944363.2020.1758191?journalCode=rjpa20.

Garcia, I., Jackson, A., Harwood, S., Greenlee, A., Lee. C., & Chrisinger, B. (2020). Like a fish out of water: Anti-racism: The experience of African American and Latinx planning students. *Journal of the American Planning Association*, 87(1), 108–122.

Garreau, J. (1984). *Edge city*. New York City, NY: Doubleday.

Garvin, A. (2013). *What makes a great city*. Washington, D.C.: Island Press.

Garvin, A. (2013) *The American city: What works and what doesn't*, 3rd ed. New York: McGraw-Hill Education.

Gates, H. (2021). Free Blacks lived in the North, right? Retrieved 1/18/21 from www.facebook.com/HenryLouisGatesJr/posts/free-blacks-lived-in-the-north-right/412618352185514/.

Gautreaux vs Chicago Housing Authority (1969). 296 F. Supp. 907 (N.D. Il. 1969).

Geddes, P. (1915). *Cities in evolution: An introduction to the town planning movement and to the study of civics*. London, GB: Williams & Norgate.

Gehl, J. (1971). *Life between buildings*. Copenhagen: Royal Danish Academy of Fine Arts, School of Architecture.

Gehl, J. (2010). *Cities for people*. Washington, D.C.: Island Press.

Gehl, J. (2015). In search of the human scale [video]. Retrieved 1/29/21 from www.youtube.com/watch?v=Cgw9oHDfJ4k.

Gehl, J. & Svarre, B. (2013). *How to study public life*. Washington, D.C.: Island Press.

Gelfand, M. (1975). *The federal government and urban America 1933–1965*. Oxford, GB: Oxford University Press.

General Transit Feed Specification (GTFS) (2021). *GTFS: Making public transit data universally accessible*. Retrieved 5/3/21 from https://gtfs.org/gtfs-background.

George, L., Feinberg, M., Wiley, K., & Strauss, L. (2018). *Rental housing for a 21st century rural America: A platform for preservation*. Washington, D.C.: Housing Assistance Council. www.ruralhome.org/storage/documents/publications/rrreports/HAC_A_PLATFORM_FOR_PRESERVATION.pdf.

George, S. & Snape, W. (2010). State Endangered Species Acts. In D. Baur & W. Irvin (eds), *Endangered Species Act: Law, policy and perspectives*, 2nd ed (pp. 344–359). American Bar Association Section on Environment, Energy, and Resources. Washington, D.C.: American Bar Association.

Gerken, H. (2010). The Supreme Court, 2009 term, foreword: Federalism all the way down. *Harvard Law Review*, 124(1), 6–74.

Gerken, H.K. (2005). Dissenting by deciding. *Stanford Law Review*, 57(6), 1745–1805.

Gibson, C. & Jung, K. (2015). *Historical census statistics on population totals by race, 1790 to 1990, and by Hispanic origin, 1970 to 1990, for large cities and other urban places in the United States*. Washington, D.C.: U.S. Bureau of the Census. Retrieved 2/24/21 from www.census.gov/library/working-papers/2005/demo/POP-twps0076.html.

Gies, E. (2018). Sponge cities. *Scientific American*, 319(6), 32–37.

Gilbert, R. & Perl, A. (2007). *Transport revolutions: Moving people and freight without oil*. Abingdon, GB and New York City, NY: Routledge.

Gilfolyle, T. (2019). *Oxford encyclopedia of American urban history*. Oxford, GB: Oxford University Press.

Gillham, O. (2002). What is sprawl? In M. Danielson & J. Doig (eds), *The limitless city: A primer on the urban sprawl debate* (pp. 3–17). Washington, D.C.: Island Press.

Giuliano, G. & Hanson, S. (eds) (2017). *The geography of urban transportation*, 4th ed. Guilford, CN: Guilford Press.

Glaab, T. & Brown, C. (1967). *A history of urban America*. New York City, NY: Macmillan.

Glaeser, E. (2012). *Triumph of the city: How our greatest invention makes us richer, smarter, greener, healthier, and happier*. New York City, NY: Penguin Books.

Global and World Cities (GaWC) (2021). GaWC website. Retrieved 2/11/21 from www.lboro.ac.uk/gawc/gawcworlds.html.

Global Planning Education Association Network (GPEAN) (2021). GPEAN website. Retrieved 1/18/21 from www.gpean.org/INDEX1.htm.

Global Planning Educators Interest Group (GPEIG) (2021). About GPEIG. Retrieved 11/22/21 from www.acsp.org/page/GPEIGAbout.

Global Research Act of 1990 (USGCRRA) (1990). P.L. 101-606, 104 Stat. 3096. Washington, D.C.: U.S. Congress. Retrieved 5/5/21 from www.govinfo.gov/content/pkg/STATUTE-104/pdf/STATUTE-104-Pg3096.pdf.

Goble, D., Scott, J., & Davis, F. (eds) (2005). *The Endangered Species Act at thirty*, vol 1: *Renewing the conservation promise*, revised ed. Washington, D.C.: Island Press.

Godfrey, B. (1988). *Neighborhoods in transition: The making of San Francisco's ethnic and nonconformist communities*. Berkeley, CA: University of California Press.

Goetz, E. (2011). Where have all the towers gone? The dismantling of public housing in U.S. cities. *Journal of Urban Affairs*, 33(3), 267–287.

Goetz, E. (2011). Gentrification in black and white: The racial impact of public housing demolition in American cities. *Urban Studies*, 48(8), 1581–1604.

Goetz, E. (2012). The transformation of public housing policy, 1985–2011. *Journal of the American Planning Association*, 78(4), 452–463.

Goetz, E.G. (2013). *New deal ruins: Race, economic justice, & public housing policy*. Ithaca, NY: Cornell University Press.

Golden vs the Town Planning Board of Ramapo (1972). 334 N.Y.S. 2d 138.

Gollin, D. (2014). The Lewis model: A 60-year retrospective. *Journal of Economic Perspectives*, 28(3), 71–88.

Goodman, A. & Hastak, M. (2015). *Infrastructure planning, engineering and economics*, 2nd ed. New York City, NY: McGraw-Hill.

Gordon, P. & Richardson, H. (2000). Critiquing sprawl's critics. *Policy Analysis*, 365, 1–18.

Gore, A. (1992). *Earth in balance: Ecology and the human spirit*. Rancho Cucaonga, CA: Houghton-Mifflin.

Gottmann, J. (1961). *Megalopolis*. Cambridge, MA: Massachusetts Institute of Technology Press.

Grafton, R., & Hussey, K. (2011). *Water resources planning and management*. Cambridge, GB: Cambridge University Press.

Gramlich, E. (2018). Getting started: First homes built with 2016 Low Income Housing Trust Fund awards. Interim summary report. Washington, D.C.: NLIHC. Retrieved 4/3/21 from https://nlihc.org/sites/default/files/NHTF_Getting-Started_2018.pdf.

Gramlich, E. (2019). Public housing. In *Advocates' guide: A primer on federal affordable housing and community development programs*. Washington, D.C.: National Low Income Housing Coalition (pp. 4–25–4–32). Retrieved 5/25/21 from https://nlihc.org/explore-issues/publications-research/advocates-guide.

Green, G. & Haines, A. (2015). *Asset building & community development*, 4th ed. Thousand Oaks, CA: Sage.

Green Climate Fund (2021). Green Climate Fund website. Retrieved 3/10/21 from www.greenclimate.fund/.

Green living ideas (2017). Top 10 list of best nonprofits fighting for climate change fixes. Retrieved 3/19/21 from https://greenlivingideas.com/2017/01/19/top-10-list-best-nonprofits-fighting-climate-change-fixes/.

Green Party US (GPUS) (2021). Greens in office. Retrieved 10/8/20 from www.gpelections.org/greens-in-office/.

Green Party US (GPUS) (2021). Platform. Retrieved 10/8/20 from www.gp.org/platform.

Greene, E. & Harrington, V. (1932). *American population before the federal census of 1790*. New York City, NY: Columbia University Press.

Greenlee, A., Jackson, A., Garcia-Zambrana, I., Lee, A., & Chrisinger, B. (2018). Where are we going? Where have we been?: The climate for diversity within urban planning educational programs. *Journal of Planning Education and Research*, 1, 1–19.

Gress., T., Cho, S., & Joseph, M. (2016) *HOPE VI data compilation and analysis. Final report*. U.S. Department of Housing & Urban Development (HUD) (September). Retrieved 3/5/21 from www.huduser.gov/portal/publications/HOPE-VI-Data-Compilation-and-Analysis.html.

Grigsby, W. (1963). *Housing markets and public policy*. Philadelphia, PA: University of Pennsylvania Press.

Gruber, N. et al. (2019).The oceanic sink for anthropogenic CO_2 from 1994 to 2007. *Science*, 363(6432), 1193–1199.

Guiot, J. et al. (2018). Impacts of 1.5°C global warming on natural and human systems. In V. Masson-Delmotte et al., *Global warming of 1.5°C*. Geneva, CH: IPCC. Retrieved 3/18/21 from www.ipcc.ch/site/assets/uploads/sites/2/2019/02/SR15_Chapter3_Low_Res.pdf.

Gunder, M., Madanipour, A., & Watson, V. (2018). *The Routledge handbook on planning theory*. Abingdon, GB and New York City, NY: Routledge.

Haar, C. (1955). In accordance with a comprehensive plan. *Harvard Law Review*, 68(7), 1154–1175.

Haar, C. (1955). The master plan: An impermanent constitution. *Law and Contemporary Problems*, 20(3), 353–418.

Habermas, J. (1971). *Knowledge and human interests*. Boston, MA: Beacon Press.

Habermas, J. (1974). *Theory and practice*. Boston, MA: Beacon Press.
Habermas, J. (1981). *The theory of communicative action*. Boston, MA: Beacon Press.
Habermas, J. (1990). *Moral consciousness and communicative action*. Cambridge, MA: Massachusetts Institute of Technology Press.
Habermas, J. (1996). *The inclusion of the other*. Cambridge, MA: Massachusetts Institute of Technology Press.
Hack, G. (2018). *Site planning international*. Cambridge, MA: Massachusetts Institute of Technology Press.
Hack, G., Birch, E., Sedway, P., & Silver, M. (2018). *Local planning*. Washington, D.C.: International City Management Association Press.
Hack, G. & Simmonds, R. (eds) (2015). *Global city regions*. Abingdon, GB and New York City, NY: Routledge.
Hagman, D. and Misczynski, D. (1978). *Windfalls for wipeouts: Land value capture and compensation*. Chicago, IL: American Society of Planning Officials (ASPO).
Halegoua, G. (2020). *Smart cities*. Cambridge, MA. Massachusetts Institute of Technology Press.
Hall, P. (1963). *London 2000*. London, GB: Faber & Faber.
Hall, P. (1966). *The world cities*. London, GB: Weidenfeld & Nicolson.
Hall, P. (1981). Enterprise zones: British origins, American adaptations. *Built Environment*, 7(1), 4–12.
Hall, P. (1982). *Great planning disasters*. Berkeley, CA: University of California Press.
Hall, P. (1988). *Cities in civilization*. New York City, NY: Random House.
Hall, P. (2007). *London voices, London lives*. Bristol, UK: Policy Press.
Hall, P. (2014 [1988]). *Cities of tomorrow*, 4th ed. New York, NY: Wiley Blackwell.
Hall, P. (2014). *Good cities, better lives: How Europe discovered the lost art of urbanism*. London, GB: Routledge.
Hall, P. & Pain, K. (2006). *The polycentric metropolis: Learning from mega-city regions in Europe*. London, GB: Earthscan.
Hall, P. & Tewdwr-Jones, M. (2010). *Urban and regional planning*, 5th ed. Abingdon, GB and New York City, NY: Routledge.
Hall, P. & Ward, C. (1998). *Sociable cities: The 21st-century reinvention of the garden city*. (1998). Abingdon, GB and New York City, NY: Routledge.
Hamdi, N. (2010). *The placemaker's guide to building community*. London, GB and New York City, NY: Routledge.
Handlin, O. (1951). *The uprooted*. Boston, MA: Little, Brown & Co.
Hanna-Attish, M. (2018). *What the eyes don't see: A story of crisis, resistance, and hope in an American city*. London, GB: One World.
Hardin, G. (1968). The tragedy of the commons. *Science*, 162(3859), 1243–1248.
Harnik, P. (2010). *Urban green: Innovative parks for resurgent cities*. Washington, D.C.: Island Press.
Harrison, J., & Hoyler, M. (eds) (2017). *Megaregions: Globalization's new frontier?* Cheltenham, GB and Northhampton, MA: Edward Elgar.
Harrison, M. (1985). *Soviet planning in peace and war 1938–1945*. Cambridge, GB: Cambridge University Press.
Hartman, C. (2002). *City for sale*. Berkeley, CA: University of California Press.
Harvard Joint Center for Housing Studies (JCHS) (2020). *The state of the nation's housing 2020*. Cambridge, MA: JCHS. Retrieved 3/5/21 from www.jchs.harvard.edu/state-nations-housing-2020.
Harvey, D. (1973). *Social justice and the city*. Baltimore, MD: Johns Hopkins University Press.
Harvey, D. (2003). *The right to the city: Social justice and the fight for public space*. Guilford, CN: Guilford Press.
Harvey, D. (2012). *Rebel cities: From the right to the city to the urban revolution*. New York City, NY: Verso.
Haub, C. (2011). How many people have ever lived on earth? Population Reference Bureau. Retrieved 4/5/21 from www.prb.org/howmanypeoplehaveeverlivedonearth/1995.
Hawken, P. (2017). *Drawdown: The most comprehensive plan ever proposed to reverse global warming*. New York City, NY: Penguin.
Hay, C. (2002). *Political analysis: A critical introduction*. New York City, NY: Palgrave
Hayden, D. (1980). What would a non-sexist city be like? Speculations on housing, urban design, and human work. *Signs*, 5(3) Supplement: Women and the American city, 170–187.
Hayden, D. (1982). *The grand domestic revolution: A history of designs for American homes, neighborhoods, and cities*. Cambridge, MA: Massachusetts Institute of Technology Press.
Hayden, D. (2002). *Redesigning the American dream: The future of housing, work, and family life*. New York City, NY: W.W. Norton.
Hayden, D. & Wark, J. (2004). *A field guide to sprawl*. New York City, NY: W.W. Norton.
Hayes, R. (1998). *The federal government and urban housing*, 2nd ed. Albany, NY: State University of New York Press.
Hays, D. (2004). What does a house weigh? *Seattle Times* (December 19).
Healey, P. (1992). Planning through debate: The communicative turn in planning theory. *Town Planning Review*, 63(2), 143–162.
Healey, P. (1997). *Collaborative planning: Shaping places in fragmented societies*. Vancouver,

CA: University of British Columbia Press. New York City, NY: Palgrave.
Healey, P. (2006). The communicative turn in planning theory and its implications for spatial strategy formation. *Environment and Planning B: Planning and Design*, 23(2), 217–234.
Healey, P. (2006). *Urban complexity and spatial strategies: Towards a relational planning for our time*. Abingdon, GB and New York City, NY: Routledge.
Healey, P. (2012). Communicative planning: Practices, concepts, and rhetorics. In B. Sanyal, L. Vale, & C. Rosan, *Planning ideas that matter* (pp. 333–355). Cambridge, MA: Massachusetts Institute of Technology Press.
Hegemann, W. & Peets, E. (1922). *The American Vitruvius: An architect's handbook of urban design*. New York City, NY. American Book Publishing Society.
Heilbroner, R. (1953). *The worldly philosophers*. New York City, NY: Simon & Schuster.
Helling, A. (1998). Collaborative visioning: Proceed with caution. *Journal of the American Planning Association*, 64(3), 335–349.
Henderson, T. (2019). *Colonias to immigrants: We need you at census time*. Washington, D.C.: Pew Research Center.
Henke, L. (1984). *Aristotle and the American Indians*. Bloomington, IN: University of Indiana Press.
Hilton, G. (1998). General Motors and the demise of streetcars: A comment. *Transportation Quarterly*, 52(2), 12–13.
Hilton, G. & Due, J. (1960). *The electric interurban railways in America*. Palo Alto, CA: Stanford University Press.
Hines, T. (2008). *Burnham of Chicago: Architect and planner*, 2nd ed. Chicago, IL: University of Chicago Press.
Hoch, C. (2015). Making plans. In R. Crane & R. Weber, *The Oxford handbook of urban planning* (pp. 241–258). Oxford, GB: Oxford University Press.
Hoffman, E. (2019). Project-based rental assistance. In National Low Income Housing Coalition (NLIHC) (ed), *Advocates' guide: A primer on federal housing and community development policy* (pp. 4–46–4–51). Washington, D.C.: NLIHC. Retrieved 6/11/21 from https://nlihc.org/sites/default/files/AG-2019/Advocates-Guide_2019.pdf.
Hoffmann, W. (2016). *Bike lanes are white lanes: Bicycle planning and urban advocacy*. Lincoln, NE: University of Nebraska Press.
Holden, J. (2019). *Water resources: An integrated approach*, 2nd ed. Abingdon, GB and New York City, NY: Routledge.
Hollander, J., Kirkwood, N., & Gold, J. (2010). *Principles of brownfield regeneration: Cleanup, design, and reuse of derelict land*. Washington, D.C.: Island Press.
Hopkins, L. (2001). *Urban development: The logic of making plans*. Washington, D.C.: Island Press.
Hou, L. (2017). Six decades of planning education in China: Those planned and unplanned. In A. Frank & C. Silver, *City and regional planning education* (pp. 81–100). Dordrecht, DE: Springer.
Housing Assistance Council (HAC) (2013). *Housing in the border colonias*. Sacramento, CA: HAC.
Housing Policy Debate (2021). *Housing Policy Debate* website. Retrieved 4/21/21 from www.tandfonline.com/toc/rhpd20/current.
Howard, E. (1898). *Tomorrow: The peaceful path to real reform*. London, GB: Swan Sonnenschein.
Howard, E. (1902). *Garden cities of tomorrow*. London, GB: Swan Sonnenschein.
Howard, E., Hall, P., & Ward, C. (2006). *Tomorrow: The peaceful path to real reform*, annotated ed. Abingdon, GB and New York City, NY: Routledge.
Hubbard, T. & Kimball, H. (1929). *Our cities today and tomorrow*. Cambridge, MA: Harvard University Press.
Hui, E. & Ho, V. (2004). Land value capture mechanisms in Hong Kong and Singapore. *Journal of Property Investment and Finance*, 22(1), 76–100.
Hunt, M. (1986). Naturally occurring retirement communities. *Journal of Housing for the Elderly*, 3(3–4), 3–22.
Hunter, F. (1953). *Community power structure*. Chapel Hill, NC: University of North Carolina Press.
Hunter, L. (1949). *Steamboats on the western rivers: An economic and technological history*. Cambridge, MA: Harvard University Press.
Hunter, R. (2012). *Mail-order homes: Sears homes and other kit houses*. New York City, NY: Shire.
Hurley, A. (2010). *Beyond preservation: Using public history to revitalize inner cities*. Philadelphia, PA: Temple University Press.
Huxley, A. (1932). *Brave new world*. New York City, NY: Harper & Row.
Huxtable, A. (2004). *Frank Lloyd Wright: A life*. New York City, NY: Viking.
Hyra, D. (2012). Conceptualizing the new urban renewal: Comparing the past to the present. *Urban Affairs Review*, 48(4), 498–527.
Ibsen, H. (1882). *An enemy of the people*. Leipzig, DE: P. Reclam.
Imhofe, J. (2012). *The greatest hoax: How the global warming conspiracy threatens your future*. Washington, D.C.: WND Books.
Immergluck, D. (2011). Critical commentary: Subprime crisis, policy response and housing

market restructuring. *Urban Studies*, 48(16), 3371–3383.

INCLUSION (2021). INCLUSION website. Retrieved 11/22/21 from www.acsp.org/page/Inclusion.

Indonesia Administrative Division (2021). *Provinces, regencies and cities*. Retrieved 2/12/21 from www.citypopulation.de/php/indonesia-admin.php.

Innes, J. (1995). Planning theory's emerging paradigm: Communicative action and interactive practice. *Journal of Planning Education and Research*, 14, 183–189.

Innes, J. (1996). Planning through consensus building: A new view of the comprehensive planning ideal. *Journal of the American Planning Association*, 62, 460–472.

Innes, J. (1998). Information in communicative planning. *Journal of the American Planning Association*, 64(1), 52–63.

Innes, J. (1998). Information in communicative planning. *Journal of the American Planning Association*, 64(1), 52–63.

Innes, J. (1999). Consensus building and complex adaptive systems. *Journal of the American Planning Association*, 65(4), 412–423.

Innes, J. (2016). Collaborative rationality for planning practice. *Town Planning Review*, 87, 1–4.

Innes, J. & Booher, D. (2010). *Planning with complexity: An introduction to collaborative rationality for public policy*. Abingdon, GB and New York City, NY: Routledge.

Institute of Transportation Engineers (ITE) & Meyer, M. (2016). *Transportation planning handbook*. Washington, D.C.: ITE.

International Association for China Planning (IACP) (2021). IACP website. Retrieved 1/22/21 from www.china-planning.org/alpha/.

International City Management Association (ICMA) (2021). *Equity and inclusion toolkit*. Washington, D.C.: ICMA. Retrieved 2/20/21 from https://icma.org/documents/icma-equity-inclusion-toolkit.

International City Management Association (ICMA) (2021). ICMA website. Retrieved 2/17/21 from http://icma.com.

International Council on Local Environmental Initiatives (ICLEI) (2021). ICLEI website. Retrieved 3/18/21 from www.iclei.org/.

International Crime Prevention Through Environmental Design (ICPTED) (2021). ICPTED website. Retrieved 1/29/21 from www.cpted.net/.

International Economic Development Council (IEDC) (2021). IEDC website. Retrieved 3/17/21 from www.iedconline.org/.

International Garden Cities Institute (IGCI) (2021). IGCI website. Retrieved 1/28/21 from www.gardencitiesinstitute.com/resources/garden-cities/letchworth-garden-city.

International Renewable Energy Administration (IRENA) (2021). *Renewable energy statistics 2019*. Abu Dhabi, AE: IRENA. Retrieved 3/10/21 from www.irena.org/Statistics.

International Society of City and Regional Planning (ISOCARP) (2021). ISOCARP website. Retrieved 1/18/21 from https://isocarp.org/.

Inter-University Consortium for Political and Social Research (ICPSR) (1997). Historical, demographic, economic, and social data: The United States, 1790–1970 [computer file]. Ann Arbor, MI: ICPSR.

Isard, W. (1956). *Location and space-economy: A general theory relating to industrial location, market areas, land use, trade, and urban structure*. Cambridge, MA: Massachusetts Institute of Technology Press and New York City, NY: Wiley.

Isard, W. (1960). *Methods of regional analysis: An introduction to regional science*. Cambridge, MA: Massachusetts Institute of Technology Press and New York, NY: Wiley.

Isard, W. (1975). *Introduction to regional science*. Englewood Cliffs, NJ: Prentice-Hall.

Isard, W. (2003). *History of regional science and the Regional Science Association*. Berlin: Springer.

Islam, S. and Winkel, J. (2017). *Climate change and social inequality*. New York City, NY: United Nations Department of Economic and Social Affairs.

Jackson, A., Garcia-Zambrana, I., Greenlee, A., & Lee, C.A. (2018). All talk no walk: Student perceptions on integration of diversity and practice in planning programs. *Journal of Planning Education and Research*, 33(5), 574–595.

Jackson, A., Garcia, I., Chrisinger, B., Greenlee, A., Lee, C., & Yerena, A. (2020). *Diversity climate survey: Moving from aspiration to action: Reorienting planners' values towards equity, diversity and inclusion*. Chicago, IL: APA & ACSP / POCIG. Retrieved 2/19/21 from https://doi.org/10.13140/RG.2.2.34937.29289.

Jackson, J.B. (1980). *The necessity of ruins*. Amherst, MA: University of Massachusetts Press.

Jackson, J.B. (1984). *Discovering the vernacular landscape*. New Haven, CN: Yale University Press.

Jackson, J.B. (1994). *A sense of place, a sense of time*. New Haven, CN: Yale University Press.

Jackson, K. (1985). *Crabgrass frontier: The suburbanization of the United States*. Oxford, GB: Oxford University Press.

Jacobs, A. (1980). *Making city planning work*. Chicago, IL: American Planning Association Press.

Jacobs, A. (1985). *Looking at cities*. Cambridge, MA: Harvard University Press.

Jacobs, A. (1993). *Great streets*. Cambridge, MA: Massachusetts Institute of Technology Press.

Jacobs, A. (2011). The civil service Giants. In A. Jacobs, *The good city* (pp. 163–171). Abingdon, GB and New York City, NY: Routledge.

Jacobs, A. (2011). *The good city: Reflections and imaginations*. Abingdon, GB and New York City, NY: Routledge.

Jacobs, A. & Appleyard, D. (1987). Toward an urban design manifesto. *Journal of the American Planning Association*, 53, 1, 112–120.

Jacobs, A., MacDonald, E., & Rofé, Y. (2002). *The boulevard book*. Cambridge, MA: Massachusetts Institute of Technology Press.

Jacobs, J. (1961). *Death and life of great American cities*. New York City, NY: Random House.

Jacobs, J. (1969). *The economy of cities*. New York, NY: Random House.

Jacobs, J. (1984). *Cities and the wealth of nations: Principles of economic life*. New York, NY: Vintage Books.

Jacobson, C. and Tarr, J. (1995). *Ownership and financing of infrastructure: Historical perspectives*. No. WPS 1466. Washington, D.C.: World Bank.

Jacobus, R. (2015). *Inclusionary housing: Creating and maintaining equitable communities*. Cambridge, MA: Lincoln Land Institute.

Jefferson, T. (1787). *Notes on the state of Virginia*. Independently published by John Stockdale.

Jeffries, R. (1977). *Crime prevention through environmental design*. Beverly Hills, CA: Sage.

Jencks, M. & Dempsey, N. (2005). *Future forms and design for sustainable cities*. Oxford, GB: Architectural Press.

John, P., Mossberger, K., & Clarke, S. (2015). *The Oxford handbook of urban politics*. Oxford, GB: Oxford University Press.

Johnson, D. (2015). *Planning the great metropolis: The 1929 regional plan of New York and its environs*. Abingdon, GB and New York City, NY: Routledge.

Johnston, D. (2015). *Divided. The perils of growing inequality:* New York City, NY: New Press.

Jojola, T. (2008). Indigenous planning: An emerging context. *Canadian Journal of Urban Research*, 17(1), 37–47.

Jones, C. (2006). Verdict on the British enterprise zone experiment. *International Planning Studies*, 11(2), 109–123.

Jones, C. & Kammen, D. (2011). Quantifying carbon footprint reduction: Opportunities for U.S. households and communities. *Environmental Science and Technology*, 45, 4088–4095. Retrieved 3/18/21 from https://pubs.acs.org/doi/abs/10.1021/es102221h.

Jones C. & Kammen, D. (2014). Spatial distribution of U.S. household carbon footprints reveals suburbanization undermines greenhouse gas benefits of urban population density. *Environmental Science and Technology*, 48, 895–902.

Jones, C., Wheeler, S., & Kammen, D. (2018). Carbon footprint planning: Quantifying local and state mitigation opportunities for 700 California cities. *Urban Planning* 3, 2, 35–51.

Journal of the American Planning Association (JAPA) (2018). Symposium: John Friedmann retrospective, 82(2).

Journal of the American Planning Association (JAPA) (2019). Fifty years since Arnstein's ladder, 85(3).

Judd, D. & Hinze, A. (2018). *City politics*, 10th ed. Abingdon, GB and New York City, NY: Routledge.

Juergensmeyer, J., Roberts, T., Salkin, P., & Rowberry, R. (2018). *Land use planning and development regulation law*, 4th ed. Eagan, MN: West Academic.

Juracek, A. et al. (2018). Housing mobility programs in the US: 2018. Washington, D.C.: Poverty & Race Research Action Council. Retrieved 4/21/21 from https://prrac.org/pdf/mobilityprogramsus2018.pdf.

Kaiser, E. & Godschalk, D. (1995). Twentieth century land use planning: A stalwart family tree. *Journal of the American Planning Association*, 3(51), 365–385.

Kanigel, R. (2016). *Eyes on the street: The life and time of Jane Jacobs*. New York City, NY: Knopf.

Kaplan, M. & Frieden B. (1975). *The politics of neglect*. Cambridge, MA: Massachusetts Institute of Technology Press.

Kasarda, J. & Lindsay, G (2011) *Aerotropolis: The way we'll live next*. New York: Farrar, Straus and Giroux.

Katz, B. & Bradley, J. (2014). *The metropolitan revolution: How cities and metros are fixing our broken politics and fragile economy*. Washington, D.C.: Brookings Institution Press.

Kauai County, Hawaii (2010). *Kauai energy sustainability plan*. Lihue, HI: Kauai County Planning Department.

Kauai County, Hawaii (2014). *Climate change and coastal hazards assessment*. Lihue, HI: Kauai County Planning Department.

Kauai County, Hawaii (2017). *Kaua'i Kakou general plan*. Retrieved 2/2/21 from http://plankauai.com/.

Kauai County, Hawaii (2017) *Kaua'i county general plan, 2019 APA Awards* [video]. Retrieved 2/9/21 from www.youtube.com/watch?v=pSYIpHdwAcQ.

Kayden, J. (2000). *Privately owned public space: The New York City experience*. New York City, NY: Wiley.

Keating, D. (2020). The right to housing. In K. Anacker, M. Nguyen, & D. Varady, *Routledge handbook on housing policy and planning* (pp. 11–22). Abingdon, GB and New York City, NY: Routledge.

Kelbaugh, D. (2019). *The urban fix: Resilient cities in the war against climate change, heat islands, and overpopulation*. Abingdon, GB and New York City, NY: Routledge.

Kelo vs New London (2005). 545 U.S. 469.

Kent, T.J. (1974). *The urban general plan*. Berkeley, CA: University of California Press.

Kidder, T. (1985). *House*. New York City, NY: Avon Books.

Kingsley, G. (2009). Appendix A: Scope and status of the HOPE VI program. In H.G. Cisneros & L. Engdahl (eds), *From despair to hope: Hope VI and the new promise of public housing in America's cities* (pp. 299–306). Washington, DC: Brookings Institution Press.

Kirkland, S. (2013). *Paris reborn: Baron Haussmann, and the quest to build a modern city*. New York City, NY: St. Martin's Press.

Kirp, D.. Dwyer, J., & Rosenthal, L. (1997). *Our town: Race, housing, and the soul of suburbia*. New Brunswick, NJ: Rutgers University Press.

Kleer, J. & Nawrot, K. (2018). *The rise of megacities: Challenges, opportunities, and unique characteristics*. London, GB: World Scientific English.

Kling, J., Lieman, J., Katz, L., & Sanbonmatsu, L. (2004). Moving to opportunity and tranquility: Neighborhood effects on adult self-sufficiency and health from a randomized housing voucher experiment. Social Science Research Network. Retrieved 1/12/22 from www.ssrn.com/index.cfm/en/.

Klosterman, R. (1990). *Community analysis and planning techniques*. Lanham, MD: Rowman & Littlefield.

Knox, J. & McCarthy, L. (2014). *Urbanization: An introduction to urban geography*, 3rd ed. New York: Pearson.

Kolbert, E. (2015). *The sixth extinction: An unnatural history*. New York City, NY: Henry Holt & Co.

Kolbert, E. (2015). *Field notes from a catastrophe*. New York City, NY: Bloomsbury USA.

Kolbert, E. (2021). *Under a white sky*. New York City: NY: Crown Publishing.

Kostoff, S. (1991). *The city shaped*. New York City, NY: Little, Brown.

Kostoff, S. (1992). *The city assembled*. New York City, NY: Little, Brown.

Krieger, A. & Saunders, W. (2009). *Urban design*. Minneapolis, MN: University of Minnesota.

Kropotkin, P. (1898). *Fields, factories and workshops: Or industry combined with agriculture and brain work with manual work*. New York City, NY: G.P. Putnam's Sons, and London, GB: Swan Sonnenschein.

Krueckeberg, D. (ed) (1982). *Introduction to planning history in the United States*. New Brunswick, NJ: Center for Urban Policy Research.

Krugman, P. (2020). *Arguing with zombies*. New York City, NY: W.W. Norton.

Krumholz, N. (1982). A retrospective view of equity planning: Cleveland, 1969–1979. *American Planning Association Journal*, 2, 163–174.

Krumholz, N. (1990). *Making equity planning work*. Philadelphia, PA: Temple University Press.

Krumholz, N. (1994). *Reinventing cities: Equity planners tell their stories*. Philadelphia, PA: Temple University Press.

Krumholz, N. (1994). Advocacy planning: Can it move the center? *Journal of the American Planning Association*, 60, 2, 150–151.

Krumholz, N., Cogger, J., & Linner, J. (1975). The Cleveland policy planning report. *Journal of the American Institute of Planners*, 41(5), 136–152.

Krumholz, N. & Hexter, K. (2019). *Advancing equity planning now*. Ithaca, NY: Cornell University Press.

Kuhn, T. (1962). *The structure of scientific revolutions*. Chicago, IL: University of Chicago Press.

LaFarge A. (ed) (2000). *The essential William Whyte*. New York City, NY: Fordham University Press.

Landis, J. & McClure, K. (2010). Rethinking federal housing policy. *Journal of the American Planning Association*, 76(3), 319–348.

Lang, R. & Dhavale, D. (2007). Beyond megalopolis: Exploring America's "new megapolitan geography". Census Report 05:01. Blacksburg, VA: Metropolitan Institute at Virginia Tech.

Langdon, P., Shibley, R., & Welch, P. (1990). *Urban excellence*. New York City, NY: Van Nostrand Reinhold.

Law, M. & Collins, A. (2015). *Getting to know ArcGIS*, 4th ed. Redlands, CA: ESRI Press.

Le Corbusier (1929). A contemporary city. In Le Corbusier, *The city of tomorrow and its planning* (pp. 163–180). New York City, NY: Payson & Clarke.

Le Corbusier (1948). *Concerning town planning*. Translated by C. Entwistle from *Propos d'urbanisme* (1946). New Haven, CT: Yale University Press.

Le Corbusier (1959). *L'Urbanisme des trois etablissements humaines* (Urban planning of the three settlements). Paris: Éditions de Minuit.

Le Corbusier. *The radiant city*. (1987). Translated by F. Etchells from *Urbanisme*, 8th ed (1933). Boulogne, FR: Éditions de l'Architecture d'Aujourd'hui.

Lee, D. (1973). Requiem for large-scale models. *Journal of the American Institute of Planners*, 39(3), 163–178.

Lees, A. (2015). *The city: A world history*. Oxford, GB: Oxford University Press.

Lefcoe, G. & Swenson, C. (2014). Redevelopment in California: The demise of TIF-funded redevelopment in California and its aftermath. *National Tax Journal*, 67(3), 719–744.

Lefebvre, H. (1992). *The production of space*. London, GB and New York, NY: Wiley Blackwell. Originally published as *La production de l'espace*. Paris, FR: Éditions Anthropos (1974).

LeFebvre, H. (1996). The right to the city. In E. Kofman, & E. Lebas, *Writings on cities: Henri Lefebvre* (pp. 147–160). Oxford, GB and Malden, MA: Blackwell. Originally published as *Le droit à la ville*. Paris, FR: Éditions Anthropos (1968).

LeGates, R. (2005). Bringing it all together in the Portland metro region. In R. LeGates, *Think globally, act regionally* (pp. 269–281). Redlands, CA: ESRI Press.

LeGates, R. (2020). How to study cities. In *The city reader*, 7th ed (pp. 1–8). Abingdon, GB and New York City, NY: Routledge.

LeGates, R. & Hudulah, D. (2014). Peri-urban planning for developing East Asia: Learning from Chengdu, China and Yogyakarta/Kartamantul, Indonesia. *Journal of Urban Affairs*, 36(S1), 1–20.

LeGates, R. & Stout F. (1998). Editor's introduction. In R. LeGates and F. Stout, *Early urban planning 1870–1940*, vol 1: *Selected essays* (pp. v–xlii). London, GB and New York City, NY: Routledge/Thoemmes Press.

LeGates, R. & Stout, F. (2020). *The city reader*, 7th ed. Abingdon, GB and New York City, NY. Routledge.

Leigh, N. & Blakeley, E. (2016). *Planning local economic development: Theory and practice*, 6th ed. Thousand Oaks, CA: Sage.

Leigh, N., French, S., Guhathakurta, S., & Stiftel, B. (eds) (2019). *The Routledge handbook of international planning education*. Abingdon, GB and New York, NY: Routledge.

Leontief, W. (1941). *The structure of the American economy 1919–1929: An empirical application of equilibrium analysis*. Cambridge, MA: Harvard University Press.

Letchworth Garden Cities Heritage Foundation (LGCHF) (2021). LGCHF website. Retrieved 1/28/21 from www.letchworth.com/who-we-are/about-us.

Levine, M. (2019). *Urban politics: Cities and suburbs in a golden age*, 10th ed. Abingdon, GB and New York City, NY: Routledge.

Levitan, S. (1969). *The Great Society's poor law*. Baltimore, MD: Johns Hopkins University Press.

Levy, J. (2017). *Contemporary urban planning*, 11th ed. Abingdon, GB and New York City, NY: Routledge.

Lewis, A. (1954). Economic development with unlimited supplies of labour. *Manchester School of Economic and Social Studies*, 22(2), 139–191.

Liebow, E. (1995). *Tell them who I am: The lives of homeless women*. London: Penguin Books.

Lindblom, C. (1959). The science of "muddling through". *Public Administration Review (PAR)*, 19(2), 79–88.

Lipman, M. (1996). *Holding ground: The rebirth of Dudley Street* [video]. Newburgh, NY: New Day Films.

Lipovská, B. & Stepankova, R. (2016). *Research methods in urban and regional planning*, 2 vols. London, GB: Koros Press.

Liptan, T. & Santen, J. (2017). *Sustainable stormwater management: A landscape-driven approach to planning and design*. Portland, OR: Timber Press.

Local Government Commission (1991). Awahnee principles for resource-efficient communities. Sacramento, CA: LGC.

Longley, P., Goodchild, M., McGuire, D., & Rhind, D. (2015). *Geographical information science*, 4th ed. New York City, NY: Wiley.

Loomis, J. (2002). *Integrated public lands management*, 2nd ed. New York City, NY. Columbia University Press.

Los Angeles City Planning. (2015). *Los Angeles general plan*. Los Angeles, CA: Los Angeles City Planning. Retrieved 4/14/21 from https://planning.lacity.org/plans-policies/general-plan-overview.

Losch, A. (1954). *The economics of location*. New Haven, CN: Yale University Press.

Lourks, D. & van Beek, E. (2017). *Water resource systems planning and management: An introduction to methods, models, and applications*. Berlin, DE & New York City, NY: Springer.

Lubove, R. (1963). *The progressives and the slums: Tenement house reform in New York City: 1890–1917*. Pittsburgh, PA: University of Pittsburgh Press.

Luccarelli, M. (1995). *Mumford and the ecological region: The politics of planning*. New York City, NY: Guilford Press.

Lundahl, R. (2013) . *The smart city: Learning from Curitiba* [video]. Retrieved 5/3/21 from http://planet-rla.com/the-smart-city-learning-from-curitiba/.

Lynch, K. (1961). *The image of the city*. Cambridge, MA: Massachusetts Institute of Technology Press.

Lynch, K. (1962). *Site planning*, 1st ed. Cambridge, MA: Massachusetts Institute of Technology Press.

Lynch, K. (1971). *Site planning*, 2nd ed. Cambridge, MA: Massachusetts Institute of Technology Press.

Lynch, K. (1972). *What time is this place?* Cambridge, MA: Massachusetts Institute of Technology Press.

Lynch, K. (1976). *Managing the sense of a region*. Cambridge, MA: Massachusetts Institute of Technology Press.

Lynch, K. (1984). *Good city form*. Cambridge, MA: Massachusetts Institute of Technology Press.

Lynch, K. & Hack, G. (1984). *Site planning*, 3rd ed. Cambridge, MA: Massachusetts Institute of Technology Press.

Lynch, K. & Southworth, M. (1990). *Wasting away*. San Francisco: Sierra Club Books.

MacDonald, E. & Larice, M. (eds) (2006). *The urban design reader*, 2nd ed. Abingdon, GB and New York City, NY: Routledge.

Madanipour, A. (2020). The new social exclusion. In R. LeGates & F. Stout (eds), *The city reader*, 7th ed. Abingdon, GB and New York City, NY: Routledge.

Madanipour, A., Cars, G., & Allen, J. (eds) (1998). *Social exclusion in European cities: Processes, experiences, and responses*. London, GB: Jessica Kingsley.

Main Street America (2020). *State of main*. Retrieved 2/15/21 from www.mainstreet.org/mainstreetamerica/stateofmain2020.

Mandel, E. (2014). *Station Eleven*. New York City, NY: Random House.

Mandelbaum, S., Mazza, L., & Burchell, R. (eds) (1996) *Explorations in planning theory*. New Brunswick, NJ: Rutgers: Center for Urban Policy Research Press.

Mandelker, D. (2017). New perspectives on planned unit developments. *Real Property, Probate and Trust Journal*, 52(2), 229–280.

Mandelker, D. et al. (2020). *Planning and control of land development: Cases and material*, 10th ed. Durham, NC: Carolina Press.

Mann, M. (2013). *The hockey stick and the climate wars: Dispatches from the front lines*. New York City, NY: Columbia University Press.

Manning, J. (1987). *Redevelopment and race: Planning a finer city in postwar Detroit*. Detroit, MI: Wayne State University Press.

Manning J. (2019). Socially responsible practice: The battle to reshape the American Institute of Planners. *Journal of Planning History*, 18(4), 258–281.

Manufactured Home Construction and Safety Standards Act of 1974 (MHCSSA) (1974). PL 93-383, 88 Stat. 700; 42 U.S.C Ch 70 s. 5401 et seq.

Marchman, P. (2012). "Little NEPAs": State equivalents to the National Environmental Policy Act in Indiana, Minnesota and Wisconsin. Arlington, VA: Federal Emergency Management Agency (FEMA).

Marcus, C. (1995). *House as a mirror of self: Exploring the deeper meaning of home*. Berkeley, CA: Conari Press.

Marcuse, P. (2012). Whose right(s) to what city? In N. Brenner, P. Marcuse, & M. Mayer, *Cities for people, not for profit*. Abingdon, GB and New York City, NY: Routledge.

Marcuse, P. et al (eds) (2011). *Searching for the just city: Debates in urban theory and practice*. Abingdon, GB and New York City, NY: Routledge.

Marsh, B. & Ford, G. (1909). *An introduction to city planning*. New York City, NY: B. Marsh and G. Ford.

Marshall, A. (2016). *Ecotopia 2121*. New York City, NY: Arcade.

Massachusetts Institute of Technology (MIT) (2021). MIT Climate change portal. Retrieved 3/13/21 from https://climate.mit.edu/.

Massey, D. (1966). *World city*. Cambridge, GB and Malden, MA: Polity Press.

Massey, D. (1984). *Spatial divisions of labour: Social relations and the geography of production*. New York City, NY: Macmillan.

Mayes, T. (2018). *Why old places matter: How historic places affect our identity and well-being*. Lanham, MD: Rowman & Littlefield.

McBrien, J. (2010). *Make no little plans: Daniel Burnham & the American city* [video]. Arlington, VA: PBS Distribution.

McClure, K. (2019). What should be the future of the Low-Income Housing Tax Credit program? *Housing Policy Debate*, 29(1), 65–81.

McElvaney, S. (2012). *Geodesign: Case studies in regional and urban planning*. Redlands, CA: ESRI Press.

McGovern, S. (2016) *Urban politics: A reader*. Washington, D.C.: CQ Press.

McHarg, I. (1969). *Design with nature*. Garden City, NJ: Doubleday & Company.

McHarg, I. (1996). *A quest for life: An autobiography*. New York City, NY: John Wiley & Sons.

McIntosh, P. (1989). White privilege: Unpacking the invisible knapsack. *Peace and Freedom*, July/August, 10–12. Retrieved 2/21/21 from www.mccc.edu/pdf/cmn214/Class%207/Unpacking%20the%20invisible%20knapsack.pdf.

McKaye, B. (1928). *The new exploration: A philosophy of regional planning*. New York City, NY: Harcourt, Brace, and Company.

McKenzie, R. (1927). The concept of dominance and world-organization. *American Journal of Sociology*, 33, 28–42.

McKibben, W. (2020). *Falter*. New York City, NY: Henry Holt and Company.

McKibben, W. (2020). *The end of nature*. Roselle, IL: Random House.

Meacham, S. (1999). *Regaining paradise: Englishness and the early garden city movement*. New Haven, CT: Yale University Press.

Medoff, P. & Sklar H. (1999). *Streets of hope: The fall and rise of an urban neighborhood*. Boston, MA: South End Press.

Meller, H. (1990). *Patrick Geddes: Social evolutionist and city planner*. Abingdon, GB and New York, City NY: Routledge.

Mendez, M. (2020). *Climate change from the streets: How conflict and collaboration strengthen the environmental justice movement*. New Haven, CT: Yale University Press.

Merrill, K. (2007). *The oil crisis of 1973–74*. New York City, NY: Bedford/St. Martin's.

Metro (Portland, OR) (2016). *Strategic plan to advance racial equity, diversity and inclusion*. Portland, OR: Metro.

Metro (Portland, OR) (2019). *2030 Regional waste plan*. Portland, OR: Metro. Retrieved 2/10/21 from www.oregonmetro.gov/regional-waste-plan.

Metro (Portland, OR) (2020). *Urban growth report: Investing in our communities 2015–2035*. Portland, OR: Metro. Retrieved 1/12/21 from www.oregonmetro.gov/urban-growth-report.

Metro (Portland, OR) (2021). Metro website. Retrieved 2/10/21 from www.oregonmetro.gov.

Metzger, J. (2000). Planned abandonment: The neighborhood life cycle theory and national urban policy. *Housing Policy Debate*, 11(1), 7–40. Washington, D.C.: Fannie Mae Foundation.

Meyers, A. (2018). Regional planning. In D. Goldfield (ed), *Encyclopedia of American urban history*. Thousand Oaks, CA: Sage.

Meyerson, H. (2014). The revolt of the cities. *American Prospect*. Retrieved 2/12/21 from http://prospect.org/article/revolt-cities.

Miller, C. (2012). *Public lands, public debates: A century of controversy*. Corvallis, OR: Oregon State University Press.

Mitsch, W. & Gosselink, J. (2015). *Wetlands*, 5th ed. New York City, NY: Wiley.

Moghadam, S., Delmastro, C., Corgnati, S., & Lombardi, P. (2017). Urban energy planning procedure for sustainable development in the built environment: A review of available spatial approaches. *Journal of Cleaner Production*, 165, 811–827.

Mohl, R. & Biles, R. (2011). *The making of urban America*, 3rd ed. New York, NY: Rowman & Littlefield.

Molotch, H. (1976). The city as a growth machine: Towards a political economy of place. *American Journal of Sociology*, 82(2), 309–332.

Molotch, H. & Logan, J. (1987). *Urban fortunes: The political economy of place*. Berkeley, CA: University of California Press.

Monkkonen, E. (1988). *America becomes urban: The development of U.S. cities and towns, 1780–1980*. Berkeley, CA: University of California Press.

Montgomery, C. (2011). *Regional planning for a sustainable America: How creative programs are promoting prosperity and saving the environment*. New Brunswick, NJ: Rutgers University Press.

Moody, W. (1911). *Wacker's Manual of the Plan of Chicago*. Chicago, IL: Chicago Plan Commission.

More, T. (1516). *Utopia*. Basel: Froben.

Moreno, C. & Miralles-Guasch, C. (2017). The bicycle as a real feeder to the transmilenio system in Bogota and Soacha. *International Journal of Transport Development and Integration*, 1(1), 92–102.

Morgan Stanley Institute for Sustainable Investing (2017). *Climate change mitigation opportunities index 2017*. Retrieved 3/18/21 from www.morganstanley.com/content/dam/msdotcom/ideas/climate-change-mitigation-index/MorganStanley_EIU-ClimateChangeIndex_Report.pdf.

Morris, A.E.J. (1979). *History of urban form before the industrial revolution*. London, GB and New York City, NY: Routledge.

Morris, C. (2008). *The two trillion-dollar meltdown: Easy money, high rollers, and the great credit crash*. New York City, NY: Public Affairs.

Moving North Carolina (2021). The horse trolley: A slow walk toward a new city. Retrieved 1/15/2021 from https://movingnorthcarolina.net/horse-trolley/.

Moynihan, D. (1969). *Maximum feasible misunderstanding: Community action in the war on poverty*. New York City, NY: Free Press.

Mueller, E. & Schwartz, A. (2008). Reversing the tide: Will state and local governments house the poor as federal direct subsidies decline? *Journal of the American Planning Association*, 74(1), 122–135.

Mumford, L. (1930). The booby prizes of 1929. *New Republic* (January 8), 190–191.

Mumford, L. (1932). The plan of New York. *New Republic*, 71, 121–126.

Mumford L. (1932). The plan of New York, II. *New Republic*, 71, 146–153.

Mumford, L. (1938). *The culture of cities*. New York City, NY: Harcourt Brace.

Mumford, L. (1962). *The city in history: Its origins, its transformations, and its prospects*. New York City, NY: Harcourt, Brace & World.

Myers, D. (1990). *Housing demography: Linking demographic structure and housing markets*. Madison, WI: University of Wisconsin Press.

Myhra, D. (1973). A-95 review and the urban planning process. *Urban Lawyer*, 56, 449–458.

Nash, G. (1986). *The urban crucible: The northern seaports and the origins of the American*

Revolution. Cambridge, MA: Harvard University Press.

Nash, G. (1991). *Forging freedom: The formation of Philadelphia's Black community, 1720–1840*. Cambridge, MA: Harvard University Press.

Nashville, Tennessee (2015, amended 2017). *Community character manual*. Retrieved 2/23/21 from www.nashville.gov/Portals/0/SiteContent/Planning/docs/CCM/2017Adopted/next_vol3_CCM-ALL_Amended2017.pdf.

Nashville, Tennessee (2016). *NashvilleNext Plan* [video]. Retrieved 2/9/21 from www.youtube.com/watch?v=FwUBSyyB2dA&feature=emb_logo.

Nashville, Tennessee (2016). *NashvilleNext Plan*. Retrieved 2/2/21 from www.nashville.gov/Government/NashvilleNext.aspx.

National Association of City and Transportation Officials (NACTO) (2013). *Urban street design guide*, 3rd ed. Washington, D.C.: Island Press.

National Association of City and Transportation Officials (NACTO) (2014). *Urban bikeway design guide*, 2nd ed. Washington, D.C.: Island Press.

National Association of City Transportation Officials (NACTO) (2021). *Urban street design guide*. Retrieved 2/20/21 from https://nacto.org/publication/urban-street-design-guide/streets/.

National Association of Housing and Redevelopment Officials (NAHRO) (2005). *The public housing capital fund*.

National Association of Local Housing Finance Agencies (NALHFA) (2021). NALHFA website. Retrieved 4/7/21 from www.nalhfa.org/page/about.

National Association of Regional Councils (NARC) (2021). NARC website. Retrieved 12/27/19 from http://narc.org/.

National Capital Planning Commission (2021). Extending the legacy: Planning America's capital for the 21st century. Washington, D.C.: National Capital Planning Commission

National Coalition for Asian Pacific Americans Community Development (National CAPACD) (2021). National CAPACD website. Retrieved 2/24/21 from www.nationalcapacd.org.

National Council of State Housing Agencies (NCSHA) (2021). NCHSA website. Retrieved 4/7/21 from www.ncsha.org/.

National Council of State Housing Finance Agencies (NCSHFA) (2020). Housing bonds. Retrieved 3/9/21 from www.ncsha.org/advocacy-issues/housing-bonds/.

National Crime Prevention Council (NCPC) (2003). *Crime prevention through environmental design guidebook*. Retrieved 1/29/21 from https://rems.ed.gov/docs/Mobile_docs/CPTED-Guidebook.pdf

National Environmental Policy Act (NEPA) (1969). Retrieved 3/14/21 from www.epa.gov/laws-regulations/summary-national-environmental-policy-act.

National Geographic Society (2020). *Biosphere*. Retrieved 3/18/21 from www.nationalgeographic.org/encyclopedia/biosphere/.

National Highway Traffic Safety Administration (NHTSA) (2021). *Overview of motor vehicle crashes in 2019*. Retrieved from https://crashstats.nhtsa.dot.gov/Api/Public/ViewPublication/813060.

National Highway Traffic Safety Administration (NHTSA) (2020). *NTHSA 2020 Report*. Retrieved 3/1/21 from https://one.nhtsa.gov/nhtsa/whatis/planning/2020Report/2020report.html.

National Historic Preservation Act (1966). 16 USC 470.

National Housing Conference (NHC) (2021). Inclusionary housing the basics in *Nexus: The NHC housing policy guide*. Retrieved 3/5/21 from https://nhc.org/policy-guide/inclusionary-housing-the-basics/.

National Housing Preservation Data Base (NHPDB) (2020). Public & Affordable Housing Research Corporation and National Low Income Housing Corporation. Cheshire, CN. Retrieved 3/8/21 from https://preservationdatabase.org/.

National League of Cities (NLC) (2021). *Cities 101: Types of local U.S. governments*. Retrieved 2/17/21 from www.nlc.org/resource/cities-101-types-of-local-governments/.

National League of Cities (NLC) (2021). *Metropolitan councils*. Retrieved 4/6/20 from https://www.nlc.org/metropolitan-councils/.

National League of Cities (NLC) (2021). NLC website. Retrieved 2/17/21 from www.nlc.org/.

National Longitudinal Land Use Survey and Data (2021). Retrieved 9/21/21 from https://datacatalog.urban.org/dataset/national-longitudinal-land-use-survey-nllus.

National Low Income Housing Coalition (NLIHC) (ed) (2020). *Advocates' guide: A primer on federal housing and community development policy*. Retrieved 2/17/21 from https://nlihc.org/explore-issues/publications-research/advocates-guide.

National Low Income Housing Coalition (2020). Washington, D.C., NLIHC. Retrieved 4/8/21 from https://reports.nlihc.org/sites/default/files/oor/OOR_2020.pdf.

National Low Income Housing Coalition (NLIHC) (2020). Analysis of President Trump's FY 2021 budget request. Retrieved 4/23/21 from https://nlihc.org/ resource/analysis-president-trumps-fy-2021-budget-request.

National Museum of African American History (NMAAH) (2021). Being antiracist. Retrieved

1/12/2021 from https://nmaahc.si.edu/learn/talking-about-race/topics/being-antiracist.

National Oceanographic and Atmospheric Administration (NOAA) (2021). Shoreline mileage of the United States. Washington, D.C. Retrieved 1/2/2021 from https://coast.noaa.gov/data/docs/states/shorelines.pdf.

National Oceanographic and Atmospheric Administration (NOAA) (2018). *National Coastal Zone Management Program Strategic Plan 2018–2023*. Washington, D.C.: NOAA. Retrieved 3/11/21 from https://coast.noaa.gov/data/docs/czm-strategic-plan.pdf.

National Oceanographic and Atmospheric Administration (NOAA) (2021). Climate change. Retrieved 3/13/21 from https://climate.gov.

National Oceanographic and Atmospheric Administration (NOAA) (2021). Global monitoring laboratory. Monthly average Mauna Loa CO_2. Retrieved 3/19/21 from www.esrl.noaa.gov/gmd/ccgg/trends/.

National Organization of Counties (NACo) (2021). NACo website. Retrieved 4/16/21 from www.naco.org/.

National Register of Historic Places (NRHP) (2021). NRHP website. Retrieved 2/20/21 from www.nps.gov/subjects/nationalregister/index.htm.

National Resources Defense Council (NRDC) (2017). The Paris agreement on climate change. Retrieved 3/19/21 from www.nrdc.org/resources/paris-agreement-climate-change.

Ndubi, F. (2014). *Ecological design and planning reader*, 3rd ed. Washington, D.C.: Island Press.

Nelson, A. (2015). Growth management and urban planning in the United States. In J. Wright (ed), *International encyclopedia of the social and behavioral sciences*, 2nd ed. Amsterdam, NL: Elsevier.

Nemeth, J., and Schmidt, S. (2007). Towards a methodology for measuring the security of publicly accessible spaces. *Journal of the American Planning Association*, 73, 283–297.

Netherlands Environmental Assessment Agency (NLEAA) (2021). Emissions database for global atmospheric research (EDGAR). Den Haag, NL: NLEAA. Retrieved 3/19/21 from https://data.jrc.ec.europa.eu/collection/edgar.

New Jersey Department of State. Office of Planning Advocacy (2001). *State plan*. Retrieved 2/2/21 from www.state.nj.us/state/planning/state-plan-cross-acceptance.shtml.

New Jersey Department of State Office of Planning Advocacy (2021). State plan: Cross acceptance. Retrieved 2/2/21 from www.state.nj.us/state/planning/state-plan-cross-acceptance.shtml.

New Jersey (1981, updated 2020). *Pineland comprehensive management plan*. State of New Jersey Pinelands Commission. New Lisbon, NJ. Retrieved 2/9/21 from www.nj.gov/pinelandsCMP.pdf/.

New York City (2013). *A stronger more resilient New York*. Retrieved 3/19/21 from http://s-media.nyc.gov/agencies/sirr/SIRR_singles_Lo_res.pdf.

Newman, O. (1972). *Defensible space: Crime prevention through urban design*. New York City, NY: Macmillan.

Newman, O. (1996). *Creating defensible space*. Washington, D.C.: U.S. Department of Housing and Urban Development (HUD). Retrieved 1/29/21 from www.huduser.gov/portal/Publications/pdf/def.pdf.

Newman, P., Beatley, T., & Boyer, H. (2017). *Resilient cities: Overcoming fossil fuel dependence*, 2nd ed. Washington, D.C.: Island Press.

Newman, P. & Isabella I. (2008). *Cities as sustainable ecosystems: Principles and practices*. Washington, D.C.: Island Press.

Newman, S. (2008). Does housing matter to poor families? A critical summary of research and issues still to be resolved. *Journal of Policy Analysis and Management*, 27(4), 895–925.

Next City (2021). Next City website. Retrieved 1/18/21 from http://nextcity.org.

Nguyen-Hoang, P. (2021). Is tax increment financing a fiscal bane or boon? *Journal of Planning Education and Research*, 18(3), 95–104. Retrieved 3/15/21 from https://journals.sagepub.com/doi/abs/10.1177/0739456X18774121.

Nolen, J. (2015). Regional planning. In J. Nolen (ed) *City planning*, 2nd ed (pp. 472–495. New York: D. Appleton and Co.

Nollan vs California Coastal Commission (1987). 483 U.S. 825.

Northeast Ohio Sustainable Communities Consortium. (NEOSCC) (2015). *Vibrant Northeast Ohio 2040 Plan*. Akron, OH: NEOSCC.

Northeast Ohio Sustainable Communities Consortium (NEOSCC) (2015). *Vibrant Northeast Ohio 2040 Plan*. Akron, OH: NEOSCC.

Oberlander, P. & Newbrun, E. (1999). *Houser: The life and work of Catherine Bauer*. Vancouver, CA: UBC Press.

Ocasio-Cortez, A. (2021). *Green New Deal*. Retrieved 3/18/21 from https://ocasio-cortez.house.gov/green-new-deal.

Office of Planning and Research (OPR) (California) (2017). *General plan guidelines*. Sacramento, CA: OPR. Retrieved 5/25/21 from ca.gov/portal/uploads/2020/10/EXEC-62-R6-2020-AS-WWW.pdf.

O'Hare, M., Bacow, L., & Sanderson, D. (1983). *Facility siting and public opposition*. New York, NY: Van Nostrand/Reinhold.

Oklahoma City (2018). *planokc 2018 APA awards* [video]. Retrieved 2/9/21 from www.youtube.com/watch?v=rXdB3oLdyAI.

Oldenberg, R. (1999). *The great good place: Cafes, coffee shops, bookstores, bars, hair salons, and other hangouts at the heart of a community*, 3rd ed. Emeryville, CA: Marlowe & Co.

Oldenberg, R. (2002). *Celebrating the third place: Inspiring stories about the "great good places" at the heart of our communities*. Boston, MA: Da Capo Press.

Olin, L., McGlade, D., Bedell, R., Sanders, L, Weiler, W., & Rubin, D. (2008). *Placemaking*. New York City, NY: Monacelli Press.

Olsen, E. (2001). *Housing programs for low-income households*. Cambridge, MA: National Bureau of Economic Research. Working paper 8208.

Olson, M. & Klein, J. (1996). *Taken for a ride* [movie]. New York City, NY: American Documentary Films.

Omi, M. & Winant, J. (1994). Racial formation. In M Omi & J. Winant, *Racial formation*, 2nd ed (pp. 9–15). Abingdon, GB and New York City, NY: Routledge.

Onaran, K. (2018). *Crafting form-based codes: Resilient design, policy, and regulation*, 1st ed. Abingdon, GB and New York City, NY: Routledge.

O'Neill, M. (1997). *Green parties and political change in contemporary Europe: New politics, old predicaments*. Aldershot, GB and Brookfield, VT: Ashgate.

Open Street Map (OSM) (2021). OSM website. Retrieved 2/27/21 from www.openstreetmap.org/#map=4/38.01/-95.84.

Opperman, J. (2017). *Floodplains: Processes and management for ecosystem services*. Berkeley, CA: University of California Press.

Oregon Department of Land Conservation and Development (DLCD) (2011). *Ballot measures 37 (2004) and 49 (2007) outcomes and effects*. Salem, OR: DLCD.

Oregon Department of Land Conservation and Development (DLCD) (2019). *Oregon's statewide planning goals and guideline*s. Salem, OR: DLCD.

Oregon measure 7 (2000). Retrieved 2/10/21 from Oregon secretary of state website: https://sos.oregon.gov/Pages/index.aspx.

Oregon measure 37 (2004). Retrieved 2/10/21 from Oregon secretary of state website: https://sos.oregon.gov/Pages/index.aspx.

Oregon measure 49 (2007). Retrieved 2/10/21 from Oregon secretary of state website: https://sos.oregon.gov/Pages/index.aspx.

Oreskes, N. (2014). *Merchants of doubt* [video]. Culver City, CA: Sony Pictures.

Oreskes, N. & Conway, E. (2011). The denial of global warming. In N. Oreskes, *Merchants of doubt: How a handful of scientists obscured the truth on issues from tobacco smoke to global warming* (pp. 169–215). London, GB: Bloomsbury Press.

Orfield, M. (2002). *American metropolitics: The new suburban reality*. Washington, D.C.: Brookings Institution Press.

Orfield, M. (2020). Metropolitics and fiscal equity. In R. LeGates & F. Stout (eds), *The city reader*, 7th ed (pp. 349–368). Abingdon, GB and New York City, NY: Routledge.

Orfield, M., Stancil, W., Luce, T., & Myott, E. (2015). High costs and segregation in subsidized housing policy. *Housing Policy Debate*, 25(3), 574–607.

Orleck, A. & Hazirjian, G. (2011). *The war on poverty*. Athens, GA: University of Georgia Press.

Orr, L., Feins, J., Jacob, R., & Beecroft, E. (2003). *Moving to Opportunity interim impacts evaluation*. Washington, D.C.: HUD Office of Policy Development and Research (PD&R).

Oshri, I., Kotlarsky, J., & Willcocks, L. (2015) *The handbook of global outsourcing and offshoring*, 3rd ed. New York City, NY: Palgrave MacMillan.

Ostergaard, P. & Sperling, K. (2014). Toward sustainable energy planning and management. *International Journal of Sustainable Energy Planning and Management*, 1, 1–6. Retrieved 3/19/21 from www.researchgate.net/publication/272704706.

O'Sullivan, A. (2018). *Urban economics*, 9th ed. New York City, NY: McGraw Hill.

Oswalt, P. (2005). *Shrinking cities*, vol 1: *International research*. Ostfildern-Ruit, DE: Hatje Cantz.

Oswalt, P. (2006). *Shrinking cities*, vol 2: *Interventions*. Ostfildern-Ruit, DE: Hatje Cantz.

Oswalt, P., Rieniets, T., & Schirmel, H. (2006). *Atlas of shrinking cities*. Ostfildern-Ruit, DE: Hatje Cantz.

Outka, U. & Warner, E. (2019). Reversing course on environmental justice under the Trump administration. Salt Lake City, UT: SJ Quinney College of Law, University of Utah. Utah Law Digital Commons. Retrieved 3/11/21 from https://dc.law.utah.edu/cgi/viewcontent.cgi?article=1173&context=scholarship.

Owen, D. (2004, October). Green Manhattan. *The New Yorker*, 111–123.

Oxford English Dictionary (OED) (2018). Region. Oxford, GB: Oxford University Press.

Pack, J. (ed) (2015). *Sunbelt / frostbelt: Public policies and market forces in metropolitan development*. Washington, D.C.: Brookings Institution.

Page, M. (2016). *Why preservation matters*. New Haven, CT: Yale University Press.

Palen, J. (2014). *The urban world*, 10th ed. Boulder, CO: Paradigm Publishers.

Pallagst, K, et al. (eds) (2009). *The future of shrinking cities: Problems, patterns and strategies of urban transformation in a global context*. Berkeley, CA: UC Berkeley Institute for Urban and Regional Development (IURD) &

the Shrinking Cities International Research Network.
Panagopoulos, T. (2020). *Nature-based solutions for restoration of ecosystems and sustainable urban development*. Basel, CH: MDPI Books.
Paris Climate Agreement (2015). United Nations FCCC/CP/2015/L.9/Rev1. Retrieved 3/19/21 from https://unfccc.int/sites/default/files/english_paris_agreement.pdf.
Parker, K. Horowitz, J., Brown, A., Fry, R., Cohn, D., & Igielnik, R. (2018). *What unites and divides urban, suburban, and rural communities*. Washington, D.C.:Pew Research Center. Retrieved 2/11/21 from www.pewresearch.org/social-trends/ 2018/ 05/22/demographic-and-economic-trends-in-urban-suburban-and-rural-communities/.
Parolek, D., Parolek, K., & Crawford, P. (2008). *Form-based codes: A guide for planners, urban designers, municipalities, and developers*. New York City, NY: Wiley.
Parr J. (1999). Growth-pole strategies in regional economic planning: A retrospective view. *Urban Studies*, 36(8), 1247–1268.
Pastor, M., Sadd, J., & Hipp, J. (2001). Which came first? Toxic facilities, minority move-in, and environmental justice. *Journal of Urban Affairs*, 23(1), 1–21.
Patch, G. (2020). American College of Sports Medicine (ACSM) (2020). *American fitness index summary report*. Retrieved 2/2/21 from https://americanfitnessindex.org/wp-content/uploads/2020/07/2020-American-Fitness-Index-Summary-Report.pdf.
Peck, J. (2011). Creative moments: Working culture, through municipal socialism and neoliberal urbanism. In E. McCann & K. Ward (eds), *Mobile urbanism: Cities and policymaking in the global age* (pp. 41–70). Minneapolis, MN: University of Minnesota Press.
Peiser, R. & Forsyth, A. (2021). *Towards 21st century new towns: Past, present, prospects*. Philadelphia, PA: Penn Press.
Pellerito, R. (2002). State Endangered Species Chart. East Lansing, MI: Michigan State University Animal Legal and Historical Center. Retrieved 9/12/21 from www.animallaw.info/article/state-endangered-species-chart.
People ex rel. Le Roy vs Hurlbut (1871). 24 Mich. 44, 52–53.
People's Republic of China (PRC) (2014). *National new style urbanization plan (2014–2020)*. Beijing, CN: People's Republic of China State Council.
Perry, A., Rothwell, J., & Harshbarger, D. (2018). *The devaluation of assets in Black neighborhoods: The case of residential property*. Washington, D.C.: Brookings Institution.
Perry, C. (1929). The neighborhood unit. In *The regional plan of New York and its environs*, vol 7: *Neighborhood and community planning*. New York City, NY: Russell Sage Foundation.
Petaluma, CA (2019). *Petaluma general plan 2025*. Petaluma, CA: City of Petaluma Planning Department. Retrieved 2/11/21 from https://cityofpetaluma.org/documents/general-plan/.
Phang, S. (2018). *Policy innovations for affordable housing in Singapore: From colony to global city*. New York City, NY: Palgrave Macmillan.
Phillips, R. & Pittman, R. (eds) (2014). *An introduction to community development*, 2nd ed. Abingdon, GB and New York City, NY: Routledge.
Piketty, T. (2015). *The economics of inequality*. Cambridge, MA: Harvard University Press.
Piven, F. (1974). Whom does the advocate planner serve? In F. Piven, S. Arnstein, & P. Davidoff (eds), *The politics of turmoil: Essays on poverty, race, and the urban crisis* (pp. 43–53). New York City, NY: Pantheon Books.
Plains CO_2 Reduction Partnership (PROC) (2021). Global carbon cycle. Retrieved 3/21/21 from https://undeerc.org/pcor/sequestration/cycle.aspx.
Planetizen (2021). *Guide to graduate urban planning programs*, 6th ed (2020). Retrieved 1/17/21 from https://store.planetizen.com/products/guide-to-graduate-urban-planning-programs-6th-edition-pdf.
Planetizen (2021). Planetizen website. Retrieved 1/20/21 from www.planetizen.com.
Planners Network (2021). Planners Network website. Retrieved 4/28/21 from www.plannersnetwork.org/.
Planners of Color Interest Group (POCIG) (2021). POCIG website. Retrieved 1/22/21 from www.acsp.org/page/POCIG.
Planning Accreditation Board (PAB) (undated). History of accredited programs. Retrieved 1/18/21 from www.planningaccreditationboard.org/index.php?id=29.
Planning Accreditation Board (PAB) (2017). *2017 accreditation standards*. New York City, NY: PAB. Retrieved 4/5/21 from www.planningaccreditationboard.org/index.php?id=217.
Planning Accreditation Board (PAB) (2017). *2017–2022 strategic plan*. Retrieved 2/23/21 from www.planningaccreditationboard.org/.
Planning Accreditation Board (PAB) (2019). Accredited planning programs. Retrieved 2/17/21 from https://planningaccreditationboard.org/~2023440.2214747/htdocs/index.php?id=30.
Planning Accreditation Board (PAB) (2021). PAB website. Retrieved 1/17/21 from www.planningaccreditationboard.org/.
Planning Advisory Service (PAS) (2021). QuickNotes archive. Chicago: American Planning Association (APA). Retrieved 1/29/21 from https://planning.org/pas/quicknotes/.

Planning Advisory Service (PAS) (2021). Reports archive. Chicago, IL: American Planning Association (APA). Retrieved 1/29/21 from https://planning.org/pas/reports/archive.htm.

Planning Advisory Service (PAS) (2021) Zoning practice archive. Chicago, IL: American Planning Association (APA). Retrieved 1/29/21 from https://planning.org/zoningpractice/.

Planning and Complexity (2021). Planning and Complexity website. Retrieved 12/7/19 from www.aesop-planning.eu/blogs/en_GB/planning-and-complexity.

Plano, Texas (2017). *Plano Tomorrow comprehensive plan*. Plano, TX: Plano Tomorrow. Retrieved from www.planotomorrow.org/.

Plano, Texas (2017). *Plano Tomorrow comprehensive plan | 2017 National Planning Excellence Award winner* [video]. Retrieved 2/9/21 from www.youtube.com/ watch?v=nllzB-YwKgk.

planokc (2018). planokc website. Retrieved 4/14/21 from http://planokc.org/.

Plumer, B. & Popovich. N. (2018, April 3). How U.S. fuel economy standards compare with the rest of the world's. *The New York Times*. Retrieved 1/19/20 from www.nytimes.com/interactive/2018/04/03/climate/us-fuel-economy.html.

Polikoff, A. (2005). *Waiting for Gautreaux*. Evanston, IL: Northwestern University Press.

Popper, F. (1981). Siting LULUs. Emmitsburg, MD: National Emergency Training Center.

Population Reference Bureau (PRB) (2020). How many people have ever lived on earth? Retrieved 5/7/21 from www.prb.org/howmanypeoplehaveeverlivedonearth/.

Porter, D. (2007). *Managing growth in America's communities*, 2nd ed. Washington, D.C.: Island Press.

Porter, M. (2008). *Competitive strategy: Techniques for analyzing industries and competitors*. New York City, NY: Free Press.

Poverty and Race Research Action Council (PRRAC) (2021). PRRAC website. Retrieved 4/28/21 from https://prrac.org/.

Prebisch, R. (1971). *Change and development: Latin America's great task*. New York City: Praeger.

Pred, A. (1977). *City systems in advanced economies*. New York City, NY: Wiley.

Pred, A. (1980). *Urban growth and city systems in the United States, 1840–1860*. Cambridge, MA: Harvard University Press.

Presidential Executive Order (EO) 12898 (1994, February 16). *Federal actions to address environmental justice in minority populations and low-income populations*. Federal Register 59, 32.

Proctor, E. (2012). The right to housing. In E. Carswell (ed), *The encyclopedia of housing*, 2nd ed (vol 2, pp. 639–642). Thousand Oaks, CA: Sage.

Project for Public Spaces (PPS) (2021). PPS website. Retrieved 1/29/21 from www.pps.org.

Prominiski, M. et al. (2012). *River. Space. Design: Planning strategies, methods, and projects for urban rivers*. Basel, CH: Birkhäuser.

Public and Affordable Housing Research Corporation (PAHRC) & National Low Income Housing Coalition (NLIHC) (2020). *2020 Picture of preservation*. Retrieved 2/17/20 from https://preservationdatabase.org/reports/picture-of-preservation/.

Public Broadcasting System (PBS) (2018–2019). *Sinking cities: A four-part series on the threat of climate change* [videos]. Arlington, VA: PBS. Retrieved from www.pbs.org/wnet/peril-and-promise/series/sinking-cities/.

Public Broadcasting System (PBS) (2020). *Kiss the ground* [video]. Retrieved 5/25/21 from https://kisstheground.com/.

Pucher, J. & Buehler, R. (2012). *City cycling*. Cambridge, MA: Massachusetts Institute of Technology Press.

Pulido, L. (2015). White supremacy vs White privilege in environmental racism. *Progress in Human Geography*, 39(6), 1–9.

Quick Guide: Canadian planning programs (2021). Retrieved 1/17/21 from https://docs.google.com/spreadsheets/d/1_cXoi54ZQROQaFDTkRdOC5U7eAMXcP2Jm5gHni3xUk/edit#gid=0.

Quigley, J. (2009). Urbanization, agglomeration, and economic development, In M. Spence, P. Annez, & R. Buckley (eds), *Urbanization and growth* (pp. 115–132). Washington, D.C.: International Bank for Reconstruction and Development/World Bank on behalf of the Commission on Growth and Development.

Raimi, D. (2017). *The fracking debate*. New York City, NY: Columbia University Press.

Randolph, J. (2011). *Environmental land use planning and management*, 2nd ed. Washington, D.C.: Island Press.

Randolph, J. & Masters, G. (2018). *Energy for sustainability: Foundations for technology, planning, and policy*, 2nd ed. Washington, D.C.: Island Press.

Rangan, H., Ng, M., Porter, L., & Chase, J. (eds) (2020). *Insurgencies and revolutions: Reflections on John Friedmann's contributions to planning theory and practice*. Abingdon, GB and New York City, NY: Routledge.

Ratcliff, R. (1949). *Urban land economics*. New York City, NY and London, GB: McGraw-Hill.

Ratcliffe, M. (2010). *A century of delineating a changing landscape: The Census Bureau's urban and rural classification, 1910 to 2010*. Retrieved 2/10/21 from https://www2.census.gov/geo/pdfs/reference/ua/Century_of_Defining_Urban.pdf.

RealClimate (2021). RealClimate website. Retrieved 3/13/21 from www.realclimate.org/.

Reclus, E. (1876–1894). *The earth and its inhabitants*. Edited by H. Keane. London, GB: Virtue & Co.

Reclus, E. (2013). *Anarchy, geography, modernity: The radical social thought of Elisée Reclus*. Edited by J. Clark and C. Martin. Lanham, MD: Lexington Books.

Rector, R. (2014). *The war on poverty: 50 years of failure*. Washington, D.C.: Heritage Foundation.

Regional Greenhouse Gas Initiative (RGGI) (2021). RGGI website. Retrieved 3/15/21 from www.rggi.org/.

Regional Plan Association (RPA) (2021). *America 2050*. New York City, NY: RPA. Retrieved 2/11/21 from https://s3.us-east-1.amazonaws.com/rpa-org/pdfs/2050-Prospectus.pdf.

Register, R. (2006). *EcoCities: Rebuilding cities in balance with nature*, revised ed. Gabriola Island, BC: New Society Publishers.

Reid vs Architectural Board of Review of City of Cleveland Heights (1963). 119 Ohio App. 65, 192 NE 2dn 74.

Reina, V., Acolin, A., & Bostic, R. (2018). Do small area fair market rent limits increase access to opportunity neighborhoods by housing choice voucher recipients? An early evaluation. *Housing Policy Debate*, 29(1), 44–61.

Ren, X. & Keil, R. (eds) (2017). *The globalizing cities reader*, 2nd ed. Abingdon, GB and New York City, NY: Routledge.

Renton vs Playtime Theaters, Inc. (1986). 475 U.S. 41.

Reps, J. (1965). *The making of urban America*. Princeton, NJ: Princeton University Press.

Resource Recovery Act (1976). 42 U.S.C. § 69012 et seq. Retrieved /14/21 from www.govinfo.gov/content/pkg/CFR-2019-title41-vol3/pdf/CFR-2019-title41-vol3-sec105-72-206.pdf.

Resources for the Future (RFF) (2021). RFF website. Retrieved 2/11/21 from www.rff.org/.

Richardson, B. (1876). *Hygeia: A city of health*. London, GB: Macmillan.

River Walk (2021). Our history. Retrieved 9/18/21 from www.thesanantonioriverwalk.com/about/our-history/.

River Walk (2021). A tribute to Robert H.H. Hugman, "Father of the River Walk" [video]. Retrieved 9/18/21 from www.thesanantonioriverwalk.com/about/our-history/.

Robinson, J. (2005). *Ordinary cities: Between modernity and development*. Abingdon, GB and New York City, NY: Routledge.

Robinson, M. (2019). *Climate justice: Hope, resilience, and the fight for a sustainable future*. New York City, NY: Bloomsbury Publishing USA.

Rodwin, L. & Sanyal, B. (eds) (2000). *The profession of city planning: Changes, images, and challenges: 1950–2000*. New Brunswick, NJ: CUPR/Transaction.

Rogelj, J. et al. (2018). Scenarios towards limiting global mean temperature increase below 1.5°C. *Nature Climate Change*, 8, 325–332.

Roman, J. (2011). *Listed: Dispatches from America's Endangered Species Act*. Cambridge, MA: Harvard University Press.

Rosan, C. (2016). *Governing the fragmented metropolis* (2016). Philadelphia, PA: Penn Press.

Roseland, M. (2012). *Toward sustainable communities: Solutions for citizens and their governments*, 4th ed. Gabriola Island, BC: New Society Publishers.

Rosenbloom, S. (2018). Introduction: John Friedmann and links to planning practice. *Journal of the American Planning Association*, 84(2), 178–179.

Ross, C. (2009). *Megaregions: Planning for global competitiveness*. Washington, D.C.: Island Press.

Ross, C. (2014). *Health impact assessment in the United States*. New York City, NY: Springer.

Ross, C. (ed) (2009). *Megaregions: Planning for global competitiveness*. Washington, D.C.: Island Press.

Ross, C. (2020). Catherine Ross's personal website. Retrieved 2/10/21 from http://catherine.ross.gatech.edu/.

Rostow, W. (1960). *Stages of economic growth*. Cambridge, GB: Cambridge University Press.

Rothberg, P. (2011) *White privilege: Essential readings on the other side of racism*, 4th ed. New York City, NY: Worth Publishers.

Rothstein, R. (2017). *The color of law: A forgotten history of how our government segregated America*. New York City, NY: Livright.

Roy, A., Negrón-Gonzales, G., Opoku-Agyemang, C., & Talwaker, C. (2016). *Encountering poverty: Thinking and acting in an unequal world*. Berkeley, CA: University of California Press.

Royal Commission on the Distribution of the Industrial Population (Barlow Commission) (1940). *Report of the Royal Commission on the Distribution of the Industrial Population*. London, GB: Royal Commission on the Distribution of the Industrial Population.

Royal Town Planning Institute (RTPI) (2021). RTPI website. Retrieved 1/18/21 from www.rtpi.org.uk/.

Rubin, H. (1988). Shoot anything that flies, claim anything that falls: Conversations with economic development practitioners. *Economic Development Quarterly*, 2(3), 236–251.

Rudy Bruner Foundation (2016). Pike Place Market. Retrieved 1/23/21 from www.rudybruneraward.org/winners/pike-place-market/pike-place-market-2/.

Rukmana, D. (2020). *The Routledge handbook of planning megacities in the global*

Ryan, B. (2012). *Design after decline: How America rebuilds shrinking cities*. Philadelphia, PA: University of Pennsylvania Press.

Ryan, B. (2017). *The largest art: A measured manifesto for a plural urbanism*. Cambridge, MA: Massachusetts Institute of Technology Press.

Ryser, J. & Franchini, T. ((2015). *International manual of planning practice*. The Hague, NL: ISOCARP.

Sachs, J. (2015). *The age of sustainable development*. New York City, NY: Columbia University Press.

Sadik-Khan, J. & Solomonow, S. (2017). *Streetfight: Handbook for an urban revolution*. New York City, NY: Penguin.

Safe Drinking Water Act (SDWA) (1974). Washington, D.C.: EPA. Retrieved 3/14/21 from www.epa.gov/sdwa.

Sagalyn, L. (2016). *Power at ground zero*. Oxford, GB: Oxford University Press.

Saint-Simon, H. (1816–1817). *L'Industrie*. France: Publisher not identified.

Saint, P., Flavell, R., & Fox., P. (1994). *NIMBY wars*. Hingham, MA: Saint University Press.

San Antonio 2020 (2021). SA2020 website. Retrieved 1/23/21 from www.sa2020.org/what-is-sa2020/.

San Francisco Bay Conservation and Development Commission (SFBCDC) (2020). *San Francisco Bay plan* (1968, updated 2020). San Francisco, CA: SFBCDC.

San Francisco General Plan (2021). San Francisco, CA: San Francisco Planning Department. Retrieved 1/12/2021 from www.sf-planning.org/ftp/General_Plan/index.htm.

San Francisco Planning Department (2021). Design review. Retrieved 2/3/21 from https://sfplanning.org/design-review.

Sandefur, T. & Sandefur, C. (2015). *Cornerstone of liberty: Property rights in the 21st century*, 2nd ed. Washington, D.C.: Cato Institute.

Sandercock, L. & Forsyth, A. (2005). A gender agenda: New directions for planning theory. In S. Fainstein & L. Servon (eds), *Gender and planning: A reader* (pp. 67–85). New Brunswick, NJ: Rutgers University Press

Sanyal, B. (2005). *Comparative planning cultures*. Abingdon, GB and New York City, NY: Routledge.

Sanyal, B. (2005). Hybrid planning cultures: The search for the global cultural commons. In B. Sanyal (ed), *Comparative planning cultures* (pp. 3–28). Abingdon, GB and New York City, NY: Routledge.

Sard, B., & Fischer, W. (2008). *Preserving safe, high quality public housing should be a priority of federal housing policy*. Washington, DC: Center on Budget and Policy Priorities. Retrieved 3/5/21 from www.cbpp.org/research/preserving-safe-high-quality-public-housing-should-be-a-priority-of-federal-housing-policy?fa=view&id=655.

Sarkar, C. & Webster, C. (2016). *Healthy cities: Public health through planning*. Cheltenham, GB and Northhampton, MA: Edward Elgar.

Sassen, S. (1991). *The global city*. Princeton, NJ: Princeton University Press.

Sassen, S. (2005). The global city: Introducing a concept. *Brown Journal of Urban Affairs*, 11(2), 27–42.

Sassen, S. (2020 [1991]). The impact of the new technologies and globalization on cities. In R. LeGates & F. Stout (eds), *The city reader*, 7th ed (pp. 613–621). Abingdon, GB and New York City, NY: Routledge.

Sassen, S. (2018). *Cities in a world economy*, 5th ed. Thousand Oaks, CA: Sage.

Saunders, W. (ed) (2009). *Urban design*. Minneapolis, MN: University of Minnesota Press.

Saunders, W. (2013). *Designed ecologies: The landscape architecture of Kongjian Yu*. Basel, CH: Birkhäuser.

Scally, C., Gold, A., Hedman, C., Gerken, M., & Dubois, N. (2018). The Low-Income Housing Tax Credit: Past achievements, future challenges. Washington, D.C.: Urban Institute. Retrieved 3/2/21 from www.urban.org/sites/default/files/publication/98761/lithc_past_achievements_future_challenges_final_0.pdf.

Schneekloth, L. & Shibley, R. (1995). *Placemaking*. New York City, NY: John Wiley & Sons.

Schön, D. (1982). *The reflective practitioner: How professionals think in action*. London, GB and New York City, NY: Routledge.

Schuetz, J., Meltzer, R., & Been, R. (2011). Silver bullet or Trojan horse? The effects of inclusionary zoning on local housing markets in the United States. *Urban Studies*, 48(2), 297–329.

Schuyler, D. (ed) (2002). *From the garden city to green cities: The legacy of Ebenezer Howard*. Baltimore, MD: Johns Hopkins University Press.

Schwartz, A. (2021). *Housing policy in the United States*, 4th ed. Abingdon, GB and New York City, NY: Routledge.

Scott, M. (1995). *American city planning since 1890*. Berkeley, CA: University of California Press.

Secrest, M. (1998). *Frank Lloyd Wright: A biography*. Chicago, IL: University of Chicago Press.

Seeley, J. (1959). The slum: Its nature, use, and users. *Journal of the American Institute of Planners*, 25(1), 7–14.

Seeley, J. (2008). What is planning? Definition and strategy. *Journal of the American Institute of Planners*, 28(2), 91–97.

Seltzer, E. (2004). It's not an experiment: Regional planning at Metro, 1990 to the present. In C. Ozawa (ed), *The Portland edge: Challenges and successes in growing communities* (pp. 35–60). Washington, D.C.: Island Press.

Seltzer, E. & Carbonell, E. (eds) (2011). *Regional planning in America: Practice and prospect.* Washington, D.C.: Lincoln Land Institute.

Senate Parks Commission (1902). *Report of the Senate Parks Commission* (The McMillan Commission). Washington, D.C.: Senate Parks Commission.

Sharp, T. (2017). Earth's atmosphere: Composition, climate, and weather. Retrieved 3/19/21 from www.space.com/17683-earth-atmosphere.html.

Shinn, M. & Khadduri, J. (2020). *In the midst of plenty: Homelessness and what to do about it.* Hoboken, NJ: Wiley Blackwell.

Shipley, R. & Newkirk, R. (1998). Visioning: Did anybody see where it came from? *Journal of Planning Literature*, 12(4), 407–415.

Shlay, A. (2006). Low-income home-ownership: American dream or delusion? *Urban Studies*, 43(3), 511–531.

Short, L. & Short, R. (2013). *Cities and nature*, 2nd ed. London, GB and New York City, NY: Routledge.

Shoup, D. (2005). *The high cost of free parking.* Abingdon, GB and New York City, NY: Routledge.

Shrank, D., Eisele, B., & Lomax, T. (2019). *Urban mobility report.* Texas A&M Transportation Institute with cooperation from INRIX.

Siegen, B. (1972). *Land use without zoning.* Lexington, MA: Lexington Books.

Silva, E., Healey, P., Harris, N., & Van den Broeck, P. (eds) (2016). *The Routledge handbook of planning research methods.* Abingdon, GB and New York City, NY: Routledge.

Simpson, M. (1982). Meliorist "versus" insurgent planners and the problems of New York, 1921–1941. *Journal of American Studies*, 16(2), 207–228.

Sitte, C. (1889). *City planning according to artistic principles*, 4th ed (2002). Originally published as *Die Städtebau nach seinen künstlerischen Grundsätzen*. Berlin, DE: Birkhäuser.

Sjoberg, G. (1960). *The pre-industrial city.* New York City, NY: Free Press.

Skillshare (2019). *A brief history of U.S. city planning* [video]. Retrieved 5/5/21 from www.youtube.com/watch?v=2Q5bICcek6s.

Slater, C. (1997). General Motors and the demise of streetcars. *Transportation Quarterly*, 51(3), 45–66.

Slotterback, C. & Laurie, M. (2019). Building a foundation for public engagement in planning. *Journal of the American Planning Association*, 85(3), 183–187.

Smith, C. (2009). *The plan of Chicago: Daniel Burnham and the remaking of the American city.* Chicago, IL: University of Chicago Press.

Solomon, R. (2005). *Public housing reform and voucher success: Progress and challenges.* Washington, D.C.: The Brookings Institution, Metropolitan Policy Program (January). Retrieved from www.brookings.edu/research/public-housing-reform-and-voucher-success-progress-and-challenges/.

Sørensen, B. (2017). *Renewable energy: Physics, engineering, environmental impacts, economics and planning*, 5th ed. New York City, NY: Academic Press.

Soule, D. (2005). *Urban sprawl: A comprehensive reference guide.* Santa Barbara, CA: Greenwood Press.

Southern Burlington NAACP vs Township of Mount Laurel (1975). Mount Laurel I. 67 N.J. 151, 336 A. 2d. 713.

Southern Burlington NAACP vs Township of Mount Laurel (1983). Mount Laurel II. 92 N.J. 158, 238.

Spain, D. (1992). *Gendered spaces.* Chapel Hill, NC: University of North Carolina Press.

Spain, D. (2002). What happened to gender relations on the way from Chicago to Los Angeles? *City & Community*, 1(2), 155–169.

Spain, D. (2014). Gender and urban space. *Annual Review of Sociology*, 40, 581–598.

Spence, M., Annez, P., & Buckley, R. (eds) (2009). *Urbanization and growth.* Washington, D.C.: World Bank.

Sperling, D. (2018). *Three revolutions: Steering automated, shared, and electric vehicles to a better future.* Washington, D.C.: Island Press.

Spirn, A. (1984). *The granite garden: Urban nature and human design.* New York City, NY: Basic Books.

Sporn, P. (2018). Detroit 48202 [video]. San Francisco, CA: Kanopy Films. Retrieved 1/18/21 from https://detroit48202.com/.

Squires, G. (2002). *Urban sprawl: Causes, consequences, and policy responses.* Washington, D.C.: Urban Institute Press.

Stalley, M. (1972). *Patrick Geddes: Spokesman for man and the environment.* New Brunswick, NJ: Rutgers University Press.

Standard and Poor's (S&P) (2021). *CoreLogic Case–Shiller home price index.* Retrieved 1/28/21 from www.spglobal.com/spdji/en/index-family/indicators/sp-corelogic-case-shiller/sp-corelogic-case-shiller-composite/#indices.

Steiner, F. (2008). *The living landscape: An ecological approach to landscape planning*, 2nd ed. Washington, D.C.: Island Press.

Steiner, F. & Butler, K. (2006). *Planning and urban design standards*, 2nd ed. New York City, San Francisco, CA: Wiley.

Steiner, F., Weller, R., McCloskey, K., & Fleming, B. (2019). *Design with nature now.* New York City, NY: Columbia University Press.

Stern, N. (2006). *The economics of climate change.* London, GB: London School of Economics Press. Retrieved 3/19/21 from https://webarchive.nationalarchives.gov.uk/20100407172811/http://www.hm-treasury.gov.uk/stern_review_report.htm.

Sternlieb, G. and Hughes, J. (1979). The post-shelter society. *The Public Interest*, 57, 39–47.

Stevens, R. (2005). From NIMBYs to DUDEs: The wacky world of plannerese. Retrieved 2/21/21 from www.planetizen.com/node/152.

Stiglitz, J. (2013). *The price of inequality: How today's divided society endangers our future.* New York City, NY: W.W. Norton.

Stiglitz, J. (2016). *The great divide: Unequal societies and what we can do about them.* New York City, NY: W.W. Norton.

Stiglitz, J. (2019). *People, power, and profits: Progressive capitalism for an age of discontent.* New York City, NY: W.W. Norton.

Stone, C. (1989). *Regime politics: Governing Atlanta, 1946–1988.* Kansas City, MO: University of Kansas Press.

Stone, C. (2015). Reflections on regime politics: From governing coalition to urban political order. *Urban Affairs Review*, 51(1), 101–137.

Stone, C. & Stoker, R (2015). *Urban neighborhoods in a new era.* Chicago, IL: University of Chicago Press.

Stout, F. (2020 [2014]). The automobile, the city, and the new urban mobilities. In R. LeGates & F. Stout (eds), *The city reader*, 7th ed (pp. 78–88). Abingdon, GB and New York City, NY: Routledge.

Strauss, L. (2020). USDA rural rental housing programs. In National Low Income Housing Coalition (NLIHC), *Advocates' guide: A primer on federal housing and community development policy* (pp. 4–74–4–78). Washington, D.C.: National Low Income Housing Coalition. Retrieved 2/17/21 from https://nlihc.org/explore-issues/publications-research/advocates-guide

Sullivan, E. (2018). *Manufactured insecurity: Mobile home parks and Americans' tenuous right to place.* Berkeley, CA: University of California Press.

Sullivan, P. (2017). *Digital zoning codes and comprehensive plans.* Chicago, IL: American Planning Association.

Sumantran, V., Fine, C., & Gonsalvez, D. (2017). *Faster, smarter, greener: The future of the car and urban mobility.* Cambridge, MA: Massachusetts Institute of Technology Press.

Susskind, L. (1996). *Dealing with an angry public.* New York City, NY: Free Press.

Susskind, L. (1999). *Using assisted negotiation to settle land use disputes.* Cambridge, MA: Lincoln Institute of Land Policy.

Susskind, L. (2014). *Good for you, great for me.* New York City, NY: PublicAffairs.

Swanke, H. (2001). *Historic preservation: project planning and estimating.* Greenville, SC: RSMeans.

Tabb, W. & Sawers L. (1984). *Marxism and the metropolis.* Oxford, GB: Oxford University Press.

Takaki, R. (1989). *Strangers from a different shore.* New York City, NY: Little, Brown & Co.

Talen E. (ed) (2013). *The charter of the New Urbanism*, 2nd ed. Washington, D.C.: CNU. Also cited as Congress for the New Urbanism (2013). *The charter of the New Urbanism*, 2nd ed.

Tax Foundation (2006). The history of the mortgage interest deduction. Retrieved 3/5/21 from https://taxfoundation.org/history-mortgage-interest-deduction.

Tax Policy Center (2021). *The Tax Policy Center's briefing book.* Retrieved 1/23/21 from www.taxpolicycenter.org/briefing-book/.

Taylor, D. (2017). Wind energy. In G. Boyle (ed), *Introducing renewable energy* (pp. 297–362). Oxford, GB and New York City, NY: Oxford University Press.

Taylor, K. (2019). Race for profit. *How banks and the real estate industry undermined Black homeownership.* Chapel Hill, NC: University of North Carolina Press.

Taylor, N. (1998). *Urban planning theory since 1945.* Thousand Oaks, CA: Sage.

Taylor, P. (2001). Specification of the world city network. *Geographical Analysis*, 33(2), 181–194.

Taylor, P. (2015). Global city network. In R. LeGates & F. Stout (eds), *The city reader*, 6th ed (pp. 92–102). Abingdon, GB and New York City, NY: Routledge.

Taylor, P. & Derudder, B. (2015.) *World city network*, 2nd ed. Abingdon, GB and New York City, NY: Routledge.

Taylor, P., Derudder, B., Saey, P., & Witlox, F. (eds) (2006). *Cities in globalization.* London, GB: Routledge.

Taylor, P. et al. (2012). *Global urban analysis: A survey of cities in globalization.* Abingdon, GB and New York City, NY: Routledge.

Taylor, P., Hoyler, M., Derudder, B., & Witlox, F. (2012). *The international handbook of globalization and world cities.* Cheltenham, GB and Northhampton, MA: Edward Elgar Press.

Teitz, M. (1996). American planning in the 1990s: Evolution, debate and challenge. *Urban Studies*, 33(4–5), 649–671.

Teitz, M. (1996). American planning in the 1990s: Part II: The dilemma of the cities. *Urban Studies*, 34(5), 775–795.

Teitz, M. (2012). Regional development planning. In B. Sanyal, L. Vale, & C. Rosan (eds), *Planning ideas that matter* (pp. 127–152). Cambridge, MA: Massachusetts Institute of Technology Press.

Thomas, J. (1997). *Redevelopment and race: Planning a finer city in postwar Detroit.* Detroit, MI: Wayne State University Press.

Thomas, J. (2008). The minority-race planner in the quest for a just city. *Planning Theory*, 7(3), 227–247.

Thomas, J. (2019). Socially responsible practice: The battle to reshape the American Institute of Planners. *Journal of Planning History*, 18(4), 258–281.

Thomson, S. (1998). *Water use, management, and planning in the United States*. Cambridge, MA: Academic Press.

Tilsley, J. (1983). *Major dams, reservoirs, and hydroelectric plants: worldwide and Bureau of Reclamation*. Denver, CO: U.S. Department of the Interior: Bureau of Reclamation.

Tortajada, C. (2018). *Integrated water resources management: From concept to implementation*. Abingdon, GB and New York City, NY.: Routledge.

Toynbee, A. (1884). *The industrial revolution*. Boston, MA: Beacon Press.

Trager, L. (2020). Risks and opportunities of climate change. Retrieved 3/19/21 from www.morganstanley.com/articles/risks-and-opportunities-of-climate-change/.

Travel and Leisure magazine (2014) The world's most visited tourist attractions. Retrieved 2/23/21 from www.travelandleisure.com/attractions/landmarks-monuments/worlds-most-visited-tourist-attractions#34.

Turenscape (2021). Turenscape website. Retrieved 3/19/21 from www.turenscape.com/en/home/index.html.

Turner, F.J. (1920). *The frontier in American history*. New York City, NY: Holt.

Tyrwitt, J. (2016). *A transnational life in planning*. Abingdon, GB and New York City, NY: Routledge.

Under2 Coalition (2021). Under2 Coalition website. Retrieved 3/16/21 from www.theclimategroup.org/under2-coalition.

United Nations (1948). *Universal declaration of human rights*. General assembly resolution 217, article 25(1). Retrieved 6/12/21 from www.un.org/en/about-us/universal-declaration-of-human-rights.

United Nations (1992). *Framework convention on climate change*. Retrieved 6/12/21 from https://unfccc.int/files/essential_background/background_publications_htmlpdf/application/pdf/conveng.pdf.

United Nations (1999). *The world at six billion*. New York City, NY: UN. Retrieved 3/19/21 from https://search.archives.un.org/uploads/r/united-nations-archives/4/b/8/4b8e1e4538ee528ec43c72fcbdd3bddb9718410f3e414240617f97ac98d388e2/S-1092-0117-01-00002.pdf.

United Nations (2009). The right to adequate housing. UN Habitat fact sheet 21. https://ohchr.org/Documents/Publications/FS21_rev_1_Housing_en.pdf.

United Nations (2015). *Transforming our world: The 2030 agenda for sustainable development*. A/RES/70/1. Seventieth session, agenda items 15 and 16. Retrieved 2/13/21 from https://sustainabledevelopment.un.org/post2015/transformingourworld/publication.

United Nations (2016). *The world's cities in 2016*. New York City, NY: United Nations.

United Nations (2017). *The new urban agenda*. Retrieved 2/13/21 from https://habitat3.org/the-new-urban-agenda/.

United Nations (2018). *Nature-based solutions for water*. New York City, NY: United Nations. Retrieved 3/19/21 from https://unesdoc.unesco.org/ark:/48223/pf0000261424.

United Nations (2019). *World population prospects 2019 revision*. New York City, NY: United Nations.

United Nations Department of Economic and Social Affairs (DESA) (2021). DESA statistics. Retrieved 3/15/21 from www.un.org/development/desa/en/key-issues/statistics.

United Nations Environment Programme (UNEP) (2020). *Emissions gap report 2020*. Nairobi, KE: UNEP. Retrieved 3/19/21 from www.unep.org/emissions-gap-report-2020.

United Nations Intergovernmental Panel on Climate Change (IPCC) (2014). *Climate change 2014: Synthesis report*. Contribution of Working Groups I, II and III to the *Fifth assessment report* of the Intergovernmental Panel on Climate Change [core writing team, R.K. Pachauri & L.A. Meyer (eds)]. Geneva, CH: IPCC.

United Nations Intergovernmental Panel on Climate Change (IPCC) (2018). *Global warming of 1.5°C*. New York, NY: IPCC. Retrieved 3/1921 from www.ipcc.ch/sr15/.

United Nations Intergovernmental Panel on Climate Change (IPCC) (2019). *Global warming of 1.5°C* (SR1.5). Geneva, CH: IPCC.

United Nations Intergovernmental Panel on Climate Change (IPCC) (2019). *Climate change and land* (SRCCL). Geneva, CH: IPCC.

United Nations Intergovernmental Panel on Climate Change (IPCC) (2019). *Special report on the ocean and cryosphere in a changing climate* (SROCC). Geneva, CH: IPCC.

United Nations Intergovernmental Panel on Climate Change (IPCC) (2021) *Climate change 2021: The physical science basis*. Washington, D.C.: United Nations.

United Nations Intergovernmental Panel on Climate Change (IPCC) (2021). IPCC website. Retrieved 3/15/21 from www.ipcc.ch.

United Nations Intergovernmental Panel on Climate Change (IPCC) (2021). Sixth assessment report. Retrieved 3/15/21 from www.ipcc.ch/assessment-report/ar6/.

United Nations Intergovernmental Panel on Climate Change (IPCC) (2021). *Climate

Change 2022: Impacts. Washington, D.C.: United Nations

United Nations Intergovernmental Panel on Climate Change (IPCC) (2021). *Climate Change 2022: Mitigation.* Washington, D.C.: United Nations

United Nations Population Division (UNPD) (2018). *Urban agglomerations.* In *World population prospects: The 2018 revise.* Retrieved 2/10/21 from https://population.un.org/wup/.

United States Bureau of Labor Statistics (2020). Life, physical, and social science occupations. Similar occupations. Washington, D.C.: BLS. Retrieved 1/15/21 from www.bls.gov/ooh/life-physical-and-social-science/urban-and-regional-planners.htm#tab-8.

United States Bureau of Labor Statistics (BLS) (2021). Current employment statistics – CES National. Washington, D.C.: BLS. Retrieved 1/18/21 from www.bls.gov/ces/.

United States Bureau of Labor Statistics (BLS) (2021). *Occupational outlook handbook.* Washington, D.C.: BLS. Retrieved 1/15/21 from www.bls.gov/ooh/life-physical-and-social-science/urban-and-regional-planners.htm.

United States Census Bureau (2002). *Measuring America: The decennial censuses from 1790 to 2000.* Washington, D.C.: U.S. Bureau of the Census. Retrieved 1/18/21 from www.census.gov/library/publications/2002/dec/pol_02-ma.html.

United States Census Bureau (2005). Historical census statistics on population totals by race, 1790 to 1990, and by Hispanic origin, 1970 to 1990, for large cities and other urban places in the United States. Retrieved 1/19/21 from www.census.gov/library/working-papers/2005/demo/POP-twps0076.html.

United States Census Bureau (2017). *American community survey 2013–2017 5-year data profile.* Retrieved 4/15/21 from https://www.census.gov/acs/www/data/data-tables-and-tools/data-profiles/2017/.

United States Census Bureau (2018). Historical estimates of world population. Revised July 5, 2018. Retrieved 1/18/21 from www.census.gov/data/tables/timeseries/demo/international-programs/historical-est-worldpop.html.

United States Census Bureau (2018). New residential construction historical data. www.census.gov/construction/nrc/historical_data/index.html.

United States Census Bureau (2018). Historical estimates of world population. Retrieved 1/18/20 https://census.gov/data/tables/time-series/demo/international-programs/historical-est-worldpop.html.

United States Census Bureau (2019). QuickFacts. Retrieved 4/15/21 from www.census.gov/quickfacts/fact/table/US/PST045219.

United States Census Bureau (2020). 2020 United States demographic analysis tables. Washington, D.C. Retrieved 9/2/21 from https://www.census.gov/data/tables/2020/demo/popest/ 2020-demographic-analysis-tables.html.

United States Census Bureau (2020). Characteristics of new housing 2019. Retrieved 3/4/21 from www.census.gov/construction/chars/highlights.html.

United States Census Bureau (2020). Historical household tables, table HH-1. Retrieved 5/3/21 from www.census.gov/data/tables/time-series/demo/families/households.html.

United States Census Bureau (2021). Glossary. Retrieved 1/18/21 from www.census.gov/glossary/.

United States Census Bureau (2021). Historical living arrangements of children. Retrieved 2/21/21 from www.census.gov/data/tables/time-series/demo/families/children.html.

United States Census Bureau (2021). Quarterly residential vacancies and homeownership, fourth quarter 2020. Retrieved 4/5/21 from www.census.gov/housing/hvs/files/currenthvspress.pdf.

United States Census Bureau (2021). Urban area facts. Retrieved 3/8/21 from www.census.gov/programs-surveys/geography/guidance/geo-areas/urban-rural/ua-facts.html.

United States Census Bureau (2021). U.S. and world population clock. Retrieved 1/19/21 from www.census.gov/popclock/.

United States Comprehensive Environmental Response, Compensation and Liability Act (CERCLA) (1980). 42 U.S.C. §§9601–9675. Retrieved 3/14/21 from www.govinfo.gov/content/pkg/USCODE-2010-title42/pdf/USCODE-2010-title42-chap103.pdf.

United States Congress (1787). An ordinance for the government of the territory of the United States, north-west of the river Ohio. Washington, D.C.: U.S. Congress. Retrieved 1/19/21 from www.loc.gov/rr/program//bib/ourdocs/northwest.html.

United States Constitution (1791). Retrieved 4/11/21 from www.refworld.org/docid/3ae6b54d1c.html.

United States Department of Agriculture (DOA) (2020). Rural development datasets: Active projects – comprehensive (04-17-2020). Retrieved 1/9/22 from www.sc.egov.usda.gov/data/MFH_section_515.html.

United States Department of Agriculture (USDA) (2021). National cooperative soil survey (NCSS). Retrieved 2/7/21 from https://websoilsurvey.sc.egov.usda.gov/App/ HomePage.htm.

United States Department of Commerce (DOC) (1928). Standard City Planning Enabling Act. Washington, D.C.: DOC.

United States Department of Defense (DOD) (2004). *National security and the threat of climate change.* Washington, D.C.: DOD.

United States Department of Defense (DOD) (2014). *An abrupt climate change scenario and its implications for United States national security* (2004). Washington, D.C.: DOD.

United States Department of Defense (DOD) (2019). *Report on effects of a changing climate to the Department of Defense.* Washington, D.C.: DOD.

United States Department of Energy (DOE) (2016). *Hydropower vision: A new chapter for America's 1st renewable energy resource.* Washington, D.C.: DOE.

United States Department of Housing and Urban Development (HUD) (1970). *Operation Breakthrough.* Washington, D.C.: HUD. Retrieved 4/12/21 from www.huduser.gov/portal//Publications/pdf/HUD%20-%20332.pdf.

United States Department of Housing and Urban Development (HUD) (1996). *Creating defensible space.* Washington, D.C.: HUD. Retrieved 1/31/21 from www.humanics-es.com/defensible-space.pdf.

United States Department of Housing and Urban Development (HUD) (2003). *Moving to Opportunity.* Washington, D.C.: HUD Office of Policy Development and Research (PD&R).

United States Department of Housing and Urban Development (HUD) (2014). *Rental burdens: Rethinking affordability measures.* Washington, D.C.: HUD. Retrieved 13/5/21 from www.huduser.gov/portal/pdredge/pdr_edge_featd_article_092214.html.

United States Department of Housing and Urban Development (HUD) (2019). *Methodology for determining section 8 income limits.* Washington, D.C.: HUD. Retrieved 3/2/21 from www.huduser.gov/portal/datasets/il/il19/IncomeLimitsMethodology-FY19.pdf.

United States Department of Housing and Urban Development (HUD) (2020). Empowerment zones. Retrieved 3/17/21 from www.hud.gov/hudprograms/empowerment_zones.

United States Department of Housing and Urban Development (HUD) (2020). Fair Housing Enforcement Office. *State of fair housing annual report to Congress FY 2018–2019.* Retrieved 1/15/2021 from www.hud.gov/sites/dfiles/FHEO/documents/FHEO%20Report%202020%20-%20Printable%20Version.pdf.

United States Department of Housing and Urban Development (2020). *Low-Income Housing Tax Credit* [data set]. Washington, D.C.: HUD. Retrieved 3/6/21 from www.huduser.gov/portal/datasets/lihtc.html.

United States Department of Housing and Urban Development (HUD) (2020). *The annual homeless assessment report (AHAR) to Congress.* Washington, DC: HUD. www.huduser.gov/portal/sites/default/files/pdf/2019-AHAR-Part-1.pdf.

United States Department of Housing and Urban Development (HUD) (2021). *A picture of subsidized households.* Retrieved 3/9/21 from www.huduser.gov/portal/datasets/assthsg.html.

United States Department of Housing and Urban Development (HUD) (2021). CDBG entitlement program eligibility requirements. Washington, D.C.: HUD.

United States Department of Housing and Urban Development (HUD) (2021). *Fair market rents.* Washington, D.C: HUD. www.huduser.gov/portal/datasets/fmr.html.

United States Department of Housing and Urban Development (HUD) (2021). HOME Investment Partnership Program. Retrieved 4/20/21 from www.hud.gov/program_offices/comm_planning/home

United States Department of Housing and Urban Development (2021). HUD allocates nearly $700 million for affordable housing. Retrieved 1/9/22 from www.hud.gov/press/press_releases_media_advisories/hud_no_21_053.

United States Department of Housing and Urban Development (HUD) (2021). *HUD's public housing program.* Retrieved 2/18/21 from www.hud.gov/topics/rental_assistance/phprog.

United States Department of Housing and Urban Development (HUD) (2021). *Moving to Work demonstration program.* Washington, D.C.: HUD. Retrieved 4/5/21 from www.hud.gov/program_offices/public_indian_housing/programs/ph/mtw/promisingpractices.

United States Department of Transportation (DOT) (2020). Congestion management process (CMP). Retrieved 3/1/21 from https://ops.fhwa.dot.gov/plan4ops/focus_areas/cmp.htm.

United States Economic Development Administration (EDA) (2021). EDA website. Retrieved 3/16/21 from http://eda.gov/.

United States Economic Development Administration (EDA) (2021). University Center Economic Development Program. Retrieved 5/6/21 from www.eda.gov/programs/university-centers/.

United States Endangered Species Act (ESA) (1973). Retrieved 3/14/21 from www.fws.gov/international/pdf/esa.pdf.

United States Energy Information Administration (USEIA) (2021). *U.S. energy facts explained.* Retrieved 7/21/20 from www.eia.gov/energyexplained/us-energy-facts/.

United States Environmental Protection Agency (EPA) (2018). *Inventory of U.S. greenhouse gas emissions and sinks 1990–2019.* Washington, D.C.: Retrieved 5/5/21 from www.epa.gov/sites/production/files/2021-04/documents/us-ghg-inventory-2021-main-text.pdf.

United States Environmental Protection Agency (EPA) (2020). *Overview of greenhouse gases.* Retrieved 3/19/21 from www.epa.gov/ghgemissions/overview-greenhouse-gases.

United States Environmental Protection Agency (EPA) (2020). *Environmental Action Agenda 2020* (EJ 2020). Retrieved 3/14/21 from www.epa.gov/sites/production/files/2016-05/documents/052216_ej_2020_strategic_plan_final_0.pdf.

United States Environmental Protection Agency (EPA) (2020). *Radioactive fallout.* Retrieved 3/19/21 from www.epa.gov/radtown/radioactive-fallout-nuclear-weapons-testing.

United States Environmental Protection Agency (EPA) (2021). EPA website. Retrieved 3/14/21 from www.epa.gov/.

United States Environmental Protection Agency (EPA) (2021). *National overview: Facts and figures on materials, wastes, and recycling.* Retrieved 3/13/21 from www.epa.gov/facts-and-figures-about-materials-waste-and-recycling/national-overview-facts-and-figures-materials#Generation.

United States Environmental Protection Agency (EPA) (2021). EPA's brownfields and land revitalization program. Retrieved 3/13/21 from www.epa.gov/brownfields/overview-epas-brownfields-program.

United States Environmental Protection Agency (EPA) (2021). Toxic release inventory. Retrieved 3/13/21 from www.epa.gov/toxics-release-inventory-tri-program.

United States Environmental Protection Agency (EPA) (2021). Summary of the Safe Drinking Water Act. Retrieved 3/11/21 from www.epa.gov/laws-regulations/summary-safe-drinking-water-act.

United States Environmental Protection Agency (EPA) (2021). Overview of the Clean Air Act. Retrieved 3/14/21 from www.epa.gov/clean-air-act-overview.

United States Environmental Protection Agency (EPA) (2021). *EPA annual environmental justice progress report FY 2020.* Washington, D.C.: EPA. Retrieved 3/14/21 from www.epa.gov/sites/production/files/2021-01/documents/2020_ej_report-final-web-v4.pdf.

United States Environmental Protection Agency (EPA) (2021). Laws and regulations. Retrieved 3/14/21 from www.epa.gov/laws-regulations.

United States Federal Highway Administration (FHWA) (1997). State motor vehicle registrations, by years, 1900–1995. Washington, D.C.: FHWA. Retrieved 4/8/20 from www.fhwa.dot.gov/ohim/summary95/mv200.pdf.

United States Federal Highway Administration (FHA) (2000). The vehicle fleet in our nation's highways 2000. Washington, D.C.: U.S. FHA.

United States Federal-Aid Highway Act of 1962 (1962). Pub.L. 87–866, 76 Stat. 1145.

United States Fish and Wildlife Service (2021). *Conservation banking.* Retrieved 3/11/21 from www.fws.gov/endangered/esa-library/pdf/conservation_banking.pdf.

United States General Accounting Office (GAO) (2003). *HUD's oversight of Hope VI sites needs to be more consistent.* GAO-03–555. Retrieved 3/6/21 from www.gao.gov/assets/240/238349.pdf.

United States Global Change Research Program (USGCRP) (2017). *Fourth national climate assessment* (NCA4), vol I: *The U.S. national climate assessment.* Washington, D.C.: USGCRP. Retrieved 10/30/20 from https://nca2014.globalchange.gov/.

United States Global Research Program (2017). *U.S. global change report.* Washington, D.C.: USGRP.

United States Green Building Council (USGBC) (2013) *Leadership in Energy and Environmental Design (LEED) green building standards v4.* Retrieved 4/15/21 from https://www.usgbc.org/leed/v4.

United States Green Building Council (USGBC) (2015). *LEED v4 for building design and construction.* Washington, D.C.: USGBC.

United States Green Building Council (USGBC) (2018). *A citizen's guide to LEED for neighborhood development.* Washington, D.C.: USGBC.

United States Green Building Council (USGBC) (2018). *LEED reference guide for neighborhood development.* Washington, D.C.: Green Building Council.

United States Green Building Council (USGBC) (2018) *LEED v4 for neighborhood development.* Washington, D.C.: USGBC. Retrieved 2/7/21 from www.usgbc.org/resources/leed-v4-neighborhood-development-current-version.

United States Green Building Council (USGBC) (2021). USGBC website. Retrieved 1/29/21 from https://usgbc.org/.

United States Homestead Act (1862). 12 Stat. 392. Retrieved 1/19/21 from www.ourdocuments.gov/doc.php?flash=false&doc=31.

United States Housing Act of 1937 (1937). Pub. L 75-412, 50 Stat. 888, enacted September 1, 1937.

United States Housing Act of 1949 (1949). Public Law 81-171, 63 Stat. 413, 414. Retrieved 5/21/21 from www.govinfo.gov/content/pkg/COMPS-10349/pdf/COMPS-10349.pdf.

United States Housing Act of 1968 (1968). Public Law 90-488.

United States Intergovernmental Cooperation Act of 1968 (1968). 42 U.S.C. 4201 et seq.

United States Internal Revenue Service (IRS) (2020). Publication 936, *Home mortgage interest deduction.* Washington, D.C.: IRS. Retrieved 3/9/21 from www.irs.gov/pub/irs-pdf/p936.pdf.

United States National Aeronautics and Space Administration (NASA) (2018). Long-term warming trend continued in 2017: NASA, NOAA. Retrieved 9/18/20 from https://climate.nasa.gov/news/2671/long-term-warming-trend-continued-in-2017-nasa-noaa/.

United States National Aeronautics and Space Administration (NASA) (2019). *Global Warming from 1880 to 2020* [video]. Retrieved 3/19/21 from https://climate.nasa.gov/climate_resources/139/video-global-warming-from-1880-to-2020/.

United States National Aeronautics and Space Administration (NASA) (2020). *Earth fact sheet*. Retrieved 3/19/21 from https://nssdc.gsfc.nasa.gov/planetary/factsheet/earthfact.html.

United States National Aeronautics and Space Administration (2021). NASA black marble image of Europe and North Africa at night. Retrieved 5/31/21 from www.nasa.gov/specials/blackmarble/2016/globalmaps/BlackMarble_2016_3km.jpg.

United States National Resources Planning Board (NRPB) (1936). *Regional planning*. Washington, D.C.: NRPB.

United States Office of Management and Budget (OMB) (1968). Circular #A-95.

United States Office of Management and Budget (OMB) (2000). *Standards for defining metropolitan and micropolitan statistical areas*. Retrieved 1/19/21 from www.federalregister.gov/documents/2000/12/27/00-32997/standards-for-defining-metropolitan-and-micropolitan-statistical-areas.

United States Office of Management and Budget (OMB) (2010). *Standards for delineating metropolitan and micropolitan statistical areas*. Washington, D.C.: U.S. Government Printing Office.

United States Office of Management and Budget (OMB) (2015). Revised delineations of metropolitan statistical areas, micropolitan statistical areas, and combined statistical areas, and guidance on uses of the delineations of these areas. Washington, D.C.: U.S. Government Printing Office.

United States Safe Drinking Water Act (1974) 42 U.S.C. § 300f et seq. Retrieved 1/9/22 from www.epa.gov/sdwa/title-xiv-public-health-service-act-safety-public-water-systems-safe-drinking-water-act-0.

United States Senate (2010). City planning: Hearings before the Committee on the District of Columbia, United States Senate on the subject of city planning. Washington, D.C.: U.S. Government Printing Office. Retrieved 1/19/21 from https://catalog.hathitrust.org/Record/007978591.

University Economic Development Association (EDA) (2021). About. Retrieved 3/17/21 from https://universityeda.org/about-us

University of California, Berkeley (1867–1977) (2021) Sanborn fire insurance maps. Retrieved 1/29/21 from http://vm136.lib.berkeley.edu/EART/snb-intr.html.

University of California, Berkeley (2021). Urban displacement project website. Retrieved 9/9/21 from www.urbandisplacement.org/.

Urban Affairs Association (UAA) (2021). UAA website. Retrieved 4/12/21 from https://urbanaffairsassociation.org/.

Utopia and Dystopia (2019). List of dystopian literature – dystopian novels. Retrieved 1/9/22 from www.utopiaanddystopia.com/dystopian-fiction/dystopian-literature-list/.

Utopia and Dystopia [website] (2019). List of utopian literature – utopian novels. Retrieved 1/9/22 from www.utopiaanddystopia.com/utopian-fiction/utopian-literature-list/.

Vale, L. (2002). *Reclaiming public housing: A half century of struggle in three public neighborhoods*. Cambridge, MA: Harvard University Press.

Vale, L. (2007). *From the puritans to the projects: Public housing and public neighbors*. Cambridge, MA: Harvard University Press.

Vale, L. (2013). *Purging the poorest: Public housing and the design politics of twice-cleared communities*. Chicago, IL: University of Chicago Press.

Vale, L. (2020 [2016]). Resilient cities: Clarifying concept or catch-all cliché? In R. LeGates & F. Stout (eds), *The city reader*, 7th ed (pp. 492–502). Abingdon, GB and New York City, NY: Routledge.

Vale, L. & Campanella, T. (2005). *The resilient city: How modern cities recover from disaster*. Oxford, GB: Oxford University Press.

Vale, L. & Freemark, Y. (2012). From public housing to public–private housing. *Journal of the American Planning Association*, 78(4), 379–402.

Van der Ryn, S. & Cowan, S. (1995). *Ecological design*. Washington, D.C.: Island Press.

Vespa, J., Armstrong, D., & Medina, L. (2021). *Demographic turning points for the United States: Population projections for 2020 to 2060*. Washington, D.C.: United States Census Bureau.

Village of Arlington Heights vs Metropolitan Housing Development Corporation (1977). 429 U.S. 252, 97 S. Ct. 555 (1977).

Vision Zero Network (2021). What is Vision Zero?. Retrieved 2/23/21 from https://visionzeronetwork.org/about/what-is-vision-zero/.

Von Hoffman, A. (2000). Why they built Pruitt–Igoe. In R. Biles & K. Szylvian (eds), *Tenements to the Taylor Homes: In search of an urban housing policy in twentieth-century America* (pp. 180–205). University Park, PA: Pennsylvania State University Press.

Von Hoffman, A. (2000). A study in contradictions: The origins and legacy of the housing act of 1949. *Housing Policy Debate*, 11(2), 299–326.

von Thünen, H. (1848). *Der isolierte Staat in Beziehuhng auf Landwirtschaft und Nationalökonomie* (The isolated state in relationship to agriculture and the national economy). Rostock, DE: von Thünen.

Waldheim, C. (2006). *The landscape urbanism reader*. Princeton, NJ: Princeton University Press.

Waldheim, C. (2016). *Landscape as urbanism*. Princeton, NJ: Princeton University Press.

Wales (2019). *National Development Framework 2020–2040, Consultation Draft 7 August–1 November 2019*. Retrieved 2/10/21 from https://gov.wales/draft-national-development-framework.

Walker, J. (2007). *Human transit: How clearer thinking about public transit can enrich our communities and our lives*. Washington, D.C.: Island Press.

Walker, R., Jojola, T., & Natcher, D. (eds) (2013). *Reclaiming indigenous planning*. Montreal, QC: McGill-Queen's University Press.

Wallace-Wells, D. (2019). *The uninhabitable earth*. New York City, NY: Tim Duggan Books.

Ward, M. (2020). Enterprise zones. London: House of Commons briefing paper 5942. Retrieved 5/5/21 from https://commonslibrary.parliament.uk/research-briefings/sn05942/.

Warner, S.B. (1962). *Streetcar suburbs*. Cambridge, MA: Harvard University Press.

Warner, S.B. (1968). *The private city*. Philadelphia, PA: University of Pennsylvania Press.

Watson, D. & Adams, M. (2010). *Design for flooding: Architecture, landscape, and urban design for resilience to climate change*. New York City, NY: Wiley.

Watson, V. (2009). Seeing from the south: Refocusing urban planning on the globe's central urban issues. *Urban Studies*, 46(11), 2259–2275.

Watson, V. & de Satgé, R. (2018). *Urban planning in the global south: Conflicting rationalities in contested urban space*. New York City, NY: Palgrave Macmillan.

Weart, S. (2008). *The discovery of global warming*, revised and expanded ed. Cambridge, MA: Harvard University Press.

Weart, S. (2021). Biosphere: How life alters climate. Retrieved 3/13/21 from https://history.aip.org/climate/biota.htm.

Weart, S. (2021). Ice sheets and rising sea levels. Retrieved 3/13/21 from https://history.aip.org/climate/floods.htm.

Weart, S. (2021). Impacts of climate change. Retrieved 3/13/21 from https://history.aip.org/climate/impacts.htm.

Weart, S. (2021). Introduction: A hyperlinked history of climate change science. Retrieved 3/13/21 from https://history.aip.org/climate/summary.htm.

Weart, S. (2021). Modern temperature trend. Retrieved 3/13/21 from https://history.aip.org/climate/20ctrend.htm.

Weart, S. (2021). Money for Keeling: Monitoring CO_2 levels. Retrieved 3/13/21 from https://history.aip.org/climate/Kfunds.htm.

Weart, S. (2021). Ocean currents and climate. Retrieved 3/13/21 from https://history.aip.org/climate/oceans.htm.

Weart, S. (202l). Other greenhouse gases. Retrieved 3/13/21 from https://history.aip.org/climate/othergas.htm.

Weart, S. (2021). Rapid climate change. Retrieved 3/13/21 from https://history.aip.org/climate/rapid.htm.

Weart, S. (2021) Roger Revelle's discovery. Retrieved 3/13/21 from https://history.aip.org/climate/Revelle.htm.

Weart, S. (2021). Simple models of climate change. Retrieved 3/13/21 from https://history.aip.org/climate/simple.htm.

Weart, S. (2021). The carbon dioxide greenhouse effect. Retrieved 3/13/21 from https://history.aip.org/climate/co2.htm.

Weart, S. (2021). The discovery of global warming. Retrieved 3/13/21 from https://history.aip.org/climate/index.htm.

Weart, S. (2021). The government view from Washington. Retrieved 3/13/21 from https://history.aip.org/climate/Govt.htm.

Weart, S. (2021). Timeline (milestones). Retrieved 3/13/21 from https://history.aip.org/climate/timeline.htm.

Weart, S. (2021). Where to find other information. Retrieved 3/13/21 from https://history.aip.org/history/climate/index.htm.

Webber, M. (1964). The urban place and the nonplace urban realm. In M. Webber et al. (eds), *Explorations into urban structure* (pp. 79–153). Philadelphia, PA: University of Pennsylvania Press.

Weber, A. (1909). *Über den Standort der Industrie* (The location of industry). Tübingen, DE: Mohr.

Weller, V. (2002). *Biopolis: Patrick Geddes and the city of life*. Cambridge, MA: Massachusetts Institute of Technology Press.

Weninger, K. (2020). European space and spatial policy. In R. LeGates & F. Stout (eds), *The City Reader*, 7th ed (pp. 252–263). Abingdon, GB and New York City, NY: Routledge.

Werner, R., Farbstein, J., Lubenau, A., & Shibley, R. (2013). Louisville Waterfront Park. Retrieved 1/29/21 from www.rudybruneraward.org/wp-content/uploads/2016/08/05-Louisville-Waterfront-Park.pdf.

Wheeler, S. (2012). *Climate change and social ecology*. Abingdon, GB and New York City, NY: Routledge.

Wheeler, S. (2021). *Reimagining sustainable cities*. Berkeley, CA: University of California Press.

Wheeler, S. & Beatley, T. (2016). *The sustainable urban development reader*, 3rd ed. Abingdon, GB and New York City, NY: Routledge.

White, M. & White, L. (1962). *The intellectual versus the city: From Thomas Jefferson to Frank Lloyd Wright*. Cambridge, MA: Harvard/MIT Joint Center for Urban Studies.

White House (2015). National security implications of a changing climate. Washington, D.C.: White House.

White House (2021). Fact sheet: The American jobs plan. Washington, D.C.: The White House. Retrieved 5/6/21 from www.whitehouse.gov/briefing-room/statements-releases/2021/03/31/fact-sheet-the-american-jobs-plan/.

Whyte, W. (1980). *The social life of small urban spaces*. New York City. NY: Project for Public Spaces.

Whyte, W. (1988). *City: Rediscovering the center*. New York City, NY: Doubleday.

Whyte, W. (1988). The social life of small urban space [video]. Santa Monica, CA: Direct Cinema.

Wilderness Act (1964). Public Law 88-577 (16 U.S.C. §§1131–1136). 88th Congress, Second Session. Adopted September 3, 1964.

Wilson, E. (1984). *Biophilia*. Cambridge, MA: Harvard University Press.

Wilson, J. (ed) (1968). *Urban renewal: The record and the controversy*. Cambridge, MA: Massachusetts Institute of Technology Press.

Wilson, J. (1987). *The truly disadvantaged*. Chicago, IL: University of Chicago Press.

Wilson, R. (2019). How to launch your planning career [video]. Retrieved 4/12/21 from www.youtube.com/watch?v=vgwb5m6xVds.

World Bank (2018). Transport. Retrieved from www.worldbank.org/en/topic/transport/overview.

World Bank (2020). Motor vehicles per 1,000 people. Retrieved 2/24/21 from http://data.worldbank.org/indicator/IS.VEH.NVEH.P3.

World Bank (2021). *World development indicators 2020*. Washington, D.C.: World Bank. Retrieved 1/18/21 from https://datatopics.worldbank.org/world-development-indicators/.

World Economic Forum (2019). These 11 sinking cities could disappear by 2100. Retrieved 3/11/21 from www.wcforum.org/agenda/2019/09/11-sinking-cities-that-could-soon-be-underwater/.

World Green Building Council (WBC) (2018). WBC rating tools. Retrieved 6/12/21 from www.worldgbc.org/rating-tools.

World Health Organization (WHO) (2015). *Global status report on road safety 2015*. Geneva, CH: WHO.

World Health Organization (WHO) (2021). Air pollution. Retrieved 3/12/21 from www.who.int/health-topics/air-pollution#tab=tab_1.

Wright, F.L. (1930). *The disappearing city*. New York City, NY: W.F. Payson.

Wright, F.L. (1935). *Broadacre City: A new community plan*. Scottsdale, AZ: Frank Lloyd Wright Foundation.

Wright, L., Kemp, S., & Williams, I. (2011). Carbon footprinting: Towards a universally accepted definition. *Carbon Management*, 2(1), 61–72.

Wright, T. (2013). The Regional Plan Association: A civic planning model for New York. *The Urbanist*, 526.

Wu, F. (2018). *Planning for growth*. Abingdon, GB and New York City, NY: Routledge.

Wulf, A. (2016). *The invention of nature: Alexander von Humboldt's new world*. Minneapolis, MN: Highbridge.

Young, I. (2005). Justice and the politics of difference. In S. Fainstein & L. Servon (eds), *Gender and planning: A reader* (pp. 86–103). New Brunswick, NJ: Rutgers University Press.

Yu, K. (2016). *Sponge city: Theory and practice*. Beijing, CN: China Architecture & Building Press.

Yu, K. (2020). *Ideal landscapes: The deep meaning of feng-shui: Patterns of biological and cultural genes*. Novato, CA: ORO Editions.

Zaferatos, N. (2015). Planning the American Indian reservation: From theory to empowerment. Syracuse, NY: Syracuse University Press.

Zeedyk, B. & Clothier, V. (2014). *Let the water do the work*, 2nd ed. White River Junction, VT: Chelsea Green Press.

Zero-Emission Vehicles Act (2020). U.S. Congress. 115th congress, 2nd session, S. 3664.

Zhang, L, Zhao, M., & LeGates, R. (2015). *Understanding Chinese urbanization*. Cheltenham, GB: Edward Elgar Press.

Zhu, J. (1999). *The transition of China's urban development: From plan controlled to market-led*. New York City, NY: Praeger.

Zhu, J. (2019). *Urban development in China under the institution of land rights*. Abingdon, GB and New York, NY: Routledge.

Zukin, S. (2011). *Naked City: The death and life of authentic urban places*. Oxford, GB: Oxford University Press.

ACRONYMS

3Cs	continuing, cooperative, and comprehensive (planning)	ATM	active transportation management
501(c)(3)	tax-exempt nonprofit corporation (USA)	AUTOSAR	Automotive Open System Architecture
A-95	U.S. Office of Management and Budget regional review	BANANA	build absolutely nothing anywhere near anything
AAA	American Anthropology Association	BATNA	best alternative to a negotiated agreement
AAG	American Association of Geographers	BCDC	(San Francisco) Bay Conservation and Development Commission
ACLU	American Civil Liberties Union	BLM	Bureau of Land Management (USA)
ACPI	American City Planning Institute	BLS	Bureau of Labor Statistics (USA)
ACS	American Community Survey	BMIR	below market interest rate (mortgage)
ACSP	Association of Collegiate Schools of Planning	BRT	Bus Rapid Transit
ADA	American with Disabilities Act	C2ES	Center for Climate and Energy Solutions
ADT	Annual Average Daily Traffic	CAD	computer-assisted design
AEA	American Economics Association	CAFE	Corporate Average Fuel Economy (standard)
AESOP	Association of European Schools of Planning	CAP	community action program
AHAR	*Annual Homeless Assessment Report* (U.S. Department of Housing and Urban Development)	CASA	Centre for Advanced Spatial Analysis
AIA	American Institute of Architects	CatEx	categorical exclusion (NEPA)
AICP	American Institute of Certified Planners	CATS	Center for Applied Transect Studies
AIP	American Institute of Planners	CAVE	citizen against virtually everything
ALEC	American Legislative Exchange Council	CBD	central business district
APA	American Planning Association	CBD	Center for Biological Diversity
APIGBV	Asian Pacific Institute on Gender-Based Violence	CBPP	Center on Budget and Policy Priorities
APO	areawide planning organization	CCC	Center for Community Change
ARC	Appalachian Regional Commission	CCS	Center for Climate and Security
ART	Autonomous Rapid Transit	CDBG	Community Development Block Grant
ASA	American Sociological Association	CDC	community development corporation
ASCE	American Society of Civil Engineers	CDC	Centers for Disease Control (USA)
ASLA	American Society of Landscape Architects	CEQ	Council on Environmental Quality (USA)
ASPO	American Society of Planning Officials		

CEQA	California Environmental Quality Act	DSNI	Dudley Street Neighborhood Initiative
CERCLA	Comprehensive Environmental Response, Compensation, and Liability Act	EA	environmental assessment
		EC	European Commission
		EDA	Economic Development Administration (USA)
CFCs	chlorofluorocarbons	EIA	Energy Information Administration (USA)
CHA	Chicago Housing Authority		
CHIP	connected, heterogeneous, intelligent, and personalized (mobility framework)	EIR	environmental impact report
		EIS	environmental impact statement
CHODO	community housing development organization	ELIHPA	Emergency Low-Income Housing Preservation Act
CIAM	Congrès Internationaux d'Architecture Moderne (International Congresses of Modern Architecture)	EPA	Environmental Protection Agency (USA)
		ESRI	Environmental Science Research Institute
CIC	complexity in cities (theory)	EU	European Union
CIP	Canadian Institute of Planners	EURA	European Urban Research Association
CIP	capital improvement program		
CNU	Congress of the New Urbanism	FAICP	Fellow of the American Institute of Certified Planners
CO_2	carbon dioxide		
COG	Council of Governments	Fannie Mae	Federal National Mortgage Association (FNMA)
ConPlan	consolidated plan		
CPB	Customs and Border Patrol (USA)	FAR	floor area ratio
CPI	consumer price index	FAST Act	Fixing America's Surface Transportation Act
CPS	Current Population Survey		
CPTED	crime prevention through environmental design	FBCI	Form-Based Code Institute
		FDI	foreign direct investment
CRS	Congressional Research Service (USA)	FDIC	Federal Deposit Insurance Corporation (USA)
CSSR	Centre for Social Studies and Reforms	FEMA	Federal Emergency Management Agency (USA)
CWA	Clean Water Act	FERA	Federal Emergency Administration of Public Works
CZMA	Coastal Zone Management Act		
CZMP	Coastal Zone Management Program	FHA	Federal Housing Administration (USA)
DARPA	Defense Advanced Research Projects Agency (USA)	FHEO	Fair Housing and Equal Opportunity Office (HUD)
DESA	Department of Economic and Social Affairs (UN)	FHFA	Federal Housing Finance Agency
		FHLMC	Federal Home Loan Mortgage Corporation (USA)
D/I	diversity/inclusion (strategy)		
DINK	double income no kids	FHWA	Federal Highway Administration
DLCD	Department of Land Conservation and Development (Oregon)	FMR	fair market rent
		FNMA	Federal National Mortgage Association (USA)
DOA	Department of Agriculture (USA)	FONSI	finding of no significant impact
DOC	Department of Commerce (USA)	FPL	federal poverty level
DOI	Department of the Interior (USA)	Freddie Mac	Federal Home Loan Mortgage Corporation (FHLMC)
DOJ	Department of Justice (USA)		
DOT	Department of Transportation (USA)	FTA	Federal Transit Administration
		FWIG	Faculty Women's Interest Group (ACSP)
DPZ	Duany Plater-Zyberk		

FWS	Fish and Wildlife Service (USA)	HUD	Department of Housing and Urban Development (USA)
FY	fiscal year		
G20	Group of Twenty (top industrialized nations)	IACP	International Association of China Planning
G7	Group of Seven (top industrialized nations)	IAPMO	International Association of Plumbing and Mechanical Officials
GAP	General Assembly Partners (UN)		
GaWC	Global and World Cities Network	ICE	U.S. Immigration and Customs Enforcement
GCA	Garden Cities Association		
GCPS	Garden City Pioneer Society	ICLEI	International Council for Local Environmental Initiatives
GDP	gross domestic product		
GFTGFY	good for them, great for you	ICMA	International City Management Association
GHG	greenhouse gas		
Ginnie Mae	Government National Mortgage Corporation (GNMC)	IEA	International Energy Administration
GIS	geographical information system (also: geographical information science)	IGCI	International Garden Cities Institute
		IPCC	Intergovernmental Panel on Climate Change (UN)
GM	General Motors		
GNC	global network connectivity	IRS	Internal Revenue Service (USA)
GNMA	Government National Mortgage Association	ISOCARP	International Society of City and Regional Planners
GPEAN	Global Planning Education Association Network	ISTEA	Intermodal Surface Transportation Efficiency Act
GPEIG	Global Planning Educators Interest Group	IWRM	integrated water resources management
GPS	Global Positioning System	Jabodetabek	Jakarta, Indonesia metropolitan region
GPUS	Green Party of the United States		
GRTA	Georgia Regional Transportation Authority	JAIP	*Journal of the American Institute of Planners*
GtCO$_2$e	gigaton of CO$_2$ equivalent	JAPA	*Journal of the American Planning Association*
GUI	graphical user interface		
HAC	Housing Assistance Council	JCHS	Joint Center for Housing Studies (Harvard University)
HALRB	Historical Affairs and Landmark Review Board		
		JPER	*Journal of Planning Education and Research*
HAMP	Home Affordable Modification Program		
		LCC	large city cluster
HCP	Habitat Conservation Plan	LCFS	low-carbon fuel standard
HCV	housing choice voucher	LEED	Leadership in Energy and Environmental Design (standards)
HDC	housing development corporation		
HFA	housing finance agency		
HHFA	Housing and Home Finance Agency (USA)	LHA	local housing authority
		LIHPRHA	Low-Income Housing Preservation and Resident Homeownership Act (1990)
HOME	Home Investment Partnership Program		
HOPE VI	Housing Opportunities for People Everywhere (program)	LIHTC	Low-Income Housing Tax Credit (program)
		Little NEPA	State Environmental Policy Act
HOV	high-occupancy vehicle	LOS	level of service
HPMS	Highway Performance Monitoring System	LULU	locally unwanted land use
		LUTAQ	land use, transportation, and air quality (planning)
HSR	high-speed rail		

M2M	Mark to Market (program)	NHC	National Housing Conference
MAP-21	Moving Ahead for Progress in the 21st Century	NHTS	National Highway Travel Survey
		NIDL	new international division of labor (theory)
MCP	Master's of City Planning		
MCRP	Master's of City and Regional Planning	NIMBY	not in my back yard
		NIMEY	not in my election year
MPO	metropolitan planning agency	NLC	National League of Cities
MSA	metropolitan statistical area	NLIHC	National Low Income Housing Coalition
MSU	Michigan State University		
MTO	Moving to Opportunity (program)	NLLUS	National Longitudinal Land Use Survey
MTW	Moving to Work (program)	NOAA	National Oceanographic and Atmospheric Administration (USA)
MUD	Master's of Urban Design		
NAA	Non-Attainment Area (permit)		
NAAQS	National Ambient Air Quality Standards	NORC	naturally occurring retirement community
NACo	National Association of Counties (USA)	NPDES	National Pollutant Discharge Elimination System
NALHFA	National Association of Local Housing Agencies	NPDWR	National Primary Drinking Water Regulations
NARC	National Association of Regional Councils	NRDC	National Resources Defense Council
NASA	National Aeronautics and Space Administration (USA)	NRPB	National Resources Planning Board
NCCP	Natural Communities Conservation Plan	NSDWR	National Secondary Drinking Water Regulations
NCFDD	National Center for Faculty Development and Diversity	NSPS	New Source Performance Standards
NCHFA	National Council of State Housing Agencies	NSR	New Source Review
		NYLON	New York and London
NCSG	National Center for Smart Growth	OAHP	Office of Affordable Housing Preservation
NCSR	New Construction/Substantial Rehabilitation (program)	OECD	Organisation for Economic Co-operation and Development
NCSS	National Cooperative Soil Survey	OEO	Office of Economic Opportunity (USA)
NCTSPM	National Center for Transportation Systems Productivity and Management		
		OMB	Office of Management and Budget (USA)
NDC	nationally determined contribution (to reducing GHG emissions)	OPEC	Organization of Petroleum Exporting Countries
		OPR	Office of Planning and Research (California)
NEC	National Electrical Code		
NEJAC	National Environmental Justice Advisory Council	OSM	Open Street Map
		OUQ	L'Ordre des urbanistes du Québec (Canada)
NEOSCC	Northeast Ohio Sustainable Communities Consortium	PAB	Planning Accreditation Board
NEPA	National Environmental Policy Act	PAS	Planners Advisory Service
		PBS	Public Broadcasting System
NESHAP	National Emissions Standards for Hazardous Air Pollutants	PD&R	Policy Development and Research
		PEO	Planners for Equal Opportunity
NFPA	National Fire Protection Association (USA)	PILOT	payment in lieu of taxes

PITI	principal, interest, taxes, and insurance	SDWA	Safe Drinking Water Act
PM2.5	2.5-micrometer particulate matter	Section 221(d)(3)	Rental Below Market Interest Rate Program (1962)
POCIG	Planners of Color Interest Group	Section 235	Below Market Interest Rate Homeownership Program (1974)
POPOS	privately owned public open space	Section 236	Below Market Interest Rate Rental Program (1974)
PPP	purchasing power parity	Section 8	Rental Housing Voucher Program (1974)
PPP	public–private partnership		
PPS	Project for Public Space	SIP	state implementation plan
PPSM	Persons per square mile	SNCC	Student Nonviolent Coordinating Committee
PRRAC	Poverty and Race Research and Action Council	SNCPC	Singapore National Crime Prevention Council
PTIA	Provincial and Territorial Institutes and Associations (Canada)	SOCS	Standard Occupational Classification System
PSB	Professional Standards Board (Canada)	SPSS	Statistical Package for the Social Sciences
PSD	Prevention of Significant Deterioration (permit)	SSPEA	Standard State Planning Enabling Act
PUD	planned unit development	SSZEA	Standard State Zoning Enabling Act
PUMA	Public Use Microdata Area	STEM	science, technology, engineering, and mathematics
PWA	Public Works Administration		
QAP	Qualified Allocation Plan	STIP	state transportation improvement program
RAD	Rental Assistance Demonstration (program)		
RC	regional council	SUM	Society for the Establishment of Useful Manufactures
RCI	Roadway Congestion Index		
RCRA	Resource Conservation and Recovery Act (USA)	SWOT	strengths, weaknesses, opportunities, and threats (analysis)
Recap	Office of Recapitalization		
RFQ	request for qualifications	TARP	Troubled Assets Relief Program
RGGI	Regional Greenhouse Gas Initiative (RGGI)	TAZ	transportation analysis zone
		TBC	The Boring Company
RLIS	Regional Land Information System	TDM	travel demand management
		TDR	transfer of development rights
RPA	Regional Plan Association (New York)	TIA	transportation impact analysis
		TIF	tax increment financing
RPAA	Regional Planning Association of America	TIP	transportation improvement project
RSA	Regional Science Association	TOPA	Tenant Opportunity to Own Assistance
RSAI	Regional Science Association International		
RTPI	Royal Town Planning Institute	TPES	total primary energy supply
S&L	savings and loan (bank)	TRB	Transportation Research Board (USA)
SA2020	San Antonio 2020		
SACRPH	Society for American City and Regional Planning History	TRI	Toxic Release Inventory
		TRI	Travel Time Index
SAFMR	small area fair market rent	TSDF	treatment, storage, and disposal facility
SBA	Small Business Administration (USA)		
		TTI	travel time index
SDSN	Sustainable Development Solutions Network (UN)	TVA	Tennessee Valley Authority
		UAA	Urban Affairs Association

UDAG	Urban Development Action Grant	UTC	urban transportation center
UDP	Urban Displacement Project (University of California, Berkeley)	VMT	vehicle miles traveled
		WCED	World Commission on Environment and Development (UN)
UGB	urban growth boundary		
ULL	urban limit line	WEF	World Economic Forum
UNEP	United Nations Environment Programme	WGBC	World Green Building Council
		WHO	World Health Organization
UNFCCC	United Nations Framework Convention on Climate Change	WMO	World Meteorological Organization
UN-Habitat	United Nations Human Settlements Programme	WMRT	Wallace McHarg Roberts & Todd
		WPA	Works Progress Administration
UPC	Uniform Plumbing Code	WPSC	World Planning Schools Conference
USGBC	United States Green Building Council		
		WQS	water quality standard
USGCRP	U.S. Global Change Research Project	WTO	World Trade Organization
		WWF	World Wildlife Fund
USGS	United States Geological Survey	ZEV	zero-emission vehicle

FIGURE CREDITS

Every effort has been made to contact copyright holders for their permission to reprint figures in this book. The publishers would be grateful to hear from any copyright holder who is not here acknowledged and will undertake to rectify any errors or omissions in future editions of this book. Following is copyright information for the figures that appear in this book.

Figure 0.1 Richard LeGates, Richard LeGates.

Figure 1.1 Multiple Flows: London Tube, Rail, and Flickr Networks. Michael Batty. Redrawn and modified from Michael Batty *Inventing Future Cities*. Cambridge, MA: Massachusetts Institute of Technology.

Figure 1.2 National Planning Commission Sketch of Urban Design for South Capital Street, Washington, D.C. Washington National Planning Commission.

Figure 1.3 U.S. City and Regional Planning Specializations, Catherine Brinkley and Charles Hoch.

Figure 1.4 Jane Jacobs, Phil Stanziola, New York World-Telegram and *The Sun Newspaper*.

Figure 2.1 Kingsley Davis's Urbanization S Curve (England), Tara Singh © 2021 Richard LeGates.

Figure 2.2 Kingsley Davis's "Family" of Urbanization S Curves, Tara Singh © 2021 Richard LeGates.

Figure 2.2a United States, Tara Singh © 2021 Richard LeGates.

Figure 2.2b China, Tara Singh © 2021 Richard LeGates.

Figure 2.2c Cambodia, Tara Singh © 2021 Richard LeGates.

Figure 2.3 Boston Harbor, 1774, Boston Public Library.

Figure 2.4 Geneva, Illinois (1869), A. Ruger, Merchant's Lithographing Co., U.S. Library of Congress.

Figure 2.5 L'Enfant Plan for Washington, D.C. (1791), Andrew Ellicott, 1792. Revised from Pierre (Peter) L'Enfant, Thackara and Valance, sc. U.S. Library of Congress.

Figure 2.6 Crowded Lodging in a Bayard Street Tenement by Jacob Riis (1889), The American YAWP, Stanford University.

Figure 2.7 Dumbbell Tenement, New York (State), *Tenement House Commission, Tenement house reform in New York, 1834–1900* (New York: Evening Post Job Printing House, 1900).

Figure 2.8 Robert Fulton's Steamboat *Clermont* (1807), George Grantham Bain Collection/Library of Congress (LC-DIG-ggbain-000005).

Figure 2.9 Horse-Drawn Streetcar (Hamilton, Virginia, circa 1874), Local History and Archives Hamilton, Virginia Public Library. Wikimedia Commons 14164495916.

Figure 2.10 "Big Red", Los Angeles Electric Streetcar (circa 1930), Oleknutlee.

Figure 2.11 Pacific Electric Railway Streetcars Awaiting Dismantling for Scrap Metal (Los Angeles, California, 1956), *Los Angeles Times*.

Figure 2.12 Patrick Geddes, The Geddes Centre, Edinburgh, Scotland.

Figure 3.1 Andrés Duany's Transect, Andrés Duany, courtesy of DPZ CoDesign.

Figure 3.2 Kevin Lynch's 5 Image of the City Elements. Drawing credit: Kevin Lynch, *The Image of the City*, 5 image form element sketches, pp. 47 and 48. © 1960 Massachusetts Institute of Technology, by permission of The MIT Press.

Figure 3.3 Strøget (Copenhagen, Denmark, 2013), *City Clock Magazine*.

Figure 3.4 Computer-Generated Street Network, created by Geoff Boeing (Boeing, 2017).

Figure 3.5 False Creek Waterfront (Vancouver, Canada), Karoline Cullen, Shutterstock Photo ID: 6480931.

Figure 3.6 Louisville Waterfront Park, Charles Mayer, courtesy of Hargreaves Associates.

Figure 3.7 Hargreaves Jones Rendering of Louisville Waterfront Park, Charles Mayer, courtesy of Hargreaves Associates.

Figure 4.1 Members of Boston's City Council (2021), courtesy of Boston City Council.

Figure 4.2 Julian Castro, U.S. Department of Housing and Urban Development.

Figure 4.3 Anti-Fracking Protest (Hollywood, California, 2014), Dan Holm/Shutterstock Photo ID: 221939047.

Figure 4.4 Pro-"Dreamers" Rally (Ann Arbor, Michigan, 2017), Susan Montgomery/Shutterstock Photo ID: 1113608147.

Figure 4.5 Protester at the United States Capitol (2006), Sergei Novikov/Shutterstock Photo ID: 1340489333.

Figure 5.1 John Friedmann, courtesy of John Friedmann.

Figure 5.2 The Rational Planning Model, Tara Singh © 2021 Richard LeGates.

Figure 5.3 Brasília, Brazil (2015), Anna Volpe/Agência Senado. Fotos produzidas pel Senado. Senado Federal do Brazil.

Figure 5.4 Miscommunication in Planning, Tara Singh © 2021 Richard LeGates.

Figure 6.1 New Lanark, Scotland, circa 1825, unknown painter, New Lanark, Scotland Visitor's Center.

Figure 6.2 New Lanark, Scotland Historic District (2021), DMC Photogallery/Shutterstock.

Figure 6.3 Ebenezer Howard's Three Magnets, public domain, from Howard (2002 [1898]).

Figure 6.4 Ebenenezer Howard's Group of Slumless Smokeless Cities, public domain, from Howard (2002 [1898]).

Figure 6.5 "The Lagoon and Agricultural Building at the World's Columbian Exhibition (Chicago, Illinois, 1893), World's Columbian Exhibition Committee (1893).

Figure 6.6 Proposed Civic Center Plaza and Buildings from the *1909 Plan for Chicago*, Charles Guérin, Chicago Commercial Club, 1909 Plan for Chicago.

Figure 6.7 Le Corbusier's Plan for a Contemporary City of 3 Million (1929), Massachusetts Institute of Technology Press.

Figure 6.8 Pudong District, Shanghai, China (2012), J. Patrick Fisher, Wikimedia Commons. File:2012 Pudong.jpg | 2012_Pudong. Copy January 4, 2012.

Figure 6.9 Frank Lloyd Wright with His Broadacre City Model (1935), Frank Lloyd Wright Foundation.

Figure 6.10 Alberto Soria y Mata's Linear City Plan (Madrid, Spain, 1894), Arturo Soria y Mata, from Arturo Soria y Mata *La Ciudad Lineal* (Madrid, 1894).

Figure 6.11 Clarence Perry's Neighborhood Unit (1929), Clarence Perry, The Neighborhood Unit, Volume 3 of the Regional Plan Association Plan of New York and Environs (New York: 1929).

Figure 6.12 North End and Downtown Vision from Boston Vision Plan (2019).

Figure 7.1 *NashvilleNext* Growth and Preservation Concept Map (Nashville, Tennessee, 2018), Metropolitan Government of Nashville and Davidson County Planning Department.

Figure 7.2 Madison County, Tennessee, Community Plan Transect Map, Madison County, Tennessee.

Figure 7.3 Madison County, Tennessee, Community Plan Transect Illustration, Madison County, Tennessee.

Figure 8.1 Allan Jacobs, courtesy of Allan Jacobs.

Figure 8.2 City of Falls Church, Virginia Zoning Map (2021), City of Falls Church, Virginia.

Figure 8.3 Typical Zoning Building Envelope, Height Limit, and Setbacks, Tara Singh © Richard LeGates.

Figure 8.4 Floor Area Ratio (FAR), Tara Singh © Richard LeGates.

Figure 8.5 Columbia Pike Form-Based Code Building Envelope Standards for Neighborhood Sites (Arlington, Virginia, 2013), Arlington County, Virginia/Dover Kohl Associates.

Figure 8.6 Gary Hack, courtesy of Gary Hack.

Figure 9.1 Sherry Arnstein's Ladder of Citizen Participation, *Journal of the American Planning Association*.

Figure 9.2 Black Lives Matter (Albany, New York, 2020), Jim Franco Photos/Shutterstock Photo ID: 1753155377.

Figure 9.3 June Thomas, courtesy of June Thomas.

Figure 9.4 1934 Map of Boston Area Showing Redlined Neighborhoods, *Cram's Street Map of the Boston Area* (1934).

Figure 10.1 Tennessee Valley Authority Dam Construction Workers (1943), Tennessee Valley Authority.

Figure 10.2 Patrick Geddes's Valley Section, Patrick Geddes.

Figure 10.3 Illustration of Central Place Theory by Walter Christaller (1933), Walter Christaller. From Walter Christaller, *Die zentralen Orte in Sud Deutschland*. Jena, Germany: Gustav Fischer (1933).

Figure 10.4 Urban Sprawl, Ryan Haggerty. United States Fish and Wildlife Service. Wikimedia Commons (8427451222).jpg.

Figure 10.5 Catherine Ross, courtesy of Catherine Ross.

Figure 10.6 Metro's 2040 Concept Map (Portland, Oregon, 1980), Metro, Portland, Oregon.

Figure 10.7 *Vibrant Northeast Ohio 2040 Plan* Workshop, Northeast Ohio Sustainable Communities Consortium.

Figure 10.8 *Vibrant Northeast Ohio 2040 Plan* Digital Dashboard Dial, Northeast Ohio Sustainable Communities Consortium.

Figure 10.9 Regional Plan Association Projected U.S. Megaregions 2050, Regional Plan Association.

Figure 11.1 United Nations World Urban Population Estimate 2020 and Projections to 2050, United Nations Department of Social and Economic Affairs.

Figure 11.2 NASA "Black Marble" Night Sky in Western Europe and Northwest Africa, U.S. National Aeronautics and Space Administration.

Figure 11.3 Hyderabad, India (2012), SNEHIT PHOTO/Shutterstock Photo ID: 147925229.

Figure 11.4 Charminar Bazaar, Hyderabad, India, Santi45 Pervaram/Shutterstock Photo ID: 1500171746.

Figure 11.5 La Défense Business District (Paris, France), Matej Kastelic/Shutterstock Photo ID: 448138693.

Figure 11.6 Ekurhuleni Aerotropolis, Ekurhuleni, South Africa, Pretoria Travel.

Figure 11.7 Global Network Connectivity according to the Global and World Cities Network, Peter Taylor © 2020 Richard LeGates and Frederic Stout.

Figure 11.8 Flooding in Jakarta, Indonesia (2013), Dani Daniar/Shutterstock Photo ID: 521794138.

Figure 11.9 Eugenie Birch, courtesy of Eugenie Birch.

Figure 12.1 Ann Forsyth, courtesy of Ann Forsyth.

Figure 12.2 Tennessee Valley Authority Programs, Tennessee Valley Authority.

Figure 12.3 Community Leaders Reviewing a Model of the Pruit–Igoe Public Housing Project (St. Louis, Missouri, circa 1953), United States Department of Housing and Urban Development.

Figure 12.4 Demolition of the Pruitt–Igoe Project (1972), United States Department of Housing and Urban Development.

Figure 12.5 Pike Place Market (Seattle Washington, 2019), EchoVisuals.

Figure 13.1 Map Layers Illustrating Ian McHarg's Design with Nature Method, Tara Singh © 2021 Richard LeGates.

Figure 13.2 Geographical Information System Map Layers, Tara Singh © 2021 Richard LeGates.

Figure 13.3 Biophilic Design, Eindhoven, the Netherlands (2021), Lea Rae/Shutterstock.

Figure 13.4 Industrial Wasteland, jfergusonphotos/Shutterstock.

Figure 13.5 Cornell Dubilier Superfund Site (South Plainfield, New Jersey), Danita Delimont/Shutterstock Photo ID: 1284280639.

Figure 13.6 U.S. Army Corps of Engineers Map Showing Areas of San Francisco Bay "Susceptible to Reclamation", U.S. Army Corps of Engineers. Future Development of the San Francisco Bay Area, 1960–2020 (1960).

Figure 14.1 Complete Streets Design, Nelson Peng HDR Partners.

Figure 14.2 Janette Sadik-Kahn, Olugbenro Ogunsemore.

Figure 14.3 New York City Pedestrianized Street at Broadway and 34th Street, Oleg Ansimov.

Figure 14.4 Bus Rapid Transit, Curitiba, Brazil (2006), Mario Roberto Duran Ortiz, Wikimedia Commons. File:Curitiba 04 2006 06 RIT.jpg | Curitiba_04_2006_06.

Figure 14.5 Ciclovia, Bogotá, Columbia (2015), Fotos593/Shutterstock Photo ID: 299174708.

Figure 14.6 Autonomous Rapid Transit System Design (2021), Nelson Peng HDR Partners.

Figure 14.7 Woonerf (Lodz, Poland, 2014), Zorro2212, Wikimedia Commons. File:First woonerf in Łódź, 6 Sierpnia Street, July 2014 01.jpg.

Figure 14.8 Magnetic Levitation Train (Shanghai, China, 2006), Alex Needham. Wikimedia Commons. File:A maglev train coming out, Pudong International Airport, Shanghai.jpg.

Figure 14.9 Proposed Sydney to Melbourne, Australia Hyperloop (2020), Zac McClelland, Vichyper.

Figure 15.1 Homeless in America, U.S. Department of Housing and Urban Development.

Figure 15.2 Sears, Roebuck and Co. Mail Order House "The Magnolia" (1926), Sears, Roebuck and Co.

Figure 15.3 Housing Efficiency, Tara Singh © 2021 Richard LeGates.

Figure 15.4 Jackson Gardens Public Housing Project (Boston, Massachusetts), courtesy of David Curtis, courtesy of Boston Housing Authority.

Figure 15.5 Robert Weaver, U.S. Department of Housing and Urban Development, Yoichi R. Okamoto, Lyndon Baines Johnson Library and Museum. Image Serial Number W341-2.

Figure 15.6 Paraisópolis, São Paulo, Brazil, Yannick Martinez/Shutterstock Photo ID: 1094704679.

Figure 16.1 Abandoned Packard Automobile Assembly Plant (Detroit, Michigan), Albert Duce, Wikimedia Commons. File: Abandoned Packard Automobile Factory Detroit 200.jpg.

Figure 16.2 Renaissance Center (Detroit, Michigan), Crisco 1492, Wikimedia Commons. File:Renaissance Center, Detroit, Michigan from S 2014-12-07.jpg.

Figure 16.3 Concert at Levitt Pavillion, SteelStacks Arts and Cultural Center

(Bethlehem, Pennsylvania, 2020), Curt Mosel, ArtsQuest Chief Administrative Officer.

Figure 16.4 Falls Church, Virginia Comprehensive Planning Opportunity Area Priority Schedule (2021), City of Falls Church, Virginia.

Figure 16.5 Canary Wharf (London, England), ZGPhotography/Shutterstock Photo ID: 1078854536.

Figure 16.6 River Walk (San Antonio, Texas), Brandon Seidel/Shutterstock Photo ID: 10965619.

Figure 17.1 Global Mean Atmospheric Temperature Increase 1880 to 2020 Relative to 1951–1980 Mean, U.S. National Aeronautics and Space Administration.

Figure 17.2 Silicon Ranch Farm Combining Solar Energy Generation and Regenerative Agriculture (Millington, Tennessee, 2020), Chris Lunghino, Cabriejo Ranch LLC.

Figure 17.3 Storm Surge Barrier (Rotterdam, Netherlands), GLF Media/Shutterstock Photo ID: 1058457203.

Figure 17.4 Kongjian Yu, Kongjian Yu, Turnescape.

Figure 17.5 Puyang River Ecological Corridor (Zhejiang Province, China), Kongjian Yu, Turnescape.

Figure 17.6 Chicago City Hall Green Roof, City of Chicago, Illinois.

INDEX

Note: Figures are indexed in *italic* page numbers. Case Studies are indexed in **bold** page numbers.

1000 Friends of Oregon 127
20/20/20 climate change targets (European Union) 409

AAA *see* American Anthropology Association
AAG *see* Association of American Geographers
AAPI *see* Asian-American and Pacific Islanders
ABAG *see* Association of Bay Area Governments
a priori reasoning 1
Abercrombie, Patrick 384
Abrams, Charles 272
Access Nashville 2040 transportation plan 139, 141, 151n2
accessibility 96, 140, 152, 311, 313–15
ACPI *see* American City Planning Institute (United States)
ACS *see* Annual Community Survey (United States)
ACSP *see* Association of Collegiate Schools of Planning (United States)
Active Transportation Management (ATM) 322
Acts and Regulations (United States) 73–4, 76, 98, 155, 158–9, 167–8, 178–9, 283, 285, 288, 303, 306, 382, 384, 390–1; Clean Air Act (CAA, 1948) *Clean Air Act* amendments, 1990) 152n10, 158, 258, 285–6, 288, 291; Clean Water Act (CWA 1948) also known as the Federal Water Pollution Control Act (FWPCA, 1948) 288; 152n10, 158, 288–289; Clean Water Act Amendments (1972) 308; Dodd-Frank Act (2010) 346; Endangered Species Act (1971) 158, 288 9; Homestead Act 1862 24, 27, 253; National Defense Housing Act (Lanham Act, 1942) 260; National Environmental Policy Act (NEPA) (1971); Resource Conservation and Recovery Act (RCRA) (1976) 300–1; Safe Drinking Water Act (1972) 288; Standard State Zoning Enabling Act (SSZEA) (1922) 28, 163, 259; Standard State Planning Enabling Act (SSPEA) (1926); Violence Against Women Act (2013) 72
Adams, Thomas 37–8, 155
adaptive reuse 375
Addams, Jane 34
adequate facilities ordinances (United States) 290
Adonis, Andrew 383
advance planning 78, 128, 145, 151
advanced producer services 233, 238, 245
advocacy planning 98, 146, 200–202

aerotropolis 235–6; *see also* Kasarda, John
AESOP *see* Association of European Schools of Planning
Affirmatively Furthering Fair Housing Rule (U.S. Department of Housing and Urban Development) 71, 72
affordable housing (United States) 70, 72, 148, 152, 167–8, 199, 271, 273, 277, 339, 343, 347, 350–2; developers 35; funding activities for 354; regional 177; units 199, 259, 350, 360
"Age of Reason" 288
agencies (United States) 70, 148–9, 192, 255, 257, 280, 286, 289, 291–2, 354, 359; designated state coastal management 305; governmental 216; public economic development 391; redevelopment 271–2, 381; social service 276; state housing finance 65
Agenda for Sustainable Development (United Nations, 2015) 362
agent-based models 100
agglomerations (as defined by United Nations Department of Economic and Social Affairs) 224, 419
agglomeration economies 233
agropolitan development 387
Agyeman, Julian 192–3, 202
AHS *see* American Historical Society (United States)
AIA *see* American Institute of Architects (United States)
AICP *see* American Institute of Certified Planners
AIP *see* American Institute of Planners (United States)
AIP *see* American Institute of Physics (United States)
air pollution 126, 143, 147, 152, 269, 285–6, 290, 317, 335, 407
air quality 67, 69, 74, 83, 136, 147, 217, 218, 283, 285, 286, 290, 311, 322, 400, 411, 419n13
Air Quality Control Regions (AQCRs) (United States) 286
air quality planning and regulation 67, 270, 285–6, 411
alcohol addiction 277, 340
ALEC *see* American Legislative Exchange Council (United States)
Albedo 173
Alioto, Joseph, Mayor of San Francisco, California 156
Aman, Willow Lung 197
Amelia Island Plantation, Florida 295

American Anthropology Association (AAA) (United States) 14
American architects 35, 49, 107, 120–21
American City Planning Institute (ACPI) (United States) 41, 280
American Historical Society (United States) 14
American Indian settlements 19, 73, 104n5
American Institute of Architects (United States) 14
American Institute of Certified Planners (AICP) 6, 9, 12–13, 97, 190, 244, 372
American Institute of Physics (AIP) (United States) 395, 418n1
American Institute of Planners (AIP) (United States) 41, 135, 184, 280, 418
American Legislative Exchange Council (ALEC) (United States) 76
American Planning Association (APA) (United States) 6, 12–13, 34, 41, 70, 133–5, 138–9, 189–90, 196–202, 221, 243–4, 254, 280, 378, 391–2
American Political Science Association (APSA) (United States) 14
American Public Transportation Association (APTA) (United States) 324; *Fact Book* (annual) 324
American Society of Civil Engineers (ASCE) (United States) 14
American Society of Landscape Architects (ASLA) (United States) 14, 318, 404
American Society of Planning Officials (ASPO) (United States) 41, 134–5, 280
American Sociological Association (ASA) (United States) 14
Americans with Disabilities Act (ADA) (United States, 1990) 312
AMI *see* Area Median Income 128
anarchism 129
Anderson, Martin 271–2
Angel, Shlomo 213, 236
Angel Island immigration station, San Francisco, California 25
Ann Arbor, Michigan 5, 80
annexation of land to a city (United States) 24, 66, 180n10, 203n7
Annie E. Casey Foundation 193, 203
Annual Community Survey (United States) 138, 174, 208–9, 374
anthropogenic (human caused) climate change 147, 270, 285, 395, 396, 398, 410, 417, 418
anti-fracking protest (Hollywood, California, 2014) 79
anti-racism 74, 193, 200, 202
ADA *see* Americans with Disabilities Act (United States, 1990)
APA *see* American Planning Association (United States)
APOs *see* Areawide Planning Organizations (United States)
Appalachia 206–7, 256
Appalachian Regional Commission 225, 256, 279
Appleyard, Donald 157, 269
APSA *see* American Political Science Association (United States)
APTA *see* American Public Transportation Association (United States)
AQCRs *see* Air Quality Control Regions (United States)

AQDs *see* Regional Air Quality Districts (United States)
aquifers 163, 215, 241, 287, 300
arable land 207, 398
ARC *see* Appalachian Regional Commission (United States)
ArcGIS 3, 9, 87, 93
architecture, vernacular 25, 27, 55, 278, 340
architects 3, 6, 10, 13, 25–7, 33–4, 37, 45–6, 55–6, 95, 155, 157, 175, 277, 279; American 35, 49, 107, 120–21
Arctic 51, 246, 398, 401, 418
Area Median Income (AMI) 340, 347, 352, 354, 365
Areawide Planning Organizations (APOs) (United States) 215
Arnstein, Sherry 74, 97, 98, 146, 202; considers serious and legitimate forms of citizen participation 185; exposes the hypocrisy of local governments 185; ladder of citizen participation 184
ASLA *see* American Society of Landscape Architects (United States)
ASA *see* American Sociological Association (United States)
ASCE *see* American Society of Civil Engineers (United States)
Asian-American and Pacific Islanders (AAPI) 25–6, 40, 190, 192, 196, 200, 253
Asian Americans 196–7, 200, 203
Asian megacities 327
ASLA *see* American Society of Landscape Architects (United States)
ASPO *see* American Society of Planning Officials (United States)
Association of American Geographers (AAG) (United States) 14
Association of Bay Area Governments (ABAG) 134–5
Association of Collegiate Schools of Planning (ACSP) (United States) 5, 7–8, 13, 190, 192–3, 196–202, 216, 243–4, 252, 254, 279–80; conferences 7, 13; Faculty Women's Interest Group (FWIG) 7, 193, 200, 202; members 7, 13; planners 190, 193, 202, 252; Planners of Color Interest Group 200; Presidential Task Force on Anti-Racism 200
Association of European Schools of Planning (AESOP) 100
ART systems *see* Autonomous Rapid Transit systems *328*
Athens Charter (*La charte d'Athènes*) 95
Atlanta (Georgia) Regional Metropolitan Planning Commission 226
ATM *see* Active Transportation Management
Australia 13n11, 90, 111, 252, 287, 332, 395
AutoCAD 2
Automotive Open System Architecture (AUTOSAR) 329
AUTOSAR *see* Automotive Open System Architecture
automobiles 31–2, 54–5, 62, 120–1, 268–9, 286, 290, 316–19, 329–31, 333–5, 400, 410, 414
autonomous vehicles 318, 327, 328, 335
Autonomous Rapid Transit systems (ART systems) *328*

back table (in negotiations) 81, 84
back-to-the-city movement 253
Balkanized local government 66, 135, 390

balloon payment mortgage 27, 267, 268
ballot box planning 76, 161
Bangkok Plan, Bangkok, Thailand 172
Bangladesh 230, 234–5, 238, 395, 401
banks 24, 74, 176, 249, 264, 267, 341, 345, 352, 381–2; chartered 267–8; federal 267; local 187, 249; regulating 346
Barlow Commission see Royal Commission on the Distribution of the Industrial Population; see *Barlow Report* 116
basic sector of an economy 370–71; *see also* primary sector of an economy and tertiary sector of an economy
BANANA see "Build Absolutely Nothing Anywhere Near Anything" syndrome
Barnett, Jonathan 45
Bassett, Edward 34, 135, 141, 147, 149–50, 258, 279
Batty, Michael 3, 100
Bauer, Catherine 37, 104, 272–4, 359; *see also* Catherine Bauer Wurster
Bay Area see San Francisco Bay Area
Bay Conservation and Development Commission (BCDC) *see* San Francisco Bay Conservation and Development Commission
BCDC *see* San Francisco Bay Conservation and Development Commission
Beasley, Larry 53
Beatley, Timothy 129, 294, 298, 306
Bell, Alexander Graham 33
Bellamy, Edward 129
Below Market Interest Rate (BMIR) housing programs 257–8, 264, 265–266, 28, 354, 364
benign neglect 73, 203n1, 253, 258
Bennett, Edward 34, 117
Berry, Brian 93, 246n5
Bethlehem, Pennsylvania 15, 373, 375–6
Bethlehem Steel Corporation 375
BethWorks Casino Gaming LLC, Bethlehem, Pennsylvania 376
BethWorks Retail shopping center complex, Bethlehem, Pennsylvania 376
Biden, President Joseph 70, 79, 286, 303, 388, 408–411, 417
bid rent curves 371
"big red", Los Angeles electric streetcar (circa 1930) *32*
Bill and Melinda Gates Foundation 102
Bill of Rights (United States Constitution) 179n3
bin Salman, Mohammed, Crown Prince of Saudi Arabia 122
biomass 400, 406–7
biophilia 125, 297
biophilic concepts (Wilson) 298
biophilic design, Eindhoven, the Netherlands (2021) *298*
Birch, Eugenie 104, 171, 243, *244*
bisexuals 198, 202
Blacks 12n1, 26–7, 137–9, 143–4, 186–92, 194, 196, 200–1, 253, 261–2, 265, 271, 274, 356, 359, 365; households 186, 191, 194, 365; migration to cities 253; and mixed-race communities 195–6, 203, 359; neighborhoods 65, 97, 196; planners 189–90; tenants in public housing 196; residential areas 97, 183, 188

Black Lives Matter Movement 188; Black Lives Matter street painting (Albany, New York, 2020) *188*
Blake, William 109
Blakeley, Edward 13, 377
blighted land 137, 272
BLM *see* Bureau of Land Management (United States)
block (United States census) 16
block group (United States census) 16
block grant 73, 152n10, 258, 271, 367, 380, 391
Bloomberg, Michael Mayor of New York City 319, 321
BLS *see* Bureau of Labor Statistics (United States)
"blue sky" visioning (Nashville, Tennessee) 141
blue sky laws (subdivisions and securities) (United States)
blue state (United States) 66
Blueprint for Oregon's Future (1000 Friends of Oregon) 127
BMIR mortgages *see* Below Market Interest Rate Mortgages
Boeing, Geoff 52–53
Bonneville Dam 207, 256
"boomburg" 138
Boring Company, The 333
Boston, Massachusetts 20–22, 31, 127, 185–6, 188, 192, 257, 260, 313, 318, 356–7; area map showing redlined neighborhoods (1934) *195*; harbor *20*; city council (2021) 69
Boston, Thomas 217
Boulton, Matthew 29
Boulevard 54, 61, 117, 156, 171, 269
Bournville, England 115
boundaries 16, 48–9, 66, 68, 89, 136, 163, 185, 205–6, 208, 225; political 5, 15–16, 214, 224; urban growth 178, 180, 219, 413
Branson, Richard 333
Brasília, Brazil (2015) *96*
Brenner, Neil 233, 236
Bridenbaugh, Carl 20, 22
British Columbia 6, 87, 90, 283, 387
Broadacre City model (1935) 120, *121*; *see also* Frank Lloyd Wright
Brooks, Michael 92, 97
Brown, Gordon 383
Brownfield 300
Bruegmann, Robert 122, 213; *see also* smart growth contrarians
Brundtland, Gro Harlem 36, 294
Brundtland Commission *see* World Commission on the Environment and Development
Bruner, Rudy 277
Brynn Mawr College 244
BTS *see* Bureau of Transportation Statistics (United States)
bubonic plague 102; *see also* pandemics
budgets 76, 148, 272, 297, 381, 390, 419
"Build Absolutely Nothing Anywhere Near Anything" people (BANANA) syndrome 81
builders 168, 173–5, 179, 341–2, 363
building codes 5, 55, 61, 148, 158, 168, 173–5, 180, 285, 290, 414–15
building envelope; sites 59, 162, 392; sizes 63;

standards 48, 152, 350; inspectors 179–80; maintenance 352; materials 25, 54
buildings 39, 45–6, 48, 50–52, 54–6, 59–63, 76–7, 117–19, 126–7, 157–8, 164–5, 167–9, 173–80, 272–3, 275, 277–8, 284–7, 321–5, 381–2, 413–15; abandoned 57; derelict 375, 388; designing 165; deteriorating 174; and districts 39, 275; efficiency of 254, 400; family 60; insulating 419; large 52, 173; maintaining 82; older 174, 271, 367, 380; public 114, 147, 161, 272, 274, 415; residential 59, 120, 168, 173–4, 176–7, 323; school 381, 389; two-story 165; value 165
building permits 177, 180n10
bulk limit (in zoning and building codes) 164, 165
Bureau of Labor Statistics (BLS) (United States) 5–6, 12–13, 374, 391
Bureau of Land Management (BLM) (United States) 299, 308
Bureau of Reclamation (United States) 299
Bureau of Transportation Statistics (United States) 315, 336
Burgess, Ernest W. 35, 235
Burnham, Daniel 10, 33–4, 107, 117, 119, 138, 155; *Plan for Chicago*, co-authored with Edward Bennett, 117; criticized as an elitist whose plans served the interests of wealthy businessmen 117; planner 33
Burnham Award 134, 138–9, 143–5, 221
Burkina Faso 408
Bus Rapid Transit, Curitiba, Brazil *325*
Bush, President George Herbert Walker 73, 84, 289, 346, 383, 392
Bush, President George W. 73, 84, 289, 303
business corporations 66
Butzner, Jane (married Robert Hyde Jacobs and changed her name to Jane Jacobs) 10

C2ES Center for Climate and Energy Solutions 409
Clean Air Act (1948) 288; Amendments (1972 and 1990) 285, 288
Clean Water Act (United States), 1948 158, 288; Amendments (1972) 152n10, 158, 288
cable car 30, 31, 268, 317, 330
Cabriejo Ranch model of solar regenerative agriculture 399
Cabrini, Frances Xavier 60, 261–2, 264, 280, 360
Cabrini–Green Homes and Pruitt–Igoe Public Housing Projects **261**
CACs *see* Citizens Advisory Committees (United States)
CAD *see* Computer-Assisted Design
Cadbury, George 114
CAFE standard, national *see* Corporate Average Fuel Efficiency standard (United States)
CAFE standard, California 286
Cahokia Mound Builder Indian site 15, 19, 104
California 33–4, 79, 96–8, 134–5, 137, 145–7, 155–6, 166, 179–80, 196–7, 199, 203, 205–6, 215, 274, 286, 307, 362, 382–3, 411–15; Air Resources Board (CARB) 411; cities 147; coastal region 205
California Environmental Quality Act (CEQA) 145, 294, 307, 412
California Global Warming Solutions Act (2006) 411
Callenbach, Ernest 107, 125, 127; *see also Ecotopia*
California *Climate Action and Adaptation Plan* **412**

Calthorpe, Peter 62
Cambodia 17, 40, 229
Camden, New Jersey 179n6, 183, 199
Canadian Institute of Planners (CIP) 6, 159, 177, 290, 313, 390
Canary Wharf (London, England) 384, *385*
cap-and-trade programs (carbon) 270, 290, 410, 411
Cape Verde Islands 186
Capital Improvement Programs (CIPs) 159, 290
capitalists 110, 114
CAPs *see* Community Action Programs (during the United States "War on Poverty") (United States)
CARB *see* California Air Resources Board
carbon 91, 98, 103, 116, 173, 395, 398–401, 405, 407–14, 416, 418–19; emissions 81, 99, 133, 146, 205, 397, 399, 408, 410–11, 416, 419; footprints 161, 175, 270, 396, 409, 411, 416; neutrality 96, 409; sinks 398–9; tax 98; zero 122
Carbon Dioxide (CO_2) 74, 175, 285–6, 333, 398, 411
Carr Lynch Associates 49; *see also* Lynch, Kevin
cars 270, 278, 285, 290, 313, 317, 319, 323–4, 327–30, 396, 399
Carson, Rachel 306
Carter, President Jimmy 73, 258
Case-Shiller Index 348
CASA *see* Centre for Advanced Spatial Analysis
Castells, Manuel 97, 198, 236–7
Castro district, San Francisco 150, 183, 198, 379
Castro, Julian 70, *71*, 72
CAT *see* Climate Action Team
categorical grant programs 73, 258, 272
Cather, Willa 199
CatEx *see* Categorical Exclusion (United States National Environmental Policy Act) (United States)
Cato Institute 158
CATS *see* Center for Applied Transect Studies
CAVs *see* Connected Autonomous Vehicles
CAVE people *see* Citizens Against Virtually Everything
Cayton, Horace 189, 203
CBD *see* Central Business District
CCP *see* Cities for Climate Protection
CDBG program *see* Community Development Block Grant program (United States)
CDC *see* Centers for Disease Control (United States)
CDCs *see* Community Development Corporations (United States)
CEDs *see* Certified Economic Developers
cellular automata models 100
census (United States) 15–16, 24–7, 40–41, 137, 139, 144–5, 192, 194, 196–7, 205, 208–9, 246, 280, 316, 364–5; blocks 16; block groups 16; Bureau 16, 84, 137, 196–7, 208–9, 250, 340, 374; designated places 208; tracts 16
Center for Applied Transect Studies (CATs) 48
Center for Climate and Energy Solutions (C2ES) 409
Centers for Disease Control 95, 102, 202, 368, 379, 381
Central Business District (CBD) 38, 235, 371
central cities 253, 272, 351, 373
Central Park (New York City) 21
central place theory 210, *211*, 246n5
Centre for Advanced Spatial Analysis (CASA) 3, 100
CEOs *see* chief executive officers

CEQ *see* Council on Environmental Quality (United States)
CEQA *see* California Environmental Quality Act
CERCLA *see* Comprehensive Environmental Response, Compensation, and Liability Act (United States)
Certified Economic Developers (CEDs) 372
Certified Local Governments (CLGs) (historic preservation) 278
Cervero, Robert 269
CHA *see* Chicago Housing Authority
Chamorros 196
Charles River (Massachusetts) 26
Charminar Bazaar, Hyderabad, India *234*
charter city 137, 142
Charter of the New Urbanism 55
CHDOs *see* Community Housing Development Organizations (United States)
Chenery, Hollis 387; *see also* over urbanization
Cheney, Vice-President Richard 419
Chernobyl nuclear reactor 407, 419
Chicago 31, 33–5, 40, 60, 62, 75, 117–19, 122, 155, 235, 237, 260–1, 263; City Hall Green Roof *415*; Commercial Club 75, 117; Housing Authority 261–3, 281, 360; Planning Commission 117
chief executive officers 70, 419
China 103, 122, 130, 206, 213–14, 229–31, 239, 246, 330–1, 386–7, 392, 399, 403–4, 407–9, 417–19
Chinatowns 25, 196
Chinese Exclusion Act (United States, 1882) 25
CHIP mobility framework *see* Connected, Heterogeneous, Intelligent, and Personalized mobility framework; *see also* Sumantran, Venkat
chlorofluorocarbons 409
CHODOS *see* Community Development Housing Organizations (United States)
Choice Neighborhoods program (United States) 264, 355–6
Christaller, Walter 210–11, 225, 246
CIAM *see* Congrès Internationaux d'Architecture Moderne
CIC *see* Complexity in Cities theory
ciclovias (bicycle roads) 325, *326*
Cincinnati, Ohio 286
CIP *see* Canadian Institute of Planners
CIP *see* Capital Improvement Program
cities 3, 6–7, 9, 12, 87, 91, 109, 113, 120, 148–9, 254–5; charter 65–6, 68, 137, 143, 218; and city planning 245, 249–50; coastal 241, 284, 401, 414; compact 21, 122, 410–11; core 31, 122, 250, 253, 271, 279, 316, 372, 392; distressed rustbelt 201, 372; ecological 404; garden 91, 107, 110–17, 119, 126, 129, 155, 383; growing 66, 325, 373; healthy 216, 252, 367, 390; historic 146, 221; incorporated 15–16, 68, 138; integrated 163; large 13, 24, 68, 78, 224, 233, 238, 359, 362, 401, 411; modern 35, 39, 87, 119; modernist 95; national 158; non-sexist 55, 194; older 36, 372; planning 1, 34–5, 39, 56, 61, 65–6, 103, 107, 134–5, 245, 249–50; and regional planning programs 8, 12–13, 87, 89, 190, 270, 279; sustainable 247; and towns 20, 40, 177, 222, 278; university 200
cities and counties 15–16, 66–9, 75–6, 135, 145, 147, 163, 165, 176–7, 205, 215, 218–19, 258–9, 360–61, 413–14; in California 147; coordinating comprehensive plans 135; development of adjoining 148; establishment of 75; grants to 136; groups of 225; growing 148, 373; managing public land 299; monitoring progress on plan implementation 149; organizations of 215; enabling legislation by state governments authorizing funding or programs 255; "development agreements" for how land is to be used in 167; regional planning 205; and state government 215
cities and regions 4, 6, 35, 37, 70, 128, 150, 213, 216–17, 370–1, 391; authority to plan 67; challenges in 287; declining 391; economy of 391; environments of 128, 213; functioning of 311; planning for 6
Cities for Climate Protection (CCP) program 409
Cities in Civilization (book by Peter Hall) 383, 384
Cities of Tomorrow (book by Peter Hall) 382
citizen participation 7, 91, 97, 98, 141, 144, 146, 157, 183, *184*, 185, 202, 219, 221, 254, 313
citizen control in Sherry Arnstein's "ladder of citizen participation" *184*, 185
citizen power in Sherry Arnstein's "ladder of citizen participation" *184*, 185
Citizens Advisory Committees (CACs) (United States) 151
Citizens Against Virtually Everything (CAVE) syndrome 80, 83, 202
Citizens Planning Institute (CPI) (Philadelphia, Pennsylvania) 146, 345
city and regional planning 1–3, 5–15, 33–5, 37–9, 62, 65–7, 73–4, 88–9, 92–3, 100, 134, 216–17, 242–3, 249, 251–2, 254–5, 286–7, 311, 372, 383; academics 103; activities 151, 306; contributions to 36; courses in 8; education 7, 35, 135; faculty and students 243; departments 4, 13, 368; and geography 383; goals 92; history 37, 111, 279; methods 9; and policy 243; process 96; research methodology 36; specializations 8, 97, 108, 141, 372, 405; students 199; topics 8, 217; and urban design 10, 171, 298
city beautiful movement 33, 34, 91, 107, 117
city planning 1, 5, 34, 45, 49, 51, 55, 70, 103, 266; commissions 65, 78, 200; conferences 34, 87; influenced by the modernist vision 119; international 243; limited 74; modern 34, 117; normative 96; physical 107; programs 270; resilient 402
city plans 34, 40, 75, 91, 145; local 77; promotion of 37; sponge 214
city planning departments 6, 78, 271, 277, 390
civil service 6, 78, 79
Civic Center Plaza and Buildings (proposed) in the 1909 *Plan for Chicago* 118
civic design 1, 35, 46, 62n1, 88, 89, 91, 93, 254, 258
Civic Design Center, Nashville, Tennessee 143
Clean Air Act (United States 1963) 152n10, 158, 258, 285–6, 288, 291; Amendments (1970) 285
Clean Water Act (United States, 1948) 152n10, 158, 288; Amendments 1972 285; *see* Federal Water Pollution Control Act (1948) 288
Clermont (Robert Fulton's steamboat) *30*; *see also* Robert Fulton; *see also* North River (Robert Fulton's steamboat)
Cleveland, Ohio 31, 97, 138, 143, 179, 201–2, 221, 226, 372–3

Cleveland Heights, Ohio 175
Cleveland State University 190, 201–2
climate action plan 76, 81, 152n10, 400, 412, 413
climate change 65–6, 72–3, 100–1, 126–7, 145–7, 161, 229–31, 239, 241–3, 247, 270–1, 303–4, 333, 388–9, 395–419; addressing 95, 175, 417; anthropogenic 270, 395, 398, 410, 417; denial 81, 417; disinformation 418; early history of 250; education 270; initiatives 198; mitigating global 175; planning and policy 56, 100, 250, 270, 335, 396, 402, 405, 409, 411, 417–18; plans to reduce carbon emissions from coal-powered plants 205, 410; policies for adaptation to 146, 409; problems 409, 417; reducing 413, 417; refugees forced to move because of 231; regional planning 411; science 398, 417; state planning 410
climate justice 416, 417
CLG see Certified Local Government (historic preservation) (United States)
Climate Change 2021 (United Nations Intergovernmental Panel on Climate Change) 396, 419n9
Climate Change and Social Ecology (book by Stephen Wheeler) 127
climate zones 396
Clinton, President William Jefferson 71, 73–5, 84, 258, 303, 387
CMP see Congestion Management Program
CNU see Congress of the New Urbanism
COAH see Council on Affordable Housing (New Jersey)
coal 29, 56, 197, 205, 207, 209, 300, 398, 406–7, 411, 419
coal mining 207, 284
coastal zone planning and management 66, 84, 284, 303–4
Coastal Zone Management Act (United States, 1972) 304, 305
Code of Ethics and Professional Conduct (American Institute of Certified Planners) 97
COGs see Councils of Governments (United States)
Collin County, Texas 138
colonial cities 19–21, 242
colonias 196, 202n8
colonies 20, 108, 242
Columbia, Maryland 82, 116
Columbia River, Oregon 207
Columbia University 23, 82, 116, 251, 307, 318, 325–6, 336, 410–11
Columbia Pike Form-Based Code and Plan (Arlington, Virginia, 2013) **169**; Building Envelope Standards for Neighborhood Sites; Special Revitalization District **169**
Columbus, Christopher 33
collaborative rationality 100
"common but differentiated responsibilities" (Paris Climate Agreement) 408
Community Action Programs (CAPs) during the "war on poverty" (United States) 256
community development 271, 367, 368
Community Development Block Grant (CDBG) program (United States) 84, 152, 258, 271, 367, 379–81; allocation formulas 392; funding 380–81; grant money 380
Community Development Corporations (CDCs) 202, 368, 379
community economic development 367, 372, 379
comprehensive plans see also general plans
conurbations 36, 110, 114
concurrency (in growth management) 176, 317
Conference of the Parties (Paris Climate Agreement) 408
Congestion Management Programs (CMPs) 322
consultation in Sherry Arnstein's "ladder of citizen participation" *184*, 185
Consumer Price Index (CPI) 345, 362
cooperative 109, 114, 115, 126
co-partnership 115
common law 99, 158, 159
communicative action planning 87, 100, 127, 202
communities 54–5, 72, 98–9, 116, 127–8, 133, 143, 145–8, 150–1, 159–61, 166–9, 174–7, 179–80, 183–4, 188–92, 197–203, 206–7, 367, 378–81, 412–13; affluent 416; coastal 304; creative 71; declining 137; disadvantaged 147, 152; distressed 392; immigrant 167, 303; indigenous 197, 308; informal 196; local 418; low-income 87, 97–8, 201–3, 206, 272, 283, 311; nonconformist 252; planned 6, 252; racial 203; renewal of 385, 392; retirement 5, 146; rural 214; scattered 418; troubled 183; upper-income 303, 416
Community Character Manual, Nashville Tennessee 143, 150
Community Housing Development Organizations (CHODOs) (United States) 365
community planning 183–203; areas 141, 151; efforts 185; indigenous 197; processes 150
community plans 136, 139, 150, 185
Community Power Structure (book by Floyd Hunter) 77
comparable properties (comps)
Complete Streets design *318*
Complexity in Cities (CIC) theory 87, 100–1, **102**, 313, 417
comps see comparable properties
Comprehensive Environmental Response, Compensation, and Liability Act (CERCLA) (United States) 302
comprehensive plans 34, 75, 133, 135, 137–8, 143, 151, 185, 258, 263, 339
Computer-Assisted Design (CAD) 2–3, 45–6, 58, 61, 93, 279
Computer-Generated Street Networks *53*; see also Boeing, Geoff
Con Plan see Consolidated Plan (Community Development Block Grant program) (United States)
Condition of the Working Class in England in 1844 (book by Friedrich Engels) 109
Conditional Use Permits (CUPs) 163, 198
congestion; management planning 315, 321–2, 324, 326, 330; management programs 322; pricing 217, 326
Congrès Internationaux d'Architecture Moderne 95, 104

Congress (United States) 23, 30, 67, 70, 159, 346, 353, 355, 359, 380, 381, 384, 392n7, 419n12
Congress of the New Urbanism 47, 55, 62, 350
Connected Autonomous Vehicles (CAVs) 327–8, 331, 334
Connected, Heterogeneous, Intelligent, and Personalized (CHIP) mobility framework for transportation planning *see also* Sumantran, Venkat
Connolly, Peter 62
conservation 55, 147, 151, 206, 290
conservative ideology 65, 73, 74
Consolidated Plan (Community Development Block Grant program) (United States) *see* (Con Plan)
Constitution (United States) 260, 262, 289
continuing, comprehensive, and coordinated (3Cs) transportation planning 290, 312
contour map 172
cool roof 1, 190, 414
CoolClimate Network 409, 416
Cooley, Thomas M. 75
Cooley Doctrine 65, 75
"Copenhagenize" 52, 61
coral bleaching 395, 401
Cornell Dubilier Superfund Site (South Plainfield, New Jersey 302
Cornell University 89, 100, 217, 251–2
Corporate Average Fuel Efficiency (CAFE) standard (United States) 47, 52–3, 119–20, 269, 286, 290, 334, 336, 388, 411, 413; *see also* Corporate Average Fuel Efficiency (CAFE) standard (California)
corporations 4, 75, 85, 138, 157, 233, 235, 253, 382, 417; auto-related 32; business 66; community development 202, 368; conservative 158; designing products 234; federal 255; large 258, 385; municipal 15, 66, 68, 75, 294; national economic development 26, 233, 237–8; nonprofit community development 379; nonprofit housing development 70, 264–5, 339, 352, 354; private 4, 70, 78, 299
corporate energy planning 416
corruption 174–5, 265
cost-burdened household 252, 339
Costonis, John 175
cosmic model of the city (Lynch) 96, 104n5
Councils of Governments (COGs) (United States) 67, 134–5, 205, 215, 217–19, 226
Council on Affordable Housing (COAH) (New Jersey) 179
Council on Environmental Quality (CEQ) (United States) 291
county (United States) 135–139, *140*, 141, *142*, 144–148, 155, 157, 159–162, 167
county boards of commissioners (United States) 135, 136
countries, developed 209, 230, 241–2, 245, 250, 318, 330, 339, 400, 407–9, 419
countries, developing 17, 39, 206, 213, 230, 233, 238, 239, 241, 242, 245, 285, 330, 340, 362, 363, 370, 386, 390, 400, 406, 407, 406, 408, 417
county planning departments 6, 68–9, 78, 128, 145, 160, 313, 390
COVID 19 pandemic 7, 101, **102**, 103, 116, 233, 238–9, 317, 362, 384

Curitiba, Brazil *325*
CPI *see* Citizens Planning Institute (Philadelphia, Pennsylvania)
CPI *see* Consumer Price Index
CPTED *see* Crime Prevention Through Environmental Design
creative class 372; *see also* Professor Richard Florida
crime 56, 59–63, 108, 186–7, 189, 239, 242, 261–2, 269, 272, 355, 357, 360, 377, 380, 382
Crime Prevention Through Environmental Design (CPTED) 45, 56, 59, 62n11, 355
critical habitat (United States Endangered Species Act) 152n10, 187, 289, 290, 297, 304
critical threshold in global climate change 402
Cross, Terry 192, 202; *see also* cultural competency
cross-acceptance policy for review of general plans (New Jersey) 136
crowded lodging in a Bayard Street tenement photograph by Jacob Riis (1889) *28*
Crystal Palace Exhibition (London, 1851) 33; *see* Great Exhibition of the Works of Industry of All Nations
Cuban Americans 196
cultural competency 192
cumulative impact (United States National Environmental Policy Act) 293, 307n7
current planning 6, 79, 81, 94, 133, 145, 254
CWA *see* Clean Water Act (United States, 1948) *and* amendments (1972 and 1990)

D-CAAP *see* Davis, California *Climate Action and Adaptation Plan* 412–13
DACA *see* Deferred Action for Childhood Arrivals program
Dahl, Robert 77
Dakota Access Pipeline 308
Dale, Chester 109
Daley, Richard, Mayor of Chicago, Illinois 359
DARPA *see* Defense Advanced Research Projects Agency (United States)
Darwin, Charles 35
Das Kapital (book by Karl Marx) 97; *see also* Karl Marx
Davidoff, Paul 74, 98, 200–202
Davis, Kingsley 16–18, 229, 294, 362, 412–13, 415; "family of S curves" to describe urbanization patterns in different countries 16–18, 229; finds urbanization generally follows an attenuated S curve 16
Davis Climate Action and Adaptation Plan (D-CAAP) 412–13; Climate Protection/Community Sustainability Strategy Framework 412; Climate Action Team (CAT) 412
de Roo, Gert 102
Death and Life of Great American Cities (book by Jane Jacobs) 10
decision analysis 77
deductive reasoning 88
Deerfield, Massachusetts 275
Defense Advanced Research Projects Agency (DARPA) (United States) 270, 327–8
defensible space 45, 56, 59, 60, 355, 356
Deferred Action for Childhood Arrivals program (United States) *see* DACA

deforestation 398
degree programs related to city and regional planning 7–9, 14, 34, 45, 62, 66, 87, 94, 136, 146, 277–9
Delaware 40–1, 178, 203
delegated power in Sherry Arnstein's "ladder of citizen participation" 185
Democratic Party (United States) 70–71, 249–50, 254, 271, 359, 388–9, 409–10
Departments of (United States): Agriculture (DOA) 173, 266, 299; Commerce (DOC) 70, 299, 304, 374, 379; Justice (DOJ) 63, 72, 360; Transportation (DOT) 33, 70, 217–18, 269, 290–1, 312, 319, 321–2, 336, 406; Housing and Urban Development (HUD) 4, 70, 71, 85n4, 97, 104n7, 184, 187, 196, 257, 258, 262, 274, 291, 299, 339, 342, 355, 358, 359, 364, 379, 380; Land Conservation and Development (DLDC) (Oregon) 136
Derudder, Benjamin 237
DESA *see* United Nations Division of Economic and Social Affairs
desertification 287, 395, 396, 405
design 4–5, 23–4, 45–7, 49, 51–63, 122–3, 151–2, 169, 171–3, 175–6, 252, 283–4, 294–8, 333, 355–6, 402–3, 419; biophilic 283, 298; of buildings 45–6, 287; cities 49; digital 61; energy-saving 173; environmental education 134–5; functional 95; guidelines 48, 172; housing program 259; hyperloop 333; neighborhood 254, 415; policies 48; projects 252; regional planning methods 47, 155, 163, 174, 178; standards 45, 61, 198; strategies 52, 56, 115, 143; urban bikeway 319
Design-Build-Finance-Operate-Maintain projects 389
Design with Nature 294–298; *see also* Ian McHarg
design review boards 61, 175
Desmond, Matthew 339, 342
Detroit, Michigan 171, 190–1, 249–50, 265, 321, 372–4
developers 5, 161–2, 167, 172, 179–80, 264–5, 288, 290–3, 307, 323–4, 342–3, 351–2, 354, 359, 361
developing countries 206, 213, 230, 233, 238–9, 241, 245, 362–3, 370, 386, 390, 400, 406–8
development 13, 46–8, 111, 147–9, 159–63, 171–2, 176–7, 187, 206–7, 212–14, 219, 270–2, 288–94, 296–7, 305–7, 318–19, 356, 367–8, 370–2, 385–7; of adjoining cities 148; agreements 163, 167; costs 259, 382; costs of public housing for low-income households 259; partnerships 376; planning 5, 207, 241, 245, 367, 374; enabling legislation for program planning and implementation authority at state and local government levels 255, 258; proposals 177; and revitalization planning 15–40, 367, 390; theory 294, 386; zones 375, 382; *see also* economic development
development era in regional planning according to Professor Michael Teitz 206, 207
developmental state 67, 386, 387
Dhavale, Dawn 226
Dillon, Judge Forest 75–6, 136, 143
Dillon's rule 75, 76, 136, 143
Dinkins, David 321
discrimination 21, 54, 168, 179, 188–9, 192, 196, 261, 263, 359–60; against Blacks 189; United States Fair Housing Act bans 168; prohibited 359
disease 22, 197, 239, 245, 285, 287–8, 298, 405

disjointed incrementalism 87, 94
district courts (federal) 180, 263, 281
District of Columbia 23, 307, 318, 336, 410–11
diversity 6, 13, 45, 54, 96, 137–8, 141, 146, 152, 192, 200; cultural 192; improving 200; racial 350, 361; social 252
DLCD *see* Oregon Department of Land Conservation and Development
DOA *see* Department of Agriculture (United States)
Doan, Petra 55, 198–9, 202
DOC *see* Department of Commerce (United States)
DOD *see* Department of Defense (United States)
Dodd-Frank Act (United States, 2010) 346
DOJ *see* Department of Justice (United States)
DOT *see* Department of Transportation (United States)
DPZ *see* Duany Plater-Zyberk urban design firm
Droughts 214, 229, 395, 405
Dreamers 80; *see* Deferred Action for Childhood Arrivals (DACA)
drinking water 288, 377
drugs 186–7, 245, 261–2, 277, 280–1, 339–40, 342, 346; dealers 187, 245, 261–2, 277, 280, 339–40, 357; illegal 186, 281, 346, 380; problems 261, 342
DSNI *see* Dudley Street Neighborhood Initiative
Du Bois, William Edward Burghardt (W.E.B.) 204
dual development model of economic development (Arthur O. Lewis) 386
Duany, Andrés 47; *see also* Duany Plater-Zyberk urban design firm (DPZ) 47
Duany Plater-Zyberk urban design firm DPZ 47
Dudley Street neighborhood 185–7
Dudley Street Neighborhood Initiative **186**
Dudley Street Triangle 187
dumbbell tenement 29; *see also* tenement
dynamic conservatism 70, 257
dystopia 107, 108, 127, 128
dystopian fiction 107, 108

early United States industrial cities **26**
earthquakes 284–5, 341
easement 161, 220, 290
East Saint Louis, Missouri 183
Ebenezer Howard's Three Magnets *112*
economic base analysis 96, 148, 370
economic development 145, 147, 150, 152, 206–7, 213, 217, 225, 241, 245, 367–92; organizations 378; planners 99, 371–2, 374; plans 371–2, 377; policies 373–4, 387, 392; practice of 391, 392; professionals 372; programs 374, 378–9, 392; projects 187, 277, 379; and revitalization planning 367–8; strategy 239; support services 378; theory and practice 392
Economic Development Administration (EDA) (United States) 378–9
economic development planning 137, 205, 367, 370, 372–4; data for 374; goal of 367; in Northeast Ohio 205; regional 207, 406; textbooks 377; theoretical literature on 370; work planners do related to 372
Ecotopia 107, **125**, 126–8; *see also* Callenbach, Ernest
ECs *see* Enterprise Communities (United States)
ECUs *see* Automotive Electronic Control Units
EDA *see* Economic Development Administration (United States)
EDF *see* Environmental Defense Fund

edge (as element of city image)
Edward Blakeley Award 7; *see also* Blakely, Edward
EHAP *see* Experimental Housing Allowance Program (United States)
EIA *see* Energy Information Agency (United States)
EIR *see* Environmental Impact Report (California)
Eisenhower, President Dwight 70, 257
EIS *see* Environmental Impact Statement (United States)
Ekurhuleni Aerotropolis, Ekurhuleni, South Africa 236; *see also* aerotropolis
Electronic Control Units (ECUs) 329
Ellicott, Andrew 24; *see also* L'Enfant Plan (Washington, D.C., 1791)
Ellis Island immigration station 25
elitist theory 77
emissions gap 397
empiricism 88
Emperor Napoleon III (France) 226
empowerment zones 158, 191, 377, 385, 392
employment multiplier 371
Empowerment Zone/Enterprise Communities (EZ/ECs) (United States) 158, 191, 382, 385, 392n8
endangered species 158, 288–9
Endangered Species Act (United States)158, 288–9
energy 26, 56, 83–4, 297, 300, 388, 398, 400, 405–8, 411, 413, 415–17, 419; planning 250, 395–417, 419; and climate change 250, 395; corporate 416; global 395; for international organizations 406; policy 395; sources 126, 395, 406–7, 410–11
Energy Information Administration (EIA) (United States) 397, 418n1
Engels, Friedrich 97, 109, 242; *see also Condition of the Working Class in England in 1844* (book by Friedrich Engels)
Enlightenment 1, 88
Enterprise Communities (United States) 158, 382, 385, 392
enterprise zones (United States) 258, 382, 384, 391–2
entitlement 162, 259, 348, 359
environmental impact assessment 292, 307
environmental design 56, 134–5, 274
Environmental Defense Fund (EDF) 409
Environmental Impact Report (EIR) (California) 293–4, 412
Environmental Impact Statement (EIS) (United States) 1, 291–4, 307, 342; *see also* National Environmental Policy Act (United States, 1971)
environmental justice 147, 284, 302–303, 308
Environmental Justice Act (2020) 303
Environmental Justice For All Act (2022) 303
environmental movement 283, 295
environmental planners 205, 213, 279
environmental planning 7–8, 84, 125, 144, 270, 283–308, 405, 412; and energy 84; and land use 284; and regulation 283, 306; and sponge city design 404
Environmental Systems Research Institute (ESRI) 9, 93
Environmental Protection Agency (EPA) (United States) 4, 70, 198, 285–6, 288–9, 300–3, 308, 376, 406, 411, 419
EPA *see* Environmental Protection Agency (United States)

equal protection clause of the fourteenth amendment (United States Constitution) 168, 179n5, 281n8, 360
equity 2, 6, 13n7, 46, 74, 91, 96, 97, 98, 137, 138, 146, 167, 183, 188, 193, 200, 201, 202, 206, 207, 238, 258, 339, 345, 350, 360, 369, 374, 377, 389
Equity and Inclusion Toolkit (International City Management Association) 193, 203n6
equity planning 97–8, 200–2; Norman Krumholz's theory of 98; practice of 138, 202
Erickson, Jennifer 192–3, 202
ESA *see* Endangered Species Act
ESRI *see* Environmental Systems Research Institute
ethanol 399, 400, 407
ethnic communities 54, 194
Etzioni, Ametai 94
EUCAR *see* European Council for Automotive Research and Development
Euclid vs Ambler Realty Company 28, 259, 179n4
Euclidean zoning 163
European Council for Automotive Research and Development (EUCAR) 318
Everglades (Florida) 215
Exactions 161, 350
exclusionary zoning 167–8
executive branch of government (United States) 67
Experimental Housing Allowance Program (EHAP) (United States) 365
extreme heat events 396
extremely low-income household 266, 347
"eyes on the street" strategy to reduce crime (Jane Jacobs) 10, 52, 60, 269, 311
EZs *see* Empowerment Zones (United States)

Fabian socialists 129
factory-built housing 343
Faculty Women's Interest Group (FWIG) (Association of Collegiate Schools of Planning) 7, 193–4
FAICP *see* Fellow of the American Institute of Certified Planning
Fainstein, Susan 5
Fair Deal 70, 257, 259
fair housing 74, 340, 358, 360; assistance program 360; complaints 360; federal 72; goals 72; organizations 360; rights 360; rules 71
Fair Housing and Equal Opportunity (FHEO), Office of (United States Department of Housing and Urban Development) 36
Fair Housing Act (1968) 179, 358–60
Fair Market Rent (FMR) 259, 267, 348, 352–3
fair share housing plans 87, 98, 168
Falcon, Mississippi 379
Falls Church, Virginia *Comprehensive Planning Opportunity Area Priority Schedule* (2021) 378; zoning map 164
False Creek waterfront (Vancouver, British Columbia, Canada) 54
Fannie Mae 268, 343, 345, 354; *see* Federal National Mortgage Association (FNMA) (United States)
FAR *see* Floor Area Ratio
Fargo, North Dakota 137
FAST Act *see* Fixing America's Surface Transportation Act (United States)
FBCI *see* Form-Based Codes Institute

FDIC *see* Federal Deposit Insurance Corporation (United States)
FDI *see* Foreign Direct Investment
Federal Aid Highway Act (United States, 1956) *see* National Interstate and Defense Highways Act (1956)
Federal Deposit Insurance Corporation (FDIC) (United States) 267
Federal Housing Finance Agency (FHFA) (United States) 348
Federal Emergency Management Agency (FEMA) (United States) 72, 285, 287
federal government (United States) 12–13, 67–8, 158–9, 179, 207, 249, 254–7, 259–60, 264–5, 267, 269, 272, 278–80, 299, 304, 312, 379–80
federal courts (United States) 158, 178, 293
Federal Highway Administration (FHWA) (United States) 268, 312, 315, 322
Federal Housing Administration (FHA) (United States) 72, 194, 261, 267, 281, 342, 345, 359
Federal Housing Finance Agency (United States) 348
federal housing programs (United States) 259, 264, 273, 280, 339–40, 351, 354
Federal Home Loan Mortgage Corporation nicknamed "Freddie Mac" (United States) 268, 345, 354
federal laws (United States) 258, 249
Federal National Mortgage Association (FNMA) nicknamed "Fannie Mae" 268, 281, 343
Federal Reserve Board (United States) 104n7, 345
Federal Road Act (United States, 1916) 269
Federal Water Pollution Control Act (United States 1948) 288; *see* Clean Water Act
feedback loop in global climate change 395, 402
Fellow of the American Institute of Certified Planning 6, 13, 372
FEMA *see* Federal Emergency Management Agency (United States)
Ferguson, Missouri 183
festival markets 276–7, 370
FHA *see* Federal Housing Administration (United States)
FHAP *see* Fair Housing Assistance Program (United States)
FHEO *see* Fair Housing and Equal Opportunity, Office of (United States Department of Housing and Urban Development) (United States)
FHFA *see* Federal Housing Finance Agency (United States)
FHWA *see* Federal Highway Administration (United States)
Filipinos 25
filtering (of housing) 348
Finding Of No Significant Impact (FONSI) (National Environmental Policy Act) (United States, 1971) 292
Fine, Charles 335
Fisher, Roger 81
Fishman, Robert 115
Fixing America's Surface Transportation (FAST) Act (United States) 312
Flint, Michigan 183
flooding in Jakarta, Indonesia (2013) *240*
floods 147, 214, 241, 285, 287, 379, 395, 401, 414, 416

flood plains, 100-year 287; 500-year 287
Floor Area Ratios (FARs) 46, 48, 76, 165–6, 336
Florida 1, 5, 19, 41, 102, 159, 162, 178, 196, 203, 226
Florida, Professor Richard 226n9, 372; *see also* creative class
FMRs *see* Fair Market Rents
FNMA *see* Federal National Mortgage Association (FNMA) nicknamed "Fannie Mae") (United States)
FONSI Finding Of No Significant Impact (National Environmental Policy Act (NEPA) (United States) 292
Ford, Henry 32
Ford, Henry II 191, 373
Ford, George B. 1, 32–4, 190, 269, 335
Foreign Direct Investment (FDI) 241, 245, 379
foreign immigrants 34
foreign worker's tax 25
Forest Service 299
Forester, John 79, 100, 252
form-based codes 1, 45, 47
Form-Based Codes Institute 48
Forsyth, Ann 104, 250, *251*
fracking (hydraulic fracturing to recover oil and natural gas) 79, 202, 284, 410, 419
fractals 100
Franklin, Benjamin 155
Freddie Mac *see* Federal Home Loan Mortgage Corporation (FNMA) (United States) 268, 345, 354
Free Blacks 21, 27, 188
free rider 100
Friends of the Market (Pike Place Market, Seattle, Washington) 276
Frieden, Bernard 187, 370
Friedmann, John 89, *90*, 91, 104, 246
Fröbel, Folker 242
frostbelt 250, 279
Fulton, Robert 29; *see also* Clermont (Robert Fulton's steamboat) and North River (Robert Fulton's steamboat)
funding 4, 37, 72–3, 247, 255, 259, 265–6, 277–9, 312–13, 348–50, 354, 365, 367–8, 379–81, 385, 389–90, 392; affordable housing 354; federal 67, 73, 217–18, 255, 260, 294, 312, 380; government 258–9, 391; for neighborhood youth 187; private 354, 370; public 311; taxpayer 256
FWIG *see* Faculty Women's Interest Group
FWS *see* Fish and Wildlife Service (United States)

Galena, Ohio 275
Garden Cities 91, 107, 110–17, 119, 126, 129, 155, 38; Association 37, 114–15; tenants co-partnership, Letchworth, England; Pioneer Society; *see also* Ebenezer Howard
Garden Cities of Tomorrow (book by Ebenezer Howard) 111, 113
Garvin, Alexander 96, 370
gated communities 360
GaWC Network *see* Globalization and World Cities Network
Gautreaux, Dorothy 262–4
Gautreaux vs Chicago Housing Authority 262
Gay Freedom parades 199
GCA *see* Garden Cities Association

GCRP *see* Global Change Research Project (United states)
GDP *see* Gross Domestic Product
Geddes, Patrick 35, *36*, 37–8, 40, 104, 117, 173, 209, 211, 239, 246; approach to studying the natural and built environment of city-regions 36–7; coined the term "world cities" 246, 246n5; conception of how cities and regions evolve 35; designs the Hebrew University in Jerusalem 37; intellectual energy scattered across multiple projects 37; physical, social and cultural approach to city planning 209; Valley Section *210*; and the Watchtower Planning Museum 36, 209
Gehl, Jan 50–2, 58, 61–2, 269; design philosophy 51; likes narrow buildings with many doors and curving, rather than straight facades 52; principles for assembling activities 62n4; research shows that 16-to-25-foot facades can contain 15–20 shops every 328 feet 62n5
GEHL Architects, Copenhagen 51
gender 34, 39, 51, 54, 55, 69, 74, 97, 107, 108, 125, 126, 128, 138, 150, 168, 183, 189, 193, 194, 252, 340, 355, 374, 377
general law city 65–6, 75
general plan *see also* comprehensive plan
Geneva, Illinois (1869) 22
gentrification 198–9, 253–4, 348; resurgent or super 199
geological hazards 284–85
Geographical Information Systems (GIS) 2–3, 7, 9, 87, 93, 206, 251, 279, 297, 298, 306, 315
George, Henry 99, 129
George Washington Bridge 218
George Washington University 77
Georgetown University 192
Getting to Yes (book by Roger Fisher, William Ury, and Bruce Patton) 81
Gerckens, Lawrence C. 244
GFTGFY *see* Good For Them Great For You
GHGs *see* Greenhouse Gases
GI Bill of Rights 250
gigaton 395, 398
Gillham, Oliver 212
Ginnie Mae (*nickname for* Government National Mortgage Association (GNMA)) 268
GIS *see* Geographical Information Systems
Glaeser, Edward 108
global cities 146, 233, 246
global era in regional planning according to Professor Michael Teitz 207
Global Mean Atmospheric Temperature 1880 to 2020 relative to 1951–1980 mean *397*
Global Network Connectivity according to the Global and World Cities Network *237*
Global North 242
Global Planning Education Association Network (GPEAN) 243
Global South 242
globalization 229, 232–3, 235, 239, 241, 245, 387
Globalization and World Cities (GaWC) Research Network 237
GMSLR *see* Gross Mean Sea-Level Rise
GNC *see* Global Network Connectivity

GNMA *see* Government National Mortgage Association nicknamed Ginnie Mae (United States)
Godschalk, David 151
Goldwater Institute 158
Gonsalvez, David 335
Good For Them Great For You (GFTGFY) 81
Good Cities, Better Lives (book by Peter Hall) 383
Gordon, Peter 122, 213; *see also* smart growth contrarians
Government National Mortgage Association "Ginnie Mae" (GNMA) 268, 281
government planning 66, 74, 373–4, 390; and investment in low-income areas 373; and neoliberal capitalist countries 4; opposed by Adam Smith 73; and the relationship of private and nonprofit planning to 65
government policies 70, 73, 369
governments 65–7, 70, 73–4, 76–7, 82, 98–9, 116, 161–2, 185, 215, 226, 273, 316–17, 330, 367–71, 373, 376–7, 382, 409–10, 416–18; state 12, 16, 76, 215, 255, 288, 318, 377, 384
GPEAN *see* Global Planning Education Association Network
Graham Foundation 62
Grand Coulee Dam 207, 256
Graphical User Interface (GUI) 2
gravity model 314
Great Exhibition of the Works of Industry of All Nations (London, England, 1851); *see* Crystal Palace Exhibition (London, England, 1851)
green street design 415
GPEAN *see* Global Planning Education Association Network
Great Famine (Ireland)
Great Depression 37, 67, 84, 116, 206, 249, 256–9, 267–9, 273, 345
"great neighborhood in America" designation by the American Planning Association (APA) 138
Great Society programs (President Lyndon Johnson) 70, 73, 84n4, 257, 259, 264
green roof 56, 270, 298, 414, *415*, 419n13
green wall 277, 298, 419n13
Green, William 261
greenbelts 35, 38, 42, 110–17, 127, 129–30, 219, 255; and large linear areas of open space 115, 219; populated 114; regional 219
Greenbelt Alliance (San Francisco Bay Area) 135
greenbelt town program (United States) 116
Greenbelt, Maryland 111, 116, 130n11, 255
Greenhills, Ohio 111, 116, 130n11, 255
Greendale, Wisconsin 111, 116, 130n11, 255
Greenpeace 409
greenhouse gases (GHGs) 1, 56, 98, 143, 146, 175, 285–6, 333, 335, 395–8, 400–401, 405, 407–408, 410–14, 416, 419
Greenwich Village 10, 379
Grigsby, William 348
Gross Domestic Product (GDP) 126, 230, 241–2, 387, 405, 411, 419
gross income 340, 347, 351
Gross Mean Sea-Level Rise 418
gross rents 348
gross vehicle weight rating (GVWR) 336

ground rents 114, 129
Group of Seven (G7) leading industrial countries 243, 247n11, 399, 417
Group of Smokeless, Slumless Cities *113*; *see also* Ebenezer Howard
Group of Twenty (G20) leading industrial countries 243, 247n11, 399, 408, 417, 419n14
growth machines 77, 372–73, 382
Guérin, Jules 117
GVWR *see* gross vehicle weight rating

Haar, Charles 150; *see also* "Impermanent constitution" (Charles Haar's characterization of comprehensive plans)
Habermas, Jürgen 100
Habitat Conservation Plans (HCPs) 1, 87, 92, 152, 205, 270, 289, 306–7, 401
Hack, Gary 61, 104, 129, 169, *171*, 172
Hall, Sir Peter Geoffrey 88–9, 91–2, 104, 113, 129, 246, 382–4
Hallidie, Andrew Smith 31
Hamilton, Alexander 26, 31
HAMP *see* Home Affordable Modification Program (United States)
Handlin, Oscar 203
Harbourfront area, Toronto, Canada 172
Hardin, Garrett 98
hard protect solution to flooding 287
Hardest Hit Fund (HHF) (United States) 346
Hargreaves Jones landscape architecture firm 57–8, *59*
Hargreaves Jones rendering of Louisville Waterfront Park *59*
Harjo, Laura 203
Hartman, Chester 201–2, 272
Harvey, David 76, 97
Hayden, Dolores 55, 194, 202, 212
Hayes, Denis 283
Hays, Harry 199
hazard insurance 343
hazardous waste 300–301
HBCUs *see* Historically Black Colleges and Universities
HCD *see* Housing and Community Development
HCPs *see* Habitat Conservation Plans
HCVs *see* Housing Choice Vouchers (United States)
HDCs *see* Housing Development Corporations
Healey, Patsy 100, 104, 202
health 126, 128, 141, 143, 145, 152, 162–3, 174–5, 238–9, 242, 252, 365, 367, 379–80; and city planning 146; and the environment 252, 303; occupational 384; planning organizations 95; risks 152, 317; *see also* public health
Health Impact Assessment in the United States (book by Catherine Ross) 217
Healthy Places Research Group (Georgia Institute of Technology) 217
heat island 143, 173, 286, 414, 419n13
Hegeman, Werner 61
height limit (in zoning and building codes) 165
Heilbroner, Robert 107, 109
Heinrichs, Jurgen 242, 246n5
heroic era in regional planning according to Professor Michael Teitz 206, 207
Hershey, Pennsylvania 379

Heseltine, Michael 383; *see also* Canary Wharf (London, England)
HFAs *see* Housing Finance Agencies (United States)
HHF *see* Hardest Hit fund (United States)
HHFA *see* Housing and Home Finance Agency (United States)
High Cost of Free Parking (book by Donald Shoup) 323
High Occupancy Vehicles (HOVs)149, 290, 315, 318, 327, 400
high-speed rail 122, 210, 235, 383
highway planning 11, 88, 313
highway revolt 11, 313
highways 82, 93, 95, 98, 205, 218–21, 235, 269, 312–14, 316, 322, 325–6, 388–9, 392
highway trust fund (United States) 269
Hills, Carla 262
Hispanics 71, 138–9, 143–4, 195–6, 253, 365; *see also* Latinx community
historic buildings 38, 55, 120, 133, 137, 176, 275–6, 278, 281, 370, 376
historic district 23, 39, 110, 150, 174, 275, 276–78
historic preservation 5, 39, 49, 55, 143, 275, 278; planning 38–9, 274–5, 277–8; projects 278; tax credits 278 (United States)
Historically Black Colleges and Universities (HBCUs) 378
Hoch, Charles 8
Holmes, Oliver Wendell 19
Home Affordable Modification Program (HAMP) (United States) 346
Home Investment Partnership (HOME) program (United States) 158, 340, 353, 364–365
home mortgage interest deduction (United States) 347, 351, 369
HOME program *see* Home Investment Partnership program (United States)
home rule 65, 75, 218
Homes for Heroes program (Great Britain) 115, 116, 130n10
homebuilding industry (United States) 339, 341–2, 363
homelessness 29, 74, 126, 133, 339–41, 347, 252, 362, 339–40, 369
homeowners 72, 167, 186, 249–50, 253–4, 339, 341–3, 345–7, 350–1, 353–4, 362–3, 365
homestead 23, 27, 253, 255, 299
Homestead Act (1862) 24, 27, 253
Hong Kong 99, 237–8, 243, 316, 382
Hoover, President Herbert 34, 269
HOPE VI program (public housing) *see* Housing Opportunity for People Everywhere VI program
horse-drawn streetcar (Hamilton, Virginia, circa 1874) 31
House of Representatives (United States) 67, 409
house prices 238, 345–6, 351
house values 267, 316
households 23–4, 29, 55, 167–8, 208–9, 250, 253–4, 259–60, 265, 267–70, 274, 315–17, 323, 339–41, 345–53, 360–1, 363–5, 413, 416; affluent 122; Black 186, 191, 194, 199, 261, 280, 365; elderly 213, 341, 345, 365; female-headed 194, 196, 261, 264; low-income 200, 202, 205, 252–3, 257, 259–60, 264–6, 339–40, 345–8, 350–5, 362, 364–5, 389; marginal

346; middle-income 62, 345; moderate-income 264, 347, 353, 355; multi-generational 197; nuclear 123; public housing 260, 262; rural 17, 266; subsidizing 351; three-person 391; two-person 391; upper-income 246, 362; utility-maximizing 368; wealthy 161
household-based subsidy 351
housing 4–7, 27, 54–6, 70–3, 96–7, 114–17, 119–20, 144–5, 147–8, 158–9, 167–8, 173–5, 179, 257–9, 262–8, 272–4, 339–43, 345–52, 354–65, 379–82; abandonment 137; assistance 72, 259, 262, 265, 348, 354; expensive 55, 254, 350; fair 74, 340, 358, 360; government-assisted 360; high-income 97; inexpensive 347; laws 74, 137, 152, 196, 360; low-cost 273; low-income 352, 363; lower density 356; luxury 376; manufactured 339, 342, 363; market rate 355; markets 29, 71, 261, 347–8, 353; mixed-income 351; moderate-income 272–3; modernist 273; multi-family 70, 177, 350; overcrowded 392; permanent 339; planners 340, 348; planning 28, 98, 104, 137, 168, 339–65; policy 28, 339–64; private market 260, 262–3, 267–8, 355, 361; programs 257–9, 350; rehabilitated 265; rural 264; sanitary 259, 267, 339, 340, 346, 363–4; single family 70; stock (United States) 144, 174, 199, 230, 252, 267, 339–40, 342; subsidies 130, 257, 273, 347–51, 354, 356, 362, 364; subsidy programs 199, 259, 264; tenement 108; terraced row in Letchworth, England 115; transitional 339, 362, 380; units 174, 176, 250, 252, 255, 259, 261, 274, 340–43, 346, 348, 361, 363–5; vouchers 72, 84, 262–3, 266–7; working-class 273
Housing Choice Vouchers (United States) 267, 340, 348, 352–3, 356, 364–5
housing element of a general plan 147, 339, 350
housing and community development 6, 147
Housing and Community Development Act (United States, 1987) 392
Housing Development Corporations (HDCs) (United States) 264, 265, 339, 354
Housing and Home Finance Agency (United States) 359
Housing and Urban Development, Department of (United States) 4, 65, 70, 71, 85n4, 97, 104n7, 184, 274, 291, 299, 339, 342, 355, 358, 364, 379, 380, 392n8
housing codes 173–4, 178
housing costs 180, 199, 253, 324, 345, 347–8, 350
Housing Development Corporations 65, 70, 264–5, 339, 352, 354
housing efficiency 349
Housing Finance Agencies (HFAs) (United States) 281, 339, 351, 354
Housing Opportunity for People Everywhere VI (HOPE VI) program (United States) 355
housing programs 249, 254–5, 257, 259, 264; affordable 364; federal 259, 264, 352, 359; inclusionary 70, 360–1; legacy 250, 266, 350; modern 273; nonprofit 354; rural rental 266; social 273; state 339, 354
housing trust funds 354, 364–5
housing units 260, 281, 340, 346, 361; deteriorated 253; distressed public 356; low-and moderate-income 141; manufactured 163, 342; middle-income 120; rehabilitated 265; rental 357; residential 346; subsidized 348, 351
housing vouchers 267; see also vouchers
HOVs see High Occupancy Vehicles
Howard, Ebenezer 35, 37–8, 82, 91, 107, 110–17, 120, 126, 128–30, 155, 383–4; crystal palace modeled on the Crystal Palace Exhibition building in Hyde Park (1851) 114; garden city vision 119; Group of Slumless Smokeless Cities *113*; legacy of 117; Jane Jacobs critique of 117; principles 38; proposed clusters of "social cities" that would form systems of social cities 112; Three Magnets *112*
Hunter, Floyd 77
Huntington, Henry E. 31, 32; see also Pacific Electric Railway (Los Angeles, California, 1956) *33*
HPMS see Highway Performance Monitoring System (United States)
HPRG see Healthy Places Research Group (Georgia Institute of Technology)
HSR see High-Speed Rail
HUD see Department of Housing and Urban Development (United States) 71, 351, 356, 360
Hughes, James 350
Hugman, Robert 388
Hunter, Floyd 77, 85
Hunter College 243, 359
Huntington, Henry E. 31–2
hurricanes 98, 105, 173, 285, 287, 341, 379, 388, 401; Katrina 287
Hwa Shan Cultural District, Taipei, Taiwan 172
hybrid vehicles 400
Hyderabad, India (2012) *234*
hydroelectric power 255, 407
hyperloops 331–34, 335
HyperVic company; see also McClelland, Zac; see also Sydney to Melbourne, Australia Hyperloop (proposed) *332*

Ian McHarg Environmental Planning Award 404; see also Ian McHarg
IAPMO see International Association of Plumbing and Mechanical Officials
International Association of Plumbing and Mechanical Officials (IAPMO) 173
Ickes, Harold L. 359
ICLEI see International Council on Local Environmental Initiatives
ICMA see International City Management Association
ideology 70, 73, 77, 241, 300, 367–8, 391; classical liberal 74; liberal, 73; neoliberal, 73; conservative 73; progressive 73–4
IEDC see International Economic Development Council
Igoe, William 60, 261–2, 264
Image of the City (book by Kevin Lynch) 45, 48, 49, *50*
IMF see International Monetary Fund
immigrants 22, 34, 41, 55, 138, 141, 203, 277, 340, 345
immigration 21–2, 41, 186, 196, 250, 253
Imperialism as the Highest Stage of Capitalism (book by Vladimir Lenin) 97; see also Lenin, Vladimir
IMF see International Monetary Fund

"Impermanent constitution" (Charles Haar's characterization of comprehensive plans)
incentives 99, 174, 180, 266, 270, 290, 324, 378, 382, 384–5, 392
implied warranty of habitability 361, 364
inclusionary zoning 74, 76, 167, 199, 254
interurban electric streetcar systems 268
indigenous planning 200, 203n10
"in-kind" contribution 272
in lieu payment 161
income 69–70, 167–8, 183, 186, 252–3, 259–60, 263–8, 340, 345–8, 352–3, 355, 360, 364–5, 374, 376; categories 347; higher 274; levels 340, 348, 363; lower 177, 348, 361; tenant 352, 356
incorporated place (United States) 16
incumbent upgraders (in gentrifying neighborhoods) 254
indigenous people 40, 190, 203, 308
inductive reasoning 10, 88
industrial cities 15, 25–6, 190, 221, 250, 303, 375, 377
industry clusters 371
informing in Sherry Arnstein's "ladder of citizen participation" 185
infrastructure 54, 56, 83–4, 141, 159–60, 176–8, 206–7, 213, 230–1, 290, 293–4, 367–8, 379–80, 384, 388–92; construction 115, 313, 390; flood control 57; funding 257; large- scale 159, 215; projects 72, 159, 218, 388, 410; planning 144, 155, 159, 216, 240, 290, 387, 389–90; in developing countries 390; regional 390; traditional transportation 315
Inner City: Urban Poverty and Economic Development in the Next Century (book by Catherine Ross and Thomas Boston) 217
Innes, Judith 100, 202
input-output analysis 371
instant cities 24
insurance 4, 179, 186, 267, 285, 287, 343, 345, 371
Integrated Water Resources Management (IWRM) 214, 288
Intelligent Transportation System (ITS) 315
interest, mortgage 340, 343
International Monetary Fund (IMF) 74, 243, 387
Intermodal Surface Transportation Efficiency Act (ISTEA) (United States) 217, 270, 312
internal structure of the city
International Association of Plumbing and Mechanical Officials (IAPMO)
International City Management Association (ICMA) 70, 193, 203, 243, 254
International Council on Local Environmental Initiatives (ICLEI) 409, 412
International Economic Development Council (IEDC) 370, 372
International Monetary Fund (IMF) 74, 243, 387
International Panel on Climate Change (IPCC) United Nations) 247, 270, 395–8, 401, 404–5, 418–19
international planning 104, 172
interstate highways (United States) 57, 257, 268–9, 312
inverse condemnation 99, 161, 176
investment 99, 166, 206, 222, 269, 350, 370, 373, 390, 411, 416
investors 115, 187, 332, 351–2, 381, 416
iPhone 229

IPCC *see* International Panel on Climate Change (United Nations)
Isard, Walter 210–11, 246, 371
ISTEA *see* Intermodal Surface Transportation Efficiency Act (United States, 1961)
Italy 230, 239, 241, 246, 295
ITS *see* Intelligent Transportation Systems
IWRM *see* Integrated Water Resources Management

Jabodetabek: The Jakarta, Indonesia, Megaregion 240
Jackson Gardens public housing project (Boston, Massachusetts) 356, *357*
Jackson, John Brinkerhoff (J.B.) 278
Jacobs Jane 9–10, *11*, 12, 52, 60, 116, 124, 269, 271, 313, 319; editor of *Amerika* 10; Greenwich Village neighborhood threatened by Robert Moses 11; joins *Architectural Forum* magazine 10; writes *Death and Life of Great American Cities* 10
Jacobs, Allan 10–11, 52–4, 61, 78, 96, 104, 117, 125, 155, *156*, 157; 1978 *Making City Planning Work* (book, 1978) 156; attributes his success with the San Francisco *Urban Design Plan* to the three-year planning process 157; constantly at odds with the San Francisco Civil Service Commission 79; San Francisco Planning Director 1967-1975 79; refuses to support San Francisco Mayor Joseph Alioto's political ambitions 156; world authority on street and boulevard design 156
Jakarta, Indonesia (flooding) (2013) *240*
Jamestown, Virginia 19, 26, 188
JAPA see Journal of the American Planning Association
Jay Chatterjee Award 190
Jeanneret, Charles-Édouard 119; *see* Le Corbusier
Jefferson, President Thomas (United States) 66, 278
Jeffries, C. Ray 59
Jim Crow laws 189
jobs 9–10, 14, 17, 96, 99, 111–12, 144–5, 258, 261, 346–7, 368, 370–3, 377, 382, 384–5; basic 371; non-basic 371; security 78, 377; state government 143
jobs-housing balance 206
Johnson, President Lyndon 73, 85, 203, 257–8, 359
Jojola, Theodore 203
Jones, Christopher 416
Journal of the American Planning Association (JAPA) **243, 251,** 280n4
Journal of Planning Education and Research (JPER) 7, 217, 254, 280
Journal of Urban Affairs (JUA) 7, 14n12
journey to work 314
judicial branch of government (United States) 67

Kaiser, Edward 151
Kammen, Daniel 416
Kasarda, John 235
Katz, Bruce 108
Kauai County, Hawaii 138, 144, 146, 149, 151–2; *Climate Change and Coastal Hazards Assessment* 146; *Kaua'I K ākou* plan 138, 144–6, 148–50, 152n11
Kemp, Jack 392
Kennedy, President John F. 73, 85, 257–8, 261, 264, 358–9
Kent, T.J. (Jack) 34, 104, 133–5, 141, 147, 149–50, 279

Kerry, John 409
King, Martin Luther Jr. 358
kit homes 342, 343
Koreans 25
Kreye, Otto 242, 246
Krier, Leon 62
Krumholz, Norman 74, 97, 201–2
Kuhn, Thomas 88

La Défense Business District (Paris, France) *235*
labor 21, 99, 111, 115, 199, 240–2, 261, 386; force 26, 107, 194, 375, 377, 386–7, 391; manual 189; rural 386–7; supply; slave 41; unions 67, 78, 110, 115
lagoon and agricultural building at the World's Columbian Exhibition (Chicago, Illinois, 1893) *118*
Lake Tahoe (California) 215, 307n4
land 16–17, 23–4, 65–7, 99, 112–15, 135–7, 160–2, 167–9, 179–80, 219–21, 260, 271–4, 280, 284, 289–90, 298–9, 303–5, 307–8, 323–4, 350; cheap suburban 31, 269; city rezoning 377; costs 213, 341, 350; dedicating 161; development 93, 299; grazing 98; homestead 299; industrial 302; prices 112, 114, 220; private 161, 220, 260, 289, 299; residential 123; rezoning 272; subdivision 78, 155, 160; temperatures 395, 401; undeveloped 23, 62, 122, 213, 219, 284; unincorporated 135, 266
Lanham Act *see* National Defense Housing Act (United States, 1940)
land value capture 99, 114, 117, 316
landfills 99, 136, 163, 270, 290, 300–301, 368, 376, 388, 392
landlords 114, 129–30, 174, 186, 260, 262, 353, 361–2, 364
landlord-tenant law 340, 361
landowners 99, 159–60, 163, 220–1, 226, 283, 285, 287, 290, 294, 307
landscape architects 33–4, 56, 62, 95, 172, 213, 270, 283–4, 295, 297, 402–4
landscape architecture 7–8, 35, 56, 58, 62, 169, 171, 284, 288, 295, 404
Landscape Architecture Frontier magazine **404**
landscapes 55–6, 99, 114, 127, 152, 213, 236, 284, 295, 402–3
landscaping 48, 60, 172, 175, 180, 272, 318, 329, 342, 388
landscape urbanism 56, 62, 254, 284, 298
landslides 165, 284–5
Lang, Robert 226; *see also* megaregions
Lanham Act *see* National Defense Housing Act (United States)
Large City Cluster (LCC) (China) 239
Larice, Michael 54
Latinos 138, 143–4, 196, 200, 365
Latinos and Planning Division, American Planning Association 200
Latinx community 12, 26–7, 39, 41, 190, 192, 194, 196, 200, 203, 253; *see also* Hispanics
Laurence Gerckens Prize 190
Lavoisier, Antoine 104
laws 5–6, 12, 23, 41, 75–6, 84, 158, 161–2, 166, 168–9, 179, 281, 293–4, 307, 410; international 66; state eviction (United States) 361; state level growth management (United States)159; state recycling (United States) 68; state subdivision (United States) 160
Laws of the Indies 23, 41n9, 203n7
LCDC *see* Oregon Land Conservation and Development Commission
Le Corbusier 119–20, 273; drafts the Athens Charter (la charte d'Athènes) 95; leads the modernist movement 107, 119; and the model of the city as a machine 104n5; *Plan for a Contemporary City of 3 Million* (1929) *95*, *119*; *see also* Radiant City
LEED standards *see* Leadership in Energy and Environmental Design standards
L'Enfant, Maj. Charles Pierre 23; *see also* L'Enfant Plan for Washington, D.C. (1792)
L'Enfant Plan for Washington, D.C. (1792) *24*; *see also* L'Enfant, Maj. Charles Pierre 23
lead agency 148, 291, 292
Leadership in Energy and Environmental Design (LEED) standards 56, 152, 283, 297, 414
LeFebvre, Henri 97
legacy federal Below Market Interest Rate (BMIR) housing programs (United States) 70, 221, 259, 264, 266, 340, 354, 357, 364, 384; 266, 357
legislative act 160, 294
legislative branch of government (United States) 67, 256
Leigh, Nancy Greene 377
Lenin, Vladimir 242; *see also Imperialism as the Highest Stage of Capitalism* (book by Vladimir Lenin)
Lerner, Jaime 325; *see also* Bus Rapid Transit, Curitiba, Brazil
Letchworth, England Garden City 82, 91, 107, 111, 114–17, 155, 255
Level of Service (LOS) 48, 148, 152, 322
Lever, William Heskith 114–15
Levitt Pavilion, SteelStacks Arts and Cultural Center (Bethlehem, Pennsylvania, 2020) *376*
Lewis, Arthur O. 386–7
LGBTQ (Lesbian, Gay, Bisexual, Transgender, Queer population) 7, 13, 39–40, 55, 138, 183, 190, 198, 200, 252
LHAs *see* Local Housing Authorities (United States)
liberal ideology 73–4, 367, 373, 391
Lichtenstein, Rachel 4
Life Between Buildings (book by Jan Gehl) 50
LIHTCs *see* Low-Income Housing Tax Credits (United States)
Lindblom, Charles 94
Line, the, proposed linear city in Saudi Arabia *see also* Bin Salman, Mohammed, Crown Prince of Saudi Arabia 122
linear city 107, 122, **123**, 128, 130n12
Linnaeus, Carl 189
listing (endangered and threated species) (Endangered Species Act (United States), 1973) 278, 288, 289
Little Italy, San Diego, California 379
little NEPAs 187, 283, 291, 293, 294, 307n4, 410
Livingston, Robert 29
local government politics 65, 74, 78, 85, 134
local governments 61–2, 66–8, 75–8, 83–4, 135–6, 158–62, 166–8, 173–6, 185, 253–5, 257–60, 270–2,

277–8, 293–4, 307, 353–4, 372–4, 377–8, 380–1, 412
Local Housing Authorities (LHAs) (United States) 9, 70
location quotients 374
Local Planning (book by Gary Hack, Eugenie Birch, Paul Sedway, and Mitchell Silver, eds) **171**
Locally Unwanted Land Uses (LULUs) 81, 183, 185, 187, 202
location theory 1, 211, 311, 370, 371, 374
Logan, John 77
London region (England) 3–4, 33, 35–6, 110–11, 115, 129–30, 233, 235, 237–8, 241, 246, 327, 329, 383–5, 401
London Voices, London Lives (book by Peter Hall) 384
LOS *see* Level of Service
Los Angeles, California (City) 20, 31, 32, 33, 137, 197, 199, 224, 226n9, 239, **270**, 286, **321**, 323, 325, **333**, 414
Louisiana Purchase 24
Louisville, Kentucky Waterfront Park *58*, *59*; Plan 56, *57*; Downtown Waterfront District 57; Waterfront Development Corporation 57–8
low-density development 212–13, 327
low-income communities 87, 97–8, 201–3, 206, 272, 283, 311, 369
low-income households 28, 362
Low-Income Housing Tax Credit (LIHTC) (United States) 348, 351–2, 355–6
Lowell, Francis Cabot 15, 25, 275; creates the model for early water-powered industry in the United States 26; mill produces cotton textiles 26
Lowell, Massachusetts 15, 25, **26**, 275; *see also* Lowell, Francis Cabot
LULUs *see* Locally Unwanted Land Uses
Lynch, Kevin 45, 48–50, 61, 91, 96, 104, 157, 169, 171–2, 254, 269

MacDonald, Elizabeth 54
MacKaye, Benton 37
macroeconomic concepts 241, 368
Madison County, Tennessee Community Plan transect illustration **142**; transect map **140**
Madrid, Spain 122–3, 130, 237, 246
magnetic levitation trains 331, *332*, 335
"The Magnolia" Sears, Roebuck and Co. Mail Order House (1926) 343, *344*
Making City Planning Work (book by Allan Jacobs) **156**
Making Home Affordable (MHA) program (United States) 346
Main Street America program (United States National Trust for Historic Preservation) (United States) 278
Maldive Islands 401
manipulation in Sherry Arnstein's "ladder of citizen participation" 185
manufactured housing 163, 339, 342, 343, 363
map change (zoning) 165
map layers illustrating Ian McHarg's "Design with Nature" method 296
Map of Boston, Massachusetts showing redlined neighborhoods (1934) *195*
MAP-21 transportation planning act *see* Moving Ahead for Progress in the 21st Century program (United States) 158, 217, 270, 312, 411
Marcus, Claire 339, 346
Marcuse, Peter 97
market failure 98, 323, 369, 391
Mariana Islands 196
market rents 362
markets 19, 21, 98, 151–2, 234, 257, 275–7, 352–3, 362, 391–2, 400; failure 98, 323, 369, 391; festivals 276–7, 370; hierarchies 78
Marsh, Benjamin Clark 34
Mayflower (ship) 15
Marx, Karl 2, 97, 109, 242; *see also Das Kapital*
Massey, Doreen 246
master plans 34, 133, 135, 151, 258–9, 268, 279, 295, 375
Master's of City and Regional Planning degree (MCRP) 7, 46
Master's of Urban Design (MUD) degree 8, 45
MAPS 3 infrastructure plan (Oklahoma City, Oklahoma) 144
MAPS 4 infrastructure plan (Oklahoma City, Oklahoma) 144
maquiladoras 196
"maximum feasible participation of the poor" during the "War on Poverty" (United States) 203n1
McClure, Kirk 351
McClelland, Zac 332
McCoy, Margarita 243
McHarg, Ian 36, 56, 58, 61, 104, 283, 287, 295–7, 306, 403; approach to landscape architecture at the University of Pennsylvania 295; "Man and the Environment" course 295; *see also* map layers illustrating Ian McHarg's "Design with Nature" method 296
McIntosh, Peggy 192–3, 202
McKenzie, Roderick 35, 246
mediation 80–1, 83
megacities 117, 120, 205, 215–216, 224–5, 229, 233, 239–41, 245–6; Asian 327
megalopolis **36**, 38, 239, 240, 246n7
megaregions 216–17, 224, 226, 239–40
magnetic levitation and hyperloops **331**
methane 398–9, 401, 410
Metro 2040 Concept Plan (Portland, Oregon) **219**
metropolitan area (United States census) 5, 38, 69, 112, 144, 168, 179n4, 215, **219**, 316, 325, 348, 352, 361, 411
Metropolitan Area Projects infrastructure plan (MAP projects) (Oklahoma City, Oklahoma) 144
Metropolitan Statistical Area (MSA) (United States) 380
megacities 117, 205, 224–5, 229, 233, 239, 241, 245
Megaregions: Planning for Global Competitiveness (book edited by Catherine Ross) **217**
merit goods 368, 369
Metropolitan Planning Organizations (MPOs) (United States) 67, 205, 215, 217–19, 224, 286, 290, 311–13, 323, 336, 411
metropolitan regions 135, 205, 213, 215, 218–19, 322
Metro's 2040 Growth Concept Map (Portland, Oregon, 1980) *220*
Mexican Americans 196

Mexico 23–4, 84, 196, 203, 226, 246, 253, 303, 389
MHA program *see* Making Homes Affordable program (United States)
Michigan State University 190
middle-income households 62, 345
mining 5, 25, 146, 207, 250, 284, 299
ministerial act 294
minority communities 1, 189–90, 192–3, 201, 353
miscommunication in planning cartoon *101*
mixed-race communities 26, 194–97
mixed scanning 87, 94, 95, 103
mobile homes 174, 339, 342–3, 363
mobility 29, 32, 38, 52, 54, **72, 216–17**, 268–70, 290, 311, 313–15, 317, 322, 328, 329, 334, 335, 340, 353, 369, **413**
mode split 314, 334
Model T Ford 25, 32, 33, 269, 317, 335
Model TT truck 317
model cities program (United States) 184, 203n1, 257
model of the city as a machine (Kevin Lynch) 96, 104n5
model of the city as an organism (Kevin Lynch) 96, 104n5
modern housing 29, 272–4
modernism 54, 87, 95, 107, 119, 254, 260, 273
modernists 95, 120, 128, 261
modular housing 343
Monks Mound, Kahokia, Illinois 15
Monterey Park, California 150, 197
Moody, Walter 119
More, Sir Thomas 107–8, 128
Morocco 407
Morse, Samuel 33
Morse code 33
mortgages 194, 249–50, 257, 264–8, 281, 339, 342–3, 345–7, 351, 354, 356–7
Mortgage Revenue Bonds (MRBs) (United States) 354, 364
Moses, Robert 11, 313, 319
motor vehicles 32, 268, 316–17, 319, 334–5, 400, 410; *see also* automobiles
motorcycles 285–6, 317–18, 333
Mount Laurel, New Jersey 168, 179
Mount Vernon 39, 281
Moving Ahead for Progress in the 21st Century transportation planning act (MAP-21) (United States) 158, 217, 270, 312
Moving to Opportunity (MTO) program (United States) 263, 355, 365
Moving to Work (MTW) program (United States) 355, 356, 365n7
MPOs *see* Metropolitan Planning Organizations (United States)
MRBs *see* Mortgage Revenue Bonds
MSAs *see* Metropolitan Statistical Areas (United States)
MSU *see* Michigan State University
MTO program *see* Moving to Opportunity program (United States)
MTW program *see* Moving to Work (MTW) program (United States)
MUD degree *see* Masters of Urban Design degree
Mumford, Lewis 11, 35, 37–8, 116, 246, 273, 326; *see also* "Design with Nature"

municipal corporation 75
municipal carbon tax 414
museums 29, 36, 114, 117, 127
municipal corporations 15, 66, 68, 75, 294
Murphy, Frank (Mayor of Detroit, Michigan) 249, 254
Musk, Elon **332–3**

NAAQS *see* National Ambient Air Quality Standards (United States)
NACo *see* National Association of Counties (United States)
NARC *see* National Association of Regional Councils (United States)
NASA *see* National Aeronautics and Space Administration (United States); "Black Marble" Night Sky in Western Europe and Northwest Africa *232*
Nash, Gary 20, 203; *see also* "web of seaport life"
Nashville, Tennessee 134, 137–41, 143, 146, 150–2
NashvilleNext Plan (Nashville, Tennessee, 2018) 134, 136, 138, **139**, 141, 143, 145–6
NashvilleNext Growth and Preservation Concept Map (Nashville, Tennessee) *139*
National Aeronautics and Space Administration (NASA) (United States) 231–2
National Ambient Air Quality Standards (NAAQS) (United States) 285
National Association of Counties (NACo) (United States) 70, 254
National Association of Real Estate Boards (United States) **274**
NAAs *see* Non-Attainment Areas (air quality)
National Association of Regional Councils (NARC) (United States) 215, 226
national building code for mobile homes and other manufactured housing (United States) 342
National Center for Faculty Development and Diversity (United States) 7
National Complete Streets Coalition (United States) 318
National Cooperative Soil Survey (United States Department of Agriculture) 173
National Defense Housing Act (United States, 1941) 260; *see* Lanham
National Electrical Code (NEC) (United States) 174
National Emissions Standards for Hazardous Air Pollutants (NESHAPs) (United States) 286
National Environmental Policy Act (NEPA) (United States) 158, 187, 258, 283, 290–1, 293–4, 307, 410, 412
National Fire Protection Association (United States) 173
National Flood Insurance Program (NFIP) (United States) 287
National Flood Insurance Act (1968) (United States) 287
National Household Travel Survey (United States) 315
National Housing Trust Fund (United States) 72, 354, 365
National Interstate and Defense Highways Act (1956) (United States) *see* Federal Aid Highway Act (1956)
National League of Cities (United States) 70, 226
Nationally Determined Commitments (NDCs) to

reduce Greenhouse Gas emissions under the Paris Climate Accord 397
National Longitudinal Land Use Survey and Data Base (United States) 162
National Marine Fisheries Service (United States) 289
National Museum of Industrial History (United States) **376**
National New Style Urbanization Plan (China) 206
National Oceanic and Atmospheric Administration (NOAA) (United States) 145, 299, 303–4, 396, 418; digital coastal sea level rise viewer 145
National Park Service (United States) 299
national planning 205–26, 256–7, 279; *see also* international planning
National Pollution Discharge Elimination System (NPDES) (United States) 288
National Primary Drinking Water Regulations (NPDWR) (United States) 288
National Secondary Drinking Water Regulations (NSDWR) (United States) 288
National Resources Planning Board (NRPB) (United States) 207, 225–6, 250, 256–7, 279
National Household Travel Survey (United States) 315
National Trust for Historic Preservation (United States) 278
natural gas 56, 79, 256, 284–5, 299–300, 398, 400, 406–7, 410–11
natural regions 205, 209, 213–14, 225
natural resources planning and management 284
Natural Resources Defense Council (NRDC) 409
natural sciences 1, 9, 88, 92, **171**, 292
Nature Conservancy 409
Navajo Nation (United States) 197
NCFDD *see* National Center for Faculty Development and Diversity (United States)
NCSC *see* National Complete Streets Coalition (United States)
NDCs *see* Nationally Determined Commitments to reduce Greenhouse Gas emissions under the Paris Climate Accord
NEC *see* National Electrical Code (United States)
negotiations 80–83, 85
Negotiation Project (Harvard Law School) 81
"Negro removal" 271; *see also* Urban Renewal Program (United States)
neighborhood, units 35, 38, 107, 122–5, 128
neighborhoods 10–11, 35–6, 55–6, 141, 150, 175, 183, 185–7, 196, 198–9, 252–3, 262–3, 265–6, 268–70, 316–17, 353, 372, 379–80, 382, 415–16; activists 271; associations 150, 186; Black 65, 97, 196; city 183, 253, 258; communities 188, 271; depressed 382; distressed 257; gay 189, 198–9; gentrifying 198–9, 253–4, 348; groups 4, 157, 185, 292; high-crime 346; higher-cost 353; low-rent bohemian 10; lower-income 186; mixed 186, 355, 359; planning 97, 150, 157, 183; residential 138; residents 123–4, 146, 185–6, 199, 202, 272, 275, 313, 381; revitalizing 199, 253, 368; urban 11, 252–3
Neighborhood Unit *124*; *see also* Clarence Perry
neo-Marxist planners 2, 97
NEOM development company, Saudi Arabia 122; *see also* "The Line"; *see also* Bin Salman, Mohammed, Crown Prince of Saudi Arabia

neoliberal ideology 73–4, 76, 242, 245, 306, 369, 373, 380, 386, 391
NEOSCC *see* Northeast Ohio Sustainable Communities Consortium
NEPA *see* National Environmental Policy Act (United States)
NESHAPs *see* National Emissions Standards for Hazardous Air Pollutants (United States)
net zero carbon emissions 81, 133, 294
network society; *see also* Manuel Castells
New Amsterdam
New Deal 27, 39, 65, 67, 206–7, 249, 254–7, 259, 267–8, 350, 358
New England 22, 26, 39–40, 98, 257
new federalism 70, 72, 258, 380
New Frontier (President John Kennedy) 70, 73, 257, 259, 264
New Harmony, Indiana 109–10
New International Division of Labor (NIDL) theory; *see also* Frobel, Folker
New Jersey 25–6, 37–8, 130, 135, 168, 178–9, 183, 199, 205, 300, 302, 307; constitution 168; Office of State Planning 136; *New Jersey Pinelands Comprehensive Management Plan* 205
New Lanark, Scotland 107–9, *110*
New Orleans, Louisiana 13n11, 31, 105n7, 150, 183, 275, 284, 287, **295**, 388, 418n6
New Source Performance Standards (NSPS) (air quality) (United States) 286
New Spain 23, 203
New Source Review (air quality) (United States) 86
new towns program (United States) Title IV of the United States Housing Act of 1968 **111**, 116, 255
New Universal Geography of Mankind and the Earth (multi-volume books by Élisée Reclus) 209, 226n3
New Urbanism 45, 55–6, 62, 356
New Urban Agenda (United Nations) 242, **243**, 247n9, 362
New York City 9–11, 13, 28–30, 37–8, 47, 171, 176, 196–7, 238–40, 319, 321, 325–6, 375, 411, 414; 19th century 82; Department of Transportation 319; Greenwich Village 10, 150, 379; housing and planning 253; Housing and Redevelopment Board 359; Housing Authority 59, 63, 355; Metropolitan Transportation Authority 336; Pedestrianized Street at Broadway and 34th Street *321*; Planning Commissioner Janette Sadik-Kahn 47, 319, 321, 244; Tenement House Act (1879) 41; tenements 29; Urban Design Group 46
New York City; commissioners 27–8
New York State 29–30, 38, 68, 158, 359, 410
Newman, Oscar 59–61, 63, 355
Newton, Sir Isaac 104
Next City website 7
NFPA 70 (United States) *see* National Electrical Code (NEC)
NHTS *see* National Household Travel Survey (United States)
Nicholas, Grand Duke of Russia 109
NIDL theory *see* New International Division of Labor theory; *see also* Frobel, Folker
NIMBY syndrome *see* "Not In My Back Yard" syndrome

NINJA loans 346
nitrogen dioxide (NO$_2$) 285
Nixon, President Richard 73, 84, 203, 253, 258, 380
NLC *see* National League of Cities (United States)
"no project" alternative (United States National Environmental Policy Act) (United States) 292
NOAA *see* National Oceanic and Atmospheric Administration (United States)
node (as element of city image) **49, 169**, 210, 235, 237, 314–15
Non-Attainment Area (NAA) for air quality (United States) 286
nonconforming use (zoning) 166
non-basic sector of an economy 371
non-participation in Sherry Arnstein's "ladder of citizen participation" 185
non-renewable energy source 175, 278, 294, 317, 406, 411
normative planning 87, 96, 97, 103, 155, **156**, 278
North Carolina 5, 27, 41, 203, 307
North Dakota 74, 137, 159, 268
North End and Downtown Vision from *Boston Vision Plan* (2019) *128*
North River (Robert Fulton's steamboat) 30; *see also* Robert Fulton; *see also* Clermont (Robert Fulton's steamboat)
Northeast Ohio Sustainable Communities Consortium 221
Northwest Ordinance (United States) 23, 27, 41n8, 222, 226n7
"Not In My Back Yard" (NIMBY) syndrome 185, 187
NPDES *see* National Pollution Discharge Elimination System (United States)
NRPB *see* National Resources Planning Board (United States)
nuclear energy 101, 407
nuisance law 99, 159, 160

O-D study *see* Origin-Destination study
OAHP *see* Office of Affordable Housing Preservation (United States Department of Housing and Urban Development)
Obama, President Barack 73, 85, 104
OECD *see* Organization for Economic Co-operation and Development
OEO *see* Office of Economic Opportunity (United States)
Office of Affordable Housing Preservation 265, 357
Office of Economic Opportunity (United States) 257
Office of Management and Budget (OMB) (United States) 4, 137, 217, 226
Office of New Americans (Nashville, Tennessee) 138, **141**
Office of Planning and Research, California Governor's 151
Office of Land Conservation and Development (Oregon) 136
oil 1, 56, 65, 197, 283–5, 300, 308, 398, 400, 406–7, 410–11
Oklahoma City, Oklahoma 138, 143, 144, 146, 150, 197
Olmsted, Frederick Law 21
Olmstead, Frederick Law Jr. 41n17
Olympia and York 384
OMB *see* Office of Management and Budget (United States)
one-stop center for processing building permits 377
one-strike eviction policy in public housing (United States) 356, 361
OPEC *see* Organization of Petroleum Exporting Countries
opportunity site (for economic development) 222, 371, 378
OPR *see* Office of Planning and Research, California Governor's
optional outdoor activity (Jan Gehl) 51
Oregon Land Conservation and Development Commission (LCDC) 206
Organization for Economic Co-operation and Development (OECD) 247
Organization of Petroleum Exporting Countries (OPEC) 406, 418
organizations 7, 74, 173, 192–3, 215, 217, 243, 247, 316, 318–19, 379, 406, 409; academic 8; conservative private property rights 158; environmental 128; grassroots 304, 414; national 134, 215, 255; non-profit 365, 375, 414; historic preservation 39, 277; professional 8, 14, 157; social 128; volunteer 186, 276
origin-destination (O-D) study 210, 311, 314, 334
Osborn, Frederick 116
O'Sullivan, Arthur 368
overlay zone 167
Owen, Robert 108–10
ownership 116, 121, 160, 199, 286, 329, 333, 342, 350, 413; cooperative 114; private 304, 307; public 29, 299; rights 27; shared 160; units 357

PAB *see* Planning Accreditation Board
Pacific Electric Railway (Los Angeles, California, 1956) *33*; *see also* Huntington, Henry
Pacific Islanders 25, 137, 144, 194, 196, 203; lacking city and regional planning special interest groups 200; migration resulting from international politics 27
Pacific Legal Foundation 158
Packard Automobile Assembly Plant (Detroit, Michigan, 1955) *373*
Page Act of 1875 25
pandemics 95, 100, **102**, 230, 239, 245
paradigm 81, 87, 88, 91–4, 98, 100, 107, 317, 327, 331, 335, 386
Paraisópolis, São Paulo, Brazil *363*
Paris Climate Agreement 395–7, 408–9, 419
Park, Robert E. 35
parks movement 21
particulate matter (2.5 milligram) 285
Parker, Barry 115–16
parking 54, 81–3, 187, 197, 313, 317, 321, 323–4, 328, 334, 369
partnership in Sherry Arnstein's "ladder of citizen participation" 185
Pastor, Manuel 303, 308n7, 308
Patterson, New Jersey 15
Patton, Bruce 81
Paul Davidoff Award 201; *see also* Paul Davidoff

payment in lieu of property tax (PILOT) in United States public housing program 260
peat 399
peatlands 398
Peets, Elbert 61
Peking University (PKU) Department of Urban and Regional Planning 404; College of Planning, Architecture, and Landscape Architecture 404
Peng, Nelson 318, 328
Penn, William 40
Penn Central Transportation Company vs New York City 178
People for Open Space (San Francisco Bay Area) **134–5**
People vs Hurlbut 75
People's Republic of China 40, 116, 125, 392
permafrost 396, 398, 404
permissive element (of a California general plan) 147
Perry, Clarence 55, 122–5; argues that schools should also function as community centers with adult education classes and cultural events in the evening 123; believes primary schools are the central institution to which families with young children relate 123; Neighborhood Unit 55, *124*; observes large patches of undeveloped land isolated by freeways that were developing haphazardly 122
Petaluma, California 176–8
Petaluma plan 177, 180n10, 180n11
PHAs *see* Public Housing Authorities (United States)
Philip II of Spain 23
physical plans 19, 91, 134–5, 137, 151, 258
Pike Place Market (Seattle: Washington) **275**, 276–7
PILOT payment *see* Payment In Lieu Of Property Tax (United States public housing program)
Pinchot, Gifford 28, 300; *see also* conservation
PITI payment *see* Principal, Interest, Taxes, and Insurance payment
Piven, Francis Fox 201
placation in Sherry Arnstein's "ladder of citizen participation" 185
placemaking 45
Planetizen website 7
planokc (Oklahoma City, Oklahoma comprehensive plan) 138, 143–5, 149–50, 151n2
Plan of the City of Chicago (1909) 34; *see also* Daniel Burnham and Edward Bennett
planned shrinkage 137, 213, 253, 372
planned unit developments (PUDs) 76, 163, 167, 174, 294
planners 1–2, 4–7, 9–13, 52–6, 80–3, 89–91, 97–8, 127–8, 133–6, 155–60, 165–7, 191–4, 198–202, 239, 245, 299–302, 311–12, 369–72, 390–1, 398–402; advocacy 146, 201; blight 38, 82, 137, 220, 257, 272, 282; of color in academic degree programs 5; contemporary 209; county 266, 284, 339; in depressed communities 377; economic development 99, 371–2, 374; environmental 205, 213, 279; female 193; and local government officials 160; minority 12; national 101, 207; neighborhood 35; neo-Marxist 2, 97; professional 12; progressive 74, 97–8, 201, 272; site 172–3; and urban designers 167; work 6, 39, 79, 224, 229, 266, 268, 277, 303, 306, 406

Planners of Color Interest Group (POCIG) (Association of Collegiate Schools of Planning) 5, 7, 190, 193, 200, 202, 252
planning 1–7, 12–15, 65, 67–9, 73–6, 87–98, 100–5, 156–9, 188–94, 196–8, 200–2, 205–7, 213–15, 229–45, 251–4, 269–73, 283–4, 311–13, 367–71, 400–2; academics 89, 306; academy (Philadelphia) 244; administration 7; authorities 75; boards and bodies 61, 256–7; budgets 178; collaborative 11, 96, 104, 146, 155, 183, 221, 254, 330, 417; commissioners 41, 78–9, 89, 134, 146, 157; commissions 5, 34, 135, 145, 162, 165, 167, 175, 258–9, 278–9, 292; conflicts 65, 81, 343; consultants 62, 89, 186–7; controversies 68; curricula 7, 200; degrees 7, 14, 155, 295; departments 145, 160, 291, 311; disputes 80, 201; ethics 7, 87, 96–7; history 7, 40, 190, 243–4; law 13, 39, 66, 74, 135, 137, 159, 162; and managing transportation 311; officials 5, 134; practice 6, 56, 65, 76, 81, 89, 92, 94, 97, 133, 136; process 57–8, 90, 96, 100, 103, 138, 145–6, 151–2, 156–7, 178, 200–1; and program implementation 279; programs 6, 35; regulations 23, 158; rural 213, 284; and urban design decisions 286, 306
Planning Accreditation Board (North America) 6–9, 13–14, 39, 45, 66, 87, 97, 196, 199–200, 202, 279, 283
Planning Advisory Service of the American Planning Association (PAS) 6; *see also* American Planning Association (APA)
"Planning and Women Division" American Planning Association 192
"Planning and the Black Community Division" American Planning Association 200
planning departments 4, 6, 9, 65–6, 68, 70, 78–80, 135, 137, 145, 160, 200, 258, 291, 311, 390; county 6, 68–9, 78, 128, 145, 160, 313, 390; local city 271
planning directors 6, 41, 78–9, 89, 135, 156, 201, 203, 280, 292
planning education 7, 35, 45, 89, 190, 200, 202, 217, 249, 254, 279–80
planning environment 93, 95, 198
Planning in the Public Domain (book by John Friedmann) 89
planning profession 5, 7, 13, 34, 38–9, 133, 192–3, 199–200, 202, 270, 279
planning programs 7, 9, 199–200, 279
planning schools 5, 12, 14, 45, 200, 254, 270
planning specializations 8, 254, 372
planning theorists 2, 91–2, 96, 100, 103, 209, 225
planning theory 7, 87–105, 107, 125, 242, 273; chronological developments in 88; city and regional 100; collaborative 104; equity 202; and European architecture 273; evolution of 88; Marxist ascendency in 242; normative 87, 96, 103; paradigm shifts in 87, 90, 107; and practice 89, 273; resilient 72; teaching 87; unified 91; urban 88, 90; the uses of according to John Friedmann 104
Plano, Texas 138, 145, 149; *see also* Plano Tomorrow comprehensive plan
Plano Tomorrow comprehensive plan 138, 143, 145, 146, 148, 152n7; *see also* Plano, Texas
plans 4, 37–8, 78–9, 82–3, 93–6, 102–4, 117–19,

133–8, 141, 143–52, 155–9, 177–8, 185–9, 205–7, 217–19, 221–2, 284–90, 304–8, 312–13, 411–14; ambitious 255, 319; building 179; draft 87, 143, 151–2; economic development 371–2, 377; local 159, 206, 417; national 396; neighborhood 150, 185; park 57–8; private sector 330; regional 141; statewide 206; town 91, 93, 222
Pilgrims 15, 19; *see also* Plimoth Plantation
Plan for Chicago 1909 (Daniel Burnham and Edward Bennett) 117, *118*, 119, 155
Plater-Zyberk, Elizabeth 47, 62
Plimoth Plantation 15, 19; *see also* Pilgrims
Plunkitt, George Washington 82
Plymouth, Massachusetts 15, 19; *see also* Pilgrims; *see also* Plimoth Plantation
POCIG *see* Planners of Color Interest Group (Association of Collegiates Schools of Planning)
point source of air or water pollution 285, 286, 396
point system in urban growth management 177, 180n10
police 56, 60, 62, 179, 183, 188, 198, 200, 369, 371, 382, 388, 392; body cameras 56; misconduct 56; protection 377; shootings 203; stations 377
police power 158, 174
policies 27–8, 69–70, 73, 82–5, 94, 116, 137–8, 146–52, 157, 192–3, 203, 206–7, 242–3, 253–4, 318–19, 323–4, 345–7, 368–70, 408–10, 417–18; anti-racist 183; civil rights 358; economic development 373–4, 387, 392; government 70, 73, 369; private sector plans and 330; redistributive 369; regional development plans and 206
political 68, 155, 224, 257, 304; activists 71; appointees 215; culture 46, 74, 83, 136, 159; horse trading 185; opposition 185, 226; orientation 68; parties 67–8, 70–1, 73, 381, 389; power 38, 66, 77, 201, 215, 224, 406; strategists 5
politicians 90, 165, 186, 260, 273–4, 359
politics 8, 65, 70, 73, 79, 83, 91, 94, 155, 172, 258; electoral 410; housing 259; international 27; liberal 257, 360, 362, 368, 380, 391; pro-climate management 411; local government 65, 74, 78, 85, 134; national 70; state-level 159; urban 13, 65, 69, 77
pollutants 214, 218, 285, 288
polluters 98, 302, 333, 416
pollution 41, 56, 62, 96, 103, 127, 143, 285–6, 295, 414, 416; air; chemical 125; exposure to 147, 152; ground level ozone 286; water 214, 224, 279, 287–8, 363
POPOS *see* Privately Owned Public Open Space
population 15–17, 19–21, 24–6, 38–9, 41, 113–15, 137–9, 143–4, 191–2, 203, 208–10, 221–2, 229–31, 239–40, 245–6, 249–51, 372–4, 380–1, 386–7, 392; Black 27, 195–6; in cities 233, 245; classifying 192; density 209, 316; gay 198, 379; growth 16–17, 143–4, 230, 239, 250, 283, 285–6; homeless in United States; 277, 340; indigenous 27, 418; projections 229; targets 110, 260; urban 40, 247, 250, 278, 387; urban growth 16, 230, 246; world 40, 229–31, 245–6, 395, 416
population growth 16–17, 143–4, 230, 250, 283, 285–6
Population Reference Bureau 246

Port Sunlight, England 114
Porter, Michael 95
post-shelter society 339, 350
post-industrial city 25, 237, 239, 249, 250, 279, 367, *375*, 387
poverty 70, 74, 137, 197, 201, 203, 207, 256–7, 352–3, 355, 381–2, 385, 392
PPP *see* Public–Private Partnership
PPP *see* Purchasing Power Parity
PPS *see* Project for Public Spaces
PRC *see* People's Republic of China
Prevention of Significant Deterioration (PSD) permits (air quality) (United States) 286
primary sector of an economy 250; *see also* secondary sector of an economy and tertiary sector of an economy
Principal, Interest, Taxes, and Insurance (PITI) payments 343, 347
private developers 41, 264, 272, 291, 294, 307, 339, 370, 388
private sector plans 330
Privately Owned Public Open Space (POPOS) 47, 165, 254
Pro-"Dreamers" Rally, Ann Arbor, Michigan 79, *80*; *see also* Deferred Action for Childhood Arrivals (DACA) program (United States)
professionals 7, 9, 82, 93, 157, 243, 372, 404; evidence-based 306; mental health 192; middle-class 198; outsider 55; skilled 80
profit 66, 165, 173, 176, 266, 345, 352, 368, 376–7, 379, 381; making subsidiaries 379; maximizing behavior 174, 277; private 306; rental 257; windfall 99, 316
programs 8, 13–14, 67, 72, 144, 146–7, 199, 254–5, 257–61, 263–6, 270–2, 281, 283, 285, 351–7, 363–5, 367–70, 379–82, 385, 391–2; academic 62; accreditation 55; adaptive reuse 375; anti-poverty 78; carbon cap-and-trade 290, 410; civic design 35; community action 203; computer 93; demand-side housing subsidy 267; distributing an annual amount of federal funding 380; educational 375; environmental 308; federal housing subsidy 340, 353–4; to fund transportation infrastructure 130; graduate city and regional planning 35; implementation 279; job training 392; low-income homeownership 265; neighborhood 185; public infrastructure 144; to resettle city dwellers 255, science 295; social safety net 257, 388–9, 391; social service 186; socialistic 130, 271–272; state coastal zone management 304; state redevelopment 271, 381; statewide rent regulation 362, 364; strategies 304; supply-side 259, 350; television 295
Program on Negotiation (Harvard Law School) 81
progressive planning 87, 97, 200, 201
Project for Public Spaces (PPS) 47, 58
projects 3–5, 57–8, 60, 157, 159, 167–9, 171–2, 186–7, 246–7, 259–61, 264–6, 271–2, 281, 290–5, 312–13, 316–17, 351–7, 370, 380–2, 388–90; community development 380, 392; controversial 293, 303; funded 271, 280, 294; infrastructure 72, 159, 218, 388, 410; landscape 404; redevelopment 271, 274, 381; regional 218; rental 257, 266; residential 59; transportation 155, 217–18, 290, 312–13, 316–17

property rights 158, 189, 202, 283
property taxes 68, 129, 177, 220, 249, 253, 260, 343, 351, 381–2
property values 97, 162, 174–5, 187, 201, 220, 249, 382
PSD permit *see* Prevention of Significant Deterioration permit (air quality) (United States)
Pruitt, Wendell O. 261
Pruitt–Igoe public housing project, St. Louis, Missouri 261–264, 281
public good 98–9, 368–9, 388
public health 9, 34, 37, 104, 143, 147, 158, 199, 203, 217, 249
public housing 59–60, 72, 74, 257–264, 271, 273–4, 339, 352–7, 361–2, 365; authorities 67, 259–61, 264, 267, 339, 348, 352–357, 361, 381; capital fund 355; development costs of 259; developments 356; federal 364; funding 355; households 260, 262; and housing choice vouchers 352; Jackson Gardens Public Housing Project (Boston, Massachusetts) 357; land for 260; in low- income neighborhoods 355; private sector investment in 72, 264, 304; inventory 356; programs 72, 74, 255, 257, 259–60, 273–4, 354, 358; project managers 260; projects 59–60, 72, 196, 205, 258–62, 264, 346, 348, 355–6; racial concentration in 355; standards 355; tenants 183, 196, 261, 264, 355, 365; units 70, 202, 257, 260–1, 264, 348, 353–6; vouchers 355; for war workers 260
public land 114, 135, 152, 283–4, 298–9, 410
public transit 69, 133, 169, 313, 327, 388, 413; agencies 316, 336, 390; management 316; oriented development 96, 122, 148–9, 254, 258, 290; public 122, 130, 144, 206–7, 250, 315, 323–5, 327, 329, 400; restructured regional 202; stations 148–9; systems 210, 327, 392
Public Works Administration (PWA) (United States) 259, 280
public works departments (local) 159, 268, 313, 390
Public–Private Partnerships (PPPs) 82, 186, 241, 370, 377, 389
Pudong District, Shanghai, China (2012) 120
PUDs *see* Planned Unit Developments
pueblo 41n9
Pueblo Bonito 19, 104n5
Puerto Ricans 196, 274
Puerto Rico 307, 318, 353
Pulido, Laura 303, 308
PUMAs *see* Public Use Microdata Area, United States Census
purchasing power parity (PPP) 241
Puyang River Ecological Corridor **403**, *404*; *see also* Yu, Kongjian
PWA *see* Public Works Administration (United States)

Qatar 408
Quakers 40, 130
Qualified Allocation Plan (QAP) for Low Income Housing Tax Credits 352
qualitative research methods 9
quantitative research methods 9
quasi-judicial act 76, 160, 294, 307n5

race 26, 56–7, 69–70, 137–8, 167–8, 177, 179, 183, 188–94, 200–1, 209, 355, 357, 359–60, 379

Race Equity Inclusion and Action Guide Annie E. Casey Foundation 193m 203n5
racial discrimination 25, 137, 186, 194, 201, 257, 261, 360
racial equity 137, 193
racism 56, 188, 193, 200; environmental 303, 416; internalized 193; overt 193; systemic 200
RAD Program (United States) *see* Rental Assistance Demonstration Program (United States)
Radburn, New Jersey 37, 42n18, 116
Radiant City 95, 119–20
rail 2, 93, 130, 324, 333, 388; corridors 149; facilities 291; local 329; region's 222; systems 32, 159, 331–2
railroads 22, 30, 41, 220, 299, 389
railways 31, 41
Railway Acts first (1862) 41n16; second (1864) (United States) 41n16
Ramapo, New York 176–7, 180n9, 180n10
Ramapo Plan 176–7, 180
rational planning model 1, 87–8, 92–5, 102–4, 143, 193, 322–3
RC program *see* Renewal City program (United States)
RCs *see* Regional Councils (United States)
RCI *see* Roadway Congestion Index
RCRA *see* Resource Conservation and Recovery Act (United States)
Reagan, President Ronald 73–4, 84, 258, 265, 300, 381, 383
Rebuild by Design Program (United States) 72
recall as way of removing local elected official from office (United States) 76
Reclus, Élisée 129n3, 209, 224, 226n3; *see also New Universal Geography of Mankind and the Earth*
recreation 75, 78, 129, 147, 299, 304–5, 308, 390, 392, 401, 403
recycling 5, 68, 125, 294, 300, 390, 392
red state (United States) 67
redevelopment 56, 149, 190, 222, 272, 324, 381–2; agencies 271–2, 381; commissions 271; London docklands 383; planning 271; programs (state) 271, 381; project areas 271; projects 271, 274, 381
Redevelopment and Race (book by June Thomas) **190**
redlining **186**, 194
regeneration 186, 271, **383–4**
regime theory 65, 77
Regime Politics (Clarence Stone) 77
regional Air Quality Districts (AQDs) (United States) 67, 285
Regional Councils (RCs) (United States) 151, 215, 217–18, 226, 382, 385, 392
regional development planning **89**, 207, 241
regional economic development and planning 207
regional economic development strategies 378
regional fair share housing coalition (United States) 87, 98
regional governments 205, 412
Regional Greenhouse Gas Initiative (United States) 410
regional land information system (RLIS), Portland, Oregon 219
Regional Plan Association (RPA) (United States) 37–8, 75, 155, 224, 244, 273; projected United States megaregions 2050 224
regional planning 38, 96, 103, 205–25; 211–12, 215,

225, 407; and the art and science of city and 1–14, 383; degree programs 6, 12–13, 87, 89; education 7, 35, 135; entities 67, 217, 256; theory 100, 209, 225; history 37, 111, 244; and national planning 205–25; politics of 65–83, 85; practice 97, 108, 141, 213; programs 6–9, 12–13, 87, 97, 190, 254, 270, 279, 283, 368, 387

Regional Plan Association (RPA) (United States) 37–8, 75, 155, 224, **244, 273**; *see also Regional Plan of New York and Its Environs* (1929)

Regional Plan of New York and Its Environs (1929) 38

Regional Planning Association of America (RPAA) 37–8, 273; *see also* Lewis Mumford

regional plans 37–8, 83, 112, 151, 169, 205, 217–18, 221, 224, 285, 287; failure to include a gender perspective 39; failure of local governments to work together to implement 225; impact on cities 39, 83, 112, 151, 192, 287, 306; and the location of manufacturing plants and transportation infrastructure 209; prepared in two main ways 192

regional science 88, 210–11, 243, 311; birth of 210; concepts 374; courses 211; in Europe 211; principles of 311

Regional Science Association (RSA) 211, 243

Regional Science Association International (RSAI) 211, 243

regional scientists 210, 225, 246, 371

regions 23, 37–8, 67, 127–8, 150, 205–9, 213–14, 216–19, 221–2, 224–6, 231, 240–1, 245–6, 255–6, 287, 370–2, 374–5, 390–1, 396–8, 405–6; agricultural 5; alpine 401; autonomous 418; geographic 416; impoverished 207; megacity 117, 205, 224–5, 229, 233, 239, 241, 245; metropolitan 135, 205, 213, 215, 218–19, 322; micropolitan 208; older industrial 221; populous 207; rural 213; underdeveloped 207; uninhabited 236

regulations (United States government) 48, 169, 173–4; environmental 5, 68, 300, 306, 410; federal 73, 255, 288, 300, 322, 334, 356; land development 48; local 27, 176; non-binding; National Primary Drinking Water 288; National Secondary Drinking Water 288; rent 361–2, 364; securities 162

regulators 328, 345, 400

Reid vs Architectural Review Board of Cleveland Heights 175

Renaissance Center (Detroit, Michigan) *374*

renewable energy 381, 395, 406–7, 409–11, 416; sources 26, 406–7, 411

rent 348, 361; control 361–2; gouging 362; payments 362; regulation 361–2, 364; stabilization 361; subsidies 266

Rental Assistance Demonstration (RAD) program 72, 264, 355–6

restrictive covenants **186**, 194–5

rental housing 116, 174, 264–5, 346–7, 352, 360, 365; affordable 350–1, 353–4; costs and affordability 348; expensive 115; low-income 354; lowest-priced 340; private 361; and section 235 home purchase programs 264

Renton vs Playtime Theaters 163

renewable energy resources 81, 270, 381, 395, 406–7, 409–11, 414, 416; *see also* non-renewable energy sources

Renewal City (RC) program (United States) 382

rent 129–30, 253, 259–60, 262–6, 281, 313, 340, 342, 345, 347–8, 352–3, 361–2, 364; cheap 277; control expensive 266; freezing 362; gross 348; high 110, 253, 266; market 362; in mobile home parks 362; in public housing 362; regulation 361–2; stabilization 361–2; statewide regulation of 362; *see also* ground rents

Reps, John 19, 27, 40, 222

Republican Party (United States) 34, 67, 70, 73, 143, 249–50, 254, 303, 381, 384, 388

required dedication of land 161

reserved powers clause (United States Constitution) 68

resilient cities 402

Resource Conservation and Recovery Act (RCRA) (United States) 300–301

resources 41, 45, 66–7, 147–50, 186–7, 192, 206–7, 209–10, 213–14, 224–5, 410, 416; biological 149; coastal zone 303; critical housing 354; environmental 144, 296–7; financial 215; forest 205; geothermal 147; nonprofit organization 225; rainwater 403; regional 305; renewable 175, 279, 294; scarce 253, 265

Resources for the Future (RFF) 207, 225

Reston, Virginia 116

retaliatory eviction defense in United States landlord-tenant law 361, 364

revitalization planning 367–8, 380, 390

RFF *see* Resources for the Future

revenue 112, 114, 219, 222, 269, 272, 275, 327, 371–2, 375–7, 382, 388, 390, 392; annual local 382, 390; discretionary 220; gambling 197; generation 374, 384; low tax 276; municipal 114, 129, 177, 272, 277, 382; public 75

Revere, Paul 20

RFF *see* Resources for the Future

RGGI *see* Regional Greenhouse Gas Initiative (United States)

Rhino 3D computer-assisted design software 2

right to housing 340, 362, 364, 365n10

right to own laws (United States) 199

Richardson, Harry W. 122, 213

right to travel 180n11

Riis, Jacob 28–9

Riley Foundation 186–7

River Clyde (Scotland) 108, 295

River Rouge automobile assembly plant 25

River Walk (San Antonio, Texas) *389*; *see also* Paseo del Rio (San Antonio, Texas); *see also* Robert Hugman

RLIS *see* Regional Land Information System (Portland, Oregon)

road diet 415

Roadway Congestion Index (RCI)

Roosevelt, President Franklin Delano 70, 225, 249, 254, 259

Roosevelt, President Theodore 28, 300

Ross, Catherine 104, 215, *216*, 217, 240

Rostow, Walt Whitman 386–7

Rothenberg ob der Tauber, Germany 115

Rotterdam, Netherlands surge barrier 401, *402*

Royal Commission on the Distribution of the Industrial Population 116; *see also* Barlow Commission

Roxbury neighborhood, Boston, Massachusetts 185, **186**
RPA *see* Regional Plan Association (United States)
RPAA *see* Regional Planning Association of America (United States)
RSAI *see* Regional Science Association International
rural areas 16–17, 152, 203, 205–6, 213–14, 221, 229, 231, 233, 236, 287–8, 343, 385–7, 392; households 17, 266; planning 213, 284
rural-urban migration 17, **111**, 386–7
Russia 109, 231, 246–7, 398–9, 406
Russian revolution 242
rustbelt 279

S curve of urbanization 16, *17*, *18*, 229; *see also* Kingsley Davis
S&Ls *see* Savings and Loan Associations
Sadik-Khan, Janette 104, 319, *320*, 321, 326
SAE *see* Society of Automotive Engineers
Safe Drinking Water Act (SDWA) (United States, 1974) 288
SAFMR *see* Small Area Fair Market Rents (United States)
Sagalyn, Lynn 370
Sagebrush Rebellion 299; *see also* "Wise Use" movement
Saint-Exupéry, Antoine de 147
SA2020 *see* San Antonio, Texas 2020
Sahel region, North Africa 206, 405
Salon d'Automne 95
Samoans 196
Sassen, Saskia 233, 235, 246n5
San Antonio, Texas 71–2, 388–9
SA2020 nonprofit organization **71**
San Diego, California 253, 379
San Francisco, California 24–5, 31, 49, 51, 76, 126, 134, 147–8, 155–7, 175–7, 198–9, 238–9, 304, 326, 357
San Francisco Bay 215, 226, 304–6, 373
San Francisco Bay Area 134, 148, 177, 304, 306
San Francisco Bay Conservation and Development Commission (BCDC) **304**
San Francisco Urban Design Plan **157**
San Jose, California 382
Santa Fe, New Mexico 23, 41n9, 281n11
Sanborn maps 173, 179n7
Santa Fe trail 23
Sanibel Island, Florida 295
Saudi Arabia 122; *see also* Bin Salman, Mohammed, Crown Prince of Saudi Arabia
Savannah, Georgia 1, 21, 40n5, 150, 183, 275
Savings and Loan Associations (S&Ls) 27, 267
SBA *see* Small Business Administration (United States)
"science of muddling through"; *see also* Charles Lindblom
scientific method
scientific revolution
"scissors" fire escape; *see also* defensible space
school buildings 381, 389
schools 7, 10, 13, 35–6, 89–90, 93, 121–4, 152, 160, 163, 171–2, 177, 180, 313–14, 371–2
Scotland 35–7, 65, 107, 109, 129, 209, 295, 408
SDSN *see* Sustainable Development Solutions Network

sea-level rise 145, 287, 304, 396, 401, 402, 414, 418n4, 418n6
Seattle-Tacoma-Bellevue metropolitan area 205
Section 8 housing certificate program (United States) 84n4, 265–7, 355–6
Section 221(d)(3) federal Below Market Interest Rate (BMIR) program (United States) 264–5, 281n9, 357, 365n8
Section 235 federal Below Market Interest Rate (BMIR) program (United States) 175, 264–5
Section 236 federal Below Market Interest Rate (BMIR) program (United States) 264–6, 354, 357, 365n8
Section 515 federal Below Market Interest Rate (BMIR) rural housing program (United States) 264, 266, 281n10
secondary mortgage market (United States) 267–8, 339, 345
self-amortizing mortgage 268, 345
Senate (United States) 67, **274**, 303, 409
setback (zoning) *165*
severely cost-burdened household (United States) 340
sexual orientation 51, 54, 55, 69, 150, 168, 183, 188, 189, 198, 359, 360, 379
Shaping the Healthy Community (Nashville, Tennessee Civic Design Center) 143
Sherry Arnstein's ladder of citizen participation *184*
shift-share analysis 374
SHPOs *see* State Historic Preservation Offices (United States)
sidewalk design 45, 52, 311
Siegen, Bernard 162
Sierra Club 409
Silicon Ranch Farm combining Solar energy generation and regenerative agriculture (Millington, Tennessee), *399*; *see also* Cabriejo Ranch model of solar regenerative agriculture
Silicon Valley, California 326, 373, 382
Simon, Herbert 92
single-parent female headed households 194, 260
site planning 45–46, 49, 56–8, 127, 148, 155, 164, 168–9, 171–3, 180, 254; professional experience in urban design and 49; and urban design 49, 172
Site Planning (books by Kevin Lynch and Gary Hack) **171**, 172
Site Planning International (book by Gary Hack) 169, **171**, 172
Site Planning and Architectural Review Committee (SPARC Committee) (Petaluma, California)180
sittable space 45, 47, 52, **58**
SketchUp computer-assisted design software 3
skip-stop elevator; *see also* defensible space 59, 281n7
slaves 188, 189, 203n3, 15, 20–21, 26–7, 41n12, 108
Small Area Fair Market Rent areas (SAFMR areas) (United States) 348, 353
Small Business Administration (SBA) (United States) 341
small business incubator 377
smart cities 329
smart growth contrarians 122, 213
smart vehicle 328
Snell, Bradford 32
state laws (United States) 16, 68, 75, 136, 162, 168

Stockholm, Sweden 231, 246n4, 369
Sociable Cities (book by Peter Hall) **383**
social cities 38, **111**, 112, 114; *see also* Ebenezer Howard
social justice 2, 5, 7, 13, 69, 76, 90, 96–7, 137, 183–202, 206, 358, 360
socialism 29, 74, 107–8, 110–11, 129n3
Society for Useful Manufactures (SUM) (United States) 26
Socrates on the importance of urban design 45
soft protect solution to flooding 152n10, 287, **403**
soil subsidence 215, 284
Soria y Mata, Arturo 107, 122, *123*, 130n12; *see also* linear city
SOCS *see* Standard Occupation Classification System (United States)
Society of Automotive Engineers (SAE) 327
solar energy 399, 407, 411
South Capitol Street, Washington, D.C. (United States) 3
Southern Burlington NAACP vs Township of Mount Laurel 1975 179n6
Southern Burlington NAACP vs Mount Laurel 1983 179n6
Soviet Union 10, 125, 407, 409, 419; *see also* Russia
SpaceX **332–3**; *see also* Elon Musk
Spain 19, 23, 123; *see also* New Spain
Spain, Daphne 55, 194, 202
Spanish flu 102
SPARC *see* Site Planning and Architectural Review Committee (SPARC Committee) (Petaluma, California)
space of flows (Manuel Castells) 237, 245
spatial mismatch 206, 311, 346
speaking truth to power 65, 82
special district 48, 65–9, 83, 221, 307n2, 410
Spirn, Anne Whiston 288, 306
sponge cities 214, 287, 402–3
Sports Utility Vehicles (SUVs) 269, 280, 317, 336
spot zoning 164
sprawl, urban 1, **36**, 55, 107, 110, **111**, 152n10, 194, 212, 213, 225, **252**, 283, 317, 324, 343, 411, 414
SSPEA *see* Standard State Planning Enabling Act (United States)
SSZEA *see* Standard State Zoning Enabling Act
staff 3, 5–6, 41, 47, 70, 72, 79, 135, 145, 247, 256–7; department 146, 157, 271, 277; full-time 292; hiring 157; of local planning departments working on historic preservation planning 39; planning 69, 78, 151, 271, 292; professional 390
stages of growth theory of economic development (Walt Whitman Rostow) 386
Standard Occupational Classification System (SOCS) (United States) 374
Standard State Planning Enabling Act (United States) 34, 134, 258, 279
Standard State Zoning Enabling Act (United States) 28, 163, 259
Starr, Roger 253
state agencies 67, 288, 291, 299, 301, 411
state courts (United States) 66, 68, 75, 178
state enabling acts (United States) 67
state governments (United States) 12, 16, 76, 215, 255, 288, 318, 377, 384

State Historic Preservation Offices (SHPOs) (United States) 278
State Implementation Plans (air quality) (United States) 286
state legislation 16, 66, 68, 74–6, 136, 158–60, 162, 168, 302, 305, 361, 364
state-level politics 159
State Transportation Improvement Programs (STIPs) (United States) 312
Statistical Package for the Social Sciences (SPSS) 2
Steagall, Henry (United States Congressman) 259
Steamboats 29, 30, 268, 331; *see also* Robert Fulton, Clermont and North River (Robert Fulton's steamboats)
SteelStacks Arts and Cultural Center (Bethlehem, Pennsylvania) **375**
Stein, Clarence 37, 42, 116
Steinbrueck, Victor 276
Stern, Nicholas 405
Sternlieb, George 350
STIPs *see* State Transportation Improvement Programs (United States)
Storm Surge Barrier, Rotterdam, Netherlands *402*
strategic planning 87, 95, 172, 200, 217, 372, 385
Stronger, More Resilient New York, A 414
Stone, Clarence 77–8
Stonewall Rebellion 198
Stonewall 50 – WorldPride NYC festival 198
strategic planning 87, 95, **216**, 372, 379
streetcars 30–31, 317, 324, 331
Street Life Project 47; *see also* William Whyte
streetcar suburb 269
street plans 54, 62, 141, 152, 159, 318
Strøget pedestrianized street (Copenhagen, Denmark, 2013) *51*
subdivision 136, **141**, 148, 155, 158–9, 160–63, 168, 291, 293, 350, 363, 377, 410
subprime mortgage crisis **72**, 339, 341, 345
subsidies 29, 74, 98, 196, 257, 259, 264–7, 339, 348–9, 351–7, 363
subways 213, 220, 268–9, 312, 316, 322, 328, 331, **332**, 388
sulfur dioxide SO_2 286
Sumantran, Venkat 335; *see also* Connected, Heterogeneous, Intelligent, and Personalized mobility framework (CHIP mobility framework)
sunbelt 250, 279, 253, 373, 407
sunrise industry 373
sunset industry 372
Sunnyside Gardens (New York City) 37, 42n18, 116
Superstorm Sandy **72**, 101, 395, 414
Supreme Court (United States)19, 23–4, 67–8, 158, 161, 163, 168, 176–7, 179–80, 255, 259, 261–2, 280
supply-side housing subsidy 264
Susskind, Lawrence 81–2, 85
suspect classification (United States constitution, fourteenth amendment) 168
Sustainable Development Solutions Network **243**
sustainable urban development 33, **36**, **125**, 270, 283, 294, **412**
SUVs *see* Sports Utility Vehicles
SDWA *see* *Safe Drinking Water Act* (United States, 1974)

Swinomish Indians 197–8, 203n10
Syrqin, Moise 387; *see also* over urbanization
systems analysis 1, 87–8, 93, 203n5
system of cities 33, 38, 93, 112
Sydney to Melbourne, Australia Hyperloop (proposed) *332*; *see also* McClelland, Zac; *see also* HyperVic company
systems, regional 93, 95, 210

Takaki, Ron 25
takings clause (United States Constitution, fifth amendment) 179n3
Taliesin Teaching Studio 49; *see also* Frank Lloyd Wright
targeting of housing subsidies 347, 364
TARP *see* Troubled Assets Relief Program (United States)
Taylor, Nigel 88
Taylor, Peter 237
tax credits 340, 351–2, 377, 392
tax incentives 384–5
Tax Increment Financing (TIF) 271, 381–2
TAZ *see* Transportation Analysis Zones (United States)
TDM *see* Travel Demand Management
TDRs *see* Transfer of Development Rights
technology 25, 29, 31, 33, 89, 91–2, 94–5, 169, 171, 173, 230–1, 240–1, 327–9, 331–3, 335; and city planning 45, 48, 96; digital 3, 12, 150–1, 233, 315, 329, 335, 387; emerging 216–17, 331; state-of-the-art 333
Teitz, Professor Michael 206–7, 225, 246
tempo control (in urban growth management) 176, 180n9
tenants 60, 63, 196, 199, 257, 259–64, 266–7, 281, 348, 352–3, 355–7, 360–2, 364–5
tenant-based housing subsidies 352
Tenant Opportunity to Purchase Assistance (TOPA) program (Washington, D.C.)
tenement house 28–9
Tenement Act (New York City 1879) 29
Tenement House Act (New York State, 1901) 41
tenement houses 28–9, 35
Tenement Museum (New York City) 29
Tennessee Valley Authority (TVA) 225, 250, 256, 279; ambitious New Deal project to build dams and new communities in much of Tennessee and parts of adjoining states 207; authorization in 1933 255; dam construction workers (1943) *208*; the most ambitious New Deal regional planning and development program 255; programs *256*
Tenochtitlan 19, 246n6
terrorism 101, 239, 245
text change (zoning) 165
Thatcher, Margaret 73–4, 258, 383–4
The House We Live In television program 295; *see also* Ian McHarg
theories of knowledge 88–8
therapy in Sherry Arnstein's "ladder of citizen participation" 185
Thomas, June 104, 130, 134, 190, *191*, 192
threatened species 288–90, 306; *see also* Endangered Species Act (United States)
Three C's (3Cs) transportation planning (United States) *see* continuing, comprehensive, and coordinated (3Cs) planning
TIF *see* Tax Increment Financing
TIPs *see* Transportation Improvement Programs (United States)
tipping point (in global climate change) 402, 404
TMAs *see* Transportation Management Areas (United States)
TOD *see* Transit-Oriented Development
tokenism in Sherry Arnstein's "ladder of citizen participation" 184
Tomorrow: The Peaceful Path to Real Reform (book by Ebenezer Howard) **111**
topographical base map (topo map) 172
tornadoes 173, 285, 341, 379
total primary energy supply (TPES) 406–7
town plans 91, 93, 222
towns 20–1, 36–7, 40, 62, 82–3, 91, 110–11, 116–17, 130, 162, 176–7, 221–2, 246, 252, 278, 383–4; and cities 20, 40, 177, 222, 278; college 146; company 146; early 19th-century New England 275; factory 379; greenbelt 116, 130, 255; industrial 107; military 19; mill 109; mining 5; policies 383; programs 111, 116, 255; residential 146; university 5, 319, 362, 412; *see also* townships
Toynbee, Arnold 25
toxic cleanup 300
Toxic Release Inventory (TRI) (United States) 301
toxic sites 283–4, 301–2, 306
toxic substances 163, 300–301
TPES *see* total primary energy supply
traffic congestion 99, 187, 276, 315, 321–2, 326–7
tragedy of the commons 98, 100, 417
train network in the United States, growth of in first half of nineteenth century *2*, *3*
Transfer of Development Rights (TDRs) 148, 175–6, 178, 290
transect 45, 47, 48, 55, 62n6, *140*, **141**, *142*, **143**, 148
transit *see* public transit
transit district 313
Transit-Oriented Development (TOD) 148, 149
transparency **11**, 65, 82–3, 221, 291
transportation 7–9, 29–30, 38–9, 72–3, 78, 93, 95–6, 126–7, 152, 216–17, 224–5, 268–9, 311–13, 315–17, 326–9, 333–4, 398–400, 411–13, 416–17; corridors 122, 220–1; costs 114, 209; data 315–16; improvement programs 10, 168, 218, 304, 312–13; infrastructure 55, 99, 141, 209, 220–21, 311–12, 316–18, 322, 327, 334–5, 339, 371; projects 155, 217–18, 290, 312–13, 316–17; public 126, 202, 311, 317, 323–5, 335–6, 369; systems 91, 152, 210, 311–12, 314–16, 334, 388; technologies 278, 312, 317, 331, 335
Transportation Management Areas (TMAs) 322
Transportation Network Companies (TNCs) 317, 329
transportation planning 6, 88, 159, 205, 210, 254, 268–9, 311–17, 319–35, 405, 411; citizen participation in 313; advanced courses in 311; creative 327; decentralized 217; developments in 290; funded 217; funding and policy guidance for 312; growth of public transit and 250; multi-modal 250, 270; policy guidance for 312; regional 215,

218; planners roles in 312; small-scale decisions 313; theoretical contributions to 311
Transportation Analysis Zones (TAZs) (United States) 16, 87, 205, 208, 316
Travel Demand Management (TDM) 315
transportation corridors 122, 220
Transportation Improvement Programs (TIPs) (United States) 218, 312
TNCs *see* Transportation Network Companies
travel demand 311, 312, 314, 316, 327, 334
Travel Demand Management (TDM) 315
Travel Time Index (TTI) 314, 336
Treasury (United States) 345
Treaty of Guadalupe-Hidalgo 24, 203n7
TRI *see* Toxic Release Inventory (United States)
"triangle trade" 220
trip assignment models 314
tribal planning 8, 197–8
Troubled Assets Relief Program (TARP) (United States) 346
Truman, President Harry 257
Trump, President Donald 73, 76, 79, 85n4, **103**, 251, 381, 405, 408, 410, 411
TTI *see* Travel Time Index
Tucson, Arizona 286
Tugwell, Rexford 130n11, 255
Turenscape landscape architecture firm, Beijing, China 287, **404**; *see also* Yu, Kongjian
TPA *see* Trust for Public Land (United States)
TVA *see* Tennessee Valley Authority (United States)

UAA *see* Urban Affairs Association
UCL *see* University College London
UCLA *see* University of California, Los Angeles
UCS *see* Union of Concerned Scientists
UDAGs *see* Urban Development Action Grants (United States)
UDP *see* Urban Displacement Project, University of California Berkeley
UEDA *see* University Economic Development Administration (United States)
UGBs *see* Urban Growth Boundaries
UK *see* United Kingdom
Ukraine 406, 410
ULLs *see* Urban Limit Lines
UN *see* United Nations
Under2 Coalition 409, 411
unearned increment in land 99; *see also* Henry George
UNFCCC *see* United Nations Framework Convention on Climate Change
Uniform Plumbing Code (United States) 173
Union of Concerned Scientists (UCS) 409
United Kingdom 4, 39, 74, 111, 114, 258, 384, 403, 409, 411
United Nations 16–17, 110, 224, 229, 239, 242–3, 246, 362, 364, 395, 404; Division of Economic and Social Affairs (DESA) 247; Educational, Scientific and Cultural Organization (UNESCO) 19, 274; Environmental Programme 395, 397, 418; Framework Convention on Climate Change 408; world population estimate 2020 and projections to 2050 230
United Nations Intergovernmental Panel on Climate Change (IPCC) 270, 395–6, 418

United States 5–9, 15–17, 21–37, 39–41, 65–70, 125–6, 195–8, 205–8, 224–6, 249–50, 278–81, 283–7, 316–19, 322–7, 339–40, 360–4, 367–73, 399–401, 405–9, 416–19; Army Corps of Engineers 215, 291, 299, **304**, *305*, 404; Chamber of Commerce **274**; Census Bureau 40, 208, 315; Coastal Zone Management Act (1972)304, **305**; Conference on City Planning (1909) 1, 34; Congress 41, 67, 85, 207, 256–8, 260, 264, 266, 268, 279, 281, 353, 355–6, 381, 392; Constitution 167; Department of Agriculture (DOA) 173; Department of Defense (DOD) 299, 405; Department of Energy (DOE) 406; Department of Housing and Urban Development (HUD) 4, 70–2, 173, 184, 187, 196, 257–8, 312, 342, 360, 405; Department of the Interior (DOI) 278, 299; Economic Development Administration (EDA) 378, 379; Environmental Protection Agency (EPA) 300; *Fair Housing Act 1968* 116, 255, 257, 259–60, 264, 267, 271, 273–4, 359–60; Fish and Wildlife Service (FWS) 289–90, 299; Geological Survey (USGS) 172; Global Change Research Project (GCRP) 395, 397, 402, 418–19; Housing Act of 1937 259; National Historic Preservation Act (1966) 278; National Safety Council 336; Office of Management and Budget (OMB) 4, 137, 217; Office of Economic Opportunity (OEO) 257
United States Green Building Council (USGBC) (United States) 56, 152, 173, 254, 283, 279, 379–80, 414
United States National League of Cities (NLC) (United States) 70, 254
United States Savings and Loan League (United States) **274**
United States Geological Survey (USGS) (United States) 172
United States vs. Certain Lands in Louisville (Kentucky) 260
University College London 3, 35, 100, 370, 383
University Economic Development Administration (UEDA) (United States) 378
University of California, Berkeley 20, 90, 252, 270, 323, 413
University of California Berkeley's Department of City and Regional Planning (DCRP) 134, 156, 274
University of California Berkeley's College of Environmental Design (CED) 134, 135, 274
University of California, Los Angeles **252**, 270, 323
University of Illinois 213
University of Maryland 77
University of Pennsylvania 295
University of Southern California 13, 52, 122, 213, 236, 303
University of Washington 276
Unwin, Raymond 115–16
urban 8–9, 35, 230, 236, 250, 342; agglomerations 224, 419; beautification projects 157; counties 162, 169, 258, 271, 380; design programs 8, 45, 56, 60–1, 89; designers 45–6, 48–52, 54–6, 58, 61–2, 155, 157, 165, 167–8, 172, 284, 287, 334–5; economics 367–8; economies 213, 387; environment 5, 48–9, 152; growth boundaries 178, 219, 413; growth management ordinances 176–7; growth management plans 176, 178; history 19, 39, 244; limit lines 178, 219, 413; neighborhoods 11, 252–3; planners 5,

12–13, 36–7, 52–3, 69, 71, 88–91, 93, 95, 122, 127–8, 201, 213–14, 251–2, 384; politics 13, 65, 69, 77; population 40, 247, 250, 278, 387; poverty 73, 217; programs 4, 67, 84, 185, 202, 254–5, 258, 274, 380, 382; renewal 10–11, 77, 97, 191, 257–8, 271–2, 274, 281, 367, 380; sprawl 1, 111, 152, *212*, 283, 324
Urban Affairs Association (UAA) 7–8, 13–14, 70, 73, 216, 226, 255, 257, 359
urban design 2, 7–8, 10, 12, 45–63, 91, 96, 133, 149, 171, 239; concepts 3; consultants 172; courses 45, 91; education 46; firms 46, 287; New York City group 46–7; planning 51–2, 58, 61, 140, 157; for reconstruction 171; and site planning 49, 172; specializations 45–6; standards 46
urban design concept for South Capitol Street, Washington, D.C. 3
Urban Development Action Grants (UDAGs) 191
Urban Displacement Project, University of California Berkeley 199
urban economics 367, 368
Urban General Plan, The (book by T.J. "Jack" Kent) 135
urban growth management 55, 155, 176–78
urban growth boundaries (UGBs) 178, 219, 413
urban limit lines (ULLs) 178, 219, 413
urban population growth 16, 230, 246n2
Urban Renewal (United States) 11, 250, 257, 271–2, 274, 359, 380–81
urbanization 2, 16–18, 55, 205, 209–10, 212, 217, 225, 229, 231
urbanization S curve 17, 18; *see also* Kingsley Davis
Ury, William 81
USC *see* University of Southern California
USDA *see* United States Department of Agriculture (United States)
USGBC *see* United States Green Building Council (United States)
USGCRP *see* United States Global Change Research Project (United States)
USGS *see* United States Geological Survey (USGS) (United States)
Utopia 107–8, 125
utopian era in regional planning according to Professor Michael Teitz 206
utopian socialists 107–8

vanishing point of rent *see also* Ebenezer Howard
Vaux, Calvert
vaccines 102–3
valley section (Patrick Geddes) *210*; *see also* Patrick Geddes
Vancouverism 53
variance 166–67
Veiller, Lawrence 29
Vehicle Travel Time (VTT) 315
Vehicle Miles Traveled (VMT) 285, 314, 317, 333, 411, 413
very low-income household 175, 252, 254, 257, 264, 277, 340, 347, 355, 365n5, 401
Veterans Administration (VA) (United States) 342
Vibrant Northeast Ohio 2040 Plan **221**; digital dashboard dial *223*; workshop 223

VicHyper company 332
Victoria and Albert Museum 4
Vieux Port, Montreal, Canada 172
Village of Euclid vs Ambler Realty Company 179n4
Violence Against Women Act (United States, 2013) 72
vision planning 71, 107, 127, 128, 146
vision statement (in comprehensive plans) 127, 135, 146, 412
Vision Zero auto safety movement 137, 141, 270, 330
VMT *see* Vehicle Miles Traveled
voters 76, 78, 81, 144, 219, 226, 293, 388
voting 76, 359
vouchers, housing 263, 266–7, 351, 353, 365
VTT *see* Vehicle Travel Time

Wacker's Manual of the Plan of Chicago 155
Walker, Jarrett 325
walking city 89
Wallace McHarg Roberts & Todd landscape architecture firm 287, 295
war 17, 27, 40–1, 108, 115, 197, 203, 229–30, 260, 362, 406
War on Poverty (United States) 70, 203n1, 257
war workers 260, 362
wartime reports (Great Britain) 116
Ward, Colin 113, 383
Wark, Jim 212
Warner, Samuel Bass 21
Washington, D.C. 3, 24, 26, 39–41, 74, 76, 159, 162, 199, 201, 203, 205, 207, 273–6, 295
Washington Consensus 74, 386, 387
Washington, President George 23, 39, 281
Washington Square 11, 313
waste management 284, 300, 377, 392n11
Watchtower Planning Museum 36, 209
water 25–6, 40–1, 57, 65–6, 69, 93, 161–2, 214–15, 283–4, 287–9, 304–5, 388–9, 402–5, 415–16, 419; distribution systems 159, 390; ocean 398, 401; planning 256, 288, 306; pollution 214, 224, 279, 285–8, 363; quality planning and regulation 67, 214, 270, 411; underground 172, 215, 241, 300
Water Pollution Control Act (1948) (United States) 288
water standards 288
waterfront 20, 53–4, 57; development 56; industrial 222; Louisville 57; transforming Chicago's 117; Washington, D.C. 275
Waterfront Development Corporations 57–8
Watt-Boulton steam engine 30
Weaver, Robert Clifton 104, 108, 274, *358*, 359
"web of seaport life" 20, 89; *see also* Gary Nash
weight, gross vehicle 336
welfare economics 87, 98, 99, 367, 368, 369
welfare state 116, 369
West Nile virus 405
Weston, William 125–6; *see also Ecotopia*
wetlands 149, 214–15, 297–8, 304, 395, 401, 403–4
Wheeler, Steven 127, 294, 306
White flight 177, 191
White privilege 26, 183, 192–3, 200, 202, 252
Whites 5, 12, 137–8, 143–4, 186, 191–4, 200, 203, 253, 261, 365
WHO *see* World Health Organization
Who Governs? (book by Robert Dahl) 77

Whyte, William Hollis 47, 52, 58, 61–2
wicked problem 239, 348
Widodo, President Joko (Indonesia) 241
Wilderness Act (United States, 1964) 299
wilderness study area 299
William Green Homes (Chicago, Illinois) 261
William Igoe Apartments (Chicago, Illinois) 261
Williamsburg neighborhood (New York City, New York) 183, 379
Williamsburg, Virginia 275
Wilson, Edward O. 297
Wilson, Harold 383
wind energy 1
windfall 316, 362
wipeout 99, 100
"Wise Use" movement 300, 306; *see also* Sagebrush Rebellion
WMRT *see* Wallace McHarg Roberts & Todd landscape architecture firm
World Commission on the Environment and Development (Brundtland Commission) 294
Wood, Edith Elmer 37
Woodlands, Texas 287, 295
woonerfs *330*
workable program for community improvement 257
Works Progress Administration 388
women 5–7, 12–13, 15, 20–1, 39, 41, 108, 138, 189–90, 192–4, 202, 216, 244, 260, 278–9; Black 186; Chinese 25; contemporary 194; inclusion of 202; liberation movement 189; and planning 6, 193–4, 200, 244; role of 216; young 22, 26
working-class 21, 115, 273; communities 274; housing 273; middle-income 77; neighborhoods 379; unplanned areas 10
Working Group on Complexity and Planning 100; *see also* Complexity in Cities (CIC) planning
working groups 221, 408, 419
workshops 21, 121, 151, 200, 222, 379
World Bank 74, 229, 243, 247n11, 387, 405
world cities 90, 229, 232–5, 237–9, 246, 383
World Cities, The (book by Peter Hall) 383
world city: network 33, 229, 232, 233, 236–39, 241, 242, 245, 312, 367, 383; hypothesis 89, 246n5; hierarchy 237, 238
World Commission on Environment and Development (WCED) 294; *see* Brundtland Commission
World Health Organization (WHO) 95, 102, 331
World Trade Center 244, 321
World Trade Organization (WTO) 229, 241–3, 247
World War I 27, 67, 115, 273, 362

World War II 25, 27, 31, 84, 88, 91, 186, 206–7, 249–50, 255–7, 260–1, 273, 275
World's Columbian Exhibition 1893 33–4, 117–18
Worldly Philosophers, The (book by Robert Heilbroner) 107
"worthy poor" 27, 260
Wozniak, Steve 281
WQS *see* water quality standards
Wright, Frank Lloyd 35, 49, 107, *120*; develops a vision of Broadacre City 120–1; envisages "a great roadside market" for retail activities 121; with his Broadacre City model (1935) *121*; considered part-time manual agricultural work a psychological and social benefit 121
Wright, Frank Lloyd, Taliesin Teaching Studio 49
Wright, Henry 37
WTO *see* World Trade Organization
Wurster, Catherine Bauer 274; *see* Catherine Bauer

yellow fever pandemic of 1793 21, 405; *see also* pandemics
Young, Coleman 191
Yu, Kongijan, 104n2, 403–404; Puyang River Ecological Corridor 404; develops the idea of "sponge cities" 402; innovative responses to flooding 402; learns how to control surface runoff during flood peaks 403

Zaferatos, Nicholas 197, 203
ZEV *see* Zero-Emission Vehicle
Zero-Emission Vehicle (ZEV) 173, 269, 327, 331, 333–5, 400, 411
Zika virus 405
zones 38, 136, 162–8, 179, 379, 382, 384–5, 405; climate 396; coastal 213, 303; economic 374; empowerment 158, 191, 377, 385, 392; enterprise 258, 382, 384, 391–2; entertainment 375; exclusionary 167–8; export processing 382; high-unemployment 368; for industry and recreation 38; low-income 373; residential 129, 163–4; trading 81
zoning 28, 45, 47–8, 67, 75, 146, 148, 150, 158–9, 161–3, 166–8, 197–8, 259, 360, 410; changes 166; districts 163, 169; eliminating single-family 361; inclusionary 74, 76, 167, 199, 254; laws 163, 285, 361; local 136, 179; mixed-use 164; ordinances 27–8, 34, 61, 69–70, 135, 160, 162–7, 169, 258–9, 268, 323; powers 179; restrictions 163; schemes 166; standards 198
Zoning Building Envelope, 165
Zoom videoconferencing software 233, 317

For Product Safety Concerns and Information please contact our EU
representative GPSR@taylorandfrancis.com
Taylor & Francis Verlag GmbH, Kaufingerstraße 24, 80331 München, Germany